Antique Trader Books

Pottery & Porcelain Ceramics Price Guide

ANTIQUE TRADER BOOKS

Pottery & Porcelain Ceramics Price Guide

Edited by
Kyle Husfloen

Contributing Editor
Susan N. Cox

An illustrated comprehensive price guide to all types of Pottery and Porcelain, American and Foreign

Antique Trader Books
P.O. Box 1050
Dubuque, IA 52004

STAFF

Assistant Editor	**Marilyn Dragowick**
Editorial Assistants	**Louise Paradis** **Ruth Willis**
Subscription Manager	**Bonnie Rojemann**
General Manager	**Ted Jones**

ISBN: 0-930625-48-X
Library of Congress Catalog Card No. 94-71387

Additional copies of this book may be ordered from:

Antique Trader Books
P.O. Box 1050
Dubuque, Iowa 52004

$14.95 plus $2.00 postage and handling.

Introduction

It has been nearly twenty-five years since The Antique Trader first issued a periodical price guide to the field of antiques and collectibles, first as a semi-annual and then as a quarterly publication and finally, in 1984, as a bi-monthly magazine. In 1985 we introduced a single annual edition which continues to be a mainstay of our publishing efforts today.

In order to broaden our coverage of all collecting fields, this year we are introducing a whole new pricing guide, ANTIQUE TRADER BOOKS POTTERY AND PORCELAIN - CERAMICS PRICE GUIDE. Although we cover a wide range of ceramic wares in our annual price guide, this new volume affords us the chance to provide even more material on a broader range of pottery and porcelain, both American and foreign.

There are dozens and dozens of categories of ceramics, from ancient to modern, which are highly collectible today and this new guide will provide the reader with an authoritative and comprehensive overview of collecting trends throughout the world of pottery and porcelain collecting. Although a large majority of such wares were produced from the mid-19th through the mid-20th century, we feel it is important to touch on a selection of rarer, earlier wares which the average collector may not often encounter as well as a few categories which remain in production today.

We have worked to gather accurate and in-depth descriptions in our expanded listings as well as provide an abundance of clear black and white photographs to illustrate the text. In addition, to help educate our readership, we are also including sketches of the factory's or maker's mark for most of the categories we list. Such markings can be key to identifying a piece. Each category begins with a brief introduction which explains the history and development of that pottery or porcelain and, when possible, we include a mention of helpful reference books for collectors who wish to do further study.

As with nearly any collecting specialty, the world of Ceramics has its own special vocabulary, we are also beginning this book with a series of sketches of common pitcher and vase forms so that as you encounter the descriptions of these in our listings you'll be better able to visualize the shape in your mind, if it is not illustrated.

For further reference we have also prepared a special "Glossary of Selected Ceramics Terms" which appears at the back of our listings. These common terms and names will appear in various categories throughout this guide. So, just in case you find a term in our listings you're not sure about, you'll have a handy reference at your fingertips. Several special Appendices have also been prepared and placed at the end of our listings which should prove helpful to anyone interested in more research or collecting information.

My staff and I have worked long and hard to prepare this new price guide and I have to thank them here for their dedication and perseverance in getting this project compiled, copy set, proofed and formatted. In addition, special thanks are due Contributing Editor Susan N. Cox, who, within the space of a few weeks, provided in depth listings and illustrations for a large number of new categories of American 20th century ceramics which we are introducing in this volume. Her expertise and dedicated support were a tremendous boon to our work. Also deserving a special note of gratitude is my longtime friend and associate Sandra Andacht, well known Orientalia expert, who helped by supplying expanded listings in several Japanese and Chinese ceramics categories. In addition to the above mentioned contributors, we will include here an extensive listing of other photographers, dealers, auctioneers and private collectors who supplied us with photographs and reference material.

It is my sincere hope that everyone who refers to *Antique Trader Books Pottery & Porcelain - Ceramics Price Guide* will find it handy, easy to use and comprehensive. We're always interested in comments from our readers, especially those of constructive critique, and we'll do all we can to provide you with the most accurate and up-to-date information on the vast and colorful work of ceramic wares from around the world.

Kyle Husfloen, Editor

Please note: Though listings have been double-checked and every effort has been made to insure accuracy, neither the compilers, editors nor publisher can assume responsibility for any losses that might be incurred as a result of consulting this guide, or of errors, typographical or otherwise.

Photography Credits

Photographers who have contributed to this issue include: Adele Armbruster, Dearborn, Michigan; Edward Babka, East Dubuque, Illinois; Stanley L. Baker, Minneapolis, Minnesota; Dorothy Beckwith, Platteville, Wisconsin; Donna Bruun, Galena, Illinois; Marie Bush, Amsterdam, New York; Susan N. Cox, El Cajon, California; J.D. Dalessandro, Cincinnati, Ohio; Jeff Grunewald, Chicago, Illinois; Louise Paradis, Galena, Illinois; Joyce Roerig, Walterboro, South Carolina; and Molly Schroeder, Danville, Illinois.

For other photographs, artwork, data or permission to photograph in their shops, we sincerely express appreciation to the following auctioneers, galleries, museums, individuals and shops:

Donna Bauerly, Dubuque, Iowa; Bell Tower Antique Mall, Covington, Kentucky; Busby Land & Auction Company, Ridge Farm, Illinois; Butterfield & Butterfield, San Francisco, California; Norm and Diana Charles, Hagerstown, Indiana; Christie's, New York, New York; Collector's Auction Services, Oil City, Pennsylvania; Collector's Sales & Services, Middletown, Rhode Island; William Doyle Galleries, New York, New York; Marilyn Dragowick, Dubuque, Iowa; DuMouchelles, Detroit, Michigan; Dunning's Auction Service, Elgin, Illinois; T. Ermert, Cincinnati, Ohio; Garth's Auctions, Delaware, Ohio; Grunewald Antiques, Hillsborough, North Carolina; Vicki Harman, San Marcos, California; Gene Harris Antique Auction Center, Marshalltown, Iowa; Doris Johnson, Rockford, Illinois; Kirsner Auctions, Minneapolis, Minnesota; Agnes Koehn Antiques, Cedar Rapids, Iowa; James Lehnhardt, Galena, Illinois; Joy Luke Gallery, Bloomington, Illinois; J. Martin, Mt. Orab, Ohio; William Miller, Rockford, Illinois; Virginia Mills, Peabody, Massachusetts; Neal Auction Company, New Orleans, Louisiana; The Nippon Room, Rexford, New York; Dave Rago, Lambertville, New Jersey; Jane Rosenow, Galva, Illinois; Shirley's Glasstiques, Brunswick, Ohio; Skinner, Inc., Bolton, Massachusetts; Sotheby's, New York, New York; Michael Strawser, Wolcottville, Indiana; Temples Antiques, Minneapolis, Minnesota; Town Crier Auction Service, Burlington, Wisconsin; Trader Lukes, Wilmington, California; Don Treadway Galleries, Cincinnati, Ohio; Lee Vines, Hewlett, New York; Doris Virtue, Galena, Illinois; Wolf's Fine Arts Auctioneers, Cleveland, Ohio; Woody Auctions, Douglass, Kansas; and Yesterday's Treasures, Galena, Illinois.

ON THE COVER: Clockwise, top left to right - A three-piece porcelain tea set marked "Carlsbad - Austria," ca. 1900; a large Niloak pottery Mission Ware vase; and a large English ironstone platter in the Farm pattern, circa 1882.

Cover design by Jaro Sebek and Tom Wallace.

Collecting Guidelines

Whenever I'm asked about what to collect, I always stress that you should collect what you *like* and want to live with. Collecting is a very personal matter and only you can determine what will give you the most satisfaction. With the wide diversity of ceramics available, everyone should be able to find a topic they will enjoy studying and collecting.

One thing that every collector does need to keep in mind is that to get the most from their hobby they must *study* it in depth, read everything they can lay their hands on, and purchase the best references available for their library. New research material continues to become available for collectors and learning is an ongoing process.

It is also very helpful to join a collectors' club where others who share your enthusiasm will support and guide your learning. Fellow collectors often become best friends and sources for special treasures to add to your collection. Dealers who specialize in a ceramics category are always eager to help educate and support collectors and many times they become a mentor for a novice who is just starting out on the road to the 'advanced collector' level.

With the very ancient and complex history of ceramic wares, it's easy to understand why becoming educated about your special interest is of paramount importance. There have been collectors of pottery and porcelain for centuries and for nearly as long, collectors have had to be wary of reproductions or 'reissues.' In Chinese ceramics, for instance, it has always been considered perfectly acceptable to copy as closely as possible the style and finish of earlier ceramics and even to mark them with period markings on the base. This was considered a way to honor the artistry of their forebears. The only problem arises when a modern collector wants to determine whether their piece, 'guaranteed' antique, was produced over two hundred years ago or barely a century ago.

With European and, to some extent, American wares, copying of earlier styles has also been going on for many decades. As far back as the mid-19th century, 'copies' and 'adaptations' of desirable early wares were finding their way onto the collector market. By the late 19th century, in particular, revivals of 18th century porcelains and even some early 19th century earthenwares were available, often sold as decorative items and sometimes clearly marked. After a hundred years, however, these early copies can pose a real quagmire for the unwary.

Again, education is the key. As you're building your store of knowledge and experience, buy with care from reliable sources.

Another area that calls for special caution on the part of collectors, especially the tyro, is that of damaged and repaired pieces. A wise collector will always buy the best example they can find and it is a good policy to save up to buy one extra fine piece rather than a handful of lesser examples. You never want to pass up a good buy. But, in the long run, a smaller collection of choice pieces will probably bring you more satisfaction (and financial reward) than a large collection of moderate quality.

Purchasing a damaged or clearly repaired piece is a judgment only the collector can make. In general I wouldn't recommend it unless the piece is so unique that another example is not likely to come your way in the foreseeable future. For certain classes of expensive and rare ceramics, especially early pottery that has seen heavy use, a certain amount of damage may be inevitable and more acceptable. The sale price, however, should reflect this fact.

Restoration of pottery and porcelain wares has been a fact of life for many decades. Even in the early 19th century before good glues were available, 'make-do' repairs were sometimes done to pieces using small metal staples and today some collectors seek out these quaint examples of early recycling. Since the early 20th century glue and repainting have been common methods used to mask damages to pottery and porcelain and these repairs can usually be detected today with a strong light and the naked eye.

The problem in recent decades has been the ability of restorers to completely mask any sign of previous damages using more sophisticated repair methods. There is nothing wrong with a quality restoration of a rare piece as long as the eventual purchaser is completely aware that such work has been done.

It can take more than the naked eye and a strong light to detect some invisible repairs today and that's where the popular 'black light,' using ultraviolet rays, can be of help. Many spots of repair will fluoresce under the 'black light.' I understand, however,that newer glues and paints are becoming available which won't show up even under the black light. The key then, especially for the beginner, is know your ceramic or know your seller and be sure you have a money-back guarantee when making a major purchase.

I certainly don't want to sound too downbeat and discourage anyone from pursuing what can be a wonderfully fun and fulfilling hobby, but starting from a position of strength, with confidence and education, will certainly pay-off in the long run for every collector.

Ceramics, in addition to their beauty and charm, also offer the collecting advantage of durability and low-maintenance. It's surprising how much pottery and porcelain from two centuries ago is still available to collect. There were literally train-cars full of it produced and sold by the late 19th century, and such wares are abundantly available and often reasonably priced. Beautiful dinnerwares and colorful vases abound in the marketplace and offer exciting collecting possibilities. They look wonderful used on today's dining tables or gracing display shelves.

A periodic dusting and once-a-year washing in mild sudsy, warm water is about all the care they will require. Of course, it's not recommended you put older pottery and porcelains in your dishwasher where the rattling and extremely hot water could cause damage. Anyway, it's more satisfying to hold a piece in your hand in warm soapy water in a rubber dishpan (for added protection) and caress it carefully with a dishrag. The tactile enjoyment of a ceramic piece brings a new dimension to collecting and this sort of T.L.C. can be nearly as satisfying as just admiring a piece in a china cabinet or on a shelf.

Whatever sort of pottery or porcelain appeals to you most, whether it be 18th century Meissen or mid-20th century California-made pottery, you can take pride in the fact that you are carrying on a collecting tradition that goes back centuries when the crowned heads of Europe first began vying for the finest and rarest ceramics with which to accent their regal abodes.

Kyle Husfloen

TYPICAL CERAMIC SHAPES

The following line drawing illustrate typical shapes found in pottery and porcelain pitchers and vases., These forms are referred to often in our price listings.

Pitcher - Barrel-shaped

Pitcher - Jug-type

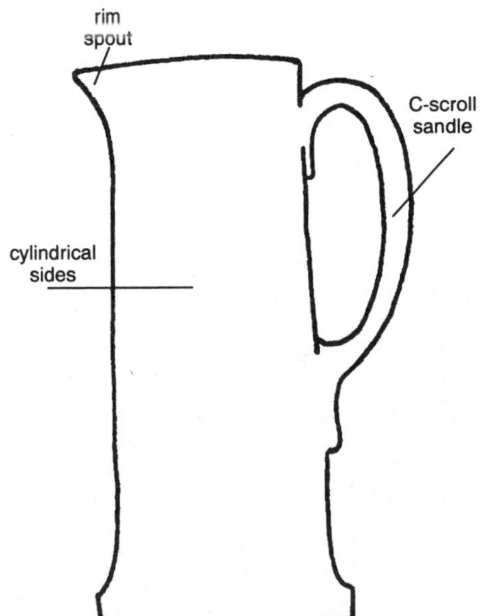

Pitcher - Tankard-type with cylindrical sides, C-scroll handle, and rim spout

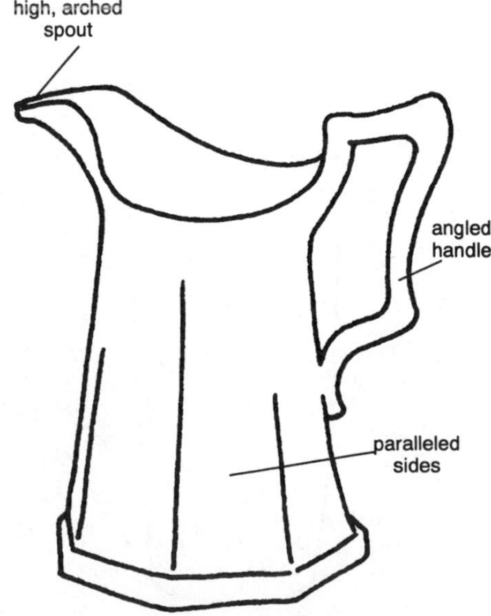

Pitcher - Tankard-type with panelled (octagonal) sides, angled handle and high, arched spout.

VASES

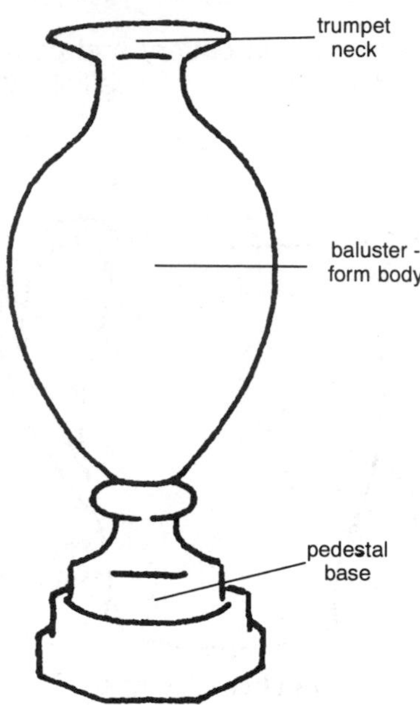

Vase - Baluster-form body with trumpet neck; raised on a pedestal base.

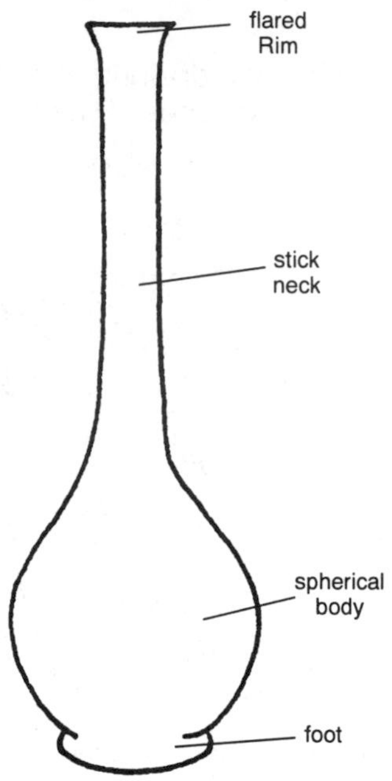

Vase - Bottle-form — Spherical footed body tapering to a tall stick neck with flared rim.

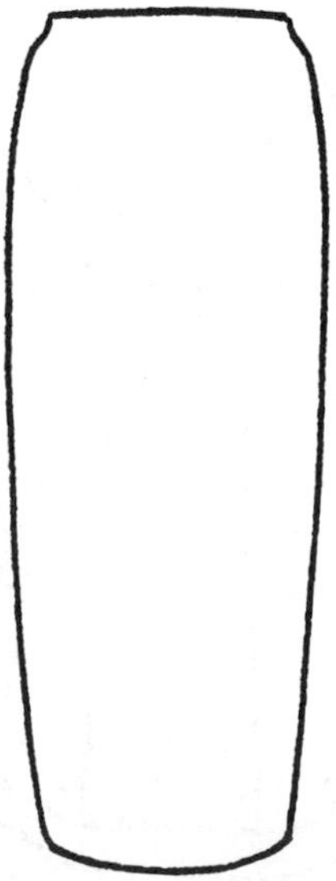

Vase - Cylindrical

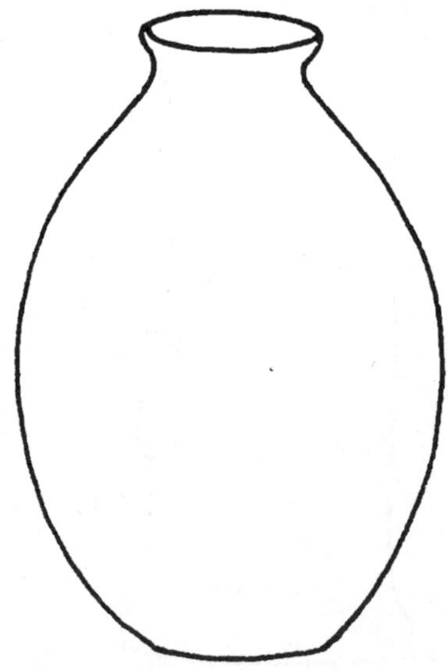

Vase - Ovoid body, tapering to a short, flared neck.

VASES (Continued)

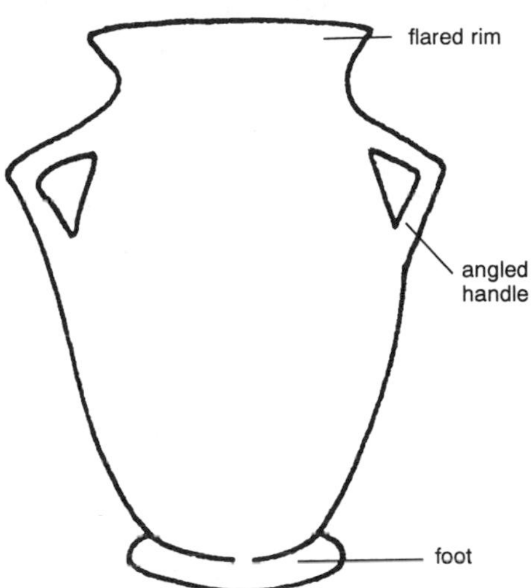

Vase - Ovoid, footed body with flared rim & angled handles.

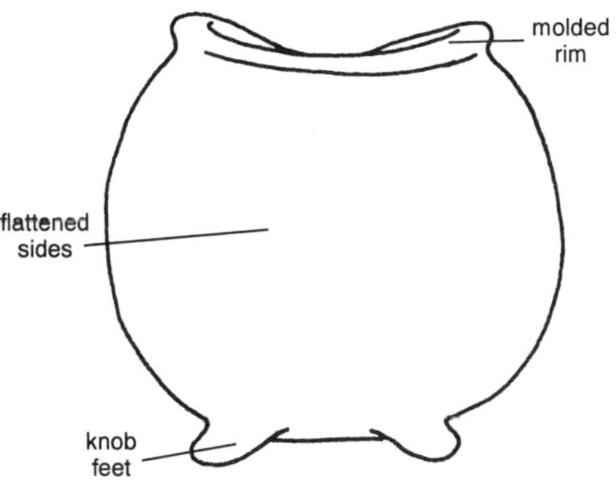

Vase - Pillow-shaped with molded rim; on knob feet.

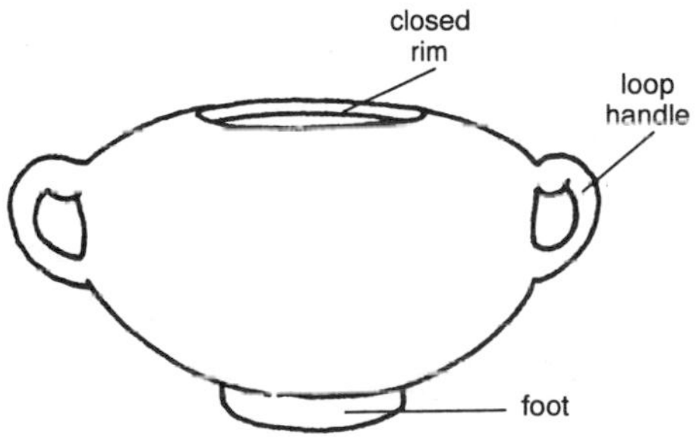

Vase or bowl vase - Spherical, footed body with closed rim and loop handles.

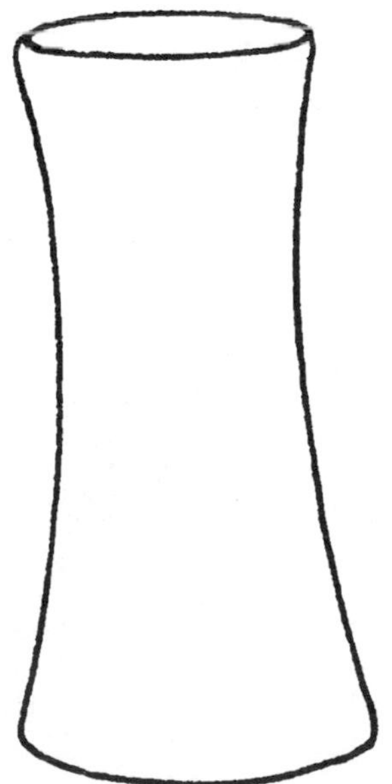

Vase - Waisted cylindrical form

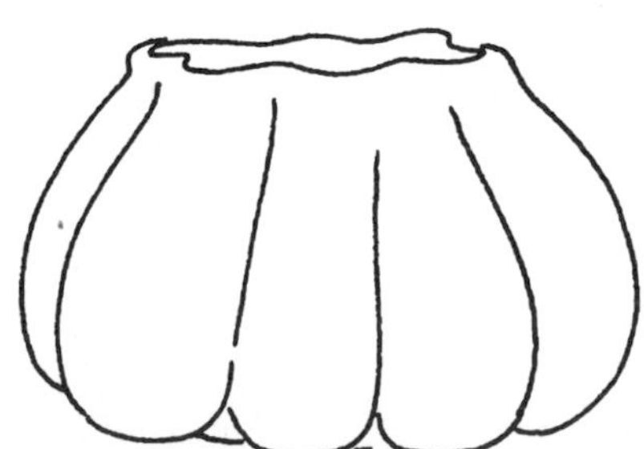

Vase - Squatty bulbous body with lobed sides

ABC PLATES

Baseball Scene ABC Plate

These children's plates were popular in the late 19th and early 20th centuries. An alphabet border was incorporated with nursery rhymes, maxims, scenes or figures in an apparent attempt to "spoon feed" a bit of knowledge at mealtime. They were made of ceramics, glass and metal. A boon to collectors is the fine book, A Collector's Guide to ABC Plates, Mugs and Things *by Mildred L. and Joseph P. Chalala (Pridemark Press, Lancaster, Pennsylvania, 1980).*

5" d., Alpine shepherd scene, black transfer scene center highlighted w/polychrome enamel & red rim stripe, embossed alphabet border, Staffordshire $60.50

6" d., adult activities, "Gathering Cotton," a central transfer-printed design of blacks working in a cotton field, embossed alphabet border, 19th c. (glaze crackling)...................550.00

6" d., "Zouaves," black transfer scene of two men w/polychrome enameling, embossed alphabet border, Staffordshire........................132.00

6¼" d., children's activities & games, "American Sports – Base Ball Running To First Base," transfer scene center of young boys playing ball, embossed alphabet border, ca. 1860-80, rim chip & edge wear (ILLUS.) ....125.00 to 150.00

7" d., adult occupations, black transfer-printed center design of a man carrying chairs titled "Chairs to Mend," blue rim stripe, embossed alphabet border (stains)...................165.00

7½" d., Nursery Rhymes, "Hey Diddle Diddle," Bavaria 75.00

ABINGDON

"Mother Goose" Cookie Jar

From about 1934 until 1950, Abingdon Pottery Company, Abingdon, Illinois, manufactured decorative pottery, mainly cookie jars, flowerpots and vases. Decorated with various glazes, these items are becoming popular with collectors who are especially attracted to Abingdon's novelty cookie jars.

Book ends, model of a horse head, black glaze, pr...............................$100.00

Compote, open, pink glaze, No. 568....30.00

Console bowl, round, blue, 9" d..............8.00

Console bowl, grey-green, 9 x 14"........18.00

Console bowl, oval, white, 18" l............18.00

Console set: No. 564 scalloped bowl & pair of No. 575 scalloped candlesticks; floral decoration, No. 33, on white ground, lavish gold trim, 3 pcs. 75.00

Cookie jar, "Aramis Bear" 25.00

Cookie jar, "Bo Peep" ....200.00 to 250.00

Cookie jar, "Choo Choo," engine ....125.00 to 150.00

Cookie jar, "Clock" (Cookie Time) 110.00

Cookie jar, "Daisy," w/"Cookies" on side 55.00

Cookie jar, "Fat Boy"..........................450.00

Cookie jar, "Hobby Horse"..................210.00

Cookie jar, "Humpty Dumpty" ....250.00 to 300.00

Cookie jar, "Jack-in-the-Box" ....250.00 to 275.00

Cookie jar, "Little Girl," w/'O's' in "Cooky" forming her eyes ....100.00 to 120.00

Cookie jar, "Little Old Lady," black woman 800.00

Cookie jar, "Little Old Lady," white......200.00

Cookie jar, "Little Old Lady," pink 225.00

Cookie jar, "Miss Muffet".....250.00 to 300.00

Cookie jar, "Money Bag".......................80.00

Cookie jar, "Mother Goose" (ILLUS.) ....300.00 to 350.00

Cookie jar, "Pineapple".........................65.00

Cookie jar, "Pumpkin" (Jack o'Lantern) ....350.00 to 400.00

Cookie jar, "Windmill" ....300.00 to 400.00

Cornucopia-vase, blue glaze, 8½" w., 4¾" h. 25.00

Figurine, kneeling nude, No. 3903, pink w/decoration............................178.00

Jardiniere, pink glaze w/decoration, No. 558 ....35.00

Model of a duck 18.50

Urn, small side handles, square foot, top w/vertical ribs, relief-molded leaf wreath decoration, rose, No. 538.........9.50

Vase, 8" h., model of a tulip, yellow......22.00

Vase/flower holder, fan-shaped, white, holder built inside lip, horizontal ribs at base, fan & scroll design, No. 491, 5 x 5 x 7" 22.00

Wall pocket, Lily patt., blue, No. 377 ....25.00

Wall shelf, yellow, cherub face, wings & neck support semi-circular shelf, No. 587, 4¼ x 7¾", 4½" h.................30.00

ADAMS

Members of the Adams family have been potters in England since 1650. Three William Adamses made pottery, all of it collectible. Most Adams pottery easily accessible today was made in the 19th century and is impressed or marked variously ADAMS, W. ADAMS, ADAMS TUNSTALL, W. ADAMS & SONS, or W. ADAMS & CO. with the word "England" or the phrase "Made in England" added after 1891. Wm. Adams & Son, Ltd. continues in operation today. Also see HISTORICAL & COMMEMORATIVE WARES and STAFFORDSHIRE TRANSFER WARES.

Adams' Rose Plate

Cup & saucer, handleless, Adams' Rose patt., impressed "A" (minor roughness) $165.00

Cup & saucer, handleless, dark blue transfer-printed design of a large flower-filled basket, ca. 1830, impressed mark (small flakes) 159.50

Plate, 7" d., Palestine patt., blue 45.00

Plate, 8¼" d., Dickensware series, transfer-printed scene titled "Mrs. Gumage casts a damp on our departure" 15.00

Plate, 8¾" d., blue transfer-printed scene entitled "Hawthornden, Edinburghshire," impressed "Adams" (small flakes & minor scratches)......115.00

Plate, 9" d., dark blue transfer-printed center design of a cupid & a maiden, floral border, impressed mark, ca. 1830 ....159.50

Plate, 9½" d., Adams' Rose patt.,

free-hand red & green w/black trim, impressed "Adams" (ILLUS.) 148.50

Platter, 15¾" l., oval, Genoa patt., light blue, impressed mark (minor stains) 137.50

Platter, 19½" oval, lightly scalloped edges, Adams' Rose patt., impressed "Adams" (pinpoints, large rim chip) 302.50

Soup plate w/flanged rim, Adams' Rose patt., red, green & black, 10¾" d. (rim repair)............................93.50

AUSTRIAN

St. Bernard Plate

Numerous potteries in Austria produced good-quality ceramic wares over many years. Some factories were established by American entrepreneurs, particularly in the Carlsbad area, and other factories made china under special brand names for American importers. Marks on various pieces are indicated in many listings. Also see ROYAL VIENNA.

Basket, long rectangular body w/anangular handle at midsection, raised on six tapering square feet, molded in low-relief w/a grid of squares about the rim & handle, glazed in mottled blue & emerald green, impressed factory mark, numbered "4990 – Austria," ca. 1920, 11¾" l., overall 5¼" h........$2,300.00

Bowl, 10" d., decorated w/red & white roses (M.Z. Austria) 150.00

Cake plate, handled, scalloped rim, scrolled relief at handles, decorated w/spray of pink & blue flowers, gold trim, 9½" d. (urn mark) 24.00

Chocolate pot, cov., decorated w/sprays of blossoms in rose, lavender & purple, enhanced w/lavish gold latticework & scrolling devices, matte finish (Carlsbad) 125.00

Cracker jar, cov., decorated w/white water lilies on green band of leaves, gold trim (M.Z. Austria) 125.00

Dessert set: 11½" d. charger & four 8½" d. plates; decorated w/a trellis bower of clustered green roses & yellow leaves in a center spray on a white ground, gold ribbon rim, 5 pcs. (Victoria Carlsbad) 115.00

Egg server, stand w/figural chicken center handle, six attached egg cups around edge, each painted inside w/little chickens (Victoria Austria) 125.00

Ewer, four-footed, rococo gold scroll handle, molded scrolls overall, decorated w/h.p. pink & yellow wild roses outlined in gold on front & back, gold rim & feet, 6" d., 11¾" h. (circle & torch mark w/"International") 155.00

Game platter, buck & four does in woodland scene, gold trim, 11¾ x 17½" 185.00

Pitcher, 10" h., left-handed type, h.p. w/multicolored floral & leaves decoration w/gold tracery, cream ground (Victoria Carlsbad).................75.00

Pitcher, pillow-shaped, 4¾ x 9", 16" h., four-footed, decorated w/giant molded scrolls & h.p. irises front & back, gold outlining, sponging & trim, reticulated handle, ivory ground, pink & gold neck spout, handle & feet (Carlsbad Austria)......360.00

Plate, 8¼" d., center decoration of children & lambs, scalloped edge, medium blue & gold border (Carlsbad Austria).............................45.00

Plate, 8½" d., red poppies decoration, curved & scalloped rim 45.00

Plate, 8½" d., decorated w/spruce branches & flowers (M.Z. Austria) 55.00

Plate, 13" d., pierced to hang, h.p. head of a St. Bernard dog in black, brown & white against a shaded blue to cream to green ground, irregular scalloped & scroll-molded gilt edge, artist-signed, marked (ILLUS.) 225.00

Plate, salad, h.p. fruit decoration, scalloped edges (H. & Co. Carlsbad) 10.50

Salt dip, pedestal base, decorated w/violets (Vienna Austria) 35.00

Vase, 5" h., two-handled, bust portrait of lovely lady w/long flowing hair against a green ground......................35.00

Vase, 5½" h., two-handled, allegorical scenes on front & back in soft pastels (beehive mark).................................60.00

Vase, 7½" h., continuous allegorical scenes w/ladies, men, cherub & flowers (beehive mark Austria) 100.00

Vase, 10" h., handled, decorated w/colorful court scenes (Victoria Carlsbad Austria) 45.00

Vase, 13" h., in the form of a tusk on a stand, decorated w/Asian figures in relief raised on a reticulated faux stand (W - R Austria) 165.00

Vase, 13" h., h.p. decoration of pink, red & yellow roses 150.00

Vase, 13½" h., 5" w. at base, four-footed, narrow neck w/flared scalloped mouth, high slender double shoulder handles, decorated w/h.p. red, yellow & white carnations, gold outlining on shaded beige-ivory ground, stylized relief-molded leaves at rim & neck, vertical ribs at base, gold trim (crown & seal "RH" Austria) 210.00

Vase, 16" h., 7" d., two-handled, swelled cylindrical body decorated w/h.p. purple violets, heavy gilt, artist-signed (crown & wreath mark)..290.00

BAUER POTTERY

The Bauer Pottery was moved to Los Angeles, California from Paducah, Kentucky, in 1909, in the hope that the climate would prove beneficial to the principal organizer, John Andrew Bauer, who suffered from severe asthma. Flowerpots, made of California adobe clay, were the first production at the new location, but soon they were able to resume production of stoneware crocks and jugs, the mainstay of the Kentucky operation. In the early 1930s, Bauer's colorfully glazed earthen dinnerwares, especially the popular Ring-Ware pattern, became an immediate success. Sometimes confused with its imitator, Fiesta Ware (first registered by Homer Laughlin in 1937), Bauer pottery is collectible in its own right and is especially popular with West Coast collectors. Bauer Pottery ceased operation in 1962.

Batter bowl, Ring-Ware patt., red $45.00

Bowl, fruit, 9" d., footed, Monterey patt., red...45.00

Bowl, 9" d., Ring-Ware patt., chartreuse 30.00

Butter dish, cov., Monterey patt., yellow 60.00

Butter dish, cov., round, Ring-Ware patt., green..75.00

Canister, cov., brown sugar, La Linda patt. 25.00

Casserole, cov., La Linda patt., green, w/metal & wooden handled holder.....35.00

Coffee server, cov., Ring-Ware patt., w/wooden handle, red.......................40.00

Coffee server, cov., Ring-Ware patt., w/wooden handle, yellow 45.00

Cornucopia-vase, double, light blue exterior, white interior, 6¼" d., 11¼" h...40.00

Creamer, La Linda patt., pink 6.00

Flowerpot, turquoise glaze, 8½" h. 25.00

Gravy boat, La Linda patt., chartreuse 15.00

Gravy boat, Monterey patt., yellow 15.00

Mixing bowl, Ring-Ware patt., yellow, No. 12 ....35.00

Mixing bowl, nest-type, Ring-Ware patt., No. 24, yellow 30.00

Pie plate, La Linda patt., metal-handled holder 18.00

Pie plate, Ring-Ware patt., cobalt blue 42.50

Pitcher, 4½" h., Ring-Ware patt., yellow....25.00

Pitcher, 6" h., Ring-Ware patt., red....45.00

Pitcher, Gloss Pastel Kitchenware patt., green, 1½ pt....14.00

Pitcher w/ice lip, Ring-Ware patt., red, ½ gal....48.00

Pitcher, Ring-Ware patt., red, 3 qt....35.00

Plate, 6" d., La Linda patt., pink....4.00

Plate, 6" d., Ring-Ware patt., black....15.00

Plate, 6" d., Ring-Ware patt., burgundy or jade green, each....8.00

Plate, 9" d., Monterey patt., yellow....10.00

Plate, 9" d., Ring-Ware patt., cobalt blue or jade green, each....15.00

Refrigerator set, stacking-type, blue, red & black, w/black lid, the set....65.00

Teapot, cov., Gloss Pastel Kitchenware patt., Aladdin lamp shape, yellow, 9 cup....85.00

Tumbler, Ring-Ware patt., cobalt blue, 12 oz....25.00

Tumbler, Ring-Ware patt., green, 12 oz....20.00

Tumbler, Ring-Ware patt., maroon, 12 oz....21.00

Tumbler, Ring-Ware patt., orange, 12 oz....25.00

Tumbler, Ring-Ware patt., yellow, 12 oz....20.00

Vase, 9" h., Ring-Ware patt., green....50.00

Vases, 13¾" h., 5 x 10¼", fan-shaped, footed, Art Deco stylized leaf-form, glossy turquoise glaze, pr....95.00

Vegetable bowl, open, Monterey patt., red., 10" oval....26.00

BAVARIAN

Ceramics have been produced by various potteries in Bavaria, Germany, for many years. Those appearing for sale in greatest frequency today were produced in the 19th and early 20th centuries. Various company marks are indicated with some listings here.

Ashtray, decorated w/pink & rose medallions, gold tracery, wide maroon border w/gold flowers & lattice, marked "Bavaria – Schumann – Arzberg Germany," 3¼ x 4¼"....$9.00

Bowl, 9¼" d., scalloped rim, pale blue, pink & orange lustre panels w/flowered sides & bright multicolored floral sprays, marked "Bavaria"....20.00

Bowl, 10¼" d., 3" h., center decoration of pastel pink & yellow roses on white ground, embossed swirls & Art Nouveau flowers on sides, scalloped rim w/green iridescent border....65.00

Bowl, 10½" d., 3" h., Art Nouveau style, h.p. scene of water nymph reaching over water lilies, w/a setting sun to one side & gilt stars against a black ground at the other, concave side panels decorated w/gilt irises, iridescent gold scalloped rim....235.00

Bowl, 10½" d., 3" h., decorated w/a pink & yellow rose spray in the center & white daisies on the sides, iridescent green rim....65.00

Butter pat, decorated w/trailing roses & buds, gold rim, "RC" crown mark & "Malmaison"....7.50

Cake stand, large floral spray decoration, scrolled blank, marked "Schumann-Artzburg, Germany," 10½" d., 4½" h....18.00

Candy dish, reticulated rim, decorated w/large h.p. roses, rose buds, leaves & festoons, 4" d....8.00

Coffee set: 9¼" h. cov. coffeepot, creamer & cov. sugar bowl; lavish multicolored floral decoration, scrolled & melon-ribbed blank, gold rim & trim, crown mark w/"Bavaria – Creidlitz – Germany," the set....125.00

Cracker jar, cov., two-handled, decorated w/a continuous landscape of green trees & grasses in the foreground, a stream, buildings & windmill in the distance, marked "Bavaria," 7¼" d., 6½" h....110.00

Cups & saucers, Winterling patt., pink roses w/gold trim, set of 8....100.00

Dinner service for twelve w/many serving pieces, gold embossed decoration on white ground, 109 pcs....495.00

Dish, figural oak leaf, decorated w/white & pink blossoms w/gold stems, marked "Old Nuremberg – Bavaria – Germany," 4½ x 11"....20.00

Dish, two-part w/center scrolled handle, fluted & scalloped rim, decorated w/medallions of Venus & Mars or Venus & Neptune surrounded by blue, gold tracery & trim, crown mark w/"Royal Bavarian – Germany," 7¾ x 11¼" 75.00

Dish, shell-shaped w/four shell lobes, pink shading to white ground, h.p. w/enameled center scenic medallion of castle, trees, snow & moon, gold trim, anchor mark & "S. Co." (Oscar Schaller & Co., 1882-1918), 12½" oval, 2½" h. 70.00

Dresser box, cov., scene of classic figures on lid, green, brown & yellow ground w/gold trim, marked "Bavaria Germany," 3½ x 5", 2" h. 65.00

Figure group, young girl w/five geese, 10" w., 10½" h. 110.00

Fish set: large platter & ten individual plates; h.p. fish & underwater scenes, 11 pcs. 525.00

Plate, 6½" d., reticulated rim, decorated w/red poppies & h.p. raised gold beading & trim, shades of pastel blue & pink in ground, gold leaves on rim, gold edge band, marked "Schumann – Arzberg Germany – Bavaria" 15.00

Plate, 8¼" d., h.p. floral decoration, artist-signed 35.00

Plates, 7½" d., fruit at centers w/two plates each of different fruits, gold tracery, border & rim, marked "Millerteich," set of 12 ....125.00

Plates, 7¾" d., decorated w/gold florals & leaves w/lattice on a wide turquoise band, crown mark & "Alka – Bavaria," set of 6 ....20.00

Vase, 9½" h., h.p. forest scene w/deer 200.00

Vase, cov., 12" h., 7" d., urn-form w/dome lid, decorated w/a large floral spray on a white ground w/gold trim, marked "Waldershof – Bavaria Handarbeit" 55.00

BELLEEK

Belleek china has been made in Ireland's County Fermanagh for many years. It is exceedingly thin porcelain. Several marks were used, including a hound and harp (1865-1880), and a hound, harp and castle (1863-1891). A printed hound, harp and castle with the words "Co. Fermanagh Ireland" constitutes the mark from 1891. Belleek-type china also was made in the United States last century by several firms, including Ceramic Art Company, Columbian Art Pottery, Lenox Inc., Ott & Brewer and Willets Manufacturing Co. Also see LENOX.

An Early Irish Belleek Mark

AMERICAN

Bowl, 7½" square, decorated w/h.p. flowers & berries (Willets) $250.00

Bowl, 8" d., 1" h., scroll decoration in silver on white ground (Willets) 90.00

Candy dish, fluted, white w/pink interior, 3½ x 4½" (Ceramic Art Company) 95.00

Chocolate cup & saucer, decorated w/a purple "W" monogram on white, gold trim & gold dragon handle (Willets) 37.00

Creamer, applied 'fishnet' decoration, knotted handle, all-white, 3¼" h. (Knowles, Taylor & Knowles) 285.00

Creamer, cylindrical, gold floral decoration, 4½" h., Ott & Brewer (light wear to gold on handle) 75.00

Creamer & open sugar bowl, gold pastel florals & brushed gold, matte finish, pr. 250.00

Cups, demitasse, Orient patt. (Morgan), set of four 175.00

Cup & saucer, demitasse, shell-shaped, gilded twig handle & trim (Ott & Brewer) 155.00

Dish, shell-shaped, on two snail shell feet, pearlescent glaze, 3" d. (Ott & Brewer) 95.00

Dish, shell-shaped, openwork twig feet, pearlescent glaze, 4" d. (Ott & Brewer) 175.00

Dish, triple shell-shaped, pale pink pearlescent glaze w/blue coral center handle, Ott & Brewer (faint hairline on one shell) 225.00

Mug, barrel-shaped, decorated w/h.p. leaves & nut pods, palette mark, 5" h., (Ceramic Art Company – Lenox) 145.00

Mug, decorated w/apples & leaves, ca. 1906, 6" h. (Ceramic Art Company) 90.00

Mug, decorated w/dainty grapes on vines on gold trellis, gold handle, 5¼" h. (Willets)................................135.00

Plate, 10½" d., floral decoration w/gold rim, marked "Coxon No. S-115" (Coxon)..........................200.00

Rose bowl, tri-footed, gold, green & brown leaves & vines decoration, beaded berries, 3¾" h. (Knowles, Taylor & Knowles)............................145.00

Salt & pepper shakers, cov., blue stylized flower decoration & gold trim on pearlized ground, pr. (Willets)...165.00

Salt dip, four-footed, decorated w/roses, 1 x 2", (Willets) 65.00

Salt dip, heart-shaped, h.p. w/gold crimped edges (Willets) 110.00

Salt dip, round w/scalloped gold edges, gold beads on white (Ceramic Art Company) 25.00

Vase, miniature, 2¾" h., blue stylized flowers & gold trim on pearlized ground (Willets) 145.00

Vase, 8" h., decorated w/bluebirds & berries, artist-signed, ca. 1906, green palette mark (Lenox).............195.00

Vase, 10" h., decorated w/black spider webs & yellow, pink, blue & orange butterflies, white pearlized ground, ca. 1906-24 (Lenox) 225.00

Vase, 12½" h., pedestal base, bulbous body w/slender neck flared at top, two gold handles at neck, yellow roses on pastel pink ground, ca. 1889 (Ceramic Art Company) 295.00

IRISH

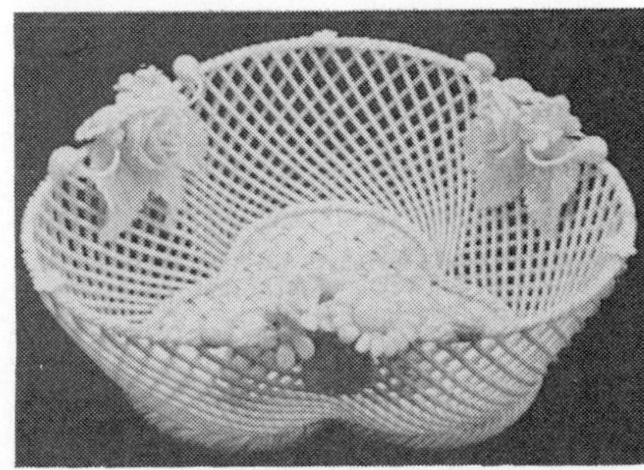

Irish Belleek Basket

Basket, Shamrock-type, four-strand, three-lobed sides w/three applied flower clusters at the rim, 6" w. (ILLUS.) ....425.00 to 475.00

Bread (or cake) plate, Neptune patt., 10" d., 3rd black mark 95.00

Bread (or cake) plate, open-handled, Shamrock-Basketweave patt., 9" d., 2nd black mark ....100.00 to 125.00

Coffee set, demitasse: cov. coffeepot, creamer, open sugar bowl & six cups & saucers; Limpet patt., 3rd black mark, 15 pcs.....................850.00

Creamer, Ivy patt., 5" h., 3rd black mark 65.00

Creamer, jug-shaped w/rope handle, 5" h., 1st black mark 450.00

Creamer, Limpet patt., 3rd black mark 95.00

Lotus Creamer

Creamer, Lotus patt., 3rd black mark (ILLUS.) 50.00

Creamer, Shamrock-Basketweave patt., large, 3" h., 3rd black mark 65.00

Creamer, Undine patt., 2nd green mark 45.00

Creamer & open sugar bowl, Cleary patt., 2nd black mark, pr. 130.00

Creamer & open sugar bowl, Irish Pot pat., 3rd black mark, pr. 65.00

Creamer & open sugar bowl, Ribbon patt., 3rd black mark, pr. 125.00

Creamer & open sugar bowl, Toy Shell patt., 1st green mark, pr............55.00

Cup & saucer, demitasse, Fan patt., w/pink trim, 2nd black mark 150.00

Cup & saucer, New Shell patt., 2nd green mark.......................................25.00

Cup & saucer, Shamrock-Basketweave patt., 3rd black mark....85.00

Cup & saucer, Tridacna patt., 2nd black mark ....75.00 to 89.00

Cardium on Coral Dish

Dish, Cardium on Coral patt., shell-shaped, 3½" h., 1st black mark (ILLUS.) 300.00

Flower holder, Nautilus on Coral patt., 9½" h., 1st black mark 750.00

Holy water font, Cherub patt., figure of a winged cherub head, 8" h., 3rd black mark 185.00

Model of a harp, decorated w/shamrocks, 8" h., 2nd green mark..225.00

Model of a pig, 3" h., 2nd black mark..230.00

Model of a swan, 3½" h., 3rd green mark..55.00

Pitcher, milk, 6" h., Shamrock-Basketweave patt., 3rd black mark..198.00

Plate, 7" d., Harp-Shamrock patt., green mark..60.00

Plate, 7" d., Hexagon patt., pink trim, 2nd black mark 30.00

Plate, 7" d., Mask patt., 3rd black mark...30.00

Plate, 7" d., New Shell patt., 1st green mark..................................60.00

Salt dip, Cleary patt., 3rd black mark....49.00

Salt dip, Hexagon patt., 2nd black mark..175.00

Salt dip, shell-shaped, Limpet patt., 1st green mark..................................25.00

Salt dip, Shamrock-Basketweave patt., 3rd black mark 35.00

Spill vase, Rock patt., small, 3rd black mark..75.00

Spill vase, Rock patt., large, 3rd green mark..95.00

Tea kettle, cov., Hexagon patt., 2nd black mark 250.00

Harp-Shamrock Teapot

Teapot, cov., Harp-Shamrock patt., green mark (ILLUS.) 135.00

Teapot, cov., Shamrock-Basketweave patt., 2nd black mark 250.00

Trinket box, cov., Cherub patt., 3½" w., 3" h., 3rd green mark 65.00

Vase, 7⅛" h., 4⅛" d., Rathmore patt., 3rd green mark 55.00

Vase, 8" h., 4½" d., Ribbon patt., applied flowers, 3rd black mark 225.00

BENNINGTON

Various Bennington Wares

Bennington wares, which ranged from stoneware to parian and porcelain, were made in Bennington, Vermont, primarily in two potteries, one in which Captain John Norton and his descendants were principals, and the other in which Christopher Webber Fenton (also once associated with the Nortons) was a principal. Various marks are found on the wares made in the two major potteries, including J. & E. Norton, E. & L.P. Norton, L. Norton & Co., Norton & Fenton, Edward Norton, Lyman Fenton & Co.,

Fenton's Works, United States Pottery Co., U.S.P. and others.

The popular pottery with the mottled brown on yelloware glaze was also produced in Bennington, but such wares should be referred to as "Rockingham" or "Bennington-type" unless they can be specifically attributed to a Bennington, Vermont factory.

Book flasks, one w/binding impressed "Kossoth," the other impressed "7," the first w/a mottled Flint Enamel glaze, the other w/a mottled brown Rockingham glaze, attributed to Lyman Fenton & Co., ca. 1850, one w/a chipped corner, 5" & $5\frac{1}{2}$" h., 2 pcs. (ILLUS. left) $357.50

Bottle, figural, barrel-shaped standing Mr. Toby, mottled dark brown Rockingham glaze, embossed "All For James Crow," impressed "1849" mark, 9" h. 395.00

Bennington Candlestick

Candlestick, slender columnar form w/flared round base, mottled dark brown Rockingham glaze, $9\frac{5}{8}$" h. (ILLUS.) 412.50

Curtain tie-backs, rosette-form, mottled brown Rockingham glaze, attributed to Lyman Fenton & Co., mid-19th c., $4\frac{1}{4}$ & $4\frac{1}{2}$" d., 2 pr. 165.00

Flowerpot, cylindrical w/slightly flaring rim, incised horizontal lines, mottled Flint Enamel glaze, attributed to Lyman Fenton & Co., star crack, 19th c., $4\frac{1}{2}$" h. (ILLUS. right) 715.00

Inkwell, cylindrical base, the lid sloping up to a ringed domed top, mottled brown Rockingham glaze, attributed to Lyman Fenton & Co., 19th c. 165.00

Rare Bennington Jar

Jar, cov., stoneware, wide ovoid body tapering to a flaring rim flanked by eared handles, inset cover, slip-quilled cobalt blue decoration of a large stag standing between a stump & a stylized fir tree w/grass below, impressed mark of J. Norton & Co., Bennington & "2," minor crack at rim, 2 gal., $11\frac{1}{2}$" h. (ILLUS.) 4,600.00

Models of poodles, standing animal holding a basket in its mouth, the tail curled over the back, applied coleslaw on the shoulders, front legs & ears, free-standing, mottled brown Rockingham glaze, attributed to Lyman Fenton & Co., 8" h., facing pair (minute losses to coleslaw) 11,000.00

Models of lions, each standing w/front paw on a ball, the tail curled over the back, w/an applied coleslaw mane, on a stepped rectangular base, mottled Flint Enamel glaze, each marked "Lyman Fenton & Co., patented 1849, Bennington, Vermont," imperfections, 11" l., 9" h., facing pair (ILLUS. of one top next column) 11,000.00

Bennington Lion

Pitcher, 7½" h., cylindrical base beneath a slightly waisted neck, mottled brown Rockingham glaze, attributed to Lyman Fenton & Co., mid-19th c. (ILLUS. center) 330.00

BERLIN (KPM)

K.P.M. Plaque

The mark, KPM, was used at Meissen from 1723 to 1725, and was later adopted by the Royal Factory, Konigliche Porzellan Manufaktur, in Berlin. At various periods it has been incorporated with the Brandenburg sceptre, the Prussian eagle or the crowned globe. The same letters were also adopted by other factories in Germany in the late 19th and 20th centuries. With the end of the German monarchy in 1918, the name of the firm was changed to Staatliche Porzellan Manufaktur and though production was halted during World War II, the factory was rebuilt and is still in business. The exquisite paintings on porcelain were produced at the close of the 19th century and are eagerly sought by collectors today.

Cuspidor, lady's, decorated w/pink roses & gold trim $78.00

Figures of putti, standing behind a scrolling draped shield-shaped device, on a circular base, 7½" h., pr. 250.00

Plaque, rectangular, depicting a young mother in a forest setting, holding a young child aloft in her arms whie another child clutches her skirt, impressed "K.P.M.," sceptre mark & "WAGNER," late 19th c., 7" w., 9⅞" h. (ILLUS.) 2,588.00

Plaque, rectangular, depicting the Assumption of the Virgin Mary, impressed "K.P.M." & sceptre mark, late 19th c., 8⅞" w., 11" h...1,955.00

Plaque, rectangular, depicting Abraham leaving the temple, impressed "K.P.M." & sceptre mark, "ZAPF" & "BKD HBO" w/paper label of Henry Bucker, Painter, 10¼" w., 12⅞" h. 3,738.00

Plaque, rectangular, depicting a winter scene of an elderly man & two young children, stamped "K.P.M." w/sceptre mark & impressed "Wagner CF," late 19th c., 10¼ x 12⅞"......................1,610.00

Plaque, rectangular, decorated w/a scene of two adult angels hovering above a small child in bed, impressed "K.P.M." & sceptre marks, late 19th c., unframed, 6½ x 13".......................................5,175.00

Lady in Courtyard Plaque

Plaque, rectangular, h.p. scene of a 16th century lady standing in a courtyard looking out over a sunset, impressed "KPM" & sceptre mark, mounted in a wide gilt-plaster frame, late 19th c., 8 x 13" (ILLUS.)................4,125.00

Plaque, rectangular, depicting semi-nude nymphs in pastel draperies flying over a pond, impressed "K.P.M." & sceptre mark, incised dimensions, late 19th c., 19" w., 11½" h. 18,400.00

Plaque, rectangular, depicting a detailed mythological scene of a prince on horseback, the devil on horseback, leaping over a maiden in pursuit of a lady holding a crown, artist-signed, labeled on back "Die Fagd nach dem Glucke von Hennberg, Berlin," in original gilded frame, 16¼ x 23¾" 9,025.00

Relish dish, composed of two oval segments centered by a handle, each section decorated w/floral sprays, insects & gilt trim, blue sceptre & "K.P.M." mark, 11" w..........77.00

Teacup & saucer, painted in shades of brown, green, yellow, blue, black & puce or iron-red on the front of the cup w/a small boy bringing a basket of flowers to a shepherd seated beside two sheep in a river landscape & in the center of the saucer w/a small boy conversing w/two travelers seated beneath a wooden sign, the center of the cup w/a puce, pale yellow, grey, iron-red & green floral sprig, the scroll-molded handle (tiny chip) heightened in gilding & the rim of each (tiny chip on saucer) w/a gilt border of demi-flowerheads, scrolls & dots, sceptre marks in underglaze-blue, gilder's numerals & impressed letter "T" on cup & on saucer, ca. 1764, cup 3⅛" d., saucer 5½" d.............1,150.00

Vase, 31" h., on stand, ovoid body w/an oval panel depicting "Clementine," heightened w/gilt on a lustre brown ground modeled w/elaborate foliate scrolled handles rising above the short flared neck, raised on an octagonal base, signed "Schunzel," sceptre mark in blue enamel & titled in red enamel, late 19th c. 14,950.00

Vases, 19" h., tall baluster-form on a pedestal base w/square foot, the flaring neck w/molded rim flanked by scrolled griffin head handles, the sides of each decorated w/a rectangular panel on each side depicting a colored view of Berlin within gilt borders, the neck decorated w/an oval leaf wreath framing floral springs & the bottom & pedestal decorated w/gilt trelliswork & gilt bands, sceptre & circular mark in underglaze-blue, mid-19th c., pr. (restorations)..............................12,650.00

Vases, 21¼" h., triple-gourd form, decorated w/chinoiserie motifs incorporating figures at various pursuits, birds & flowers in multicolors on a red ground, first quarter 19th c., pr. 5,750.00

BISQUE

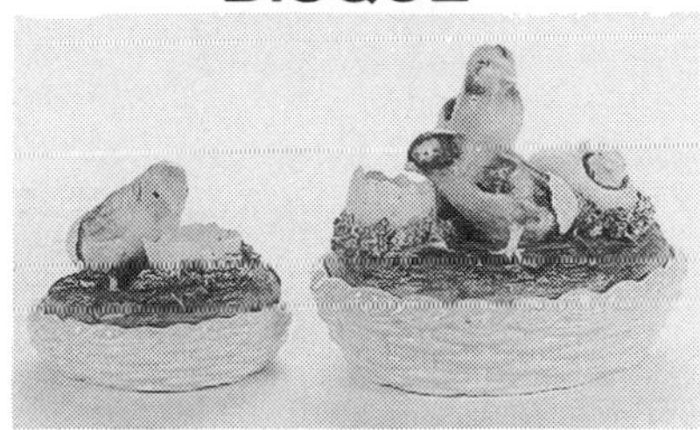

Bisque Animal Dishes

Bisque is biscuit china, fired a single time but not glazed. Some bisque is decorated with colors. Most abundant from the Victorian era are figures and groups, but other pieces from busts to vases were made by numerous potteries in the U.S. and abroad. Reproductions have been produced for many years so care must be taken when seeking antique originals.

Animal covered dish, a realistic model of a chick in brown w/its broken shell on the domed green grass cover, white basketweave base (ILLUS. left)...........................$500.00

Animal covered dish, two realistic chicks, one in tan & the other in tan & black, w/their shells on the domed green grass cover, pale yellow basketweave base (ILLUS. right) 625.00

Dog on Basketweave Base Dish

Animal covered dish, dog reclining on a green blanket on the lid, the white shaggy animal w/brown & black head & tail, on an oval gold basketweave base, blue bisque maker's seal under the lid, France, 19th c., 5¾ x 8¼", 5⅜" h. (ILLUS.) $550.00

Bust of Victorian girl leaning on log, chin held in hand, playful flirting expression, deep molded sculpturing, Heubach "sunburst" mark, 6" h. 595.00

Bust of "Winter," modeled as a young girl w/lavender scarf on her head, wearing a sad look, on a socle base, signed "L. Kley," France, 9½" h. 350.00

Figure of a Bathing Beauty, Germany, 3½" l. 120.00

Figure of baby lying on its back w/toe in mouth, lying in glazed bathtub, Heubach mark, 4½" l., 3½" h. 395.00

Figure, Happifat boy, Germany, 3½" h. 375.00

Figure, Happifat girl, Germany, 3½" h. 375.00

Figure of baby & egg, artist-signed, Heubach, 5" h. 250.00

Figure of Oriental boy w/green umbrella, signed "Heubach," 5" h. ... 295.00

Figure of a monk, standing wearing brown robe, holding a snuff box in one hand & a pinch of snuff in the other, a jug behind him, 3" w., 7" h. ... 79.00

Figure of a young girl holding an oversized pipe, a basket on a bench beside her, a castle in the background, artist-signed, Germany, 7½" h. (tiny flake on basket) 175.00

Figure of a girl dressed in bunny costume, eyes turned to the side, hands outstretched, standing in front of large pink egg, marked "Heubach," 7½" h. 595.00

Figure of pouty character, intaglio eyes, No. 7602, Heubach "sunburst" mark, 10" h. 395.00

Figure of a young woman w/lovely serene face, holding a small book, marked "Heubach," 10¼" h. 295.00

Figure of a Blackamoor, the standing woman wearing a short blue tunic & a feathered turban, holding a basket her upraised hand, on a round socle of flowers to one side & a parrot on

Lady Blackamoor Figure

base, fine detailing & pastel coloring, France, 19th c., 3⅝" d., 11¼" h. (ILLUS.) 550.00

Figure of 18th century man, Heubach "sunburst" mark, 12" h. 375.00

Figure of little blond-haired boy holding rabbit in arms & by ear, marked "Heubach," 12" h. 395.00

Blue Boy Bisque Figure

Figure of a young boy standing and wearing a Van Dyke-style pale blue outfit w/lavender florals & gold trim, holding a feathered hat to his side, he carries posies in one hand, on a round base, 3¼" d., 12" h. (ILLUS.) 175.00

Figure of young boy wearing lavender suit & holding a monkey on his arm w/hand outstretched as if begging, Heubach mark, 13" h. 375.00

Figure of a young boy standing & carrying a basket, wearing a

Fine Bisque Figurines

lavender coat & short blue striped pants, his puffed blue hat w/pink ribbons, on a tan stone-work base, 5¼" d., 14" h. (ILLUS. right) 200.00

Figure of a toddler standing in a small attached bisque tub, signed "Heubach," 15" h. 1,795.00

Figure of a young woman w/hands behind her back, dressed in a peacock blue & pink costume w/lavish gold decorations, marked "2920, RW," 18" h. 1,295.00

Figures of little blond boy & girl standing in detailed brown & beige outfits, girl holding a shoe she wants the boy to buy, Germany, 11" h., pr. 295.00

Figures of a young blonde lady & gentleman, each wearing detailed pink costumes w/broad-brimmed hats, she carries a tambourine & he carries a small horn, French-style, 19th c., 3¾" d., 12¼" h., pr. (ILLUS. left) 295.00

Figures of a young lady w/a dog in her apron & a young man carrying a water dish & leash, in cream, blue, red, green & brown, Germany, 4½" w., 13" h., pr. 325.00

Figures of a blond-haired man & woman in pink & blue floral-decorated Empire era costumes, Germany, 18" h., pr. 475.00

Figure group, Dutch boy & girl in brown & green clothes, standing back to back, signed "Heubach," 5" h. 275.00

Figure group, a little girl holding two kittens in her skirt, a dog & cat flanking her on each side, 8½" h. 145.00

Game dish, cov., model of two birds on the cover, one w/wings down, the other w/wings out, basketweave base, 7½" d., 6¾" h. (wing on one bird restored) 100.00

Game Dish with Rabbits

Game dish, cover & underplate, the cover modeled w/two white rabbits on a grassy mound, round basket-weave base on a separate underplate, underplate minor chip, underplate 9" d., dish 7¼" d., 7¼" h., the set (ILLUS.) 470.00

Piano baby, lying on tummy holding dog in arm, Handwerck mark, 5½" h. 125.00

Piano baby, lying w/head on pillow & pacifier in its mouth, a dog reclining on its back, Handwerck mark, 6½" h. 175.00

Piano baby, crawling on tummy, wearing a white gown w/blue bow, head turned to side, Heubach "sunburst" mark, 8" h. 495.00

Snow baby & girl wearing a skirt on a sled 235.00

Snow baby on ice skates 210.00

Snow baby on skis 175.00

Snow baby riding a polar bear 185.00

Snow baby seated w/candleholder, 1" h. 165.00

Snow baby, girl w/brown Snow bear on sled 285.00

BLANC-DE-CHINE

This ware is a fine white Chinese porcelain with a rich clear glaze. It became popular in France in the early 18th century and remained popular in Europe and America through the 19th century. Fine figural pieces are most often found and the earlier examples bring the highest prices.

Figure of a Chinese Dignitary

Figure of Guanyin, modeled w/long flowing robes trailing over the rockworth plinth, the arms resting on the raised right knee, below the head w/gentle features & chignon piled high, now mounted as a lamp, China, 18th c., 11" h. (head repaired) $880.00

Figure of a Chinese dignitary, the man standing on a reticulated rockwork plinth wearing long flowing robes falling in elegant folds to reveal his feet, sashed around the waist w/a broad cloth incised w/circlet flowerheads & foliage, one exposed hand grasping a leafy peach fruit, the round head w/pierced chin, moustache, furrowed brows & small cap, all under an ivory-tinted glaze, China, Kangxi period (firing cracks, chips) 16⅛" h. (ILLUS.) 3,105.00

Figure of Guanyin, modeled standing in a slightly swayed position, wearing a beaded necklace & long robes falling in elegant folds toward the base & billowing out in back, leaving her hands exposed, her rounded face framed by a chignon piled high & secured w/a pin, the back w/an impressed mark, China, 18th c., 18¼" h. (crack, loss) 4,370.00

Figure group, a standing Dutchman wearing a tricorn hat & a buttoned coat & holding a fan, a standing youth beside him wearing similar coat & holding a baton, before them a flowering plant in a jardiniere beside a recumbent dog on a mound base, China, 1690-1710, 3⅝" h. (two chips on man's hat) 1,725.00

Blanc-de-Chine Vase

Vase, 7¼" h., dragon-type, shouldered ovoid body, the sides tapering to the slightly splayed base, molded in high-relief w/a dragon clambering around the tall, lipped neck, ivory-tinted clear glaze, China, Kangxi period (ILLUS.) 4,370.00

BLUE & WHITE POTTERY

Dutch Children Kissing Pitcher

The category of blue and white or blue and grey pottery includes a wide variety of pottery, earthenware and stoneware items widely produced in this country in the late 19th century right through the 1930s. Originally marketed as inexpensive wares, most pieces featured a white or grey body molded with a fruit, flower or geometric design and then trimmed with bands or splashes of blue to highlight the molded pattern. Pitchers, butter crocks and salt boxes are among the numerous items produced but other kitchenwares and chamber sets are also found. Values vary depending on the rarity of the embossed pattern and the depth of color of the blue trim; the darker the blue, the better. The pattern names used with our listings are taken from two references, Blue & White Stoneware, Pottery, Crockery by Edith Harbin (Collector Books, 1977) and Blue & White Stoneware by Kathryn McNerney (Collector Books, 1981).

Bowl, 9" d., embossed Apricots w/Honeycomb patt. ....$85.00 to 125.00

Butter crock, cov., embossed Butterfly patt. 96.00

Butter crock, cov., embossed Draped Windows patt., w/bail handle, 9" d., 8" h. ....165.00 to 195.00

Canister, cov., embossed Basketweave patt., "Tea" 150.00

Cuspidor, embossed Peacock (at Fountain) patt. 345.00

Mug, embossed Basketweave patt.....150.00

Mug, embossed Windy City patt., marked on bottom "Robinson Clay Pottery Co., Akron, Ohio," 5½" h. ....225.00 to 250.00

Pitcher, 7¾" h., 6½" d., cylindrical, embossed Peacock patt. 550.00

Pitcher, 8" h., embossed Grape Cluster on Trellis patt.......175.00 to 200.00

Pitcher, 8½" h., embossed Cow patt. ....150.00 to 175.00

Pitcher, 9" h., 6½" d., embossed Columns & Arches patt. 350.00

Pitcher, 9" h., embossed Good Luck (Swastika)......200.00 to 250.00

Pitcher, 9" h., 6" d., embossed Dutch Children Kissing patt. (ILLUS.) ....150.00 to 200.00

Pitcher, 9" h., embossed Windmill & Bush patt. 235.00

Pitcher, embossed Windy City (Fannie Flagg) patt., Robertson Co., Ohio ....375.00 to 425.00

Rolling pin, blue band decoration 150.00

Rolling pin, swirl design w/diffused blues 675.00

Wildflower Pattern Rolling Pin

Rolling pin, printed Wildflower patt., 7" l. (ILLUS.) 190.00

Salt box, cov., hanging-type, embossed Apricot patt. 200.00

Salt box, cov., hanging-type, embossed Eagle w/Shield & Arrows patt. 300.00

Soap dish, embossed Cat's Head patt. ....125.00 to 150.00

Soap dish, embossed Rose patt.........125.00

Toothpick holder, figural Swan patt. 60.00

BLUE RIDGE DINNERWARES

The small town of Erwin, Tennessee was the home of the Southern Potteries, Inc., originally founded by E.J. Owen in 1917 and first called the Clinchfield Pottery.

In the early 1920s Charles W. Foreman purchased the plant and he revolutionized the company's output, developing the popular line of hand-painted wares sold as "Blue Ridge" dinnerwares. Free-hand painted by women from the surrounding hills, these colorful dishes in many patterns, continued in production until the plant's closing in 1957.

Bonbon, flat shell-shape, Easter Parade patt. $50.00

Bonbon, flat shell-shape, French Peasant patt. 95.00

Bonbon, flat shell-shape, Nove Rose patt. 50.00

Bowl, cereal, Ribbon Plaid patt...............8.00

Bowl, cereal, Sunny patt., Colonial shape 8.00

Box, cov., Dimity patt., Sherman Lily shape 395.00

Butter pat, Valley Violet patt. 35.00

Cake plate, maple leaf-shaped, Calico patt. 40.00

Cake plate, maple leaf-shaped, Chintz patt. 75.00

Cake plate, maple leaf-shaped, Verna patt. 44.00

Candy box, cov., Rose Marie patt 128.00

Casserole, cov., Julie patt. 35.00

Celery dish, leaf-shaped, Chintz patt....46.00

Celery dish, leaf-shaped, French Peasant patt. 90.00

Celery dish, leaf-shaped, Rose of Sharon patt. 52.00

Celery dish, leaf-shaped, Serenade patt. 30.00

Celery dish, leaf-shaped, Summertime patt. 35.00

Cigarette box, cov., Sailboat patt..........50.00

Creamer & open sugar bowl, pedestal foot, French Peasant patt., pr. 240.00

Cup & saucer, demitasse, Emalee patt. 25.00

Cup & saucer, demitasse, Magic Carpet patt. 35.00

Cup & saucer, demitasse, Tulip Row patt. 25.00

Cup & saucer, Christmas Tree patt. 40.00

Cup & saucer, Valley Violet patt. 20.00

Egg cup, double, Valley Violet patt.......30.00

Egg plate, Rooster patt. 78.50

Pitcher, 6" h., vitreous china, figural chick, floral decoration 87.50

Pitcher, 8¼" h., vitreous china, Chintz patt., Milady shape 125.00

Pitcher, 7" h., Tralee Rose patt., Spiral shape 55.00

Pitcher, 8½" h., French Peasant patt., Milady shape 229.00

Pitcher, 8¾" h., earthenware, figural Betsy 150.00

Pitcher, jug-type, Paul Revere patt.....600.00

Plate, 8½" d., Blackbird patt., Songbirds series, Astor shape 75.00

Plates, 8½" d., County Fair patt., red rim, set of 4 ....35.00

Plate, 9½" d., Fruit Fantasy patt. 6.00

Plate, 9½" d., Grandmother's Garden patt. 6.00

Plate, 10" d., Christmas Tree patt.........65.00

Plate, 10" d., Mickey patt. 7.00

Platter, 15" l., Bluebell Bouquet patt.....16.00

Platter, 15" oval, French Peasant patt. 195.00

Platter, Thanksgiving Turkey patt. 165.00

Relish dish, vitreous china, heart-shaped, Buttons & Forget-Me-Nots patt. 30.00

Relish dish, deep, shell-shaped, Chintz patt. 60.00

Relish dish, leaf-shaped, French Peasant patt., 10" l. 87.50

Relish, shell-shaped, Nove Rose patt. 65.00

Relish dish, leaf-shaped w/loop handle, Serenade patt. 48.50

Salt & pepper shakers, Blossom Time patt., pr. 32.00

Salt & pepper shakers, Calico patt., Blossom Top shape, pr. 30.00

Salt & pepper shakers, figural chickens, model of a hen & rooster, hen 4" h., rooster 4¾" h., pr. 120.00

Salt & pepper shakers, Garden Lane patt., pr. 35.00

Salt & pepper shakers, Mallard patt., male 4" h., female 3½" h., pr. 250.00

Salt & pepper shakers, tall, footed, Paper Roses patt., pr. 40.00

Salt & pepper shakers, Valley Violet patt., Blossom Top shape, pr. 35.00

Smoking set: cov. cigarette box & four ashtrays; Rooster patt., 5 pcs. 150.00

Smoking set: cov. cigarette box & four ashtrays; Sailboat patt., 5 pcs. 150.00

Smoking set: cov. cigarette box & four ashtrays; Violets patt., 5 pcs.....135.00

Snack tray, three-section, Rose Parade patt., Martha shape 69.50

Sugar bowl, open, breakfast size, Valley Violet patt. 40.00

Sugar bowl, cov., w/pedestal base, French Peasant patt. 68.50

Teapot, cov., Crab Apple patt., Colonial shape, brown trim 60.00

Teapot, cov., Delta Daisy patt., Colonial shape 50.00

Teapot, cov., Flounce patt., Colonial shape 50.00

Teapot, cov., Kate patt., Colonial shape 50.00

Teapot, cov., Spiderweb patt. 50.00

Teapot, cov., Sunbright patt. 75.00

Toast plate, cov., Valley Violet patt. 85.00

Vase, 8" h., boot-shaped, Gladys patt. 95.00

Vase, 9" h., ruffled rim, tapered, Delphine patt. 60.00

Vegetable bowl, open, round, French Peasant patt. 67.50

BOCH FRERES

Boch Freres Jardiniere

The Belgian firm, founded in 1841 and still in production, first produced stoneware art pottery of mediocre quality, attempting to upgrade their wares through the years. In 1907, Charles Catteau became the art director of the pottery and slowly the influence of his work was absorbed by the artisans surrounding him. All through the 1920s wares were decorated in distinctive Art Deco designs and are now eagerly sought along with the hand-thrown gourd-form vessels coated with earthtone glazes that were produced during the same time. Almost all Boch Freres pottery is marked, but the finest wares also carry the signature of Charles Catteau in addition to the pottery mark.

Jardiniere, wide ovoid body w/flared mouth, decorated w/a wide band of stylized cream blossoms outlined in black against a shaded brown opaque-glazed ground, cobalt blue & cream highlights, Gres Keramis marks, ca 1890, 11" d., 9⅜" h. (ILLUS.)....$825.00

Pitcher, 4½" h., white w/black & red geometric decoration 35.00

Vase, 6¼" h., 4¾" d., wide ovoid shouldered body w/a short flaring neck, decorated w/a band of stylized antelope in blue & green against an ivory crackled background, marked 302.50

Vase, 6½" h., ovoid body tapering to straight collar, decorated w/h.p. Art Deco style flowers 240.00

Vase, 6¾" h ., 4" d., semi-ovoid shouldered body w/short neck, incised yellow, orange & green fruit w/brown foliage against a thick white crackled ground, marked "MADE IN BELGIUM, BOCH Fes, LA LOUVIERE, FABRICATION BELGE, D. 745, ct." 192.50

Vase, 9½" h., stylized leaves in matte yellow, blue & white on a black ground, designed by Charles Catteau, artist-signed, stamp mark, ca. 1925 ....467.50

Vase, 12⅝" h., slender ovoid body tapering to a small neck w/widely flared rim, decorated w/stripes of stylized leaf & berry bands up the sides in safron yellow, ochre & white against a ground of alternating cobalt blue & copper green horizontal bands, designed by Charles Catteau, stamped company mark & facsimile signature, ca. 1930 ....1,035.00

Vase, 12⅞" h., elongated ovoid, decorated on four sides w/stylized bouqets of flowers in shades of blue & highlighted by yellow & rust on a cream crackle ground, outlined in black, impressed & stamped marks, ca. 1925 ....357.50

Boch Freres Polar Bear Vase

Vase, 16" h., shouldered ovoid body w/a short wide neck, painted w/five panels depicting a polar bear in various poses, the base & neck decorated w/waves & spots in greenish grey against an amber & brown ground, painted signature "Ch. Catteau" & marked "B.F.K.," inscribed "1020 B Gres" (ILLUS.) 6,900.00

Vase, 18" h., tall baluster-shaped body, crackled glaze decorated w/floral medallions in greens & blues, designed by Charles Catteau, printed company mark & painted "Ch. Catteau MADE IN BELGIUM" 230.00

BOEHM PORCELAINS

Although not antique, Boehm porcelain sculptures have attracted much interest as Edward Marshall Boehm excelled in hard porcelain sculptures. His finest creations, inspired by the beauties of nature, are in the forms of birds and flowers. Since his death in 1969, his work has been carried on by his wife at the Boehm Studios in Trenton, New Jersey. In 1971, an additional studio was opened in Malvern, England, where bone porcelain sculptures are produced. We list both limited and non-limited editions of Boehm.

ANIMALS

Boehm Hunter Horse

Chipmunk, 1980, 3" w., 3¼" h. $65.00

Colt, No. 41023, all-white 400.00

Dog, American Cocker, brown & white, No. 104, 1951-59, 6½" h..............................225.00 to 250.00

Dog, Poodle, reclining, white bisque, green collar, 1959-61, No. 133, 5" l. 450.00

Dog, Whippet, female, bisque, No. 120, 1954-61, 7¾" h. 1,000.00

Dog, Whippet, male, bisque, decorated, No. 120, 1954-61, 7¾" h. 1,000.00

Horse, Hunter, No. 203, 1952-62, 14 x 14" (ILLUS.) 1,500.00

Lioness, glazed, decorated, No. 508, 1952-59, 15" l., 6" h. 2,500.00

Panda, Giant Panda Cub, reclining on bamboo, No. 400-47, introduced in 1975, 6½ x 8"..................................695.00

Percheron Stallion, white, galzed decoration of ribbons & roses, No. 201, 1951-59, 12" l., 9½" h.....2,500.00

Black-Capped Chickadee

BIRDS

Baby Blue Jay, No. 436, introduced in 1957, 4½" h.................175.00 to 225.00

Baby Crested Flycatcher, No. 458E, 1962-72, 5" h. 239.00

Baby Woodthrush, No. 444, 1958- , 4¼" h. 90.00

Black-Capped Chickadee, perched on holly leaves, No. 438, 1957-73, 9" h. (ILLUS.) 450.00

Black-Throated Blue Warbler, Male on Mountain Laurel, No. 441, 1958-66, 5" l., 10½" h..................................1,500.00

Blue Grosbeak w/Oak Leaves, RPC No. 1078-02, 1967-76, 11" h.........1,000.00

Blue Jays on Strawberries, No. 1057-01, 1962-66, male 14" h., female 12" h., pr...........................8,000.00

Bobolink w/Corn Stubble, No. 475, 1964-71, 8" l., 14½" h. 1,250.00

California Quails, male & female, No. 433, 1957-68, female 7½" h., male 8½" h., pr. 2,000.00

Cardinals, Male & Female w/grapes, No. 415, 1955-66, 15" h., pr. 2,100.00

Catbird w/Hyacinth, No. 483, 1965-73, 7½" l., 14½" h. ....1,200.00 to 1,600.00

Crested Flycatcher on Sweet Gum, No. 488, 1967-74, 18½" h. 2,000.00

Downy Woodpeckers on Trumpet Vine, No. 427, 1957-69, 5½" l., 13" h. ....1,400.00 to 1,600.00

Fledgling Canadian Warbler w/Monarch Butterfly, No. 490, 1967-73, 8½" h. 1,100.00

Golden Crowned Kinglets w/Oriental Poppies. No. 419, 1956-68, 13" h. ....1,000.00 to 1,200.00

Goldfinches on Scottish Thistle, No. 457, 1961-68, 5" w., 11½" h. 1,000.00

Green Jays with Black Persimmon, 1966-74, 18" h., pr. 1,800.00

Hooded Mergansers, No. 496, 1968-76, 10½" h., pr. ....2,000.00 to 2,500.00

Hummingbird, Male on Cactus, No. 440, 1958-75, 8½" h. 398.00

Jenny Wren, bird on rocks w/white flowers, Malvern Studio, England, No. 2001, introduced in 1971, 4 x 6" ....350.00 to 450.00

Boehm Kestrels

Kestrels, Male & Female, No. 492, 1968-78, male 14" h., female 16½" h., pr. (ILLUS.) 2,100.00

Lesser Prairie Chickens, No. 464, 1962-74, 10" h., pr. 1,700.00

Meadowlark w/Mushroom, No. 435, 1957-64, 7½ x 8½" 1,750.00

Nonpareil Buntings on Flowering Raspberry, No. 446, 1958-67, 5 x 8½" 650.00

Northern Water Thrush w/Ferns & Cladonia, No. 490, 1967-73, 10½" h. 700.00

Oven Bird w/Indian Pipe, No. 400-04, 1970-75, 7 x 11" 1,500.00

Owls on Books, No. 453, 1960-70, decorated eyes & beak only, 9" h., pr. 500.00

Parula Warblers w/Morning Glories, No. 484, 1965-73, 9" w., 14½" h. 1,800.00

Prothonotary Warblers, Female w/Eggs & Fledgling, No. 445, 1958 - discontinued, 5½" h. 400.00

Red-Breasted Grosbeaks, bisque, No. 405, 1952-59, 6" h., pr. 750.00

Red-Breasted Grosbeaks, glazed, decorated, No. 405, 1952-59, 6" h., pr. 1,500.00

Red-Winged Blackbirds on Cattails, Male & Female, No. 426, 1957-64, 17" h., pr. 3,500.00

Road Runner w/Horned Toad, No. 493, 1968-76, 10½" l., 14" h. ....2,000.00 to 2,200.00

Rufous Hummingbirds on Icelandic Poppy, 1966-73, 9" w., 14" h. 1,000.00

Song Sparrows w/Tulips, No. 421, 1956-60, 9 x 17", pr. 22,000.00

Sugarbirds, No. 460, 1961-66, 11 x 25½" pr. 8,000.00

Tree Sparrow, No. 468, 1963-75, 8" h. ....300.00 to 350.00

Tufted Titmice w/Sumac, No. 482, 1965-72, 6" w., 13" h. ....1,000.00 to 1,250.00

Tumbler Pigeons, No. 416, 1955-70, 10½" h., pr. 600.00

Varied Buntings w/Crown Imperial, No. 481, 1965-74, 14 x 18" 3,000.00

Western Bluebirds w/Wild Azaleas, No. 1088-01, 1969-76, 12½ x 20" 5,000.00

Woodcock, No. 413, 1954-66, 10" h. 1,000.00

Young American Bald Eagle, No. 498B, 1969-74, 6 x 9½" 795.00

MISCELLANEOUS FIGURALS

Apollo, No. RPC-711-02, Babyhood of the Gods series, 1953-59, 7½" h. 250.00

Immaculate Conception, No. 614, 1956-60, 10" h. 300.00

Letter opener, porcelain eagle, made for 1976 Bicentennial 95.00

Madonna (La Pieta), undecorated bisque, No. RPC 605-02, artist-signed, 11" h. ....125.00 to 175.00

Pigtail Angel, bisque, No. 604, 1953-57, 4½" h. 100.00

Romantic Moments, ballerina, bisque, 11¾" h. 80.00

St. Maria Goretti, glazed, decorated, No. 608, 1952, 6½" h. 500.00

BOW PORCELAIN

Early Bow Figure

The Bow China Works was established in London about 1747 by Thomas Frye and was in operation for approximately three decades. Some fine porcelain was produced but attribution is often difficult.

Early Bow marks included an incised or painted anchor or a painted crescent mark.

Candlesticks, figural, modeled affronté, each as a Cupid w/rose, yellow & iron-red wings, wearing colorful floral garlands & striped rose or patterned yellow drapery, kneeling beside a brown-spotted recumbent or seated hound & a blue & gold quiver or torch amid flowers & leaves on the turquoise, rose & gilt-trimmed scroll-footed base, & reaching toward a colorful bird perched on a flowering branch of a small, lush bocage behind, surmounted by pierced foliate bobeches & candle nozzles trimmed in underglaze-blue & gold, ca. 1765, Anchor & Dagger marks, 9¼" & 9⅜" h., pr. (chips on bocages, bobeches reattached, each candle nozzle w/a repaired chip, left wing repaired, firing flaw in left wrist) $1,035.00

Figure of a Blackamoor, standing wearing a yellow & white turban (plume missing), a white shirt (neck repaired), a purple-edged yellow jacket sashed in iron-red, a blue skirt, pink leggings & yellow boots, holding an iron-red & green-sprigged teabowl & saucer on a scalloped tazza (tiny chips), standing amid green leaves (florettes missing) on a puce-trimmed scroll-molded tripod base, based on a Meissen model, ca. 1760, 6 9/16" h. (ILLUS.) 2,013.00

Figure of a boy dancing, wearing a gilt-edged purple hat, a gilt-edged white collar & purple-laced yellow doublet over a burgundy jacket, white breeches striped in yellow, turquoise, rose & burgundy, & iron-red shoes, his hands behind his back above a tree stump base applied w/colorful floral clusters & green leaves, & his right foot raised above the rose- and gilt-trimmed tall scroll-footed base, ca. 1765, 7¾" h. (repair on hat, right arm repaired, chips on leaves) 920.00

Figure of Minerva, the standing woman wearing a gilt-edged blue helmet (plumes missing), an underglaze-blue cuirass patterned w/gilt scalework, tied w/an iron-red sash & pendant w/gilt-fringed iron-red, yellow & turquoise ribbons, a rose-lined purple skirt & yellow & turquoise gaiters, modeled w/her left hand resting on a gilt-edged pale blue shield molded w/a lady's mask & standing amid colorful florettes (one missing) & green leaves on a rose-marbleized diamond-shaped base, iron-red Anchor & Dagger mark & an "X" in underglaze-blue, ca. 1760, 6¾" h. 1,320.00

Sauceboat, fluted body & loop handle, decorated in puce, yellow, blue & green w/loose bouquets & scattered sprigs, the interior w/scattered sprigs beneath a puce border, ca. 1765, 7⅜" l. (minute rim chips, chip on footring)....................................462.00

Sweetmeat dish, figural, modeled as a seated Turkish lady wearing a tall purple headdress, a yellow-lined coat patterned w/iron-red, blue & green floral sprigs, a white-sashed rose robe, iron-red & purple striped white pantaloons & iron-red shoes, seated on a cairn & holding to her side a large brown-edged shell-form bowl decorated on its interior w/a floral spray & sprig, above a green 'mossy' mound applied w/iron-red, salmon & purple shells & coral, ca. 1760, 5⅝" h. (left shoe missing) 1,380.00

Vases, 9⅜" h., tall hexagonal baluster-form, painted in a Kakiemon palette of iron-red, blue, green, yellow, black & gold on three sides w/a phoenix bird perched on a flowering branch, & on the alternating sides w/a stylized flowering peony plant, the neck w/floral sprigs, the slightly flared foot w/an iron-red band border, ca. 1755, pr. (repaired neck chips, border band touched up).........................6,325.00

BRAYTON LAGUNA POTTERY

Brayton Mammy Cookie Jar

Durlin E. Brayton began his operation in Laguna Beach, California in 1927. After his marriage a short time later to Ellen Webster Grieve, who also became his business partner, the venture became a successful endeavor. One of the most popular lines was the Childrens' series *which featured a rubber stamp-like mark with the first name of the child followed underneath with a line which separates the words "Brayton Pottery." Both white clay and pink clay were used during Brayton's production. More than 150 people, including approximately twenty designers, were employed by Brayton. Sometimes on items too small for a full mark, designers would incise their initials. It was not until after World War II and the mass importation of pottery products into the United States that Brayton's business declined. Operations ceased in 1968.*

Brayton Laguna Pottery

COPYRIGHT 1943 BY BRAYTON LAGUNA POTTERY

BRAYTON'S

Ashtray, w/one cigarette rest, round, turquoise glaze, incised 'Brayton Laguna Pottery,' 4¼" d. $12.00

Candleholder, figural, Blackamoor in seated position, colorful glazes w/lots of gold trim, designed by Ruth Peabody, 5" h. 75.00

Cookie jar, figural black Mammy, bright blue dress, white apron w/yellow, black, green & blue trim, red bandana on head, yellow earrings, marked examples only (being reproduced), 12⅝" h. (ILLUS.) 425.00

Creamer & open sugar bowl, round, eggplant glaze, incised mark, 2½" h., pr. 27.00

Figure of a black baby w/diaper, sitting, 3¾" h. 25.00

Figure of a black baby w/diaper, crawling, 4¼" l..................................30.00

Figure. Childrens' series, "Ann," girl seated w/legs apart, knees bent, 4" h...100.00

Figure, Childrens' series, "Butch," boy standing w/present under each arm, short pants w/suspenders, 7½" h.......70.00

Figure, Childrens' series, "Dorothy," girl seated w/legs together & straight, hands by her sides, hair w/pigtails & tied w/ribbons, 4¼" l., 4" h...95.00

Figure, Childrens' series, "Ellen," girl standing w/pigtails & a hat tied at neck, arms bent & palms forward, one leg slightly twisted, 7¼" h............75.00

Figure, Childrens' series, "Emily," girl standing & holding purse which sometimes has her name on it, & w/a hair bow usually the same color as her socks, 7" h. 65.00

Figure, Childrens' series, "Eugene," boy standing, wearing short pants & shirt w/hankie pinned on, arms behind back holding flower, 6¾" h.....65.00

Figure, Childrens' series, "Ida," girl standing w/one arm wrapped around full-sized doll, both w/matching hats, 6¾" h..50.00

Figure, Childrens' series, "Jon," boy standing & carrying basket in one hand, rooster in other, 8¼" h. 75.00

Brayton Laguna "Millie" Figure

Figure, Childrens' series, "Millie," girl bent over w/legs apart, head between legs, scarce, 3¾" h. (ILLUS.) 155.00

Figure, Childrens' series, "Miranda," girl standing, wearing coat & hat, decorations on shoes, many assorted glazes available, sometimes unmarked, 6½" h. 55.00

Figure, Childrens' series, "Pat," girl standing, freckles on her face, wearing a hat w/tie around neck & short dress, holding full-sized doll in back between her legs, 7" h. (hard to find) 85.00

Figure, Childrens' series, "Petunia," black girl standing w/basket of flowers, wearing a pinafore, 6¼" h...130.00

Figure, Childrens' series, "Sambo," black boy standing w/chicken under one arm, 7½" h. 145.00

Figure, Gay Nineties lady, holding up her dress w/one hand, umbrella in other hand, ruffled flowing skirt, hat, high-top shoes, ca. 1930, 9½" h. 105.00

Figure, "Tweedle Dee," character from Alice in Wonderland, non-Disney, 3" h..28.00

Figures of dice players w/dice, black boys on hands & knees, 4¾" l., 3½" h., set of 3................................195.00

Flower holder, figural, "Francis," girl standing & holding small planter in front, blonde hair w/snood & flower, 8" h..35.00

Model of a bear, seated, light blue, underglaze mark 'Brayton's Laguna, Cal.,' Model No. T-1, 3½" h...............18.00

Model of a duck, textured bisque body, glossy glazed green face, Model No. 4138, 5½" l., 5" h. 35.00

Model of a swan, grey & white glossy glaze, marked 'Copyright 1940 By Brayton Laguna Pottery,' 6" l., 4½" h...20.00

Planter, figural, Dutch girl pushing a cart, girl w/yellow hair, blue dress, white apron & hat, black shoes, grey cart, ca. 1950, 8" h............................15.00

Salt & pepper shakers, figural man & woman, he w/hands in his pockets, she w/arms folded across her waist, he wears a brown jacket & pants trimmed w/yellow & white hearts & flowers, she wears a white scarf over her head & white apron, touches of yellow & green hearts & flowers, both w/brown stained faces & hands, Model No. K26, 6½" h., pr...45.00

Tile, decorated w/a Mexican man taking a siesta under tree w/cacti nearby, blue, green, white, incised mark, ca. 1928, 6½" sq. 95.00

BUFFALO POTTERY

Buffalo Pottery was established in 1902 in Buffalo, New York, to supply pottery for the Larkin Company. Most desirable today is Deldare Ware, introduced in 1908 in two patterns, "The Fallowfield Hunt" and "Ye Olden Days," which featured central English scenes and a continuous border. Emerald Deldare, introduced in 1911, was banded with stylized flowers and geometric designs and had varied central scenes, the most popular being from "The Tours of Dr. Syntax." Reorganized in 1940, the company now specializes in hotel china.

DELDARE

Deldare Candleholder

Bowl, cereal, 6½" d., The Fallowfield Hunt $275.00

Bowl, fruit, 9" d., 3¾" h., Ye Village Tavern.............................450.00 to 500.00

Bowl, fruit, 9" d., The Fallowfield Hunt - The Death.....................................550.00

Bowl, soup, 9" d., The Fallowfield Hunt 495.00

Bowl, soup, 9" d., Ye Olden Days - Ye Village Street.............................475.00

Candleholder, shield-back, Village Scenes, 7" h. (ILLUS.) 895.00

Candlesticks, Ye Olden Days - Ye Village Street, 9½" h., pr. 1,000.00

Card tray, tab handles, Mr. Pickwick Addresses the Club, 7" d. 900.00

Card tray, The Fallowfield Hunt - The Return, 7¾" d............350.00 to 375.00

Card tray, Ye Olden Days - Ye Village Street, 7¾" d..................495.00

Creamer, hexagonal, The Fallowfield Hunt - Breaking Cover 200.00

Cup & saucer, The Fallowfield Hunt - The Return.......................................250.00

Cup & saucer, Ye Olden Days - Ye Village Street..............250.00 to 300.00

Dresser tray, Dancing Ye Minuet, 1909, 9 x 12"....................................650.00

Fern bowl, Ye Olden Days - Ye Village Street, 8" d. 675.00

Hair receiver, cov., Ye Village Street..............350.00 to 400.00

Humidor, cov., bulbous, There was an Old Sailor, etc., 8" h. 1,250.00

Humidor, cov., octagonal, Ye Lion Inn, artist-signed, 1909, 7" h. 800.00

Mug, The Fallowfield Hunt, 2½" h...............................500.00 to 550.00

Fallowfield Hunt Deldare Mug

Mug, The Fallowfield Hunt, 3½" h. (ILLUS.) ....350.00 to 400.00

Mug, The Fallowfield Hunt, artist-signed, 4½" h. ....450.00 to 500.00

Mug, Ye Olden Days - Ye Lion Inn, 4½" h...............................400.00 to 425.00

Nut bowl, Ye Lion Inn, 1909, 8" d., 3¼" h..700.00

Pin tray, Ye Olden Days, 3½ x 6¼"..250.00

Pitcher, 6" h., octagonal, The Fallowfield Hunt, artist-signed, ca. 1908 ....775.00

Pitcher, 6" h., octagonal, Their Manner of Telling Stories - Which He Returned with a Curtsey ....450.00 to 550.00

Pitcher, 7" h., The Fallowfield Hunt - Breaking Cover................450.00 to 500.00

Pitcher, 7" h., octagonal, To Spare an Old, Broken Soldier - To Advise Me in a Whisper, 1923...........550.00 to 600.00

Pitcher, 8" h., octagonal, The Fallowfield Hunt - The Return........................700.00 to 800.00

Deldare Octagonal Pitcher

Pitcher, 9" h., octagonal, With a Cane Superior Air - This Amazed Me (ILLUS.) 775.00

Pitcher, tankard, 12½" h., The Fallowfield Hunt - The Hunt Supper ....900.00 to 950.00

Deldare Tankard Pitcher

Pitcher, tankard, 12½" h., Vicar of Wakefield, All you have to do to teach the Dutchman English - The Great Controversy (ILLUS.) ....1,000.00 to 1,500.00

Plaque, pierced to hang, The Fallowfield Hunt - Breakfast at the Three Pigeons, 12" d................................600.00 to 650.00

Plate, 7¼" d., Ye Village Street, 1908................................125.00 to 175.00

Plate, 8¼" d., Ye Town Crier 175.00

Plate, 9½" d., Ye Olden Times, artist-signed, 1909 ....175.00 to 200.00

Plate, 10" d., The Fallowfield Hunt - Breaking Cover, artist-signed 325.00

Plate, 10" d., Ye Village Gossips ....150.00 to 175.00

Plate, chop, 14" d., An Evening at Ye Lion Inn, artist-signed, ca. 1908 ....700.00 to 800.00

Plate, chop, 14" d., The Fallowfield Hunt - The Start ....900.00 to 950.00

Powder jar, cov., Ye Village Street ....450.00 to 500.00

Relish tray, Ye Olden Times, artist-signed, 1908, 6½ x 12" 695.00

Sugar bowl, cov., The Fallowfield Hunt - Breaking Cover .....250.00 to 300.00

Teapot, cov., The Fallowfield Hunt - Breaking Cover ....350.00 to 400.00

Teapot, cov., Scenes of Village Life in Ye Olden Days, 5¾" h. ....400.00 to 450.00

Tea tile, The Fallowfield Hunt - Breaking Cover, artist-signed, 6" d..295.00

Deldare Tea Tray

Tea tray, Heirlooms, 1908, 10½ x12" (ILLUS.) ....700.00 to 750.00

EMERALD DELDARE

Bowl, fruit, 9" d., 3¾" h., Dr. Syntax Reading His Tour.............850.00 to 900.00

Bowl, fruit & undertray, octagonal, Art Nouveau floral & geometric designs, tray 14" w., bowl 10" w., 6¾" h., 2 pcs................................1,450.00

Card tray, handled, Dr. Syntax Robbed of his Property, 7" d. 550.00

Cup & saucer, Dr. Syntax at Liverpool, 1911 ....650.00

Humidor, cov., Doctor Syntax returned Home, artist-signed, 1911, 6¼" d., 7" h. 1,750.00

Mug, Dr. Syntax scenes, "I give to the law that are owing, etc.," 2¼" h........795.00

Mug, Dr. Syntax again filled up his glass ..., 4¼" h. ....675.00 to 700.00

Plate, 7¼" d., Dr. Syntax Soliloquising....................................595.00

Plate, 8¼" d., Art Nouveau stylized geometric designs............................465.00

Plate, 8½" d., Dr. Syntax - Misfortune at Tulip Hall ....450.00 to 550.00

Plate, 10" d., Dr. Syntax Making a Discovery 1,100.00

MISCELLANEOUS

Campbell Kids Feeding Dish

Bowl, 4" d., 2¼" h., Blue Willow patt., design on interior & exterior.................5.00

Bowl, 5" d., Blue Willow patt...................5.00

Christmas plate, 1955...........................48.00

Christmas plate, 1960...........................35.00

Christmas plate, 1962, designed for the exclusive use of Hample Equipment Company, Elmira, New York 250.00

Creamer, Abino Ware.........................635.00

Cup & saucer, Blue Willow patt., 1905..35.00

Cup & saucer, Gaudy Willow patt.........80.00

Feeding dish, Campbell Kids decoration, Grace Drayton design, 7¾" d. (ILLUS.)..................................85.00

Fish set, platter & six fish plates, artist-signed 295.00

Mug, Abino Ware, sailboat decoration, ca. 1912, 4¼" h.............395.00

Mug, Abino Ware, windmill & boat decoration, artist-signed, 1913, 4¼" h...875.00

Pitcher, jug-type, 6" h., The Buffalo Hunt (ILLUS.)...................................325.00

Buffalo Hunt Pitcher

Pitcher, jug-type, 6" h., Holland patt., scenes of Dutch children around the body, rural landscape band around the rim 345.00

Pitcher, jug-type, 6" h., Whaling City, souvenir of New Bedford, Massachusetts, 1907.......................650.00

Pitcher, 7" h., jug-type, Gaudy Willow patt..335.00

Pitcher, jug-type, 7½" h., George Washington, blue decoration, gold trim, 1905...565.00

Buffalo Sailors Pitcher

Pitcher, 9¼" h., waisted tankard shape, two sailors on one side, lighthouse on rocky shore reverse, blue decoration, 1906 (ILLUS.)........500.00

Plate, 7½" d., commemorative, Faneuil Hall, Boston, blue-green 30.00

Plate, 8¼" d., Gaudy Willow patt., ca. 1908 ....90.00

Plate, 9¼" d., Arts & Crafts style stylized rose decoration in cobalt blue on a white ground, ink stamped "BUFFALO POTTERY CO." (minor surface nicks)....................................77.00

Plate, 9" d., scalloped rim, The Gunner scene, deep blue-green 125.00

Plate, 10" d., Abino Ware, windmill scene 925.00

Plate, 12" d., Rouge Ware, Breakfast at the Three Pigeons, 1930s............595.00

Platter, 12" l., Lune Ware, Cairo patt., blue 55.00

Platter, 11 x 14" rectangle, buffalo hunting scene 425.00

Platter, 14" l., Blue Willow patt., oval 145.00

Relish dish, Vienna patt.......................34.00

Tray, Abino Ware, scenic decoration of windmill & boat, artist-signed, 1911, 10½ x 13¾" .....1,000.00 to 1,500.00

CALIENTE POTTERY

Caliente Dancing Lady

Virgil K. Haldeman opened his pottery in Burbank, California in 1933. He created satin matte glazes and blended colors while Andrew Hazelhurst, chief designer until 1941, used his talents to produce a variety of merchandise. The business moved to Calabasas, California in 1947 and closed in 1953.

Early pieces have a strong Catalina Pottery influence, probably because Virgil Haldeman worked about three years for that company. Molded pieces (numbers under 100), hand-made pieces (200 numbers), figures, mostly animals and fowl (300 numbers), dancing girls (400 numbers), a continuation of hand-made pieces (500-549), and molded pieces with roses added (550 and over numbers) were created. Since incised numbers are on many of the Caliente pieces, this system aids in their identification. Almost without exception, Caliente items have a solid bottom. A few dancing girls, especially the #401, have been reproduced. The reproductions have a hole *in the bottom, are lighter weight and many have hand-painted flowers on the dresses.*

Caliente used several marks over the years with the "Made in California" mark in block letters the most commonly found. A mold number was included on many of the pieces. Paper labels were also used.

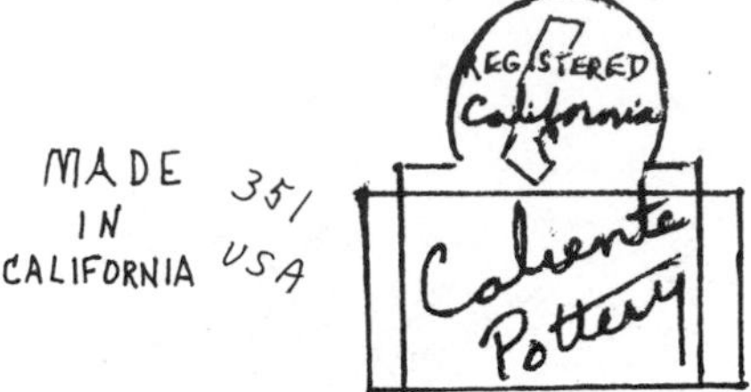

Candleholder, model of a lily pad, pale green glaze, 5" l., 2" h. $10.00

Figure of a dancing lady, head tilted, back arched, left arm holding up edge of her dress, right arm across body touching left elbow, deep green glaze, script incised on white clay "Calif. 401," 6¾" h.......................40.00

Figure of a dancing girl in bloomers, a scarf in each hand & draping to the floor, head bent & slightly tilted, face features indistinct, left hand resting on waist, Model No. 406, hard-to-find, 6½" h. (ILLUS.) 65.00

Dancing Lady on Tiptoes

Figure of a dancing girl on base, right elbow pointed upward w/hand resting under chin, left leg bent back w/left hand holding up edge of her dress, right leg straight w/foot on tiptoes, ivory glaze, face features indistinct, weighs less than 4 ounces, Model No. 400, 4½" h. (ILLUS.) 60.00

Flower frog, model of a sailboat, white w/light blue glaze, Model No. 73, 5" h. 25.00

Caliente Deer

Model of a deer, standing, four legs separated & on an oval base, right front leg slightly bent, ivory glaze w/five tan brushed spots on body, Model No. 351, 5" h. (ILLUS.) 26.00

Model of a goose, head up, light green, Model No.303, 4¼" h. 15.00

Model of a Scottie dog & fire hydrant, dog standing w/left rear leg raised, tail up, black glaze, Model No. 311, 3½" h.; hydrant, black glaze, Model No. 352, 3½" h., set of two.................55.00

Vase, 3½" h., 3¼" d., globular shape, trefoil opening, in-relief leaves on both sides of a single rose 34.00

Vase, 5¾" h., Art Deco design, rectangular base w/two buttresses on each side flaring upward to a thin lip 30.00

CALIFORNIA FAIENCE

Chauncey R. Thomas and William V. Bragdon organized what was to become the California Faience pottery in 1916, in Berkeley, California. Originally named after its owners, it later became The Tile Shop, finally adopting the California Faience name about 1924. Always a small operation whose output was a simple style of art pottery, primarily designed for the florist shop trade, it also made colorfully decorated tiles. During the mid-1920s, California Porcelain was produced by this firm for the West Coast Porcelain Manufacturers of Millbrae, California. The great Depression halted art pottery production and none was produced after 1930 although some tiles were made for the Chicago World's Fair about 1932. Collectors now seek out these somewhat scarce pieces that always bear the incised mark of California Faience.

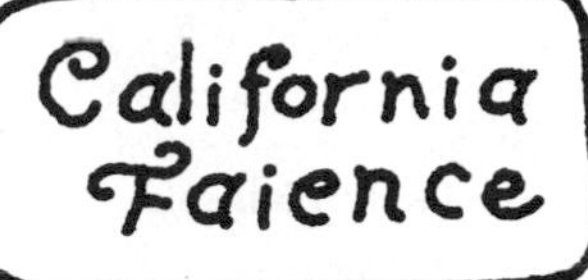

Bowl, 6" d., 2½" h., fluted, glossy blue over turquoise glaze exterior, turquoise glaze interior $165.00

Tea tile, decorated w/large stylized yellow poppies against a turquoise ground w/a black framing band, worked in the squeezebag technique w/a fine matte veined glaze, impressed "California Faience," paper label "CALIFORNIA FAIENCE MADE AT THE TILE SHOP - BERKELEY," 5½" d. 880.00

Tea tiles, round, each decorated in the center w/a stylized basket of flowers in blue, green, deep red, pink & yellow, one basket against a black ground the other against a dark blue ground, one w/a wide border band of dark blue, the other w/a wide yellow band, glossy & matte glazes, matted & framed, each 5¼" d., pr.................................660.00

Vase, 5½" h., bulbous, glossy turquoise glaze 185.00

Vase, 6" h., decorated w/doves, relief-molded arrows, turquoise glaze.......750.00

Vase, 8 x 9", persimmon decoration on two-colored blue glaze................795.00

CANTON PORCELAIN

This ware has been decorated for nearly two centuries in factories near Canton, China. Intended for export sale, much of it was originally inexpensive blue-and-white hand decorated ware. Late 18th and early 19th century pieces are superior to later ones and fetch higher prices.

Basket & undertray, deep oval flaring reticulated sides, on a conforming undertray, 19th c., basket 10¾" l., 2 pcs. (ILLUS. of part)....................$920.00

Canton Basket

Bowl, 7¼" d., shallow scalloped sides, 19th c. 550.00

Creamer, baluster-form body on a circular foot, 19th c., 3½" h. 207.00

Dinner service: fifty 7¾" & 9¾" plates, four small dishes & 14 soup spoons; each piece decorated w/variations of the river landscape scene w/pagodas, figures, bridges & boats, 19th c., 68 pcs. (chips, hairlines) 2,588.00

Dish, cov., almond-shaped w/flared sides & flat rim, low domed cover w/knob finial, faintly marked on base "China," 10½" l. (minor edge flakes) 93.50

Dish, elongated oval w/shaped sides, 10¾" l. 495.00

Dish, oval, 11⅜" l. 302.50

Garden seats, barrel-shaped, painted on the front & back w/a landscape scene w/sailboats & pagodas in a river within a rectangular panel flanked on the sides by pierced cash medallions surrounded by prunus blossoms & tied w/whorl-patterned ribbons between horizontal bands of molded bosses & undulating borders forming panels of beribboned objects around the rim or prunus branches around the foot, the top w/a similar river scene interrupted by another pierced cash medallion within a prunus-patterned roundel & the rim w/dashed scallop & trellis diaper bands, 19th c., 19¼" h., pr. (some fritting & firing flaws) 9,200.00

Hot water dish, round, 19th c., 8½" d...132.00

Pitcher, 7½" h., wide ovoid body tapering to a flaring rim w/a wide arched spout, slender highly arched strap handle, 19th c. 935.00

Pitcher, 15¾" h., footed tall ovoid body tapering to a wide arched spout, long arched C-scroll handle, 19th c. 1,155.00

Platter, 12½" l., rectangular w/cut corners 385.00

Platter, 12¾" oval, w/indented well & tree in the center, 19th c. 605.00

Platter, 16¾" l. oblong octagon, orange peel glaze (edge chips) 330.00

Platter, 17¼" oval, 19th c...................495.00

Sauce tureen, cov., oval-form w/a pair of rabbit's head end handles, 19th c., 6¼" l. 322.00

Canton Sauce Tureen

Sauce tureen, cover & undertray, the oblong squared deep body w/boar's head handles, the low domed cover w/stem finial, on a conforming dished undertray, 19th c., tureen 6½" l. (ILLUS. of tureen) 550.00

Serving dish, cov., oblong almond-shaped w/a flanged rim, low domed cover w/pine cone finial, 19th c., 11¼" l...467.50

Soup tureen, cov., rectangular, 19th c., 12¼" l. 1,265.00

Sugar bowl, cov., wide cylindrical body w/twisted loop handles, the domed cover w/a fruit finial, 19th c., 6" h...495.00

Teapot, cov., bulbous tapering cylindrical body w/a wide, flat base, an angled twig handle & swan's neck spout, the low domed cover w/a flanged rim & small knob finial, 19th c., 6" h. 275.00

Teapot, cov., wide oval cylindrical body w/a rounded shoulder tapering to a small top opening w/a fitted cover w/knob finial, angled handle & nearly straight swan's neck spout, 19th c., 6¼" h. 412.50

Teapot, cov., footed ovoid pear-shaped body w/C-form handle & swan's neck spout, the domed cover w/flanged rim & knob finial, 19th c., 8" h...522.50

Tile, square, 19th c., 4¾" w................357.50

Tureen, cover & undertray, deep oval flaring sides above a flaring foot & w/boar's head handles, the domed cover w/stem finial, on a conforming undertray, 19th c., tureen 10¼" l......770.00

Umbrella stand, tall cylinder decorated w/large Chinese landscapes, 19th c., 24½" h..........1,430.00

Vegetable dish, cov., rectangular w/cut corners, 8" l. 291.50

Vegetable dish, cov., almond-shaped, 9" l...330.00

Vegetable dish, cov., almond-shaped, 10¼" l..330.00

CAPO DI MONTE

Production of porcelain and faience began in 1736 at the Capo-di-Monte factory in Naples. In 1743 King Charles of Naples established a factory there that made wares with relief decoration. In 1759 the factory was moved to Buen Retiro near Madrid, operating until 1808. Another Naples pottery was opened in 1771 and operated until 1806 when its molds were acquired by the Doccia factory of Florence, which has since made reproductions of original Copo-di-Monte pieces with the "N" mark beneath a crown. Some very early pieces are valued in the thousands of dollars but the subsequent productions are considerably lower.

Bowl, cov., 6" d., 3½" h., multicolored allegorical scenes, molded figures around bowl & lid, lion finial, three paw feet, marked "Italy" $125.00

Box, cov., shaped oval, scene on cover of armor making, sides decorated w/a central bust portrait & florals in polychrome enamel & gilt, gilt brass fittings, 9" l. 247.50

Casket w/hinged lid, top & sides decorated w/panels of Bacchic scenes, 5 x 8" 525.00

Figure group, two ladies in 18th c. costume seated on the ground, one holding a lute & the other an open music book, floral-decorated gowns & applied flowers on the oval base, "N" & crown mark, 19th c., 6½ x 9½"..225.00

Plates, 8" d., the center w/a small colored floral bouquet framed by colorful scroll bands & a wide, outer border band w/small cherub figures, crowned "N" mark, pr. 77.00

CARLTON WARE

The Staffordshire firm of Wiltshaw & Robinson, Stoke-on-Trent, operated the Carlton Works from about 1890 until 1958, producing both earthenwares and porcelain. Specializing in decorative items like vases and teapots, they became well known for their lustre-finished wares, often decorated in the Oriental taste. The trademark Carlton Ware *was incorporated into their printed mark. Since 1958, a new company,* Carlton Ware Ltd.*, has operated the Carlton Works at Stoke.*

Bowl, oval, two-handled, Bleu Royale, king-fisher decoration $195.00

Box, cov., ball-footed, decorated w/enameled & gilt kingfisher & willow tree, mottled red ground........200.00

Creamer & sugar bowl, Rouge Royale, Nautilus shape, pr...............125.00

Dish, Rouge Royale, Art Deco style decoration, 11" d..............................125.00

Figurine, h.p. man in apron w/Wallaby in pocket, 4" h. 195.00

Figurine, standing ostrich, "My Goodness, My Guinness" 195.00

Vase, 4¼" h., ovoid, everted rim, gilt handles, kingfisher decoration...185.00

Vase, 6" h., footed, baluster-form, decorated w/enameled & gilt kingfisher & willow tree, mottled red ground...200.00

CATALINA ISLAND POTTERY

The Clay Products Division of the Santa Catalina Island Co. produced a variety of wares during their brief ten-year operation. The brainchild of chewing-gum magnate, William Wrigley, Jr., owner of Catalina Island at the time, and his business associate D.M. Retton, the plant was established at Pebbly Beach, near Avalon in 1927. Its two-fold goal was to provide year-round work for the island's residents and building material for Wrigley's ongoing development of a major tourist attraction at Avalon. Early production consisted of bricks and roof and patio tiles. Later, art pottery, including vases, flower bowls, lamps and home accessories, were made from a local brown-based clay and, about 1930, tablewares were introduced. These early wares carried vivid glazes but had a tendency to chip readily and a white-bodied, more chip-resistant clay, imported from the mainland, was used after 1932. The costs associated with importing clay eventually caused the Catalina pottery to be sold to a California mainland competitor in 1937. These wares were molded and are not hand-thrown but some pieces have hand-painted decoration.

CATALINA
MADE IN
U.S.A.
POTTERY

Charger w/wide flanged rim, Submarine Garden patt., a round center scene of deep red & yellow & blue & yellow jellyfish among green & red sea plants & shells against a medium blue ground, the wide border band in dark blue, matte & glossy glazes, marked, ca. 1930, 10 3/8" d. $660.00

Charger, painted w/a banjo player in green, yellow & blue against an ivory ground, early clay body, die-stamped "CATALINA," 12 1/2" d. 400.00

Charger, painted w/a galleon on the sea in shades of green, yellow & orange against a satin sky-blue ground, early clay body, die-stamped "CATALINA," 14" d. 400.00

Pitcher, cov., w/wooden handle, Toyon red, brown clay, hand-incised mark 100.00

Platter, 13" l., turquoise glaze 75.00

Vase, 8 1/2" h., handled, Avalonware, Toyon red, w/paper label 300.00

CERAMIC ARTS STUDIO OF MADISON

Founded in Madison, Wisconsin in 1941 by two young men, Lawrence Rabbitt and Reuben Sand, this company began as a "studio" pottery. In early 1942 they met an amateur clay sculptor, Betty Harrington and, recognizing her talent for modeling in clay, they eventually hired her as their chief designer. Over the next few years Betty designed over 460 different pieces for their production. Charming figurines of children and animals were a main focus of their output in addition to models of adults in varied costumes and poses, wall plaques, vases and figural salt and pepper shakers.

Business boomed during the years of World War II when foreign imports were cut off and, at its peak, the company employed some 100 people to produce the carefully hand-decorated pieces.

After World War II many poor-quality copies of Ceramic Arts Studio figurines appeared and when, in the early 1950s, foreign imported figurines began flooding the market, the company found they could no longer compete. They finally closed their doors in 1955.

Since not all Ceramic Arts Studio pieces are marked, it takes careful study to determine which items are from their production.

Bo Peep Figurine

CERAMIC ARTS
STUDIO

Bank, figural, Mr. Blankety Bank $85.00

Bank, figural, Mrs. Blankety Bank.........95.00

Bell, figural, Lillibelle 50.00

Candleholder, two-light, figural Triad woman kneeling 69.50

Figurine, Accordion Boy, 5" h. 45.00

Figurine, Angel, praying on knees, 4½" h. 35.00

Figurine, Aphrodite, black & tan, 7¾" h. 120.00

Figurine, Bali-Gong, 5½" h. 35.00

Figurine, Balinese Dancer, 9½" h. 42.00

Figurine, Beth, modern dancer 20.00

Figurine, Bo Peep, 5¼" h. (ILLUS.) ....20.00 to 25.00

Figurine, Boy Blue 27.00

Figurine, Boy in Chair, blue, green & brown, 2¼" h. 15.00

Figurine, Colonial Boy, dancing 20.00

Figurine, Colonial Man..........................27.50

Figurine, Comedy, grey gown w/blue mask, 10" h. 46.00

Figurine, Cuban girl, shades of green...32.50

Figurine, Drummer Girl, 4¼" h.............78.00

Figurine, Gay 90 Woman, No. 1, artist-signed, 6½" h. 52.00

Figurine, Girl in Chair, 2¼" h. 15.00

Figurine, Guitar Boy, 5" h. 45.00

Figurine, Isaac, 10½" h. 79.00

Figurine, Jill, 4¾" h. 18.00

Figurine, Little Jack Horner, 4½" h. 58.00

Figurine, Miss Muffet 45.00

Figurine, Pioneer Susie, standing girl w/broom, 5½" h. 35.00

Figurine, Pixie Boy, riding worm ....25.00 to 30.00

Figurine, Pixie Girl, kneeling, 2½" h......28.00

Figurine, Pixie under Toadstool 35.00

Figurine, Promenade Lady, 7¾" h........53.00

Figurine, Rebekah, 10⅛" h. 79.00

Figurine, Running girl 15.00

Figurine, Saxophone Boy, blue, 5½" h..35.00

Figurine, Shadow Dancer, 7" h. 65.00

Figurine, Shepherdess, 8½" h. 40.00

Figurine, Southern Belle, blue, 7" h. 24.00

Figurine, Spanish Dance Woman 48.00

Figurine, Sultan on pillow, 4¾" h. 29.00

Figurine, Summer Sally 62.00

Figurine, Winter Willie, kneeling boy w/snowball 50.00

Figurines, Beth & Bruce, dancers, 5" & 6½" h., pr. 60.00

Figurines, Black Sambo & Tiger, 5" l., 3½" h., pr. 150.00

Figurines, Cinderella & her Prince, green costume, pr. 150.00

Figurines, Colonial Dancing Boy & Girl, 5" & 5¼" h., pr. 42.00

Figurines, Comedy & Tragedy, 10" h., pr..115.00

Figurines, Encore Man & Lady, 8¼" & 8¾" h., pr. 175.00

Figurines, Gypsy Tambourine Girl & Violin Boy, pr.................................165.00

Figurines, Lu-Tang & Wing-San, 6¼" h., pr. 70.00

Figurines, Peter Pan & Wendy, on bases w/tall leafy plants, pr. 60.00

Figurines, Polish Boy & Girl, orange pants, skirt & caps, unmarked, 5½" h., pr. 50.00

Figurines, Spanish Dancers, Man & Woman, 7" & 7½" h., pr. 140.00

Figurines, Square Dance Boy & Girl, 6" & 6½" , pr. 55.00

Figurines, Temple Dancer, gold trim, pr..178.50

Figurine, shelf-sitter, Farmer Girl, blue clothes 35.00

Figurine, shelf-sitter, Harmonica Boy..62.00

Figurine, shelf-sitter, Pierrette 40.00

Figurines, shelf-sitters, Colonial Boy & Girl, on bench, pr. 85.00

Figurines, shelf-sitters, Dutch Boy & Girl, pr. 37.00

Figurines, shelf-sitters, Fishing Boy & Farm Girl, pr........................85.00 to 90.00

Figure group, Hansel & Gretel, 7" h..30.00

Lamps, Fire Man & Fire Woman, on bases, pr. 250.00

Model of Archibald the Dragon 125.00

Model of a cat, kitten playing w/ball of yarn 25.00

Model of a cat, kitten scratching, white, 2" h. 15.00

Model of a cat, Tom 25.00

Model of cat, Mother, shelf-sitter 35.00

Model of a dog, Gingham Dog.............17.00

Model of a hare, 1¾" h. 15.00

Model of lovebirds ,joined, pr. 25.00

Model of a skunk, Baby Boy 22.00

Model of a skunk, Baby Girl 25.00

Model of a skunk, Daddy 24.00

Model of a skunk, Mother 26.00

Model of a rooster, stylized bird w/long neck 68.50

Models of Mother Skunk & Baby, pr. 45.00

Pitcher, jug-type, Adam & Eve, boy & girl w/apple 30.00

Pitcher, jug-type, 5½" h., brown w/monk decoration, artist-signed 400.00

Planters, models of heads, Manchu & Lotus, pr. 160.00

Salt & pepper shakers, figural Chihuahua & dog house, pr. 78.00

Salt & pepper shakers, figural deer & fawn, pr. 50.00

Salt & pepper shakers, figural Dutch boy & girl, pr. 32.00

Salt & pepper shakers, figural elephants, pr. 45.00

Salt & pepper shakers, figural Gingham Dog & Calico Cat, pr. 65.00

Salt & pepper shakers, figural Mr. & Mrs. Penguin, pr. 50.00

Salt & pepper shakers, figural monkeys, pr. 60.00

Salt & pepper shakers, figural mother & baby cow, pr. 70.00

Salt & pepper shakers, figural mother & baby polar bears, pr. 55.00

Salt & pepper shakers, figural mouse & cheese, pr. 25.00

Salt & pepper shakers, figural native boy on an alligator, pr. 180.00

Salt & pepper shakers, figural ram & ewe, polka dot decoration, pr. 60.00

Salt & pepper shakers, figural Wee Chinese Boy & Girl, pr. 28.00

Salt & pepper shakers, figural Wee Elephants, pr. 47.00

Salt & pepper shakers, figural Wee Eskimos, pr. 37.00

Salt & pepper shakers, figural Wee French Boy & Girl, pr. 48.00

Salt & pepper shakers, figural Wee Indians, pr. 47.50

Salt & pepper shakers, figural Wee Pigs, pr. 48.00

Figural Salt & Pepper Shakers

Salt & pepper shakers, figural Wee Scots boy & girl, black & yellow outfits, 3½" h., pr. (ILLUS.) 45.00

Salt & pepper shakers, model of covered wagon & oxen, pr. 50.00

Vases, triple-bud, figures of Lu-Tang & Wing-Sang standing in front of bamboo-form cylinders, pr. 52.00

Wall plaque, pierced to hang, figural ballet dancer, Greg 47.50

Wall plaque, pierced to hang, model of a cockatoo 39.50

Wall plaques, pierced to hang, figural ballerinas, Arabesque & Attitude, pr. 98.00

Wall plaques, pierced to hang, figural Dutch boy & girl dancing, pr. 72.00

Wall plaques, pierced to hang, figural Harlequin & Columbine, pr. 112.50

Wall plaques, pierced to hang, figural Zor & Zorina, pr. 95.00

CHELSEA SPRIG WARE

The name for this ware is misleading since the design is thought to have originated at the Coalport, England porcelain factory in the early 19th century, long after the closing of the Chelsea factory. In this attractive pattern, small grape clusters or sprigs are raised in relief and colored in light blue or purple lustre on a white ground. It was popular from the mid-19th century into the early 20th century and is often referred to as "Grandmother's Ware."

Butter pat $12.00

Cup & saucer 30.00

Plate, 6¼" d. 12.00

Plate, 8¼" d. 15.00

Teapot, cov., ca. 1850, 9" h. 150.00

Waste bowl 40.00

CHELSEA

Chelsea Coffee Cup & Saucer

This ware was made in London from 1754 to 1770 in England's second porcelain factory. From 1770 to 1783 it was operated as a branch of the Derby Factory. Its equipment was then moved to Derby. It has been reproduced and ceramics made elsewhere are often erroneously called Chelsea.

Various painted and impressed anchor markings were most often used on early pieces.

Coffee cup & saucer, a footed bell-shaped cup & wide, shallow saucer each painted in shades of rose, iron-red, yellow, blue, green & brown w/a floral bouquet & scattered sprigs beneath the brown-edged rim, ca. 1755, Red Anchor mark, saucer 5" d., cup 2 7/16" h. (ILLUS.) $1,495.00

Figure of a Canoness of Cologne, the woman standing wearing a black trailing veil, a white cowl, ruff-and-lace-edged surplice which she gathers up in her right hand to reveal a yellow skirt painted in iron-red, purple, blue & green w/Oriental flowers above a pointed brown slipper, & standing on a low circular mound base applied w/black-centered iron-red florettes & green leaves, modeled by Joseph Willems, ca. 1754, 6½" h. (restored chip on veil, left hand restored at wrist, nose touched up) 1,035.00

Figure of Pantaloon, the grey-bearded actor wearing a black cap & long black coat, a gold-buttoned orange jacket & breeches & yellow shoes, a gold-handled black knife thrust into his tan belt, & modeled slightly bent forward, his right hand tucked into a pocket, his left extended, & standing amid yellow-and-black-centered pink & blue florettes & green leaves on a low circular mound base, ca. 1755, Red Anchor mark, 5⅝" h. (right arm restored, left hand replaced) 1,495.00

Plates, 8⅜" d., botanical-type, each painted w/a pair of shaded purple figs & grey-veined green leaves, an iron-red apple & four rose hips, a green leaf sprig & three brown nuts within a russet & turquoise feather-molded rim, ca. 1760, Brown Anchor mark, pr. (some touched-up stacking wear) 6,613.00

Platter, 14⅜" l., oval, painted in shades of rose, blue, yellow, iron-red, purple, brown, green & grey w/two floral bouquets & scattered sprigs within a brown-edged raised & scalloped rim, ca. 1755, Red Anchor mark 4,025.00

Sugar bowl, cov., the yellow ground painted in shades of rose, puce, green & grey around the cylindrical body w/a sprig of roses, sweet peas & a poppy & around the gilt rocco-scroll knop on the domed cover w/a small rose sprig, honeysuckle, trailing myrtle & bellflowers, each within a gilt dentil-edged rim, the interior of the bowl w/a tooled gilt floral spray & sprig, ca. 1765, Gold Anchor mark, 5 3/16" h. 7,188.00

Sweetmeat dish, 'Blind Earl' type, rounded & molded w/two sprays of brown-veined chartreuse & yellow leaves & two chartreuse & puce rosebuds issuing from a twig handle shaded in chartreuse & yellow & trimmed w/brown & pale turquoise knots, the scalloped rim edged in gilding, Red Anchor mark, ca. 1755, 5 11/16" w. (one leaftip restored) 2,013.00

Tray, shallow leaf-shaped form, the center painted in shades of iron-red & green w/a flowering leafy branch & molded w/rose-trimmed veins issuing from the yellow- and rose-tipped curled stem handle (small

Early Chelsea Leaf-Shaped Tray

hairline), the crinkled rim shaded from green to pale yellow, minor imperfections, puce Anchor mark, ca. 1758, 11" l. (ILLUS.)................4,888.00

CHILDREN'S MUGS

The small sized mugs used by children first attempting to drink from a cup appeal to many collectors. Because they were made of such diverse materials as china, glass, pottery, graniteware, plated silver and sterling silver, the collector can assemble a diversified collection or single out a particular type around which to base a collection. We list only ceramic examples here.

Staffordshire pottery, pearlware, cylindrical, black transfer-printed bird titled "A Pretty Bird," polychrome enamel trim, 2" h. (wear, small chips, short hairline in base)...$99.00

Staffordshire pottery, cylindrical, black transfer-printed large "Y" on one side & "Z" on the other w/an interior scene of a lady & children at a table in the center, 2⅜" h. (hairlines in handles) 176.00

Staffordshire pottery, cylindrical, brown transfer-printed scene of a lumberjack kneeling & surveying felled trees, scene titled "Franklin Maxims - Little Strokes Fell Great Oaks," polychrome enamel trim, 2½" h. (glaze wear on handle) 170.50

Staffordshire pottery, cylindrical, transfer-printed large & small "A" & "B" against a landscape background in brown w/red enamel trim, 2½" h. (hairline in handle, old repair on bottom edge)...................................165.00

Staffordshire pottery, black transfer-printed scene of men standing by a horse titled "John Gilpin...," 2½" h. (rim chip)...104.50

Staffordshire pottery, cylindrical, black transfer-printed design of a boy riding a large dog & a sheep, titled "Boy and Dog" & "Sheep," 2½" h. (pinpoint flakes) 132.00

Staffordshire pottery, cylindrical, black transfer-printed large "I" on one side & "J" on the other w/an interior scene of a workman in the center, green & orange enamel trim, 2½" h...170.50

Staffordshire pottery, cylindrical, black transfer-printed design of a child in a dog cart, polychrome enamel trim, 19th c., 2⅝" h. 137.50

Staffordshire pottery, cylindrical, brown transfer-printed design of a cat & three kittens w/polychrome enamel trim, 2⅝" h. (flakes on base)...110.00

Staffordshire pottery, cylindrical, black transfer-printed alphabet on the front & a cottage scene & flowers on the back, polychrome trim, 2¾" h. (wear, stains) 137.50

Staffordshire pottery, cylindrical, brown transfer-printed design of children riding early bicycles & the letters "J K L," 19th c., 2¾" h. 137.50

Staffordshire pottery, cylindrical, brown transfer-printed w/children on early cycles & "STU," w/polychrome enameled trim, 2⅞" h. 115.50

Staffordshire pottery, cylindrical, red transfer-printed outdoor sporting scene titled "Cricket," 19th c., 2⅞" h...126.50

Staffordshire pottery, transfer-printed design of mother & child sitting near an open hearth, verse for February on other side 135.00

CHINESE EXPORT

Large quantities of porcelain have been made in China for export to America from the 1780s, much of it shipped from the ports of Canton and Nanking. A major source of this porcelain was Ching-te-Chen in the Kiangsi province but the wares were also made elsewhere. The largest quantities were blue and white. Prices fluctuate considerably depending on age, condition, decoration, etc.

CANTON and ROSE MEDALLION export wares are listed separately.

Chinese Export Square Bowl

Basket, blue "Fitzhugh" patt., oval w/deep reticulated sides, the interior decorated w/pine cone, dragon & trellis diaper medallion within a border of spearheads & dumbbells & surrounded by four clusters of flowers & precious objects, the sides pierced w/fretwork & the rim w/a trellis diaper border edged in spearheads & dumbbells & interrupted by underglaze-blue upright scroll handles (one w/repaired chip, the other repaired), ca. 1810-20, 9 7/16" l. $1,035.00

Baskets, miniature, horizontally ribbed & painted w/a border of pink rose sprays, the interiors w/flowering branches in iron-red & gilt, gilt-striped ropetwist handles, ca. 1760, 2 7/8" h., pr. (slight rubbing).............2,420.00

Bowl, 9 7/8" w., square w/notched corners, decorated on the exterior front & back w/a landscape scene of a Chinese man in a sampan on a river & on the sides w/flowering plants separated by bats on the corners, the interior w/a central reserve of a landscape scene w/a flautist & companion in a sampan near a rocky shore, below a pavilion within a cell diaper-bordered square, the outer rim w/a trellis diaper & patterned panel band, ca. 1810, some chips & fritting (ILLUS.) 690.00

Bowl, 10 3/8" d., deep rounded sides raised on a wide footring, *famille rose* palette, painted w/an iron-red bird flying toward another perched on a salmon & *grisaille* rock amid brown-stemmed pink & green peonies & green leaves beneath a *grisaille* & gold foliate-scroll & blossom border around the rim, ca. 1745...1,093.00

Fitzhugh Pattern Bowl

Bowl, 10 9/16" d., blue "Fitzhugh" patt., shallow sides w/a scalloped rim, the interior decorated w/four flowers & precious objects panels within a trellis diaper border edged in spearheads & dumbbells, late 19th c. (ILLUS.)................................920.00

Box, cov., 'clobbered' blue "Fitzhugh" patt., rectangular w/flat cover, the cover w/a central medallion surrounded by four clusters of flowers & precious objects washed in worn gilding & painted between Canton *famille rose* enamels & sprigs of flowers & fruits, the sides of the base w/a gilt-trimmed trellis diaper border repeated around the cover edge, the base also w/a band of spearheads & dumbbells & further enameled w/a border of butterflies, flowers & fruit, the interior w/a central divider, ca. 1875, 7 1/4" l.........345.00

Candleholders, modeled in the form of a reclining lap dog, looking forward w/open mouth & pink tongue, spotted fur markings in sepia w/gilt details, the tall nozzle decorated w/green & iron-red leaf tips, ca. 1800, 6 1/4" l., pr. (slight wear)........5,500.00

Chamberstick, the floriform candle socket trimmed in blue & rising from an octafoil shallow dish painted in the center w/a flautist & companion on a sampan near a pavilion in a river landscape within a trellis diaper-bordered roundel, the rim w/a border of patterned panels, butterflies & unfurled landscape scrolls interrupted at one side by the stem-form loop handle, its thumbpiece a flattened flowerhead, ca. 1790, 5½" w. 2,070.00

Charger, armorial-type, vividly enameled in the center w/a coat-of-arms, possibly Dutch, beneath a prancing horse crest, the scalloped rim painted w/three autumnal flowering branches in early *famille rose* colors, early Qianlong period, 12¾" d. (tiny rim chips, short hairline) 1,870.00

Charger, *famille rose* palette, painted in rose, yellow, blue, turquoise, green, brown & gold in the center w/a basket of peonies on the cavetto w/a brown & gold trellis diaper border reserved w/four floral panels, & on the rim within a pink trellis diaper band interrupted w/yellow & blue demiflowerheads, ca. 1740, 14⅛" d...1,840.00

Chocolate pot, cov., the tapering cylindrical lighthouse form body w/gilt & blue enamel decoration at neck & base, centering the arms of the State of New York on both sides, the flat lid w/strawberry finial edged w/gilt & blue enamel, w/applied interlacing handle & tapering straight spout, ca. 1790-1810, 7¼" d., 8" h...4,400.00

Coffee cup & saucer, armorial-type, each w/the arms of Browne quartering Fitzalan, Neville, Montagu, Monthermer & Plantagenet, w/the supporters of Browne, Viscount Montagu, probably for Anthony Browne, sixth Viscount Montagu, all beneath gilt spearhead borders, ca. 1755 (tiny chips) 1,100.00

Coffeepot, cov., armorial-type, painted on each side w/the arms of Coys or Quoys of Essex in gilt & enamel colors beneath a gilt spearhead border, ca. 1755, 8⅝" h. (knop restuck) 1,760.00

Creamer, helmet-shaped, w/flaring lip decorated w/sepia & gilt banding w/meandering bead & flower over a polychrome arms of the State of New York above a spreading circular foot, w/tapering bamboo-molded handle, ca. 1790-1810, 5" h..825.00

Dinner service: eight dinner plates, nine dessert plates, a 12¾" oval platter, 11¾" oval platter, pair of scalloped sauceboats, circular potted meat dish & cover, & two soup plates; Nanking 'Two Birds' patt., each piece decorated w/a central landscape scene of a sampan on a river between banks w/pagodas, the cavetto w/a cell diaper border & rim w/a trellis diaper border edged in spearheads & dumbbells, late 18th - early 19th c., 24 pcs. (various small chips, repairs & hairlines) 3,738.00

Fitzhugh Shell-Shaped Dish

Dishes, blue "Fitzhugh" patt., shell-shaped, each decorated w/a central medallion surrounded by four panels of flowers & precious objects all within a trellis diaper, spearhead & dumbbell border w/gilt bands (worn), a lightly molded wide handle at one side decorated w/salmon & brown & trimmed w/gilt, one handle w/repaired chip, ca. 1820, 10⅜" l., pr. (ILLUS. of one) 1,955.00

Ecuelles (handled bowls), covers & underplates, blue "Fitzhugh" patt., deep rounded footed bowl w/entwined strap side handles & a low domed cover w/flat rim & fruit sprig finial, the interior decorated w/a central medallion beneath the trellis diaper, spearhead & dumbbell border, the exterior w/four clusters of flowers & precious objects, all trimmed w/gilt, ca. 1810, 6⅞" to 7⅞" d., underplates 8$\frac{5}{16}$" to 8½" d., set of 4 (one w/a rim chip, one w/rim hairline, three w/a chip or fritting, varous wear, three saucer rims w/chips & one of these w/three hairlines) 2,013.00

Egg cup, blue "Fitzhugh" patt., the U-shaped bowl painted on the front & back w/a pine cone, dragon & trellis diaper medallion edged w/spear-heads & dashes, on either side w/two clusters of flowers & precious objects & on the interior w/a trellis diaper band beneath the gilt edge, the conical base w/four swastikas above a base band, 19th c., 2⅜" h. 403.00

Nanking Egg Cups

Egg cups, Nanking "Inclined Pines" patt., U-shaped cups w/an almost continuous river landscape, the funnel foot w/two swastika devices & a trellis diaper band around the base, mid- to late-19th c., 2⅝" to 2¾" h., set of 4 (ILLUS.) 805.00

Eye cup, the shallow ovoid cup painted on the interior w/two Chinese men & a dog near pavillions in a river landscape within a scallop-and-dot border beneath the rim & on the exterior w/two flowering branches, the slender knopped stem (fritted) rising from a domed octagonal foot painted w/fruit, flowers & foliate scrolls, ca. 1775, 2⅜" h. (repaired rim chips).....575.00

Chinese Export Fish Bowl

Fish bowl, a wide ovoid body w/a flattened molded rim, decorated around the exterior w/two scaly dragons in pursuit of the flaming pearls amid clouds above a lappet border around the base & beneath a border of *ruyi* heads & prunus blossoms & a Greek key band below the rim, the flat top of the rim w/a demi-prunus blossoms border, 16 1/16" d., 13½" h. (ILLUS.)............1,495.00

Fruit basket & undertray, reticulated basket w/flaring sides & raised rim handles, sepia "Fitzhugh" patt., 10½" l., 5½" h...................................935.00

Fruit stand, boat-shaped, "Tobacco Leaf" patt., the ogee-shaped bowl w/gilt-trimmed incurved scroll handles at the ends above a flaring oval foot, painted overall the exterior & upper half of the interior w/rose, iron-red, blue, yellow & green blossoms & sprigs superimposed on a profusion of yellow, blue, turquoise, spring green, shaded salmon & brown leaves veined in grey, rose or gold & edged in gilt & the rim & footrim also edged in gilt, the sides reserved in the center w/a gilt-edged leaf-shaped panel initialed in gold "RL" between small rose, blue, yellow & green floral swags, ca. 1810-20, 12 9/16" l. (slight wear to gilt rim, one handle repaired) 4,888.00

Fitzhugh Pattern Garden Seat

Garden seat, hexagonal, blue "Fitzhugh" patt., the slightly swelling body painted on four sides with the characteristic medallion within four clusters of flowers & precious objects, & on the other two sides w/two similar clusters beneath a pair of pierced cash medallions, all between diaper bands edged in spearheads & dumbbells within molded bosses & floral lappet borders around the rim (chip) & footrim, the top w/another pierced cash medallion surrounded by four clusters of flowers & precious objects within a trellis diaper border edged in spearheads & dumbbells, late 19th c., 18⅜" h. (ILLUS.) 2,875.00

Goblets, decorated in blue enamel & gilt w/sprays of fruit & flowers below a leafy floral garland & a band of swags, the band repeated on the interior rim, the pedestal gadroon foot painted w/upright leaf tips & supported on a square base, ca. 1800, 5⅜" h., set of 8 (one broken & restored, one w/rim chip, the others w/slight wear) 4,620.00

Nanking Hot Water Dish & Platter

Hot water dish, cov., Nanking "Inclined Pines" patt., the deep sided oval dish w/end spouts, decorated in underglaze-blue w/a central landscape scene of a Chinese man crossing a bridge near another in a sampan on a river w/numerous buildings on the banks interrupted at the top of the base & on either side of the pine cone finial of the domed cover w/the gilt initial "P" within a beribboned oval, the cavetto of the base w/a trellis diaper border repeated on the rim of each within a band of spearheads & dumbbells, the base w/lotus & peony sprigs, ca. 1810-20, cover slightly small & w/repaired edge chips, 18$^{13}/_{16}$" l. (ILLUS. front) 1,495.00

Jardiniere, very wide ovoid body tapering to a flaring mouth w/flattened rim, decorated around the sides w/the 'Hundred Antiques' design between a lappet border around the foot & a peony & *ruyi*-lappet border, the flat rim w/a swastika-diaper border, 19th c., star cracks, 21½" d. (ILLUS.) 1,725.00

Chinese Export Jardiniere

Jardiniere, blue & white, scene depicting a mountainous riverscape w/small boats at sail & villas on the shore, below *ruyi* head borders & w/a pair of biscuit lion mask handles, Qianlong period, 24½" d. (handles touched up) 8,250.00

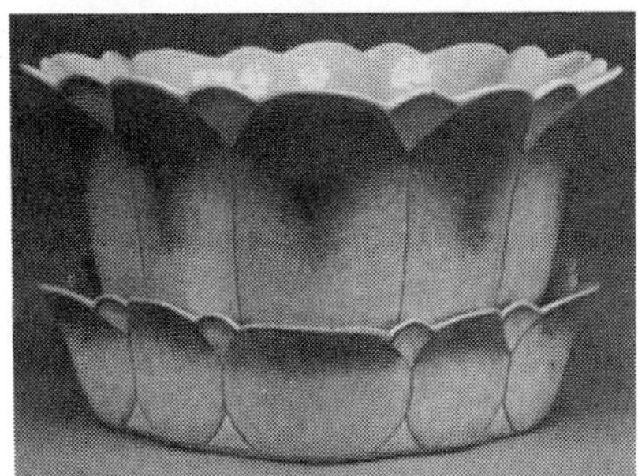

Lotus-Form Jardiniere

Jardinieres & undertrays, lotus-form, the blossom-form jardiniere w/scalloped & ruffled rim decorated w/shaded enamels, resting in a matching undertray, late 19th c., 11" d., 6" h., pr. (ILLUS. of one)....4,888.00

Jardinieres & undertrays, hexagonal, each piece decorated w/a continuous landscape scene of a Chinese man & his water buffalo crossing a bridge toward other figures & buildings on a river bank w/sampans plying the waters before distant hills, the flat rims decorated w/foliate scrolls & dots within the molded edge, 19th c., 7⅞" h., pr. (ILLUS. of one top next column) ...2,875.00

Chinese Export Jardiniere & Undertray

Model of a hawk, *famille rose* palette, perched on blue rockwork w/head cocked, his breast & head iron-red w/gilt feather details, his folded wings richly enameled w/overlapping feathers in pink, yellow, iron-red, black, blue, sepia & green, Qianlong period, 6½" h. (slight flaking to enamels of beak & feathers) 6,050.00

Model of a rabbit, the seated animal naturalistically modeled w/ears pricked back, their interiors washed in salmon, brown-glazed biscuit eyes & well defined white-spotted brown coat, late 18th - early 19th c., 5¼" h. (one ear repaired, one foot restored) 3,450.00

Models of doves, perched w/a slightly turned head, white body, brown-glazed biscuit eyes, incised wing & tail feathers & biscuit feet showing traces of red cold paint, the low rocky base covered in a lustrous *cafe-au-lait* glaze, 19th c., 6¾" h., facing pr. (some minor chips) 1,725.00

Chinese Export Mustard Pot

Mustard pots, cov., barrel-shaped, decorated in the Kangxi style w/three mounted horsemen in pursuit of a fleeing stag beneath a trellis diaper border at the rim reserved w/four panels of peonies, the reeded entwined strap handle w/blossom & foliate terminals, each mounted w/a Dutch silver hinged cover engraved w/flowers & foliage, pot w/underglaze-blue luo (conch shell) mark, silver w/collection marks & Dutch control marks for the early 19th c., early 19th c., 3⅝" h., pr. (ILLUS. of one) 1,035.00

Fitzhugh Toddy Pitchers

Pitchers, cov., toddy, 10¹³⁄₁₆" h., blue "Fitzhugh" patt., barrel-shaped, each painted beneath the spout (one w/a chip issuing a hairline) w/a pine cone, dragon & trellis diaper medallion bordered in spearheads & dumbbells & flanked by four clusters of flowers & precious objects, the underglaze-blue reeded entwined strap handle w/gilt trim, the low domed cover w/further decoration & a gilt recumbent kylin figural finial, one finial w/chipped tail, ca. 1810-20, pr. (ILLUS.) 5,175.00

Plate, 8½" d., octagonal, armorial-type, the arms of Maitland quartering Lauder, 18th c. (minor imperfections) 880.00

Plate, 9⅜" d., the lobed edge decorated w/underglaze-blue & gilt decoration, centering a blue enamel & gilt oval containing a sepia & gilt flower, ca. 1790-1810 .... 110.00

Plate, 9¾" d., orange "Fitzhugh" patt., large spread-winged eagle w/shield in the center, 19th c. (ILLUS.) 4,180.00

Plates, pudding, 7¾" d., blue "Fitzhugh" patt., each decorated w/the usual central medallion surrounded by four flower & precious objects panels all within a spearhead & dumbbell border, worn gilt edges, 19th c., set of 18 (two w/a repaired chip) 805.00

Fitzhugh Plate with Eagle

Plates, dessert, 8" d., blue "Fitzhugh" patt., decorated w/the usual central medallion surrounded by four flower & precious objects panels all within a spearhead & dumbbell border, 19th c., set of 13 (hairlines & chips) 575.00

Plates, 8⅞" d., armorial-type, each w/a large English coat-of-arms in the center & a hand grasping heart crest on the rim, the wells w/a band of diaper pattern & the rims finely 'pencilled' w/four profusely flowering boughs, two flowering branches on each back, decorated in underglaze blue, ca. 1725, set of 4 ....4,180.00

Plates, 9½" w., octagonal, *famille verte* palette, painted w/a Chinese pheasant in flight above another perched on a fence beneath a pine tree amid flowers, the cavetto w/an iron-red demi *ruyi* head band, the rim w/a black-stippled green-ground border of phoenixes & peonies beneath an iron-red whorl band, the edge molded w/gilt-trimmed iron-red gadrooning, 1710-20, pr. (one broken & restored, other w/restored chip) 550.00

Plates, 9½" w., octagonal, *famille verte* palette, painted w/a Chinese pheasant in flight above another perched on a fence beneath a pine tree amid flowers, the cavetto w/an iron-red demi *ruyi* head band, the rim w/a black-stippled green-ground border of phoenixes & peonies beneath an iron-red whorl band, the edge molded w/gilt-trimmed iron-red gadrooning, 1710-20, pr. (one broken & restored, other w/restored chip) 550.00

Plates, dinner, 9⅝" d., blue "Fitzhugh" patt., each decorated w/a central pine cone, dragon & trellis diaper medallion encircled w/spearhead & dumbbells & surrounded by four clusters of flowers & precious objects within a trellis diaper border edged in spearheads & dumbbells around the rim, one with a gilt rim, 19th c., set of 10 (hairlines, repaired chips) 1,150.00

Plates, dinner, 9¾" d., rose "Fitzhugh" patt., each painted in shades of rose in the center w/a gilt-edged roundel (worn) depicting two figures in a rowboat before a large European building w/trees in the foreground, the rim w/a characteristic border of patterned panels, butterflies, fret devices & floral sprigs, ca. 1825, pr. (one w/three small hairlines at edge)...2,875.00

Platter, 9⅞ x 12⅞", armorial-type, green "Fitzhugh" patt., 19th c........1,760.00

Platter, 14⅝ x 17⅜", armorial-type, green "Fitzhugh" patt., w/reticulated insert, 19th c., 2 pcs. (rim repair on platter)..2,090.00

Platter, 21" l., oval, blue "Fitzhugh" patt., 19th c. (minor rim chips) 825.00

Platter, 21⅜" l., oval, Nanking "Inclined Pines" patt., decorated w/a central landscape of a Chinese man carrying a parasol across a bridge near another in a sampan on a river w/various buildings on the banks, the cavetto w/a trellis diaper border interrupted by four panels of beribboned objects, the rim w/a trellis diaper border edged in spearheads & dumbbells, ca. 1810-20 (ILLUS. back)..................1,035.00

Punch bowl, *famille rose* palette, deep rounded sides on a wide footring, painted around the exterior predominantly in shades of soft pink, green, turquoise, yellow, aubergine, white & black w/two small birds flying amid large lotus blossoms & pads (some enamel chips), the interior (some wear) w/a butterfly flitting above a vase of peonies & other flowers beneath a pink- and yellow-edged black-ground border of pink, yellow, white & green flowering vines interrupted by six blue-edged panels of flowering plants at the gilt-edge (worn) rim (two hairlines & small touched-up chips), ca. 1740,

15 7/16" d. 2,875.00

Salt cellars, blue "Fitzhugh" patt., oval tapering cylindrical base below a flattened rim around the well, each decorated w/a medallion within a trellis diaper border edged in spearheads & dumbbells, the base w/clusters of flowers & precious objects, ca. 1800-10, 4 1/8" l., pr. (each w/a hairline, one w/touch-up chip, other w/glaze flaw) 460.00

Fitzhugh Sauce and Soup Tureens

Sauce tureen, cover & undertray, blue "Fitzhugh" patt., the deep footed oval body decorated w/pine cones, dragons & trellis diaper medallions w/spearhead & dumbbell border, the domed cover w/a large flowerhead knop, entwined strap handles on the base, ca. 1810-20, tureen 7 3/8" l., undertray 8 1/16" l., the set (ILLUS. right)..1,265.00

Soup plates w/flanged rims, armorial-type, each painted in the center in brown, *grisaille*, pale yellow, blue, turquoise & shades of green w/a European tower building, possibly Fort St. George, in a river landscape within a gilt quatrefoil above the iron-red & gilt arms of Pole on the cavetto & bottom of the rim (some chips), the top of the rim w/the brown falcon rising crest, & the sides w/gilt-edged panels depicting Plymouth Sound & the Pearl River, ca. 1745, 9" d., pr..........................2,875.00

Soup plates, blue "Fitzhugh" patt., decorated w/the usual central medallion surrounded by four flower & precious objects panels all within a spearhead & dumbbell border, three w/worn gilt rims, 9 3/4" d., set of 15 (most w/hairlines, chips, & one w/rim repair)....................................575.00

Soup tureen, cov., oblong, the body painted in underglaze-blue, iron-red, gold & shades of green on either side w/peonies, bamboo, a fungus & rocks surrounding a pine tree in a fenced garden beneath an

Chinese Export Soup Tureen

underglaze-blue scroll-and-tassel border at the rim (hairline), the ends w/gilt-spotted iron-red dog's-head handles (slight fritting), the domed cover painted in iron-red, gold & shades of green w/five sprays of peonies & hibiscus encircling the iron-red recumbent dog finial (slight fritting) above an underglaze-blue trellis diaper border around the rim (shallow chip), ca. 1750, 14" l. (ILLUS.) 3,450.00

Soup tureen, cov., blue "Fitzhugh" patt., the footed deep oval body painted on either side w/a pine cone, dragon & trellis diaper medallion encircled by spearheads & dumbbells & flanked by pairs of clusters of flowers & precious objects above a trellis diaper border around the foot edged also in spearheads & dumbbells & repeated on the domed, gilt-edged cover rim (small chips & glaze flaw) beneath four further clusters of flowers & precious objects encircling the gilt-trimmed flowerhead knop, the reeded entwined strap handles on the base also w/traces of gilt, ca. 1810-20, 14 1/16" l. (ILLUS. left) 2,588.00

Soup tureen, cover & undertray, *Mandarin palette*, oblong w/chamfered corners, the tureen w/deep rounded sides above a wide flaring foot & rabbit-head end handles, each piece painted on either side or in the center w/a scene of Mandarin figures in a fenced garden in a hilly river landscape within black scroll-edged panels between similarly edged floral or bird panels & iron-red landscape vignettes, all reserved on an iron-red, black & gold Y-diaper ground, the cover surmounted by an iron-red, turqoise & gilt floral sprig knop (losses & restoration), & the tureen & cover rims (all w/small chips & fritting) edged in iron-red, ca. 1785, 13½" & 13¹¹⁄₁₆" l., the set 4,600.00

Spoon tray, blue "Fitzhugh" patt., fluted hexafoil form, a central medallion & a band of 'onion' devices & a border of feathering w/worn gilt trim, ca. 1815, 4¾" l. 230.00

Sugar bowl, cov., the molded bowl of globular form w/symmetric applied interlaced handles, blue banding at neck & foot centering gilt & sepia floral decoration, the molded domed lid w/shaped rim & waving band of blue enamel & gilt stars & husk band centering a strawberry finial, ca. 1790-1810, 6" w., 5¾" h. 132.00

Tea caddy, cov., upright rectangular form, painted in iron-red, salmon, black, gold & green w/a strolling European couple on one side, another side w/their hound beneath a leafy branch, a third side w/a flowering plant & a tree behind a garden fence, & the fourth side w/flowers & a pierced rock beneath a leafy branch, the flat shoulders w/an iron-red & gilt cell diaper ground reserved at the corners w/oval panels of peony sprigs (some fritting & a small chip inside the neck), the round brass cap w/milled edge, 1720-30, 4¼" h. 3,450.00

Teacups & saucers, the faceted cups w/sepia & gilt guilloche, a sepia & gilt flower at bottom of cup & winged trumpeting putti w/motto, "A moi vincit omnia," scrolled handle, the matching faceted saucers w/sepia & gilt guilloche banding, centering two putti w/trumpets bearing standard w/the motto, cups 2½" w., 2" h., saucers 5" w., 2 sets 660.00

Teapot, cov., pear-shaped w/long slightly curved spout & ear-shaped loop handle, applied on either side w/a blue-edged pierced floral quatrefoil medallion surrounded by shaded pink peonies above a row of lightly molded chrysanthemum petals shaded in rose, the handle & gilt-edged spout issuing applied aubergine branches of pink & gold prunus blossoms, rose & yellow buds & blue leaves (tiny chips), the stepped & domed cover applied w/a blue-edged turquoise pierced floral quatrefoil medallion surmounted by a gilt pierced ball knop & surrounded by four peony sprigs above an iron-red diaper border around the gilt-edged scalloped & barbed rim, ca. 1740, 4¾" h. 1,610.00

Teapot, cov., the molded cylindrical body w/gilt & blue enamel banding & decoration at neck, tapering shoulders & center polychrome arms of the State of New York on both sides, the molded circular lid centering a gilt strawberry finial, w/gilt & blue enamel banding & decoration at edge, w/applied interlacing handle & tapering spout, ca. 1790-1810, 6" h. 1,210.00

Teapot, cov., footed spherical body w/a short neck supporting the domed cover w/a pointed acorn finial, a short straight spout & C-loop handle, white w/a polychrome crest depicting a spread-wing eagle within a leaf cartouche & floral wreath on the body, polychrome floral sprays & scrolling gilt foliage on the cover, ca. 1750, 6¼" h. 605.00

Teapot stand, oval, armorial-type, the center painted in iron-red, gold & *grisaille* w/the arms of Jennings or Jenyns within gold, brown & rose scrollwork issuing rose, blue & green floral sprays, the narrow flat rim w/an iron-red & gilt spearhead border at the worn gilt edge, ca. 1785, 7⅛" l. 690.00

Tea set: cov. teapot, cov. sugar bowl & creamer; orange "Fitzhugh" patt., early 19th c., teapot 6½" h., 3 pcs. (imperfections) 3,850.00

Tureen, cov., oval, blue "Fitzhugh" patt., decorated w/the crest of the Beale family, 19th c., 10¾" l. 1,980.00

Tureens, covers & lobed circular undertrays, blue & white, the large pomegranate-shaped dish slightly lobed & decorated on either side & in the center of the undertray w/a landscape scene of Chinese men in sampans on a river between dwellings on the banks surrounded by a narrow cell diaper border around the cavetto & rim, the bases w/a blossom handle on one end & a short leafy stem handle on the other each trimmed w/gilt, the cover decorated w/three pagoda vignettes around the three iron-red & gilt-trimmed molded pomegranates issuing from the gnarls & leaf stem-form handle, the cover & undertray w/an elaborate wide border of patterned panels, cash medallions, scrolls & blossoms within a fish-roe band at the edge, ca. 1785, tureen 6½" l., undertray 9⁹⁄₁₆" pr. (one finial leaf chipped, one undertray w/hairline) 6,613.00

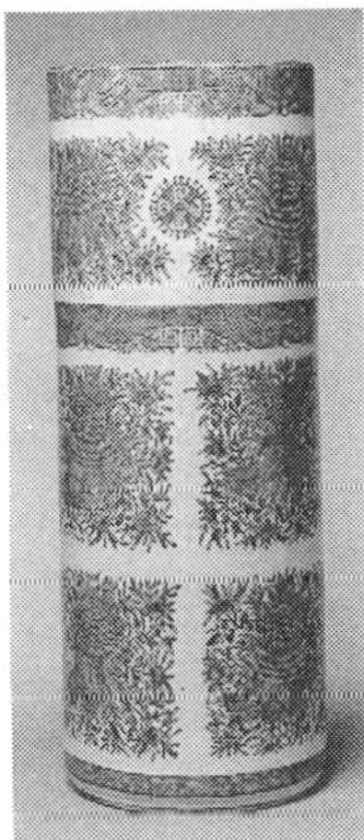

Fitzhugh Umbrella Stand

Umbrella stand, cylindrical, green "Fitzhugh" patt., painted on both sides in the upper third w/a peony, beast & trellis diaper medallion encircled by spearheads & dumbbells flanked by pairs of clusters of flowers & precious objects between characteristic borders around the rim & around the mid-section above two rows of four further clusters of flowers & precious objects, the base (star crack) w/a trellis diaper border, late 19th - early 20th c., hairline in body, 23½" h. (ILLUS.) 1,438.00

Vases, 11¼" h., square bottle-form, blue & white, each side painted w/a court scene, including dancers performing before noblewomen & mounted huntresses outside a fortress, borders of crosshatch & diaper, flowering branches on the square neck, ribbon-tied artemesia leaf marks in recessed squares on the base, Kangxi period, pr. (one neck w/restoration, some fritting) 3,300.00

Vases, cov., 13½" h., wide baluster-form body w/a short cylindrical neck topped by a domed cover w/flanged rim & pointed ball finial, decorated w/a continuous scene of Chinese figures in pastel tones, 19th c., pr. (ILLUS. of one, top next column) ..1,438.00

Vegetable dishes, cov., blue "Fitzhugh" patt., the oval body w/a wide flat flanged rim w/chamfered corners, the domed cover w/entwined branch handle, the interior & either side of the cover decorated w/a medallion & w/a wide border band of spearheads & diaper, the covers w/gilt trim, some fritting, chip on underside of one rim, gilt worn, ca. 1810, 14⅜" l., pr. (ILLUS. of one) 2,300.00

Chinese Export Covered Vase

Chinese Export Vegetable Dish

Vegetable dish, cov., blue "Nanking" patt., rectangular w/chamfered corners, low domed cover w/figural pine cone knop (ILLUS.) 403.00

Nanking Pattern Vegetable Dish

Wine coolers, *famille rose* palette, footed fluted cylindrical body w/scalloped rim & applied loop handles, painted on the front & reverse in shades of rose, blue, yellow, green, tuquoise, white & gold

Famille Rose Wine Cooler

w/a flowering branch, & on the sides w/a smaller flowering branch or a sprig of dianthus beneath the iron-red & worn gilt-trimmed handles (one restored), the rim (some fritting, one touched up) w/a molded ridge bordered in iron-red & gold, the round foot w/a similar border, 1755-65, 10" d., 8" h., pr. (ILLUS. of one) 5,500.00

CLARICE CLIFF DESIGNS

Clarice Cliff Centerpiece

Clarice Cliff was a designer for A.J. Wilkinson, Ltd., Royal Staffordshire Pottery, Burslem, England when they acquired the adjoining Newport Pottery Company whose warehouses were filled with undecorated bowls and vases. About 1925 her flair with the Art Deco style was incorporated into designs appropriately named "Bizarre" and "Fantasque" and the warehouse stockpile was decorated in vivid colors. These hand-painted earthenwares, all bearing the printed signature of designer Clarice Cliff, were produced until World War II and are now finding enormous favor with collectors.

Note: Reproductions of the Clarice Cliff "Bizarre" marking have been appearing on the market recently.

Bowl, 6¼" d., octagonal flanged rim on the rounded body, Woodland patt., stylized landscape w/trees in orange, green, black, blue, purple & yellow, marked $253.00

Bowl, 8" d., 3¾" h., "Bizarre" ware, deep gently rounded sides tapering to a foot ring, Original Bizarre patt., a wide band of block & triangles around the upper half in blue, orange, ivory & purple, purple band around the bottom section, marked 440.00

Bowl, 9" d., Alpine patt., shallow rounded sides, decorated w/a band of stylized fir trees in polychrome banded in orange, marked 207.00

Bowl, 9" d., deep rounded sides, the upper half w/a wide band in polychrome featuring large stylized cottages w/pointed orange roofs beneath arching trees, lime green banding, marked 322.00

Bowl, 9¼" d., "Bizarre" ware, Rhodanthe patt. 875.00

Butter dish, cov., "Bizarre" ware, Crocus patt., a wide shallow base w/low, upright sides fitted w/a shallow, flat-sided cover w/a slightly domed top & flat button finial, the top decorated w/purple, blue & orange blossoms on an ivory ground, marked, 4" d., 2¾" h. 302.50

Candleholders, figural, modeled as a kneeling woman w/her arms raised high holding the candle socket modeled as a basket of flowers, My Garden patt., orange dress & polychrome trim, marked, 7¼" h., facing pr. 403.00

Candlestick, loop-handled, Tonquin patt., red 30.00

Centerpiece, "Bizarre" ware, model of a stylized Viking longboat, raised on trestle supports & w/a frog insert, glazed in orange, yellow, brown & black on a cream ground, printed factory marks, ca. 1925, restored, 15¾" l., 9⅝" h., 2 pcs. (ILLUS.)........345.00

Coffee service: cov. coffeepot, creamer, open sugar bowl, pitcher & six cups & saucers; Crocus patt., serving pieces w/slightly tapering cylindrical bodies, cylindrical cups w/shallow saucers, all pieces decorated w/stylized blossoms in orange, blue & purple, marked, coffeepot 7½" h., the set 483.00

Coffee service: cov. coffeepot, creamer, open sugar bowl, five cake plates & six cups & saucers; Ravel patt., creamer & sugar w/pointed conical bodies supported by buttress legs, other serving pieces w/flaring cylindrical bodies, marked, coffeepot 6" h., the set 748.00

Cup & saucer, "Bizarre" ware, Autumn Crocus patt., Athens shape 175.00

Demitasse set: cov. cylindrical coffeepot, creamer, open sugar bowl & six cylindrical demitasse cups & saucers; "Honey-glaze," each body in deep orange, the angled handles in black & dark green, all marked, coffeepot 6" d., 6¼" h., the set (chip inside pot cover, minor flake on sugar bowl) 3,190.00

Figures, "Bizarre" ware, flat cup-outs, comprising two groups of musicians & two groups of dancing couples, all highly stylized & glazed in red-orange, yellow, lime green, cream & black, printed factory marks "HAND PAINTED - Bizarre - by - Clarice Cliff - A. J. Wilkinson Ltd. - NEWPORT POTTERY - ENGLAND," ca. 1925, 5⅝" to 7" h., 4 pcs......18,400.00

Jam pot, cov., Trees & House patt., swelled cylindrical body w/a slightly domed inset cover molded w/two cherries as finials, orange, green & black decoration, marked, 3½" h. 173.00

Jam pot, cov., Secrets patt., cylindrical w/inset flat cover w/angled knob finial, polychrome landscape decoration w/quaint cottages tucked among hills, green & yellow banding on the cover, marked, 3¾" h...........230.00

Jam pot, cov., Blue Firs patt., flat-sided round form on small log feet, domed cover w/flat round knob, stylized landscape w/trees, marked, 4¼" h...253.00

Jardiniere, "Fantasque" line, Melon patt., Dover shape, deep cylindrical sides on three small tab feet, decorated w/Cubist-style fruits in orange, yellow, blue, green & amber against a cream ground, orange base & rim bands, marked, 6¼" d., 6¼" h. (minor inside paint wear) 1,540.00

Clarice Cliff Lemonade Set

Lemonade set: 8" h. tankard pitcher & four cylindrical tumblers; each decorated in an abstract geometric pattern in orange, blue, purple, green & yellow, marked, the set (ILLUS.) 690.00

Pitcher, 5¾" h., "Fantasque" line, Melon patt., wide conical body w/solid triangular handle, orange & thin black bands flanking a wide central band of stylized melons in yellow, blue, green & orange, marked, ca. 1930 (tiny glaze nicks at rim & base, faint scratch in lower orange band) 715.00

Pitcher, jug-type, 7" h., 6" d., "Bizarre" ware, Lotus shape, Coral Firs patt., wide ovoid body w/a wide flat rim, heavy applied loop handle, decorated w/a wide landscape band in brown, orange, yellow, brown & grey on an ivory ground, marked 770.00

Pitcher, 7" h., 9" d., "Bizarre" ware, Rhodanthe patt., a squatty bulbous base tapering to a wide flaring rim, heavy strap handle, decorated w/large stylized flowers in brown, yellow, orange & powder blue on an ivory ground 495.00

Pitcher, 7⅛" h., "Fantasque" line, Athens shape, Lily Orange patt., ovoid octagonal body on a flaring octagonal foot, loop handle, wide orange band & black stripes flank a wide central band of stylized orange leaves w/green veins against a black ground, white foot & handle, marked, ca. 1929 (small chip at base) 770.00

Bulbous Clarice Cliff Pitcher

Pitcher, 7¼" h., footed bulbous spherical body tapering to a flat rim w/an angled handle, Poppy Delecia patt., decorated in orange, pink & yellow, marked (ILLUS.) 633.00

Pitcher, 9¾" h., 8" d., "Bizarre" ware, Isis shape, Farmhouse patt., the ovoid body decorated at the top & bottom w/alternating red, orange & yellow bands, the stylized farm landscape in shades of orange, black, green & red, marked (bruise to base, some paint wear) 1,650.00

Pitcher, jug-type, 10" h., 7" d., bulbous ovoid body w/thick applied handle, "Fantasque" line, Isis shape, Gay-day patt., a wide central band of stylized blossoms in orange, purple, red, blue & green against an ivory ground, die-stamped "Fantasque by Clarice Cliff - Lawley's Regent Street" 1,210.00

Pitcher, 10" h., ovoid body tapering to a flat rim, Isis shape, decorated w/a wide central band of large triangles separating stylized blossoms w/plain bands above & below, all in shades of green, orange, blue & yellow,marked 920.00

Pitcher, 11½" h., jug-type w/an ovoid body molded w/overall rings, Lotus shape, Autumn patt., polychrome stylized landscape w/trees, banded in orange & green, marked 1,265.00

Pitcher, 12" h., jug-type w/ovoid body w/overall fine molded banding, Lotus shape, Nasturtium patt., colorful stylized floral band w/a yellow band at the top & orange band around the base, marked 460.00

Lotus Pitcher with Sunrise Pattern

Pitcher, 12" h., jug-type w/ovoid body w/overall fine molded banding, Lotus shape, Sunrise patt., decorated in bright yellow & orange, marked (ILLUS.) 920.00

Plate, 9¾" d., Forest Glen patt., a stylized cottage in a woodland scene in orange, ivory & green, die-stamped "Clarice Cliff - Newport Pottery - England" 550.00

Plate, 10" d., round w/narrow molded rings, Forest Glen patt., polychrome stylized forest scene, marked 92.00

Plate, 10" d., transfer-printed Rural Scenes patt., color image of wood-cutters in center, brown harvest bounty rim, Royal Staffordshire Dinnerware, ink mark.........................27.50

Plate, 10⅜" d., Devon patt., poly-chrome decoration of tall curved trees & stylized flowers, banded in yellow & green, marked 437.00

Plate, 10¾" d., rounded w/four double-lobe protrusions around the sides, Autumn patt., polychrome stylized landscape w/trees framed by yellow & green rim banding, marked 368.00

Plate, 10¾" d., rounded w/four double-lobe protrusions around the sides, Sunrise patt., colorful center stylized sunrise design banded in orange & green, marked (ILLUS top next column.) 253.00

Sugar shaker, Autumn patt., sharply pointed conical shape w/rows of small holes pierced around the top, decorated in pastel autumn colors, marked, 5½" h.................................368.00

Tumbler, Sunray patt., conical form, polychrome decoration of a stylized

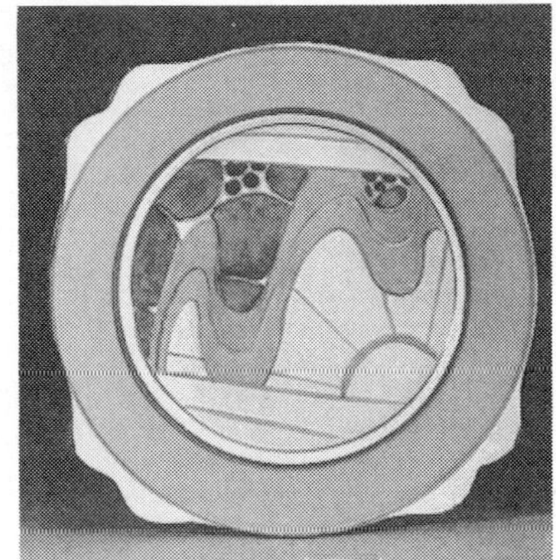

Sunrise Pattern Plate

sun, orange banding, marked, 3" h. 230.00

Vase, 6¼" h., 3¼" d., "Fantasque" line, Shape No. 196, Trees and House patt., a cylindrical body w/a widely flaring & rolled rim, decorated w/a wide central landscape band in black, orange & green against an ivory ground, marked 880.00

Vase, 6⅝" h., "Bizarre" ware, Bon Jour shape, Green Japan patt., flat-sided egg-shaped body w/closed rim & raised on small "log" feet, decorated w/a stylized lakeside landscape in pale green, yellow, rose, blue & white, marked (factory grinding on one foot) 440.00

Vase, 8" h., 5½" d., "Fantasque" line, Blue Chintz patt., bulbous ovoid body tapering to a ringed neck w/flaring rim, decorated w/stylized green, blue & pink flowers against an ivory ground, blue & green rim & base bands, marked "Fantasque - Hand Painted Bizarre by Clarice Cliff - Newport Pottery, England - 358bx" 1,210.00

Vase, 8" h., 5¾" d., "Bizarre" ware, Shape No. 358, Secrets patt., wide ovoid body w/heavy molded rings at the neck, decorated w/a stylized landscape in yellow, green & brown on an ivory ground, die-stamped "Fantasque - Bizarre by Clarice Cliff" 880.00

Vase, 8¼" h., cylindrical w/flared rim, multicolored landscape scene on a stippled cafe-au-lait yellow ground 368.00

Vase, 9" h., Inspiration patt., baluster-form body w/a short slightly flaring neck, scrolling abstract design in blue, turquoise, lavender, yellow & beige, marked 437.00

Vase, 9" h., 4½" d., "Bizarre" ware, baluster-shaped w/a short, wide slightly flaring neck, decorated on the upper half w/a wide band of triangles alternating w/quadrilateral blocks in blue, yellow & purple on an orange ground, Shape No. 14D, marked 1,430.00

Vase, 9⅝" h.,"Fantasque" line, Isis shape, Umbrella and Rain patt., wide ovoid body tapering to a flat flaring rim, decorated around the middle w/a wide band divided into panels each w/three large stylized 'blossoms' or 'umbrellas' in black, red & blue & divided by white bars, yellow bands at top & base, marked (small glaze nicks at rim, small ground off glaze bubble on base) 2,530.00

Vase, 11¾" h., 10" d., "Bizarre" ware, Lotus shape, Geometric patt., urn-form, handled, decorated w/a wide maroon base band & wide green neck band flanking a wide central band of triangular devices in a row in cream, purple, blue, maroon & green, black, blue & cream rim bands & cream handles, marked 2,200.00

Vase, 12" h., ovoid body w/lightly molded rings tapering to a flat rim flanked by loop handles, Lotus shape, Garland patt., polychrome bands of stylized flowers in orange, yellow, purple & blue, marked 805.00

CLEMINSON

Cleminson Comic Mug

Betty Cleminson began her home-based business, named "Cleminson Clay" in

1941. Within two years it was necessary to move to larger facilities in El Monte, California and the name was changed to "The California Cleminsons." Originally, Mrs. Cleminson concentrated on creating butter dishes, canisters, cookie jars - mostly kitchen related items. After the move, and with up to 150 employees, she was able to expand her lines with giftware such as vases, wall plaques, cups and saucers, cleanser shakers and a full line of tableware called Distlefink. The incised, stylistic "BC" mark was the first mark used; the California Cleminson mark can be found with or without the boy and girl on each side. The company went out of business in 1963.

Ashtray, model of a fish, two cigarette rests at bottom edge, hole for eye, light & dark ocean blue inside w/pale grey outside, second mark without boy & girl, ca. 1950, 7½" d., 2¾" h...$24.00

Butter dish, cov., figural, model of a Distlefink sitting in an oblong base, bird's head turned toward back, brown glossy glaze w/dark brown & rust accents, 7½" l., 5¾" h. 35.00

Cleanser shaker, figure of a woman standing, yellow hair, pink scarf over head, pink & white dress w/grey trim, five holes in top of head, 6½" h. 18.00

Mug, cov., man's face w/hangover expression, model of water bag forms cover, irregular shaped mug & rim, reverse of mug w/lettering "Morning after" & inside bottom of mug lettering, "Never again," white mug w/blue, dark pink, green & black accents, grey water bag bottom w/black rim & yellow top, second mark without boy & girl, 4½" d., 5" h. (ILLUS.) 26.00

Pie bird, figural, model of a bird, white body decorated in pink, green & blue, first mark, ca. 1941, 4½" h. 22.00

Pitcher, 10½" h., figural, model of a Distlefink, beak forms head, tail is handle, white body w/brown & green accents 30.00

Plate, 7" d., scalloped pale blue edge, pink & purple flowers, green leaves, light & dark pink butterflies, two holes for hanging, second mark without boy & girl 15.00

Razor blade holder, model of a man's face w/hand holding razor, slot in top for used blades, solid unglazed bottom w/stamped mark, 3¼" d., 3¼" h. 18.00

Child's Soup Mug

Soup mug, juvenile, straight sides w/one round knob on each side at rim, Native American boy & his dog playing & encircled by a white ring, pale pink body w/green, brown & white glazes for dog & boy, second mark w/boy & girl on each side, 4" d., 4¼ h. (ILLUS.) 36.00

Tea bag holder, model of a teapot w/words, "Let me hold the bag," yellow, blue & black glazes over white body, teapot open handle can be used for hanging, stamped mark, 4¼" h. 10.00

Wall plaque, h.p. girl w/green, white & brown dress holding bouquet of flowers, butterflies, two holes at top for hanging, first mark, ca. 1941, 3½" d., 4¾" h. 15.00

Wall pocket, model of a teapot, pale green body w/dark green lid, heart-shaped motif w/words "Kitchen bright & a singing kettle make home the place you want to settle," bail handle w/round wood center decorated w/painted flowers, 9" d., 6" h. 24.00

Wall pocket, model of a kettle w/three feet, black body w/white heart decorated w/words, "The kitchen is the heart of the home," bail handle, 4½" d., 4¼" h. 22.00

CLEWELL WARES

Small Clewell Vase

Though Charles W. Clewell of Canton, Ohio, didn't operate a pottery, he is responsible for a category of fine art pottery through his development of a unique metal coating placed on pottery blanks obtained from Owens, Weller and others. By encasing objects in a thin metal shell, he produced copper- and bronze-finished ceramics. Later experiments led him to chemically treat the metal coating to attain the blue-green patinated effect associated with copper and bronze. Although he produced metal-coated pottery from 1902 until the mid-1950s, Clewell's production was quite limited for he felt no one else could competently recreate his artwork and, therefore, operated a small shop with little help.

Bowl, 3⅛ h., wide flat bottom below the low rounded & incurved sides, mottled natural copper & coppery green patina, base marked "Clewell 422-2-6," early 20th c....................$247.50

Lemonade set: tankard pitcher & four mugs; each w/a footed ovoid body tapering to a wide flat rim, loop handles, the pitcher w/a wide & long rim spout, each piece w/a body clad in riveted rectangular copper plating w/a dark natural patina, each piece stamped "Clewell Canton Ohio," ca. 1910, pitcher 10" h., the set (one mug w/copper tear glued down) 715.00

Vase, 3¾" h., 4" d., squatty bulbous body w/a wide shoulder to a flat mouth, copper-clad w/a reddish brown & verdigris patina, hand-incised "Clewell - 343 - 26" 220.00

Vase, 4½" h., 3½" d., footed ovoid body w/a very wide, flaring mouth, copper-clad w/a fine verdigris & brown patina, hand-incised "Clewell 11 - 330-2-9 - UYX" 440.00

Vase, 5" h., 3" d., ovoid body tapering to a wide, flat mouth, copper-clad w/a bronze & verdigris patina, hand-incised "Clewell - 324-26" 357.50

Vase, 6" h., 4¾" d., footed ovoid shouldered body w/a wide molded low neck, copper-clad faceted body in brown & green w/raised bands of upright scrolls, fine patina, unmarked (copper peeling on inside) ..485.00

Vase, 7" h., ovoid body tapering to a short narrow ringed neck w/a widely flaring rolled rim, streaky light & dark green coppery patina, base incised "Clewell 435-1-6" & "CW"..............1,100.00

Vase, 7" h., 4½" d., tapering ovoid body w/a wide shoulder to a very small flared neck, copper-clad, medium brown patina, hand-incised "Clewell - 338-4" (ILLUS.) 357.50

Vase, 7" h., 4¾" d., tapering base, rounded shoulder & tiny mouth, copper jacket w/fine brown & verdigris patina, hand-incised "Clewell 388-2-9" 880.00

Clewell Floor Vase

Vase, 11⅜ h., baluster-form body

w/short flaring neck, copper-clad w/a mottled natural copper & coppery green patina, base incised "Clewell 302-2-6," ca, 1940 (moderate wear to patina) 605.00

Vase, 16" h., tall baluster-form copper-clad body w/flared rim on the short neck, mottled coppery blue patina, base inscribed "Clewell 277-6," on a Weller blank (minor scratches & abrasions on patina).. 1,540.00

Vase, 21½" h., 10" d., floor-type, milk can-shaped, copper-clad w/a reddish dark brown & verdigris patina, hand-incised "Clewell - 450-26" (ILLUS. top next column) 2,750.00

CLEWS, J. & R.

James and Ralph Clews established this pottery in Cobridge, England in 1814 and operated it until 1836 when it was taken over by Wood & Brownfield. Some of the wares have been reproduced. Also see HISTORICAL & COMMEMORATIVE.

Cup plate, "The Errand Boy," Wilkie series, flowers & scrolls border, dark blue transfer, 3½" d................$302.50

Pitcher, 6⅜" h., pearlware, bulbous ovoid body w/a wide spout & C-scroll handle, h.p. w/large stylized peony-like blossoms & scrolling leaves in blue, dark blue rim band, impressed mark (edge chips, hairlines) 192.50

Plate, 9" d., "The Valentine," Wilkie series, flowers & scrolls border, dark blue transfer....................................290.00

Plate, 10" d., "Picturesque View Nr. Fishkill, Hudson River," black transfer..195.00

Plate, 10" d., scene of Troy from Mt. Ida, black transfer 195.00

Plate, 10" d., Coronation patt., medium blue transfer-printed design of a floral bouquet, fruits & a small bird..181.50

Plate, 10½" d., Oriental landscape scene, dark blue transfer, impressed mark...137.50

Soup plate, "Sancho Panza at the Boar Hunt," floral border, dark blue transfer, 9¾" d. 192.50

Soup plate w/flanged rim, "Doctor Syntax mistakes a gentleman's house for an Inn," floral border, dark blue transfer, 9⅞" d.........................165.00

Toddy plate, blue feather-edged design, impressed mark, 4¾" d. (pinpoint flakes, in-the-making hairline) 71.50

Vegetable dish, "Dr. Syntax Sells Grizzle," molded ribbon handles, flowers & scrolls border, dark blue transfer, 8 x 11½" (wear & small surface flakes) 550.00

CLIFTON POTTERY

William A. Long, an organizer of the Lonhuda Pottery, and Fred Tschirner, a chemist, established the Clifton Art Pottery in Newark, New Jersey, in 1905. The first art pottery produced was designated the Crystal Patina line and was decorated with a subdued pale green crystalline glaze which was later also made in shades of yellow and tan. Indian Ware, introduced in 1906, was patterned after the pottery made by the American Indians. These two lines are the most notable in the pottery's production though Tirrube and Robin's-egg Blue lines were also produced. After 1911, production shifted to floor and wall tiles and by 1914 the pottery's name was changed to Clifton Porcelain Tile Company to better reflect this production.

Bowl-vase, compressed globular body tapering to a small mouth, fine matte green flambé glaze over a crystalline apple green glaze, marked "Clifton 1906," ca. 1906, 8" d., 4" h. $605.00

Humidor, cov., Indian Ware, unglazed brick red exterior w/geometric Indian relief-molding at rim & on lid, black matte incised & h.p. decoration around center, glazed interior 95.00

Teapot, cov., compressed squatty bulbous sides w/a low rim supporting a flattened cover w/button finial, a short cylindrical angled spout on one side & long loop handle on opposite side, mottled greyish green Crystal Patina glaze, stamped "271-30," ca. 1910, 3⅜" h. 165.00

Teapot, cov., a tall wide funnel base tapering up & continuing to form the squatty bulbous body w/a short flaring cylindrical spout & a heavy loop handle, a low domed cover w/button finial, pale mottled green Crystal Patina glaze, ca. 1910, company mark & "272-42," 5⅜" h. ...302.50

Teapot, cov., Indian Ware, impressed decoration on mottled yellow lustre w/gold trim, 7½" h. 50.00

Vase, 2½" h., 3½" d., squatty bulbous body raised on three small curved tab feet, the closed rim molded w/stylized lily pads, matte green glaze, incised "Clifton - 146" 385.00

Vase, 3½" h., 3½" d., spherical body tapering to a tiny, short neck, the sides molded in high-relief w/swirling fish, matte green glaze, incised "Clifton - CAP - 1906 - 108," dated 1906 ....495.00

Vase, 3¾" h., a very wide squatty compressed body centered by a short neck supporting a swelled rim pulled into two wide loop handles curving down to attach to the shoulder, mottled pale green & bluish green Crystal Patina glaze, marked & dated "1905" & "113" 165.00

Vase, 5¾" h., 5" d., Indian Ware, squatty bulbous base tapering to a short cylindrical neck, decorated around the lower body w/wide black & ivory intertwining bands against the brick red unglazed ground, two black & ivory sawtooth bands around the neck, die-stamped mark "Clifton" & incised "Arkansas 238" ...357.50

Vase, 6" h., 7¼" d., squatty spherical body on a narrow footring, tapering to a short, narrow mouth, fine Crystal Patina pale green & gold satin glaze, incised "Clifton - CAP - 161 - 1905," dated 1905 ....330.00

Vase, 6¾" h., squatty bulbous base tapering to a wide cylindrical neck w/flared rim, creamy crystalline Crystal Patina glaze w/yellow around the neck, decorated around the body w/silver overlay in an ornate looping & scrolling vine design w/large blossoms above, silver band around the rim, overlay work by Electrolytic of Trenton, New Jersey, company mark, dated "1906" & incised "171" 880.00

Vase, 6¾" h., 4¾" d., Crystal Patina line, expanding cylinder w/closed-in mouth, embossed decoration of large poppy blossoms & stems cascading down the sides, light green glaze w/white showing through, impressed "#173"...............522.50

Vase, 8¼" h., 5½" d., bottle-shaped w/a squatty bulbous body tapering to a tall cylindrical neck, Crystal Patina light green & brown shaded crystalline glaze, incised "Clifton - CAP - 106 - 164," 1906....................357.50

Vase, 8½" h., 5" d., bottle-shaped w/compressed globular base & long slender neck, greenish gold speckled glaze w/green drips, marked "Clifton, 1906," ca. 1906 .....247.50

COALPORT

Japan Pattern Coalport Platter

Coalport Porcelain Works operated at Coalport, Shropshire, England, from about 1795 to 1926 and has operated at Stoke-on-Trent as Coalport China, Ltd., making bone china since then.

Bough pots, D-shaped, each painted in shades of iron-red, rose, purple, green & yellow w/anemones, ranuculus & roses or poppies, convolvulus, ranunculus & roses against a black ground in a rectangular panel flanked by lightly fluted pilasters, the sides w/slightly recessed panels painted in rose against the gold ground w/neo-classical foliate scrolls issuing from demi-eagles above urns in ovals, & raised on four gilt ball feet, now fitted w/brass covers pierced w/three large & four small circular apertures, ca. 1810, 8$\frac{11}{16}$" l., pr. (one w/footrim chip, small hairline in back, small rim chip, star crack on base).......$9,200.00

Dessert service: pair oval fruit stands, pr. scalloped lozenge-shaped dishes, pr. square dishes, pr. shell-shaped dishes & 12 plates; 'Rock and Tree' patt., each piece painted in an expanded Imari palette of underglaze-blue, iron-red, green, salmon & gold w/an acacia tree & peonies growing by a double rock in a fenced garden, the rim w/a 'brocade' border of floral, foliate & cell diaper panels within a gilt edge, ca. 1805-10, fruit stands 11$\frac{7}{8}$" & 12$\frac{1}{8}$" l., 20 pcs. 7,475.00

Dish, undulating reticulated rim, decorated w/stylized bird & flowers center w/floral medallions at rim, 9" d..214.50

Inkstand, the drum-shaped body w/a pale pink ground patterned w/gilt-centered white dots, reserved on the front w/a gilt-edged chamfered rectangular panel colorfully painted w/peasants cooking & conversing in a hilly landscape, & interrupted at the sides w/gilt foliate-bordered semicircular wells, & at the back w/two gilt quill holders flanking a gilt handle forming a taperstick, the slightly dished top w/a gilt palmette border (slight wear) pierced w/three quill holes & encircling a removable inkpot, ca. 1815, 6$\frac{3}{8}$" w. (some wear at gilt edges) 550.00

Platter, 21$\frac{3}{8}$" l., oval, Japan patt., painted w/a central gilt blossom on a field of green & yellow foliage surrounded by gilt-dashed under-glaze-blue trees, iron-red, green & yellow blossoms, berries & leaves, & iron-red ground panels of underglaze-blue & gilt stylized plants bearing yellow leaves, the wavy rim edged w/a gilt band, wear to gilt band, ca. 1805 (ILLUS.)................1,495.00

Vase, 8$\frac{13}{16}$" h., 'Church Gresley' patt., decorated around the flaring cylindrical neck w/a colorful floral garland between gilt hatched & berried foliate band borders repeated in variation around the shield-shaped body & flaring circular foot & enclosing an elaborate pattern of yellow hexagons reserved w/gilt ovals painted w/cornflowers & surrounded by rose sprigs in diamond-shaped panels alternating w/rectangular panels of green & iron-red ovals, the front reserved w/a gilt-edged floral panel, the lower body w/a gilt border of arches & sprigs above the knopped ankle & the integral square base fully gilded, painted probably in the London studio of James Giles, ca. 1805 (ankle repaired).............................1,150.00

COOKIE JARS

All sorts of charming and whimsical cookie jars have been produced in recent decades and these are increasingly collectible today. Many well known American potteries such as McCoy, Hull and Abingdon, produced cookie jars and their products are included in those listings. Below we are listing cookie jars produced by other companies.

Current reference books for collectors include: The Collector's Encyclopedia of Cookie Jars, *by Fred and Joyce Roerig (Collector Books, 1991);* Collector's Encyclopedia of Cookie Jars, Book II *by Fred and Joyce Roerig (Collector Books, 1994) and* The Complete Cookie Jar Book *by Mike Schneider (Schiffer, Ltd., 1991).*

AMERICAN BISQUE

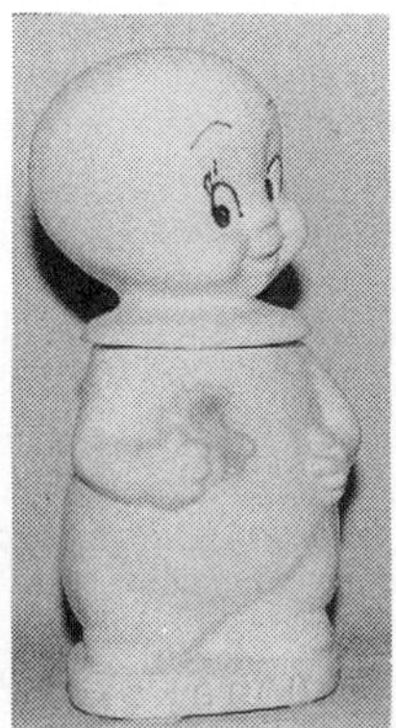

Casper Cookie Jar

Baby Elephant $105.00

Bear with Cookies....35.00

Bear with Hat....60.00

Bear with Honey, flasher-type....350.00 to 400.00

Blackboard Boy....400.00

Blackboard Clown....250.00 to 300.00

Blackboard Girl....300.00 to 350.00

Boy Bear w/blue pants....75.00

Casper, the Friendly Ghost (ILLUS.)..850.00

Cheerleaders, flasher-type....275.00 to 300.00

Chef....210.00

Chick with yellow & brown coat....48.00

Churn....35.00

Clown on Stage, black curtains, flasher-type....250.00 to 300.00

Coffeepot....25.00

Coffeepot, with "Cookies"....45.00

Collegiate Owl....50.00 to 75.00

Cookie Barrel....35.00

Cookie Truck....50.00 to 75.00

Cowboy Boots....175.00 to 200.00

Davy Crockett Cookie Jar

Davy Crockett, standing, name across chest (ILLUS.)....450.00

Dutch Boy....70.00

Dutch Girl....70.00

Elephant w/Baseball Cap....75.00 to 100.00

Fred Flintstone, Dino finial (ILLUS. top next column)....900.00 To 1,200.00

French Poodle, blue decoration....85.00

Girl Bear w/Cookie....75.00

Grandma....100.00 to 125.00

Fred Flintstone Cookie Jar

Hot Chocolate Mug....50.00

Kids Watching TV, "Sandman Cookies," flasher-type....300.000

Kitten and Beehive....50.00

Kittens on Ball of Yarn....40.00

Lady Pig....85.00

Majorette....350.00 to 400.00

Milk Wagon, with "Cookies & Milk"....95.00

Pennsylvania Dutch Girl....350.00 to 375.00

Pig Dancer....30.00

Pig-in-Poke....65.00

Pig w/Hands in Pockets....95.00

Pig w/Straw Hat....75.00

Pinky Lee Head, blue hat....550.00

Rabbit in Hat....65.00

Recipe Jar....75.00

Ring the Bell for Cookies....50.00 to 75.00

Rubbles House....850.00

Saddle Blackboard....165.00

Saddle, without blackboard....200.00 to 225.00

Santa Head, laughing....300.00

Schoolhouse w/bell lid, "After School Cookies"....40.00 to 50.00

Spaceship, w/"Cookies Out of This World"....300.00 to 350.00

Train Engine, gold trim....195.00

Treasure Chest....110.00

Tugboat, blue, light brown & green....95.00

Umbrella Kids....350.00 to 375.00

Yarn Doll....75.00 to 100.00

Yogi Bear Cookie Jar

Yogi Bear (ILLUS.) ....350.00 to 450.00

BRAYTON - LAGUNA

Granny...389.00

Lady, floral top...................................645.00

Mammy, blue dress 1,200.00

BRUSH - MC COY

Davy Crockett Cookie Jar

Cinderella Pumpkin ....175.00 to 225.00

Circus Horse, green, brown & white trim ....900.00 to 1,000.00

Clown bust.........................350.00 to 400.00

Clown w/brown pants ....175.00 to 200.00

Cookie House ....50.00 to 75.00

Covered Wagon.................................750.00

Cow, w/Cat finial, brown ....75.00 to 100.00

Cow, w/Cat finial, purple & white ....1,200.00 to 1,400.00

Davy Crockett, brown (ILLUS.) ....350.00 to 400.00

Davy Crockett, gold decoration ....875.00 to 900.00

Elephant w/Ice Cream Cone, wearing baby hat...425.00

Fish, 1971 ....550.00

Formal Pig ....250.00 to 275.00

Granny, green dress...........450.00 to 500.00

Granny, white w/blue polka dots on dress 450.00

Happy Bunny, grey ....200.00 to 250.00

Hillbilly Frog 5,000.00

Humpty Dumpty w/Beanie ..250.00 to 275.00

Humpty Dumpty w/Peaked Hat ....175.00 to 200.00

Little Red Riding Hood, large..............600.00

Nite Owl ....100.00 to 150.00

Old Woman's Shoe..............................95.00

Owl, not stylized, yellow 110.00

Panda Bear..125.00

Peter Pan Cookie Jar

Peter Pan, large (ILLUS.) ....700.00 to 1,000.00

Peter Pumpkin Eater (Pumpkin w/Lock on Door)..............300.00 to 400.00

Puppy Police.......................600.00 to 650.00

Red Riding Hood 595.00

Sitting Pig 425.00

Smiling Bear ....375.00 to 425.00

Squirrel on Log ....75.00 to 100.00

Squirrel w/Top Hat.............250.00 to 300.00

Stylized Owl, brown 350.00

Teddy Bear, feet together...100.00 to 125.00

Three Bears, tree stump finial ....75.00 to 100.00

Treasure Chest....................................95.00

CALIFORNIA ORIGINALS

Cookie Monster Cookie Jar

Bert & Ernie Fine Cookies, No. 977 ....250.00 to 300.00

Big Bird, No. 976 ....100.00

Christmas Tree ....125.00 to 150.00

Cookie Monster (ILLUS.) 50.00

The Count...........................450.00 to 500.00

Donald Duck Cookie Jar

Donald Duck & Pumpkin (ILLUS.) 275.00

Dumbo's Greatest Cookies on Earth ..125.00

Eeyore 395.00

Ernie ....50.00 to 75.00

Oscar the Grouch, No. 972 (ILLUS. top next column.) 75.00

Rabbit on Stump, No. 2620 ....65.00

Raggedy Ann......................................60.00

Santa Claus, standing, No. 871 ....150.00

Sheriff w/Hole in Hat..............50.00 to 70.00

Tiger 115.00

Tigger 155.00

Oscar the Grouch Cookie Jar

Winnie the Pooh, No. 907.....75.00 to 100.00

Woody Woodpecker in Tree House, copyright by Walter Lantz 625.00

DORANNE OF CALIFORNIA

Cat w/Bow Tie 45.00

Cookie Cola, bottle-shaped 55.00

Cow Jumped Over the Moon.............175.00

Duck w/Basket of Corn 75.00

Elephant, seated..................................40.00

Owl, wearing mortar board hat 110.00

Pig w/Barrel of Pork.............................85.00

Pinocchio Head, non-Disney, marked "CJ46" 250.00

FITZ & FLOYD

Rio Rita..95.00

Santa Claus on Motorcycle w/Side Car ....300.00 to 375.00

Santa Claus & Plane (Spirit of St. Nicholas) 185.00

MADDUX OF CALIFORNIA

Humpty Dumpty.................................225.00

Raggedy Andy ....200.00 to 250.00

MAURICE OF CALIFORNIA

Gigantic Clown 250.00

Kittens in Shoe, tan tones, gold trim...120.00

METLOX POTTERIES

Barrel of Apples 65.00

Bear with Bow, "Beau"..........75.00 to 100.00

Bear on Roller Skates........................125.00

Bear with Sombrero (Pancho) 85.00

Bunch of Grapes Jar

Bunch of Grapes (ILLUS.) ....175.00 to 200.00

Calico Cat, lime green 85.00

Chicken (Mother Hen) 75.00

Clown, standing, black & white outfit ....150.00 to 175.00

Cookie Girl, matte glaze 125.00

Cow with Butterfly, purple...400.00 to 600.00

Daisies, globe-shaped w/pedestal base 50.00

Dinosaur, "Mona"....................150.00 to 175.00

Dog, Fido 75.00

Duck with Raincoat (Puddles) ....75.00 to 100.00

Dutch Boy ....150.00 to 175.00

Gingham Dog 74.00

Humpty Dumpty by Metlox

Humpty Dumpty (ILLUS.) ...250.00 to 275.00

Kitten Head w/Hat, "meows" when hat tipped ....100.00 to 125.00

Koala Bear ....100.00 to 125.00

Lamb's Head w/Hat 100.00

Lion, seated ....175.00 to 200.00

Mammy, yellow polka dots 495.00

Mouse, Chef Pierre....................75.00 to 100.00

Orange....................89.00

Panda Bear....................100.00

Pelican Coach (U.S. Diving Team).....125.00

Penguin (Frosty) 120.00

Rabbit on Cabbage....................154.00

Raccoon, Cookie Bandit....................95.00

Raggedy Andy ....200.00 to 225.00

Raggedy Ann....................130.00

Rose Blossom Cookie Jar

Rose Blossom (ILLUS.) 450.00

Scottie Dog, black....................175.00 to 200.00

Sir Francis Drake (duck)....................50.00

Slenderella (pig) ....100.00 to 125.00

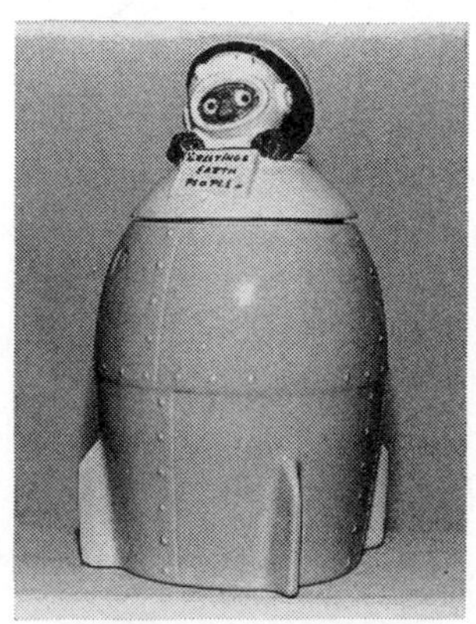

Metlox Spaceship

Spaceship (ILLUS.) ....400.00 to 450.00

Squirrel on Pine Cone ....75.00 to 100.00

Strawberry ....75.00 to 85.00

Topsy, blue & white polka dots...........450.00

Wheat Sheaf w/Ribbon.........................25.00

MOSIAC TILE

Mammy, blue dress ....650.00 to 700.00

Mammy, white dress & apron w/blue & yellow trim 1,500.00

NAPCO

Little Red Riding Hood

Cinderella 125.00

Dog, "Alpo Dan"...................................45.00

Little Bo Peep 250.00

Little Red Riding Hood (ILLUS.) 225.00

PEARL CHINA

Black Chef w/"Cooky" on front.................................450.00 to 500.00

Black Chef, w/gold trim.......................700.00

Mammy..............................700.00 to 900.00

POTTERY GUILD

Elsie the Cow Jar

Balloon Lady..65.00

Dutch Boy ....60.00 to 80.00

Dutch Girl...80.00

Elsie the Cow (ILLUS.) ....275.00 to 325.00

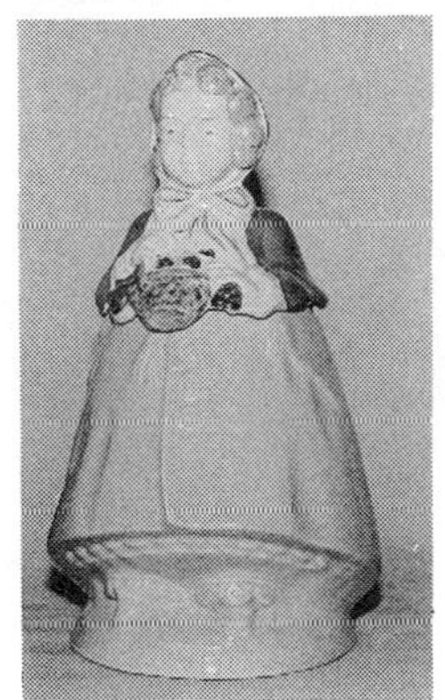

Little Red Riding Hood

Little Red Riding Hood (ILLUS.) ....125.00 to 150.00

Rooster 75.00

REGAL CHINA

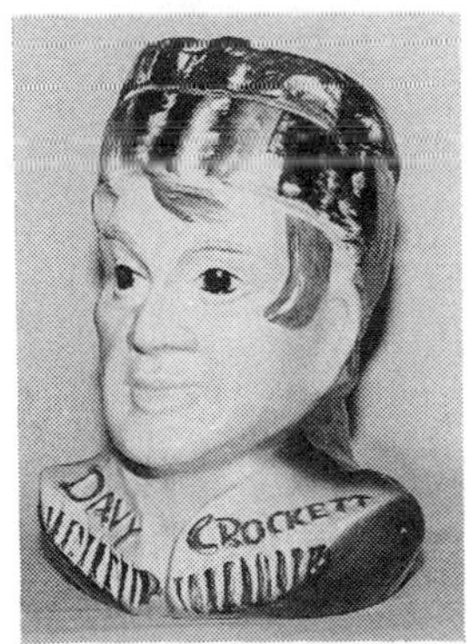

Regal Davy Crockett Jar

Barn, Old MacDonald line...400.00 to 450.00

Churn Boy...275.00

Davy Crockett (ILLUS.).......................375.00

French Chef........................200.00 to 250.00

Goldilocks ....300.00 to 350.00

Hubert the Lion 850.00

Humpty Dumpty..................300.00 to 350.00

Kraft-T-Bear (Kraft Marsh-mallows)..........................200.00 to 250.00

Little Miss Muffet (ILLUS .top next column) ....200.00 to 250.00

Little Red Riding Hood.......................295.00

Regal Little Miss Muffet

Pig in Diaper ....400.00 to 500.00

Quaker Oats Canister.........100.00 to 150.00

ROBINSON RANSBOTTOM

Cow Jumped Over Moon Jar

Chef with Bowl of Eggs.......200.00 to 225.00

Cow Jumped Over Moon [Hi Diddle Diddle] (ILLUS.) ....200.00 to 225.00

Dutch Girl............................175.00 to 225.00

Hootie Owl (Wise Bird) ....50.00 to 75.00

Jocko the Monkey...............375.00 to 400.00

Sailor Jack 200.00

Sheriff Pig ....100.00 to 115.00

World War II Soldier (Bud) ....150.00 to 200.00

TWIN WINTON

Bambi, beside stump 90.00

Barn, "Cookie Barn" 40.00

Churn & Kittens (ILLUS. top next column)..................................60.00 to 80.00

Chipmunk 65.00

Churn & Kittens Cookie Jar

Cookie Time Clock Jar

Cookie Time Clock, button lid (ILLUS.) ....125.00 to 175.00

Cookie Time Clock, mouse on lid ....22.50 to 27.50

Cooky Catcher Truck............................65.00

Cow ....65.00 to 75.00

Dutch Girl...............................50.00 to 75.00

Elf Bakery Tree Stump ....45.00 to 55.00

Friar Tuck 50.00

Hotei (Buddha) 175.00

Ole King Cole Cookie Jar

Ole King Cole (ILLUS.) ....150.00 to 175.00

Persian Kitten 65.00

Raccoon 75.00

Ranger Bear ....45.00 to 55.00

Rooster 60.00

Sailor Elephant ....55.00 to 65.00

Squirrel on Nut, "Cookie Nut" ....35.00 to 45.00

Turtle, seated..........................70.00 to 90.00

Walrus Cookie Jar

Walrus (ILLUS.) 95.00

VANDOR

Betty Boop, standing ....725.00 to 750.00

Howdy Doody, head 375.00

Howdy Doody in Bumper Car 250.00

Juke Box, Auxiliary wall box ....100.00 to 150.00

Popeye, head ....425.00 to 475.00

WISECARVER

Angel 70.00

Mixing Bowl Mammy...........175.00 to 200.00

Rumpelstiltskin 125.00

MISCELLANEOUS COMPANIES

Butler (Carol Gifford) 145.00

Daisy Mae in Barrel (Imperial Porcelain, Paul Webb design) 795.00

Dog House w/Cat on Roof (Starnes of California) 250.00

Donald Duck w/Hand in Cookie Jar (Hoan Ltd.) 75.00

Humpty Dumpty (Puriton Pottery Co.) 425.00

Kooky-K-Egg (Green Products)..........200.00

Liberty Bell (House of Webster)............25.00

Mickey Mouse w/Chef's Hat & Rolling Pin (Hoan Ltd.) 50.00

Nun, "The Lord Helps Him Who Helps Himself" (Deforest of California).......275.00

Pirate on Chest (Starnes of California) 395.00

R2-D2 Cookie Jar

R2-D2, Roman Ceramics (ILLUS.) 200.00

Smoky Bear head (Norcrest) 450.00

Snoopy (Holiday Designs) 60.00

Snowman (B.C. - Made in U.S.A.)........55.00

Tasmanian Devil (Warner Bros., Inc., The Good Co.) ....300.00 to 350.00

Trolley with People (Otagiri) ...30.00 to 40.00

Young Lady, head (Lefton Co.) 75.00

COPELAND & SPODE

Early Spode Dinner Service

W.T. Copeland & Sons, Ltd., have operated the Spode Works at Stoke, England, from 1847 to the present. The name Spode was used on some of its productions. Its predecessor, Spode, was founded by Josiah Spode about 1784 and became Copeland & Garrett in 1843, continuing under that name until 1847. Listings dated prior to 1843 should be attributed to Spode.

Bouillon cups & underplates, red, navy & green floral decoration, ribbed body, scalloped rims, ca. 1900-10, four sets, 8 pcs. $200.00

Cake plate, pedestal base, Spode's Tower patt., pink 125.00

Coffeepot, cov., Queen's Bird patt......140.00

Coffeepot, cov., straight-sided, Spode's Italian patt., blue, 9" h. 175.00

Cup & saucer, demitasse, Mayflower patt., decorated w/mulberry flowers & scrolls on the exterior, h.p. red flowers decoration on the interior, ornate handle, gadrooned rim, marked "Copeland - Spode - England - Mayflower".........................23.00

Dinner service: 14⅝" l. oval soup tureen, cover & 17³⁄₁₆" l. undertray, a pair of 9⅜" w. square cov. vegetable dishes, an 18⁷⁄₁₆" l. chamfered rectangular platter, a 16¹¹⁄₁₆" l. platter, a pair of 14⅝" platters, a pair of 12⁷⁄₁₆" l. platters, an 11¹⁄₁₆" l. platter & a 10¼" l. platter & a 15" l. pierced oval strainer, a pair of oval sauce tureens, underplates & one cover, eight octagonal soup plates, 20 octagonal dinner plates & 16 octagonal dessert plates; pearlware, Italian patt., blue transfer-printed landscape design, impressed "SPODE" marks, ca. 1820, together w/a modern milk pitcher, three breakfast cups & saucers, a teabowl & seven teacups & saucers marked "COPELAND - SPODE'S ITALIAN - ENGLAND," & a similar early sauce-boat, various damages, the set (ILLUS. of part) 4,313.00

Ginger jar, cov., Spode's Tower patt., pink 300.00

Plate, 8¼" w., cabinet-type, squared w/notched corners, painted in the center in shades of rose, iron-red, purple, yellow & green w/an arrangement of flowers in a yellow urn behind a sprig of pink roses on a brown marbleized ledge against a shaded brown ground, the cavetto w/a gilt band, & the gilt-edged rim w/a tooled gilt border of flower-filled baskets alternating w/pairs of eagles flanking a flaming torch & all conjoined by foliate scrollwork, marked "SPODE" in worn gilt, ca. 1825...1,495.00

Plate, 10½" d., decorated w/basket of colorful flowers & fruit, marked "Copeland - England".........................90.00

Plates, 9⅞" d., armorial-type, scalloped rim, each painted in the center in black, grey, gold & iron-red w/the arms & crest of Dent of Dent near Newcastle upon Tyne, impaling another within a gilt scroll-and shell border on the cavetto beneath the spring green ground rim, molded edge trimmed in gilt, one marked "SPODE" in iron-red, the other w/the wreathed "Spode Felspar Porcelain" mark in purple, ca. 1825, pr. 805.00

Punch bowl, Spode's Tower patt., blue, 15½" d....................................200.00

Soup plates, ironstone, dark blue transfer-printed floral bouquet in the center & six floral clusters around the rim, overall polychrome enamel & gilt trim, marked "Copeland," 9" d., set of 6 (one w/rim chip) 132.00

Spill vase, cylindrical, the front painted in shades of iron-red, blue, yellow, rose & grey w/three shells, coral & seaweed against a shaded drab-brown ground within a gilt-edged rectangular panel, the reverse decorated in gold w/two birds drinking from a fountain between urns supported on foliate scrolls pendent w/floral garlands, the rim & flaring foot w/gilt borders, ca. 1820, "Spode" mark in iron-red, 3" h. (slight border wear)..........................690.00

Teapot, cov., Spode's Tower patt., pink 400.00

CORDEY

Founded by Boleslaw Cybis in Trenton, New Jersey, the Cordey China Company was the forerunner of the Cybis Studio, renowned for its fine porcelain sculptures. A native of Poland, Boleslaw Cybis was commissioned by his government to paint "al fresco" murals for the 1939 New York World's Fair. Already a renowned sculptor and painter, he elected to remain and become a citizen of this country. In 1942, under his guidance, Cordey China Company began producing appealing busts and figurines, some decorated by applying real lace dipped in liquid clay prior to firing in the kiln. Cordey figures were assigned numbers that were printed or pressed on the base. The Cordey line was eventually phased out of production during the 1950s as the porcelain sculptures of the Cybis Studios became widely acclaimed.

Candleholder, three-light, a slender arched scroll-molded strip applied w/flowers, applied w/three upright flower spirals staggered along the arch & serving as the candleholders, lavender & other colors w/gold trim, No. 8013, 12" l. $80.00

Figure of a Chinese goddess, tall standing female w/a tall purple headdress w/blue trim & red roses w/cinnamon leaves & yellow lace, lavender long outer gown w/dark figure work & a big blue medallion, flat blue lace trim on the long open sleeves, inner gown w/panels of gold over quilting & green & yellow flat lace, one shoe pokes out, on a high scroll-molded & gilt-trimmed base, No. 5073, 12" h. 125.00

Figure of a Colonial man, standing wearing a long black coat over a yellow & black striped tunic, lace jabot, cuffs & trim, yellow britches & white stockings w/black shoes, curly hair, on a scroll base w/a tree stump w/applied roses & leaves, No. 4047, 13" h...165.00

Figure of a male harvester, standing wearing a mauve & cherry red hat & vest, mauve shirt & orange britches, No. 305, 16" h. 80.00

Figure of a man, standing wearing a large hat w/four pink leaves & white lace trimmed w/gold in bows & streamers, a long pink lace cape w/drapes & folds & white lace top ruffle & shoulder drape, a creamy figured blouse w/many gathers & turned-back cuffs & gold-trimmed pink lace streamer down the front, skin-tight pink britches flared & w/bows just below the knees, scrolled uprights on the round base trimmed w/flowers & leaves, No. 4153, 14" h. (one cape fold w/tiny crack, one leaf point off) 115.00

Figure of a Neopolitan boy, standing wearing a colorful outfit, on a scroll-molded base w/applied leaves & flowers, No. 5046, 9½" h....................85.00

Figure of a woman, standing & wearing ornate 18th c. costume w/ruffled paniers & lacy trim, her hair piled high on her head & trimmed w/applied roses, on a scroll-molded base, colorful decoration, No. 5084, 11¼" h...85.00

Figure of a Yorkshire girl, standing & balancing a jug on her left shoulder & holding grapes in the folds of her skirt w/her right hand, lace-like sleeves & skirt ruffles, nicely decorated, No. 5047, 10" h. 85.00

Figures of a lady & gentleman, standing & wearing 18th c. costumes, she w/a low-cut blouse w/ruffles, bustle & petticoat w/ruffles & a hat w/bow, holding a fan, decorated in shades of green w/some mauve, he wearing a waistcoat & shirt w/ruffles, a hat & pantaloons & holding a bouquet of flowers, same colors as the lady, lady No. 300, 15½" h., pr. 145.00

Figure group, courting couple, a lady & gentleman in ornate costumes, he standing & holding a mandolin, she seated, his outfit w/profuse folds of pink lace at the top, elbows & knees, she w/ringlets in her hair & her entire skirt & bodice trimmed w/ornate lace, the base applied w/flowers & leaves, gold trim, No. 4129A, 6¼" d., 11" h. (minor lace damage).............275.00

Lamp base, a bust of Madame DuBarry, her piled hair w/large center-part curls & a long curl down one shoulder, all trimmed w/applied flowers & ribbons, wearing a swagged lace-trimmed bodice w/a large applied ribbon at one shoulder, raised on a tall, angled scroll-molded base & set on a separate lamp base, lovely colors & gold trim, No. 8039, bust 14¼" h. 225.00

Model of a bird on a pedestal-form stump base, the chubby bird w/a black neck & head w/a short, sharp beak, russet breast & grey & black body w/long black folded wings, the stump base w/applied green leaves & pink trim, gold banding on the base, No, 2037, 8½" h. 110.00

Model of a lamb, ears extended, on a scrolled base w/a tree stump & applied leaves & flowers, No. 6025 .....135.00

Wall shelf, model of a cornucopia, half-round, flat shelf above the twisted & curled horn applied w/a large cupid figure on one side & applied blossoms, lavender scrolls, mauve roses, green leaves & buds & gilt trim, No. 7028, 8" h. 95.00

COWAN

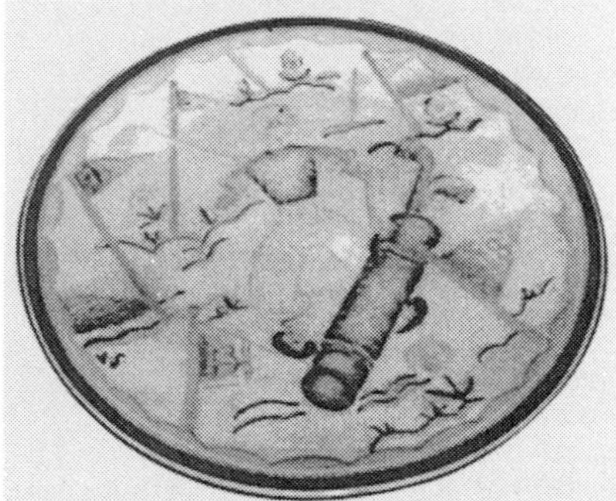

Golf Pattern Charger

R. Guy Cowan first opened a studio pottery in 1913 in Cleveland, Ohio. The pottery continued to operate almost continuously, at various locations in the Cleveland area, until it was forced to close in 1931 due to financial problems. This fine art pottery, which was gradually expanded into a full line of commercial productions, is now sought out by collectors.

Bowl, 9¼" d., pedestal base, ribbed sides, scalloped rim, ivory glaze w/green interior $34.00

Candlesticks, scalloped rim, orange lustre glaze, 3¾" h., pr. 32.00

Charger, round, the flat front incised w/the Tennis patt. featuring stylized abstract tennis rackets & a net, all-white glaze, designed by Viktor Schreckengost, marked on the back, artist-initialed in the design, ca. 1930, 11¼" d................................1,210.00

Charger, round, the flat surface decorated w/the stylized Fox Hunt patt., hunters on horseback & dogs & birds in pastel shades of purple, green, yellow & red on a cream crackle ground, designed by Viktor Schreckengost, marked & artist-initialed, ca. 1930, 11⅜" d................797.50

Charger, round, the flat front decorated w/the Golf patt. featuring a stylized golfer w/bag of clubs & various flags in the grassy background, decorated in pastel shades of yellow, green, purple & red against a cream crackled ground, marked on the back & artist-initials in the design, ca. 1930, 11½" d.(ILLUS.) 1,320.00

Console set: three-light candlesticks & center bowl; floral scroll design, mint green glaze, 3 pcs. 225.00

Flower frog, figural nude w/scarf, white glaze, 6½" h...........................135.00

'Jazz' Punch Bowl

Punch bowl, 'Jazz Bowl,' deep flaring bell-form sides on a small foot, geometric abstract designs with "JAZZ" in a large circle on the side, glazed in glossy blue & black, designed by Viktor Schreckengost, ca. 1931, 13⅝" d., 8½" h. (ILLUS.) 16,500.00

Vase, 7½" h., simple classical shape, blue lustre glaze, ink stamped mark ..50.00

Vase, 8" h., fan-shaped w/figural sea horse base, yellow matte glaze 85.00

Vase, 11" h., melon-ribbed w/flared rim, Sunrise glaze 225.00

Vase, 11⅛" h., figural, the oblong plinth base supporting a figural stylized Oriental pheasant which supports a flaring ribbed trumpet-form vase on its back, pale celadon green frothy glaze, die-stamped mark, ca. 1929 ....330.00

CUP PLATES (Earthenware)

Like their glass counterparts, these small plates were designed to hold a cup while the tea or coffee was allowed to cool in a saucer before it was sipped from the saucer, a practice that would now be considered in poor taste. The forerunner of the glass cup plates, those listed below were produced in various Staffordshire potteries in England. Their popularity waned after the introduction of the glass cup plate in the 1820s.

Staffordshire (unmarked), medium blue transfer-printed scene of a man standing by a rail fence, 3⅝" d.........$82.50

Staffordshire (unmarked), dark blue transfer-printed scene w/three children, 3¾" d. 82.50

Staffordshire (unmarked), black transfer-printed Alpine scene, 3⅞" d..........33.00

Staffordshire (unmarked), dark blue transfer-printed English country scene, floral border w/pink lustre wash, 3⅞" d. (pinpoint on table ring)..77.00

Staffordshire (unmarked), medium blue transfer-printed scene of soldier & girl, 3⅞" d. (pinpoint on table ring)...88.00

Staffordshire, black transfer-printed scene entitled "Flower Gatherers" depicting two young children, molded floral border, shield mark, 4¼" d. (wear) 55.00

Staffordshire, blue transfer-printed Willow patt., 4" d. 33.00

Staffordshire (unmarked), medium blue transfer-printed Quadrupeds patt., hyena depicted, 4" d. (pinpoints on table ring) 148.50

Stevenson, dark blue transfer-printed floral design, impressed mark, 4" d..126.50

CYBIS

Though not antique, fine Cybis porcelain figures are included here because of the great collector interest. They are produced in both limited edition and non-numbered series and thus there can be a wide range available to the collector.

Madonna with Bird

Abigail Adams, No. 487, 1976, 10" h..$725.00

Alice, seated child, No. 4006, 1978, 7¾" h..............................225.00 to 250.00

Allegra, No. 4005, 1978, 9½" h...........225.00

Baby Boy Head, No. 453, 1967-68, 11" h...600.00

Baby Bust, No. 456, 1968, limited edition of 500, 11" h. 600.00

Baby Girl Head, No. 452, 1967-68, 11" h.Ï..600.00

Baby Owl, No. 334, 1957, 4½" h...................................80.00 to 90.00

Ballerina, "On Cue," No. 423, 1963-69, color, 12½" h.....400.00 to 425.00

Ballerina, "On Cue," No. 423, 1963-69, white, 12½" h....400.00 to 425.00

Bathsheba, No. 4097, 1984, 14" h...1,500.00

Berengaria, No. 4015, 1979-81, 15" h...2,000.00

Blue Headed Vireo "Building Nest," No. 340, 1960-65, 8½" h. 450.00

Buffalo, No. 640, 1968-78, 5 x 5¾"............................100.00 to 125.00

Bunny, "Mr. Snowball," No. 611, 1962, 4" h......................................75.00 to 85.00

Calla Lily, No. 515, 1968-74, 16½" h.............................800.00 to 850.00

Carolina Male Paroquet, No. 355, 1962-65, 8" h. 475.00

Carousel Lion, No. 647, 1974-83, 12½"..360.00

Chinese Goddess "Kwan Yin," No. 467, 1972-76, 13½" h. 70.00

Christmas Rose, No. 514, 1965, limited edition of 500, 7½" h.............500.00

Colts, "Darby & Joan," No. 648, 1969-73, 9 x 9½"..............................285.00

Emily Ann, No. 4070, 1982, 6½" h......195.00

Eskimo Child Head, "Snow Bunting," No. 466, 1972, 10½" h. 225.00

Folk Singer, No. 449, 1967-74, 13" h...500.00

Goldilocks & Panda Bears, No. 471, 1973-75, 6" h. 300.00

Head of Girl, No. 436, 1963-70, white, on wooden pedestal, 10" h. 500.00

Holiday Child, 1980, 5½" h. 250.00

Jogger, male, 1980, 14" h. 350.00

Karina, ballerina, No. 4053, 1981,

5½" h...450.00

Kitty Fisher, No. 4075, 1983, 9" h.........80.00

Little Boy Blue, No. 4000, 1978, 6 x 9"................................300.00 to 400.00

Little Match Girl, No. 4067, 1983, 5¾" h...............................150.00 to 200.00

Little Miss Muffet, No. 4008, 1980, 7¼" h...300.00

Little Red Riding Hood, No. 473, 1973-75, 6½" h. ....250.00 to 275.00

Madame Butterfly, No. 4090, 1983, 13½" h.......................1,500.00 to 2,000.00

Madonna, Queen of Angels, No. 2093, 1950s, 11" h. ...125.00 to 150.00

Madonna with Bird, colored, No. 2148, 1956, 11" h. (ILLUS.) ....225.00 to 275.00

Madonna with Lace Veil, decorated, No. 2080, early 1960s......................100.00

Magnolia, No. 391, 1963, 8" h. 350.00

Melissa, No. 486, 1976,

10" h................................300.00 to 325.00

Mushroom, "Jack-O-Lantern," No. 521, 1970-72, 7" h.....150.00 to 200.00

Onondaga "Hiawatha," No. 701, 1969, limited edition of 500, 11½" h........1,800.00

Pandora, No. 454, 1967-83, 5" h..................................150.00 to 175.00

Pansies, "China Maid" (yellow) with Butterfly, No. 523Y, 1972-74, 5" l., 7" h...375.00

Pierre, The Performing Poodle, 4½" h...............................250.00 to 275.00

Pollyanna, No. 465, 1971-75, 7½" h...............................250.00 to 350.00

Priscilla, No. 489, 1976, 14" h.............................800.00 to 1,000.00

Queen Esther, No. 480, 1974, 13½" h..1,100.00

Raccoon, "Raffles," No. 636, 1965, 7½" h...............................200.00 to 250.00

Rapunzel (lilac), No. 468L, 1978, 8½" h...............................750.00 to 775.00

Scarlett, No. 459, 1968-74, 13" h. ...1,400.00

Turtle, The "Baron," No. 820, 1975-79, 5" l., 3" h. 100.00

Unicorn, No. 664, 1969-74, 10 x 13" ..225.00

Wankan Tanka, "The Great Spirit," No. 704, 1979, limited edition of 200, 17" h.....................................2,500.00

Yankee Doodle Dandy, boy riding horse toy, No. 484, 1975-77, 9" h...240.00

DEDHAM

Crackleware Center Bowl

This pottery was organized in 1866 by Alexander W. Robertson in Chelsea, Massachusetts, and became A. W. & H. Robertson in 1868. In 1872, the name was changed to Chelsea Keramic Art Works and in 1891 to Chelsea Pottery, U.S.A. About 1895, the pottery was moved to Dedham, Massachusetts, and was renamed Dedham Pottery. Production ceased in 1943. High-fired colored wares and crackle ware were specialties. The rabbit is said to have been the most popular decoration on crackle ware in blue.

Since 1977, the Potting Shed, Concord, Massachusetts, has produced quality reproductions of early Dedham wares. These pieces are carefully marked to avoid confusion with original examples.

Ashtray, square w/indentations in each side, Rabbit patt., marked & dated "1943," 6" w. $1,540.00

Bell, curved conical form w/knob top, Rabbit patt., unsigned, 4" d., 4" h. ...770.00

Candle snuffer, tapering cylinder w/flattened ball end, Rabbit patt., 2" h. 660.00

Center bowl, Crackle Ware, oval w/deep scallop on sides & toothed scallops at each end, decorated w/h.p. blue flowers against a white ground, blue "registered" mark, 4 x 8¾" (ILLUS.) 660.00

Coffeepot, cov., conical body, domed cover, angled handle, Rabbit patt., inscribed "first one made," dated "4/1/14," blue stamp mark & exhibition label, 8½" h. 1,430.00

Cracker jar, cov., wide ovoid body w/a flared rim inset w/a low-domed cover w/a wide knob handle, Elephant patt., stamped & incised mark, 6" h. 1,760.00

Cracker jar, cov., wide ovoid body w/a flared rim inset w/a low-domed cover w/a wide knob handle, Poppy patt., marked & dated "1931," 6¼" h. 3,300.00

Creamer & cov. sugar bowl, Rabbit patt., No. 1, stamped mark, bowl overall 4¾" h., pr. 357.50

Cup plates, one Elephant patt., one Azalea patt., two Horsechestnut patt., marked, 4⅜" d., set of 4..........660.00

Cup & saucer, Elephant patt., stamp registered mark, saucer 6" d. 770.00

Cup & saucer, Polar Bear patt., marked & exhibition label, saucer 6" d. 357.50

Demitasse cups & saucers, Rabbit patt., marked, saucer 4½" d., cup 2¼" h., set of 6...............................550.00

Flower frog, figural, a model of a standing rabbit atop a domed base pierced w/holes, stamped mark & dated "1931," 6¼" h. 880.00

Humidor, cov., decorated w/two elephants, clamp-type fastener, inscribed "Dedham Pottery - May 1917 - #79," 7" h. 1,980.00

Knife rests, figural, model of a rabbit, marked, 3½" l., pr. (one w/glaze roughness) 660.00

Model of a boot, miniature, high-topped & low-heeled w/blue band around top, unmarked, 2¼" h. 550.00

Mug, tall tapering cylindrical sides, angled handle, Elephant patt., marked, 5¼" h. 605.00

Paperweight, figural, model of a small frog, by Charles F. Davenport, inscribed in pencil & initialed by artist, 2" l. 605.00

Paperweight, figural, model of an elephant standing on a flat oval foot, stamped mark & exhibition label, 6" l., 4" h. 7,700.00

Pitcher, 8⅜" h., Rabbit patt., w/one rabbit leaping over lower handle, No. 3, initialed "P," impressed & stamp mark 1,320.00

Plate, 6" d., Dolphin in Surf patt., marked & exhibition label.................330.00

Plate, 6¼" d., Dolphin patt., marked 1,100.00

Plate, 6½" d., Chick patt., marked....2,530.00

Plate, 7½" d., Crab patt., marked 357.50

Plate, child's, 7¾" d., Rabbit patt., stamped mark & exhibition label...1,650.00

Plate, 8¼" d., Tapestry Lion patt., marked 1,320.00

Plate, 8⅜" d., Fish patt., marked & dated "1931," exhibition label........1,870.00

Plate, 8⅜" d., Reverse Poppy patt., marked 495.00

Plate, 8½" d., Iris patt. 175.00

Plate, 8½" d., raised Pineapple patt., impressed "CPUS - EE - X" 275.00

Plate, 8½" d., Poppy patt., impressed mark, stamp & inscribed cross.........495.00

Plate, 8½" d., Rabbit patt....................275.00

Plate, 8½" d., Swan patt., marked ...1,100.00

Plate, 8⅞" d., scalloped rim, molded Putti & Goat patt., marked 605.00

Plate, 9¾" d., Azalea patt., marked 440.00

Plate, 9¾" d., Rose Spray patt., inscribed on back "From Nature - by HR," decorated by Hugh C. Robertson, exhibition label (surface glaze burst) 1,430.00

Plate, 10" d., Elephant patt., marked 715.00

Plate, 10" d., "Golden Gate SF," depicting sun setting on water, inscribed on reverse to M. Shepherd, designed by Hugh Robertson, artist's cipher, impressed mark & enhanced blue stamp (chipping on foot, glaze bursts) 2,750.00

Lion & Owl Plate

Plate, 10" d., Lion & Owl patt., bisque ground, artist-initials by Hugh C. Robertson, impressed mark (ILLUS.) 1,540.00

Plate, chop, 12" d., Rabbit patt., impressed mark twice & stamp........275.00

Plates, 8¾" d., Lobster patt., impressed & stamped mark, set of 5 (foot chip) 1,650.00

Platter, 12" d., Lobster patt., stamped & impressed marks & exhibition label 715.00

Platter, 12" d., Sailing Ship patt. in center, by Charles F. Davenport, marked & dated "1927," w/exhibition label 2,640.00

Tea tile, round, Rabbit patt., 6" d. 235.00

Tureen, cov., 9" d., 5½" h., Rabbit patt., figural rabbit finial on cover, marked & exhibition label (minor staining & peppering).......................935.00

Vase, 6½" h., 4¾" d., slightly globular base w/short thick neck, 'Volcanic' glaze, red, orange & green lustered glaze, designed by Hugh Robertson, hand-incised "Dedham Pottery - HCR"...3,080.00

Vase, 7" h., 4¼" d., 'Volcanic' glaze, cylindrical, covered in a sage green glaze dripping over a metallic copper colored base, restoration to hairline at rim, incised "Dedham Pottery - HCR" (ILLUS. top next column) 1,760.00

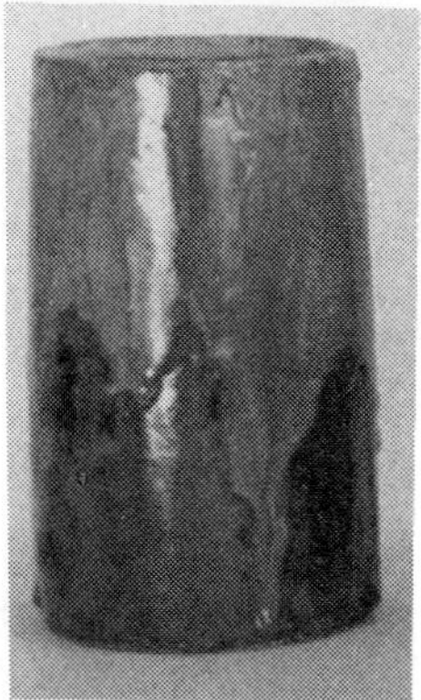

Volcanic Glaze Vase

Vase, 7½" h., ovoid body tapering toward the base & to a flat rim, experimental iridescent oxblood drip glaze, by Hugh C. Robertson, incised "Dedham Pottery" & artist's initials 880.00

Vase, 7½" h., 4½" d., 'Volcanic' glaze, slightly swelling cylindrical body tapering at the shoulder to a flat rim, flowing glossy glaze in brown, green & blue, by H.C. Robertson, incised "Dedham Pottery - HCR - 136" 825.00

Vase, 7¾" h., ovoid body tapering to a short neck w/flat rim, experimental 'Volcanic' drip glaze in shades of brown w/white, olive & opalescent highlights, by Hugh C. Robertson, incised company mark & artist's cipher...2,970.00

Vase, 8" h., 5¼" d., swollen-form, covered in a multicolored mottled lustered glaze, by Hugh Robertson, hand-incised "Dedham Pottery - HCR" 2,970.00

Vase, 8" h., 5½" d., 'Volcanic' glaze, wide baluster-form body w/flat mouth, thick *sang-de-boeuf* glaze dripping over a dark green ground w/blue accents, by Hugh Robertson, marked 2,630.00

Vase, 8¼" h., 5" d., Crackle Ware, slightly swollen cylinder, decorated w/large blue poppy blossoms & pods against a white ground, painted "Dedham III - 15"...........2,860.00

Vase, 8½" h., 5½" d., swollen body w/short wide neck, covered in an active reddish orange, green, blue & black dripping flambé glaze, by Hugh Robertson, hand-incised "Dedham Pottery - HCR" 3,300.00

Vase, 9" h., 5" d., swollen cylinder w/short wide mouth, covered in a fine mottled dripping opaque glossy green glaze, by Hugh Robertson, hand-incised "Dedham Pottery - HCR" 1,650.00

Vase, 10" h., 5" d., ovoid base w/wide short neck, 'Volcanic' glaze, covered in a thick brown glaze dripping over an olive green base, full of bubbles, by Hugh Robertson, hand-incised "Dedham Pottery - B.W. - HCR" 1,980.00

DELFT

English Delft Charger

In the early 17th century Italian potters settled in Holland and began producing tin-glazed earthenwares, often decorated with pseudo-Oriental designs based on Chinese porcelain wares. The city of Delft became the center of this pottery production and several firms produced the wares throughout the 17th and early 18th century. A majority of the pieces featured blue on white designs, but polychrome wares were also made. The Dutch Delftwares were also shipped to England and eventually the English copied them at potteries in such cities as Bristol, Lambeth and Liverpool. Although still produced today, Delft peaked in popularity by the mid-18th century.

Bowl, 6½" d., wide rounded body w/flattened rim, decorated in polychrome w/a scene of a house in a landscape w/a fence, trees & rocks within an iron-red & blue scale band & a border band of ovals & diamonds, Lambeth, England, ca. 1730 (cracked) $2,640.00

Bowl, 8¾" d., deep rounded sides on a thick footring, decorated in polychrome w/iron-red flowers w/green leaves & blue tendrils beneath an iron-red & blue scalloped diaper border band suspending tassels, the interior w/a blue flowerhead, Bristol, England, ca. 1730 (cracks at rim, chips on footring) 2,420.00

Charger, decorated in blue on white w/figures of Adam & Eve holding yellow fig leaves & standing beneath a large apple tree w/green-sponged leaves, yellow fruit & a yellow serpent coiled in the branches, within a blue-dash & flowerhead border, Bristol, England, ca. 1670, 13" d...4,950.00

Charger, Tulip patt., painted in blue, green, yellow & iron-red w/a large central tulip, two flanking buds & tall leaves within blue lines around the top & bottom of the cavetto, the flanged rim w/five leaves alternating w/five stylized bud sprigs, Bristol, England, 1730-40, repaired rim w/restored chips, 13" d. (ILLUS.) 863.00

Charger, colorfully decorated w/a well-done equestrian portrait of King Charles I in blue armor astride a rearing manganese war horse in a green & yellow landscape w/a blue & yellow church in the distance & a blue line & dash border, Lambeth, England, ca. 1640, 16¼" d. (rim chips) 99,000.00

Flower brick, upright rectangular form w/three rows of round holes & two rectangular openings in the top edge, painted in blue on white on the front & back w/a landscape scene of a man in a punt on a river before two buildings & trees, & on the ends w/another building, raised on short bracket feet w/traces of cold gilding, Bristol, England, 1750-60, 5 13/16" l. (chip on one corner) 575.00

Bristol Delft Loving Cup

Loving cup, cov., footed bulbous body tapering to a flaring neck flanked by large loop handles, the high domed cover w/flanged rim & flattened disc finial, painted in blue, iron-red & yellow on the front & back of the body & around the cover finial w/panels of stylized flowering plants, the neck w/an iron-red & blue border of leaves, the cover rim w/a chain border, the handles w/blue stripes, Bristol, England, 1720-30, various wear, chips & hairlines, 7 7/16" h. (ILLUS) 5,175.00

Plate, 8¼" w., octagonal, decorated in blue on white w/a round central reserve of a couple in period costume having tea in a garden, the wide edge border w/a stylized Fitzhugh-like design, the back inscribed "E/WQ," Bristol, England, ca. 1770 (rim chips) 3,850.00

Plate, 9" d., Fazackerly-type, decorated in green, yellow & purple across the center w/stylized flower branches in a garden w/a trellis fence, Liverpool, England, ca. 1760, (rim chips) 275.00

Plate, 9" d., polychrome decoration, painted in the center in blue, pale iron-red & olive green w/a stag leaping over a fence between trees on a plateau within a roundel, the rim w/a border of blue leaves, probably London, England, mid-18th c. (minor glaze chips)............1,035.00

Plate, 10¼" d., decorated at one side in blue on white w/the initials "B/FM - 1698" within a tasseled cartouche, Holland (rim chip, slight flaking).......825.00

Posset pot, cov., squatty bulbous body tapering to a flared rim, C-scroll applied handle & a swan's-neck spout, the domed cover w/a flat button finial, decorated in blue on white in the 'Transitional' style w/Chinamen seated in landscapes w/trees, Lambeth, England, ca. 1690, 6¾" h. (base cracked, rim chips, cover rim restored) 6,600.00

Punch bowl, *bianco-sopra-bianco* (white-on-white) style, deep flaring rounded sides on a thick footring, decorated w/manganese & blue Chinese pavilions in a landscape on the exterior, the interior w/white-on-white diaper & floral panels, the center w/manganese flowers issuing from rocks, Bristol, England, ca. 1760, 11¾" d. (rim chips, hairline crack) 3,080.00

Punch bowl, deep rounded sides on a thick footring, the exterior decorated w/a continuous Chinese landscape w/houses & pavilions, bridge & lake in blue, the interior decorated w/a large blue sailing ship flying a red & blue union jack flag on a pea green sea, within a Fitzhugh-type blue border, Liverpool, England, ca. 1760, 20" d. (broken & restored) 10,450.00

Sauceboat w/attached undertray, the oblong bowl w/a wide scalloped spout at each end & handles at the center of the sides, decorated in blue on white w/stylized flowering branches, reserved w/leaves on the spouts, each handle in the form of a standing fox, the interior w/stylized flowering branches beneath a diaper border, Bristol, England, ca. 1760, 8⅞" l. (cracked, handles & rim chipped) 2,860.00

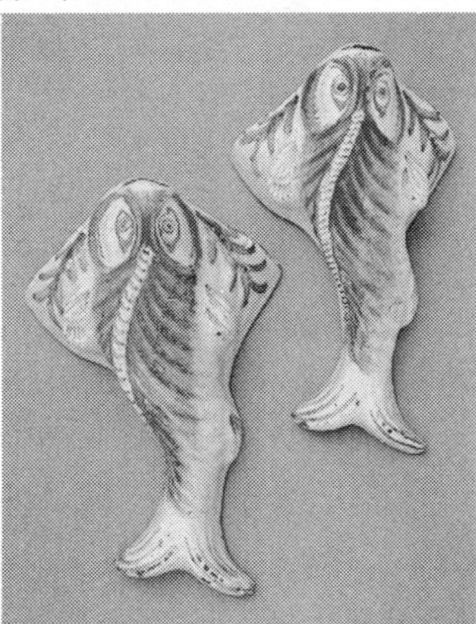

English Delft Wall Pockets

Wall pockets, modeled as a fish in blue & green w/iron-red spines, fins & tails & green seaplants flanking the head, Liverpool, England, ca. 1770, one cracked & reglued, some glaze flaking, 8" h., pr. (ILLUS.) 8,800.00

DERBY & ROYAL CROWN DERBY

William Duesbury, in partnership with John and Christopher Heath, established the Derby Porcelain Works in Derby, England, about 1750. Duesbury soon bought out his partners and in 1770 purchased the Chelsea factory and six years later, the Bow works. Duesbury was succeeded by his son and grandson. Robert Bloor purchased the business about 1814 and managed successfully until illness in 1828 left him unable to excerise control. The "Bloor" Period, however, extends from 1814 until 1848, when the factory closed. Former Derby workmen then resumed porcelain manufacture in another factory and this nucleus eventually united with a new and distinct venture in 1878 which, after 1890, was known as Royal Crown Derby.

A variety of anchor and crown marks have been used since the 18th century.

Early Derby Harlequin Figure

Coffeepot, cov., tall footed pear-shaped body w/domed cover w/acorn finial, swan's-neck spout & S-scroll handle, painted in naturalistic shades of brown, blue, purple, iron-red, yellow & green on one side w/a bird in flight above another perched on a branch near a strutting peacock, on the reverse w/a finch perched on a leafy branch, & on the cover w/four insects above the brown-edged rim, the foliate-molded spout trimmed in green & puce, the handle decorated w/puce diamond designs & puce feathering at its join to the body, ca. 1760-65, 8 7/16" h. (repaired rim chips, spout tip restored, repairs to foot) $1,150.00

Creamer & sugar bowl, narcissus decoration, wide apple green borders, dated 1933, pr. 55.00

Cup & saucer, demitasse, Imari-style decoration, artist-signed, 20th c.........85.00

Dessert set: cup & saucer & 10½" d. plate; Imari patt., 20th c., 3 pcs. 200.00

Figure of Harlequin, standing wearing a white-plumed pink hat, a black mask, a gilt-buttoned motley costume checkered in iron-red, black, turquoise, yellow, pink & white, turquoise shoes & a gold-buckled iron-red belt through which is thrust the tan slapstick in his left hand, his right hand dramatically touching his heart, & standing against a green & brown mottled leafy tree stump on a green & tan mound base applied w/iron-red & yellow florettes & green leaves, incised model number "N199" & letters "G" & "J," 1769-75, usual chips on base & leaves, 5⅞" h. (ILLUS.). 2,300.00

Model of a bullfinch, miniature, the small bird w/a salmon breast, a black head, wings & tail, a blue back & a grey beak, modeled perched above clusters of yellow, rose & blue flowers & green leaves on a light green tree stump, ca. 1820, 2½" h. (small tail chips & chips on leaves) 690.00

Models of sheep, recumbent animals modeled as a white fleecy ewe & grey-horned ram w/shaded iron-red spots, grey eyes, iron-red mouths & black hooves, lying before a green leafy bocage covered w/white, yellow & iron-red flowers, on a green mound base applied w/three florettes, ca. 1775, each incised "0," 3⅝ & 3 11/16" h., pr. (usual chips on bocage) 1,380.00

Plate, 9 5/16" d., botanical-type, painted in the center w/a large sprig of rose, green & brown w/two moss rose blossoms & a bud all within a wide gilt-edged cobalt blue-ground rim decorated w/a border of delicate gilt cornucopias issuing berries, flowers & foliage, 1810-15, Crowned Derby

Botanical Plate

Crossed Batons & D mark (ILLUS.) 1,150.00

Tea tray, oblong quatrefoil-shaped, the center w/a conforming gilt quatrefoil within a gilt foliate vine at the lower edge of a wide border of gilt dots superimposed w/clusters of gilt-bound shaded green grasses on the slightly dished rim, the end affixed w/gilt-striped foliate-scroll handles, ca. 1800, Crowned Crossed Batons & D mark (some wear) 345.00

Vine-Molded Derby Tray

Tray, oblong w/lightly ruffled rim, painted in the center w/shades of rose, iron-red, blue, yellow, purple & green w/floral sprays & sprigs, & molded around the sides w/a cluster of pink grapes pendent from a brown & green vine bearing brown-veined green & yellow leaves, the ends & the middle of each side w/a turquoise-trimmed rococo scroll device, 1760-65, two repaired rim chips, 10¾" l. (ILLUS.) 805.00

DOROTHY DOUGHTY BIRDS

Cardinal

These magnificent porcelain birds were created by the talented artist Dorothy Doughty for the Royal Worcester Porcelain Factory in Worcester, England, beginning in 1935. They are life-sized, beautifully colored and crafted with the greatest artistry.

Bewick's Wrens and Yellow Jasmine, ca. 1955, 9⅓" h., pr........................$385.00

Blue-Grey Gnatcatchers, ca. 1955, 10¾" h., pr. (leaf damage) 467.50

Blue-Tit Cock and Pussy Willow in Spring, ca. 1984, 7¾" h., pr..275.00

Cactus Wrens and Prickly Pear, ca. 1958, 10¼" h., pr. (thorn missing) 550.00

Canyon Wrens with Wild Lupin, ca. 1959, 6¾" h., pr. 550.00

Cardinals, ca. 1950, 9½" h., pr. (ILLUS. of one) 495.00

Cerulean Warblers and Red Maple, ca. 1965, 8½" h., pr.........................440.00

Chiff Chaff on Hogweed, ca. 1964, 17" h..330.00

Downy Woodpeckers and Pecans, ca. 1959, 10" h., pr. 440.00

Hooded Warblers and Cherokee Rose, ca. 1961, 10½" h., pr. (minor chips) 550.00

Indigo Buntings and Blackberry Sprays, ca. 1955, 8" h., pr. 275.00

Kingfisher and Autumn Beech, ca. 1964, 11½" h..................................330.00

Lark Sparrow with Red Gild and Twinpod Growing in Volcanic Ash, ca. 1966, 5¾" h...............................220.00

Lesser White Throats and Wild Rose, ca. 1964, pr. 412.50

Magnolia Warblers and Magnolia, ca. 1957, 13" h., pr. 990.00

Mocking Birds and Peach Blossoms, ca. 1940, 10" h., pr. (minor chips)....330.00

Mountain Bluebirds and Spleenwort Niger, ca. 1959, 8¾" h., pr. 302.00

Oven Birds with Crested Iris and Lady's Slipper, ca. 1960, 9¾" h., pr. 605.00

Parula Warbler and Sweet Bay

Parula Warblers and Sweet Bay, one w/base crack, ca. 1957, 8¼" h., pr. (ILLUS. of one) 330.00

Phoebes and Flame Vine, ca. 1958, 10" h., pr. (base hairline, branch off)...440.00

Red-Eyed Vireos and Swamp Azalea, ca. 1954, 7¾" h., pr..........................440.00

Red Start on Gorse

Redstarts on Gorse, ca. 1968, 10¼" h., pr. (ILLUS. of one) 880.00

Robin, ca. 1964, 6½" h. 220.00

Ruby-Throated Hummingbirds

Ruby-Throated Hummingbirds and Fuchsia, ca. 1954, 9¼" h., pr. (ILLUS.) 935.00

Scarlet Tanagers and White Oak, ca. 1956, 11½" h., pr. 330.00

Scissor-Tailed Flycatcher, ca. 1962, 24" l. 330.00

Yellow Throats and Water Hyacinth, ca. 1959, 11" h., pr..........................550.00

DOULTON & ROYAL DOULTON

Doulton & Co., Ltd., was founded in Lambeth, London, about 1858. It was operated there till 1956 and often incorporated the words "Doulton" and "Lambeth" in its marks. Pinder Bourne & Co., Burslem was purchased by the Doultons in 1878 and in 1882 became Doulton & Co., Ltd. It added porcelain to its earthenware production in 1884. The "Royal Doulton" mark has been used since 1902 by this factory, which is still in

production. Character jugs and figurines are commanding great attention from collectors at the present time.

ANIMALS

Royal Doulton Dogs

Cat, sitting licking hind paw, HN 2580 .... $60.00

Cat, kitten sitting, surprised, tan, HN 2584 .... 50.00

Cat, Siamese, sitting, HN 2655 .... 110.00

Dog, Airedale, "Cotsford Topsail," HN 1023, medium 140.00

Dog, Bulldog, HN 1075 .... 275.00

Dog, Bulldog Pup, sitting, K 2, 1¾" h. .... 75.00 to 100.00

Dog, Cocker Spaniel, HN 1000 .... 400.00

Dog, Cocker Spaniel, "Lucky Star of Ware," black,HN 1020, 5" .... 80.00 to 100.00

Dog, Cocker Spaniel, dark brown spots & ears, HN 1036, 6¾" l., 5¼" h. (ILLUS. right) 165.00

Dog, Cocker Spaniel, liver & white, HN 1037, small 75.00

Dog, Cocker Spaniel puppy in basket, HN 2585, 2" h. 60.00

Dog, Cocker Spaniel & Pheasant, red & white, HN 1029, small 135.00

Dog, Collie, "Ashstead Applause," HN 1059, 3½" 125.00

Dog, Dachshund, "Shrewd Saint" HN 1128, 4" .... 125.00 to 150.00

Dog, French Poodle, HN 2631, 5¼" .... 125.00 to 150.00

Dog, Irish setter, HN 1056, small .... 100.00 to 130.00

Dog, Pekinese, "Biddee of Ifield," HN 1012, small 98.00

Dog, Pekinese, HN 1040, brown & tan w/black trim, 3⅛" h., 3¾" l. (ILLUS. left) 195.00

Dog, Pekinese, sitting, K 6, miniature, 2" h. .... 50.00 to 75.00

Fox, "Huntsman," HN 6448, 1½" 135.00

Salmon, leaping, "Veined Sung Flambé" glaze, 12¼" h. 220.00

CHARACTER JUGS

The Cavalier Jug

'Ard of 'Earing, small, 3½" h. .... 600.00 to 700.00

'Arriet, "A" mark, miniature, 2¼" h. 135.00

'Arriet, small, 3½" h. 95.00

'Arriet, large, 6" h. .... 175.00 to 200.00

'Arry, "A" mark, miniature, 2¼" h. 165.00

'Arry, miniature, 2¼" h. 57.50

'Arry, small, 3½" h. 100.00

Athos, large, 6" h. 95.00

Auld Mac, "A" mark, miniature, 2¼" h. 38.50

Auld Mac, miniature, 2¼" h. 40.00

Auld Mac, "A" mark, small, 3½" h. 42.00

Auld Mac, "A" mark, large, 6¾" h. 89.00

Bacchus, small, 3½" h. 55.00

Beefeater, small, w/GR on handle, 3½" h. 60.00

Blacksmith, large, 6" h. 75.00

(Sergeant) Buz Fuz, small, 3½" h. 80.00

Cap'n Cuttle, "A" mark, small, 3½" h. 95.00

Cap'n Cuttle, small, 3½" h. 97.00

Capt. Ahab, small, 3½" h. 45.00

Captain Henry Morgan, small, 3½" h. 40.00

Captain Henry Morgan, large, 6" h. 75.00

Captain Hook, miniature, 2¼ h. 365.00

Captain Hook, large, 6" h., No. D6597 ....525.00

Cardinal, miniature, 2¼" h. 50.00

Cardinal, "A" mark, miniature, 2¼" h. 57.00

Cardinal, "A" mark, small, 3½" h. 85.00

Cavalier, "A" mark, small, 3½" h. 77.50

Cavalier, small, 3½" h. 65.00

Cavalier, large, 6" h. (ILLUS.) ....125.00 to 150.00

Cliff Cornell, blue, large ......275.00 to 300.00

Cliff Cornell, brown, large 400.00

Dick Turpin, mask on face, horse handle, small, 3½" h. 65.00

Dick Turpin, mask on hat, gun handle, "A" mark, miniature, 2¼" h. 65.00

Drake, small, 3½" h. 75.00

Drake Jug

Drake, large, 5⅝" h. (ILLUS.) 340.00

Farmer John, small, 3½" h. 92.50

Farmer John, "A" mark, large, 6" h. 95.00

Fat Boy, tiny, 1¼" h. ....75.00 to 100.00

Fat Boy, small, 3½" h. 115.00

Fortune Teller, miniature, 2¼" h. ....325.00 to 350.00

Fortune Teller, small, 3½" h. 340.00

Friar Tuck, large, 6" h. 375.00

Gaoler, small, 3½" h. 68.00

Gaoler, large, 6" h. 120.00

Gardener, large, 6" h. 175.00

Gondolier, large, 6" h. 650.00

Gone Away, large, 6" h. 125.00

Granny, large, 6¼" h. 80.00

Guardsman, small, 3½" h. 50.00

Gulliver, miniature, 2¼" h. 365.00

Gulliver, small, 3½" h. 350.00

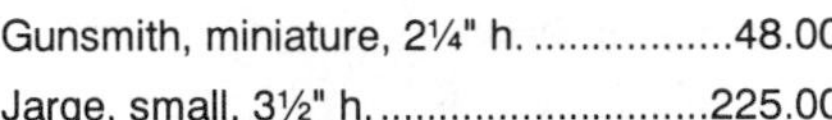

Gunsmith, miniature, 2¼" h. 48.00

Jarge, small, 3½" h. 225.00

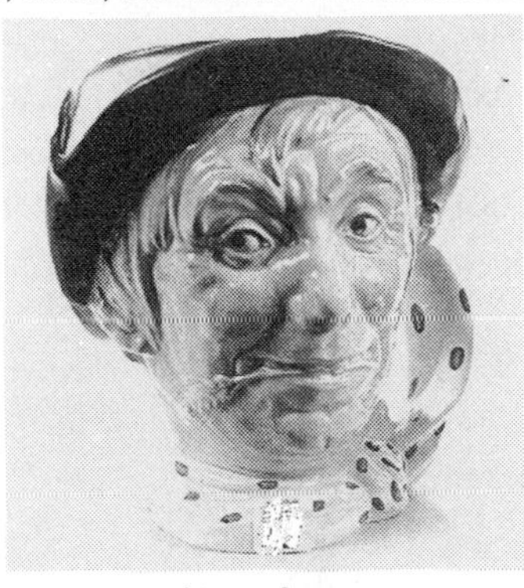

Jarge Jug

Jarge, large, 6½" h. (ILLUS.) ....325.00 to 350.00

Jockey, large, 6" h. ....350.00 to 400.00

John Barleycorn, small 70.00

John Barleycorn Jug

John Barleycorn, "A" mark, large (ILLUS.) 175.00

Johnny Appleseed, large, 6" h. ....300.00 to 325.00

John Peel, tiny, 1¼" h. 200.00

John Peel, miniature, 2¼" h. 50.00

John Peel, small, 3½" h. 85.00

Lumberjack Jug

Lumberjack, small, 3½" h. (ILLUS.)......55.00

Lumberjack, large, 6" h.......................105.00

Mad Hatter, large, 6" h........................110.00

Mine Host, miniature, 2¼" h. 30.00

Mine Host, small, 3½" h........................42.00

Mine Host, large, 6" h. 80.00

Mr. Micawber, tiny, 1¼" h. 95.00

Mr. Micawber, "A" mark, miniature, 2¼" h...55.00

Mr. Micawber, small, 3½" h. 70.00

Mr. Pickwick, tiny, 1¼" h.....200.00 to 225.00

Mr. Pickwick, "A" mark, small, 3½" h...95.00

Old Charley, "A" mark, miniature, 2¼" h...65.00

Old Charley, "A" mark, small, 3½" h...55.00

Old Charley, small, 3½" h. 52.00

Old Charley Jug

Old Charley, "A" mark, large, 6" h. (ILLUS.) 72.50

Old King Cole, large, 6" h. 350.00

Paddy, tiny, 1¼" h................................75.00

Paddy, "A" mark, large, 6" h. 160.00

Paddy, large, 6" h. 130.00

Parson Brown, "A" mark, large, 6" h...175.00

Pied Piper, small, 3½" h. 47.00

Punch & Judy Man, small, 3½" h..............................300.00 to 350.00

Sairey Gamp, tiny, 1¼" h......................95.00

Sairey Gamp, "A" mark, miniature, 2¼" h. (ILLUS. top next column)........55.00

Sairey Gamp, "A" mark, small, 3½" h...62.50

Sairey Gamp, "A" mark, large, 6" h.................................100.00 to 125.00

Sam Weller, tiny, 1¼" h. 100.00

Sairey Gamp Jug

Sam Weller, small, 3½" h...............................125.00 to 150.00

Sam Weller, "A" mark, large, 6" h.......130.00

Sam Weller, large, 6" h.......................150.00

Sancho Panza, large 70.00

Santa Claus, doll & drum handle, large 100.00

Santa Claus, reindeer handle, large...110.00

Scaramouche, small, 3½" h. 415.00

Simon the Cellarer, large, 6" h............130.00

Smuggler, small, 3½" h.........................58.00

Tam O'Shanter, miniature, 2¼" h. 45.00

Tam O'Shanter, small, 3½" h................55.00

Tam O'Shanter, large 125.00

Toby Philpots, miniature, 2¼" h............45.00

Toby Philpots, "A" mark, small, 3½" h...65.00

Tony Weller, "A" mark, miniature, 2¼" h...55.00

Tony Weller, miniature, 2¼" h. 50.00

Tony Weller, "A" mark, small, 3½" h...95.00

Tony Weller, "A" mark, large...............200.00

Tony Weller, extra large 275.00

Touchstone, "A" mark, large, 6" h.......205.00

Town Crier, small, 3½" h. .....75.00 to 100.00

Trapper, small, 3½" h. 55.00

Trapper, large, 6" h. 90.00

Veteran Motorist, small, 3½" h..............55.00

Vicar of Bray, "A" mark, large (ILLUS. top next column) 225.00

Viking, large, 6" h. ....175.00 to 200.00

Walrus & Carpenter, small, 3½" h. 50.00

Walrus & Carpenter, large, 6" h..........110.00

Vicar of Bray Jug

W.C. Fields, large, 6" h.......................125.00

Yachtsman, large, 6" h. 125.00

FIGURINES

Autumn Breezes

Afternoon Tea, HN 1747, pink dress, 1935-82...350.00

Alexandra, HN 2398, 1970-76...........................150.00 to 185.00

Aragorn, HN 2916, tan costume, 1981-84...100.00

Artful Dodger, M 55, 1932-83 ....70.00

Autumn Breezes, HN 1911, peach dress, green jacket, 1939-76 (ILLUS.) 250.00

Autumn Breezes, HN 1913, green dress, blue jacket, 1939-71...........................200.00 to 250.00

Ballerina, HN 2116, 1953-73 ....265.00

Balloon Seller (The), HN 583, green shawl, cream dress, 1923-49...........650.00

Basket Weaver (The), HN 2245, 1959-62...........................350.00 to 375.00

Belle O' the Ball, HN 1997, 1947-79...300.00

Bernice, HN 2071, 1951-53 ....1,050.00

Biddy, HN 1513, red dress, blue shawl, 1932-51 ....225.00 to 250.00

Blacksmith of Williamsburg, HN 2240, white shirt, brown hat, 1960-83...........................200.00 to 250.00

Blithe Morning, HN 2021, blue & pink dress, 1949-71 ....150.00 to 200.00

Blithe Morning, HN 2065, red dress, 1950-73..235.00

The Bride

Bride (The), HN 2166, pale pink dress, 1956-76 (ILLUS.) ....175.00 to 200.00

Bridesmaid (The Little), M 12, multicolor gown, 1932-45................370.00

Bridesmaid (The LIttle), HN 2196, white dress, pink trim, 1960-76........125.00

Broken Lance (The), HN 2041, 1949-75..400.00

Bunny, HN 2214, 1960-75.................150.00

Camellia, HN 2222, 1960-71 ....200.00

Carpet Seller (The), HN 1464, 1931-69...........................275.00 to 325.00

Child from Williamsburg, HN 2154, blue dress, 1964-83........................135.00

Claribel, HN 1951, red dress, 1940-49...550.00

Cookie, HN 2218, 1958-75................185.00

Curly Locks, HN 2049, 1949-53...........................350.00 to 375.00

Dainty May, M 67, pink skirt, blue overdress, 1935-49.........................400.00

Delight, HN 1772, red dress, 1936-67...150.00

Delphine

Delphine, HN 2136, 1954-67 (ILLUS.) ....250.00 to 275.00

Dulcie, HN 2305, white skirt, white bodice w/ red, yellow & white designs, trimmed in blue, 1981-84...250.00

Enchantment, HN 2178, 1957-82.......160.00

First Steps, HN 2242, 1959-65...........275.00

Forty Winks

Forty Winks, HN 1974, 1945-73, (ILLUS.) ....175.00 to 200.00

The Gaffer

Gaffer (The), HN 2053, 1950-59 (ILLUS.) 445.00

Giselle, The Forest Glade

Giselle, The Forest Glade, HN 2140, 1954-65 (ILLUS.) 360.00

Good Morning, HN 2671, 1974-76 .....190.00

Grand Manner, HN 2723, 1975-81............................200.00 to 225.00

Granny's Shawl, HN 1647, red cape, 1934-49..385.00

Harmony, HN 2824, grey dress, 1978-84...170.00

He Loves Me, HN 2046, 1949-62...145.00

Honey, HN 1910, green dress, blue jacket, 1939-49 ....760.00

Ibrahim, HN 2095, earthenware, 1952-55...600.00

Innocence, HN 2842, 1979-83............135.00

Irene, HN 1621, pale yellow dress, 1934-51 ....225.00

Ivy, HN 1768, pink hat, lavender dress, 1936-79..................................85.00

Jack, HN 2060, 1950-71 ....125.00

Janet, M 69, pale green skirt, green overdress, 1936-49..........................340.00

Janice, HN 2022, green dress, 1949-55............................350.00 to 400.00

Jersey Milkmaid (The), HN 2057,1950-59 (ILLUS top next column) ....250.00 to 275.00

Jill, HN 2061, 1950-71 ....125.00 to 150.00

Julia, HN 2705, 1975-90.....150.00 to 175.00

Karen, HN 1994, red dress, 1947-55...450.00

Kate, HN 2789, white dress, 1978-87...225.00

The Jersey Milkmaid

Katrina, HN 2327, 1965-69............................225.00 to 250.00

Ko-Ko, HN 2898, yellow & blue, 1980-85...475.00

Lady April

Lady April, HN 1958, red dress, 1940-59 (ILLUS.) ....275.00 to 300.00

Lady Charmian, HN 1948, green dress, red shawl, 1940-73 ....195.00

Lady Charmian

Lady Charmian, HN 1949, red dress, green shawl, 1940-75 (ILLUS.)........235.00

Lady from Williamsburg, HN 2228, 1960-83...160.00

Lady Jester, HN 1222, 1927-38, black & white 1,300.00

Lady of the Georgian Period (A), HN 41, gold & blue, 1914-38 ....1,250.00

Lambing Time, HN 1890, 1938-80 .....190.00

Leading Lady, HN 2269, 1965-76.......190.00

Legolas, HN 2917, 1981-84.................67.00

The Leisure Hour

Leisure Hour (The), HN 2055, mottled green & peach dress, 1950-65 (ILLUS.) 440.00

Lights Out, HN 2662, blue trousers & yellow spotted shirt, 1965-69...........276.00

Lilac Time

Lilac Time, HN 2137, 1954-69 (ILLUS.) ....225.00 to 250.00

Lily, HN 1798, white shawl, pink dress, 1936-49................125.00 to 150.00

Lisa, HN 2310, violet & white dress, 1969-82...120.00

Loretta, HN 2337, rose-red dress, yellow shawl, 1966-80 .....125.00 to 150.00

Lorna, HN 2311, green dress, apricot shawl, 1965-85 ....125.00 to 150.00

Love Letter, HN 2149, pink & white dress, blue dress, 1958-76 ....335.00

Lucy Ann, HN 1502, red gown, 1932-51 ....150.00

Lucy Locket, HN 524, yellow dress, 1921-49..425.00

Lunchtime, HN 2485, 1973-80............150.00

Madonna of the Square, HN 2034, light green-blue costume, 1949-51 ..650.00

Margaret, HN 1989, 1947-59............................350.00 to 375.00

Marguerite, HN 1928, pink dress, 1940-59............................350.00 to 400.00

Marietta, HN 1314, black costume, red cape, 1929-49............................795.00

Marjorie, HN 2788, blue & white dress, 1980-84................................225.00

Mary Mary, HN 2044, 1949-73 ....125.00

Masque, HN 2554, 1973-82 ....175.00

Maureen

Maureen, HN 1770, red dress, 1936-59 (ILLUS.) ....275.00 to 300.00

Mayor (The), HN 2280, 1963-71............................400.00 to 450.00

Melanie, HN 2271, 1965-81................165.00

Melody, HN 2202, 1957-62................195.00

Memories, HN 2030, green & red dress, 1949-59................400.00 to 450.00

Meriel, HN 1931, pink dress, 1940-49..1,300.00

Midsummer Noon, HN 2033, 1949-55..595.00

Minuet

Minuet, HN 2019, white dress, floral print, 1949-71 (ILLUS.) ....250.00 to 300.00

Miss Muffet, HN 1936, red coat, 1940-67............................200.00 to 225.00

Mr. Pickwick, HN 1894, 1938-42..195.00

Mrs. Fitzherbert, HN 2007, 1948-53...725.00

Monica, M 66, shaded pink skirt, blue blouse, 1935-49...............................425.00

Nina, HN 2347, 1969-76.....135.00 to 165.00

Noelle, HN 2179, 1957-67..................365.00

Old King Cole, HN 2217, 1963-67......300.00

Olga, HN 2463, 1972-75.....................179.00

Omar Khayyam, HN 2247, 1965-83...140.00

Once Upon a Time, HN 2047, pink dotted dress, 1949-55......................330.00

The Orange Lady

Orange Lady (The), HN 1759, pink skirt, 1936-75 (ILLUS.).....................210.00

Orange Lady (The), HN 1953, light green dress, green shawl, 1940-75...........................200.00 to 250.00

Orange Vendor (An), HN 1966, purple cloak, 1941-49 ....800.00

Paisley Shawl, M 4, green dress, dark green shawl, black bonnet w/red feather & ribbons, 1932-45 ....300.00

Paisley Shawl, HN 1392, white dress, red shawl, 1930-49 ....485.00

Paisley Shawl, HN 1987, cream dress, red shawl, 1946-59 ....190.00

Paisley Shawl, HN 1988, cream & yellow skirt, red hat, 1946-75...........170.00

Pantalettes, M 16, red skirt, red tie on hat, 1932-45.....................................280.00

Pearly Boy, HN 1482, red jacket, 1931-49..310.00

Pearly Boy, HN 2035, red jacket, w/hands clasped, 1949-59...............150.00

Pearly Girl, HN 1483, red jacket, 1931-49..275.00

Pecksniff, HN 2098, black & brown, 1952-67..175.00

Peggy, HN 2038, red dress, green trim, 1949-79....................................100.00

Pensive Moments, HN 2704, blue dress, 1975-81 ....175.00

Pied Piper (The), NH 2102, brown cloak, grey hat & boots, 1953-76.....275.00

Polka (The), HN 2156, pale pink dress, 1955-69.................275.00 to 325.00

Polly Peachum, HN 550, red dress, 1922-49...350.00

Regal Lady, HN 2709, 1975-83..........150.00

Reverie, HN 2306, peach dress, 1964-81............................225.00 to 275.00

Rosabell, HN 1620, 1934-38 ....1,450.00

Rosamund, M 32, yellow dress tinged w/blue, 1932-45 ....450.00

Royal Governor's Cook, HN 2233, 1960-83, dark blue, white & brown ..400.00

St. George, No. 2051, 1950-85 ....400.00

St. George

St. George, HN 2067, purple, red & orange blanket, 1950-79 (ILLUS.) 3,150.00

Sairey Gamp, HN 2100, white dress, green cape, 1952-67........................275.00

Samwise, HN 2925, 1982-84..............425.00

Silversmith of Williamsburg, HN 2008, green jerkin, 1960-83.......125.00 to 150.00

Skater (The), HN 2117, red & white dress, 1953-71 ....325.00

Sleepyhead, HN 2114, 1953-55.........................950.00 to 1,000.00

Soiree, HN 2312, white dress, green overskirt, 1967-84............150.00 to 175.00

Spring Flower, HN 1807, green skirt, grey-blue overskirt, 1937-59............................275.00 to 300.00

Stephanie, HN 2807, yellow gown, 1977-82..200.00

Stitch in Time (A), HN 2352, 1966-80..125.00

Summer, HN 2086, red gown, 1952-59..350.00

Summer's Day

Summer's Day, HN 2181, 1957-62 (ILLUS.) 275.00

Suzette

Suzette, HN 2026, 1949-59 (ILLUS.) 290.00

Sweet & Twenty

Sweet & Twenty, HN 1298, red & pink dress, 1928-69 (ILLUS.) ....250.00 to 300.00

Sweet Anne, M 5, cream to red skirt, shaded red & blue jacket, 1932-45 ..255.00

Sweet Anne, HN 1496, pink & purple dress & hat, 1932-67 ....210.00

Sweeting

Sweeting, HN 1935, pink dress, 1940-73 (ILLUS.) 140.00

Sweet Sixteen, HN 2231, 1958-65 .....260.00

Thanksgiving, HN 2446, blue overalls, 1972-76...250.00

Top O' the Hill, HN 1833, green dress,1937-71 (ILLUS. top next column) ....175.00 to 200.00

Toymaker (The), HN 2250, 1959-73...265.00

Uriah Heep, HN 554, black jacket & trousers, 1923-39.............................600.00

Victorian Lady, M 1, red-tinged dress, light green shawl, 1932-45...............385.00

Top O' the Hill

Victorian Lady (A), HN 728, red skirt, purple shawl, 1925-52 .....275.00 to 300.00

Virginia, HN 1693, yellow dress, 1935-49...500.00

Votes For Women, HN 2816, 1978-81...140.00

Windflower, M 79, blue & green, 1939-49...550.00

Winsome, HN 2220, red dress, 1960-85...165.00

Winter, HN 2088, shaded blue skirt, 1952-59...335.00

MISCELLANEOUS

Jackdaw of Rheims Charger

Ashpot, figural bust, Auld Mac ....100.00 to 125.00

Ashpot, figural bust, Farmer John 95.00

Ashtrays, figural bust, Artful Dodger, Sam Weller, Mr. Micawber & Tony Weller, 1⅞ x 2⅝", set of 4................150.00

Bowl, 8½" d., 5½" h., stoneware, squatty bulbous body on a footring, the rounded sides tapering to narrow molded rim bands & a sterling silver rim flanked by angled loop handles, decorated w/a wide band of floral clusters flanked by narrower bands of scallops, all in earthtones, marked "Doulton Lambeth - 1880" 440.00

Bowl, 9"d., Shakespeare Characters series, "Romeo" 125.00

Bowl, 10" d., Gaffers series, "Zunday Zmocks" 145.00

Bowl, 10½" d., Shakespeare Characters series, "Juliet" 100.00

Charger, Jackdaw of Rheims series, 13½" d. (ILLUS.) 175.00

Creamer, stoneware, wide flat-bottomed tapering ovoid body w/a flared short neck, decorated w/a small band of stylized florals on a mottled ground, in shades of blue & brown, marked "Doulton Lambeth - 1876," 4 3/16" h. 220.00

Cup & saucer, demitasse, Granthan patt., No. D5477 ....15.00

Cup & saucer, Coaching Days series ...50.00

Flask, "Dewars," Kingsware, bust of Night Watchman, 8" h. 150.00

Humidor, cov., Chang Ware, the squat lidded jar molded w/four ribs about the sides, flat inset lid w/large domical finial, glazed in brilliant shades of red, blue, yellow & white w/thick cracqueler, designed by Charles Noke, signed in overglaze "Chang - Royal - Doulton" & "NOKE" w/monogram, ca. 1925 ....1,955.00

Jardiniere, stoneware, bulbous body on a flaring foot & tapering to a narrow flared rim, the body decorated w/ a band of line-drawn farm animals between brightly decorated incised bands in cobalt blue, brown & ivory, by Hannah Barlow, marked "Doulton-Lambeth 1883, BHB 346, JLB 391, EM, Ob," 9" d., 7" h. 1,210.00

Jardiniere, flow blue, Babes in the Woods series, mother & child w/basket picking flowers, 9½" d., 8" h. 695.00

Jardiniere, decorated w/blue daffodils on white ground, gold rim, ca. 1890s, Doulton - Burslem mark, 10" h. 300.00

Jugs, squared upright body w/rounded shoulder to a small flaring neck, an angled handle from rim to shoulder, molded ribbing in brown around sides w/blue & white molded bands around the shoulder, one handle initialed "I.W.," the other "S.W.," molded base mark "Doulton Lambeth - 1882," 7¾" h., pr. 451.00

Pitcher, 6" h., Coaching Days series, "Innkeeper Talks to Driver" 195.00

Pitcher, 6" h., flow blue, Babes in the Woods series, scene of a girl holding a guitar 285.00

Pitcher, 6" h., Shakespeare Characters series, "Wolsey" 165.00

Pitcher, 10½" h., tankard-type, stoneware, incised cobalt blue & bluish grey floral decoration on tan ground, initialed "H.B." (Hannah Barlow), dated 1875, Doulton - Lambeth mark 700.00

Plate, 6¾" d., Coaching Days series 75.00

Plate, 7½" d., Robin Hood series (Under the Greenwood Tree), scene of Robin Hood 60.00

Plate, 8½" d., flow blue, Babes in the Woods series, girl w/ basket 485.00

Plate, 10" d., Gaffers series, "Zunday Zmocks" 65.00

Plate, 10" d., Historic England series, "Henry VIII" 55.00

Plate, 10" d., Monks series, "Fishing, Tomorrow will be Friday," signed "Noke" & dated "1911" 165.00

Plate, 10" d., Sir Roger deCoverly series 85.00

Plate, 10" d., rack-type, "The Doctor" ...65.00

Plate, 10" d., rack-type, "The Mayor" 65.00

Plate, 10" d., rack-type, "The Parson" ...65.00

Plate, 10" d., rack-type, "Sir Francis Drake" 55.00

Plate, 10" d., rack-type, "The Squire" 95.00

Plate, 10½" d., Night Watchman series, watchman in blue-grey w/blue boots, tan background w/fine speckling, "With compliments of P. McIntosh & Co. Grocers," on back ...100.00

Punch bowl, deep rounded bowl on a pedestal foot, decorated around the upper half w/a continuous comical scene of late 18th c. figures ice skating, titled "Pryde Goeth Before A Fall," 16" d. (ILLUS. top next column) 385.00

Tray, Robin Hood (Under the Greenwood Tree), "King of Archers" scene, 6 x 7¾" 125.00

Royal Doulton Punch Bowl

Tumbler, stoneware, slightly tapering cylindrical form, molded w/taverns & hunt scenes around the sides, dark brown glazed rim band above a tan body, applied sterling silver rim band w/a London hallmark, late 19th c., 4⅝" h. 110.00

Vase, 4¼" h., 3¼" d., footed ovoid body w/swelled neck, decorated w/white flowers, berries & green leaves, tan & beige shaded ground, gold feet & trim on sides, Doulton - Burslem mark 95.00

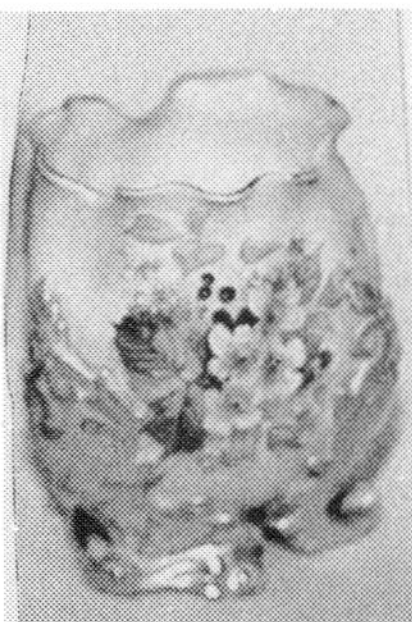

Small Doulton Vase

Vase, 4¼" h., 3¼" d., ovoid body w/ruffled, flaring rim, supported by gilt scroll feet, decorated w/white flowers, black berries & green leaves on a shaded tan & beige ground, Doulton Burslem mark (ILLUS.) 95.00

Vase, 5⅞" h., stoneware, footed bulbous ovoid body tapering to a short wide flaring neck, applied on one side w/a large branch of white cherry blossoms, the other side w/applied geese, sparrows, fish & snakes, all on a light tan ground, Doulton Lambeth mark, ca. 1890..... 330.00

Vase, 6" h., Chang Ware, footed very squatty bulbous base w/the wide shoulder tapering to a short cylindrical neck, glazed in rich ruby decorated w/thick white crackle glaze trimmed w/ochre & blue, signed "Chang - Royal - Doulton - ENGLAND - Noke," original paper label, ca. 1925 .... 2,588.00

Vase, 6¼" h., flow blue, Babes in the Woods series, children playing Blind Man's Buff 495.00

Vase, 6½" h., flow blue, Babes in the Woods series, girls under tree ... 535.00

Vase, 7¾" h., 3" d., tapering cylindrical body w/flared rim, bands of green & periwinkle blue beading & short ribs around the top half w/mottled green on the lower half, stamped "Royal Doulton England - MW - 8128" 302.50

Vase, 8" h., Rouge Flambé glaze, landscape decoration 495.00

Vase, 8¼" h., 5½" d., Rouge Flambé glaze, ovoid body tapering to a short cylindrical neck, large ship on the front & back 195.00

Vase, 10½" h., handled, flow blue, Babes in the Woods series, mother & child scene, ornate gold handles 750.00

Vase, 11½" h., two-handled, decorated w/gold-outlined flowers in yellow, brown & pale blue, artist-initialed, Doulton - Burslem mark..... 190.00

Vase, 13½" h., Chang Ware, slightly swelled cylindrical body tapering to a flared rim, brilliant flambé red glaze decorated w/white, yellow, blue & green textured overglaze, printed factory marks & "Chang" & "NOKE," ca. 1925 .... 2,588.00

Fine Doulton Vase

Vase, 20" h., wide baluster-form body w/a short rolled neck, raised on a short pedestal on a square foot, decorated w/delicate birds & flowering branches on a creamy ground, ca. 1880 (ILLUS.) 715.00

Vases, 4" h., Silicon Ware, decorated w/ornate relief-molded design in white, aqua & chocolate brown on tan ground, pr. (one w/tiny firing crack) 110.00

DRESDEN

Figural Dresden Compote

Dresden-type porcelain evolved from wares made at the nearby Meissen Porcelain Works early in the 18th century. "Dresden" and "Meissen" are often used interchangeably for later wares. "Dresden" has become a generic name for the kind of porcelains produced in Dresden and certain other areas of Germany but perhaps should be confined to the wares made in the city of Dresden.

Bowl, 9" d., h.p. pink & lavender wildflowers $100.00

Bowl, 9¼" d., 2¼" h., wide reticulated sides decorated overall w/small flowers, Dresden patt. in the center, signed "Schumann" only, early 95.00

Bowl, 10½" d., three dolphin feet, reticulated sides, tiny h.p. pastel floral decoration in center 395.00

Candelabra, two-light, the candle-sockets supported by ornately scroll-molded arms raised on a tall conical pedestal base ornately molded w/scrolls & trimmed w/applied pink & yellow roses, the whole w/gilt trim, 10" h., pr. 395.00

Card tray, footed, applied flowers, cupid & cornucopia decoration, 10" sq. 550.00

Celery dish, elongated oval w/raised scalloped rim, interior & exterior decorated w/h.p. flowers & gold accents, 5 x 13" 195.00

Center bowl, boat-shaped, on four square feet, h.p. floral interior, applied flowers on exterior, artist-signed, 7½ x 17" 350.00

Charger, ornate reticulated border, tiny h.p. pastel floral decoration in center on white ground, ca. 1893, 11½" d. 395.00

Clock, table model, a circular enameled dial within a scrolled rococo-style case w/four applied putti representing the four seasons, glazed in pale blue & pink, the putti brightly decorated, ca. 1880, 18" h. (minor breakage to extremities, age lines) 825.00

Compote, open, 12¼" h., circular bowl w/flaring reticulated scalloped rim, raised base w/full-figure men & women in peasant attire encircling the flower-decorated standard, late 19th c. (ILLUS.) 605.00

Compote, open, 10 x 11", 13" h., shaped oval bowl decorated w/polychrome florals & gilt trim, raised on a standard applied w/flowers & cherubs, marked "Dresden" (small chips) 220.00

Compote, open, 14" h., cornucopia-shaped bowl w/handles, reticulated latticework sides w/relief-molded flowers & h.p. cherub decoration, artist-signed, ca. 1890-1906 ....750.00

Desk set, pair of covered bulbous inkwells on a scalloped rectangular tray w/shaped ends, decorated overall w/small pastel flowers on a white ground, 3 pcs. 295.00

Dessert plates, reticulated edges, decorated w/florals & gilt trim, 7¼" d., set of 4 ....121.00

Ewer, ovoid, openwork maroon lustre & gold base & top, one side decorated w/a h.p. scene of two ladies in a garden w/cupid, the reverse w/a scene of children playing blindman's buff, elaborate openwork handle in lavish dull gold, marked "Wissman Dresden," ca. 1890, 5½" d., 11¾" h. (ILLUS. top next column) 695.00

Figure of a ballerina wearing a lace dress w/applied flowers, 3¼" h. 110.00

Ornate Dresden Ewer

Figure of a ballerina w/outstretched arms, brown hair, wearing blue ruffled lace dress w/applied flowers, white bodice w/lace trim, gold slippers, marked "Dresden" in blue, crown & "T & K," 6" h. 145.00

Figure of a ballerina wearing an ornate tiered lacy dress, shown standing w/one leg forward & one hand holding her skirt as she bows, her other arm extended back, raised on an oval plinth base, "Dresden" mark under base, ca. 1890, 11" h....525.00

Figure of a lady wearing a crinoline gown & seated on a settee holding an open book & talking to a parrot perched on one arm of the settee, applied flowers & much lace trim, ca. 1895, 7 x 8½" (only slight lace damage)..425.00

Figure group, peasant man leaning over his sleeping lady surrounded by a lamb, kid, birds, bee & playful children, 10" h. 650.00

Figure group, a couple in 18th c. dress, the lady sitting on a settee holding a music book, the gentleman behind her playing a violin & wearing a green coat, on an oblong scroll-molded base, 10½" l., 10" h...850.00

Figure group, two lovers in 18th c. peasant dress seated on a large scroll-molded base, crown mark in blue, 19th c., 13¼" h. 385.00

Figure group, two Cavalier musicians & a barmaid, one man playing a lute, the other a bagpipe, the barmaid holding a jug & dancing, on an oval base, 9" w., 14½" h. 1,250.00

Figure group, lady & man playing chess, man in green coat & pants, lady in dress trimmed w/lace & roses, maroon bodice, gold trim, unmarked.......................................345.00

Lamp, table-type, waisted lower portion surmounted by a baluster-form upper portion, applied w/figural cupids holding birds & flowers, the whole decorated w/applied flowers, electrified, unmarked, 16" h. plus base fittings.....................................450.00

Lamps, table-type, a tall ovoid body tapering to a wide flaring neck & raised on a tall pedestal above a stepped block base, the sides of the body flanked by tall, narrow loop handles, the front decorated w/a scene of classical lovers in a landscape trimmed below w/an applied swag of encrusted blossoms, the block base w/a scene of a single figure above a similar applied swag, the reverse w/colorful floral sprays, gilt band trim on body & base, fitted for electricity, ca. 1890, 16" h., pr. ...495.00

Plate, 9" d., reticulated cobalt & gold border w/center scene of a Victorian couple 195.00

Plates, 6½" d., reticulated rim, center w/polychrome floral decoration, marked "Dresden, Germany," set of 6...115.50

Plates, 8⅜" d., ivory ground w/a yellow & green border & a large floral bouquet in the center & gold trim, marked "Dresden," set of 14 ....231.00

Vases, 9½" h., bulbous body w/straight top, two white figural panels & two gold panels w/floral decoration, ca. 1860, entwined "AP" mark, pr...250.00

FIESTA

Fiesta dinnerware was made by the Homer Laughlin China Company of Newell, West Virginia, from the 1930s until the early 1970s. The brilliant colors of this inexpensive pottery have attracted numerous collectors. On February 28, 1986, Laughlin reintroduced the popular Fiesta line with minor changes in the shapes of a few pieces and a contemporary color range. The effect of this new production on the Fiesta collecting market is yet to be determined.

Fiesta Carafe

fiesta
HLC USA

Ashtray
- chartreuse $52.00
- cobalt blue 38.00
- red 41.00
- turquoise 33.00
- yellow 32.00

Bowl, individual, 4¾" d.
- cobalt blue 21.50
- forest green 20.00
- ivory 19.50
- rose 23.50

Bowl, individual fruit, 5½" d.
- forest green 28.00
- light green 19.50
- yellow 16.50

Bowl, dessert, 6" d.
- chartreuse 37.00
- cobalt blue 33.00
- ivory 33.50
- rose 38.00

Bowl, individual salad, 7½" d.
- turquoise 55.00
- yellow 55.00

Bowl, nappy, 8½" d.
- grey 38.50
- light green 23.00
- medium green 79.00
- red 39.00

Bowl, nappy, 9½" d.
- cobalt blue 40.00
- rose 50.00
- yellow 38.50

Bowl, salad, 9½" d.
- ivory 28.00
- turquoise 27.50

Bowl, fruit, 11¾" d.
- cobalt blue 116.00
- turquoise 150.00

Bowl, cream soup
- forest green 45.00
- grey 58.00
- medium green 46.50
- red 43.50

Bowl, salad, large, footed
- ivory 240.00
- red 280.00
- yellow 140.00

Cake plate, 10" d.
- turquoise 605.00

Candleholders, bulb-type, pr.
- light green 57.00
- red 79.00

Candleholders, tripod-type, pr.
- cobalt blue 392.00
- ivory 236.00
- light green 340.00
- yellow 262.00

Carafe, cov.
- turquoise 160.00
- yellow (ILLUS.) 151.00

Casserole, cov., two-handled, 10" d.
- chartreuse 177.00
- forest green 231.00
- light green 94.00
- medium green 440.00
- turquoise 100.00

Coffeepot, cov., demitasse, stick handle
- cobalt blue 305.00
- ivory (ILLUS.top next column) 289.00
- light green 200.00
- red 230.00

Fiesta Demitasse Coffeepot

Coffeepot, cov.
- cobalt blue 150.00
- forest green 210.00
- grey 200.00
- ivory 120.00
- yellow 92.00

Compote, 12" d., low, footed
- cobalt blue 132.00
- red 120.00
- turquoise 111.00

Compote. sweetmeat, high stand
- light green 37.50
- red 64.00
- yellow 40.00

Creamer, individual size
- red 138.00

Creamer, stick handle
- ivory 25.00
- turquoise 35.00
- yellow 24.00

Fiesta Creamer

Creamer
- grey 23.00
- ivory (ILLUS.) 14.00
- light green 13.50
- rose 23.50

Cup & saucer, demitasse, stick handle
- cobalt blue 55.00
- grey 273.00
- ivory 54.00
- turquoise 52.50

Cup & saucer, ring handle
- chartreuse 31.00
- forest green 34.50
- medium green 46.00
- red 29.00
- yellow 19.00

Egg cup
- cobalt blue 49.00
- light green 32.00
- rose 100.00
- yellow 33.00

Fork (Kitchen Kraft)
- red 56.00

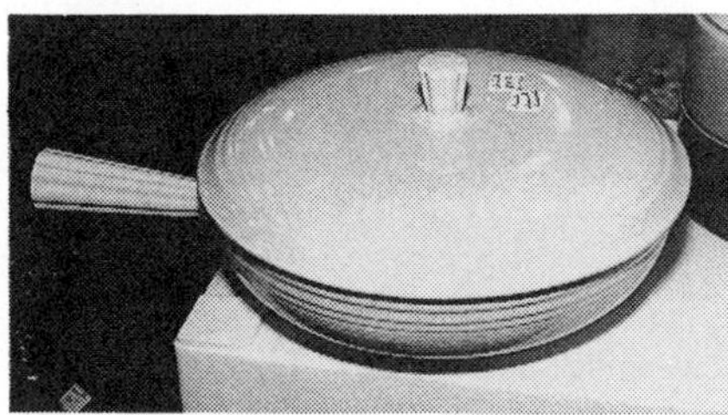

Fiesta French Casserole

French casserole, cov., stick handle
- yellow (ILLUS.). 162.00

Gravy boat
- chartreuse 50.00
- cobalt blue 41.00
- grey 59.00
- ivory 38.00

Lid for mixing bowl, size No. 1
- light green 695.00

Marmalade jar, cov.
- cobalt blue 160.00
- red 186.00

Mixing bowl, nest-type

Size No. 1, 5" d.
- ivory 55.00
- turquoise 50.00

Size No. 2, 6" d.
- cobalt blue 69.00

red 67.50
Size No. 3, 7" d.
light green.....................................60.00
turquoise.......................................75.00
Size No. 4, 8" d.
ivory...65.00
turquoise.......................................60.00
Size No. 5, 9" d.
light green.....................................91.00
yellow 81.00
Size No. 6, 10" d.
ivory...106.00
yellow 90.00
Size No. 7, 11½" d.
turquoise.....................................141.00

Mug
chartreuse 56.00
grey 65.00
light green.....................................42.00

Mug, Tom & Jerry style
forest green 58.00
ivory/gold 55.00
light green.....................................42.00
yellow 38.00

Mustard jar, cov.
cobalt blue 175.00
light green..................................150.00
yellow 132.00

Onion soup bowl, cov.
light green..................................425.00
red 650.00

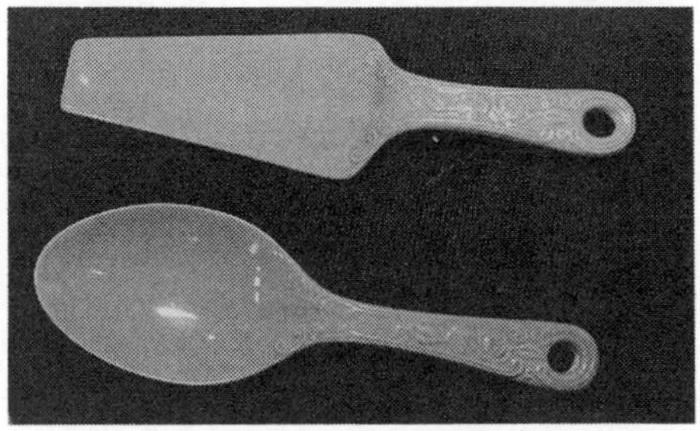

Fiesta Pie Server and Spoon

Pie server, (Kitchen Kraft)
light green (ILLUS. top) 45.00
red 85.00

Pitcher, jug-type, 2 pt.
chartreuse 96.00
ivory...48.00
red 75.00
turquoise (ILLUS.) 40.00
yellow 42.50

Fiesta Two-Pint Pitcher

Pitcher, juice, disc-type, 30 oz.
light green.....................................90.00
red 392.00
yellow 37.50

Pitcher, water, disc-type
cobalt blue 152.00
grey 200.00
ivory...95.00
medium green 725.00
red 118.00
rose 177.00
yellow 85.00

Fiesta Ice Lip Pitcher

Pitcher, w/ice lip, globular, 2 qt.
ivory...85.00
light green.....................................80.00
yellow (ILLUS.) 85.00

Plate, 6" d.
cobalt blue 8.00
grey 8.00
light green.......................................5.00
medium green 14.00
red 7.00
rose 8.00
yellow 4.00

Plate, 7" d.
chartreuse 11.00

forest green 9.00
ivory 6.50
light green......................................8.50
medium green 22.50
red 8.00
rose 10.00

Plate, 9" d.
chartreuse 16.00
forest green 14.00
ivory 11.00
light green......................................9.50
medium green 40.00
rose 18.00
turquoise...8.50
yellow 9.00

Plate, 10" d.
chartreuse 34.00
grey 48.00
ivory 22.50
light green....................................20.00
medium green 80.00
yellow 22.00

Plate, grill, 10½" d.
cobalt blue 35.00
light green....................................23.00
red 50.00
rose 45.00
turquoise.......................................20.00

Plate, grill, 11½" d.
cobalt blue 50.00
light green....................................38.00

Plate, chop, 13" d.
chartreuse 50.00
grey 50.00
ivory 23.00
red 85.00
turquoise.......................................26.00
yellow 22.50

Plate, chop, 15" d.
chartreuse 100.00
forest green 60.00
ivory 35.00
light green....................................35.00
red 48.00
yellow 28.00

Platter, 12" oval
chartreuse 40.00
cobalt blue 24.00
grey 40.00
light green....................................20.00
red 60.00
yellow 19.00

Relish tray w/five inserts
ivory 100.00
multi-colored..............150.00 to 200.00
turquoise.....................................185.00
yellow 165.00

Salt & pepper shakers, pr.
forest green 40.00
grey 32.00
light green....................................18.00
medium green 105.00
turquoise.......................................16.00
yellow 14.50

Soup plate w/flanged rim, 8" d.
cobalt blue 33.00
forest green 35.00
light green....................................28.00
red 46.00
rose 35.00
yellow 24.50

Spoon (Kitchen Kraft)
red (ILLUS. bottom) 85.00

Sugar bowl, cov.
chartreuse 37.00
cobalt blue 47.00
grey 44.50
light green....................................26.00
red 37.00
rose 42.00
yellow 25.00

Syrup pitcher w/original lid
cobalt blue ....225.00 to 250.00
light green...................175.00 to 200.00
red 220.00
turquoise.....................................222.00

Fiesta Medium Size Teapot

Teapot, cov., medium size (6 cup)
chartreuse 180.00
ivory 150.00
light green (ILLUS.) 112.00
red 138.00
rose 325.00
turquoise.....................................101.00

Teapot, cov., large size (8 cup)
red 156.00
turquoise.....................................105.00
yellow 45.00

Tray, Figure 8
turquoise.....................................250.00

Tumbler, juice, 5 oz.
cobalt blue 31.00

grey 250.00
light green....................27.00
turquoise....................19.50
yellow 25.00

Tumbler, water,10 oz
cobalt blue....................49.00
ivory....................42.00
light green....................41.00
turquoise....................47.00
yellow 42.00

Utility tray
ivory....................27.50
light green....................28.00
red 32.00
turquoise....................21.50
yellow 20.00

Vase, bud, 6½" h.
ivory....................46.00
light green....................43.00
yellow 50.00

Vase, 8" h.
cobalt blue 422.00
ivory....................275.00 to 300.00
light green....................310.00
turquoise....................334.00
yellow 325.00

Vase, 10" h.
cobalt bluc 475.00
light green....................400.00 to 425.00
red 600.00

Vase, 12" h.
cobalt blue ....550.00 to 600.00
red ....500.00 to 600.00

FLORENCE CERAMICS

Florence "Memories" Figure

Florence Ward began her successful enterprise in 1939. By 1946 she had moved her home workshop into a small plant in Pasadena, California. About three years later it was again necessary to move to larger facilities in the area. Semi-porcelain figurines, some with actual lace dipped in slip, were made. Figurines, such as fictional characters and historical couples, were the backbone of her business. To date, almost two hundred figurines have been documented. For about two years, in the mid-1950s, Betty D. Ford created what the company called 'stylized sculptures from the Florence wonderland of birds and animals.' Included were about a half dozen assorted doves, several cats, foxes, dogs and rabbits. Several marks were used over the years with the most common being the circle with 'semi-porcelain' outside the circle. The name of the figurine was almost always included with a mark. A "Floraline" mark was used on floral containers and related items. There was also a script mark and a block lettered mark as well as paper labels. The company was sold to Scripto Corporation in 1964 but only advertising pieces were made such as mugs for the Tournament of Roses in Pasadena, California. The company ceased all operations in 1977.

Floraline
BY
FLORENCE CERAMICS INC
PASADENA, CALIFORNIA

Candlestick, feathered effect overall in white w/gold trim, marked "Floraline by Florence Ceramics Pasadena, CA," Model No. R6, 6" h. $20.00

Figure of a boy, "Mike," standing w/head thrown back & arms straight up & back, palms up, 6½" h. 125.00

Figure of a boy, standing w/legs apart & right leg slightly bent, holding a package in right hand, white shoes, jacket & shirt, pale blue socks, pants & hat, brown hair, 6¼" h. 105.00

Figure of a girl, "Joy," standing w/green hat, yellow dress w/white & green collor, 6" h. 85.00

Figure of a girl standing in front of rectangular planter w/left arm resting on top of planter, blond hair, green & brown hat, white coat w/green buttons, green & brown gloves, 6" h. 35.00

Figure of a girl standing w/feet slightly apart, sand pail in right hand & left arm bent at elbow holding shovel to shoulder, black bathing suit w/yellow polka-dots, matching scarf tied around her short blond hair w/bow at top, 7" h. 85.00

Figure of a Grandmother sitting in chair reading, "Memories," white w/22k gold trim (ILLUS.) 155.00

Figure of a mermaid, "Jane," shelf sitter-type w/arms at shoulders, elbows bent, Model No. M2, 7" h. 170.00

Florence "Amelia" Figure

Figure of a woman, "Amelia," standing w/left elbow bent & right hand at waist, red brocade floor length dress w/low scalloped neckline & short sleeves, Model No. F204, 7½" h. (ILLUS.) 155.00

Figure of a woman, "Roberta," standing, one arm behind back, one hand holding skirt, head tilted, blonde hair in an upsweep, yellow floor length dress, brown gloves, 8¾" h. 135.00

Model of a dove on a base, flying position w/tail up, wings back, head down, porcelain bisque, brown w/white, designed by Betty Davenport Ford, Model No. B-6, 8" l., 11" h. 95.00

Wall plaque, rectangular w/scalloped edges, molded-in-relief full-sized girl holding fan, beige plaque w/green clothing, Model No. P-3, 6½" l. 9" h. 115.00

FLOW BLUE

Flowing Bue wares, usually shortened to Flow Blue, were made at numerous potteries in Staffordshire, England and elsewhere. They are decorated with a blue that smudged lightly or ran in the firing. The same type of color flow is also found in certain wares decorated in green, purple and sepia. Patterns were given specific names, which accompany the listings here.

ACME (Probably Sampson Hancock & Sons, ca. 1900)

Bowl, 8½ x 11", 2" h., scalloped gilt edge $150.00

Bowl, 11" d., scalloped rim 125.00

Creamer & sugar bowl, pr. 110.00

Pitcher, milk 95.00

Sauce ladle 195.00

Tea tile 95.00

ALASKA (W.H. Grindley, ca. 1891)

Butter pat 34.00

Plate, 9" d. 45.00

Vegetable bowl, cov. 200.00

Vegetable bowl, open, 7½ x 10¼" 105.00

ALBANY (W.H. Grindley, ca. 1899)

Gravy boat 80.00

Plate, 8¾" d. 50.00

Vegetable bowl, open, 6¼ x 8" 65.00

AMOY (Davenport, dated 1844)

Amoy Plate

Bowl, cereal, 7¼" d. 120.00

Chamber pot....195.00
Creamer (professional repair)....475.00
Cup, handleless....95.00
Cup & saucer, handleless....150.00
Cup plate....110.00
Honey dish....75.00
Pitcher, 7¼" h., bulbous, 1½ qt. (minor professional repair)....700.00 to 750.00
Plate, 7½" d....85.00
Plate, 8¼" d. (ILLUS.)....97.50
Plate, 9" d....125.00
Plate, 9¾" d....130.00
Plate, 10½" d....160.00
Platter, 16" l....495.00
Platter, 20" l. (professional repair)....995.00
Sauce dish, 5" d....75.00
Soup plate w/flanged rim, 9" d....145.00
Soup plate w/flanged rim, 10½" d....195.00
Sugar bowl, cov. (professional repair)....625.00
Teapot, cov. (professional repair)....625.00
Vegetable bowl, cov., 12" d....1,195.00
Vegetable bowl, open, 10½" d....425.00
Waste bowl, large (edge flakes)....345.00

ANGLESEA (J.G. Meakin, ca. 1912)

Platter, 17" l....195.00
Sauce tureen, underplate & ladle, 3 pcs....200.00
Vegetable dish, cov....225.00

ARABESQUE (T.J. and J. Mayer, ca. 1845)

Plate, 7½" d....80.00
Sauce dish, 5" d....80.00
Sugar bowl, cov....550.00

ARGYLE (W.H. Grindley, ca. 1896)

Argyle Platter

Bowl, soup, 8¾" d....62.50
Butter pat....35.00
Charger, 15" d....165.00
Creamer....225.00
Gravy boat & undertray, 2 pcs....275.00
Plate, 7" d....37.50
Plate, 8¾" d....75.00
Platter, 8¾ x 12¾" (ILLUS.)....250.00
Platter, 12 x 17½"....395.00
Platter, 13¼ x 19"....545.00
Sauce dish....38.00
Soup plate w/flanged rim, 8¾" d....75.00
Toothbrush holder....295.00
Vegetable bowl, cov....325.00

ASTORIA (Johnson Bros., ca. 1900)

Butter pat....35.00
Cup & saucer....75.00
Plate, 10" d....75.00
Sauce dish....35.00

AYR (W. & E. Corn, ca. 1900)

Plate, 9" d....65.00
Platter, 8 x 11¼"....95.00
Vegetable bowl, open, 6¾ x 8½"....85.00

BAMBOO (Samuel Alcock & Co., ca. 1845)

Plate, 10¼" d....135.00
Platter, 14 x 16¾"....595.00
Soup plate w/flanged rim, 10" d....100.00
Tureen, cover & undertray, twisted twig handles & bud finial, 3 pcs....425.00

BEAUFORT (W.H. Grindley, ca. 1903)

Butter dish, cov....270.00
Cup & saucer....72.50
Gravy boat....95.00
Platter, 10 x 14"....150.00
Platter, 11¼ x 16¼"....175.00
Vegetable bowl, cov....215.00

BEAUTIES OF CHINA (Mellor, Venables & Co., ca. 1845)

Bowl, soup, 8¼" d....90.00

Cake plate 225.00

Platter, 16" l. 595.00

BLUE DANUBE, THE (Johnson Bros., ca. 1900)

Butter pat 32.00

Cake plate, 10½" 130.00

Pitcher, 8½" h. 325.00

Plate, 10" d. 75.00

Platter, 13½ x 18" 350.00

Sauce dish, 5" d. 30.00

Soup tureen, cov. 315.00

Vegetable bowl, cov. 195.00

Vegetable bowl, open, 7½ x 9¾" 65.00

BURLEIGH (Burgess & Leigh, ca. 1903)

Bowl, cereal 25.00

Butter pat 33.50

Plate, 9¾" d. 65.00

Platter, 10½ x 14" 200.00

Sauce tureen, cover & underplate, 3 pcs. 275.00

BUTE (Ford & Sons, ca. 1900)

Cheese dish, cov. 395.00

Relish tray, three-part 495.00

Sauce tureen, cover & underplate, 3 pcs. 395.00

BYZANTIUM (Brown, Westhead, Moore & Co., ca. 1900)

Plate, 9" d. 38.00

Plate, 10" d. 48.00

Sauce dishes, set of 6 ....75.00

CALIFORNIA (Podmore, Walker & Co., ca. 1849)

Bowl, 10" d. 225.00

Platter, 16" l. 250.00

Tea set, cov. teapot, creamer & cov. sugar bowl, 3 pcs. 695.00

CANDIA (Cauldon Ltd., ca. 1910)

Butter pat 32.00

Plate, 10¼" d. 75.00

Platter, 8¾ x 10½" 135.00

Soup plate w/flanged rim, 7½" d. 58.00

CARLTON (Samuel Alcock, 1850)

Compote, fruit 795.00

Creamer 390.00

Plate, 7¼" d. 73.00

Plate, 8½" d. 90.00

Plate, 9½" d. 125.00

Platter, 8½ x 11" 250.00

Sauce dish 60.00

Sauce tureen, cover & underplate, 3 pcs. 495.00

Vegetable bowl, open, 9¼" d. 250.00

CASHMERE (Ridgway & Morley, G.L. Ashworth, et al., 1840s on)

Cashmere Soup Plate

Compote, sauce (professional repair) 825.00

Plate, 9½" d. (under rim chip) 140.00

Plate, dinner, 10½" d. 250.00

Soup plate w/flanged rim, 10½" d. (ILLUS.) 260.00

Vegetable bowl, open, 6½ x 8½" 775.00

Waste bowl 875.00

CHAPOO (John Wedge Wood, ca. 1850)

Creamer 550.00

Plate, 7¼" d. 95.00

Plate, 8½" d. 125.00

Plate, 9½" d. 140.00

Chapoo Platter

Platter, professional repair, 10½ x13½" (ILLUS.) 350.00
Platter, 16" l. 500.00
Platter, 17¾" l. 795.00
Teapot, cov. (minor flaw) 895.00

CHEN-SI (John Meir, ca. 1835)

Cup & saucer, handleless 155.00
Platter, 12¼ x16" 775.00
Sauce dish, 5" d. 135.00

CHINESE (Wedgwood & Co., ca. 1908)

Bone dish 48.00
Plate, 6¾" d. 35.00
Sugar bowl, cov., child's size 175.00

CHUSAN (J. Clementson, ca. 1840)

Creamer 575.00
Plate, 8¼" d. 80.00
Plate, 10½" d. 100.00

CIRCASSIA (J. & G. Alcock, ca. 1840)

Cup & saucer, handleless 90.00
Pitcher, water, 8" h. 400.00
Relish dish, shell-shaped, 9" l. 175.00
Vegetable bowl, open, 9" oval 200.00
Waste bowl 200.00

CLARENCE (W.H. Grindley, ca. 1900)

Butter dish, cov. 275.00
Cup & saucer 75.00
Gravy boat 95.00
Soup tureen, cov. 495.00
Vegetable bowl, cov. 225.00

CLOVER (W.H. Grindley, ca. 1910)

Bowl, cereal, 6¾" d. 35.00
Plate, 8" d. 45.00
Platter, 16" l. 180.00
Vegetable bowl, cov. 150.00

COBURG (John Edwards, ca. 1860)

Creamer, footed 595.00
Gravy boat 350.00
Pitcher, 6" h., 1 pt. 575.00
Plate, 9" to 10" d. .... 110.00 to 125.00
Platter, 20" l. 1,250.00
Teapot, cov. 825.00

COLONIAL (J. & G. Meakin, ca. 1891)

Butter dish, cov. 125.00
Butter pat 29.00
Cup & saucer 65.00
Gravy boat & undertray, 2 pcs. 125.00
Plate, 10" d. 75.00

CONWAY (New Wharf Pottery, ca. 1891)

Cup & saucer 68.00
Plate, 9" d. 65.00
Plate, 10" d. 80.00
Platter, 7¾ x 10¾" 120.00
Soup plate w/flanged rim, 9" d. 75.00
Vegetable bowl, open, 8¾" 85.00

CORINTHIAN FLUTE (Cauldon, ca. 1905)

Butter pat 27.50
Plate, 6" d. 25.00
Plate, 7½" d. 30.00
Plate, 10" d. 50.00
Platter, 9 x 10½" 85.00
Sauce dish, 6½" d. 20.00

DAINTY (John Maddock & Son, ca. 1896)

Butter pat 18.00
Cup & saucer, large 75.00
Egg cup 115.00
Gravy boat 120.00
Plate, 8" d. 50.00
Plate, 9½" d. 55.00
Vegetable bowl, cov., 11½" oval 200.00

DAISY (Burgess & Leigh, ca. 1897)

Platter, 12 x 16" 250.00

Tea set, cov. teapot, cov. sugar bowl & creamer, 3 pcs....550.00

Vegetable dish, individual, 4 x 5¾" 25.00

DELAMERE (Henry Alcock, ca. 1900)

Bowl, 9"' d., 2" h. 100.00

Butter pat....25.00

Cup & saucer....75.00

Plate, 6¾" d....30.00

Plate, 7¾" d....38.00

Plate, 8" d. 45.00

Plate, 9" d. 60.00

Platter, 16" l. 295.00

Sauce dish....28.00

Vegetable bowl, cov. 210.00

DELAWARE (J. & G. Meakin, ca. 1890)

Dinner service for eight w/serving pieces including teapot, 106 pcs...5,000.00

DELFT (Mintons, ca. 1871)

Drainer, 8¼" d....250.00

Egg cup 55.00

Plate, 10½" d. 68.00

Teapot, cov....395.00

Vegetable bowl, cov., oval....295.00

DUCHESS (W.H. Grindley, ca. 1891)

Bone dish....25.00

Butter pat....35.00

Creamer & cov. sugar bowl, pr. 295.00

Gravy boat....75.00

Plate, 7" d. 35.00

Platter, 10½ x 12¼" 110.00

Sauce dish....40.00

Soup plate w/flanged rim, 9½" d. 55.00

Vegetable bowl, cov. 150.00

Vegetable bowl, open, oval 50.00

Waste bowl 95.00

DUNDEE (Ridgways, ca. 1910)

Bone dish....30.00

Cup & saucer....75.00

Gravy boat....110.00

Plate, 9" d. 50.00

FAIRY VILLAS - 3 Styles (W. Adams, ca. 1891)

Fairy Villas Plate

Bone dish....110.00

Butter pat....35.00

Creamer....130.00

Cup & saucer....95.00

Gravy boat....95.00

Plate, 9" d. (ILLUS.)....87.50

Platter, 5 x 8¼" 120.00

Platter, 15" l. 185.00

Sauce dish, 5" d....32.00

Soup plate w/flanged rim, 8¾" d. 75.00

Vegetable bowl, cov. ....450.00 to 500.00

Vegetable bowl open, 9" d....125.00

Vegetable bowl, open, 10" d....95.00

FLORIDA (W.H. Grindley, ca. 1891)

Butter pat....37.50

Cake plate 95.00

Creamer....185.00

Gravy boat & undertray, 2 pcs. 185.00

Plate, 6" d. 45.00

Plate, 7" d. 50.00

Plate, 9" d. 60.00

Plate, 10" d. 75.00

Vegetable bowl, open, 9¾" l. 110.00

FLORIDA (Johnson Bros., ca. 1900)

Butter pat....................35.00
Platter, 11 x 16½"....................250.00
Sauce dish....................32.50
Vegetable bowl, cov. 200.00

GAINSBOROUGH (Ridgways, ca. 1905)

Bowl, 9½" d....................110.00
Butter pat....................34.00
Gravy boat....................80.00
Plate, 9" d....................85.00
Platter, 12 x 16"....................135.00
Tureen, cov., octagonal....................325.00

GENEVA (Royal Doulton, 1906 & 1907)

Cup & saucer....................65.00
Pitcher & bowl set, 2 pcs. 1,000.00
Plate, 7½" d. 38.00
Plate, 10½" d. 65.00
Soup plate w/flanged rim....................140.00
Soup tureen, cov. 395.00
Vases, 5½" h., pr. 350.00

GEORGIA (Johnson Bros., ca. 1903)

Butter dish, cov. (hairline)....................325.00
Plate, 8¾" d....................45.00
Sauce dish, 5" d....................35.00

GIRONDE (W.H. Grindley, ca. 1891)

Gironde Cup & Saucer

Bone dish....................45.00
Bowl, soup, 7¾" d. 40.00
Cup & saucer (ILLUS.) 70.00
Gravy boat & undertray, 2 pcs....................145.00
Pitcher, milk....................225.00
Plate, 6½" d. 35.00
Plate, 8" d. 45.00
Plate, 9" d. 55.00
Plate, 10" d. 70.00
Platter, 10¾ x 15¼"....................150.00
Platter, 12 x 17"....................265.00
Sauce dish....................30.00
Soup tureen, cov. 300.00
Vegetable bowl, cov. 230.00
Vegetable bowl open, 9" d....................85.00

GOTHA (Joseph Heath, ca. 1850)

Creamer....................175.00
Plate, 10¾" d....................95.00
Platter, 10¼ x 13½"....................195.00

GOTHIC (Jacob Furnival, ca. 1850)

Plate, 6½" d. 37.50
Plate, 10½" d. (small under rim chip)..130.00
Soup plate w/flanged rim, 8½" d....................95.00
Soup tureen, cover & ladle....................3,500.00

GRACE (W.H. Grindley, ca. 1897)

Bowl, 6¼" d....................36.00
Butter pat....................35.00
Cup & saucer....................70.00
Gravy boat....................95.00
Plate, 7" to 8" d....................40.00 to 45.00
Plate, 9" d. 58.00
Sauce dish, 5⅜" d. 30.00
Tureen, cover & underplate, oval,
the set....................150.00
Vegetable bowl, open, 10½" d....................110.00
Vegetable bowl, open, 7¾ x 10⅛"......125.00

GRENADA (Henry Alcock & Co., ca. 1891)

Butter pat....................32.50
Creamer & cov. sugar bowl, pr. 300.00
Cup & saucer....................75.00
Platter, 12 x 17"....................125.00

HADDON (W.H. Grindley & Libertas, ca. 1891)

Butter pat....................35.00

Cup & saucer 75.00

Plate, 10" d. 75.00

Soup plate w/flanged rim, 10" d. 85.00

Vegetable bowl, cov. 200.00

HAMILTON (John Maddock & Sons, ca. 1896)

Pitcher, 6½" h. 225.00

Platter, 12½" l. 110.00

Platter, 10½ x 15" 225.00

Sauce tureen, cover & undertray, 3 pcs. 225.00

HINDUSTAN (John Maddock, ca. 1855)

Bowl, 9½" d. 195.00

Plate, 6¼" d. 55.00

Plate, 10¾" d. 135.00

Platter, 7¾" l. 195.00

Platter, 13½" l. 325.00

HOFBURG, THE (W.H. Grindley, ca. 1891)

Bone dish 30.00

Dinner service, twelve each dinner plates, salad plates, soup bowls, cups & saucers, butter pats, eleven berry bowls, one each gravy boat & underplate, cov. butter dish w/drainer, oval vegetable bowl, 10" platter & 16" platter, the set (vegetable bowl chipped) 4,500.00

Gravy boat 45.00

Plate, 10" d. 52.00

HOLLAND, THE (Alfred Meakin, ca. 1891)

Bone dish 35.00

Bowl, cereal 25.00

Chocolate cups, pedestal base, set of 5 ....225.00

Plate, 8" d. 40.00

Plate, 9" d. 45.00

Plate, 10" d. 75.00

Platter, 12½" l. 128.00

Platter, 14" l. 145.00

Sauce dish, 5" d. 10.00

Soup plate w/flanged rim, 7¾" d. 35.00

HOLLAND (Johnson Bros., ca. 1891)

Cake plate, 10½" d. 165.00

Holland Plate

Creamer & cov. sugar bowl, pr. 300.00

Egg cup 105.00

Gravy boat 110.00

Plate, 6½" d. 35.00

Plate, 9" d. 47.00

Plate, 10" d. (ILLUS.) 78.00

Sauce dish, 4¾" d. 30.00

Soup tureen, cov. 395.00

Vegetable bowl, open, 8½" d. 95.00

Vegetable bowl, open, 9½" oval 65.00

HONG KONG (Charles Meigh, ca. 1845)

Platter, 15⅝" x 20¼" (minor back hairline) 750.00

Sauce tureen, cov. (hairline) 275.00

Teapot, cov. 750.00

Toothbrush holder, cov. 895.00

HUDSON (J. & G. Meakin, ca. 1890)

Butter dish, cov. 250.00

Dinner service, eight each 9" d. plates, 7" d. plates, cups & saucers & sauce dishes plus seven serving pieces, 47 pcs. (slight damage) 1,495.00

Vegetable tureen, cov., oval flaredscalloped base & fancy handles,11⅜" d. 230.00

IDRIS (W.H. Grindley, ca. 1910)

Butter pat 18.00

Cup & saucer (ILLUS. top next column) 65.00

Pitcher, milk 185.00

Idris Cup & Saucer

Plates, 6" d., set of four 80.00
Plate, 10" d. 38.00
Vegetable bowl, cov. 150.00

INDIAN (possibly F. & R. Pratt, ca. 1840)

Creamer, 5" h. ....350.00 to 400.00
Cup & saucer, handled 125.00
Cup & saucer, handleless..................140.00
Pitcher, 8" h. (professional repair) 495.00
Plate, 7" d. 40.00
Plate, 8¼" d. 78.00
Plate, 9¾" d. 100.00
Platter, 12" l. 295.00
Platter, 11¾ x 15" 325.00
Relish 175.00
Sauce dish 55.00
Soup plate w/flanged rim, 10¾" d. 165.00
Teapot, cov., bulbous (oversize) 1,095.00

INDIAN JAR (Jacob & Thos. Furnival, ca. 1843)

Creamer 295.00
Plate, 7¼" d. 65.00
Platter, 10½ x 13½" 295.00
Platter, 12 x 16" 375.00
Syllabub cup, pedestal base, ring handle 145.00

INDIAN STONE (E. Walley, ca. 1850)

Plate, 7½" d. 70.00
Plate, 10½" d. 125.00
Vegetable bowl, cov. 450.00

IRIS (Arthur Wilkinson - Royal Staffordshire Potteries, ca. 1907)

Bowl, soup, 8" d. 30.00
Cup & saucer 65.00
Egg cup 75.00
Plate, 6" d. 35.00
Teacup & saucer 60.00

JANETTE (W.H. Grindley, ca. 1897)

Janette Sugar Bowl

Butter pat 30.00
Plate, 8¾" d. 45.00
Sugar bowl, cov., 6½" h. (ILLUS.) 130.00
Vegetable dish, 4¼ x 6" 35.00
Vegetable tureen, cov. 225.00

KAOLIN (Podmore & Walker, ca. 1850)

Plate, 7½" d. 55.00
Plate, 9¼" d. 75.00
Teapot, cov. (minor professional repair to spout tip) 750.00

KELVIN (Alfred Meakin, ca. 1891)

Butter pat 32.50
Creamer 175.00
Platter, 11½ x 15¾" 225.00
Sauce ladle 225.00
Soup tureen, cover & undertray, the set 550.00

KIN SHAN (Edward Challinor, ca. 1855)

Plate, 7½" d. 62.00
Soup plate w/flanged rim, 10½" d. 195.00
Waste bowl 250.00

KYBER (John Meir & Son, ca. 1870; W. Adams & Co., ca. 1891)

Kyber Plate

Pitcher, 7" h., 1 qt. 425.00
Pitcher & bowl set, 2 pcs. 2,250.00
Plate, 7" d. 35.00
Plate, 8" d. (ILLUS.) 80.00
Plate, 9" to 10" d. ....75.00 to 95.00
Platter, 10" l. 160.00
Platter, 11 x 14½" 275.00
Sauce dish 45.00
Vegetable bowl, open, 9" d. 135.00

LA BELLE (Wheeling Pottery, ca. 1900)

La Belle Chop Plate

Bowl, 9" sq., 2" h. 125.00
Bowl, 13½" d., helmet-shaped 395.00
Butter pat 45.00
Celery dish 210.00
Charger, 12¾" d. 335.00
Pitcher, 5" h. design at top only 95.00
Pitcher, 7" h 450.00
Plate, 6¼" d. 30.00
Plate, chop, 11½" d. (ILLUS.) 165.00
Platter, 18⅜" l. 375.00
Sauce dish 30.00
Soup plate w/flanged rim, 9½" d. 45.00
Syrup pitcher & underplate, 2 pcs. 325.00
Vegetable bowl open, leaf-shaped, 9" l. 195.00

LADAS (Ridgways, ca. 1905)

Gravy boat w/underplate 150.00
Plates, 8" d., set of 6 ....300.00
Plates, 9" d., set of 9 ....540.00
Platter, 12 x 16" 225.00
Soup plates w/flanged rim, 9" d., set of 12 ....720.00
Vegetable bowl, cov., oval 225.00

LAKEWOOD (Wood & Sons, ca. 1900)

Butter pat 32.00
Cup & saucer 85.00
Plate, 7¾" d. 45.00

LANCASTER (New Wharf Pottery, ca. 1891)

Cup & saucer 75.00
Pitcher, 5" h. 175.00
Plate, 7¾" d. 65.00
Plate, 9" d. 55.00

LEAF & SWAG (unknown maker, early, brush-stroke painted)

Cup & saucer 60.00
Plate, 9½" d. 135.00
Waste bowl 125.00

LE PAVOT (W.H. Grindley, ca. 1896)

Dinner service, five each 9" d. soup plates, 8" d. plates, 6½" d. saucers, six each 9" d. plates, 7" d. plates, 5" d. sauce dishes, plus individual vegetable bowl, 7½ x 10½" platter, 8¾ x 9½" oval handled vegetable bowl & 8⅝" d., 2¼" h. handled vegetable bowl, the set 1,200.00
Soup plate w/flanged rim, 9" d. 44.00

LINDA (John Maddock & Sons Ltd., ca. 1896)

Bone dish....55.00

Creamer, 5¼" h. 125.00

Cup & saucer, demitasse 60.00

Gravy boat....95.00

Pitcher, 5½" h. 195.00

Plate, 6" d. 35.00

Plate, 8" d. 40.00

Plate, 9½" to 10" d. 65.00

Platter, 9¼ x 13" 66.00

Punch cup....55.00

Vegetable bowl, cov. 190.00

LOIS (New Wharf Pottery, ca. 1891)

Cup & saucer....80.00

Plate, 9¾" d. 95.00

Vegetable bowl, open, 9" d. 100.00

Vegetable, open, 10" d. 125.00

LORNE (W.H. Grindley, ca. 1900)

Bowl, soup....65.00

Butter pat....33.00

Gravy boat....92.00

Plate, 6½" d. 25.00

Plate, 8" d. 40.00

Plate, 8¾" d. 55.00

Plate, 10" d. 70.00

Platter, 7 x 10" 110.00

Platter, 8 x 11" 130.00

Platter, 9 x 12" 155.00

Platter, 11½ x 16⅛" 225.00

Relish tray, 9" l. 98.00

Soup plate w/flanged rim, 7¾" d. 40.00

Soup tureen, cov. (professional repair) 650.00

Sugar bowl, cov. 155.00

Vegetable bowl, cov., oval....295.00

Vegetable bowl, open, 7 x 9¾" 110.00

Waste bowl....55.00

LORRAINE (Ridgways, ca. 1905)

Bone dish....30.00

Butter pat....25.00

Mush cup & saucer....185.00

Plate, 9¾" d. 45.00

Waste bowl....75.00

LOTUS (W.H. Grindley, ca. 1910)

Butter dish, cover & drain insert, 3 pcs. 135.00

Cup & saucer....30.00

Vegetable bowl, cov. 175.00

LUGANO (Ridgways, ca. 1910)

Butter pat 35.00

Dinner service for twelve w/serving pieces, 94 pcs. 3,500.00

Plate, 8" d. 38.00

Vegetable bowl, cov., 7¼" x 9⅝" 150.00

MADRAS (Doulton & Co., ca. 1900)

Cup & saucer....75.00

Dinner service: six 10½" d. plates, six 9½" d. plates, six 7½" d. plates, 13 x 15¼" platter, 10" d. open vegetable bowl, oblong cov. vegetable bowl, round cov. vegetable bowl & two 9" d. cake plates, 25 pcs. 1,500.00

Gravy boat....82.50

Pitcher, 7" h. 195.00

Plate, 5½" to 6½" d. ....35.00 to 45.00

Plate, 7" d. 45.00

Plate, 8½" d. 80.00

Plate, 9½" to 10½" d. 85.00

Platter, 13¾" l. 150.00

Platter, 15¾" l. 255.00

Sauce dish, 4¾" d. 35.00

Sauce dish, 5¾" d. 38.00

Vegetable bowl, cov., oblong....200.00

Vegetable bowl, cov., round 215.00

Vegetable bowl, open, 8½" oval....120.00

MANILLA (Podmore, Walker & Co., ca. 1845)

Bowl, soup....195.00

Plate, 8¾" d. 100.00

Plate, 9" d. 112.50

Plate, 9½" d. 110.00

Plate, 10" d. 160.00

Platter, 16" l. 725.00

Platter, 18" l. 895.00
Relish dish 260.00

MARECHAL NIEL (W.H. Grindley, ca. 1895)

Bone dish...42.50
Butter pat 37.00
Cup & saucer 55.00
Gravy boat 135.00
Plate, 10" d. 95.00
Platter, 11¾" x 15½"..........................225.00
Platter, 18" l. 325.00
Sauce dish 37.00
Soup plate w/flanged rim 50.00
Vegetable bowl, cov., oval.................285.00

MARGUERITE (W.H. Grindley, ca. 1891)

Bone dish..23.00
Butter pat 35.00
Cup & saucer 65.00
Plate, 8¾" d. 55.00
Sauce dish 30.00
Sauce tureen, underplate & ladle 375.00
Vegetable bowl, cov. 225.00

MARIE (W.H. Grindley, ca. 1891)

Butter dish, cov. 290.00
Creamer..165.00
Gravy boat & underplate, 2 pcs. 145.00
Plate, 10" d. 75.00
Vegetable bowl, cov. 230.00

MARQUIS, THE (W.H. Grindley, ca. 1906)

Bowl, 5½" d..35.00
Plate, 6" d. 35.00
Sauce dish, 6¼" d................................27.00

MELBOURNE (W.H. Grindley, ca. 1900)

Bowl, 6¼" d..36.00
Butter dish, cov. 225.00
Butter pat 30.00
Creamer..155.00
Cup & saucer 65.00
Gravy boat & underplate, 2 pcs. 125.00
Plate, 6¾" d. 40.00
Plate, 8" to 9" d. ....45.00 to 55.00
Plate, 10" d. 78.00
Platter, 8½ x 12" 130.00
Platter, 10 x 14" 140.00
Platter, 11½ x 16½" 205.00
Saucer, 5¾" d. 15.00
Soup plate w/flanged rim, 10" d. 85.00
Sugar bowl, cov. 225.00
Vegetable bowl, cov., 12¼" oval.........295.00
Vegetable bowl, open, 9" oval 95.00
Vegetable bowl, open, 9¾" oval.........115.00

MELROSE (Doulton, ca. 1891)

Creamer, 4" h. 105.00
Platter, 8 x 11" 120.00
Platters, nested, 8½ x 12", 10 x 14", 12 x 16" & 13 x 18", set of 4............650.00
Sauce tureen & underplate, 2 pcs. 395.00
Vegetable bowl, cov. 175.00

MILAN (W.H. Grindley, ca. 1893)

Plate, 8" d. 40.00
Plate, 9" d. 45.00
Plate, 10" d. 65.00
Sauce dish 32.00
Soup plate w/flanged rim, 8¾" d. 40.00

MONGOLIA (Johnson Bros., ca. 1900)

Cup & saucer 75.00
Gravy boat, 3 x 4" 70.00
Plate, 7¼" d. 50.00
Plate, 9" d. 65.00
Platter, 12 x 16 oval 300.00
Soup plate w/flanged rim, 10" d. 55.00

MURIEL (Upper Hanley Potteries, ca. 1895)

Creamer...115.00
Gravy boat 95.00
Plate, 10" d. 75.00
Vegetable bowl, open, 10" d. 115.00

NANKIN (Ashworth, ca. 1865)

Cake plate 150.00
Plate, 8" d. 65.00

Platter, 21½" l., w/well & tree (professional repair) 790.00

Sauce tureen w/underplate 425.00

NEOPOLITAN (Johnson Bros., ca. 1900)

Bone dish 35.00

Butter pat 30.00

Dinner service, eight each 10", 9" & 7" d. plates, butter pats, bone dishes & cups & saucers, seven sauce dishes & one each cov. butter dish w/drain insert, round cov. vegetable bowl, oval cov. vegetable bowl, 9" d. open vegetable bowl, cov. sauce tureen w/underplate, relish dish, 8 x 10½" platter, 9 x 12¼" platter & 11 x 14¼" platter, the set 2,975.00

Plate 10" d. 70.00

Platter, 10½ x 14" 150.00

NON PAREIL (Burgess & Leigh, ca. 1891)

Non Pareil Plate

Bowl, 6½" d. 47.00

Butter dish, cov. (base hairline) 275.00

Butter pat 35.00

Cake plate, 11" d. 245.00

Creamer, 5" h. 235.00

Cup & saucer 105.00

Egg cup 195.00

Gravy boat 160.00

Ladle holder 225.00

Pitcher, 1 qt. 475.00

Plate, 7¾" d. 50.00

Plate, 8½" d. 56.00

Plate, 9¾" d. (ILLUS.) 90.00

Plate, 11" d., two-handled 210.00

Platter, 13¾" l. 295.00

Platter, 12¼ x 15½" 370.00

Sauce tureen, cover & undertray, the set (professional repair to finial) 750.00

Saucer 18.00

Sauce ladle 475.00

Soup plate w/flanged rim, 8¾" d. 65.00

Sugar bowl, cov. 295.00

Teapot, cov. 375.00

Vegetable bowl, cov., rectangular 390.00

Vegetable bowl, cov., octagonal 390.00

Vegetable bowl, open, 8½" d. 115.00

Waste bowl 110.00

NORMANDY (Johnson Bros., ca. 1900)

Bowl, soup, 7½" d. 75.00

Butter pat 41.00

Creamer & cov. sugar bowl, pr. (very minor chip on inside rim of creamer) 300.00

Cup & saucer 72.00

Plate, 6" d. 30.00

Plate, 10 d. 80.00

Platter, 9½ x 12½" 125.00

Sauce dish 32.50

Sugar bowl, cov. 140.00

Vegetable bowl, cov., oval 315.00

OAKLAND (John Maddock, ca. 1895)

Butter pat 25.00

Sauce dish, 6" sq. 25.00

Soup plate, w/flanged rim, 8¾" d. 35.00

OPHIR (E. Bourne & J.E. Leigh, ca. 1891)

Dinner service: four each 9¼" d. plates,8" d. plates, 9¼" d. soup plates w/flanged rim, 5" d. sauce dishes,butter pats, cups & saucers, two 10" oval cov. casseroles, one each gravy boat & undertray, 14½" l. platter, 12" l. platter, creamer & cov. sugar bowl,36 pcs. 3,160.00

OREGON (T.J. & J. Mayer, ca. 1845)

Plate, 5" to 6" d. 100.00

Plate, 9¾" d. 125.00

Platter, 12 x 16" 425.00

Sauce dish...75.00

Soup plate w/flanged rim, 10½" d.......185.00

Teapot, cov...750.00

Vegetable bowl, cov. 995.00

Vegetable bowl, open, 10⅜" d. 350.00

ORIENTAL (Ridgways, ca. 1891)

Charger, 12½" d. 125.00

Cup & saucer.......................................60.00

Plate, 6½" d. 30.00

Plate, 7¾" d..50.00

Plate, 8¾" d..60.00

Plate, 9½" d. 75.00

Relish dish, self-handled, 5 x 8½" oval 85.00

Sugar bowl, cov. 165.00

Tureen, cov., 6½ x 9 x 10½"..............325.00

Waste bowl 95.00

ORMONDE (Alfred Meakin, ca. 1891)

Platter, 11⅛" l. 140.00

Platter, 14⅛" l. 180.00

Platter, 18" l. 200.00

Sauce dish, oblong 30.00

Soup plate w/flanged rim 65.00

Vegetable bowl, cov., footed 275.00

OSBORNE (W.H. Grindley, ca. 1900)

Bone dish...45.00

Bouillon cup & saucer..........................85.00

Butter pat 32.00

Cup & saucer.......................................85.00

Gravy boat & underplate, 2 pcs..........125.00

Platter, 10½" l. 55.00

Platter, 12½" l. 90.00

Platter, 13½" x 18"............................395.00

Vegetable bowl, cov. 200.00

Vegetable bowl, open, 8¼" oval 60.00

Vegetable bowl, open, 10" oval 48.00

OSBORNE (Ridgways, ca. 1905)

Bone dish...40.00

Bouillon cup & saucer..........................85.00

Butter pat 42.00

Plate, 9½" d. 60.00

Relish dish, 9" oval 95.00

Soup plate w/flanged rim, 9" d.............50.00

Soup tureen, cov. 450.00

Vegetable bowl, cov., clover-shaped..240.00

Vegetable bowl, open, 8¼" oval 72.00

Vegetable bowl, open, 7¼ x 9½".........80.00

Vegetable bowl, open, 10" oval 60.00

OVANDO (Alfred Meakin, ca. 1891)

Dinner service, six each 8" & 6¾" d. plates, 5" d. bowls, butter pats & cups & saucers, five 9" d. plates, three each 6¼" d. bowls, bone dishes, 9" d. soup plates & 6" d. waste bowls, plus oval cov. vegetable bowl, 14" oval platter, round open vegetable bowl & cov. teapot, the set 2,900.00

Vegetable bowl, cov., oval 265.00

OXFORD (Johnson Bros., ca. 1900)

Butter pat 35.00

Gravy boat 65.00

Plate, 6¼" d. 35.00

Plate, 10" d. 72.00

Sauce dish, 5⅜" d. 45.00

PARIS (New Wharf Pottery and Stanley Pottery Co., ca. 1891)

Butter pat 35.00

Dinner service, eight each 9", 8" & 7" d.plates, cups & saucers & sauce dishes plus cov. butter dish w/drain insert, 9" d. open vegetable bowl, 9" oval open vegetable bowl & an 8 x 10½" platter, 52 pcs. 2,395.00

Plate, 7⅛" d. 35.00

Plate, 8" d. 46.50

PEKING (Podmore, Walker & Co., ca. 1850)

Tea set, cov. teapot, cov. sugar bowl & creamer, 3 pcs.............................850.00

Waste bowl 295.00

PELEW (E. Challinor, ca. 1840)

Creamer...425.00

Cup & saucer, handleless..................175.00

Plate, 9¾" d. 130.00

Platter, 16" l. 495.00

Sauce dish 70.00

Vegetable bowl, cov. 795.00

PERSIAN MOSS (Utzchneider & Co., ca. 1891)

Celery tray 65.00

Creamer 65.00

Platter, 10¾ x 16½" 155.00

Vegetable bowl, cov. 165.00

Vegetable bowl, open, 8¼" d. 50.00

Waste bowl 65.00

PORTMAN (W.H. Grindley, ca. 1891)

Butter pat 30.00

Gravy boat 110.00

Plate, 6¾" d. 25.00

Relish dish 38.00

PROGRESS (W.H. Grindley, ca. 1894)

Bone dish 37.50

Butter pat 25.00

Cup & saucer 75.00

Dinner service, child's, six each 4" & 3" d. plates plus cov. vegetable bowl, gravy boat, 3 x 4" platter & 3¾ x 5"platter, 16 pcs. 750.00

Vegetable dish, divided, individual size, 5½" oval 40.00

RHINE (Thomas Dimmock, dated May 7, 1844)

Cup & saucer, handleless 115.00

Plate, 9½" d. 60.00

Platter, 12½" octagonal (two small hairlines on back) 260.00

Waste bowl 135.00

RHODA GARDENS (Hackwood, ca. 1850)

Cup & saucer, handleless 165.00

Soup plate w/flanged rim, 9¼" d. 95.00

ROSE (W.H. Grindley, ca. 1893)

Butter dish, cov. 140.00

Gravy boat 65.00

Plate, 9" d. 45.00

Platter, 11 x 15¾" 145.00

Sauce dish, 5⅛" d. 32.00

Soup plate w/flanged rim, 8¾" d. 35.00

Vegetable bowl, open, 8" d. 52.00

ROSEVILLE (John Maddock & Sons, ca. 1891)

Bowl, 9¾" d. 90.00

Butter pat 28.00

Chocolate pot, cov. 575.00

Vegetable bowl, cov., 11" l. 260.00

SABRAON (Unknown, probably English, ca. 1845)

Pitcher, milk 575.00

Plate, 9¼" d. 95.00

Plate, 10½" d. 170.00

Platter, 16" l. 425.00

Platter, 18¼" l. 750.00

SAVOY (Johnson Bros., ca. 1900)

Savoy Plate

Butter pat 35.00

Creamer 175.00

Cup & saucer 70.00

Plate, 7" d. 35.00

Plate, 9" d. (ILLUS.) 55.00

Plates, 10½" d., set of 4 ....220.00

Platter, 12¼ x 16" 155.00

Sauce dish, 5⅛" d. 31.00

SCINDE (J. & G. Alcock, ca. 1840 and Thomas Walker, ca. 1847)

Scinde Plate

Bowl, 6½" d., 3¾" h. 195.00
Bowl, 10½" d. 200.00
Butter dish, cover & liner
(professional repair to finial) 1,275.00
Cake plate, scalloped rim, 10½" d. 70.00
Cup & saucer, handleless 195.00
Gravy boat 405.00
Ladle holder 175.00
Plate, 7" d. 50.00
Plate, 8¼" d. 65.00
Plate, 9" d. 85.00
Plate, 10½" d. (ILLUS.) 205.00
Platter, 9¾" l. 215.00
Platter, 11" l. 395.00
Platter, 10¼ x 13½" 450.00
Platter, 15½" l. ....675.00 to 725.00
Platter, 14 x 18" 890.00
Relish dish, mitten-shaped 295.00
Sauce tureen, cov. 895.00
Sugar bowl, cov. ....600.00 to 650.00
Teapot, cov. 985.00
Undertray for sauce tureen 325.00
Vegetable bowl, cov., 10 x 13" (minor
professional repair) 795.00
Vegetable bowl open, 10¾"
octagon 225.00

SEVILLE (New Wharf Pottery, ca, 1891 and Wood & Son)

Butter pat 35.00
Creamer 180.00
Plate, 7" d. 60.00
Soup plate w/flanged rim 85.00
Vegetable dish, cov. 250.00

SHANGHAE (J. Furnival, ca. 1860)

Cup, handleless 52.00
Plate, 9" d. 115.00
Platter, 20" l. 615.00
Teapot, cov. 795.00
Vegetable bowl, cov. 495.00

SHELL (Wood & Challinor, ca. 1840; E. Challinor, ca. 1860)

Cup & saucer, handleless 165.00
Gravy boat 175.00
Plate, 8½" d. 75.00
Plate, 9¾" d. 77.50
Plate, 10½" d. 135.00
Sugar bowl, cov. 325.00

SHUSAN (F. & R. Pratt & Co., ca. 1855)

Creamer 395.00
Gravy boat 275.00
Platter, 16" l. 495.00

SPINACH (Libertas, ca. 1900, brush-painted)

Spinach Bowl

Bowl, 8" d. (ILLUS.) 65.00
Cup & saucer 75.00
Plate, 7¾" d. 55.00
Sauce dish 40.00
Waste bowl 150.00

TIVOLI (Thomas Furnival, ca. 1845)

Cup & saucer, handleless....................100.00
Gravy boat....................150.00
Platter, 12½ x 16"....................250.00

TOGO (F. Winkle, ca. 1900)

Togo Plate

Gravy boat....................69.00
Plate, 10" d. (ILLUS.)....................55.00
Platter, 9 x 12"....................110.00
Platter, 14½" l....................195.00
Tray, 5 x 6¼"....................52.00

TONQUIN (W. Adams & Son., ca. 1845)

Plate, 7½" x 8½" d....................75.00
Plate, 9¾" d....................125.00
Teapot, cov. (professional repair)....................925.00
Waste bowl....................150.00

TONQUIN (Joseph Heath, ca. 1850)

Creamer....................475.00
Plate, 8½" d....................50.00
Plate, 9½" d. (some glaze wear)....................85.00
Platter, 10 x 13¼"....................365.00
Platter, 16" l....................595.00
Vegetable bowl, cov....................975.00

TOURAINE (Henry Alcock, ca. 1898 and Stanley Pottery, ca. 1898)

Bone dish....................84.00
Butter dish, cov....................515.00
Butter pat....................47.00
Creamer & cov. sugar bowl, pr....................480.00

Touraine Plate

Cup & saucer....................85.00 to 100.00
Gravy boat & underplate, 2 pcs....................235.00
Pitcher, 6" h....................395.00
Pitcher, 6½" h....................475.00
Pitcher, 8" h....................750.00
Pitcher, 2 qt....................695.00
Plate, 6½" d....................40.00
Plate, 7½" d....................45.00
Plate, 8¾" d....................60.00
Plate, 10" d. (ILLUS.)....................85.00
Platter, 9 x 10"....................225.00
Platter, 12½" l....................150.00
Platter, 15" l....................250.00
Salt dip....................48.00
Sauce dish, 6¼" d....................52.00
Saucer....................20.00
Soup plate w/flanged rim, 7½" d....................80.00
Sugar bowl, cov....................300.00
Vegetable bowl, cov., 11¾" d....................375.00
Vegetable bowl, open, 9¼" d....................135.00
Vegetable bowl, open, 9" oval....................125.00
Vegetable bowl, open, 10" d....................92.50
Waste bowl....................175.00

TRILBY (Wood & Sons, ca. 1891)

Cake plate, open handled, 10½" d....................95.00
Toothbrush holder....................165.00
Vegetable bowl, open, 9½" d....................70.00
Wash bowl, large....................350.00

VERMONT (Burgess & Leigh, ca. 1895)

Bone dish....................30.00

Butter pat 35.00

Dinner service, eight each 9" & 8" d. plates, 5" d. bowls, 9" d. soup plates, cups & saucers & butter pats, 6½" x 9" & 7 x 9¼" open vegetable bowls, 7 x 10½" cov. vegetable bowl, 7½" x 10", 8½ x 11½" & 11¾ x 16" (small chip) platters, 5 x 8" relish dish, gravy boat & 4" h. pitcher, 65 pcs. 2,800.00

Pitcher, 5¼" h. 125.00

Plate, 9¾" d. 42.00

Plate, 10" d. 79.00

Platter, 12¼ x 16½" 185.00

Sauce tureen, cover & underplate, 3 pcs. 300.00

Vegetable bowl, cov. 175.00

Vegetable bowl, open, 7½ x 10" 110.00

VERONA (Wood & Son, ca. 1891)

Cup & saucer 95.00

Pitcher, 2 qt. 435.00

Platter, 9 x 12¾" 130.00

Soup plate w/flanged rim 85.00

VINRANKA, PERCY (Cefle, Upsala, Ekeby, Sweden, ca. 1968)

Cup & saucer 48.00

Plate, 7½" d. 20.00

Plate, 10¼" d. 45.00

Platter, 11¼" l. 60.00

Sauce dish, 5" d. 15.00

Soup plate w/flanged rim, 9½" d. 45.00

Sugar bowl, cov. 100.00

Vegetable bowl, open, 9¼" oval 60.00

WALDORF (New Wharf Pottery, ca. 1892)

Waldorf Cup & Saucer

Bacon platter, oval 135.00

Bowls, cereal, 6" d., set of four 140.00

Bowl, 9" d. 85.00

Creamer 150.00

Cup & saucer (ILLUS.) 85.00

Plate, 6" d. 35.00

Plate, 9" d. 70.00

Plate, 10" d. 80.00

Platter, 9 x 10¾" 110.00

Potato bowl 9" d. 100.00

Sauce dish 38.00

Soup plate w/flanged rim 110.00

Vegetable bowl, open, 9" d. 87.50

Vegetable bowl, open, 10" d. 125.00

Waste bowl 160.00

WARWICK (Podmore, Walker & Co., ca. 1850)

Plate, 8½" d. 58.00

Sauce dish 30.00

Teapot, cov. 450.00

Wash bowl (faint hairline) 595.00

WARWICK PANSY (Warwick China Co., ca. 1900)

Chocolate pot, 9¼" h., large 875.00

Pitcher, large, bulbous, 2 qt. 595.00

Plate, 9½" d. 65.00

WATTEAU (Doulton & Co., ca. 1900)

Bowl, cereal 35.00

Butter pat 25.00

Egg cup 100.00

Ewer, 12½" h. 500.00

Plate, 6½" d. 35.00

Plate, 9½" d. 50.00

Plate, 10½" d. 72.00

Platter, 14 x 17½" 375.00

Soup plate w/flanged rim 75.00

WATTEAU (New Wharf Pottery, ca. 1891)

Bowl, 10¼" d. 185.00

Cup & saucer 75.00

Plate, 9" d. 45.00

Platter, 8 x 11" 100.00

Platter, 9 x 10¾", scalloped rim..........235.00

Vegetable bowl, open, 9" d..................75.00

WAVERLY (W.H. Grindley, ca. 1891)

Creamer..125.00

Plate, 6¾" d...30.00

Vegetable bowl, open, 10" d..............125.00

WELBECK (J.H. Weatherby & Sons, Ltd., ca. 1905)

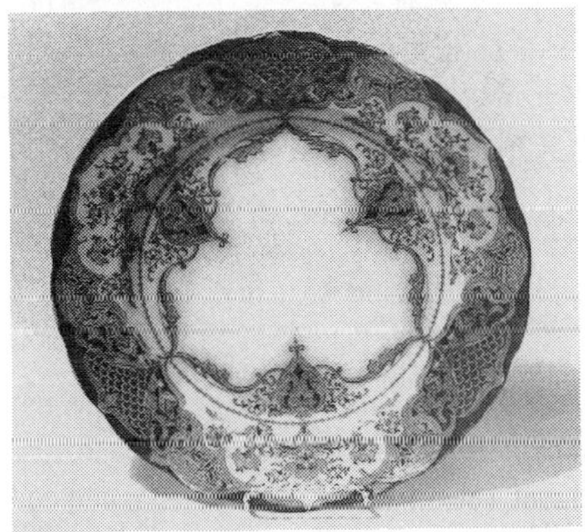

Welbeck Plate

Creamer..95.00

Plate, 7½" d..65.00

Plate, 9½" d. (ILLUS.)...........................75.00

Platter, 12" l.......................................155.00

Platter, 14" l.......................................175.00

Platter, 17" l.......................................235.00

Soup plate w/flanged rim, 10" d...........65.00

YEDO (Ashworth & Bros. Ltd., ca. 1870)

Plate, dinner, 10⅜" d...........................95.00

Platter, 9¼ x 10¼" oval......................115.00

Soup plate w/flanged rim, 10¼" d.......110.00

(End of Flow Blue Section)

FRANCISCAN WARE

A product of Gladding, McBean & Company of Glendale and Los Angeles, California, Franciscan Ware was one of a number of lines produced by that firm over its long history. Introduced in 1934 as a pottery dinnerware, Franciscan Ware was produced in many patterns including "Desert Rose," introduced in 1941 and reportedly the most popular dinnerware pattern ever made in this country. Beginning in 1942 some vitrified china patterns were produced under the Franciscan name also.

After a merger in 1963 the company name was changed to Interpace Corporation and in 1979 Josiah Wedgwood & Sons purchased the Gladding, McBean & Co. plant from Interpace. American production ceased in 1984.

FRANCISCAN WARE
MADE IN CALIFORNIA U.S.A.

Bowl, salad, 4½ x 8", crescent-shaped, Apple patt., ca. 1940..........$22.00

Bowl, fruit, 5¼" d., Desert Rose patt., ca. 1941 ....8.00

Bowl, soup, 5½" d., 2¼" h., footed, Desert Rose patt., ca. 1941 ....21.00

Bowl, cereal or soup, 6" d., Cafe Royal patt..15.00

Bowl, cereal or soup, 6" d., Desert Rose patt., ca. 1941..........................10.00

Bowl, cereal, El Patio Table Ware, 1934-54...10.00

Bowl, cereal, Hacienda patt., green glaze, ca. 1964 ....5.00

Bowl, 7" d., Madeira patt., ca. 1967........6.00

Bowl, 7¾" d., Coronado Table Ware, ivory glaze, 1936-56 ....9.00

Bowl, salad, 10" d., 3¼" h., Desert Rose patt., ca. 1941...........................65.00

Bowl, salad, 11" d., Coronado Table Ware, coral satin glaze, 1936-56.......30.00

Bowl, salad, 11¼" d., Ivy patt., ca. 1948..95.00

Butter dish, cov., Apple patt., ca. 1940, ¼ lb...35.00

Butter dish, cov., Cafe Royal patt., ¼ lb. 35.00

Butter dish, cov., Coronado Table Ware, ivory glaze, 1936-56................65.00

Butter dish, cov., El Patio Table Ware, 1934-54 ....45.00

Butter dish, cov., Ivy patt., ca. 1948, ¼ lb. 40.00

Butter dish, cov., Tiempo patt., ca. 1949 ....40.00

Candleholders, Desert Rose patt., ca. 1941, 3" h., pr. 76.00

Casserole, cov., round, handled, Apple patt., ca. 1940, 1½" qt., 6¾" d., 3" h. 75.00

Casserole, cov., round, handled, Ivy patt., ca. 1948, 1½ qt., 8" d., 4" h.....110.00

Coffeepot, cov., demitasse, Coronado Table Ware, ivory glaze, 1936-56....125.00

Coffeepot, cov., Apple patt., ca. 1940, 7½" h. 110.00

Coffeepot, cov., Desert Rose patt., ca. 1941 ....88.00

Compote, open, footed, Coronado Table Ware, ivory glaze, 1936-56......45.00

Cookie jar, cov., Apple patt., ca. 1940, 9¼" h. ....150.00 to 200.00

Cookie jar, cov., Desert Rose patt., ca. 1941, 9¼" h. ....200.00 to 250.00

Creamer, Coronado Table Ware, golden glow satin glaze, 1936-56 ......12.50

Creamer, El Patio Table Ware, redwood brown glaze, 1934-54 ....8.00

Creamer, Ivy patt., ca. 1948, 4" h. 15.00

Cup & saucer, demitasse, Desert Rose patt., ca. 1941 ....37.50

Cup & saucer, demitasse, El Patio Table Ware, 1934-54 ....25.00

Cup & saucer, Apple patt., ca. 1940.....12.00

Cup & saucer, Cafe Royal patt. 18.00

Cup & saucer, Desert Rose patt., ca. 1941 ....14.00

Cup & saucer, El Patio Table Ware, 1934-54 ....11.00

Cup & saucer, Madeira patt., ca. 1967 ....6.00

Cup & saucer, Oasis patt., ca. 1954.......7.50

Egg cup, Apple patt., ca. 1940, 3¾" h. 15.00

Egg cup, Desert Rose patt., ca. 1941, 3¾" h. 20.00

Ginger jar, cov., Cafe Royal patt. 85.00

Gravy boat w/attached undertray, Apple patt., ca. 1940, 8¼" l., 3½" h. 35.00

Gravy boat w/attached undertray, Desert Rose patt. 35.00

Gravy boat, footed, El Patio Table Ware, golden glow gloss glaze, 1934-54 ....20.00

Gravy boat w/attached undertray, Ivy patt., ca. 1948, 9" l., 5" h. 35.00

Gravy boat w/attached undertray, Starburst patt., ca. 1954 ....25.00

Ladle, Apple patt., ca. 1940, 10" l. 20.00

Marmalade jar, cov., Desert Rose patt., ca. 1941 ....85.00

Mixing bowl, Apple patt., ca. 1940, 7½" d., 4¼" h. 22.00

Mug, Apple patt., ca. 1940, 12 oz., 4¼" h. 35.00

Mug, Desert Rose patt., ca. 1941, 12 oz. 58.00

Napkin ring, Desert Rose patt., ca. 1941, 1½" h. 25.00

Napkin rings, Cafe Royal patt., set of four in original box 85.00

Pepper mill, Apple patt., ca. 1940 ....67.00

Pitcher, milk, 6½" h., Apple patt., ca. 1940, 1 qt. ....75.00 to 85.00

Pitcher, 7¼" h., Starburst patt., ca. 1954 ....30.00

Pitcher, syrup, 6¼" h., Desert Rose patt., ca. 1941, 1 pt. 65.00

Pitcher, water, 8¾" h., Desert Rose patt., ca. 1941, 2½ qt. 125.00

Plate, 6" d., Coronado Table Ware, yellow satin, ca. 1936 ....4.00

Plate, 6¼" d., Coronado Table Ware, ivory glaze, 1936-56 ....3.00

Plate, bread & butter, 6¼" d., Ivy patt., ca. 1948 ....8.00

Plate, bread & butter, 6½" d., Apple patt., ca. 1940 ....10.00

Plate, 7" d., Oasis patt., ca. 1954 ....6.00

Plate, salad, 4½ x 8", crescent-shaped, Apple patt., ca. 1940 ....35.00

Plate, salad, 4½ x 8", crescent-shaped, Desert Rose patt., ca. 1941 ....24.00

Plate, 8¼" d., El Patio Table Ware, coral satin glaze, 1934-54 ....6.00

Plate, salad, 8½" d., Apple patt., ca. 1940 ....7.50

Plate, salad, 8½" d., Cafe Royal patt....14.00

Plate, luncheon, 9¼" d., Ivy patt., ca. 1948 ....16.00

Plate, luncheon, 9½" d., Apple patt., ca. 1940 ....8.00

Plate, 9½" d., Coronado patt., turquoise 8.00

Plate, luncheon, 9½" d., Desert Rose patt., ca. 1941 ....10.00

Plate, 9½" d., Coronado Table Ware, maroon gloss glaze, 1936-56 ....8.00

Plate, 10" d., Oasis patt., ca. 1954 ....8.00

Plate, dinner, 10¼" d., Ivy patt., ca. 1948 ....12.00

Plate, dinner, 10½" d., Apple patt., ca. 1940 ....16.50

Plate, dinner, 10½" d., Cafe Royal patt. 20.00

Plate, dinner, 10½" d., Desert Rose patt., ca. 1941 ....12.50

Plate, dinner, 10½" d., El Patio Table Ware, coral satin glaze, 1934-54 ....9.00

Plate, dinner, 10½" d., Hacienda patt., green glaze, ca. 1965 ....7.00

Plate, dinner, 10½" d., Madeira patt., ca. 1967 ....7.00

Plate, grill, 10⅞" d., Apple patt., ca. 1940 ....55.00

Plate, buffet, 11" d., Ivy patt., ca. 1948 ....24.50

Plate, chop, 12" d., Apple patt., ca. 1940 ....55.00

Plate, chop, 12" d., Cafe Royal patt. 40.00

Plate, cake, 13" d., Ivy patt., ca. 1948 ....35.00

Plate, chop, 14" d., Apple patt., ca. 1940 ....125.00

Plate, chop, 14" d., Ivy patt., ca. 1948 ....125.00

Platter, 11" l., oval, coupe steak, Desert Rose patt., ca. 1941 ....42.00

Platter, 11½" l., oval, Ivy patt., ca. 1948 ....35.00

Platter, 8½ x 12¾" oval, Apple patt., ca. 1940 ....30.00

Platter, 8½ x 12¾" oval, Desert Rose patt., ca. 1941 ....20.00

Platter, 13" l., oval, Coronado Table Ware, ivory satin glaze, 1936-56 ....16.50

Platter, 13" l., oval, El Patio Table Ware, 1934-54 ....18.00

Platter, 13" l., oval, Starburst patt., ca. 1954 ....40.00

Platter, 10¼ x 14" oval, Apple patt., ca. 1940 ....30.00

Platter, 10¼ x 14" oval, Cafe Royal patt. 45.00

Platter, 13¼ x 19" oval, Apple patt., ca. 1940 ....185.00 to 200.00

Relish dish, oblong, three-part, Apple patt., ca. 1940, 11¾" l. 30.00

Relish dish, oblong w/end handle, Coronado Table Ware, ivory glaze, 1936-56, 9" l. 15.00

Relish dish, oval, three-part, Desert Rose patt., ca. 1941, 12" l. 60.00

Salt & pepper shakers, Apple patt., ca. 1940, tall, 6¼" h., pr. 45.00

Salt & pepper shakers, Desert Rose patt., ca. 1941, tall, 6¼" h., pr. 35.00

Salt & pepper shakers, Madeira patt., ca. 1967, pr. 10.00

Sherbet, footed, Desert Rose patt., ca. 1941, 2½" h. 20.00

Soup plate w/flanged rim, Apple patt., ca. 1940, 8½" d. 16.00

Soup plate w/flanged rim, Desert Rose patt., ca. 1941, 8¼" d. 20.00

Soup plate w/flanged rim, Ivy patt., ca. 1948, 8½" d. 21.00

Soup tureen, cov., three-footed, Apple patt., ca. 1940, 7½" d., 5¼" h. 325.00

Sugar bowl, cov., Coronado Table Ware, yellow glaze, 1936-56 ....15.00

Sugar bowl, cov., El Patio Table Ware, maroon gloss glaze, 1934-54 ....18.00

Sugar bowl, open, individual, Desert Rose patt., ca. 1941, 2" h. 21.00

Teapot, cov., Apple patt., ca. 1940, 4¾" h. 85.00

Teapot, cov., Desert Rose patt., ca. 1941 ....85.00

Tidbit tray, two-tier, Ivy patt., ca. 1948 ....75.00

Tumbler, Ivy patt., ca. 1948, 10 oz., 5¼" h. 28.00

Tumbler, water, Apple patt., ca. 1940, 10 oz., 5¼" h. 25.00

Vase, bud, 6" h., Cafe Royal patt., w/original box 95.00

Vegetable bowl, open, round, Apple patt., ca. 1940, 7¾" d., 2" h. 40.00

Vegetable bowl, open, oval, divided, Cafe Royal patt., 7 x 10¾" 40.00

Vegetable bowl, open, round, Desert Rose patt., ca. 1941, 8" d., 2¼" h. 20.00

Vegetable bowl, open, round, Desert Rose patt., ca. 1941, 9" d. 32.00

Vegetable bowl, open, round, El Patio Table Ware, lettuce green gloss glaze, 1934-54, 8½" d. 20.00

Vegetable bowl, open, oval, divided, Ivy patt., ca. 1948, 12" l. 60.00

Vegetable bowl, oval, Starburst patt., ca. 1954 ....15.00

Vegetable dish, cov., Apple patt. 65.00

FRANKOMA

1969 Nixon-Agnew Mug

John Frank began producing and selling pottery on a part-time basis during the summer of 1933 while he was still teaching art and pottery classes at the University of Oklahoma. In 1934, Frankoma Pottery became an incorporated business that was successful enough to allow him to leave his teaching position in 1936 to devote full time to its growth. The pottery was moved to Sapulpa, Oklahoma in 1938 and a full range of art pottery and dinnerwares were eventually offered. In 1953 Frankoma switched from Ada clay to clay found in Sapulpa. Since John Frank's death in 1973, the pottery has been directed by his daughter, Joniece. In early 1991 Richard Bernstein became owner and president of Frankoma Pottery which was renamed Frankoma Industries. Joniece Frank serves as vice president and general manager. The early wares and limited editions are becoming increasingly popular with collectors today.

Book ends, Bucking Bronco, No. 423, Prairie Green glaze, 5½" h., pr. $175.00

Bottle-vase, V-6, 1974, aqua glaze, 13" h. 55.00

Bottle-vase, V-7, 1975, Desert Gold glaze w/Coffee colored cover & base, 13" h. 60.00

Bottle-vase, No. V-8, 1976, Freedom Red & white, 13" h. 60.00

Bottle-vase, No. V-9, 1977, white w/black base & stopper, 13" h. 60.00

Bottle-vase, V-14, 1982, Flame Red body on black base, 11" h. 60.00

Bowl, 10½" d., Wagon Wheel patt., Prairie Green glaze 12.00

Candleholders, double, No. 304, pr......22.00

Candleholders, Oral Roberts, "Christ the Light of the World," pr. 18.50

Centerpiece bowl, green & brown glaze, scalloped, leaf forms center medallion, No. 200, 8¾ x 13" oval 22.00

Christmas card, 1965 ....70.00

Christmas card, 1967 ....42.50

Christmas card, 1968 ....42.50

Christmas card, 1969 ....30.00

Christmas card, 1970 ....22.50

Christmas card, 1971, profile of Franks portraits ....20.00 to 30.00

Christmas card, 1972 ....25.00

Christmas card, 1973 ....22.00

Christmas card, 1974 ....28.00

Christmas card, 1976 ....20.00

Christmas card, 1977 ....15.50

Christmas card, 1978 ....20.00

Christmas card, 1979 ....19.00

Christmas card, 1980 ....18.50

Christmas card, 1981 ....20.00

Christmas card, 1982 ....18.50

Christmas card, 1983 ....15.50

Christmas card, 1984 ....15.50

Cornucopia-vase, No. 56, Ada clay, 7" h. 25.00

Cornucopia-vase, green glaze, No. 57, 9½" l. 12.00

Creamer, Wagon Wheel patt., Prairie Green glaze 8.00

Creamer & cov. sugar bowl, Mayan-Aztec patt., grey & brown, Nos. 7A & 7B, 3⅝" h., pr. 15.00

Cup & saucer, Mayan-Aztec patt., Woodland Moss glaze 4.50

Cup & saucer, Wagon Wheel patt., Prairie Green glaze 9.00

Dish, clover-shaped, Plainsman patt., bronze glaze, No. 223, 6½" d. 6.50

Dish, leaf-shaped, Prairie Green glaze, 12½" l. 12.00

Figure of a Fan Dancer, No. 113, green on red brick clay, 1955, 8½ x 13½" ....200.00 to 225.00

Figure, Indian Chief, No. 142, brown matte glaze, 8" h. 15.50

Figures, Dreamer Girl, No. 427, Onyx Black glaze, Ada clay, 5⅜" h., pr. 182.00

Flask, Mayan-Aztec patt., green & brown, leather thong through ceramic loops, 2 x 6 x 6¼" 18.00

Flower holder, model of an elephant, No. 180, 1942, 3½" h. 89.50

Model of a circus horse, No. 138, Desert Gold glaze, 4½" h. 75.00

Model of a puma, seated, No. 114, Ada clay, green glaze, 7½" h. 69.50

Model of a swan, miniature, No. 168, black glaze, 3" h. 38.00

Model of a swan, miniature, No. 168, Desert Gold glaze, 3" h. 35.00

Mug, 1968 (Republican) elephant, white glaze 65.00

Mug, 1969 (Republican) elephant, Nixon-Agnew, flame-red glaze (ILLUS.) 80.00

Mug, 1970 (Republican) elephant, blue glaze 35.00

Mug, 1973 (Republican) elephant, Nixon-Agnew, Desert Gold glaze.......30.00

Mug, 1975 (Democratic) donkey, Autumn Yellow glaze 19.00

Mug, 1977 (Democratic) donkey, "Carter-Mondale," pink glaze 21.50

Mug, 1978 (Democratic) donkey, blue glaze 16.50

Mug, 1979 (Republican) elephant, brown satin glaze w/white interior......15.00

Mug, 1980 (Democratic) donkey, terra cotta glaze 18.50

Mug, 1980 (Republican) elephant, terra cotta glaze 15.00

Mug, 1981 (Republican) elephant, "Reagan-Bush," Celery Green glaze 20.00

Mug, 1982 (Republican) elephant, robin's egg blue glaze 25.00

Mug, Plainsman patt., Desert Gold glaze, 16 oz., 5⅜" h. 6.00

Mug, Woodland Moss glaze, No. C5, 3¾" h. 5.00

Pitcher, jug-type, 7" h., Plainsman patt., Desert Gold glaze, No. 8 ....8.50

Planter, boat-shaped, white glaze, No. 211, 5 x 12½" 12.00

Plate, 6½" d., scalloped, Plainsman patt., Woodland Moss glaze 2.50

Plate, 6½" d., Wagon Wheel patt., Prairie Green glaze 5.00

Plate, 7" d., Mayan-Aztec patt., Woodland Moss glaze 3.50

Plate, 7½" d., "Easter," made for Oral Roberts, 1972 ....15.00

Plate, 8½" d., Christmas, 1965, "Good Will Towards Men," depicts Mary, Joseph & Jesus 225.00

Plate, 8½" d., Christmas, 1968, "Flight Into Egypt" 26.00

Plate, 8½" d., Christmas, 1972, "Seeking The Christ Child" 22.50

Plate, 8½" d., Christmas, 1973, "The Annunciation" 22.50

Plate, 10" d., Wagon Wheel patt., Prairie Green glaze 8.00

Sugar bowl, cov., Mayan-Aztec patt., Woodland Moss glaze 8.50

Sugar bowl, cov., Wagon Wheel patt., Prairie Green glaze 13.00

Teapot, cov., Wagon Wheel patt., Prairie Green glaze, small, 2 cup.......15.00

Tea set: cov. teapot, creamer & cov. sugar bowl; Plainsman patt., gold-bronze, teapot, No. 5T, creamer & sugar bowl, Nos. 5A & 5B, w/original label, 3 pcs. 32.00

Trivet, round, "Seals of the Five Civilized Tribes of Indians in Oklahoma," 1971-79 ....10.00 to 15.00

Vase, 6" h., figural Flower Girl, No. 700, 1942-51, blue glaze............35.00

Vase, 7⅜" h., 2⅞ x 5" rectangular, Mayan-Aztec patt., Woodland Moss glaze, No. 63Z 20.00

Vase, 8½" h., fan-shaped, green-bronze leaf forms, No. 74 ....30.00

Wall masks, bust of Indian Maiden, No. 132, ivory glaze, Ada clay, w/original sticker, 4⅛" h. 60.00

Wall masks, bust of Afro Man, No. 125, & Afro woman, No. 124, black glaze, man 6¾" h., woman 6½" h.,pr. 145.00

Wall masks, bust of Afro Man, No. 125, & Afro woman, No. 124, ivory glaze, man 6¾" h., woman 6½" h., pr.........145.00

Wall pocket, model of a cowboy boot, No. 133, white glaze, unmarked, 6½" h....................................10.00 to 20.00

Wall pocket, Wagon Wheel patt., Prairie Green glaze, Ada clay 35.00

Wash bowl & pitcher, blue & brown glaze, oval bowl 1½ x 5 x 6", pitcher 4½" h., No. 40B, 2 pcs. 10.00

FULPER

Exceptional Fulper Articles

The Fulper Pottery was founded in Flemington, New Jersey, in 1805 and operated until 1935, although operations were curtailed in 1929 when its main plant was destroyed by fire. The name was changed in 1929 to Stangl Pottery, which continued in operation until July of 1978, when Pfaltzgraff, a division of Susquehanna Broadcasting Company of York, Pennsylvania, purchased the assets of the Stangl Pottery, including the name.

Book ends, mission bell-type, modeled as upright double-tiered mission bell towers in taupe over black & w/two figural bells in mustard yellow,unmarked, ca. 1915, 7¾" h., pr. $605.00

Book ends, figural, a peacock w/a large, fanned tail perched between tapering uprights, khaki & blue flambé glaze, vertical ink mark, 4" w., 5¾" h., pr. (restoration to one beak) 412.50

Book ends, Ramses II patt., green matte glaze, 10" h., pr. 850.00

Bowl, 6½" d., 3¼" h., deep flaring sides molded as a large morning glory blossom, glossy grey, cobalt blue & caramel flambé interior glaze, grey, bluish purple & rose flambé matte exterior glaze, rectangular ink mark 467.50

Bowl, 8" d., fluted rim, crystalline black glaze 550.00

Bowl, 5 x 13", handled, ivory & mahogany flambé glaze, Panama-Pacific 1915 label............................675.00

Bowl-vase, squatty spherical body w/closed rim, 'artichoke' type w/molded overlapping leaves decorated w/a viscous crystalline mottled green & yellow glaze over brown, marked, 5¼" h. (stilt pull on foot) 880.00

Bowl-vase, footed spherical form w/closed rim, covered in a yellow & grey satin glaze dripping over a speckled matte mustard base, early rectangular stamp & "P," 6½" d., 5¾" h...770.00

Bowl-vase, 'Norse' design, three scrolled handles holding a vessel w/'hammered' surface, copper dust crystalline glaze, raised vertical mark, 11½" w., 11" h. (ILLUS. right)..3,575.00

Bulb bowl, ten-sided, shallow, mottled mulberry glaze over dark rose, 9" d..195.00

Candle sconce, matte blue glaze w/blue, yellow & green leaded slag glass inserts, oval vertical ink stamp, 5" w., 10¾" h. (ILLUS. left)............1,045.00

Candlesticks, round cushion foot tapering to a slender swelled shaft below the flared socket, leopard skin glaze, vertical box ink mark, 6" d. foot, 8½" h., pr. 357.50

Candlesticks, the tall cylindrical shaft supporting a flaring bell-form socket & raised on a widely flaring stepped round base, cat's-eye mirror black & caramel flambé glaze, vertical oval ink mark, 10½" h., pr. 302.50

Candlesticks, heavy twist stem supporting a flaring socket & raised on a flaring foot, crystal patina glaze, incised vertical oval mark, 11" h., pr. 165.00

Center bowl, deep lobed & rounded sides w/a wide, flattened & scalloped rim, raised on a short pedestal w/a high domed foot, curdled light green & caramel semi-matte glaze, incised vertical mark, 11" d., 6½" h. 302.50

Centerpiece, a round shallow bowl w/inverted rim supported by three effigy figures kneeling on a stepped disc base, the bowl w/a glossy dark blue, khaki & lavender flambé glaze, the base w/a matte green & blue glaze, vertical ink mark, 10¼" d., 7¼" h...550.00

Console bowl, shell-shaped, widely lobed sides w/one lobe folded inward & flattened & pierced w/holes to form a flower frog, fine green, blue, yellow & brown glossy flambé glaze, vertical box mark, 11¾" w., 4" h...247.50

Doorstop, figural, Bulldog in seated position w/open front legs, blue & caramel flambé glaze, unmarked, 10½" w., 7½" h. (minor restoration).....................................715.00

Doorstop, figural, cat in reclining position w/tail curled around body, matte pink to mirrored black flambé glaze, vertical rectangular ink stamp mark, 9" l., 5½" h. (minor restoration to ear) 770.00

Dresser box, cov., figural, the cylindrical base w/a low, domed cover mounted w/a large figure of a kneeling Egyptian maiden w/hand-decorated trim, matte glaze, impressed marks, overall 8½" h.......302.50

Flower bowl, very compressed squatty bulbous sides raised on a narrow footrim, the wide shoulder tapering up to a wide short cylindrical neck, glossy caramel body, rectangular ink mark, 10½" d. flambé glaze over a matte mustard , 4" h...495.00

Flower frog, model of a scarab, ochre & green glaze...................................75.00

Jardiniere, footed, matte green glaze, early ink mark, 5" h...............125.00

Jug, very wide & bulbous ovoid body w/a wide shoulder to the short cylindrical neck, a high arched strap handle from neck to edge of shoulder, overall copperdust glaze, raised vertical mark & original paper label, ca. 1915, 11⅜" h. (handle repaired) 385.00

Perfume lamp, figural lady, pink glaze 235.00

Vases, bud, 5½" h., blue & brown flambé glaze over speckled blue, pr..245.00

Vase, 5¾" h., 8" d., slightly rounded sides tapering toward the top, angular handles from midsection to rim, wisteria matte mottled purple glaze over a grey ground, vertical incised mark...................................715.00

Vase, 6" h., 8¾" d., squat gourd-shaped body w/angular handles, fine mottled apple green & gunmetal flambé glaze, vertical box ink mark 715.00

Vase, 6½" h., 6" d., bulbous ovoid body tapering sharply to short neck & heavy molded rim, upright loop handles at the shoulder, ivory, crystalline blue & gun-metal flambé semi-gloss glaze, incised vertical mark 660.00

Vase, 6½" h., 8½" d., a low foot supporting a very wide squatty bulbous body tapering to a short cylindrical neck flanked by three small loop handles, overall fine leopard skin crystalline glaze, incised vertical oval mark................605.00

Vase, 6½" h., 8½" d., flattened globular form w/a short upward neck, mottled matte green glaze, incised oval vertical mark................467.50

Vase, 6¾" h., 4" d., ovoid body w/a short wide neck, ivory, mahogany & blue flambé glaze, vertical incised mark 192.50

Vase, 6¾" h., 8½" d., wide bulbous ovoid body w/a wide shoulder to a short flaring neck, cucumber green matte flambé glaze, incised vertical oval mark 275.00

Vase, 7¼" h., urn-shaped, small side

handles, widely flaring mouth, dark blue & green drippy glaze over brown, die-impressed mark 170.00

Vase, 7½" h., 7¼" d., bulbous w/flattened shoulder & tapering base, bluish-grey crystalline flambé glaze over a clear caramel base, incised vertical oval mark................522.50

Vase, 8½" h., 10½" d., very wide squatty bulbous shouldered body tapering to a wide cylindrical neck w/molded flat ribs & flanked by loop handles, the neck w/a brown crystalline glaze, the base w/a shaded matte green to purple glaze, raised vertical oval mark 715.00

Vase, 9½" h., hexagonal ovoid body w/flat mouth, decorated w/a green over rust, blue & cream flambé glaze, vertical ink mark 605.00

Vase, 9½" h., 4½" d., tall cylindrical body w/two square cut-out windows in the sides above a relief-molded base band of stylized mushrooms, finely shaded ivory to elephant's breath flambé glaze, vertical ink mark & paper label..........................825.00

Vase, 9½" h., 6" d., bulbous w/rounded shoulder & ridged flaring neck, lustered bluish green, green & cobalt blue flambé glaze over a blue & grey matte crystalline base, vertical oval ink mark 412.50

Vase, 10" h., 6" d., tapering base, indented shoulder & flaring rim, cream, brown & blue flambé crystalline glaze, No. 523, shaved off mark..495.00

Vase, 10¾" h., 5½" d., hexagonal baluster-form body, fine Chinese blue flambé glaze, incised vertical oval mark 385.00

Vase, 11" h., 5¼" d., six-sided baluster-form, milky blue, purple, ochre & green crystalline flambé glaze, No. 660, incised vertical oval mark..550.00

Vase, 11" h., 5½" d., tall waisted cylindrical body w/a flat mouth flanked by angular loop buttress handles, overall leopard skin crystalline glaze, vertical rectangular mark..467.50

Vase, 11½" h., 8" d., wide baluster-form body w/flaring neck, overall mottled matte purple glaze, vertical oval ink-stamp mark........................275.00

Vase, 11¾" h., 4¾" d., tall slender footed baluster-form body w/flaring neck, overall fine Chinese blue flambé glaze, die-stamped vertical oval mark 302.50

Vase, 11¾" h., 11½" d., wide footed ovoid body tapering to a short wide neck w/rolled rim, small loop handles at the shoulder, 'hammered' ground decorated w/a crystalline tiger's eye glaze, vertical oval ink mark & several paper labels...........660.00

Vase, 12¼" h., 11" d., wide ovoid body tapering to a rounded, stepping neck w/a flat rim, mirrored black to sky blue flambé glaze, raised vertical oval mark 2,200.00

Vase, 12¼" h., 11¼" d., wide bulbous ovoid footed body tapering to a short, wide cylindrical neck w/heavy molded rim, loop handles at the shoulder, overall textured leopard skin green crystalline & gun-metal glaze, vertical oval ink mark 1,650.00

Vase, 12½" h., 7½" d., tall footed ovoid body tapering to a closed rim, heavy ring handles near the rim, mottled iridescent green & purple glaze over matte rose pink base, factory hole in base, unmarked.......385.00

Vase, 12¾" h., 7½" d., tall tapering ovoid body w/a narrow closed rim, gun-metal black over copperdust flambé glaze, raised vertical mark 1,760.00

Vase, 13" h., 7½" d., squatty bulbous base on footring below a tall trumpet-form neck, mottled glossy brown, purple & mint green flambé glaze, oval incised mark & two paper labels....................................935.00

Vase, 13¼" h., 3¼" d., cylindrical, pigeon-feathered light yellowish green & purple glaze over a caramel ground, No. 57, incised vertical mark & paper label.............522.50

Vase, 15½" h., 5" d., tall slender cylindrical body slightly swelled at the top & tapering to a flat rim, fine semi-matte light green to light yellow flambé glaze, raised vertical mark 1,320.00

Vase, floor-type, 17" h., 9" d., wide baluster-form body w/low, flaring neck, brown, grey, green & cream flambé glaze, drilled base & factory wire hole on side, raised vertical mark & paper label 660.00

Wall pocket, Art Deco design, brown & caramel glaze, vertical stamp 375.00

GALLE´ POTTERY

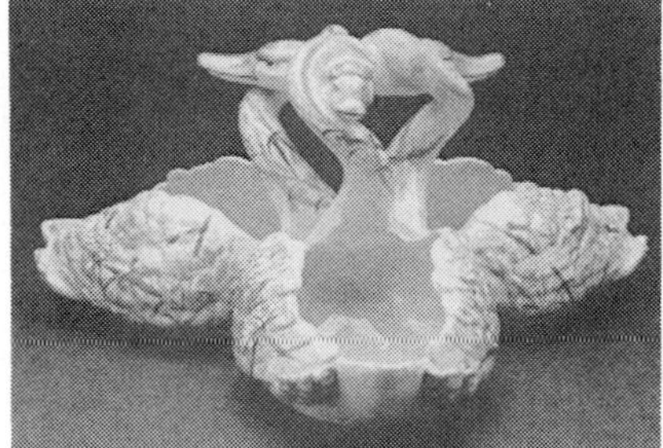

Gallé Figural Center Bowl

Fine pottery was made by Emile Gallé, the multi-talented French designer and artisan, who is also famous for his glass and furniture. The pottery is relatively scarce.

Center bowl, figural, modeled as three geese w/their necks intertwined, open backs serving as dishes or flower bowls, colorful polychrome decoration of butterflies & stylized grasses & flowers, gold trim, signed on base "E. Gallé - Nancy - E (cross) G Déposé," very minor glaze wear, 15" w., 6½" h. (ILLUS.) $2,090.00

Centerpiece, figural, modeled as a large mother swan, her body forming a bowl, her head twisted down to two baby swans at her side, glazed white & decorated w/small nosegays of roses & wildflowers in various colors, shaded w/grey & trimmed in gilt, impressed factory mark, ca. 1885, 12¼" l., 9" h...........770.00

Jars, cov., tall baluster-form, one molded in high-relief w/a stealthily crawling cat up the side amid blossoming orchid branches furtively eyeing the figural mouse finial on the domed cover, the other molded w/a cat standing at the base & rubbing itself against the side of the jar, again w/blossoming orchid branches & w/a figural mouse finial on the cover, rich polychrome glazes trimmed w/gilding, painted signature "E. Gallé Nancy," 13" h., pr...9,350.00

Model of a dog, a seated Pug in yellow patterned w/a random blue dot & heart design, brown glass eyes, painted signature "e. Gallé Nancy," 12½" h. 2,640.00

Gallé Owl

Model of an owl, the large bird perched on a circular socle, enameled in naturalistic colors, set w/green glass eyes, signed in the mold & enameled "Emile Gallé fec," 13¼" h. (ILLUS.) 4,025.00

Pitcher, 7⅞" h., C-shaped w/molded handle, patinated bronze color ground w/an enameled window representing an outdoor view w/two men sitting on a bench & listening to a third one standing on a tun & playing bagpipes, enameled signature "e. Gallé Nancy E.G. déposé"...920.00

Plates, 9½" d., round w/laced rim, the white glaze decorated w/flowers & insects, one w/the inscription "Cet age est sans pitié," the other w/"Florian, pour vivre heureux vivons caché E.G.," one marked "Gallé Nancy St. C. - déposé," the other "Gallé a Nancy Déposé" w/Saint-Clement marks, pr. 935.00

Vase, 5¾" h., gourd-shaped, flowing lustred body decorated w/enameled ferns & leaves, crickets & a bee, signed "Emile Gallé" 1,650.00

Wall pocket, figural, modeled as a broad-brimmed lady's straw hat decorated w/winged insects, bugs & a caterpillar & blossoms &

Gallé Figural Wall Pocket

suspended from a ribbon bow, signed "E. Gallé Nancy," minor glaze wear at edges, 12" h. (ILLUS.) 1,540.00

GAUDY DUTCH

Gaudy Dutch Toddy Plate & Creamer

This name is applied to English earthenware with designs copied from Oriental patterns. Production began in the 18th century. These copies flooded into this country in the early 19th century. The incorporation of the word "Dutch" derives from the fact that it was the Dutch who first brought the Oriental wares into Europe. The ware was not, as often erroneously reported, made specifically for the Pennsylvania Dutch.

Creamer, War Bonnet patt., minor stains & wear w/small flakes in enamel, 4½" h. (ILLUS. right) $962.50

Cup & saucer, handleless, Single Rose patt. (small hairline in saucer) 450.00

Cup & saucer, handleless, Urn patt. (minor wear, small rim chip on saucer, pinpoints on table ring)........247.50

Cup & saucer, handleless, War Bonnet patt. (in-the-making hairlines, minor wear & pinpoint flakes) 605.00

Plate, 6¾" d., Single Rose patt. (flaked enamel) 302.50

Gaudy Dutch Plate & Waste Bowl

Plate, 8½" d., Dove patt., minor wear & small flakes in the enamel (ILLUS. left) 715.00

Soup plate w/flanged rim, War Bonnet patt., 8⅛" d. (minor wear) 715.00

Toddy plate, Grape patt, small flakes in enamel, 5¼" d. (ILLUS. left).........302.50

Toddy plate, Urn patt., 5⅝" d. (wear, small flakes, short rim hairline) 357.50

Waste bowl, Dove patt., stains, wear & pinpoint flakes, 5⅝" d., 2¾" h. (ILLUS. right) 715.00

GAUDY WELSH

Gaudy Welsh Creamer & Plate

This is a name for wares made in England for the American market about 1830 to 1860, with some examples dating much later. Decorated with Imari-style flower patterns, often highlighted with copper lustre, it should not be confused with Gaudy Dutch wares whose colors differ somewhat.

Creamer, Lotus patt., underglaze-blue & polychrome enamel, lustre trim, 4¾" h. (ILLUS. left) $121.00

Creamer, jug-type, Oyster patt., underglaze-blue & polychrome enamel, lustre trim, 4½" h. 104.50

Cup & saucer, over-sized, Hexagon patt., underglaze-blue & polychrome enameling, lustre trim 82.50

Cups & saucers, Buckle patt., underglaze-blue & polychrome enamel, lustre trim, set of 6 ....99.00

Mug, child's, cylindrical w/molded base, C-scroll handle, Grape IV patt., 2¼" h. (wear, small chips).......104.50

Pitcher, 5⅝" h., footed bulbous ovoid body w/shallow molded paneling tapering to a wide mouth w/a high arched spout, S-scroll handle, Begonia patt. (minor wear & stains) 192.50

Pitcher, 6⅝" h., the baluster-form paneled octagonal body molded around the lower section w/a band of large diamonds, wide long spout, long C-scroll handle, Gwent patt. (wear, stains, chips).........................220.00

Plate, 8½" d., Oyster patt., underglaze-blue & polychrome enamel, lustre trim, some wear(ILLUS. right)...104.50

Sugar bowl, cov., six-footed, ornate handles & finial, Tulip patt., underglaze-blue & polychrome enameling, lustre trim, 7" h. (stains) 209.00

Peach Pattern Teapot

Teapot, cov., Peach patt., underglaze-blue & polychrome enamel, lustre trim, crow's foot, 6" h.......................330.00

Teapot, cov., paneled sides & flaring foot, Vine patt., underglaze-blue & polychrome enamel, lustre trim, 9¼" h. (stains, chips & short hairlines) 220.00

Tea set: cov. teapot, creamer, waste bowl, 9" d. plate & ten cups & saucers; Peppermint patt., underglaze-blue & polychrome enamel, lustre trim, teapot 7½" h., 24 pcs. (teapot stained, some hairlines) 764.50

GEISHA GIRL WARES

The beautiful geisha, a Japanese girl specifically trained to entertain with singing or dancing, is the featured decoration on this Japanese china which was cheaply made and mass-produced for export. Now finding favor with collectors across the United States, the ware varies in quality. The geisha pattern is not uniform - Butterfly, Paper Lanterns, Parasol, Sedan Chair and other variations are found in this pattern that is usually colored in shades of red through orange but is also found in blue and green tones. Collectors try to garner the same design in approximately the same color tones.

Collectors will find helpful The Collector's Encyclopedia of Geisha Girl Porcelain, *by Elyce Litts (Collector Books, 1988).*

Bread plate, Chinese Coin patt., maroon trim.....................................$10.00

Chocolate set: 9½" h. cov. chocolate pot & six cups & saucers; decorated w/Teahouse & Parasols design, red trim, 13 pcs. 105.00

Creamer & cov. sugar bowl, Chinese Coin patt., pr. 42.00

Sugar bowl, cov., Chinese Coin patt., medallions on green background.......45.00

Tea set: 3" h. cov. teapot & six cups & saucers; Fan patt., lavish gold trim, 13 pcs. 95.00

Toothpick holder, Chinese Coin patt., blue trim 24.00

Vase, 4¾" h., squatty, two-handled, three-footed, Fan patt., lavish gold trim 50.00

GIBSON GIRL PLATES

Miss Babbles, the Authoress....

The artist Charles Dana Gibson produced a series of 24 drawings entitled "The Widow and Her Friends," and these were reproduced on plates by the Royal Doulton works at Lambeth, England. The plates were copyrighted by Life Publishing Company in 1900 and 1901. The majority of these plates usually sell within a price range of $85.00 to $125.00 today.

Miss Babbles, the Authoress, Calls and Reads Aloud, No. 6 (ILLUS.) ..$125.00

Mrs. Diggs is Alarmed at Discovering... (No. 7) 82.50

She Goes to the Fancy Dress Ball as "Juliet" (No. 15) 115.00

She Looks for Relief Among Some of the Old Ones (No. 19)........................85.00

GOLDSCHEIDER

Goldscheider Dancer Figure

The Goldscheider firm, manufacturers of porcelain and faience in Austria between 1885 and the present, was founded by Friedrich Goldscheider and carried on by his widow. The firm came under the control of his sons, Walter and Marcell, in 1920. Fleeing their native Austria at the time of World War II, the Goldscheiders set up an operation in the United States. They were listed in the Trenton, New Jersey, City Directory from 1943 through 1950 and their main production seems to have been art pottery figurines.

Box, cov., the cover w/a figural finial of a large German Shepherd's head w/its tongue out, shaded green & brown glaze, 4 x 5½" $85.00

Bust of a woman, earthenware, modeled w/curly reddish orange hair & lips, a yellow blossom w/green foliage at her neck, stamped & incised marks, ca. 1925, 8" h...........357.50

Bust of a woman w/a hand holding an apple, painted in naturalistic tones, in collaboration w/Myott Sone Co., on a black base, stamped company mark, 8¼" h.....................................230.00

Candelabra, three-light, each in the form of a dancing maiden enclosed by a circular ring set w/three candle supports, raised on a shaped standard above an oval base, the figures in clear glaze, the supports in dark brown decorated about the base & ring w/multicolored dashes, each w/printed factory marks "Goldscheider - Wien - MADE IN AUSTRIA," impressed "5366/148/11" & "5366/156/18" respectively, w/overglaze marks "D5/XXVIII./F." & "D.5/IV" respectively, ca. 1925, 19" h., pr. (now electrified) 3,450.00

Figure of an Art Deco lady dressed as a vamp, Austria, 18" h......................880.00

Figure of a butterfly girl, the dancer clad in a costume resembling the outspread wings of a butterfly in shades of mauve, blue, yellow & black, standing by a flower-filled urn, mounted on a black-glazed oval base, printed factory mark "Goldscheider - Wein - MADE IN AUSTRIA - Lorenzl," inscribed "6204," impressed "4" & "5A," ca. 1925, 12" h...................................2,070.00

Figure of a dancer, a female dancer in Arabian-inspired costume, glazed in lavender, yellow, red, blue & green, printed, inscribed & impressed factory marks, ca. 1925, 17⅞" h. (ILLUS. top next column) 2,300.00

Figure of a dancer, the young maiden in twirling gown w/one hand at her hip & the other at the hem of her gown, glazed in cream matte & pale blue, raised on a swag-decorated marks & numbers, ca. 1900, 20¾" h. 1,150.00

Figure of Juliet w/doves, rose, grey, cobalt & pale blue, 12¼" h. 225.00

Figure of a lady w/muff, wearing plumed green & lavender hat, flowered cream underskirt, incised "BCV," impressed "802/5/10," 8¼" h. 90.00

Figure of a lady w/parasol, leaning back, green & brown skirt, emerald muff, bodice & bustle trimmed w/ermine, 11" h. 175.00

Figure of a nude female dancer, one arm extended forward, the other backward, all-white on a domed black-glazed round base, after a design by Lorenzl, impressed mark "Goldscheider - Wein - MADE IN AUSTRIA - Lorenzl" & "5802 -464," ca. 1925, 11" h. 805.00

Figure of Sing Lo, young Oriental lady holds bird up, fancy yellow tunic, green trousers, long queue, w/pagoda & birdhouse, 7¼" h. 32.00

Figure of a Southern Belle, blue ruffled dress & hat, 8" h. 75.00

Figurines, "Chinese Teahouse," kneeling Oriental figures in pink & green brocaded robes, man eats from rice bowl, woman plays lute, designed by Helen Lindhoff, 5 x 6¾", pr. 60.00

Figure group, modeled as a woman in plaid sunsuit w/straw hat over her shoulders & holding her wire-haired terrier by the front paws as if dancing w/him, glazed in shades of maroon, white, yellow, brown & black, raised on a black oval base, after a design by Dakon, impressed "Goldscheider - Wein - MADE IN AUSTRIA - Dakon" & "7194/66/19," ca. 1925, 12½" h. 4,025.00

Goldscheider Lamp Base

Lamp base, figural, a belly dancer leaning against a composite column, raised on a rectangular base w/rounded corners, printed "Goldscheider" & "MADE IN AUSTRIA," ca. 1930s, 16¾" h. (ILLUS.) 1,035.00

Mask, hanging-type, modeled as a woman's head, a hand holding an orange-glazed eye mask, the face glazed in white & the hair in bluish green, stamped company mark & "MADE IN AUSTRIA," 10½" h. 345.00

Figural Goldscheider Wall Plaque

Plaque, pierced to hang, figural, modeled as the stylized head of a woman turned to the left & holding a rose blossom in her hand, glazed in white, green, orange & yellow, factory mark & "4490," repaired, ca. 1925, 10½" h. (ILLUS.) 690.00

Plaque, pierced to hang, Madonna & Child, artist-signed, gold sticker, 15" h. 695.00

Allegorical Wall Plaque

Plaques, pierced to hang, allegorical, rectangular w/crown-form crest above a low-relief landscape centered by a high-relief female figure, one representing Summer & the other Winter, titled at the base "HIVER" or "ÉTÉ," painted in shades of amber, ochre, green & ivory, decorated by Chere, one impressed "REPRODUCTION RESERVÉE - Frederich Goldscheider - Wien," Austria, ca. 1900, drill holes, 28½" h., pr. (ILLUS. of Winter)......2,300.00

GOUDA

Gouda Plaque & Vase

While tin-enameled earthenware has been made in Gouda, Holland since the early 1600s, the productions of modern factories are attracting increasing collector attention. The art pottery of Gouda is easily recognized by its brightly colored peasant-style decoration with some types having achieved a "cloisonne" effect. Pottery workshops located in, or near, Gouda include Regina, Zenith, Plazuid, Schoonhoven, Arnhem and others. Their wide range of production included utilitarian wares, as well as vases, miniatures and large outdoor garden ornaments.

MADE IN ZUID-HOLLAND

PLAZUID GOUDA HOLLAND

Bowl, 8⅞" d., 4" h., Art Deco style, the interior w/a stylized large central flowerhead & a squiggled edge line all in green, gold, rust, blue & white, the exterior w/deep green w/blue & white bands, satin finish, Gouda - Holland mark..................................$135.00

Candleholder, shield-back type, Art Nouveau designs in dark colors.........67.00

Humidor, cov., colorful designs in cobalt blue, beige, yellow & orange, artist-signed, 5" h. 265.00

Lamp, blue & rust stylized leaves on black ground, base 12" h. 195.00

Pitcher, 5" h., stylized tulip blossom & foliage against an off-white ground, Royal Zuid mark & paper label 39.00

Plaque, rectangular, polychrome enamel decoration of a village harbor scene, mounted in a wide oak frame, artist-signed, house symbol for Zuid, plaque 12¼ x 16¼" (ILLUS. left) 770.00

Vase, 4" h., 6" d., decorated w/peacock feathers on a black satin ground, house mark, "Zwaro" 90.00

Vase, 5" h., bulbous-form, decorated w/Art Nouveau florals & a scene w/windmill & sailboat in lake on an eggshell ground, marked 50.00

Vase, 13" h., two-handled, Art Nouveau-style glossy multicolored stylized iris decoration, Zuid-Holland house mark 450.00

Vases, 15½" h., tall baluster-form, decorated w/flowers & vines in purple, blue, green & gold on a white ground, painted factory marks "Holland Gouda N.P. S8" for New Porcelain, Zuid, ca. 1910, pr. (ILLUS. of one, right) 1,320.00

Vase, 17" h., tall ovoid body tapering to a slender trumpet-form neck flanked by slender round loop handles, deep umber ground decorated w/stylized blossoms, stems & foliage in violet, yellow, blue & green, painted mark "213 B.O. GOUDA HOLLAND," & incised "213" 1,100.00

Vase, 19" h., stylized roosters in blue & mustard on bright green background, leaf decoration in mustard around neck 750.00

Vase, 20½" h., 9¾" d., floor-type, the tall ovoid body tapering to a short wide neck, decorated around the body w/long panels alternating w/stylized daisies & slender scrolls, bands of rounded arches around the base & shoulder & a scalloped band of half sunbursts at the top, plain dark bands at the very base & rim, in polychrome, marked "106 - Daisy - Z. Holland - Gouda," early 20th c. 1,210.00

GRUEBY

Grueby Four-sided Bowl

Some fine art pottery was produced by the Grueby Faience and Tile Company, established in Boston in 1891. Choice pieces were created with molded designs on a semi-porcelain body. The ware is marked and often bears the initials of the decorators. The pottery closed in 1907.

GRUEBY

Bowl, 5¼" d., 2¼" h., squatty bulbous sides w/a wide shoulder to a rolled rim, molded w/wide, rounded leaves, matte green glaze, artist-initialed & dated "1906" $467.50

Bowl, 7¼" sq., 3¾" h., large tooled & applied leaves around sides, thick organic matte green glaze exterior, clear green glaze interior, restoration to tip of one leaf, designed by Ruth Erickson, marked "GRUEBY POTTERY, BOSTON U.S.A., RE, 102, 10-12-08," 1908 (ILLUS.) 660.00

Bowl-vase, squatty bulbous body on a small footring, the wide shoulder tapering to a short, flared mouth, lightly molded w/wide ribs, covered in an organic matte yellow glaze, 9" d., 6½" h. 1,980.00

Candleholder, low dished round base tapering to short flaring candle socket flanked by small loop handles, matte speckled dark blue glaze, impressed circular mark, 6" d., 2" h. 247.50

Candleholder, shallow dished base w/a low, flaring candle socket in the center joined to the rim by two arched handles, dark matte blue glaze, circular impressed mark & original paper label, 6" d., 2" h. 357.50

Fireplace surround, composed of seven large rectangular tiles, the top three decorated w/a continuous landscape scene of a farmer w/oxen pulling a cart piled w/logs in shades of brown, white, yellow, blue & green, the lower tiles in dark green, probably designed by Addison Le Bouthillier, made for "Dreamwold," a Cohasset, Massachusetts home, ca. 1902, unmarked, 60½" l., 36½" h. (some small edge chips, repaired crack in one tile) 21,450.00

Humidor, cov., tall slightly waisted cylindrical body w/a flat inset cover w/knob finial, decorated around the rim w/a narrow band of oyster white blossoms against a French blue ground, impressed "Grueby Pottery, Boston USA - F.E. - 4-21-07," 4½" d., 8¼" h. (minor chips inside cover) 1,430.00

Grueby Jardiniere

Jardiniere, slightly canted sides, narrow shoulder & rounded rim, decorated w/tooled & applied flowers & curled leaves, thick matte green glaze, horizontal "Boston" mark, minor glaze flecks to rim & high points, 8¼" h., 8" d. (ILLUS.) 1,650.00

Jardiniere, wide bulbous spherical body w/a wide mouth & short everted rim, the sides applied w/long stylized vertical leaves, decorated by Kiichi Yamada, marked, 19½" d., 15" h. 20,700.00

Lamp base, squatty bulbous base molded w/wide curl-tipped leaves below the wide cylindrical neck fitted w/metal electric fixture, veined green matte glaze, 5" d., 5½" h. 715.00

Lamp base, cylindrical, long tooled & applied leaves under a fine matte green glaze, impressed circular mark "GRUEBY FAIENCE - BOSTON U.S.A.," 7½" d., 12¼" h. 3,300.00

Paperweight, model of a scarab beetle, leathery deep blue glaze, impressed "Grueby Pottery Boston USA," 2¼" l., 3¼" h. (very minor base nick) 247.50

Trivet, a square tile decorated in cuenca w/seagulls & a buoy on the ocean, fitted in a hammered copper frame w/button feet, signed "M.C.," 4" sq. 385.00

Vase, 3½" h., 5½" d., very compressed bulbous base tapering to a wide, short neck w/heavy rolled rim, leathery blue glaze, impressed "Grueby Pottery Boston USA - 95" 550.00

Vase, 4" h., 5½" d., squatty bulbous base w/a wide shoulder to a short, cylindrical neck molded w/thin rings, deep cucumber green glaze, impressed "Grueby Faience - 92B" 522.50

Vase, 4½" h., 5" d., squatty bulbous footed body tapering to a short, flared neck, tooled & applied wide leaves under an organic matte cucumber green glaze interspersed w/yellow lily blossoms around the neck, impressed circular mark "Grueby Pottery Boston USA - FH - 17-6" 2,530.00

Vase, 5" h., 3½" d., squatty bulbous base below a wide cylindrical neck w/flared rim, matte green veined glaze, unmarked 385.00

Vase, 5½" h., ovoid body w/a wide, tri-lobed rim, the sides molded w/three wide leaves separated by slender stems topped by a small yellow bud, deep green matte glaze, decorated by Ruth Erickson, company mark & artist's initials, ca. 1907................2,090.00

Vase, 5¾" h., 6¾" d., squatty bulbous body w/a wide shoulder tapering to a short cylindrical neck, wide lightly molded leaves around the sides, dark green matte glaze, unsigned 880.00

Vase, 7¼" h., 4¾" d., bulbous w/flaring neck, five round tooled leaves w/curled edges, applied to the bottom & covered in a medium matte green glaze, alternating w/buds atop long stems, under a deep matte cucumber green glaze, impressed circular mark "GRUEBY FAIENCE CO BOSTON U.S.A.," original paper label w/waterlily "GRUEBY POTTERY PAN AMERICAN EXPOSITION 1901," rectangular sales label "GRUEBY - POTTERY - PRICE (obliterated) - CON. NO. '5410'" hand-written in ink 1,980.00

Vase, 7¼" h., 7" d., squatty bulbous shouldered body w/a short, wide & slightly flaring neck, alternating narrow & wide molded leaves around the body, deep cucumber green glaze, marked (rim repair) ..1,210.00

Vase, 7⅜" h., ovoid body tapering to a wide, flat mouth, the sides molded w/wide leaves w/curled tips separated by slender stems topped by small molded buds around the rim, light matte green glaze, by Ruth Erickson, ca. 1908, signed...........1,045.00

Grueby Vase with Ruffled Rim

Vase, 7½" h., 4¼" d., slightly rounded cylinder w/star-shaped opening, w/tooled & applied leaves alternating w/buds, matte green glaze, by Florence Liley, marked "GRUEBY - FAIENCE Co. BOSTON U.S.A., F.L., 75," two glaze chips to base (ILLUS.)...............................1,045.00

Vase, 7½" h., 4¾" d., bulbous base tapering to a short neck, tooled & applied broad leaves w/curled-up edges, interspersed w/buds on tall stems, fine matte green glaze, designed by Ruth Erickson, marked "GRUEBY POTTERY, BOSTON U.S.A., RE." 1,540.00

Vase, 7¾" h., 3¾" d., ovoid body tapering to a gently flaring mouth, molded w/four full-length wide leaves, cucumber green glaze, marked 1,210.00

Vase, 8" h., simple ovoid body w/a wide, flat mouth, matte green glaze, impressed mark & paper label 605.00

Vase, 8½" h., 5" d., slightly expanding cylinder w/flat narrow shoulder, covered w/ superimposed full-length tooled & applied leaves, under a rich tactile & uneven matte green glaze, by Florence Liley, impressed circular mark "GRUEBY FAIENCE CO. BOSTON U.S.A." 2,320.00

Vase, 8⅝" h., wide ovoid body tapering to a short flaring neck, molded around the body w/a band of tall, wide & pointed overlapping leaves, green glaze, impressed marks 1,210.00

Vase, 9½" h., 6¼" d., bulbous spherical base below a slender cylindrical neck w/slightly flared rim, molded around the lower body w/an overlapping band of lily pads w/curled edges, smooth matte light green glaze, signed (minor restoration to edge of one leaf) 1,870.00

Vase, 9½" h., 7¼" d., barrel-shaped, tooled & applied wide leaves alternating w/long leaves, under a thick curdled white glaze, impressed "GRUEBY FAIENCE U.S.A." 1,980.00

Vase, 12" h., 6¼" d., tall ovoid body, molded w/wide, tall pointed leaves up the sides to the narrow shoulder & the short, flaring neck, leaves alternate w/slender stems topped by small yellow buds around the shoulder, veined matte green glaze, incised medallion mark & "255" 3,850.00

Vase, 12½" h., 5½" d., slightly bulging cylinder, gently flaring rim, w/tooled & applied full-length rectangular leaves w/curled tips, under a very deep cucumber green matte glaze, horizontal die-stamped "GRUEBY - BOSTON, MASS.," ca. 1895-1900...5,225.00

Vase, 12⅞" h., bulbous squatty base below a wide ring-molded neck w/a flaring rim, rich curdled green matte glaze, stamped mark & numbered "32," ca. 1904 (small burst glaze bubble, some very minor glaze skips) 1,980.00

Vase, 13" h., 8½" d., gourd-shaped, clear glaze over a curdled cobalt to light blue dripping over a light grey flambé glaze, showing a buff body, impressed circular mark "GRUEBY POTTERY BOSTON U.S.A." 6,050.00

Grueby Vase with Flowers

Vase, 13¼" h., bulbous spherical base tapering to a tall, cylindrical neck, molded w/alternating foliate & floral decoration highlighted by repeating yellow three-petal flowers around the top, matte green glaze, incised artist's initials & impressed mark, minor base chip (ILLUS.) 2,970.00

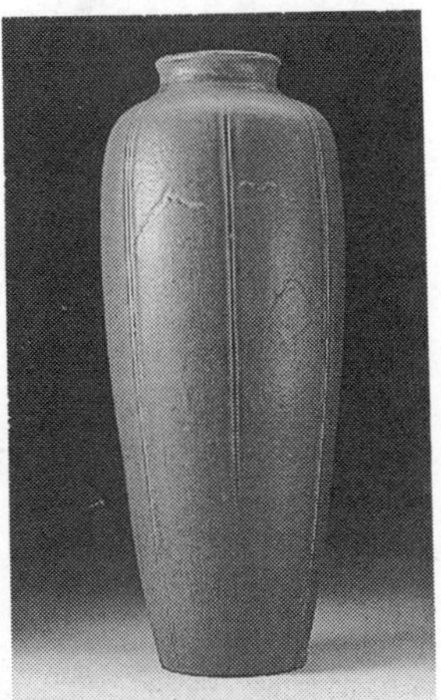

Tall Grueby Vase

Vase, 22½" h., slightly expanding cylinder w/narrow sloping shoulder, the body finely carved w/stylized leaves, green glaze, decorated by Kiichi Yamada, impressed w/monogram "KY," impressed company mark (ILLUS.) 8,970.00

HALL

Founded in 1903 in East Liverpool, Ohio, this still-operating company at first produced mostly utilitarian wares. It was in 1911 that Robert T. Hall, son of the company founder, developed a special single-fire, lead-free glaze which proved to be strong, hard and non-porous. In the 1920s the firm became well known for their extensive line of teapots (still a major product) and in 1932 they introduced kitchenwares followed by dinnerwares in 1936 and refrigerator wares in 1938.

The imaginative designs and wide range of glaze colors and decal decorations have led to the growing appeal of Hall wares with collectors, especially people who like Art Deco and Art Moderne design. One of the firm's most famous patterns was the "Autumn Leaf" line, produced as premiums for the Jewel Tea Company. For listings of this ware see "Jewel Tea Autumn Leaf."

Helpful books on Hall include , The Collector's Guide to Hall China *by Margaret & Kenn Whitmyer, and* Superior Quality Hall China - A Guide for Collectors *by Harvey Duke (An ELO Book, 1977).*

Batter pitcher, Sundial shape, Blue Blossom patt. $165.00

Batter pitcher, Sundial shape, Blue Garden patt. ....150.00 to 175.00

Bean pot, cov., single handle, Crocus patt. 225.00

Bean pot, cov., single handle, Orange Poppy patt. 70.00

Bowl, cereal, 6" d., Red Poppy patt., Radiance shape 12.00

Bowl, 8" d., straight-sided, Silhouette (Taverne) patt. 24.00

Bowl, salad, 9" d., Rose Parade patt. ...30.00

Bowl, salad, 9" d., Royal Rose patt. 16.50

Bowl, salad, 9" d., Silhouette (Taverne) patt. 23.00

Butter dish, cov., Zephyr shape, Blue Garden patt. 300.00

Canisters, cov., Radiance shape, Orange Poppy patt., set of three...1,200.00

Casserole, cov., Clover patt., w/gold trim 28.50

Casserole, cov., Radiance shape, Pastel Morning Glory patt. 35.00

Casserole, cov., Sundial shape, No. 4, Chinese Red, 8" d. 25.00

Casserole, cov., Thick Rim shape, Royal Rose patt. 32.50

Casserole, cov., Westinghouse line, canary yellow 20.00

Casserole, cov., Pert shape, Rose White patt. 40.00

Coffeepot, cov., Drip-o-lator, Cactus patt. 55.00

Coffeepot, cov., drip-type, all-china, Pert shape, Tulip patt., complete 100.00

Coffeepot, cov., w/insert, china, Wildfire patt. 50.00

Cookie jar, Sundial (Saf-Handle) shape, marine blue 325.00

Cup & saucer, Orange Poppy patt. 32.00

Custard cup, Crocus patt. 30.00

Custard cup, straight-sided, Pert patt., Chinese Red 9.00

Drip jar, cov., Clover patt. 40.00

Leftover dish, cov., Crocus patt., square 60.00

Mug, Silhouette (Taverne) patt. 35.00

Pepper shaker, handled, Blue Blossom patt. 10.00

Pie baker, Red Poppy patt. 32.00

Pitcher, 5" h., Five Band shape, Chinese Red 16.00

Pitcher, 6¼" h., Radiance shape, Red Poppy patt., No. 5 ....35.00

Pitcher, ball-type, Pastel Morning Glory patt. 40.00

Pitcher, ball-type, Silhouette (Taverne) patt., maroon, No. 5 ....24.00

Plate, 7" d., Orange Poppy patt. 15.00

Plate, 9" d., Crocus patt. 12.00

Pretzel jar, cov., china, Crocus patt. ...215.00

Pretzel jar, cov., Pastel Morning Glory patt. 100.00

Pretzel jar, cov., Silhouette (Taverne) patt. 85.00

Punch set: footed punch bowl, twelve cups & ladle; Old Crow patt., mint in box, 14 pcs. 125.00

Salt & pepper shakers, loop handles, Orange Poppy patt., pr. 45.00

Salt & pepper shakers, handled, Radiance shape, Red Poppy patt., pr. 30.00

Salt & pepper shakers, Pert shape, Rose White patt., large, pr. 22.00

Teapot, cov., Airflow shape, blue w/gold 60.00

Teapot, cov., Aladdin shape, turquoise, 6-cup size, w/infuser 75.00

Teapot, cov., Aladdin shape, yellow w/gold 35.00

Teapot, cov., Automobile shape, ivory w/gold trim 750.00

Teapot, cov., Cleveland shape, forest green 45.00

Teapot, cov., Doughnut shape, Chinese Red 150.00

Teapot, cov., Doughnut shape, cobalt blue 125.00

Teapot, cov., Globe shape, dripless, w/turn-down spout, Addison grey & gold, 6-cup size 35.00

Teapot, cov., Kansas shape, yellow w/gold trim 190.00

Teapot, cov., Los Angeles shape, yellow, black & white 30.00

Teapot, cov., Manhattan shape, green 39.50

Teapot, cov., Melody shape, Orange Poppy patt. 175.00

Teapot, cov., Nautilus shape, maroon, 6-cup size 275.00

Teapot, cov., Parade shape, canary yellow w/gold trim 55.00

Teapot, cov., Parade shape, Delphinium Blue 40.00

Teapot, cov., Pert shape, Rose Parade patt., 6-cup size 30.00

Teapot, cov., Star decoration, yellow & gold 79.00

Teapot, cov., Streamline shape canary yellow 19.00

Teapot, cov., Sundial (Saf-Handle) shape, cobalt blue 165.00

Teapot, cov., Sundial (Saf-Handle) shape, turquoise 125.00

Teapot, cov., Surfside shape, emerald green 135.00

Teapot, cov., T-Ball, silver, round ....125.00 to 150.00

Teapot, cov., Twin-spout shape, black & gold 79.00

Teapot, cov., Windshield shape, maroon w/gold trim 35.00

Tea tile, Silhouette (Taverne) patt., round 120.00

HAMPSHIRE POTTERY

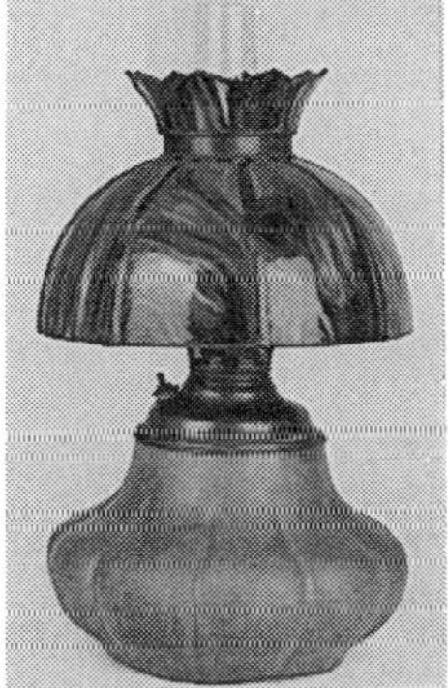

Lamp Designed by Robertson

Hampshire Pottery was made in Keene, New Hampshire, where several potteries operated as far back as the late 18th century. The pottery now known as Hampshire Pottery was established by J.S. Taft shortly after 1870. Various types of wares, including Art Pottery, were produced through the years. Taft's brother-in-law, Cadmon Robertson, joined the firm in 1904 and was responsible for developing over 900 glaze formulas while in charge of all manufacturing. His death in 1914 created problems for the firm and Taft sold out to George Morton in 1916. Closed during part of World War I, the pottery was later reopened by Morton for a short time and manufactured white hotel china. From 1919 to 1921, mosaic floor tiles became the main production. All production ceased in 1923.

Bowl, 5" d., 3" h., squatty bulbous form molded overall w/artichoke leaves, veined green matte glaze, unmarked $192.50

Bowl, 6" d., 4¼" h., squatty body w/rolled rim, decorated w/embossed cattails, matte green glaze, marked "Hampshire, 112" 275.00

Bowl-vase, squatty bulbous form w/a flattened angled shoulder deeply embossed w/pairs of ovals & tapering up to a molded, rolled rim, smooth matte green glaze, stamped "HAMPSHIRE - 32," 7¾" d., 4" h. 302.50

Ewer, the wide squatty bulbous footed base w/a wide shoulder tapering to a cylindrical neck flaring to a long arched spout & incurved tab attached to the top of the slender S-scroll handle, matte green glaze, marked "J.S.T. & Co. - KEENE, N.H.," 9½" d., 9½" h. 247.50

Inkwell, low cylindrical form, the flat top pierced w/pen holes centering the small domed cap w/button finial, ceramic liner, smooth matte green glaze, marked & numbered "26," 4¼" d., 3½" h. 165.00

Lamp, table model, lobed compressed globular base, matte green glaze, designed by Cadmon Robertson, w/bent panel green slag glass shade, impressed "006," overall 19" h. (ILLUS.) 605.00

Lamp base, kerosene table-type, the wide tapering bulbous body w/an overall matte green glaze, angular loop handles at the sides, fitted w/a cylindrical metal canister font w/an electrified burner, paper label & impressed marks, ca. 1907, 7½" h...330.00

Lamp base, kerosene table-type, the wide bulbous ovoid body tapering to a wide flat rim inset w/a metal kerosene font w/burner, the sides incised w/tight scrolled "bull's-eyes" connected by slender lines about the middle, overall mottled bluish green glaze, marked, ca. 1907, 9⅜" h. (one small burst glaze bubble) 880.00

Lamp base, table model, slightly tapering cylinder w/narrow shoulder, relief-molded long leaves, smooth matte green glaze, factory-drilled hole in base, marked "Hampshire Pottery M," 9½" d. 15" h..................990.00

Lamp base, table model, deep wide-mouth bowl-form, relief-molded large heart-shaped leaf design around sides, matte green glaze, designed by Cadmon Robertson, impressed marks, w/canister lamp insert, 19" h. 605.00

Pitcher, tankard, 11¾" h., 6¼" d., tall cylindrical body flared at the base w/a molded panel band at rim & base, angled handle w/scrolled tips, feathered matte green glaze, impressed mark "44" (hairline in base) ..88.00

Vase, 6½" h., 4½" d., globular base & wide slightly flaring neck, deeply crackled matte green glaze, unmarked 192.50

Vase, 6¾" h., 4" d., expanding cylinder w/rounded shoulder, relief-molded leaf decoration, rich curdled & marbleized bluish green matte glaze, marked "33, Hampshire Pottery" 412.50

Vase, 7" h., 3¾" d., compressed flaring bulbous base tapering to a cylindrical body ending in a small shoulder & short neck flanked by angled loop handles, matte green glaze, incised "Hampshire Pottery - 114"..165.00

Vase, 7¼" h., 4¾" d., wide ovoid body tapering to a wide, flat mouth, a band of embossed stylized flowers around the shoulder above slender stems down the sides, mottled blue glaze, incised "123 - M - Hampshire Pottery" 357.50

Vase, 9" h., 4½" d., ovoid, relief-molded elongated oval leaves, matte veined taupe glaze, marked "Hampshire Pottery"........................302.50

Vase, 9" h., 4¾" d., ovoid body tapering to a flaring neck, molded w/a band of tall, narrow pointed leaves, chocolate brown matte glaze, marked 275.00

Vases, 9½" h., 7" d., compressed globular base & long neck w/flaring rim, base decorated w/relief-molded leaves, matte dark blue glaze, marked "124, Hampshire Pottery, M," pr. 770.00

Vase, 11" h., 6¼" d., footed baluster-form w/flaring neck, the shoulders applied w/square loop handles, smooth matte green glaze, die-stamped mark 385.00

Vase, 15" h., 5" d., tall ovoid body tapering to a narrow short neck w/a widely flaring rim, small loop handles from rim to shoulder, matte green glaze, marked "J.S.T. & Co." 495.00

HARLEQUIN

The Homer Laughlin China Company, makers of the popular "Fiesta" pottery line, also introduced in 1938 a less expensive and thinner ware which was sold under the "Harlequin" name. It did not carry the maker's trade-mark and was marketed exclusively through F.W. Woolworth Company. It was produced in a wide range of dinnerwares in assorted colors until 1964. Out of production for a number of years, in 1979 Woolworth requested the line be reintroduced using an ironstone body and with a limited range of pieces and colors offered. Collectors also seek out a series of miniature animal figures produced in the Harlequin line in the 1930s and 1940s.

Ashtray, basketweave, turquoise........$21.00

Bowl, 36s, 4½" d., red..........................12.00

Bowl, 36s, 4½" d., rose........................12.00

Bowl, fruit, 5½" d., maroon 8.00

Bowl, fruit, 5½" d., red 8.00

Bowl, fruit, 5½" d., rose..........................8.00

Bowl, oatmeal, 6½" d., chartreuse........20.00

Bowl, individual salad, 7" d., blue 22.00

Bowl, individual salad, 7" d., turquoise 20.00

Bowl, individual salad, 7" d., yellow......20.00

Butter dish, cov., red.............................95.00

Candleholders, yellow, pr. 155.00

Casserole, cov., maroon....................135.00

Creamer, individual size, spruce green...17.00

Creamer, forest green 12.00

Creamer, red 15.00

Creamer, turquoise...............................6.00

Creamer, novelty, ball-shaped, maroon...48.00

Creamer, novelty, ball-shaped, red 30.00

Creamer, novelty, ball-shaped, rose.....38.00

Creamer & cov. sugar bowl, yellow, pr...25.00

Cream soup, handled, blue 21.00

Cream soup, handled, grey 12.00

Cream soup, handled, light green 11.00

Cream soup, handled, rose 10.00

Cream soup, handled, turquoise 14.00

Cup, demitasse, light green.................45.00

Cup & saucer, demitasse, blue............65.00

Cup & saucer, demitasse, chartreuse 135.00

Cup & saucer, demitasse, maroon 165.00

Cup & saucer, demitasse, red 125.00

Cup & saucer, demitasse, rose 65.00

Cup & saucer, demitasse, spruce green...165.00

Cup & saucer, demitasse, turquoise.....45.00

Cup & saucer, demitasse, yellow 45.00

Cup & saucer, grey..............................10.50

Cup & saucer, medium green..............25.00

Cup & saucer, rose 6.00

Cup & saucer, turquoise 6.00

Cup & saucer, yellow.............................6.00

Egg cup, single, blue 21.50

Egg cup, single, grey 19.00

Egg cup, single, maroon.......................22.50

Egg cup, single, spruce green 30.00

Egg cup, single, turquoise 20.00

Egg cup, double, forest green 20.00

Egg cup, double, grey..........................28.00

Gravy boat, blue 15.00

Gravy boat, maroon.............................25.00

Marmalade jar, cov., turquoise 155.00

Nappy, 9" d., red.................................16.00

Nappy, yellow 30.00

Nut dish, individual size, basketweave interior, red...9.00

Nut dish, individual size, basketweave interior, turquoise 7.00

Nut dish, individual size, basketweave interior, yellow 7.00

Pitcher, 9" h., ball-shaped w/ice lip, red..54.00

Pitcher, 9" h., ball-shaped w/ice lip, spruce green......................75.00 to 100.00

Pitcher, 9" h., ball-shaped w/ice lip, turquoise 35.00

Pitcher, 9" h., ball-shaped w/ice lip, yellow 45.00

Pitcher, cylindrical, 22 oz., chartreuse..40.00

Pitcher, cylindrical, 22 oz., grey...........54.00

Pitcher, cylindrical, 22 oz., light green..37.00

Pitcher, cylindrical, 22 oz., red.............37.00

Pitcher, cylindrical, 22 oz., rose...........39.50

Plate, 7" d., grey 6.50

Plate, 9" d., grey 11.00

Plate, 9" d., medium green 28.50

Plate, 9" d., yellow 10.00

Platter, 11" l., oval, turquoise...............13.00

Platter, 13" l., oval, red 22.00

Spoon rest, turquoise 172.50

Sugar bowl, cov., rose 15.00

Sugar bowl, cov., turquoise 15.00

Sugar bowl, cov., yellow 15.00

Teapot, cov., chartreuse.....................110.00

Teapot, cov., forest green.....................72.00

Teapot, cov., red...................................58.00

Teapot, cov., rose.................75.00 to 100.00

Tumbler, blue..35.00

Tumbler, red 38.00

Tumbler, turquoise................................35.00

Tumbler, yellow 25.00

HARLEQUIN ANIMALS

Model of a cat, maroon.......................125.00

Model of a donkey, maroon 75.00

Model of a duck, gold 24.00

Model of a fish, maroon......100.00 to 125.00

Model of a fish, yellow 72.00

Model of a penguin, yellow 85.00

HAVILAND

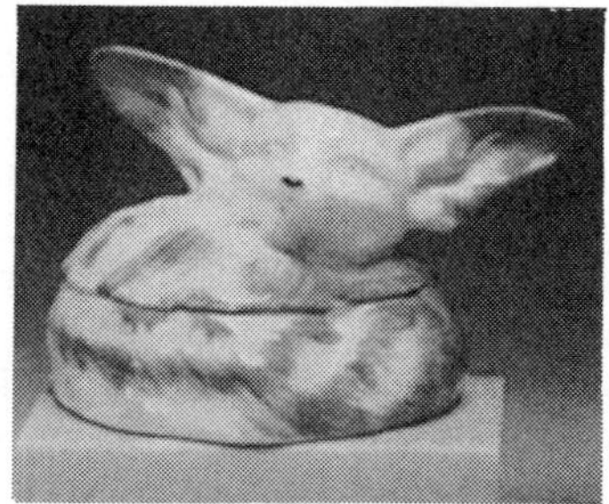

Haviland Figural Box

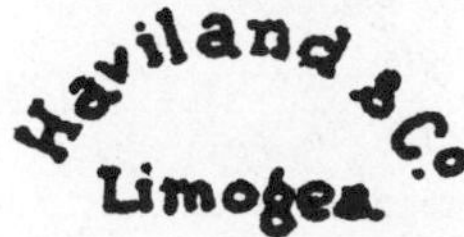

Haviland porcelain was originated by Americans in Limoges, France, shortly before the mid-19th century and continues in production. Some Haviland was made by Theodore Haviland in the United States during the last World War. Numerous other factories also made china in Limoges, which see.

Bone Dish, No. 1 Ranson blank $20.00

Bone dish, decorated w/lavender & pink roses, gold trim, Blank No. 22 ......8.00

Bouillon cup & saucer, two-handled, No. 1 Ranson blank 18.50

Bouillon cup & saucer, two-handled, Rosalinde patt., Theodore Haviland 30.00

Bowl, 9", serving-type, unusual shape, Baltimore Rose patt. 75.00

Bowl, cream soup, handled, w/underplate, Yale patt., Blank No. 103, 2 pcs. 35.00

Bowl, oyster, Clover Leaf patt., Blank No. 98C...65.00

Box, cov., figural, modeled in the form of a recumbent fox, his ears outspread, glazed in chocolate brown against a white ground, designed by Gérard Sandoz, ca. 1925, enameled factory marks & "G.M. Sandoz SC," & incised numerals, 6¼" d. (ILLUS.) 690.00

Butter pat, decorated w/lavender & pink roses, gold trim, Blank No. 22 ....15.00

Butter pat, Princess patt. 15.00

Butter pat, Silver Anniversary patt., Blank No. 19 ....12.00

Cake plate, open-handled, decorated w/sprays of vivid red & pink roses, gold scallops, embossed mark, 16" d...125.00

Chocolate pot, cov., Silver Anniversary patt. 200.00

Chocolate set: cov. chocolate pot & six cups & saucers; Baltimore Rose patt., 13 pcs........................1,500.00

Chocolate set: tankared-shaped cov. chocolate pot & six cups & saucers; embossed & decorated w/tiny pink roses & green leaves, gold handles & trim, 13 pcs. 295.00

Coffeepot, cov., Autumn Leaf patt., gold trim 225.00

Creamer & cov. sugar bowl, Springtime patt., pr....................................115.00

Creamer & cov. sugar bowl, Yale patt., Blank No. 103, pr. 95.00

Cup & saucer, demitasse, decorated w/blue flowers & green leaves, gold rims, marked "CFH-GDM" 20.00

Cup & saucer, demitasse, Clover Leaf patt., Blank No. 113 ....25.00

Cup & saucer, demitasse, decorated w/royal blue & yellow flowers, pale blue leaves & royal blue medallions, cream ground, gold handles & trim, Blank No. 561 ....25.00

Cup & saucer, demitasse, figural butterfly handle, factory-decorated 42.50

Cups & saucers, demitasse, pink morning glories decoration, gold brushed trim, set of 6 ....125.00

Cups & saucers, demitasse, applied gold handles, cream ground decorated w/pale blue leaves & royal blue & yellow flowers, set of 8 ....350.00

Cup & saucer, Athena patt. 45.00

Cup & saucer, Charonne patt., Blank No. 501 ....35.00

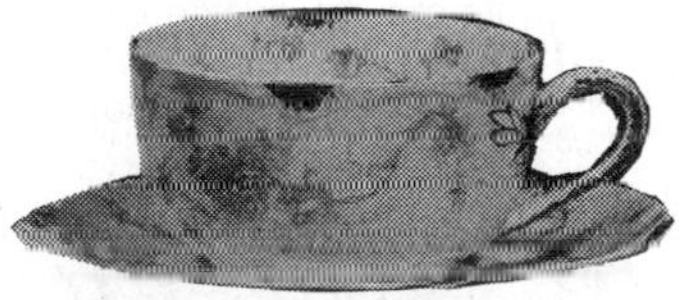

Princess Pattern Cup & Saucer

Cup & saucer, Princess patt. (ILLUS.) 45.00

Cup & saucer, decorated w/lavender & pink roses, gold trim, Blank No. 22 ....22.00

Cup & saucer, No. 1 Ranson blank 30.00

Cup & saucer, Silver Anniversary patt., Blank No. 19 ....34.00

Cup & saucer, Yale patt., Blank No. 103 ....32.50

Dinner service: including soup tureen, cov. butter, cov. vegetable bowl, platters; decorated w/large morning glories in shades of pink & lavender, 34 pcs. 850.00

Dinner service for 12 & extra pieces, Auberge patt., 63 pieces 875.00

Dish, leaf-shaped, decorated w/pink roses, green leaves, gold trimmed edge, Limoges, France, 7" l. 29.00

Fish set: 24" l. platter, twelve 7½" sq. plates & gravy boat w/underplate; h.p. fish decoration on each piece, the set (two plates w/minor rim chips, gravy boat w/hairline) 450.00

Game plate, h.p. game bird center, gold decorated border, 9¾" d. 30.00

Gravy boat w/attached underplate, octagonal, interior decorated w/gold parrots on cobalt blue ground, gold trim, Theodore Haviland (speck of gold missing on edge) 75.00

Gravy boat w/attached underplate, double pouring spouts, decorated w/pink flower sprays, marked "Theodore Haviland, Limoges - France" 65.00

Gravy boat, Yale patt., Blank No. 103 ..95.00

Oyster plate, decorated w/sprays of blue flowers, rose, wine, brown, pink lustre accent shells, marked "H.C.-L."Ï 105.00

Oyster plate, factory decorated w/small yellow roses, brown leaves & stems, gold trim, four oyster wells, round, Charles Field Haviland - GDM 45.00

Plate, bread & butter, 5" d., No. 24 Ranson blank w/gold 16.50

Plate, dessert, 5½" d., decorated w/lavender & pink roses, gold trim, Blank No. 22 ....7.00

Plate, 6¼" d., decorated w/lavender & pink roses, gold trim, Blank No. 22 ......7.00

Plate, salad, 7½" d., No. 24 Ranson blank w/gold.......................................18.50

Plate, salad, 7½" d., Silver Anniversary patt., Blank No. 19 ....16.50

Plate, salad, 7½" d., Yale patt., Blank No. 103 ....16.50

Plate, luncheon, 8½" d., No. 1 Ranson blank 14.50

Plate, luncheon, 8½" d., No. 24 Ranson blank w/gold 16.00

Plate, dinner, 9½" d., Athena patt.........45.00

Plate, dinner, 9½" d., Princess patt. 28.00

Plate, dinner, 9½" d., No. 1 Ranson blank 19.00

Plate, dinner, 9½" d., No. 24 Ranson blank w/gold.......................................22.00

Plate, dinner, 9½" d., Silver Anniversary patt., Blank No. 19 ....18.50

Plate, dinner, 9½" d., Yale patt., Blank No. 103 ....18.50

Plate, 11½" d., Drop Rose patt...........275.00

Plate, chop, 12½" d., self-handled, decorated w/bouquets of tiny pink roses, Ranson gold border, gold trimmed handles 115.00

Platter, 11½" l., Yale patt., Blank No. 103 ....40.00

Platter, 10 x 13¾", self-handled, Autumn Leaf patt., scalloped, gold handles 95.00

Platter, 14" l., Athena patt. 195.00

Platter, 14" l., decorated w/lavender & pink roses, gold trim, Blank No. 22 ....45.00

Platter, 16" l., decorated w/relief-molded sprays of bamboo & leaves, scalloped, lavish gold trim 125.00

Sauce tureen, cov., decorated w/butterflies & birds, ca. 1890s 150.00

Soup bowl & underplate, bowl w/applied handles, Rosalinde patt., the set 75.00

Soup plate w/flanged rim, Silver Anniversary patt., Blank No. 19 ....24.00

Soup tureen, Drop Rose patt., lavender & gold 225.00

Vegetable dish, cov., decorated w/butterflies & birds, ca. 1890s, 12" l. 150.00

Vegetable dish, cov., round, Yale patt., Blank No. 103 ....90.00

Vegetable dish, open, Athena patt. 135.00

Vegetable dish, open, oval, Yale patt., Blank No. 103 ....60.00

HEDI SCHOOP

Cowboy & Lady Figure Group

Hedi Schoop began producing ceramics in 1940 in Hollywood, California. Practically all figurines from then until 1958, when a fire resulted in the closing of the pottery, were designed and modeled by Hedi Schoop even though almost fifty decorators worked at her studio. A variety of items was made including animals, ashtrays, bowls, boxes with lids, candlesticks, figurines, lamps, planters, and wall plaques. Hedi Schoop products range from those with crude characteristics to those with intricate details to others with delicate, fragile traits. Almost all items are marked. There were a variety of marks ranging from the stamped or incised Schoop signature to the hard-to-find Hedi Schoop sticker. The words "Hollywood, Cal." or "California" can also be found in conjunction with the Hedi Schoop name.

Hedi
Schoop

HEDI SCHOOP
HOLLYWOOD, CALIF.

Hedi Schoop
HOLLYWOOD CAL.

Bowl, 10½" l., 6" h., figural, duck sitting w/body forming bowl, dark brown w/gold trim $45.00

Bowl, 10¾" d., 3" h., low round sides w/fluted edges, woman sitting in middle w/one flower in her hands, dress sleeves have h.p. flowers, hair w/rough texture 75.00

Bust of a child, angel-like w/finger at mouth indicating 'quiet,' pink, white, blue decorations, 8" h. 45.00

Figure of a ballet dancer, pink w/platinum trim, platinum ring on each arm, one leg extended, other slightly bent, 10" h. 155.00

Figure of a clown standing, legs crossed, one hand to head, other hand to mouth, bucket & mop at his side, 10½" h. 95.00

Figure of a clown w/legs apart, one hand over head holding barbell, other hand on waist, turquoise & pink w/platinum trim, 13" h. 110.00

Figure of a girl standing, bell-shaped skirt w/scalloped edges, sunflower-shaped face & yellow hair, green blouse, yellow skirt, Model No. 703, 9" h. 38.00

Figure of a girl standing holding holding bowl over her head, one leg raised slightly, the other leg on base, white glossy overall glaze w/blue & green striped skirt, blue scarf around head & tied at neck, blue shoes, 13" h. 85.00

Figure of a woman on a base w/an oval upright mirror behind her, reflecting her back, all black except white hair, blouse, purse & trim on hat & dress, w/mirror in good condition, 4¾" l., 8" h. 160.00

Figure group, cowboy & lady, dancing, bisque faces & hands, he has hat & kerchief, she is holding up her long ruffled dress w/right hand & has bow in hair at back, green, black & yellow glazes, 11" h. (ILLUS.) 175.00

Schoop Girl & Tree Figure

Figure group, girl & tree on a base, girl w/head up looking at top of tree w/her arms raised, rough texture, mint green w/white glaze, brown leaves on girl's skirt, 7½" l., 11½" h. (ILLUS.) 105.00

Lamp, figural, TV-type, Comedy & Tragedy masks on a base w/full Comedy, part Tragedy conjoined, dark green w/gold trim, ca. 1954, 10¾" l., 12" h. 325.00

Model of a cat, reclining, two bells in-relief on collar, bow on collar forms two small pots at side of head, rough textured white w/dark brown pots & yellow bells, 7¼" l., 5¾" h. 50.00

Model of a cat, sitting, two bells in-relief on collar, bow on collar forms two small pots at back of head, rough textured white w/dark brown pots & yellow bells, 4½" l., 7½" h. 55.00

HISTORICAL & COMMEMORATIVE WARES

Arms of Delaware Platter

Numerous potteries, especially in England and the United States, made various porcelain and earthenware pieces to commemorate people, places and events. Scarce English historical wares with American views command highest prices. Objects are listed here alphabetically by title of view.

Most pieces listed here will date between about 1820 and 1850. The maker's name is noted in parenthesis at the end of each entry. Also see ADAMS, CLEWS, RIDGWAY and WOOD (Enoch).

Arms of Delaware platter, flowers & vines border, spoked wheels equidistant around border, dark blue, 16¾" l., T. Mayer, faint scratches (ILLUS.) $1,650.00

Arms of Georgia platter, flowers & vines border, spoked wheels equidistant around border, dark blue, 12¾" l., T. Mayer (restored crack, reglazed) 4,125.00

Arms of Massachusetts Platter

Arms of Massachusetts platter, flowers & vines border, spoked wheels equidistant around border, dark blue, 9½" l., T. Mayer (ILLUS.) 4,675.00

Arms of Maryland Punch Bowl

Arms of Maryland punch bowl, flowers & vines border, spoked wheels equidistant around border, dark blue, 11¾" d., 5" h., T. Mayer (ILLUS.) 9,350.00

Arms of New York plate, flowers & vines border w/spoked wheels equidistant around, dark blue, 10" d. (Mayer) 660.00

Arms of North Carolina platter, flowers & vines border, spoked wheels equidistant around border, dark blue, 14½", T. Mayer (restored, reglazed) 2,420.00

Arms of Rhode Island plate, flowers & vines border w/spoked wheels equidistant around, dark blue, 8½" d. (Mayer) 440.00

Arms of Rhode Island plate, flowers & vines border w/spoked wheels equidistant around, medium blue, 8½" d., Mayer (wear, scratches, pinpoint flake) 220.00

Arms of South Carolina dish, leaf-shaped, flowers & vines border, spoked wheels equidistant around border, dark blue, 5¾" l., T. Mayer (restoration to rim) 3,025.00

Arms of Virginia compote, flowers & vines border, spoked wheels equidistant around border, dark blue, 4½ x 12¼" oval, T. Mayer (restored, reglazed) 4,125.00

Baltimore & Ohio Railroad (Inclined) plate, shell border, dark blue, 9⅛" d. (Enoch Wood & Sons) 660.00

Battle Monument, Baltimore plate, long-stemmed roses border, purple, 9" d. (Jackson) 85.00

Belleville on the Passaic River soup tureen, cov., shell border & circular center w/trailing vine around outer edge of center, dark blue, 14½" w. (Enoch Wood & Sons) 4,675.00

Boston State House bath pitcher, floral border, dark blue, pouring handle under spout, 11" d., 13" h., John Rogers (restored, spider crack in base) 1,045.00

Boston State House plate, flowers & leaves border, medium blue, 10" d., Rogers (chip on rim back)................220.00

Boston State House platter, flower & leaves border, medium dark blue, 16⅞" l., John Rogers & Son (stains, scratches) 880.00

Cadmus cup plate, trefoil border, dark blue, 3⅝" d. (Wood) 264.00

Cadmus plate, shell border w/irregular center, dark blue, 10" d. (Wood)......440.00

Caius College, Cambridge (England) soup tureen, cover & St. Peter's College, Cambridge undertray, floral scrolls border, medium blue, 15" l., the set (stains) 1,375.00

Capitol, Washington Platter

Capitol, Washington platter, flowers within medallions border, dark blue, 20½" l., J. & W. Ridgway (ILLUS.) 2,200.00

Castle Garden, Battery, New York cup plate, abbreviated border, dark blue, 3¾" d. (Wood)................................357.50

Castle Garden, Battery, New York cup plate, shells border, circular center w/trailing vine around outer edge of center, dark blue, 3⅝" d. (Wood).....413.00

Cattskill (sic) Mountain House plate, flowers, shells & scrolls border, red, 10⅜" d., Adams (minor glaze flakes on rim)...170.50

Cave Castle, Yorkshire (England) plate, dark blue, 8½" d. (Enoch Wood) 135.00

Christ Church, Oxford (England)

plate, medium blue, 10" d. (small flake on table ring) 99.00

Christmas Eve creamer, flowers & scrolls border, dark blue, Wilkies Designs series, 5½" h., Clews (edge chips) 247.50

Christmas Eve plate, flowers & scrolls border, dark blue, Wilkies Designs series, ca. 1830, 9" d. (Clews) 375.00

City Hall, New York plate, flowers within medallions border, dark blue, 10" d. (Ridgway) ....200.00 to 225.00

City Hall, New York plate, long-stemmed roses border, black, 10½" d., Jackson (chips on table ring) 110.00

City Hotel, New York plate, acorns & oak leaves border, dark blue, 8½" d. (Stevenson) 302.50

Clarence Terrace, Regents Park (London, England) platter, wide vintage grape border, dark blue, 10¾" l. 412.50

Columbus (Ohio) platter, groups of flowers & scrolls border, dark blue, 14½" l., Clews (old chips & hairline, minor wear & stains) 880.00

Commodore MacDonnough's Victory plate, shell border, dark blue, 6½"d., Enoch Wood & Sons (minor wear & stains, pinpoint flakes) 330.00

Commodore MacDonnough's Victory plate, shell border, dark blue, 8" d., Enoch Wood (wear, stains, scratches & pinpoint flakes) 412.50

Commodore MacDonnough's Victory plate, shell border w/irregular center, dark blue, 10" d., Enoch Wood & Sons (imperfections) 137.50

Commodore MacDonnough's Victory sugar bowl, cov., floral border, irregular center, dark blue, 6⅞" h., Enoch Wood & Sons (chips) 660.00

Conway Castle, Carnavonshire (England) platter, large flowers in border, dark blue, ca. 1830, 15" oval 467.50

Cornwall Terrace, Regents Park, London (England) platter, leafy tree border, dark blue, ca. 1830, 19⅜" l. 715.00

Culford Hall, Sussex (England) cup & saucer, handleless, dark blue (Stevenson) 110.00

Deaf and Dumb Asylum, Hartford, Connecticut pitcher & bowl set, bowl w/Lawrence Mansion, Boston, vining leaf border, dark blue, bowl 14" d., pitcher 10" h., the set, R. Stevenson (ILLUS.) 2,760.00

Deaf & Dumb Asylum Pitcher & Bowl

Denton Park, Yorkshire (England) pitcher, dark blue, early 19th c., 6¾" h., John & Richard Riley (wear, chips, stains) 247.50

Detroit platter, flower & scroll border, dark blue, 18½" l. (Clews) 3,500.00

Diorama View of Houghton Conquest House, Bedfordshire (England) platter, wide floral border, dark blue, 21¼" l. (minor wear, stains) 687.50

Doctor Syntax Mistakes a Gentleman's Home for an Inn plate, floral border, dark blue, ca. 1830, 10¼" d. (Clews) 175.00

Doctor Syntax Mistakes a Gentleman's House for an Inn soup plate, floral border, dark blue, ca. 1830, 9⅞" d. (Clews) 165.00

Doctor Syntax Reading His Tour plate, floral border, dark blue, ca. 1830, 10¼" d. (Clews) 175.00

Doctor Syntax Sells Grizzle vegetable dish, molded ribbon handles, flowers & scrolls border, dark blue, ca. 1830, 8 x 11½", Clews (wear & small surface flakes) 550.00

Doctor Syntax Taking Possession of His Living plate, floral border, dark blue, ca. 1830, 10¼" d.. (Clews) 175.00

Errand Boy (The) cup plate, flowers & scrolls border, dark blue, Wilkies Designs series, ca. 1830, 3½" d. (Clews) 302.50

Fair Mount Near Philadelphia plate, spread eagles amid flowers & scrolls border, medium blue, 10" d., Stubbs (table ring chips, wear, stains) 165.00

General W. H. Harrison, Hero of the Thames 1813 plate, black, Philadelphia importer's mark, 9½" d. (ILLUS. top next column) 2,365.00

General Harrison Plate

General W. H. Harrison, Hero of the Thames 1813 plate, green, Philadelphia importer's mark (stains)....1,980.00

General Jackson, Hero of New Orleans plate, molded feather edge w/pink lustre trim, black, 8¾" d. (minor wear).................................1,155.00

Hartford, Connecticut soup plates, long-stemmed roses border, red, 10½" d., Jackson, set of 4 (two w/very minor flakes on table rings) ..440.00

Hartford State House custard cup, handled, flowers & leaves border, medium dark blue, Andrew Stevenson (minute flake on rim) 1,400.00

Harvard Hall, Massachusetts plate, floral border, brown, 6¾" d. (Jackson) 90.00

Hawthornden, Edinburghshire (England) plate, dark blue, ca. 1830, 8¾" d., Adams (small flakes & minor scratches) 115.00

Hoboken in New Jersey plate, spread eagles amid flowers & scrolls border, dark blue, 7¾" d. (Stubbs)........176.00

Hudson, Hudson River platter, birds, flowers& scrolls border, purple, 13½" l., Clews (short hairlines, minor stains & some glaze flakes on back) 275.00

Insane Hospital, Boston plate, flowers within medallions border, dark blue, 7¼" d. (Ridgway) 247.50

Italian Scenery - Ponte Del Palazzo platter, dark blue, 16¾" l. (minor imperfections) 605.00

Lafayette at Franklin's Tomb coffeepot, cov., baluster-form w/scrolled handle & spout, domed lid w/beehive knop, floral border, dark blue, overall 12" h., Wood, short hairline, small chips, finial reglued (ILLUS. top next column)....770.00

Lafayette at Franklin's Tomb Coffeepot

Lafayette at Franklin's Tomb pitcher, floral border, dark blue, 9½" h., Enoch Wood & Sons (imperfections) 770.00

Lafayette at Franklin's Tomb teapot, cov., floral border, dark blue, 7½" h., Enoch Wood (foot chips, finial reglued) 1,045.00

Lafayette at Washington's Tomb platter, floral border, dark blue, 14½" l. (Wood) 1,600.00

Landing of General Lafayette at Castle Garden, New York, 16 August, 1824 plate, floral & vine border, dark blue, 9" d. (Clews)..275.00

Landing of General Lafayette at Castle Garden, New York, 16 August, 1824 plate, floral & vine border, dark blue, 10" d. (Clews)............................300.00 to 350.00

Landing of General Lafayette at Castle Garden, New York, 16 August, 1824 tray, floral & vine border, dark blue, rectangular w/rounded corners & end handles, 6" l., Clews (chips on table ring & back of one handle) 1,237.50

Landing of General Lafayette at Castle Garden, New York, 16 August, 1824 covered tureen, floral & vine border, oval w/flared rim & scrolled end handles, the stepped, domed cover w/florette finial, dark blue, 14¾" l., Clews (flakes) 4,675.00

Landing of General Lafayette at Castle Garden, New York, 16 August, 1824 open vegetable dish, floral & vine border, dark blue, 10 x 12", Clews (wear, scratches, old chips on back)............................412.50

Letter of Introduction platter, flowers & scrolls border, blue, Wilkies Designs series, 12⅜" l., Clews (glaze wear & flakes on edge of rim) 577.50

Library, Philadelphia plate, flowers within medallions border, dark blue, 8" d., Ridgway (minor stains, crazing, pinpoint flakes) 170.50

Log Cabin cup & saucer, handleless, saucer border w/oval medallions of Major General Wm. H. Harrison alternating w/floral urns, red, Adams (small flakes & short hairline in saucer) 385.00

London Views - George's Chapel Regent Street platter, grape border, dark blue, 18¾" l., Enoch Wood & Sons (some imperfections) 770.00

Marine Hospital, Louisville, Kentucky plate, shell border, dark blue, 9" d., Wood (wear, pinpoint flakes, scratches) 385.00

Mitchell & Freeman's China and Glass Warehouse, Chatham Street, Boston plate, foliage border, dark blue, 10" d. (Adams) 770.00

Montevideo, Connecticut, U.S. plate, flowers, shells & scrolls border, pink, 7" d. (Adams) 80.00

Mount Pleasant Classical Institution, Amherst, Mass. plate, flowers w/large scrolls border, dark blue, 10½" d. (Clews) 8,000.00

Nahant Hotel, Near Boston plate, spread eagles amid flowers & scrolls border, dark blue, 8½" d., Stubbs (minor scratches, chip on table ring) 330.00

Near Fort Miller, Hudson River plate, birds, flowers & scrolls border, grey, 9" d. (Clews) 65.00

Oriental Scenery - Tomb of the Emperor Shah Jehan platter, dark blue, 18" l. (J. Hall & Sons) 660.00

Park Theatre, New York plate, acorn & oak leaves border, dark blue, 10" d., Stevenson (minor glaze flakes) 275.00

Peace & Plenty platter, oval, wide band of fruit & flowers border, dark blue, 19" l., Clews (small surface flakes, minor wear) 880.00

Penn's Treaty plate, latticework design border, Penn standing, attendant kneeling, Indians standing, medium blue, 8¼" d. (Thomas Green)..125.00

Portrait Medallion Pitcher

Portrait Medallion pitcher, oval portraits of Washington, Jefferson, Lafayette & Clinton, floral border, dark blue, R. Stevenson & Williamson (ILLUS.)...............................12,100.00

The Rabbit on the Wall platter, large flowers & scrolls border, dark blue, Wilkies Designs series, 10¾" l., Clews (minor edge wear)................880.00

Residence of the Late Richard Jordan, New Jersey platter, flowers or dual line border, purple, 19½" l., J. Heath & Co. (minor spot of glaze wear)...962.50

Sancho Panza at the Boar Hunt soup plate, floral border, dark blue, ca. 1830, 9¾" d. (Clews) 192.50

Sandusky (Ohio) platter, floral border, medium dark blue, 16¾" l., Clews (very minor glaze flakes)..............3,960.00

Shannondale Springs, Virginia plate, flowers, shells & scroll border, pink, 8" d. (Adams) 85.00

Southhampton, Hampshire (England) plate, shell border, dark blue, 7⅝" d., Wood (minor stains, tiny edge flakes) 220.00

States series plate, building & fishermen w/net, names of states in festoons separated by five-point stars border, dark blue, 10½" d., Clews (minor hairline) 247.50

States series plate, building & fishermen w/net scene, names of fifteen states in festoons on border separated by five- or eight-point stars, dark blue, 10½" d., Clews (ILLUS. top next column) 300.00

States series plate, building, sheep on lawn, names of fifteen states in festoons on border, separated by

State Series Plate

five- or eight-point stars, dark blue, 8¾" d., Clews (minor wear, hairline, pinpoint flakes on table ring) 220.00

States series platter, mansion, foreground a lake w/swans, border w/names of fifteen states in festoons separated by five-point stars, dark blue, 16¾" l. (gap in transfer shows up as a ⅜ x 1¾" white area in pattern, minor wear, stains & old pinpoint flakes) 1,045.00

Staughton's Church, Philadelphia plate, flowers in medallions border, dark blue, 8¼" d. (Ridgway) 220.00

Sulpher Springs, Delaware, Ohio plate, floral cluster & scalloped swag border, medium blue border & black central scene, 9½" d. (minor wear) .. 198.00

Texian Campaigne - Battle of Buena Vista plate, symbols of war & "goddess-type" seated border, purple, 8½" d., Anthony Shaw (stains) 203.50

Texian Campaigne - Battle of Chapultepec plate, symbols of war & a "goddess-type" seated border, mulberry, 9½" d. (Shaw) 350.00

Union Line plate, shells border, dark blue, 10½" d., Wood (minor glaze wear) 440.00

Valentine (The) plate, flowers & scrolls border, dark blue, Wilkies Designs series, ca. 1830, 9" d. (Clews) 290.00

View of Liverpool (England) soup plate, shell border, dark blue, 8⅜" d. (Wood) 275.00

View of New York from Weehawk platter, flowers between leafy scrolls border, dark blue, 18½" l. (Andrew Stevenson) 2,640.00

View Near Conway N. Hampshire, U.S. plate, floral wreath border, red, 9" d. (Adams) 85.00

Villa in the Regents Park, London (England) plate, leafy trees frame center scene, dark blue, 10" d., Adams (minor edge flakes) 115.00

Washington & Lafayette plate, flower & scroll border, dark blue, 10⅛" d., Stevenson & Williams (tiny rim flake) 1,300.00

Welcome Lafayette the Nation's Guest and Our Country's Glory plate, flowers & scrolls border, blue, 8¾" d., Clews (minor wear & pinpoint flakes) 632.50

West Point, Hudson River plate, scrolls & flowers border, Picturesque Views series, brown, 7⅞" d., Clews (wear, minor stains, pinpoint flakes) 104.50

Windsor Castle Platter

Windsor Castle, Berkshire (England) platter, floral border, dark blue, 18¾" l., William Adams, minor imperfections (ILLUS.) 715.00

Winter View of Pittsfield, Mass.(A) plate, floral border w/medallions of center view border, dark blue, 8" d.(Clews) 357.50

Yale College & State House, New Haven vegetable dish, floral border, black, oblong w/scalloped edges & loop end handles, 12¾" l., Jackson (very minor edge flakes) 302.50

HOUND-HANDLED PITCHERS

Pitchers and jugs with handles formed as hunting hounds comprise a unique collecting category. For the most part, these pitchers had a hunting scene molded in relief on the body. Listed below by maker or type of glaze, these pitchers usually command a high price.

Rockingham-glazed Pitcher

Majolica, the footed ovoid body cast w/hanging game tapering to a high arched spout, a long-legged hound handle w/molded detailing, glazed in shades of brown, blue & green, 19th c., 8½" h. $440.00

Rockingham-glazed, miniature, wide slightly tapering cylindrical body below a narrow shoulder & cylindrical neck w/wide spout, hound's head resting on the front paws, mottled dark brown glaze, relief-molded hunting scene around the sides, 3⅛" h. (pinpoint edge flakes) 280.50

Rockingham-glazed pottery, flat-bottomed tapering cylindrical body molded w/hanging game & a molded eagle spout, simple hound handle w/hound's head resting on front paws, mottled dark brown glaze, probably Ohio, 9½" h. (hairline in base) 137.50

Rockingham-glazed, slightly swelled cylindrical body w/wide arched spout, molded w/a boar, eagle & stag hunt scene, the hound-handle w/hound's head resting on upper paws, mottled dark brown glaze, late 19th - early 20th c., 10" h. (ILLUS.) ...99.00

HULL

This pottery was made by the Hull Pottery Company, Crooksville, Ohio, beginning in 1905. Art Pottery was made until 1950 when the company was converted to utilitarian wares. All production ceased in 1986.

Reference books for collectors include Roberts' Ultimate Encyclopedia of Hull Pottery *by Brenda Roberts (Walsworth Publishing Company, 1992), and* Collector's Guide to Hull Pottery - The Dinnerware Lines *by Barbara Loveless Gick-Burke (Collector Books, 1993).*

Little Red Riding Hood Standing Bank

Ashtray, Serenade patt., pink, No. S23, 10½ x 13" $70.00

Baker, cov., oval "nest" base w/figural hen cover, dark brown glaze, House 'n Garden line, 13⅜" l., 11" h. 50.00

Bank, figural Corky Pig, blue & pink, 5" h. 70.00

Bank, figural pig, pink bow, 7" l. 70.00

Bank, figural pig, orange w/a bright blue bow, 14" l. 100.00

Bank, standing-type, Little Red Riding Hood patt., 7" h. (ILLUS.) 615.00

Bank, wall-type, Little Red Riding Hood patt., 9" h. 1,100.00

Basket, Blossom Flite patt., No. T-2, 6" h. 32.00

Basket, Blossom Flite patt., No. T-8, 8¼ x 9¼" 65.00

Basket, Bow-Knot patt., blue to pink, No. B-25-6½", 6½" 160.00

Basket, Bow-Knot patt., pink & blue, No. B-12-10½", 10½" h. 525.00

Basket, Butterfly patt., cream & turquoise, No. B13, 8 x 8" 85.00

Basket, triple-handle, Butterfly patt., matte glaze, No. B 17, 10½" h. 265.00

Basket, Capri patt., mottled maroon & dark green, No. 48, 6 x 12¼" 50.00

Basket, Continental patt., persimmon glossy glaze, No. C55, 12½" h...........81.00

Basket, Dogwood patt., center handle, blue & pink, No. 501-7½", 7½".........175.00

Basket, Ebb Tide patt., model of a large shell w/long fish handle, No. E-11, 16½" l...............................175.00

Basket, Magnolia Gloss patt., No. H-14-10½", 10½".......................145.00

Basket, Magnolia matte patt., No. 10-10½", 10½" h........................120.00

Basket, Mardi Gras (Granada) patt., No. 32-8", 8" l..................................110.00

Basket, Mardi Gras patt., No. 65-8, 8" h...135.00

Basket, Parchment & Pine patt., No. S-3, 6" l.......................................42.50

Basket, Parchment & Pine patt., No. S-8, 16½" l..................................60.00

Basket, Rosella patt., No. R-12-7", 7" h...140.00

Basket, Royal Woodland patt., turquoise, W22, 10½" l.......................70.00

Basket, Tokay patt., No. 6, 8" h...........55.00

Basket, Tokay patt., round "Moon" form, white, No. 11, 10½" h. 95.00

Basket, Tulip patt., pink & blue, No. 102-33-6", 6" h. 160.00

Basket, Water Lily patt., No. L14-10½", 10½" h......................175.00

Basket, hanging-type, footed bulbous body, Woodland patt., rose & cream, No. W12-7½", 7½" h. 350.00

Woodland Gloss Basket

Basket, Woodland Gloss patt., No. W9-8¾", 8¾" h. (ILLUS.)...........168.00

Basket, fan-shaped, Woodland Gloss patt., yellow & pink, No. W22-10½", 10½" h...125.00

Batter pitcher, side pour, Little Red Riding Hood patt., 7" h....................370.00

Bean pot, cov., House 'n Garden Ware, 6½" h. 20.00

Book ends, Orchid patt., pink & blue, No. 316-7", pr...............................1,050.00

Bowl, 6¼" d., 3" h., Imperial patt., relief-molded leaf decoration, dark green, No. F8 ....8.00

Bowl, 6½ x 8½", Imperial patt., pink, melon ribbed, No. 154-8½" 12.00

Bowl, 9" d., Imperial patt., dark green, basketweave, No. 117 ....12.00

Bowl, fruit, 10 x 11½", 7" h., pedestal base, two upturned sides, Serenade patt., pink, No. S-15-11½"................100.00

Butter dish, cov., House 'n Garden Ware 7.00

Little Red Riding Hood Butter Dish

Butter dish, cov., Little Red Riding Hood patt. (ILLUS.) 315.00

Candleholder, Bow-Knot patt., cornucopia-form, No. B17, 4" h..........75.00

Candleholder, Butterfly patt., glossy white, No. B22, 2½" h. 22.00

Candleholders, Dogwood patt., cornucopia-form, peach & turquoise, No. 512, 3¾" h., pr..........................115.00

Candleholders, Ebb Tide patt., No. E-13, 2¾", pr. 50.00

Candleholders, Magnolia Matte patt., No. 27-4", 4" h., pr. 125.00

Candleholders, Open Rose patt., model of a dove, No. 117-6½", 6½" h., pr. 215.00

Candleholders, Water Lily patt., glossy white, No. L-22, 4½" h., pr. 55.00

Candleholders, Wildflower patt., No. W-22, 2½" h., pr. 95.00

Candy dish, urn-shaped, Butterfly patt., No. B6, 5½" h. 55.00

Canister, cov., "Flour," Little Red Riding Hood patt. ....650.00 to 700.00

Canister, cov., "Nutmeg," Little Red Riding Hood patt. 875.00

Canister, cov., "Salt," Little Red Riding Hood patt. 850.00

Canister, cov., "Tea," Little Red Riding Hood patt. 630.00

Casserole, cov., Debonair patt., No. 0-17, 8½" 45.00

Casserole, cov., Sunglow patt., No. 51-7½", 7½" d. 22.50

Coffeepot, cov., House 'n Garden patt. 25.00

Console bowl, Blossom Flite patt., No. T10, 16½" l. 135.00

Console bowl, Bow-Knot patt., No. B-16-13½", 13½" l. 215.00

Console bowl, three-footed, Butterfly patt., No. B21, 10" d. 75.00

Console bowl, Magnolia Gloss patt., pink, No. H-23-13", 13" l. 47.50

Console bowl, Orchid patt., No. 314-13", 13" l. 250.00

Console bowl, Water Lily patt., No. L-21-13½", 13½" l. 200.00

Console set: console bowl & pair of candleholders; Ebb Tide patt., bowl No. E12-15½", candleholders No. E-13, deep wine, 3 pcs. 200.00

Cookie jar, cov., Barefoot Boy, made for Hull by Gem Refractories, 13" h. ....350.00 to 375.00

Cookie jar, cov., figural apple, Novelty Line 40.00

Cookie jar, Little Red Riding Hood 365.00

Cornucopia-vase, Bow-Knot patt., No. B-5-7½", 7½" h. 115.00

Bow-Knot Cornucopia-vase

Cornucopia-vase, double, Bow-Knot patt., No. B-13-13", 13" h. (ILLUS.) 210.00

Cornucopia-vase, Butterfly patt., matte cream w/blue interior, No. B2, 6¼" h. 22.00

Cornucopia-vase, Calla Lily patt., blue, peach & tan, No. 570-33-8", 8" h. 75.00

Cornucopia-vase, Fiesta patt., yellow, No. 49, 8¼" h. 27.00

Cornucopia-vase, double, Magnolia Matte patt., tan, No. 6-12", 12" w. 115.00

Cornucopia-vase, Tokay patt., green & white, No. 10, 11" l ....45.00 to 55.00

Cornucopia-vase, double, Water Lily patt., No. L27-12", 12" l. 100.00

Cornucopia-vase, Wildflower patt., matte finish, No. W10-8½", 8½" h. 75.00

Cracker jar, cov., Little Red Riding Hood patt., 8½" h. 560.00

Creamer, Bow-Knot patt., blue & pink, B-21-4", 4" h. 85.00

Creamer, House 'n Garden Ware 7.00

Creamer, side pour, Little Red Riding Hood patt. 125.00

Creamer & cov. sugar bowl, House 'n Garden Ware, pr. 14.00

Creamer & cov. sugar bowl, Little Red Riding Hood patt., head pour creamer, pr. 650.00

Cup & saucer, House 'n Garden Ware ...9.00

Dish, leaf-shaped, Capri patt., No. C63, 10½ x 14" 35.00

Dish, leaf-shaped, Tuscany patt., No. 19, 14" l. 28.00

Dish, pedestal base, Imperial patt., dark green, 4¼ x 6½", 2½" h., No. F53 ....8.00

Ewer, Blossom Flite patt., No. T13, 13½" h. 95.00

Bow-Knot Ewer

Ewer, Bow-Knot patt., No. B-1-5½", 5½" h. (ILLUS.) 110.00

Ewer, Butterfly patt., No. B15-13½", 13½" h....................100.00

Ewer, Calla Lily patt., No. 506-10", 10¾" h....................235.00

Ewer, Classic patt., No. 6-6", 6" h. 17.00

Ewer, Dogwood patt., No. 505-6½", 8½" h....................235.00

Ewer, Granada patt., No. 66-10", 10" h....................100.00

Ewer, Iris patt., No. 401-13½", 13½" h....................350.00

Ewer, Magnolia Gloss patt., No. H-3-5½", 5½" h....................25.00

Ewer, Magnolia Gloss patt., pink, No. H-19-13½", 13½" h....................250.00

Ewer, Magnolia Matte patt., No. 5-7", 7" h....................65.00

Ewer, Magnolia Matte patt., pink & blue, No. 18-13½", 13½" h....................350.00

Ewer, Open Rose patt., No. 105-7", 7" h....................195.00

Ewer, Pine Cone patt., green, 13½" h....................95.00

Ewer, Tulip patt., blue, No. 109-8", 8" h....................195.00

Ewer, Tuscany patt., No. 21, 14" h.....135.00

Wildflower Ewer

Ewer, Wildflower patt., W-11-8½", 8½" h. (ILLUS.) 115.00

Ewer, Wildflower patt., pink & blue, No. W-19-13½", 13½" h....................316.00

Ewer, Woodland Gloss patt., glossy glaze, No. W24-13½", 13½" ....150.00 to 175.00

Ewers, Mardi Gras/Granada patt., No. 66-10", 10" h., pr. 305.00

Flower dish, Continental patt., green, No. 51, 15½" l. 38.00

Flowerpot w/attached saucer, Bow-Knot patt., No. B-6-6½", 6½" h....................87.00

Flowerpot w/attached saucer, Sueno Tulip patt., blue, No. 116-33-6", 6" h....................95.00

Gravy boat, House 'n Garden Ware, dark brown glaze 14.00

Grease jar, cov., figural apple, Novelty Line 15.00

Grease jar, cov., Sunglow patt., No. 53, 5¼" h....................65.00

Honey jug, Blossom Flite patt., No. T1-6", 6" h. 26.00

Jardiniere, Bow-Knot patt., blue, No. B-18-5¾", 5¾" h....................100.00

Jardiniere, Early Art Stoneware, relief-molded honeycomb & flowers, brown exterior & green interior, No. 550-7", 6 x 7¼"....................58.00

Jardiniere, Imperial line, green, horizontal ribs, No. 418, 5" h....................12.00

Jardiniere, two-handled, Orchid patt., No. 310-9½", 9½" h....................350.00

Jardiniere, Sueno Tulip patt., No. 117-30-5", 5" h. 95.00

Lamp, Little Red Riding Hood patt. ....2,000.00 to 2,500.00

Lamp-planter, model of a seated kitten beside a cylindrical flowerpot, ca. 1948 ....80.00

Lavabo & base, Butterfly patt., Nos. B24 & B25, overall 16" h. 125.00

Match box, hanging-type, Little Red Riding Hood patt., 5¼" h....................700.00

Mug, barrel-shaped, embossed "Happy Days Are Here Again," green glaze, No. 497, 5" h. 22.50

Mug, House 'n Garden Ware, No. 526, 16 oz. 7.00

Pie baker, Nuline Bak-Serve patt., blue 20.00

Pie plate, House 'n Garden Ware, 9¼" d....................20.00

Pitcher, milk, 6¾" h., House 'n Garden Ware 22.00

Pitcher, milk, 8" h., Little Red Riding Hood patt. 250.00

Pitcher, 9½" h., House 'n Garden Ware 25.00

Pitcher, Cinderella Kitchenware, Blossom patt., No. 29-16 oz. 30.00

Pitcher, Cinderella Kitchenware, Bouquet patt., No. 29-32 oz. 35.00

Pitcher, Sunglow patt., yellow, No.52-24 oz. 35.00

Madonna & Child Planter

Planter, bust of the Madonna & Child, pink, No. 26, 7" h. (ILLUS.) 25.00

Planter, Imperial patt,. four-footed, vertical rib, yellow, No. F39, 4½ x 7" oval 8.50

Planter, Imperial line, goblet-shaped, bead stem, dark green spiral bowl, No. F5, 4¾" h. 7.50

Planter, wall-type, Little Red Riding Hood patt., 9" h. 415.00

Planter, model of a goose, No. 80 ....18.00

Planter, model of a swan, white, No. 23, 10" h. 38.00

Plate, dessert, 6½" d., House 'n Garden Ware 4.00

Salt & pepper shakers, figural apple, Novelty Line, pr. 15.00

Salt & pepper shakers, mushroom-shaped, House 'n Garden Ware, 3¾" h., pr. 15.00

Salt & pepper shakers, Little Red Riding Hood patt., medium, 4½" h., pr. 800.00

Salt & pepper shakers, Little Red Riding Hood patt., large, 5½" h., pr. ....125.00 to 150.00

Salt & pepper shakers, Sunglow patt., pink, No. 54, pr. 18.00

Spice jar, cov, "Cinnamon," Little Red Riding Hood patt. 675.00

Steak platter, House & Garden Serving Ware, w/well & tree...............25.00

Steins, Early Utility, Alpine drinking scene, No. 492, 6¼" h., set of 5.......125.00

String holder, Little Red Riding Hood patt., 9" h. 2,550.00

Sugar bowl, cov., Cinderella Kitchenware, Blossom patt., No. 27-4½", 4½" h. 22.00

Sugar bowl, cov., Crescent Kitchenware, pink & maroon, No. B14, 4½" h. 12.00

Little Red Riding Hood Sugar Bowl

Sugar bowl, open, crawling figure, Little Red Riding Hood patt. (ILLUS.) 215.00

Teapot, cov., Butterfly patt., No. B18....95.00

Teapot, cov., Dogwood patt., No. 507-6½", 6½" h. 185.00

Teapot, cov., Ebb Tide patt., No. E-14..80.00

Teapot, cov., House 'n Garden Ware ...17.50

Little Red Riding Hood Teapot

Teapot, cov., Little Red Riding Hood patt., 8" h. (ILLUS.) ....300.00 to 350.00

Teapot, cov., Serenade patt., pink, No. S17 ....110.00

Tea set: cov. teapot, creamer & cov. sugar bowl; Ebb Tide patt., 3 pcs. ...135.00

Tea set: cov. teapot, creamer & cov. sugar bowl; Magnolia Matte patt., yellow & brown, 3 pcs. 250.00

Tea set: cov. teapot, creamer & cov. sugar bowl; Serenade patt., pink glaze, 3 pcs. 275.00

Tea set: cov. teapot, creamer & cov. sugar bowl; Water Lily patt., 3 pcs. 145.00

Vase, 5" h., Calla Lily patt., chocolate brown, No. 530/33-5" 58.00

Vase, 5½" h., Water Lily patt., brown, No. L-2-5½" 40.00

Vase, 6" h., Calla Lily patt., No. 504-6" 70.00

Vase, 6" h., suspended-type, Sueno Tulip patt., blue, No. 100-33-6" 120.00

Vase, 6¼" h., two-handled, Magnolia Matte patt., No. 4-6¼" 40.00

Bow-Knot Vase

Vase, 6½" h., Bow-Knot patt., pink & blue, No. B-3-6½" (ILLUS.) 95.00

Vase, 6½" h., Parchment & Pine patt., green, No. S-1 ....15.00

Vase, 6½" h., Water Lily patt., No. L-4-6½" 40.00

Vase, 7" h., twin fish, Ebb Tide patt., green & pink, No. E-2-7" 55.00

Vase, 8" h., Sunglow patt., No. 94-8" ...30.00

Vase, double bud, 8" h., Woodland Gloss patt., No. W15-8" 62.00

Vase, 8½" h., Bow-Knot patt., No. B-7-8½" 97.00

Vase, 8½" h., Bow-Knot patt., blue & pink, No. B-8-8½" 145.00

Vase, 8½" h., Dogwood patt., blue & pink, No. 503-8½" 90.00

Vase, 8½" h., two-handled, Magnolia Matte patt., pink & blue, No. 3-8½" 50.00

Vase, 8½" h., Magnolia Matte patt., pink & blue, No. 7-8½" 115.00

Vase, 8½" h., Morning Glory patt., No. 61-8½" 200.00

Vase, 8½" h., Serenade patt., No. S-6 ....40.00

Vase, 8½" h., Tropicana patt., flat-sided, No. T53-8½" ....350.00 to 375.00

Vase, 8½" h., Water Lily patt., No. L-8-8½" 90.00

Vase, 8½" h., Wildflower patt., brown & cream, No. W-9-8½" 70.00

Vase, 9" h., Mardi Gras/Granada patt., pink & blue, No. 48-9" 48.00

Vase, 9½" h., Water Lily patt., No. L-10-9½" 100.00

Vase, 9½" h., Wildflower patt., No. W-12 ....100.00

Vase, 9½" h., Wildflower patt., No. W-13-9½" 135.00

Vase, 10" h., Orchid patt., No. 302-10" ....250.00 to 275.00

Vase, 10" h., Sueno Tulip patt., blue, No. 100-33-10" 150.00

Vase, 10½" h., Bow-Knot patt., pink & blue, No. 10-10½" 315.00

Vase, 10½" h., Butterfly patt., No. B14 ....52.00

Vase, 10½" h., Open Rose (Camelia) patt., pink & blue, No. 139-10½" 400.00

Vase, 10½" h., Serenade patt., yellow, No. S11 ....60.00

Vase, 10½" h., Water Lily patt., pink, No. L-13-10½" 115.00

Vase, 12" h., Tokay patt., No. 12 ....47.50

Vase, 12½" h., Bow-Knot patt., blue, No. B-14-12½" 1,165.00

Vase, 13" h., Calla Lily patt., No. 560\33-16" 285.00

Vase-candleholders, Continental patt., orange & gold, 10¼" h., pr. 60.00

Wall pocket, model of a sad iron, Bow-Knot patt., No. B-23, 6¼" h. ....175.00 to 200.00

Wall pocket, Bow-Knot patt., model of a whisk broom, blue, No. B-27-8", 8" h. 115.00

Wall pocket, Imperial line, model of a goose, pink & green, No. 67, 6½" h. ..35.00

Wall pocket, Poppy patt., No. 609-9", 9" h. 230.00

Wall pocket, model of goose in flight, Novelty Line 30.00

Wall pocket, Woodland Gloss patt., No. W-13-7½", 7½" h. (ILLUS.) 55.00

Window box, Butterfly patt., glossy glaze, No. B-8, 4¾ x 12¾" 27.50

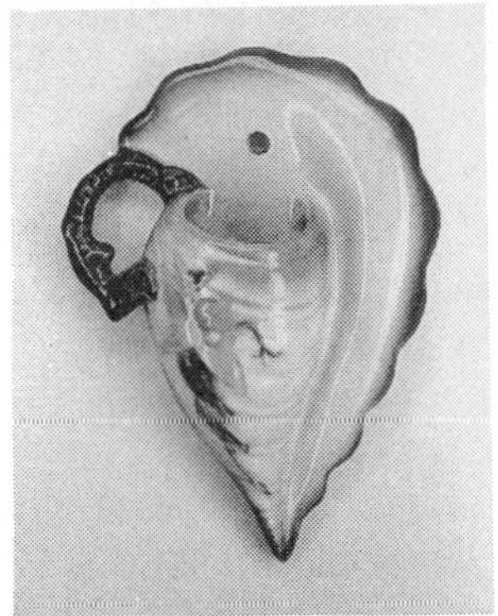

Woodland Gloss Wall Pocket

Window box, Dogwood patt., No. 508-10½" l. 105.00

Window box, Imperial line, "Fantasy," scalloped, glossy blue exterior, yellow interior, No. 153, 12½" l. 25.00

HUMMEL FIGURINES & COLLECTIBLES

"Boots"

The Goebel Company of Oeslau, Germany, first produced these porcelain figurines in 1934 having obtained the rights to adapt the beautiful pastel sketches of children by Sister Maria Innocentia (Berta) Hummel. Every design by the Goebel artisans was approved by the nun until her death in 1946. Though not antique, these figurines with the "M.I. Hummel" signature, especially those bearing the Goebel Company factory mark used from 1934 and into the early 1940s, are being sought by collectors though interest may have peaked some years ago.

Crown Mark

Full Bee Mark

Last Bee Mark

Accordion Boy, full bee mark, 1940-57, 5" h. $185.00

Accordion Boy, stylized bee mark, 1956-68, 5" h. 118.00

Accordion Boy, last bee mark, 1972-79, 5" h. 100.00

Adoration, crown mark, 1934-49, 6¼" h. ....600.00 to 750.00

Adoration, 1972-79, 6¼" h.................150.00

Adoration, 1956-68, 9" h.....................410.00

Angel Cloud font,1940-57, 2¼ x 4¾"..375.00

Angel Duet candleholder, 1940-57, 5" h. 250.00

Angel Duet candleholder, 1972-79, 5" h 105.00

Angelic Song, 1934-49, 4" h. 330.00

Angelic Song, 1940-57, 4" h..................................150.00 to 175.00

Angel Lights candleholder, 1972-79...185.00

Angel Serenade, 1934-49, 5½" h 460.00

Angel Shrine font, 1940-57, 3 x 5"........80.00

Angel with Accordion, 1956-68, 2¼" h...50.00

Angel with Trumpet, 1956-68, 2½" h...40.00

Apple Tree Boy, 1934-49, 4" h. 225.00

Apple Tree Boy, 1940-57, 4" h. 160.00

Apple Tree Boy, 1956-68, 4" h. 80.00

Apple Tree Boy, 1972-79, 4" h. 58.00

Apple Tree Boy, 1940-57, 6" h. 260.00

Apple Tree Boy, 1956-68, 6" h. 185.00

Apple Tree Boy, three line mark, 1963-71, 30" h. ....7,000.00 to 10.000.00

Apple Tree Boy, 1972-79, 6" h. 125.00

Apple Tree Girl, 1934-49, 4" h. 255.00

Apple Tree Girl, 1934-49, 6" h. 380.00

Apple Tree Girl, 1940-57, 6" h. 275.00

Apple Tree Girl, 1956-68, 6" h. 175.00

Apple Tree Girl, 1972-79, 10" h. 625.00

Apple Tree Girl table lamp, 1940-57, 7½" h. 360.00

Apple Tree Boy & Girl, 1956-68, 4" h., pr. 210.00

Artist (The), 1963-71, 5½" h. ....350.00 to 425.00

Artist (The), 1972-79, 5½" h. 130.00

Auf Wiedersehen, 1934-49, 5" h. 725.00

Auf Wiedersehen, 1956-68, 5" h. ....150.00 to 175.00

Auf Wiedersehen, 1956-68, 7" h. ....125.00 to 175.00

Auf Wiedersehen, 1972-79, 7" h. 170.00

Baker, 1934-49, 4¾" h. 315.00

Baker, 1956-68, 4¾" h. ....150.00 to 200.00

Baker, 1963-71, 4¾" h. 120.00

Baker, 1972-79, 4¾" h. 100.00

Barnyard Hero, 1940-57, 4" h. ....150.00 to 175.00

Barnyard Hero, 1956-68, 4" h. 110.00

Barnyard Hero, 1963-71, 5½" h. 170.00

Begging His Share, 1940-57, 5½" h. ....300.00 to 350.00

Begging His Share, w/candle hole, 1956-68, 5½" h. 185.00

Begging His Share, without candle hole,1956-68, 5½" h. 155.00

Begging His Share, 1972-79, 5½" h. ..115.00

Be Patient, 1940-57, 4¼" h. 190.00

Be Patient, 1956-68, 4¼" h. 175.00

Be Patient, 1963-71, 4¼" h. 150.00

Be Patient, 1940-57, 6¼" h. 300.00

Bird Duet, 1956-68, 4" h. 115.00

Bird Duet, 1972-79, 4" h. 96.00

Bird Watcher, 1972-79, 5" h. 105.00

Birthday Serenade, 1940-57, 4¼" h. ..345.00

Birthday Serenade, 1940-57, 5¼" h. ..300.00

Birthday Serenade, reverse mold, 1940-57, 5¼" h. ....550.00 to 650.00

Birthday Serenade table lamp, 1972-79, 7½" h. 215.00

Birthday Serenade table lamp, 1972-79, 9¾" h. 290.00

Blessed Event, 1963-71, 5½" h. 280.00

Blessed Event, 1972-79, 5½" h. 175.00

Book Worm, 1956-68, 4" h. 165.00

Book Worm, 1972-79, 4" h. 125.00

Book Worm, 1956-68, 8" h. ....750.00 to 850.00

Book Worm, 1972-79, 8" h. ....625.00 to 700.00

Book Worm book end, 1940-57, 5½" h. 300.00

Book Worm book end, 1956-68, 5½" h. 150.00

Book Worm book end, 1972-79, 5½" h. 120.00

Boots, 1934-49, 5½" h. (ILLUS.) ....375.00 to 475.00

Boots, 1940-57, 5½" h. 185.00

Boots, 1956-68, 5½" h. 115.00

Boots, 1972-79, 6½" h. 125.00

Boy with Horse, 1972 -79, 3½" h. 38.50

"Boy with Toothache"

Boy with Toothache, 1963-71, 5½" h. (ILLUS.) 130.00

Brother, 1956-68, 5½" h. 120.00

Brother, 1972-79, 5½" h. ....100.00 to 125.00

Carnival, 1963-71, 6" h. 165.00

Carnival, 1972-79, 6" h. 110.00

Celestial Musician, 1956-68, 7" h. 200.00

Celestial Musician, 1963-71, 7" h. 170.00

Chef, Hello, 1940-57, 6¼" h. ....225.00 to 275.00

Chef, Hello, 1956-68, 6¼" h. ....150.00 to 175.00

Chef, Hello, 1972-79, 6¼" h. 110.00

Chef, Hello, 1940-57, 7" h. 350.00

"Chick Girl"

Chick Girl, 1934-49, 3½" h. (ILLUS.) ....375.00 to 425.00

Child in Bed plaque, 1940-57, 2¾" d. 125.00

Chimney Sweep, 1956-68, 4" h. ....75.00 to 125.00

Chimney Sweep, 1934-49, 5½" h. 415.00

Chimney Sweep, 1956-68, 5½" h. 125.00

Christ Child, 1934-49, 2 x 6" 195.00

Christ Child, 1940-57, 2 x 6" 125.00

Christmas Angel, 1956-68 ....6,000.00

Cinderella, eyes open, 1972-79, 5½" h. ....750.00 to 775.00

Cinderella, eyes closed, 1972-79, 5½" h. 150.00

"Close Harmony"

Close Harmony, 1963-71, 5½" h. (ILLUS.) ....225.00 to 250.00

Confidentially, 1940-57, 5½" h. 5,000.00

Congratulations (no socks), 1940-57, 6" h. 220.00

Congratulations (w/socks), 1956-68, 6" h. 95.00

Congratulations (no socks), 1956-68, 6" h. 165.00

Congratulations (w/socks), 1972-79, 6" h. 100.00

"Congratulations"

Congratulations, 1934-49, 8¼" h. 6,500.00

Congratulations, 1956-68, 8¼" h. 3,900.00

Coquettes, 1940-57, 5" h. ...250.00 to 300.00

Coquettes, 1956-68, 5" h ...150.00 to 175.00

Crossroads, 1972-79, 6¾" h. 235.00

Culprits, 1956-68, 6¼" h. 200.00

Culprits, 1963-71, 6¼" h. ....225.00 to 250.00

Culprits, 1972-79, 6¼" h. 155.00

Culprits lamp base, 1963-71, 9½" h. ..170.00

Dealer display plaque, 1963-71, 4 x 5½" 250.00

Doctor, 1940-57, 4¾" h. 175.00

Doctor, 1956-68, 4¾" h. ......100.00 to 125.00

Doll Bath, 1963-71, 5" h. 165.00

Doll Bath, 1972-79, 5" h. 115.00

Doll Mother, 1940-57, 4¾" h. ....275.00 to 350.00

Doll Mother, 1972-79, 4¾" h. 120.00

Duet, 1940-57, 5" h. ....225.00 to 275.00

Duet, 1972-79, 5" h. 140.00

Eventide, 1940-57, 4¼ x 4¾" ....350.00 to 450.00

Eventide, 1956-68, 4¼ x 4¾" ....225.00 to 250.00

Eventide, 1972-79, 4½ x 4¾" 185.00

Farewell, 1956-68, 4¾" h. ...200.00 to 250.00

Farewell, 1972-79, 4¾" h. 130.00

Feeding Time, 1956-68, 4¼" h. 135.00

Feeding Time, 1963-71, 4¼" h. 125.00

Festival Harmony, w/mandolin, 1934-49, 11" h. 1,100.00

Flitting Butterfly plaque, 1940-57, 2½ x 2½"..125.00

Flower Madonna, white, 1940-57, 13" h................................250.00 to 300.00

For Father, 1956-68, 5½" h. 150.00

For Father, 1963-71, 5½" h. 135.00

For Mother, 1963-71, 5" h..................105.00

Friends, 1940-57, 10¾" h. 1,465.00

Globe Trotter, 1940-57,

5" h.................................225.00 to 250.00

Globe Trotter, 1972-79, 5" h. 110.00

Going to Grandma's, 1934-49 4¾" h...400.00

Going to Grandma's 1940-57, square base, 4¾" h. 300.00

Good Friends table lamp, 1972-79, 7½" h..195.00

Good Friends & She Loves Me, She Loves Me Not book ends, 1956-68,

5¼" h., pr. 210.00

Good Hunting, 1956-68, 5¼" h. 630.00

Good Shepherd, 1940-57, 6¼" h........195.00

Good Shepherd, 1940-57, 7½" h.....6,000.00

Goose Girl, 1956-68, 4¾" h. 145.00

Goose Girl, 1972-79, 4¾" h. 125.00

Goose Girl, 1972-79, 7½" h. 280.00

Guardian Angel font, 1934-49,

2½ x 5⅝," 1,300.00

"Happiness"

Happiness, 1956-68,4¾" h. (ILLUS.) 92.00

Happy Days, 1940-57, 4¼" h.............210.00

Happy Days, 1972-79, 4¼" h................83.00

Happy Days, 1972-79, 6" h................255.00

Happy Days table lamp, 1972-79,

7¾" h..............................200.00 to 250.00

Happy Days table lamp, 1940-57, 9¾" h...700.00

Happy Pastime candy box, 1956-68, 6" h. 125.00

Hear Ye, Hear Ye, 1940-57, 5" h.................................175.00 to 200.00

Hear Ye, Hear Ye, 1972-79, 5" h.................................100.00 to 125.00

Heavenly Song candleholder, 1934-49, 3½ x 4¾"........................7,000.00

Herald Angels candleholder, 1934-49, 2¼ x 4".............................495.00

Herald Angels candleholder, 1940-57, 2¼ x 4".............................175.00

"Home From Market"

Home From Market, 1940-57, 5¾" h. (ILLUS.) 265.00

Joyful ashtray, 1940-57, 3½ x 6"..205.00

Joyous News, 1934-49, 4¼ x 4¾"...1,750.00

Joyous News, Angel w/accordion

candleholder, 1940-57, 2¾" h. 120.00

Joyous News, Angel w/accordion candleholder, 1956-68, 2¾" h. 32.00

Just Resting, 1963-71, 4" h. 105.00

Just Resting, 1963-71, 5" h. 145.00

Just Resting table lamp, 1972-79, 9½" h...225.00

Latest News, 1940-57, inscribed "Panama American," 5¼" h...........1,500.00

Latest News, 1956-68, inscribed "Munchener Presse", 5¼" h. 210.00

Let's Sing ashtray, 1940-57,

3½ x 6¾"..435.00

Let's Sing candy box, 1956-68, 6" h...125.00

Letter to Santa Claus, 1963-71, 7" h...350.00

Little Band candleholder, 1972-79 3 x 4¾"...145.00

Little Bookkeeper, 1963-71, 4¾" h. 185.00

Little Bookkeeper, 1972-79, 4¾" h. 125.00

Little Cellist, 1934-49, 6" h..................................400.00 to 450.00

Little Cellist, 1940-57, 6" h.................220.00

Little Cellist, 1956-68, 6" h.................145.00

Little Cellist, 1963-71, 6" h.................135.00

Little Drummer, 1972-79, 4¼" h............82.50

Little Fiddler, 1934-49, 4¾" h..............330.00

Little Fiddler, 1963-71, 4¾" h.............175.00

Little Fiddler, 1956-68, 10¾" h...........850.00

Little Fiddler, 1972-79, 12¼" h...........750.00

Little Fiddler plaque, 1972-79, 4½ x 5"...120.00

Little Fiddler plaque, 1956-68, 4¾ x 5⅛"...115.00

Little Gabriel, 1940-57, 5" h...............165.00

Little Gabriel, 1934-49, 6" h.............................2,000.00 to 3,000.00

Little Gardener, 1934-49, 5" h. 200.00

Little Goat Herder, 1956-68, 4½" h.....130.00

Little Goat Herder, 1963-71, 4¾" h.....110.00

Little Goat Herder, 1956-68, 5½" h.....160.00

Little Goat Herder, 1963-71, 5½" h.....140.00

Little Guardian, 1956-68, 4" h............100.00

Little Hiker, 1940-57, 4¼" h. 110.00

Little Pharmacist, 1963-71, 6" h..........265.00

Little Scholar, 1940-57, 5½" h. 200.00

Little Scholar, 1956-68, 5½" h. 130.00

Little Sweeper, 1956-68, 4½" h. 90.00

Lost Sheep, 1963-71, 4½" h.................85.00

Lost Sheep, 1956-68, 5½" h..............150.00

Lost Sheep, 1963-71, 5½" h.................95.00

Lullaby candleholder, 1972-79 6 x 8" (ILLUS. top next column).......230.00

Madonna, seated, brown cloak, 1940-57, 12" h. 9,500.00

The Mail is Here, 1963-71, 4¼ x 6"....360.00

March Winds, 1972-79, 5" h. 88.00

Max & Moritz, 1940-57, 5" h. 240.00

"Lullaby" Candleholder

"Meditation"

Meditation, 1972-79, 4¼" h. (ILLUS.) ...70.00

Meditation, 1956-68, 5¼" h................110.00

Meditation, 1972-79, 5" h...................110.00

Merry Wanderer, 1956-68, 4¾" h. 115.00

Merry Wanderer, 1956-68, 6¼" h. 135.00

Merry Wanderer plaque, 1956-68, 4¾ x 5⅛"..110.00

Mischief Maker, 1972-79, 5" h. 115.00

Mother's Helper, 1956-68, 5" h...........145.00

Mother's Helper, 1963-71, 5" h...........120.00

Mountaineer, 1963-71, 5" h. 160.00

Mountaineer, 1972-79, 5" h. 97.00

Nativity set, 1972-79, 12 pcs. 950.00

Not for You, 1963-71, 6" h. 150.00

Out of Danger, 1956-68, 6¼" h. (ILLUS. top next column) 220.00

Out of Danger table lamp, 1963-71, 9½" h...225.00

Photographer, 1972-79, 5¼" h. 125.00

"Out of Danger"

Playmates, 1940-57, 4" h. 165.00

Playmates, 1956-68, 4" h. ..100.00 to 125.00

Playmates candy box, 1972-79, 6¼" h. 115.00

Prayer Before Battle, 1956-68, 4¼" h. 115.00

"Puppy Love"

Puppy Love, 1956-68, 5" h. (ILLUS.) 200.00

Retreat to Safety, 1972-79, 4" h. 80.00

Retreat to Safety, 1934-49, 5½" h. 575.00

"Retreat to Safety"

Retreat to Safety,1940-57, 5½" h. (ILLUS.) ....$350.00 to 400.00

Retreat to Safety plaque, 1972-79, 4¾ x 5" 110.00

"Ring Around the Rosie"

Ring Around the Rosie, 1956-68, 6¾" h. (ILLUS.) ....2,500.00 to 3,000.00

School Boy, 1940-57, 4" h. 130.00

School Boy, 1956-68, 5½" h. 116.00

"School Boys"

School Boys, 1963-71, 7½" h. (ILLUS.) ....775.00 to 850.00

"School Girl"

School Girl, 1956-68, 4¼" h. (ILLUS.) 110.00

School Girl, 1972-79, 4¼" h..................70.00

"School Girls"

School Girls, 1956-68, 7½" h. (ILLUS.) ....750.00 to 850.00

Sensitive Hunter, 1972-79, 5½" h. ....100.00 to 125.00

Sensitive Hunter, 1940-57, 7½" h. 610.00

Sensitive Hunter, 1972-79, 7½" h. 185.00

"Serenade"

Serenade, 1934-49, 4¾" h. (ILLUS.) 280.00

She Loves Me, 1963-71, 4¼" h. 115.00

She Loves Me table lamp, 1956-68, 7½" h...240.00

Shepherd's Boy, 1956-68, oversized 130.00

Signs of Spring, 1972-79, 4" h.............90.00

Signs of Spring, 1956-68 5½" h. ....175.00 to 225.00

Signs of Spring, 1963-71, 5½" h.........135.00

Signs of Spring, 1972-79, 5½" h.........145.00

Silent Night candleholder, w/black child at left, 1940-57, 5½" l., 4¾" h...9,000.00

Silent Night candleholder, 1963-71, 5½" l., 4¾" h....................................180.00

"Singing Lesson"

Singing Lesson, 1940-57, 2¾" h. (ILLUS.) ....125.00 to 150.00

Singing Lesson candy box, 1956-68, 5¼" h..125.00

Sister, 1940-57, 5½" h.......................140.00

"Sister"

Sister, 1956-68, 5½" h. (ILLUS.) 135.00

Smiling Through plaque,1972-79, 5¾" d. 82.00

Spring Cheer, 1956-68, 5" h..................180.00

Spring Cheer, 1963-71, 5" h...100.00 to 125.00

Spring Cheer, 1972-79, 5" h...125.00 to 175.00

"Star Gazer"

Star Gazer, 1963-71, 4¾" h. 135.00

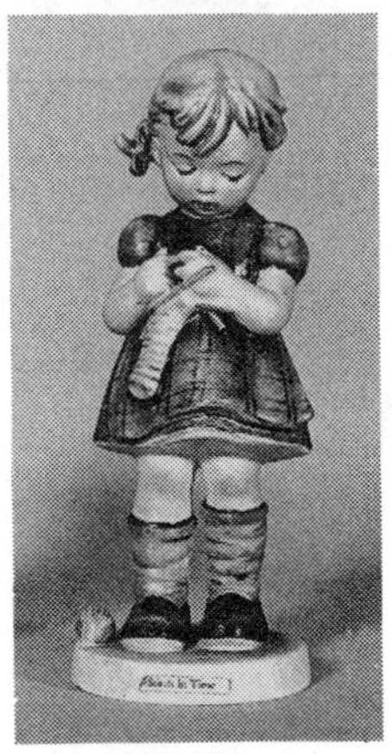

"Stitch in Time"

Stitch in Time, 1956-68, 6¾" h. (ILLUS.) 190.00

Street Singer, 1972-79, 5" h. .... 100.00 to 125.00

Strolling Along, 1956-68, 4¾" h. 150.00

Surprise, 1934-49, 4¼" h. 385.00

Surprise, 1940-57, 4¼" h. 155.00

Surprise, 1940-57, 5½" h. 250.00

Surprise, 1956-68, 5½" h. ... 150.00 to 175.00

Surprise, 1972-79, 5½" h. 125.00

Sweet Music, 1972-79, 5¼" h. 115.00

Telling Her Secret, 1940-57, 5¼" h. .... 300.00 to 350.00

Telling Her Secret, 1963-71, 5¼" h. (ILLUS. top next column) 165.00

To Market, 1940-57, 5½" h. 250.00

"Telling Her Secret"

Trumpet Boy, 1956-68, 4¾" h. 110.00

Tuneful Goodnight plaque, 1956-68, 4¾ x 5" 200.00

Umbrella Boy, 1956-68, 4¾" h. 475.00

Umbrella Boy, 1972-79, 4¾" h. 260.00

"Umbrella Boy" & "Umbrella Girl"

Umbrella Boy & Umbrella Girl, 1956-68, 4¾" h., pr. (ILLUS.) 900.00

Umbrella Girl, 1963-71, 4¾" h. .... 350.00 to 400.00

Valentine Gift, 1972-79, 5¾" h. 380.00

Valentine Joy, 1972-79, 5¼" h. 160.00

Village Boy, 1934-49, 4" h. 175.00

Village Boy, 1956-68, 5" h. 80.00

Village Boy, 1963-71, 5" h. 68.00

Village Boy, 1972-79, 5" h. 62.00

Village Boy, 1934-49, 6" h. .... 325.00 to 375.00

Village Boy, 1972-79, 7¼" h. .... 150.00 to 175.00

Visiting an Invalid, 1972-79, 5" h. 105.00

Volunteers, 1940-57, 5" h. 285.00

Waiter, 1972-79, 7" h. 145.00

Wall vase, Boy, 1956-68, 4½ x 6¼" 190.00

Wall vase, Girl, 1956-68, 4½ x 6¼" 190.00

Wash Day, 1963-71, 5¾" h.................165.00

"Wash Day"

Wash Day, 1972-79, 5¾" h. (ILLUS.) 125.00

Wayside Devotion, 1940-57, 7½" h................................400.00 to 475.00

Wayside Harmony, 1963-71, 3¾" h......96.00

Wayside Harmony, 1956-68, 5" h.......150.00

Wayside Harmony, 1972-79, 5" h.......140.00

Wayside Harmony lamp, 1963-71, 7½" h..210.00

Wayside Harmony lamp,1972-79, 9½" h..225.00

Weary Wanderer, 1956-68, 6" h.........155.00

Weary Wanderer, 1972-79, 6" h.........105.00

We Congratulate, 1940-57, 4" h.........265.00

We Congratulate, 1963-71, 4" h..........88.00

"Which Hand?"

Which Hand?, 1963-71, 5¼" h. (ILLUS.) 130.00

"Whitsuntide"

Whitsuntide, 1934-49, 7¼" h. (ILLUS.) 1,050.00

Whitsuntide, 1972-79, 7¼" h. 170.00

IMARI

Imari Charger

This is a multicolor ware that originated in Japan, was copied by the Chinese, and imitated by the English and European potteries. It was decorated in overglaze enamel and underglaze-blue. Made in Hizen Province and Arita, much of it was exported through the port of Imari in Japan. Imari often has brocade patterns.

Beaker-vase, panels of cranes & bamboo on a ground filled w/peony blossoms & chrysanthemums, 18th c., 12" h...........$1,500.00 to 2,200.00

Bottle, bulbous form w/elongated neck painted w/underglaze-blue peony sprays, 18th c., 13" h. (base cracked) ....3,000.00 to 4,000.00

Bottle-vase, bulbous w/long cylindrical neck, profusely decorated w/fan shapes & medallions on a floral ground, late 19th c., 15" h..........................2,000.00 to 3,000.00

Bowl, 4½" d., Kakiemon-style, exterior in underglaze-blue w/pine, prunus & birds, 18th c. ....600.00 to 800.00

Bowl, 7" d., Kenjo, molded chrysanthemum in center, the interior & exterior w/petals decorated w/repetitive patterns, late 18th c., 7" d...............2,500.00 to 3,500.00

Bowl, 7½" d., crane & curling wave design, late 19th c.............75.00 to 100.00

Bowl, 8" d., landscape in center surrounded by dragons & flowers, late 19th c. ....200.00 to 300.00

Charger, three-color & gilt decoration w/passion flower in center surrounded by birds & baskets, early 20th c., 15½" d................300.00 to 400.00

Charger, underglaze-blue birds, iris & peony sprays, ca. 1900, 16" d................................150.00 to 225.00

Charger, underglaze-blue, red & gilt, the panels w/figures & carp, exotic birds & other mythical beasts, the underside painted w/underglaze-blue foliate scrolls, late 19th c., 24½" d. (ILLUS.) 2,090.00

Dish, scallop shell-form w/flower cart design, ca. 1900, 6½" l. ...125.00 to 150.00

Dish, fish-form, three-color, ca. 1900, 10" l................................400.00 to 600.00

Plate, 8½" d., paulownia in center surrounded by hydrangea, late 19th c. ....50.00 to 75.00

Plate, 9" d., designs of birds & flowers in a mountainscape, late 19th - early 20th c. ....100.00 to 150.00

Stemcup, dove & ribbon design, late 19th c., 6" d., 5" h............100.00 to 150.00

Vase, cov., 17" h., ovoid form boldly painted in underglaze-blue w/phoenix & flowers, late 17th c. (damaged) ....1,375.00 to 1,700.00

IRONSTONE

The first successful ironstone was patented in 1813 by C.J. Mason in England. The body contains iron slag incorporated with the clay. Other potters imitated Mason's ware and today much hard, thick ware is lumped under the term ironstone. Earlier it was called by various names, including graniteware. Both plain white and decorated wares were made throughout the 19th century. Tea Leaf Lustre ironstone was made by several firms.

Turner's Patent Bowl

GENERAL

Bowl, 11" d., deep rounded & slightly flaring sides on a thick footring, decorated in the 'Japan' patt., painted in underglaze-blue, iron-red, green, brown, yellow, rose & gold around the exterior w/sprays of stylized Oriental flowers & scrolling foliage, decorated on the interior w/a central Kakiemon-style chrysanthemum & wheat sheaf design beneath a wide underglaze-blue border patterned w/gilt diaperwork & reserved w/four trefoils of flowering plants, printed "Turner's Patent" mark, early 19th c., gilt wear on edge (ILLUS.) $1,840.00

Creamer, bulbous paneled base & tall paneled & flaring neck, "gaudy" Imari-style decoration, molded serpent handle, marked "Mason's Patent Ironstone," ca. 1850 (wear)..148.50

Cup & saucer, handleless, miniature, paneled sides, "gaudy" Urn patt. in polychrome, mid-19th c................231.00

Cup & saucer, handleless "gaudy" Seeing Eye patt. 165.00

Cup & saucer, handleless, paneled sides, "gaudy" decoration of an urn & blossoms in underglaze-blue trimmed w/polychrome enamel & lustre, ca. 1850 ....192.50

Cup plate, "gaudy" Urn patt. 375.00

Garden seats, hexagonal, Canton-style, each w/a celadon ground printed in black & enameled in shades of pink, green, yellow, white, grey & black w/birds & insects amid a profusion of chrysanthemum sprigs, peaches, pomegranates & peonies between wide borders of blue & white key-fretwork superimposed w/further pink, white, yellow & turquoise blossoms & scrolling foliage & edged w/worn gilt molded bosses, the top w/a pink & white Greek key border & pierced in the center w/a gilt-edged 'cracked-ice and prunus' patterned 'cash medallion,' the sides w/similarly pierced & decorated double 'cash medallions,' probably by G. L. Ashworth & Bros., late 19th c., 18 13/16" h., pr. (enamel chipping) 2,875.00

Gravy tureen, cov., two-handled, footed, paneled sides, red, blue & copper lustre decoration, 7" h. (minor stains) 104.50

Mug, paneled cylindrical sides w/flaring base & molded serpent handle, "gaudy" Imari-style floral decoration w/pink lustre trim, marked "Ironstone China," mid-19th c., 3 7/8" h. 269.00

Plate, 8¼" w., ten-sided, "gaudy" floral decoration 165.00

Plate, 8⅜" w., 12-sided, "gaudy" decoration of colorful blossoms & large underglaze-blue leaves w/lustre trim, impressed "Ironstone," ca. 1850 (wear)...............................115.00

Plate, 8⅜" w., 12-sided, "gaudy" Morning Glory patt., underglaze-blue w/lustre trim, ca. 1850......................104.00

Plate, 8½" d., "gaudy" floral design in underglaze-blue w/polychrome enamel & lustre, impressed registry mark & "E. Walley, Niagara shape"..126.50

Plate, 8½" w., paneled sides, "gaudy" Strawberry patt., underglaze-blue w/polychrome & lustre trim, ca. 1850 (wear, chip on footring) 148.50

Plate, 8⅝" d., free-hand blue Morning Glory patt., mid-19th c. (wear) 104.50

Plate, 8¾" w., paneled sides, "gaudy" cornucopias & flowers decoration in underglaze-blue w/red & green & lustre trim, impressed "T. Walker," ca. 1850 (flakes)................203.50

Plate, 8¾" w., paneled sides, "gaudy" stylized tulip & berry cluster in the center w/three similar clusters on the border, underglaze-blue trimmed w/red, green & black (stains) 148.50

Plate, 8¾" d., polychrome transfer scene of rural England, blue rim, marked "Pratt & Co., Fenton" (rim worn)..27.50

Plate, 8⅞" d., "gaudy" urn decoration in underglaze-blue & polychrome enamel, lustre trim (wear & flaking) 192.50

Plate, 9" d., "gaudy" grapevine decoration in underglaze-blue trimmed w/red & green & gold lustre, ca. 1860 ....115.50

Japan Pattern Dinner Plate

Plates, dinner, 10 3/16" to 10 5/16" d., 'Japan' patt., painted in an Imari palette of underglaze-blue, iron-red, salmon, yellow & gilding w/a vase of flowers on a balustraded terrace within an elaborate border of *ruyi*-shaped floral lappets alternating w/three roundels of birds interrupting foliate scrolls & 'clouds' on the fluted rim, two w/a chip & another w/a riveted crack, G.L. Ashworth & Bros., impressed "REAL IRONSTONE CHINA" marks, Royal Arms & "IRONSTONE CHINA" above the retailer's mark of Higginbotham Grafton St. Dublin & letter "P" printed in maroon, 1965-75, set of 11 (ILLUS. of one) 1,380.00

Platter, 16" w., 20½" l., transfer-printed w/an architectural & figural landscape in an Imari palette, Mason's, early 19th c.......................495.00

Punch bowl on collared base, Lily of the Valley patt., all-white, marked "W.E. Corn," 8" d., 6" h. 150.00

Punch bowl, deep rounded sides raised on a thick footring, transfer-printed design in black & enameled in a *famille rose* palette of pink, green, yellow, iron-red, blue, turquoise, white & gold on the exterior w/three scenes of five

Mason's Punch Bowl

Chinese figures in a garden within pink-diapered unfurled scrolls reserved on a black whorl-patterned ground embellished w/large blossoms & leaves, the interior w/a larger version of the same scene similarly reserved on a flowered whorl ground further reserved w/three panels of precious objects near the orange lustre trimmed edge, marked w/Mason's crowned "PATENT IRONSTONE CHINA" banner in black & green, ca. 1820, interior crackled & worn, rim cracked, 13⅜" d. (ILLUS.)................460.00

Sugar bowl, cov., transfer-printed blue Canton-style Oriental decoration, Mason's, 6" d., 5¾" h. 60.00

Syrup pitcher, cov., h.p. pale apricot wild rose & foliage, white body, ornate pewter top, Knowles, Taylor, Knowles mark 95.00

Teapot, cov., transfer-printed blue Canton-style Oriental decoration, Mason's, 19th c., 9½" d., 6" h. (minor nick inside rim, minor spout roughness) 80.00

Toddy plate, Franklin Maxim, farm scene w/"Make Hay While the Sun Shines..." around the edge, black transfer w/polychrome enamel, molded floral & wheat border w/green rim stripe, Alfred Meakin, 5⅜" d...88.00

Toddy plate, central black transfer-printed scene of a monkey & cat entitled "Take your time Miss Lucy" within a molded hops border w/red stripe, Alfred Meakin, 6" d...............104.50

Tureens, covers & undertrays, hexagonal, each piece decorated in underglaze-blue, iron-red, green, turquoise, yellow & gold w/stylized Oriental flowers repeated as borders on the orange lustre-edged scalloped & barbed rims, the handles formed as underglaze-blue & gilt dragons' heads & scrolls & on the cover finial molded as a floral

Large Mason's Tureen

sprig, the undertrays impressed "MASON'S PATENT IRONSTONE CHINA," ca. 1820-25, reglued chip on one undertray, small chip on one handle, one finial w/small chip, undertray 11¾" w., 11

Vase, cov., 30½" h., octagonal baluster-form w/gilt-trimmed yellow dragon-scroll handles at the sides of the neck & similarly decorated double-dolphin knop finial, each part transfer-printed in underglaze-blue & decorated in yellow & gold w/overall rococo scrolling foliage & patterned panels surrounding on the front & back of the vase an urn of lilies on a pedestal, all against a bright blue ground, the rims gilt-edged, marked w/a pattern number "5742," ca. 1835-50 (knop finial repaired, gilt wear)..2,013.00

Staffordshire Gilt-decorated Covered Vase

Vases, cov., 26⅝" h., quadrangular baluster-form, cobalt blue ground decorated in gilding on the front & sides w/Oriental flowering shrubbery & on the reverse w/butterflies, the cover similarly decorated, the dragon handles on the sides of the neck & the seated kylin knop on the cover (one w/small chips) washed in gilding, the rim (one w/a chip on a back corner) & footrim (worn) w/wide gilt borders (some chips on the interior rims), Staffordshire, possibly Mason's, 1820-30, pr. (ILLUS. of one) 2,875.00

Vegetable bowl, cov., shallow oval flaring bowl on a scalloped flaring raised foot, the domed cover w/a loop handle, Victoria patt., brown transfer-printed design w/polychrome & gilt trim, 19th c., 11½" l. 93.50

TEA LEAF IRONSTONE

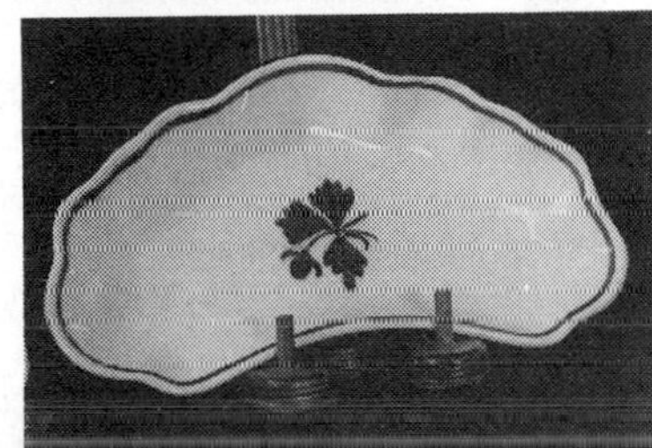

Tea Leaf Crescent-Shaped Bone Dish

Apple bowl, footed, Alfred Meakin......450.00

Baker, oval, Lily of the Valley patt., Anthony Shaw, 9" l............................60.00

Baker, rectangular, Mellor, Taylor & Co., 7 x 9½", 2½" h. 40.00

Bone dish, crescent-shaped, Red Cliff, ca. 1960s 45.00

Bone dish, scalloped rim, Anthony Shaw 70.00

Bone dishes, scalloped crescent shape, Alfred Meakin, set of 3 (ILLUS. of one) 90.00

Bowl, serving, 10" w. hexagonal, Anthony Shaw...................................95.00

Brush box, cov., oblong, Lily of the Valley patt., Anthony Shaw.............725.00

Brush box, cov., oblong, Red Cliff, ca. 1960s 135.00

Butter dish, cov., rectangular, Iona patt., gold lustre, Powell & Bishop 50.00

Butter dish, cover & liner, Fish Hook patt., Alfred Meakin, 3 pcs. 80.00

Butter dish, cover & liner, Iona patt., gold lustre, Powell & Bishop, 3 pcs. 100.00

Cake plate, handled, square, Daisy patt., Arthur Wilkinson......................120.00

Cake plate, round, scroll-embossed handles, Thomas Furnival & Sons.....90.00

Cake plate, open-handled, square on square pedestal base, Red Cliff, ca. 1960s 150.00

Cake stand, Edge Malkin...................250.00

Canister, cov., footed spherical body, Kitchen Kraft line, Homer Laughlin, ca. 1930s 7½" d. 60.00

Casserole, cov., round w/flanged rim, inset slightly domed cover w/recessed knob finial, Kitchen Kraft line, Homer Laughlin, ca. 1930s 55.00

Chamber pot, cov., Llon's Head patt.,Mellor, Taylor & Co. (cover hairline) 175.00

Chamber pot, cov., Square Ridged patt., Mellor, Taylor & Co. 155.00

Coffeepot, cov., Bamboo patt., Alfred Meakin 110.00

Coffeepot, cov., Plain Round shape, W. & W. Corn 200.00

Coffeepot, cov., 9" h., Plain Round shape, Alfred Meakin 185.00

Coffeepot, cov., Simple Square patt., Wedgwood & Co. 80.00

Compote, open, 10" d., Henry Burgess..160.00

Compote, open, 10" w., square shallow bowl on square pedestal w/squared domed base, Alfred Meakin 300.00

Compote, open, 10" w., Square Ridged patt., Henry Burgess..............90.00

Creamer, child's, Mellor, Taylor & Co...95.00

Creamer, demitasse size, Empress patt., Micratex by Adams, ca. 1960s 120.00

Creamer, Basketweave patt., Anthony Shaw 130.00

Creamer, Chelsea patt., Johnson Bros. 140.00

Creamer, Fish Hook patt.,Alfred Meakin (ILLUS.) 60.00

Creamer, square tapering shape, East End Pottery 65.00

Creamer, square, Arthur Wilkinson 120.00

Tea Leaf Fish Hook Creamer

Creamer, Square Ridged patt., Wedgwood & Co., 6" h....................150.00

Creamer & cov. sugar bowl, Square Ridged patt., Red Cliff, ca. 1960s......95.00

Cup & saucer, child's, Lily of the Valley patt., Anthony Shaw (slight flake on saucer base rim) 350.00

Cup & saucer, demitasse, handled, Empress patt., Micratex by Adams, ca. 1960s 55.00

Cups & saucers, gold lustre, Powell & Bishop, set of 4 ....80.00

Cups & saucers, handled, cone-shaped cups, gold lustre, large size, Powell & Bishop, set of 6................130.00

Cup plates, Anthony Shaw, set of 3..120.00

Dish, Square Ridged patt., Arthur Wilkinson, 19" w................................55.00

Doughnut stand, round, pedestal base, Anthony Shaw........................185.00

Gravy boat, Chelsea patt., Johnson Bros. 55.00

Gravy boat, Chelsea patt., Alfred Meakin 60.00

Gravy boat, Daisy patt., Arthur Wilkinson 45.00

Tea Leaf Fish Hook Gravy Boat

Gravy boat, Fish Hook patt., Alfred Meakin (ILLUS.) 60.00

Gravy boat, oval body, Mayer China Co., Beaver Falls, Pennsylvania........25.00

Gravy boat & undertray, Bamboo patt., Alfred Meakin, 2 pcs. (slight wear)..65.00

Ladle, sauce, gold lustre, Powell & Bishop 100.00

Mixing bowl, Kitchen Kraft line, Homer Laughlin, ca. 1930s, 8¾" d. 45.00

Mush bowl, footed, Alfred Meakin 70.00

Pitcher, 7" h., Bamboo patt., Alfred Meakin..................................130.00

Pitcher, 7" h., embossed design, Cartwright Bros. 60.00

Pitcher, hot water, Edge Malkin (rim flake) 525.00

Plate, 6" d., Wilkinson.............................5.00

Plate, 8" sq., Alfred Meakin 45.00

Plate, 9" d., Alfred Meakin 10.00

Plates, child's, Knowles, Taylor & Knowles, set of 3 ....100.00

Plates, child's, Mellor, Taylor & Co., set of 5 ....190.00

Platter, 11" l., rectangular, Alfred Meakin 15.00

Platter, 10 x 14", rectangular, Wedgwood & Co...............................40.00

Platter, 10½ x 14½", rectangular. Anthony Shaw..................................35.00

Platter, 16" oval, Lily of the Valley patt., Anthony Shaw...........................80.00

Posset cup, footed, Lily of the Valley patt., Anthony Shaw.............400.00

Punch bowl, footed, Alfred Meakin (hairlines) 600.00

Punch bowl, deep rounded bowl on low domed base, Anthony Shaw 537.50

Relish dish, mitten-shaped, Cable patt., Thomas Furnival & Sons 50.00

Relish dish, rectangular, handled, Fish Hook patt., Alfred Meakin...........20.00

Relish dish, rectangular, Square Ridged patt., Wedgwood & Co. 60.00

Salt & pepper shakers, Empress patt., Micratex by Adams, ca. 1960s, pr. ..250.00

Salt & pepper shakers, footed spherical body, Kitchen Kraft line by Homer Laughlin, ca. 1930s, pr...........70.00

Sauce dishes, square scalloped shape, Anthony Shaw, set of 4 ....60.00

Sauce tureen, cover & ladle, Bullet

patt., Anthony Shaw, 3 pcs. (leg nick) 250.00

Sauce tureen, cover, undertray &ladle, Bamboo patt., Alfred Meakin, the set 325.00

Tea Leaf Chinese Shaving Mug

Shaving mug, Chinese patt., Anthony Shaw (ILLUS.) 150.00

Shaving mug, Lily of the Valley patt., Anthony Shaw....................215.00

Soap dish, cov., Victory (Dolphin) patt., John Edwards 155.00

Soap dish, cover & liner, Square Ridged patt., Mellor, Taylor & Co., 3 pcs. (manufacturer's defect) 110.00

Soup plate, child's, Lily of the Valley patt., Anthony Shaw....................100.00

Soup plates w/flanged rims, Alfred Meakin, set of 6 ....120.00

Soup plates w/flanged rims, Red Cliff, ca. 1960s, set of 6 ....160.00

Soup tureen, cover, ladle & undertray, gold lustre, Henry Burgess, 3 pcs....450.00

Sugar bowl, cov., child's, Knowles, Taylor & Knowles 110.00

Sugar bowl, cov., demitasse size, Empress patt., Micratex by Adams, ca. 1960s 50.00

Sugar bowl, cov., Bamboo patt., Alfred Meakin....................65.00

Sugar bowl, cov., Empress patt., Micratex by Adams, ca. 1960s...........50.00

Sugar bowl, cov., Fish Hook patt., Alfred Meakin....................60.00

Sugar bowl, cov., Simple Square patt., Wedgwood & Co....................90.00

Sugar bowl, cov., Simple Square patt., Arthur Wilkinson....................80.00

Sugar bowl, cov., Square Ridged patt., Henry Burgess 110.00

Teapot, cov., child's, Knowles, Taylor & Knowles....................60.00

Teapot, cov., Cable patt., Anthony Shaw 165.00

Teapot, cov., Chinese patt., Anthony Shaw 425.00

Teapot, cov., Fish Hook patt., Alfred Meakin, small 100.00

Teapot. cov., Simple Square patt., Wedgwood & Co 120.00

Tea Leaf Toothbrush Holder

Toothbrush holder, upright square footed form, Anthony Shaw (ILLUS.) 200.00

Tureen, cover, underplate & ladle, Iona patt., gold lustre, Powell & Bishop, the set 90.00

Vegetable dish, cov., Iona patt., gold lustre, Powell & Bishop, 6¾" l. 90.00

Vegetable dish, cov., square, Iona patt., gold lustre, Powell & Bishop,7¼" w. 60.00

Vegetable dish, cov., Simple Square patt., gold lustre, Powell & Bishop, 8½" w. 45.00

Vegetable dish, cov., rectangular, Bamboo patt., Alfred Meakin, 9" l. 65.00

Vegetable dish, cov., round, pedestal foot, Cable patt., Anthony Shaw, 10" d....................170.00

Vegetable dish, cov., oblong, Chelsea patt., Alfred Meakin, 10" l. 130.00

Vegetable dish, cov., rectangular, Fish Hook patt., Alfred Meakin, 10" l. 95.00

Vegetable dish, cov., Gentle Square patt., Thomas Furnival & Sons, 10" l. 80.00

Vegetable dish, cov., oval, Lily of the Valley patt., Anthony Shaw, 10" l.....280.00

Vegetable dish, cov.,

Lion's Head patt., Mellor, Taylor & Co., 10" l. 80.00

Vegetable dish, cov., rectangular, ribbed base, Iona patt., gold lustre, Powell & Bishop, 11¼" l. 55.00

Vegetable dish, cov., rectangular, Fish Hook patt., Alfred Meakin, 12" l. 90.00

Vegetable dish, cov., rectangular, Square Ridged patt., Mellor, Taylor & Co., 12" l. 95.00

Vegetable dish, open, footed square ribbed shape w/handles, gold lustre, Powell & Bishop, 10" w. 20.00

Washbowl & pitcher set, Bamboo patt., Alfred Meakin, 2 pcs. (rim flakes on bowl) 275.00

Wash pitcher, Square Ridged patt., Bishop & Stonier 90.00

Waste bowl, child's, Mellor, Taylor & Co. 160.00

Waste bowl, ribbed base, Grindley & Co. 130.00

TEA LEAF VARIANTS

Bowl, serving, fluted, Teaberry patt., J. Clementson 230.00

Coffeepot, cov., Pepper Leaf patt. 200.00

Creamer, miniature, porcelain, Cloverleaf patt., gold lustre 45.00

Creamer, porcelain, footed ovoid body, Cloverleaf patt., gold lustre 30.00

Creamer, Gothic shape, Lustre Band decoration, Red Cliff, ca. 1960s 70.00

Creamer, high spout, Morning Glory patt., Elsmore & Forster (hairline) 220.00

Creamer, Gothic shape, Pinwheel patt., 6½" h. 150.00

Creamer, simple ovoid body, lustre trim on embossed handle scrolls, Teaberry patt., J. Clementson 475.00

Cups & saucers, handleless, Ceres patt., Lustre Band trim, Elsmore & Forster, two sets 140.00

Cup plate, Laurel Wreath patt., lustre trim, Elsmore & Forster 160.00

Cuspidor, Tobacco Leaf patt., Elsmore & Forster (professional rim repair) 525.00

Egg cup, porcelain, Cloverleaf patt., gold lustre, Three Crown China 40.00

Egg cup, Teaberry patt. 475.00

Pitcher, 8" h., ovoid body, angled handle, Pepper Leaf patt. 140.00

Pitcher, 9" h., Morning Glory patt., Elsmore & Forster (spout flake) 290.00

Platter, 10 x 14" oval, Teaberry patt., J. Clementson 80.00

Punch bowl, footed, simple rounded bowl w/Lustre Band trim, J. Clementson 260.00

Punch bowl, footed, loop handles w/lustre trim, Teaberry patt., J. Clementson (hairline) 1,700.00

Relish dish, oblong diamond shape, Pepper Leaf patt. 130.00

Shaving mug, Tobacco Leaf patt. 400.00

Soup plate w/flanged rim, Teaberry patt., New York shape, J. Clementson 55.00

Sugar bowl, cov., Square Ridged patt., Henry Burgess 80.00

Sugar bowl, cov., simple ovoid shape w/domed cover, lustre trim on handles & cover, Teaberry patt., J. Clementson 185.00

Teapot, cov., porcelain, ovoid body, Cloverleaf patt., gold lustre 40.00

Teapot, cov., Morning Glory patt. 250.00

Washbowl, Morning Glory patt., Elsmore & Forster 195.00

Washbowl, Tobacco Leaf patt., Elsmore & Forster 150.00

ISPANKY FIGURINES

"Cleopatra"

Though not antique, the exquisite limited edition porcelain figures created by Lazlo Ispanky have attracted numerous collectors.

Betsy Ross, introduced 1971............$300.00

Cinderella, 1972-74............................250.00

Cleopatra, introduced 1979 (ILLUS.)..1,700.00

Diann, 1974-75...................................400.00

Drummer Boy....................................400.00

Elizabeth, introduced 1969.................150.00

Huck Finn, 1967-77............................250.00

Lancelot..............................165.00 to 200.00

Mary...................................135.00 to 175.00

Peter Pan, 1967-74............................250.00

Pioneer Woman (bisque), 1967-74.....125.00

Reverie, girl sitting w/legs bent beneath body, salmon shirt w/yellow top, salmon scarf, 1970..................150.00

Storm, 1969-77...................................700.00

JASPER WARE (Non–Wedgwood)

German Jasper Ware Plaque

Jasper ware is fine-grained exceedingly hard stoneware made by including barium sulphate in the clay and was first devised by Josiah Wedgwood, who utilized it for the body of many of his fine cameo blue-and-white and green-and-white pieces. It was subsequently produced by other potters in England and Germany, notably William Adams & Sons, and is in production at the present. Also see WEDGWOOD - JASPER.

Creamer, bulbous body w/short cylindrical neck, band of white relief classical figures on a dark blue ground, marked "Adams," 3¼" h..................$44.00

Plaque, pierced to hang, round, white relief figure of lady & mandolin on green, white relief floral border, Germany, 4⅝" d. (ILLUS.).................40.00

Jasper Ware Plaque with Cupid

Plaque, pierced to hang, round, white relief figure of cupid holding an umbrella over a bird on a blue ground, white relief small white leaf border, Germany, 4⅝" d. (ILLUS.)......55.00

Plaque with Musical Couple

Plaque, pierced to hang, oblong, white relief figure of seated lady w/guitar, man placing wreath on her head on blue ground , Germany, 3⅝ x 5½" (ILLUS.).............................45.00

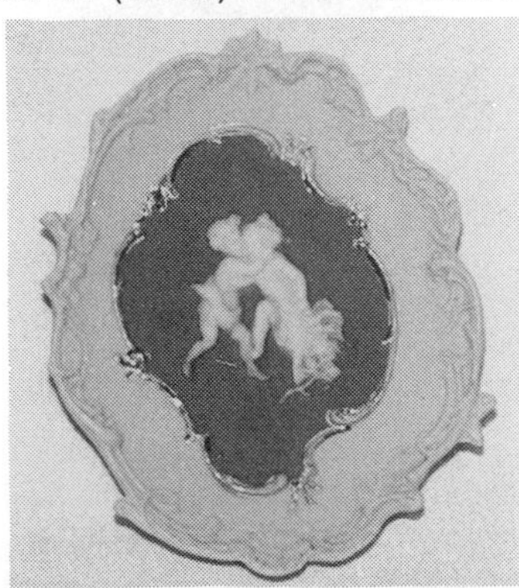

Ornate Plaque with Children

Plaque, pierced to hang, oblong w/scalloped rim, pale green around rim, blue center w/white relief figure of young boy kissing young girl, light gold trim around center scene, Germany, 4⅜ x 5⅝" (ILLUS.) 65.00

Cupid & Heart on Plaque

Plaque, pierced to hang, round white relief cupid holds broken arrow w/heart at his side on green ground, white relief leaves & flowers on border, Germany, 5⅜" d. (ILLUS.) 65.00

Plaque with Lohengrin & Elsa

Plaque, pierced to hang, round w/scalloped rim, white relief figures of Lohengrin & Elsa w/a swan nearby on a blue ground, white relief floral border, Germany, 5⅞" d. (ILLUS.) 85.00

Plaque, pierced to hang, round, white relief bust of Psyche w/a figure of Cupid on green ground, wide white relief floral border, Germany, 6" d. (ILLUS.) 75.00

Psyche & Cupid Plaque

Plaque with Game Bird

Plaque, pierced to hang, round w/deeply scalloped scroll-molded rim, white relief center scene w/a large wild game bird perched in a tree on a green ground, white relief scroll border, 6⅜" d. (ILLUS.) 70.00

Vase, 5" h., white relief scene of man, woman & dog on green ground 50.00

JEWEL TEA AUTUMN LEAF

Though not antique this ware has a devoted following. The Hall China Company of East Liverpool, Ohio, made the first pieces of Autumn Leaf pattern ware to be given as premiums by the Jewel Tea Company in 1933. The premiums were an immediate success and thousands of new customers, all eager to acquire a piece of the durable Autumn Leaf pattern ware, began purchasing Jewel Tea products. Though the pattern was eventually used to

we include only the Hall China Company items in our listing,.

Autumn Leaf Cereal Bowl

Bean pot, two-handled, 2¼ qt. ....$100.00 to 120.00

Bowl, fruit, 5½" d. 5.50

Bowl, cereal, 6½" d. (ILLUS.) 10.50

Autumn Leaf Salad Bowl

Bowl, salad, 9" d. (ILLUS.) 16.00

Bowl, cream soup, two-handled 22.50

Bowls, stacking-type, 18, 24 & 34 ounce, w/cover, 10" h., set of 3 ....95.00

Butter dish, cov., ¼ lb. ....175.00 to 225.00

Butter dish, cov., 1 lb. 310.00

Cake plate, 9½" d. ....20.00 to 25.00

Candy dish w/"Goldenray" metal base ....425.00 to 525.00

Casserole, cov., round, 1½ qt. ....30.00 to 35.00

Coffee maker, cov., all-china, 5 cup 300.00

Coffeepot, cov., dripolator-type, 4 pcs. 45.00

Cookie jar, cov., large eared handles, Ziesel, 1957-69 ....150.00 to 175.00

Creamer & cov. sugar bowl, pre-1940 ....38.00

Cup & saucer 10.00

Cup & saucer, St. Denis style 32.50

Gravy boat 22.00

Marmalade jar, cov., w/spoon, 3 pcs. 50.00

Autumn Leaf Mixing Bowl

Mixing (or utility) bowl, nest-type, "Radiance," 6½" d. (ILLUS.) 10.00

Mixing (or utility) bowl, nest-type, "Radiance," 9" d. 15.00

Mixing utility or bowls, nest-type, "Radiance," set of 3 ....45.00

Pickle dish, oval, 9" l. 28.00

Pitcher w/ice lip, ball-type, 5½ pt. ....40.00 to 55.00

Plate, 9" d. 7.50

Platter, 13½" l. 20.00

Range set: handled salt & pepper shakers & cov. grease jar; pre-1940, 3 pcs. 58.00

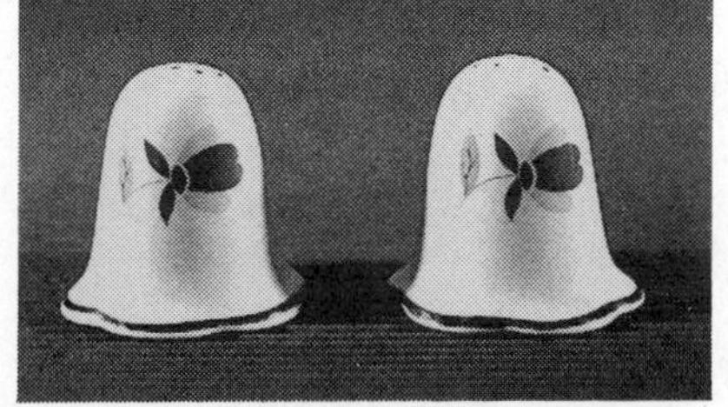

Small Autumn Leaf Salt & Pepper

Salt & pepper shakers, bell-shaped, small, pr. (ILLUS.) 24.00

Salt & pepper shakers, handled, range size, pr. 32.00

Sugar bowl, cov., new style 10.50

Teapot, cov., Aladdin lamp shape 73.00

Teapot, cov., Newport style ....150.00 to 175.00

Vegetable bowl, open, divided, oval, 10½" l. 68.00

KAY FINCH CERAMICS

Figure of a Madonna

Kay Finch
CALIFORNIA

Kay Finch
CALIFORNIA

K.Finch
Calif.

Kay Finch Ceramics began in 1939 in Corona del Mar, California. Animals were always the mainstay of the enterprise which employed over twenty-five decorators, all trained by the owner, Katherine Finch. George Finch, son of Katherine and Braden Finch, designed and modeled most of the utilitarian items such as ashtrays, bowls, planters, and vases. It was in 1963, following Braden's death, that the business ceased operations. The Freeman-McFarlin Potteries purchased Mrs. Finch's molds and in the mid-seventies commisioned her to model dog figurines. This arrangement lasted until 1980. Collectors will find varying marks such as incised, impressed, ink-stamped and hand-painted. Kay Finch died on June 21, 1993 at the age of eighty-nine.

Figure of lady standing, head down, Godey fashion attire, blue skirt w/purple dots around edge & flowers in front, pink w/dark pink flower at bottom in back, white cape w/rose neck closure & white muff w/rose, pink hat w/purple deco-ration, incised "K. Finch Calif.," 7¼" h.........$70.00

Figure of a man standing, slightly turned head, one arm behind him & other arm over waist holding bouquet of flowers, Godey fashion attire, mauve trousers w/purple stripe on each side, pink & purple hat, deep purple shoes, 8" h. 75.00

Figure of a Madonna kneeling, hands together on chest w/head bowed, blonde hair, overall pink clay, blue & purple mantilla w/flowers over her head & shoulders, incised "K. Finch" & stamped in script "Kay Finch" w/"California" in block letters, 6½" h. (ILLUS.) 95.00

Model of a bird, perched on a branch w/two leaves in-relief at right foot, head turned to left, feathers out slightly & tail down, matte white, incised "Kay Finch," ca. early 1950s, 4" h.,...45.00

Model of a camel, walking, ivory body w/grey & tan accents, 5¼" l., 5" h. 85.00

Model Of A Cat

Model of a cat, standing, stylized w/sgraffito-type decorations, head turned slightly, brown glossy glaze, incised "K. Finch," 5" l., 5" h. (ILLUS.) 75.00

Model of a dog, poodle in playful pose, crouching on front legs, back legs almost straight, mouth open, light & dark grey w/gold trim, 11" l., 7½" h. 280.00

Model of a duck, sitting, white high glaze body w/medium green tail & top of head, dark green front feet, bill, eyes & a few back feathers, marked "Kay Finch California," 3¾" l., 3" h. 34.00

Model of a hen, "Biddy," white body w/green accents, Model No. 176, 5" l., 5½" h. 75.00

Model of a lamb, kneeling, pink body, white & dark pink accents, 2½" l., 2¼" h. 27.00

Model of "Winkie" Pig

Model of a pig, "Winkie," tail & right ear up, right eye winking, left ear down, 4" l., 3¾" h. (ILLUS.) 50.00

Planter, egg w/irregular rim depicting 'broken' egg, mint matte green, 3¼" d., 4" h. 18.00

Plate, 6½" d., Santa face, 1st edition, 1950, pale pink background, white beard, dark pink hat 85.00

Powder jar w/lid, cherry blossom in-relief on lid, sea green body, 3½" d., 3" h. 25.00

Wall plaque, goldfish, light blue matte w/gold, 7¼" l., 6¾" h. 55.00

KUTANI

Kutani Charger

This is a Japanese ware from the area of Kutani, a name meaning "nine valleys," where porcelain was made as early as about 1675. The early wares are referred to as "Ko-Kutani" and "Ao-Ko Kutani."

Bowl, 9" d., peach-shape molded w/three leaves, w/panels of ladies, marked "Dai Nihon Kutani Sei," early 20th c. ....$600.00 to 800.00

Bowl, 10" d., porcelain, red-orange & gilt design of ladies picknicking, late 19th c. ....200.00 to 300.00

Charger, Ao Kutani, panels of leaves, birds & Daikoku, the reverse w/grapes & foliage, signed "Kutani" (Nine Valleys), ca. 1890, 14" d. ....1,200.00 to 1,500.00

Charger, Ao Kutani, figural landscape w/sages, the exterior w/cherry blossoms, signed "Kutani," Taisho period, 18" d. (ILLUS.) ...1,000.00 to 1,500.00

Cups, footed, exterior design of Japanese poets, interior w/calligraphy, ca. 1925, 3" h. & 3½" h., pr. ....200.00 to 300.00

Figure of Kannon, polychrome & gilt, impressed Kutani mark on base, ca. 1955, 8" h. ....100.00 to 200.00

Plate, rust red, decorated w/the Seven Gods of Good Luck, ca. 1900 ....400.00 to 600.00

Sake bottle, design of poets, polychrome & gilt, ca. 1930, 6½" h. ....100.00 to 175.00

Sake cups, red & gilt w/birds & flowers, base marked "Kutani" in English, ca. 1955, set of 5 ....25.00 to 50.00

Stemmed sake cups, each w/one of the seven household gods of good luck, each signed "Kutani," ca. 1930, set of 7 ....275.00 to 375.00

Tazza, figural design of sages, polychrome & gilt, 5½" d...............................250.00 to 350.00

Teapot, cov., design of 1000 cranes, colors & gilt, ca. 1955 ......100.00 to 175.00

Teaset: cov. teapot, cov. sugar bowl, creamer & eight cups & saucers & two cake plates; early 20th c., the set ....200.00 to 250.00

Vase, 10" h., Ao Kutani, pear-shaped w/detailed landscapes, marked "Kutani," ca. 1900 ....250.00 to 350.00

Vases, 12" h., design of ducks, mounted as lamps, early 20th c., mirror image pr. ....400.00 to 600.00

LEEDS

The Leeds Pottery in Yorkshire, England, began production about 1758. It made, among other things, creamware that was highly competitive with Wedgwood's. In the 1780s it began production of reticulated and punched wares. Little of its production was marked. Most readily available Leeds ware is that of the 19th century during which time the pottery was operated by several firms.

Cup & saucer, handleless, pearlware, 'gaudy' style decoration, a band of large rounded blossoms connected by leaf sprigs in blue, green, brown, yellow & ochre, early 19th c. (chips on table rings, wear on cup) $93.50

Plate, 9¾" d., pearlware, blue feather-edged design, h.p. in the center in blue w/a stylized Oriental landscape w/a large pagoda (small rim & tablering chips) 192.50

Platter, 13" l., pearlware, blue feather-edged border, h.p. central gaudy floral decoration in blue, green, yellow & yellow-ochre (minor stains & very minor edge wear) 1,870.00

Platter, 15⅜" l., oval, pearlware, blue feather-edged design, h.p. in the center in blue in a stylized Oriental land-scape w/delicate scrolly trees, early 19th c. 467.50

LENOX

The Ceramic Art Company was established at Trenton, New Jersey, in 1889 by Jonathan Coxon and Walter Scott Lenox. In addition to true porcelain, it also made a Belleek-type ware. Re-named Lenox Company in 1906, it is still in operation today.

Bowl, 9" d., shell-shaped, pink w/gold trim $86.00

Cup & saucer, demitasse, embossed gold border, made for S.& G. Gump Co., San Francisco, California 75.00

Cup & saucer, demitasse, Mystic patt., black Wreath mark 35.00

Model of a swan, open, white, green Wreath mark, 4" h. 30.00

Model of a swan, pink, green Wreath mark, 3½ x 4½" 45.00

Punch bowl & base, h.p. blue plums on blue background, green Palette mark, 15½" d., 12" h., 2 pcs. 985.00

Vase, 4½" h., 8" d., squatty bulbous base w/small neck, h.p. nasturtiums on a cream ground, unsigned 125.00

Vase, 9" h., overall design of relief-molded Phoenix Birds in flight, Ming trees & flower blossoms, white ground, green Wreath mark 95.00

Vase, bud, 10" h., decorated w/black spider webs w/butterflies in yellow, pink, blue & orange on white pearlized background, ca. 1906-1924 ....245.00

Vase, 11½" h., 4¼" d., tall cylindrical body w/a wide, flat mouth, decorated w/abstract stylized blossom clusters on long, angular stems, in green, yellow & red on an ivory ground, Palette mark 192.50

LIMOGES

Numerous factories produced china in Limoges, France, with major production in the 19th century. Some pieces listed below are identified by the name of the maker or are identified by the name of the maker or the mark of the factory. Although the famed Haviland Company was located in Limoges, wares bearing their marks are not included in this listing. Also see HAVILAND.

An excellent reference is The Collector's Encyclopedia of Limoges Porcelain, Second Edition, *by Mary Frank Gaston (Collector Books, 1992).*

Hand-Painted Limoges Bowl

Bowl, 8⅝" d., 1¾" h., fluted body w/scalloped rim, h.p. flowers on ivory ground, further decorated w/gold scrolls & sponging, L S & S Limoges, France $35.00

Bowl, 8½" d., ramekin-type & 11½" d. matching underplate, lavish pink roses decoration on green ground, 2 pcs., T & V (Tresseman & Vogt) ...110.00

Bowl, 9⅜" d., 4½" h., interior w/h.p. red strawberries & yellow & green leaves against a cream & rust ground, exterior similarly decorated, heavy gold edge & foot, artist signed, Julius Brauer Co. (ILLUS.) .325.00

Bowl, 9½" d., 5¼" h., footed, h.p. strawberries against cream & rust ground, heavy gold scalloped edge, gold pedestal foot, artist-signed.......325.00

Box, cov., purple violets decoration on gold, 8½" w. 225.00

Butter pat, decorated w/lavender floral sprays (Charles Ahrenfeldt - France) 10.00

Cake plate, h.p. orange poppies decoration, artist-signed, 10½" d., T & V 45.00

Cake plate, open-handled, decorated w/spray of mountain laurel blossoms, gold handles, artist-signed, 13" d. T & V - Limoges 95.00

Cake plate, open-handled, decorated w/giant speckled orchids, lavish gold scrolls, dated "1898," J.P.L. (Jean Pouyat - Limoges) 95.00

Center bowl, open-handled, paneled, decorated w/pink flowers & lily pads, scenic center panel, heavy gold handles, 14" d. 350.00

Charger, decorated w/giant pink h.p. roses w/green foliage on a pastel ground, scalloped rim w/rococo gilded leaf scrolls, 12¾" d., T & V Limoges 185.00

Chocolate pot, cov., decorated w/flowers & butterflies, wide gold ribbons entwine handle 145.00

Chocolate set: cov. chocolate pot & six cups & saucers; decorated in cobalt blue, gold & white, Jean Pouyat mark, ca. 1910, 13 pcs. 450.00

Chocolate set: cov. chocolate pot & eight cups & saucers; decorated w/blue starlings in flight against a white ground, gold handles, 17 pcs. 425.00

Cider set: 8" h., 6" d. pitcher & five cups; berries & leaves decoration, gold trim, 6 pcs. 165.00

Cracker jar, cov., branch handle, decorated w/yellow mums & brushed gold 110.00

Cup & saucer, demitasse, blue floral sprays, gold trim, A/L - Limoges, France & anchor mark 26.00

Cup & saucer, demitasse, gilded cup interior & handles, embossed gilt around saucer & cup rims, cobalt blue ground, artist-signed 50.00

Decanter, whiskey, w/original stopper, factory-decorated w/pink & red roses highlighted w/gold trim, artist-signed, 6⅜" h., T & V 195.00

Dessert set: cov. coffeepot, creamer, cov. sugar bowl, six 7¼" d. plates & six cups & saucers; h.p. sprays of tea roses against a two-toned pastel ground, further decoration on cup interiors, artist-signed, 21 pcs. T & V 700.00

Dinner service: fifteen 8¾" d. plates & a large oval tray; decorated w/different pairs of birds within peach colored & gilt borders, tray 18" l., the set 880.00

Dish, leaf-shaped, multicolored h.p.

floral center, gold scrolls, matte pink border, gold rim & stem, Limoges, France, 4½ x 5" 18.00

Dish, rectangular w/scalloped rim, decorated w/blue flowers, green & grey leaves, gold rim, 4 x 9", Limoges, France 18.00

Dish, loop handle, h.p. pink wild roses & green foliage on pale pastel ground, molded scrolls, signed "M. A. Thaw," 6½ x 10¾" 95.00

Dish, three-section, single heavy gold branch handle from center to rim, russet shading to white w/heavy gold branches & flowers in each section, scalloped gold edge, 11½" d., marked Limoges, France...165.00

Limoges Three-Section Dish

Dish, three-section w/center handle, irregular gold edge, each section decorated w/pink roses & green leaves outlined in fine gold, ornate gold handle, 13" d., 4½" h. (ILLUS.) 165.00

Ornate Triple Sectioned Dish

Dish, three-section w/interior handle, each section decorated w/pink, lavender & blue flowers & heavy gold leaves against a soft peach shading to white ground, ornate gold trimmed edge, marked, 12 x 13¼" (ILLUS.) 175.00

Dish, two-sectioned w/gold trimmed handled, scene of man & maiden on one half & cavalier & lady on other, shaded soft salmon pink to white ground w/ornate gold trimmed irregular edges, unmarked, 8½ x 14½", 4" h...............................165.00

Dresser jar, cov., h.p. purple pansies against a light green ground 85.00

Dresser tray, h.p. courting scene of elegantly dressed Colonial couple, reticulated border w/raised pink lustre grapes, 8 x 13" 165.00

Dresser tray, rectangular, decorated w/large h.p. sprays of light blue flowers, green leaves, pink buds on shaded pastel ground, beaded scalloped blank, artist-signed, 8¼ x 10½", W. G. & Co., Limoges, France (William Guerin) 60.00

Dresser tray, rectangular, decorated overall w/flowers & edged in gold, 8 x 13" 45.00

Dresser tray, handled, shaded purple decorated w/violets, 13¾" d. 150.00

Fish set: 23" l. platter & twelve 8" plates; h.p. fish decoration, gold scalloped rim, artist-signed, 9 pcs. ..475.00

Game plate, pierced to hang, h.p. deer & dog, artist-signed, 10" d. 115.00

Game plate, pierced to hang, h.p. colorful male pheasant w/female pheasant against grassy ground, heavy dull Roman gold irregular scalloped edge, artist-signed, 10" d., Coronet 195.00

Game Plate with Pheasants

Game plate, pierced to hang, h.p. colorful male pheasant in foreground, the female in background, heavy gold irregular edge, 10¾" d., Coronet, Limoges (ILLUS.) 165.00

Game platter, fowl & chick, gold rim, artist-signed, 12 x 19", Coronet 225.00

Game platters, h.p. large quail on one & colorful male pheasant on the other, each against a pastel natural setting w/flowers & foliage, heavy dull Roman gold edges, artist-signed, 10¾ x 16¼", pr., Limoges, France 450.00

Game set: 18" l. platter & five 9" plates; h.p. game scene on each, scalloped borders w/lavish gold trim, 6 pcs. 995.00

Game set: twelve plates & matching deep platter; h.p. bird on each, artist-signed, 13 pcs., red wreath circle mark 1,450.00

Ice cream set: 16" serving plate & five individual plates; gold floral branches on a white ground, scalloped rims decorated w/cobalt blue & light blue, ca. 1891, decorators marks for A. Lanternier, 6 pcs. 595.00

Letter holder, desk-type, four gold feet, h.p. forest scene on one side, full lion face on other side, green ground, stationary gold ring handle on each side, France, 3½ x 6½ x 8½" h. 70.00

Mug, decorated w/h.p. green grapes, leaves & brown vines on pastel green to tan ground, gold handle, 4" d., 5⅝" h., T & V - Limoges - France 95.00

Pitcher, cider, 5½" h., 6½" d., h.p. red cherries & leaves on pastel ground, gold handle & trim, artist-signed, marked "Limoges - France" 165.00

Pitcher, cider, 5¾" h., 6¾" d., h.p. swags of large pink roses & vines around the top on a beige ground, lavish gold handle & rim, WG & Co., Limoges, France 150.00

Pitcher, tankard, 13½" h., twisted scroll handle, decorated w/h.p. bunches of cherries & foliate branches in ivory, gold & shades of red, wide gold bands at top & bottom, J.P. L. - France 390.00

Plaque, pierced to hang, h.p. purple grapes & peaches w/green leaves against a dark & light green ground, heavy gold irregular border, artist-signed, 10¼" d., Coronet, Limoges (ILLUS.) 125.00

Plaque with Grapes & Peaches

Plaque, pierced to hang, Dutch scene decoration, gold rococo border, artist-signed, 12½" d. 245.00

Plaque, pierced to hang, h.p. fruit decoration, gold rococo border, artist-signed, 13¼" d. 185.00

Plaques, pierced to hang, decorated w/French landscape scenes w/buildings on pastel backgrounds, heavy irregular Roman gold edges, unmarked, 13⅜" d., pr. 395.00

Limoges Hunting Scene Plaque

Plaques, pierced to hang, h.p. w/hunter leaning on gun visiting w/a pretty maiden sitting on a wall, a dog in the foreground, against a wooded landscape, the other w/a man holding a fishing pole talking to a girl seated on a wall, against a wood landscape, in brilliant blues, golds, greens & browns, heavy gold scalloped edges, facing pair, 13¾" d., pr. (ILLUS. of one) 495.00

Plate, 8" d., h.p. birds & roses 30.00

Plate, 8½" d., decorated w/plums. artist-signed 45.00

Plate, 9" d., ornate scrolled gilt rim, decorated w/roses, artist-signed, T & V 125.00

Plate, serving, 9½" d., fancy decoration of bright flowers & gold trim, Royal Limoges 45.00

Plate, 10¼" d., decorated w/apples, berries & leaves, gold rococo rim, artist-signed 85.00

Plate, 10¼" d., two pheasants decoration, gold rococo rim, artist-signed 125.00

Plates, dessert, 9" d., floral decoration on pink & white ground, set of 6, Elite 150.00

Plates, 10¼" d., decorated w/bright colored flowers, dark blue border, ca. 1919, set of 12 ....250.00

Plates, 11¼" d., wide gold encrusted floral design rim, center filled w/polychrome flowers against a white ground, marked "Limoges, France," set of 12.............................146.00

Plates, dessert, h.p. daisies on peach ground, set of 6................................135.00

Platter, 14" l., decorated w/gold, cream & yellow roses & green leaves, T & V - Limoges.....................70.00

Powder jar, cov., decorated w/stylized gold leaf fronds & lines on eggshell ground, Limoges, France 30.00

Punch bowl, h.p. violets on white ground interior & exterior, w/gold trim,12½" d., T & V - Limoges - France..450.00

Teapot, cov., oval body, h.p. floral decoration, 9" h., T & V......................65.00

Tip tray, Perrier advertisement w/scene of girl on bar stool 75.00

Tray, handled, ornate gilt scalloped rim, decorated w/roses, artist-signed, 11" l., T & V 195.00

Tray, decorated w/h.p. lilacs & autumn foliage on pastel ground, beaded scalloped gold rococo rim & tab handles, artist-signed, crown mark, Coronet, Limoges, France, 9¼ x 12½".......................................145.00

Trivet, three button feet, decorated w/h.p. yellow roses & foliage on pastel ground, artist-signed, 6½" d., T & V Limoges 48.00

Vase, pillow-type, 2½ x 4½ x 6", footed, decorated w/h.p. magenta chrysanthemums on one side, h.p. purple flowers on other side, scrolled handles, scalloped foot & rim, lavish gold trim, D & Co., France (R. Delinieres & Cie.) 60.00

Vase, pillow-type, 3 x 6½ x 9", gold twig feet w/encrusted berries, gold shoulder handles w/molded flowers & berries, gold rim, h.p. orange blossoms on one side & violet clusters on other, artist-signed, ca. 1882-96...350.00

Vase, 12" h., decorated w/dahlias & chrysanthemums in pastels on a dark green ground 385.00

Vase, 13" h., fancy scroll handles, decorated w/pink & red roses w/lilacs 310.00

Vase, 13" h., portrait of woman w/long brown hair wearing sheer pink gown, light green lustre ground 550.00

Vase, 13½" h., h.p. bird & tree w/foliage on front, green, brown & light grey ground, T & V 300.00

LIVERPOOL

Early 19th Century Liverpool Pitcher

Liverpool is most often used as a generic term for fine earthenware products, usually of creamware or pearlware, produced at numerous potteries in this English city during the late 18th and early 19th centuries. Many examples, especially pitchers, were decorated with transfer-printed patriotic designs aimed specifically at the American buying public.

Mug, cylindrical, a sepia transfer-printed design of a central oval reserve w/inscription below crossed flags centered by a Liberty cap & above a banner inscribed "Independence," early 19th c., 5" h. (flakes on base) $1,540.00

Pitcher, jug-type, 4⅞" h., black transfer-printed Seal of the United States, silver lustre highlights (some slight crazing)................................3,250.00

Pitcher, jug-type, 6¾" h., creamware, decorated on the front w/a black transfer-printed design of a three-masted ship flying an American flag, the reverse w/a pastoral scene, early 19th c. (minor imperfections) ..660.00

Pitcher, jug-type, 7⅝" h., creamware, black transfer-printed & enamel-trimmed portraits of "proscribed patriots" Samuel Adams & John Hancock, the reverse w/a three-masted sailing ship & "Success to Trade," under the spout an American eagle & the date "1802," trimmed in blue, red, yellow & green enamel, early 19th c. (repaired spout & minor imperfections) 2,750.00

Pitcher, jug-type, 8" h., creamware, one side w/a black transfer-printed oval medallion enclosing a bust of Washington flanked by figures of Justice, Liberty & Victory, the other side w/a large oval medallion w/an inscription to Washington below crossed banners & a Liberty cap & w/a banner reading "Independence" below, an American eagle under the spout, ca. 1800 ....1,650.00

Pitcher, jug-type, 8⅜" h., creamware, black transfer-printed portrait of Washington w/inscription "He In Glory & America In Tears," the other side w/George Washington memorial urn encircled w/verse, beneath the spout, "A Man Without Example - A Patriot Without Reproach," black line border (professional restoration to base, the side [into the Washington transfer], the handle and the base rim) 1,700.00

Pitcher, jug-type, 8⅞" h., creamware, black transfer-printed design of a memorial monument to George Washington below "Washington in Glory," the reverse w/"The Cordwainers Arms," under the spout a wreathed cypher, early 19th c. (imperfections) 1,100.00

Pitcher, jug-type, 9" h., creamware, the ovoid body decorated on one side w/a transfer-printed monument to George Washington, the obverse w/an eagle w/a shield at its breast under sixteen stars within a floral wreath, under the spout inscribed "Pretty Dick," early 19th c. (glaze imperfections, flake at spout, crack at handle) 550.00

Pitcher, jug-type, 9⅛" h., creamware, one side w/a black transfer-printed oval reserve w/a scene of Classical figures flanking L'Enfant's "Plan of the City of Washington," the other side w/"Peace, Plenty and Independence," the American eagle under the spout, wear at spout, small base flakes (ILLUS.)............2,860.00

Pitcher, jug-type, 9⅞" h., creamware, black transfer-printed scene of shipbuilding on one side, the other side w/an oval medallion & banner reading "Washington in Glory," Seal of the United States under the spout, early 19th c. (professional repair to upper rim, base & handle, handle & base reglazed)...............1,600.00

"Defense of Stonington" Pitcher

Pitcher, jug-type, 10" h., creamware, black transfer-printed scene entitled "Defense of Stonington, Connecticut," the reverse w/"American Eagle" & cypher "GLP," a wreath beneath the spout, old repair, break to spout, flakes & spider cracks, early 19th c. (ILLUS.) 7,700.00

Pitcher, jug-type, 10" h., creamware, decorated on one side w/a black transfer-printed oval reserve showing a standing figure of Washington beside a large oval world map, the reverse w/a scene of Independence, early 19th c. (repair) 935.00

Pitcher, jug-type, 10" h., creamware, one side w/an oval transfer-printed reserve w/Classical figures flanking

Liverpool Pitcher with Washington

a bust of George Washington over the inscription "First President of The U.S. of America, " the other side w/a scene of the three-masted sailing ship 'Amelia' flying an American flag & trimmed w/green, yellow, red, blue & black enamel above the inscription "Amelia of New York - William S. Brooks, Commander of New-York," a wreathed monogram under the spout, early 19th c. (ILLUS.) 4,950.00

Pitcher, jug-type, $10\frac{1}{2}$" h., creamware, black transfer-printed & enamel-decorated design of the three-masted sailing ship "Carpenter" flying an American flag & trimmed in red, blue, green, brown & yellow, the reverse w/an oval panel showing a memorial to George Washington, under the spout an American eagle & a foliate monogram, early 19th c. (hairlines, chips at rim & spout) 1,870.00

Pitcher, jug-type, 11" h., creamware black transfer-printed monument to George Washington in a landscape, the reverse w/"Peace, Plenty and Independence," under the handle the inscription "A man without example - a patriot without reproach," the rim & spout w/floral swags, all trimmed w/gold, early 19th c. (discoloration, flakes on base) 2,200.00

Teapot, cov., slightly ovoid body painted in shades of rose, blue, iron-red, purple & green on either side w/an Oriental-style floral spray & scattered sprigs beneath an iron-red scalloped line around the neck repeated on the cover rim beneath further floral sprays & sprigs, the spout rim & knop dashed in iron-red, Pennington's factory, ca. 1780, $6\frac{5}{8}$" h. (small footrim chip, small hairlines & chips in cover flange) 345.00

LLADRO

Spain's famed Lladro porcelain manufactory creates both limited and non-limited edition figurines as well as other porcelains. The classic simple beauty of the figures and their subdued coloring makes them readily recognizable and they have an enthusiastic following of collectors.

LLADRÓ

Andean Flute Player, No. 2174, matte finish $275.00

Boy with Dog, No. 4522, matte finish, $7\frac{1}{2}$" h. 175.00

Can I Play?, No. S7610 ....300.00

Carnival Couple, No. 4882, $9\frac{1}{2}$" h. 200.00

Clown with Concertina, No. 1027, 18" h. 430.00

Court Jester, No. 405 ....1,295.00

Debbie with Doll, No. 1379, 11" h.......700.00

Elephant, large, w/calf, on base, No. 1150, 15" h. 250.00

Feeding the Ducks, No. 4849, matte finish, $6\frac{1}{2}$" h. 230.00

Feeding the Pigeons, No. 5428 ....590.00

Flower Song, No. S7607 ....435.00

Garden Classic, No. 7617 ....325.00

Girl carrying Lamb, No. 4584, $10\frac{1}{4}$" h. 110.00

Girl Shampooing, No. 1148, $8\frac{1}{4}$" h.....300.00

Girl w/Cats, No. 1309, $9\frac{1}{2}$" h. 190.00

Girl w/Geese, No. 4815, $12\frac{1}{2}$" h. 295.00

Girl w/Mandolin, No. 4633, 8" h. 75.00

Girl w/Mother's Shoe, No. 1084, $7\frac{1}{2}$" h. 300.00

Girl w/Puppies in Basket, No. 1311, $9\frac{3}{4}$" h. 210.00

Group of Angels, caroling, No. 4542, $6\frac{1}{2}$" h. 150.00

Gymnast Balancing Ball, No. 5332.....200.00

Island Girl, No. 2171 ....170.00

Joy in a Basket, No. 5595....................170.00

Juggler Sitting, No. L1382..................485.00

Little Eagle Owl, 2020Gr......................350.00

Little Traveler, No. S7602...................900.00

Lovers in the Park, No. 1274, 11½" h..850.00

Motoring in Style, No. 5884.............3,200.00

Oriental Girl, kneeling Japanese girl arranging flowers, No. 4840, 7½" h..250.00

Pekingese Sitting, No. 4641...............450.00

Picture Perfect, No. S7612.................300.00

Puppet Maker, No. 5396.....................700.00

School Girl, No. 1313, 11" h. 400.00

Spring Bouquets, No. S7603........................500.00 to 550.00

Suzy & Her Doll, No. 1378, 11½" h..500.00

Tinker-Bell, No. 7518,......................2,195.00

Voyage of Columbus, No. 5847.......1,450.00

LONGWY

Longwy Charger

This faience factory was established in 1798 in the town of Longwy, France and is noted for its enameled pottery which resembles cloisonne. Utilitarian wares were the first production here but by the 1870s an Oriental style art pottery that imitated "cloisonne" was created through the use of heavy enamels in relief. By 1912, a modern Art Deco style became part of Longwy's production and these wares, together with the Oriental style pieces, have made this art pottery popular with collectors today. As interest in Art Deco has soared in recent years, values of Longwy's modern style wares have risen sharply.

Box, cov., footed, decorated w/colorful enameled flowers & gold trim, 5" sq. $125.00

Bowl, 14¾" d., round flaring sides, white crackled glaze decorated w/Cubist stylized vine in blue, green, yellow & grey, the exterior glazed in blue, stamped "PRIMAVERA LONGWY FRANCE" & artist's signature, ca. 1920s 528.00

Center bowl, a twelve-sided flaring bowl on a conforming base, glazed in turquoise blue crackle w/stylized floral borders in pink, brick red & cobalt blue, trimmed in gold, printed factory mark, ca. 1925, 13⅜" d., 6" h...1,495.00

Charger, the shallow circular dish molded in low-relief w/stylized black & white nude ladies in a tropical beach landscape in eggplant, mustard yellow & shades of blue, stamped "PRIMAVERA LONGWY FRANCE," 14½" d.........................1,650.00

Charger, circular, painted w/a white stork surrounded by yellow, pink & salmon blossoms against a blue & green ground, decorated by R. Rizzi, stamped company mark & "DECOR de R. Rizzi," numbered "33/60," ca. 1920s, 14¾" d..............660.00

Charger, round, decorated in the Limoges-style, large pink & white roses w/green leaves on a blue ground w/gold highlights, the work of E. Killiert, incised signature & impressed mark "Longwy D - 1182" in a circle, 17" d. (ILLUS.) 880.00

Plaque w/hanger, cloisonne-style enamel decoration of a spread-winged parrot on colorful blossoming branches against a blue ground, 9" d. 275.00

Tray, Art Nouveau design, w/enameled black nude figure decoration, artist-signed, made for W.W. Atelier d'Art Bon Marche,

4⅞ x 6¼" 75.00

Trivet in metal mount decorated w/sparrow on floral branch, early marks, 6½" sq. ....150.00 to 200.00

Vases, 6½" h., 3" d., baluster-form, decorated in the Chinese style w/multicolored flowers & foliage enameled against a Chinese Blue ground, stamped "Decore A La Main - Longwy France - Made In France," w/original price tags from La Samaritaine, pr. 225.00

Vase, 9" h., tubular shape, enameled florals in blue, yellow & red 300.00

Vase, 10⅞" h., footed cylinder w/everted rim, decorated w/a Cubist landscape in rust, grey & moss green over a crackled glaze, enhanced w/black, stamped "Atelier primavera LONGWY FRANCE" & w/artist's signature, ca. 1920s (some restoration at rim)..................605.00

Vase, 11½" h., gourd-shaped, decorated w/stylized naked women on a waterside among stylized vegetation, in various tones of blue trimmed w/green & black, stamped "PRIMAVERA LONGWY FRANCE," ca. 1920s 2,640.00

Longwy Vase

Vase, 13⅜" h., bell-shaped, a band of stylized flowers & fruits in mustard & cherry around the lower portion, the octagonal upper portion w/defined ribbing ascending to rim, over a crackled glaze, stamped "SOCIETE DES FAIENCERIES LONGWY FRANCE" w/company logo (ILLUS.) 935.00

LUSTRE WARES

Lustred wares in imitation of copper, gold, silver and other colors were produced in England in the early 19th century and onward. Gold, copper or platinum oxides were painted on glazed objects which were then fired, giving them a lustred effect. Various forms of lustre wares include plain lustre – with the entire object coated to obtain a metallic effect, bands of lustre decoration and painted lustre designs. Particularly appealing is the pink or purple "splash lustre" sometimes referred to as "Sunderland" lustre in the mistaken belief it was confined to the production of Sunderland area potteries. Objects decorated in silver lustre by the "resist" process, wherein parts of the objects to be left free from lustre decoration were treated with wax, are referred to as "silver resist."

Wares formerly called "Canary Yellow Lustre" are now referred to as "Yellow-Glazed Earthenwares" which see.

COPPER

Copper Lustre Pitcher

Creamer, canary yellow band w/white reserves decorated w/brown transfer scenes of woman & children highlighted in polychrome enamel, 4¾" h. (some wear)........................$165.00

Pitcher, 5¾" h., globular lower section, wide neck, C-scroll handle, overall polychrome floral decoration (minor wear).....................................71.50

Pitcher, 6½" h., commemorative, footed bulbous body w/a flaring cylindrical neck w/long spout, C-scroll handle, a wide canary yellow middle band w/white oval reserves printed in black, one w/"LaFayette," the other w/"Cornwallis," early 19th c. (spout chip) 385.00

Pitcher, 6¾" h., jug-type, tapered body on a short foot, a raised beaded band around the rim, squared handle, a wide yellow band around the middle decorated w/a black transfer-printed bust portrait of Andrew Jackson on both sides, titled "General Jackson - The Hero of New Orleans" 1,100.00

Pitcher, 7¼" h., cylindrical w/narrow neck & flaring top, decorated w/polychrome floral enameling (some wear) 137.50

Pitcher, 7½" h., footed bowl-form lower body below a sloping shoulder to the high cylindrical neck w/arched mask spout & angled & scalloped serpent handle, painted blue bands around the lower body & a wide blue band around the neck w/molded blossoms decorated in polychrome 126.50

Pitcher, 8⅞" h., footed conical body w/a narrow angled shoulder to the short cylindrical neck w/long arched spout & angled handle, the middle w/a wide blue band w/an applied scene of cherubs in a chariot trimmed in polychrome enamels & purple lustre (ILLUS.) 220.00

Sugar bowl, cov., urn-shaped w/saucer base, ram's head handles, 5¼" h. 104.50

Teapot, cov., floral spray decoration w/blue trim, 6" h. 250.00

SILVER & SILVER RESIST

Bowl, 9¼" d., 4¼" h., deep rounded sides on thick footring, silver lustre resist w/large grape clusters & leaves spaced along wavy band, early 19th c. (wear, hairlines in foot) 165.00

Creamer, wide ovoid body w/a short wide cylindrical rim & angled handle, silver resist decoration of a large bird in a tree, 4⅝" h. (wear) 132.00

Pitcher, 5½" h., jug-type, bulbous ovoid body tapering to a flat rim w/pinched spout, angled handle, silver lustre resist w/a neck band of grapevines, the body w/a large "farmer's arms" design (wear) 137.50

Pitcher, 5⅝" h., pearlware, jug-form w/wide ovoid body & angled handle, silver resist decoration w/scenes of a Dalmatian dog & dog in a flowery landscape, early 19th c. (wear, scratches, chip on spout) 104.50

Pitcher, 5¾" h., jug-type, spherical w/shaped rectangular handle, canary yellow w/wide silver resist band of stylized florals & foliage 660.00

Pitcher, 5⅞" h., jug-type, molded mask sides, canary yellow ground decorated w/polychrome highlighted w/silver resist accents 495.00

SUNDERLAND PINK & OTHERS

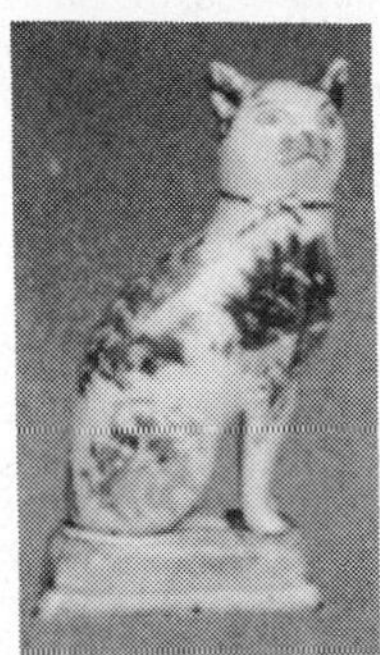

Cat Figure with Pink Lustre

Bowl, 8½" d., 4¼" h., deep rounded sides above a wide footring, black transfer-printed hunt scenes & verse on one side & a bridge scene titled "Cast iron Bridge over the River Wear" on the other, polychrome enamel trim & Sunderland lustre ground, impressed mark "Moore & Co.," 19th c. (minor wear & stains) 203.50

Butter tub w/attached undertray, cov., wide & low cylindrical body, the sides & edge of undertray w/wide white bands between thin pink lustre bands, lavish gold florals & trim, scalloped rim, marked "C.T." w/an eagle in blue, Germany, 6½" d., 4½" h. 125.00

Creamer, bulbous ovoid body tapering to a short cylindrical neck, C-scroll handle, brown transfer-printed front inscription "Ladies all I pray make free - and tell me how you like your tea," red & green enamel & pink lustre trim & a Sunderland lustre band around the neck, early 19th c., 2⅞" h. (small chips) 71.50

Jar, cov., wide cylindrical body w/applied horizontal loop side handles, low domed cover w/button finial, decorated w/a black transfer-printed scene w/polychrome trim titled "Sailors Farewell," pink lustre trim, 5½" d., 4½" h. (wear, stains, pinpoint flakes) 148.50

Models of cats, seated white animal decorated w/splotches of pink lustre, England, 19th c., 7" h., pr. (ILLUS. of one) 467.50

Pitcher, 4½" h., jug-type, wide bulbous body w/a wide cylindrical neck & angled handle, pink lustre resist w/a vintage grape design & blue rim & base stripes (chips) 220.00

Pitcher, 4¾" h., jug-type w/wide ovoid body & C-scroll handle, molded in relief around the body w/a hunting scene w/a large dog below an upper band of flower vines, green enamel & pink lustre trim, early 19th c. (wear, chips & enamel flakes)..........104.50

Pitcher, 6⅝" h., pearlware, jug-form w/wide ovoid body & angled handle, h.p. w/a wide upper band of stylized florals w/large round blossoms enclosing four petals alternating w/large serrated leaves & scattered small leaves in red, yellow, green & black w/pink lustre trim, early 19th c. (wear, minor stains & enamel flakes) 115.50

Pitcher, 7⅛" h., jug-type, commemorative, wide ovoid body w/a short cylindrical neck, simple "C" handle, each side w/a large oval reserve transfer-printed in dark brown, one w/"Iron Bridge at Sunderland," the other w/a scene of two sailors drinking, the scenes trimmed in polychrome, the background w/splashed pink lustre, early 19th c. (wear, hairlines & small chips) 385.00

Pitcher, 11½" h., black transfer-print of "Ship Caroline" on one side & "The Shipwright Arms" on the other, pink lustre trim 137.50

Plaque, pierced to hang, scroll-molded shaped rim w/pink lustre trim forming a shadow box effect & framing a black transfer scene highlighted w/polychrome enameling, marked "Waverley, S. Moore & Co., Sunderland," 7⅞ x 8½"..255.00

MAJOLICA

Majolica, a tin-enameled glazed pottery, has been produced for centuries. It originally took its name from the island of Majorca, a source of figuline (potter's clay). Subsequently it was widely produced in England, Europe and the United States. Etruscan majolica, now avidly sought, was made by Griffen, Smith & Hill, Phoenixville, Pa., in the last quarter of the 19th century. Most majolica advertised today is 19th or 20th century. Once scorned by most collectors, interest in this colorful ware so popular during the Victorian era has now revived and prices have risen dramatically in the past few years. Also see SARREGUEMINES and WEDGWOOD,.

Reference books which collectors will find useful include: The Collector's Encyclopedia of Majolica, *by Mariann Katz-Marks (Collector Books, 1992);* American Majolica, 1850-1900, *by M. Charles Rebert (Wallace-Homestead Book Co., 1981);* Majolica, American & European Wares, *by Jeffrey B. Snyder & Leslie Bockol (Schiffer Publishing, Ltd., 1994); and* Majolica, British, Continental and American Wares, 1851-1915, *by Victoria Bergesen (Barrie & Jenkins, Ltd., London, England, 1989).*

ETRUSCAN

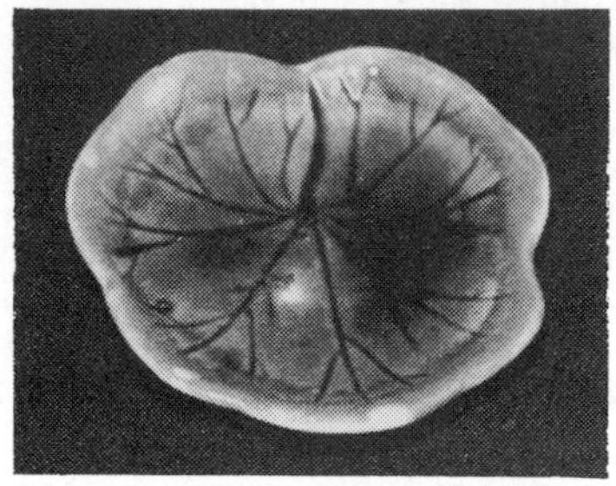

Geranium Pattern Butter Pat

Bowl, 8½" d., Shell & Seaweed patt...$275.00

Butter pat, Geranium patt., green & brown (ILLUS.)...................................70.00

Coffeepot, cov., Shell & Seaweed patt..................................650.00 to 700.00

Creamer, Corn patt............................110.00

Pitcher, 4½" h., Bamboo patt.............165.00

Pitcher, 8½" h., Corn patt. 170.00

Plate, 5½" d., Cauliflower patt. 55.00

Plate, 7½" d., Cauliflower patt. 98.00

Saucer, 6" d., Albino, Shell & Seaweed patt....................................50.00

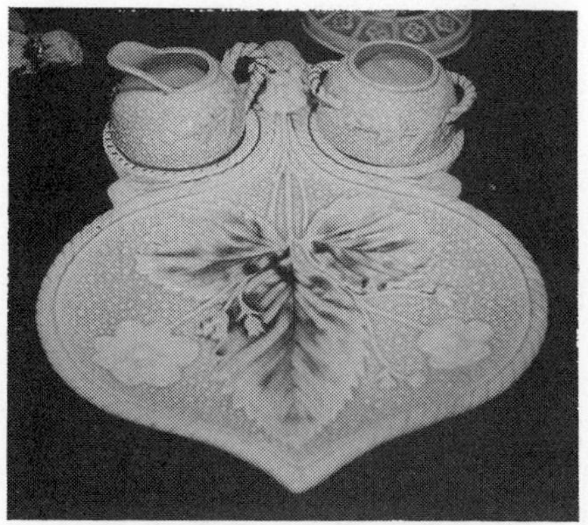

Etruscan Strawberry Serving Set

Strawberry serving set: spade-shaped undertray-dish w/a small open sugar bowl & creamer; strawberry blossoms & leaf sprig on a lavender ground, rope borders, the set (ILLUS.) 900.00

Teapot, cov., Shell & Seaweed patt. ....525.00 to 550.00

GENERAL

Majolica Basket

Basket, slightly canted sides, decorated w/white flowers & green leaves against a basketweave ground, the twisted handle w/bows at the terminals, 8½" l., 8" h. (ILLUS.) 425.00

Bottle, model of a duck w/straight neck, beak forms pouring spout, France, 14" h. 100.00

Bowl, 8" d., 2½" h., footed, Pond Lily patt., George Jones, England 500.00

Bowl, 11" d., Pond Lily patt., J. Holdcroft, England 250.00

Bowl, lemonade, 12" d., footed, Avalon Ware, Blackberry patt., D.F. Haynes & Co., Baltimore 180.00

Bulb bowls, the sides molded as brown wooden planks covered w/green rose vines, a gold band around the sides tying the planks together, blue interior, Minton, England, ca. 1870, 2¼ x 10½", 2" h., pr. 900.00

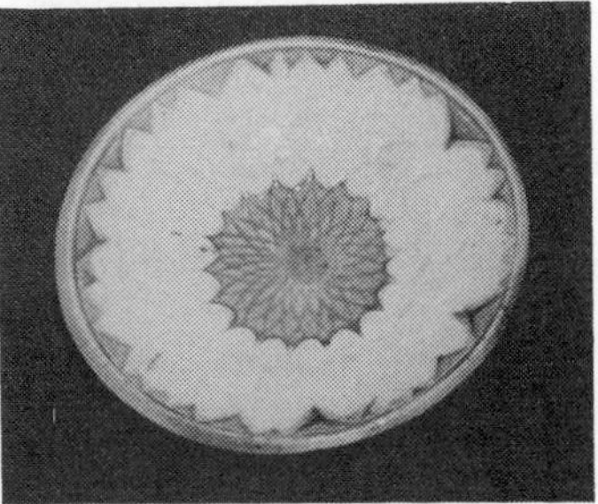

Aster Pattern Butter Pat

Butter pat, Aster patt., Wedgwood, England (ILLUS.) 130.00

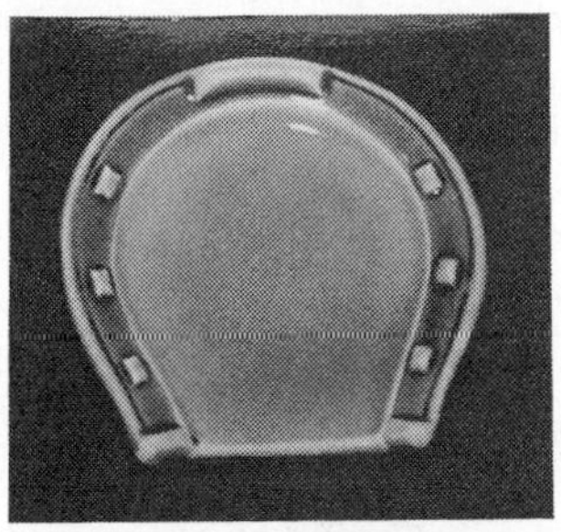

Horseshoe Pattern Butter Pat

Butter pat, Horseshoe patt., Wedgwood, England (ILLUS.) 225.00

Charger, 12" d., decorated w/fruit on gold leaf ground, Sarreguemines.......85.00

George Jones Cheese Keeper

Cheese keeper, cov., Dogwood & Woven Fence patt., George Jones, England, 11½" d., 10½" h. (ILLUS.) 2,500.00

Cheese Keeper with Trout

Cheese keeper, cov., domed cover molded w/large grey & pink trout on a cobalt blue ground, arched fish handle on top, possibly J. Roth, London, England, chip on underplate (ILLUS.) 1,700.00

Compote, open, two-handled, Flower & Basketweave patt. 185.00

Creamer, birds & grapevines decoration on blue ground 15.00

Creamer, Corn patt., 4" h......................30.00

Cup, Shell & Seaweed patt................150.00

Cuspidor, Basketweave & Fern patt. ..165.00

Dessert dish, fan-shaped, Fan & Bow patt., 6½" l. 125.00

Dessert set: large open-handled platter & four matching plates; hibiscus flower decoration on a basketweave ground, incised number, Germany, 5 pcs. 375.00

Dish, Cabbage Leaf patt., Sarreguemines, France, 6½" l. 35.00

Ewer, cov., Art Nouveau w/white flowers & green leaves on a dark olive green ground, hinged pewter cover, 10" h. 350.00

Ewer, molded flower in scrolled reserves in cobalt blue, brown & yellow against a molded fishscale ground, England 280.00

Tavern Scene Figure Group

Figure group, tavern scene w/a seated gentleman at a table looking across at a standing barmaid, on a rectangular footed platform base, 21" h. (ILLUS.) 880.00

Game dish, cov., two-handled, game bird nestled in a grassy setting on cover, the sides decorated w/rabbits amid ferns, restored, white glazed liner, George Jones, England, 13" w., 7" h. (ILLUS. top next column) 4,000.00

Game Dish by George Jones

Humidor, cov., figural, model of a Pug dog, brown glaze, 9" h. 895.00

Jardiniere & pedestal, each decorated w/a scallop & scroll design w/large leafy scrolls glazed in green, brown, pink & blue, overall 32" h., 2 pcs......330.00

Jardiniere & stand, Art Nouveau style, globular swirl-molded jardiniere w/ornate molded leaf & flower design around rim & pierced handles, the tripod stand w/twist-molded legs & ornate molding at top & base, Dressler, Austria, 15½" d., overall 42¼" h., 2 pcs. 1,600.00

Majolica Model of a Whippet

Model of a Whippet dog, the handsome animal modeled in a seated position w/collar around its neck, amber & white glaze, repairs, 31" h. (ILLUS.) 1,870.00

Pedestal, scrolled triangular form above a baluster body, decorated w/floral cartouches reserved on a cobalt ground w/yellow & gold floral sprays, impressed mark, England, 19th c., 40½" h...............................742.50

Pitcher, 4½" h., Corn patt. 75.00

Pitcher, 4½" h., Dogwood patt. 70.00

Pitcher, 5½" h., Pineapple patt. 100.00

Pitcher, 5¾" h., pink & white flowers

w/green leaves on a turquoise ground, registration mark on base (minor roughness at base)..............110.00

Pitcher, 6" h., floral decoration on basketweave ground..........................65.00

Pitcher, 6" h., bulbous, Wild Rose on Tree Bark patt. 70.00

Pitcher, 6½" h., green palm tree decoration on textured brown ground...125.00

Pitcher, 8" h., bird on flowering branch against a basketweave ground, yellow, brown & green 180.00

Pitcher, water, 8" h., decorated w/pink flowers & green leaves 80.00

Figural Fish Pitcher

Pitcher, 11" h., figural fish, tail forms handle, lavender interior, attributed to Morley & Co., Wellsville, Ohio (ILLUS.) 175.00

Pitcher, cov. tankard, 12½" h., 5¼" d., footed cylindrical body w/applied handle, green & gold raised circles on a brown ground, hinged pewter cover 245.00

Planter, hour glass-shaped, Corn patt., 6" h...120.00

Plaque, pierced to hang, depicting a castle scene, 6½" h............................88.00

Plate, 7" d., fruit decoration, Sarreguemines 65.00

Plate, 7½" d., blossoms & leaf decoration 85.00

Plate, 7½" d., U.S. Eagle decoration, green...55.00

Plate, 8" d., decorated w/scene of birds on branches, light blue ground, Germany 35.00

Plate, 8" d., dog & deer decoration.....110.00

Plate, 8" d., figural maple leaf..............90.00

Plate, 8" d., Pond Lily patt., George Jones 300.00

Plate, 8½" d., decorated w/cherries on a limb, St. Clemens, France mark 65.00

Plate, 8½" d., decorated w/pomegranates on a limb, St. Clemens, France mark.....................................50.00

Plate, 8½"d., Lettuce Leaf patt., New Milford Pottery "Lettuce Leaf" mark 55.00

Plate, 9" d., scenic decoration of a cottage in the forest, Zell, Germany...45.00

Plate, 9" d., Water Lily patt., Zell, Germany 55.00

Plate, 10" d., Blackberry patt. 110.00

Plate, 10" d., decorated w/an apple, grapes & gold leaves 30.00

Plate, 11¼" d., decorated w/maple leaves on branch 75.00

Plates, 9" d., Bird & Fan patt., artist-signed & dated, set of 6 ....795.00

Smoking set, figural brown lion w/white ruff & chest standing in front of cups for cigarettes and matches, striker on side, green ground 250.00

Stand, the circular base supported by three large dolphins w/curling tails & fins, their snouts & ears w/long whiskers, glazed in cream, green, amber & brown, 19th c., 18" d., 34" h..440.00

Syrup pitcher, Albion Ware, morning glory design on sides, ca. 1885, Bennet's Patent, 6¼" h. 175.00

Teapot, cov., globular w/straight spout & wedge-shaped handle, four scrolled feet, sides decorated w/relief-molded swallows 140.00

Teapot, cov., wild rose decoration on gold ground, gold overglaze accents, 4½" h. 175.00

Trivet, Art Nouveau style, the tile decorated w/blue & white flowers on a green vine against a bluish green ground, Hampshire Pottery, in wire frame...90.00

Urn, Palissy-type, ovoid w/slender open-work neck, figural snake handles rising from shoulders to rim, body decorated w/relief-molded frogs, lizards, bees & beetles, 14" h...550.00

Vase, 4⅜" h., Buttercup patt., Avalon line, Haynes & Co., Baltimore............60.00

Vase, 5½" h., double-handled, Art Nouveau style, decorated w/pink flowers 45.00

MARBLEHEAD

Marblehead Bowl with Indian Design

This pottery was organized in 1904 by Dr. Herbert J. Hall as a therapeutic aid to patients in a sanitarium he ran in Marblehead, Massachusetts. It was later separated from the sanitarium and directed by Arthur E. Baggs, a fine artist and designer, who bought out the factory in 1916 and operated it until its closing in 1936. Most wares were hand-thrown and decorated and carry the company mark of a stylized sailing vessel flanked by the letters "M" and "P."

Bowl, 3¼" d., 1¾" h., bulbous form tapering gently to a wide, flat rim, smooth matte dark blue glaze, w/separate matching flower frog, bowl w/ship mark & paper label, 2 pcs. $220.00

Bowl, 5½" d., 3½" h., rounded base below flat cylindrical sides, decorated w/an incised wide band of abstract U-form devices in black against a fine shimmering matte green ground, impressed ship mark 1,210.00

Bowl, 7" d., 2" h., compressed bulbous incurved sides, decorated around the rim w/a band of stylized blue berries & grey foliage on a matte grey ground, impressed ship mark 880.00

Bowl, 7¼" d., 3¾" h., squatty bulbous body gently tapering to a flat mouth, matte sand-colored ground incised w/an Indian scroll design in brown, artist-initialed & impressed mark (ILLUS.) 1,870.00

Bowl, 7½" d., 5" h., canted sides & flaring rim, matte dark blue exterior & lighter blue interior, marked..........302.50

Plain Marblehead Bowl

Bowl, 8¾" d., 4½" h., deep flaring sides, smooth matte speckled grey glaze, impressed mark (ILLUS.) 302.50

Bowl-vase, bulbous w/narrow flaring rim, incised floral decoration in blue, red & green against a dark matte blue ground, marked, 4½" d., 3¾" h. 825.00

Bowl-vase, squatty bulbous body w/a molded mouth, the base tapering to a flared foot, matte dark blue glaze, impressed ship mark, 6¼" d., 4¼" h. 247.50

Candlestick, turned round base tapering to a double-ringed slender shaft w/a flared rim, matte green glaze, impressed mark, 7⅝" h. 302.50

Candlesticks, cylindrical standard w/broad flaring base & flaring rim, smooth matte speckled green glaze, impressed ship mark & paper label, 6" d.,14¼" h., pr. 1,870.00

Cider set: pitcher & four mugs; slightly tapering cylindrical form w/angled handles, smooth speckled matte green ground w/black handle & incised stripe, incised "MP" w/ship & "AB/T/MADE FOR H.P. HUGHES AUG. '07," by Arthur Baggs, 1907, pitcher 8½" h., 8¼" d., the set.......1,210.00

Console bowl, wide shallow form w/incurved rounded sides, matte grey speckled glaze, stamped ship mark, 13½" d.................................330.00

Lamp base, tapering base & closed-in

rim, dripping satin dark blue & green glaze, factory drilled hole, 7" d., 11½" h. 770.00

Vase, 3¼" h., squatty bulbous body w/wide closed mouth, overall speckled matte green glaze decorated w/an incised black band at the rim & repeating stylized floral medallions around the shoulder, impressed mark, ca. 1907 ....440.00

Vase, 3¼" h., 4¾" d., spherical body w/flat rim, decorated w/stylized swirling grey flower sprigs against a smooth matte speckled grey ground, by Hannah Tutt & Arthur Baggs, impressed ship mark & artists' initials 1,045.00

Vase, 3¼" h., 5" d., compressed spherical form w/closed rim, smooth matte green speckled glaze, ship mark 467.50

Vase, 3½" h., 2½" d., slightly ovoid body w/wide, flat rim, speckled matte mustard yellow glaze, ship mark 330.00

Vase, 3½" h., 3¼" d., tapering ovoid body w/a flat molded rim, decorated w/a band of stylized yellow roses w/green leaves & brown stems against a smooth matte speckled ochre ground, by Hannah Tutt, marked (prominent firing crack inside) 495.00

Vase, 3½" h., 4" d., bulbous tapering ovoid body w/a narrow flared rim, incised w/stylized full-length trees in green against a smooth dark matte blue ground, by Hannah Tutt, signed 935.00

Vase, 3¾" h., 4¼" d., very bulbous ovoid body tapering to a narrow flared rim, decorated w/a band of large incised leaf-like medallions in dark green on a smooth matte dark blue ground, impressed mark 605.00

Vase, 4" h., 5" d., bulbous form w/closed mouth, smooth matte dark blue glaze, ship mark 357.50

Vase, 4⅜" h., wide ovoid body w/wide flat mouth, matte grey ground decorated w/a repeated design of tall stems supporting branched stylized blossoms around the top in blue, tan & grey-green, decorated by Hannah Tutt, marked, ca. 1918 ....1,320.00

Vase, 4½" h., simple tapering ovoid body w/a wide flat rim, the blue speckled matte glazed ground decorated w/repeating 'candelabra' -form stylized branched florals in dark grey, blue & two shades of brown, by Hannah Tutt, impressed company mark & artist's initials, ca. 1909 ....880.00

Vase, bud, 5" h., 2" d., slender slightly tapering cylindrical body, smooth matte green glaze, impressed ship mark 385.00

Vase, 5" h., 3" d., slightly swollen cylindrical body, smooth matte green glaze w/grey speckles, impressed mark 220.00

Vase, 5¼" h., wide ovoid body w/a wide flat mouth, a deep yellow ground decorated w/a spaced band of stylized trees w/double slender brown trunks & ruffled green tops, marked, ca. 1917 (small glaze bubble on side, tiny glaze skip at base) 1,760.00

Vase, 5¾" h., 3¼" d., footed ovoid body w/a wide gently flaring neck, smooth matte dark blue exterior & a sky blue glossy interior, ship mark 220.00

Vase, 6" h., 5" d., wide ovoid body tapering to a flared rim, fine mottled green & brown glaze, impressed ship mark 550.00

Vase, 6¼" h., 5¼" d., tapering ovoid body w/rolled rim, decorated w/a wide band of stylized blossoms on twig branches in varied shades of bluish grey against a lighter grey speckled ground, impressed ship mark & paper label 2,090.00

Vase, 6¾" h., tall ovoid body w/wide flat mouth, blue ground decorated w/five black-outlined stylized trees w/green leaves, red berries & brown trunks extending to border above & below, impressed mark (flat kiln chip under base) 1,100.00

Vase, 7" h., 4" d., slightly ovoid, decorated w/a repeated pattern of stylized grape vines w/green leaves, blue berries & brown narrow tree trunks against a smooth speckled matte ochre ground, artist-initialed "HT," Hannah Tutt, & impressed ship mark w/"M/P" 4,950.00

Vase, 7" h., 4" d., slightly waisted cylindrical body, smooth matte heavily speckled dark blue glaze,ship mark (ILLUS. top next column) 357.50

Simple Marblehead Vase

Vase, 7¼" h., 3¾" d., slightly swelled cylindrical body w/a flat mouth, incised w/tall stylized trees in green & red w/blue trunks against a matte blue ground, impressed ship mark & paper label 1,980.00

Vase, 8" h., 7" d., narrow base expanding to a bulbous shoulder, feathered matte mustard glaze, marked 440.00

Vase, 9½" h., 5¼" d., cylindrical body rounded at the bottom & at the closed rim, smooth matte dark blue speckled glaze, ship mark 605.00

Vase, 9¾" h., cylindrical form w/closed rim, subtle repeating decoration of five conventionalized tree clusters in shades of green, brown & greyish black against a misty greyish blue ground, impressed mark, blue artist initials & date "1913" 5,500.00

Vase, 11" h., 4½" d., slightly ovoid, decorated around the top portion w/incised stylized pine cones in dark brown against a matte olive ground, "M" crossed by seagull mark, A. Baggs monogram 7,700.00

MARTIN BROTHERS POTTERY

Martinware, the term used for this pottery, dates from 1873 and is the product of the Martin brothers - Robert, Wallace, Edwin, Walter and Charles - often considered the first British studio potters. From first to final stages, their hand-thrown pottery was completely the work of the team. The early wares may be simple and conventional, but the Martin brothers built up their reputation by producing ornately engraved, incised or carved designs as well as rather bizarre figural wares. The amusing face-jugs are considered some of their finest work. After 1910, the work of the pottery declined and can be considered finished by 1915, though some attempts were made to fire pottery as late as the 1920s.

Martin Brothers Jar

RW Martin & Brothers
London & Southall

Jar, cov., modeled as a strange whimsical bird w/very expressive face, the cover formed by the head, glazed in bluish green & brown tones, mounted on a wooden base, incised on base & head "Martin Bros - London T Southhall - 11-1889," dated 1889, bird 3¾" d., 9" h. $7,000.00

Jar, cov., modeled as a grotesque bird, the head w/closed eyes & a laughing expression to the open beak, glazed in browns, beige & deep blues, signed & dated "7-1892" (head) & "10-1891" (body), minor nick on beak, 4¼" w., 10½" h. (ILLUS.) 6,875.00

Jar, cov., modeled as a strange bird, the cover formed by the head, naturalistic coloring, the base & cover incised "Martin Bros. London Southall RW," & base "71890," & cover "7V890," 15" h. (beak restored) 7,475.00

Model of a grotesque bird, standing w/molded wings & feathers, blue & brown glaze, artist-signed, dated 1893 (or 98), 3" h. 715.00

Pitcher, 8⅛" h., jug-type, bulbous

ovoid body w/short neck, pulled spout & applied handle, molded in low-relief w/a smiling grotesque face & incised w/clusters of grapes pendent from leafy vines, further decorated in black, chrome green & iron slips under a rich textured salt glaze, inscribed "Martin Bros - London & Southall - 2-1892," dated 1892 ....3,575.00

Pitcher, 8⅝" h., jug-type, the bulbous ovoid body w/short cylindrical neck, pulled spout & applied handle, molded in low-relief w/a smiling grotesque face amid incised clusters of raspberries & leafage, decorated in black slip under textured salt glaze, inscribed "Martin Bros. - London & Southall - 2-1892," dated 1892 ....3,850.00

Martin Brothers 'Sun' Pitcher

Pitcher, 9½" h., jug-type, the spherical body tapering at one side of the top to a raised spout opposite a long loop handle, molded in relief on each side w/a smiling 'Sun' face w/radiating rays glazed in pale olive, the face in dark reddish brown, inscribed "Martin Bros - London & Southall - 6-1897," ca. 1897 (ILLUS.) 6,038.00

Vase, 5¼" h., 3½" d., ovoid lobed body w/a short, molded neck, overall semi-gloss speckled brown glaze, marked "Martin Bro. - London & Southall - 1x2 - 1-1901" 412.50

Vase, 5½" h., 2" d., bottle-form, vertical ridges under a curdled green & brown glaze, dark blue glossy neck, marked "Martin, London"........165.00

Vase, 5¾" h., 2¼" d., cylindrical body, incised decoration of two bluebirds on a branch against a beige ground, marked "R. W. Martin, Southall 11. 1877," 1877 (line around underside of base)...550.00

Vase, 6¾" h., 3¼" d., bulbous footed base below a tall, slender cylindrical neck w/flared rim, the base w/looped panels decorated w/stylized 'faces' in light & dark blue against a beige ground, the tall neck w/stylized palm leaves in the same colors, marked "R.W. Martin - London - 15" 770.00

Vase, 8" h., 6" d., bulbous base below a tall, wide & slightly tapering neck flanked by loop handles down the sides, the base w/staggered blue vertical ribbing on a tan ground, the neck w/bluish green fanned & spiky leaves in a zigzag pattern on a tan ground, brown rim & handles, marked "Martin London & Southall 29-6-82" 770.00

Vase, 8⅛" h., footed bulbous ovoid body tapering to a short flared neck, decorated w/several small flying & perched birds on flowering branches in shades of brown, tan, grey & white, all against a speckled & shaded brown & tan ground, base incised "4-1887-R-W Martin & Bros London & Southall," dated 1887 ....2,530.00

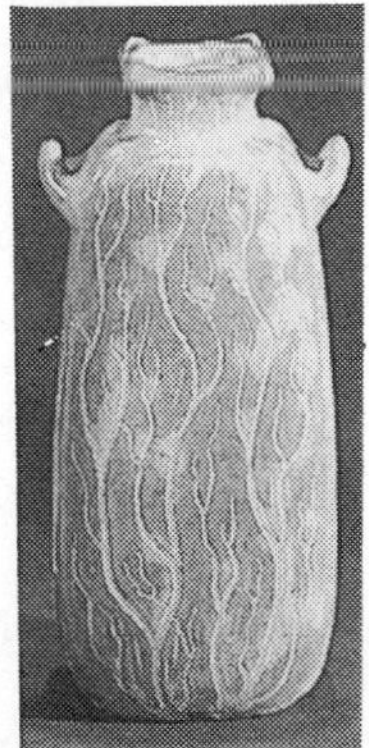

Martin Brothers Vase

Vase, 9" h., 4" d., slightly tapering cylindrical body w/a short neck w/squared rim, upturned loop handles at the shoulder, decorated w/coral-like branches in sgraffito on a brown ground, script mark & "N5 - 7-1903" (ILLUS.) 1,210.00

Vase, 9¼" h., 6½" d., footed bulbous ovoid body tapering to a wide flaring neck, covered in vivid incised & modeled swirls, brown & black satin glaze, script signature & "1-1-1903" 1,210.00

CLEMENT MASSIER

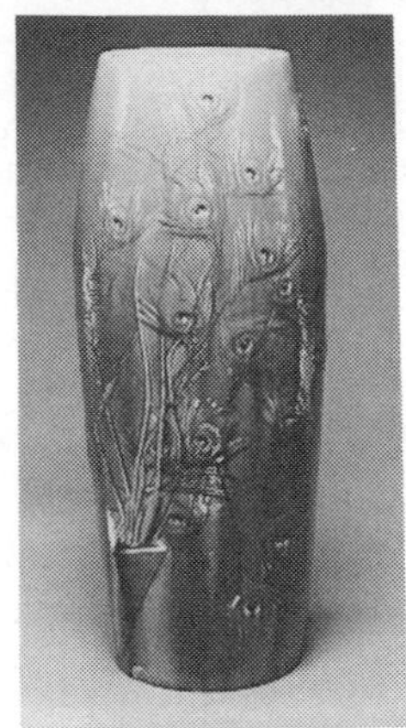

Clement Massier Umbrella Stand

Clement Massier was a French artist potter who worked in the late 19th and early 20th centuries creating exquisite earthenware items with lustre decoration.

Clement-MASSIER
Golfe Juan AM

Plate, 8" d., a yellow lustre ground decorated w/four blue flowers on leafy stems & connected by scrolling blue leafy vines, signed in slip on the back "C.M. 1888" & stamped "Clement Massier, Golfe Juan" (two chips on back rim edge)..................$247.50

Plate, 10¼" d., footed, decorated overall w/a landscape by the water & a setting sun in green, gold & burgundy iridescent glaze, signed "Massier"..935.00

Umbrella stand, slightly swelled cylindrical form, molded w/an applied pocket near the base, the pocket issuing applied & carved peacock feathers wrapping around the sides, green glaze shaded w/charcoal-over-white underglaze, impressed mark "CLEMENT MASSIER - Golfe Juan - A.M.," ca. 1900, chips to base & rim, 26" h. (ILLUS.) 1,438.00

Vase, 4¾" h., gentle tapering cylindrical body w/a wide square mouth, scattered stylized flowers & leaves all in iridescent shades of green, base marked "MCM Golfe. Juan (AM)" & stamped circular logo mark (minor rim roughness).............495.00

Clement Massier Vase

Vase, 12¾" h., gently tapering ovoid body w/a flat mouth, green-glazed body w/pink iridescent decoration of three grasshoppers in intaglio amid stalks of wheat, painted mark "M. CLEMENT MASSIER GOLFE JUAN A.M." & incised "MCM GOLFE - JUAN" (ILLUS.).............................4,620.00

Vase, 22" h., 10" d., tall baluster-form w/a cylindrical neck, molded around the shoulder w/a row of lion medallions among overall scrolling gilded florals, the lower half w/large stylized flowers & angled bars, impressed "CLEMENT MASSIER - GOLFE JUAN"..............................1,100.00

MC COY

Caboose Cookie Jar

Collectors are now seeking the art wares of two McCoy potteries. One was founded in Roseville, Ohio, in the late 19th century as the J.W. McCoy Pottery, subsequently becoming Brush-McCoy Pottery Co., later Brush Pottery. The other was founded also in Roseville in 1910 as Nelson McCoy Sanitary Stoneware Co., later becoming

Nelson McCoy Pottery. In 1967 the pottery was sold to D.T. Chase of the Mount Clemens Pottery Co. who sold his interest to the Lancaster Colony Corp. in 1974. The pottery shop closed in 1985. Cookie jars are especially collectible today.

A helpful reference book is The Collector's Encyclopedia of McCoy Pottery, *by the Huxfords (Collector Books), and* McCoy Cookie Jars From the First to the Latest, *by Harold Nichols (Nichols Publishing, 1987).*

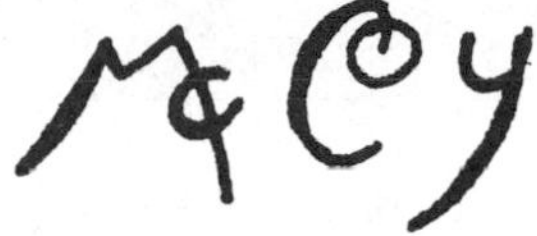

Ale set: tankard pitcher & two mugs; relief-molded Buccaneer figure on sides, green glaze, 3 pcs $55.00

Bank, barrel-shaped, "Drydock Savings Bank, That's my Bank" 22.00

Bank, Bowery money chest, green glaze, unsigned 25.00

Bank, figural sailor w/large duffle bag over his shoulder, "Seaman's Bank for Savings" 32.00

Bank, figural, model of a spread-winged American eagle on a rectangular base, made for Immigrant Industrial Savings Bank 29.00

Bank, model of an owl, Woodsy Owl .... 55.00 to 65.00

Barbeque set: cov. coffee server w/warmer, four cups, chuck wagon cov. food warmer & candle, iced tea dispenser & soup tureen w/sombrero cover; El Rancho Bar-B-Que line, ca. 1960s, 8 pcs 950.00

Basket, hanging-type, round relief-molded loop handles, basketweave design on turquoise ground, 4¼" h. 35.00

Basket, hanging-type, half-round shape, molded ivy leaves around the sides on a finely ribbed ground, pale green glaze, ca. 1950 .... 18.00

Basket, hanging-type, spherical body w/wide flat rim & three-toed base, shaded brown & green matte glaze, Nelson McCoy Sanitary Stoneware Co., ca. 1926 .... 20.00

Bulb bowl, oblong, horizontal ripple rim band above wide vertical ribs, white glaze, 3¾ x 4½" 4.00

Candleholder-book end, upright cluster of molded leaves, white glaze, ca. 1940, 5½" h. 15.00

Cookie jar, Apple, red, 1950-64 .... 62.50

Cookie jar, Apple, yellow or green, 1950-64, each 30.00

Cookie jar, Apollo, 1970-71 .... 900.00 to 950.00

Cookie jar, Asparagus, 1977 .... 37.00

Cookie jar, Astronaut, 1963 .... 650.00

Cookie jar, Barnum's Animals (Nabisco Wagon), 1972-74 .... 300.00 to 325.00

Cookie jar, Barrel w/"Cookies" on finial, black, 1969-72 .... 27.00

Cookie jar, Basket of Potatoes, 1978-80 .... 35.00

Cookie jar, Bear (Cookie in Vest), 1943-45 .... 75.00

Cookie jar, Bean Pot, black, 1939-43 .... 40.00

Cookie jar, Bear (Hamm's Bear), 1972 .... 200.00 to 225.00

Cookie jar, Bear & Beehive, 1978-86 .... 50.00 to 60.00

Cookie Jar, Betsy Baker, 1975-76 .... 350.00 to 400.00

Cookie jar, Bobby the Baker, 1974-79 .... 40.00 to 60.00

Cookie jar, Boy on Baseball, 1978 .... 250.00 to 300.00

Cookie jar, Boy on Football, 1978 .... 275.00

Cookie jar, Bunch of Bananas, 1948-52 .... 80.00 to 100.00

Cookie jar, Caboose, "Cookie Special," 1961 (ILLUS.) 145.00

Cookie jar, Chef (Bust), w/"Cookies" on hat band, 1962-64 .... 100.00 to 125.00

Cookie jar, Chilly Willy, 1986-87 .... 55.00

Cookie jar, Chinese Lantern ("Fortune Cookies") 1967 .... 52.00

Cookie jar, Chipmunk, 1960-61 .... 100.00

Cookie jar, Christmas Tree, 1959 .... 1,100.00

Cookie jar, Circus Horse, black, 1961 .... 175.00 to 200.00

Cookie jar, Clown bust, 1945-47 .... 52.00

Cookie jar, Clown in Barrel, 1953-56 (ILLUS. top next column) .... 75.00 to 100.00

Clown in Barrel Cookie Jar

Cookie jar, Clyde Dog, 1974 ....150.00 to 175.00

Cookie jar, Coalby Cat, 1967-68 ....350.00 to 400.00

Coffee Grinder Cookie Jar

Cookie jar, Coffee Grinder, brown, 1961-68 (ILLUS.) 30.00

Cookie jar, Coffee Mug, 1963-66..........45.00

Cookie jar, Coke Jug, 1986 ....60.00

Cookie jar, Colonial Fireplace, 1967-68..........85.00 to 95.00

Cookie jar, Cookie Cabin (log cabin),1956-60..........60.00

Cookie jar, Cookie Churn, 1977-87 ......29.00

Cookie jar, Cookie House, 1958-60 (ILLUS. top next column) 100.00

Cookie jar, Country Stove (Pot Belly Stove), black, 1963 ....33.00

Cookie jar, Country Stove (Pot Belly Stove), white, 1970-72..........50.00

Cookie House Cookie Jar

Covered Wagon Cookie Jar

Cookie jar, Covered Wagon (Cookie Wagon), 1959-62 (ILLUS.)..........75.00

Cookie jar, Davy Crockett, 1957 ....500.00 to 550.00

Cookie jar, Dog on Basketweave, 1956-57 ....55.00

Cookie jar, Duck, w/leaf in bill, 1964...110.00

Cookie jar, Dutch Boy, 1946..........45.00

Cookie jar, Early American (Frontier Family), plain knob finial, 1964-71 .....48.00

Cookie jar, Early American Chest (Chiffonier), 1965-68..........72.00

Cookie jar, Elephant, whole trunk, 1953 ....100.00 to 125.00

Cookie jar, Engine, black, 1962-64..........125.00 to 150.00

Cookie jar, Forbidden Fruit, 1967-68..........65.00

Cookie jar, Globe, 1960 (ILLUS. top next column) ....200.00 to 225.00

Cookie jar, Grandma, white w/color trim, 1974-75..........80.00

Globe Cookie Jar

Cookie jar, Happy Face, 1972-79.........35.00

Cookie jar, Hen on Nest, 1958-59........85.00

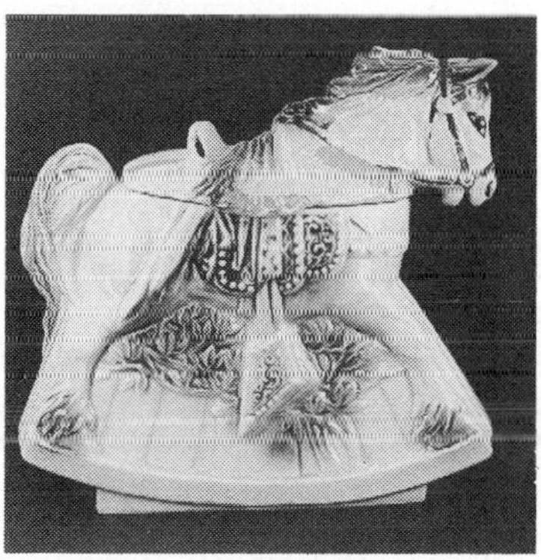

Hobby Horse Cookie Jar

Cookie jar, Hobby Horse, 1948-53 (ILLUS.) ....150.00 to 200.00

Cookie jar, Hobnail pattern, almostheart-shaped, w/flat sides, 7-pint, 1940.....................................450.00

Cookie jar, Hocus Rabbit, 1978-79.......69.00

Cookie jar, Holly Hobbie, 1980.............45.00

Cookie jar, Honey Bear (on Side of Tree), 1953-55...................75.00 to 100.00

Cookie jar, House (two story), No. 161, 1980s 395.00

Cookie jar, Hot Air Balloon, 1985-86....28.00

Cookie jar, Hound Dog (Thinking Puppy), 1977-79 ....27.50

Cookie jar, Indian Head, 1954-56(ILLUS. top next column) ....325.00 to 350.00

Cookie jar, Kangaroo w/Joey in pouch, matte blue finish, after 1965................................200.00 to 250.00

Indian Head Cookie Jar

Kangaroo Cookie Jar

Cookie jar, Kangaroo w/Joey in pouch, tan finish, 1965 (ILLUS.) 450.00

Cookie jar, Keebler Tree House, 1986-87................................50.00 to 75.00

Cookie jar, Kettle, hammered bronze finish, 1961-67 ....35.00

Cookie jar, Kitten on a Coal Bucket, 1983..350.00

Cookie jar, Kittens (Two) in a Low Basket, 1950s 800.00

Cookie jar, Kittens (Three) on Ball of Yarn, 1954-55 ....110.00

Cookie jar, Koala Bear, 1960-77..............................75.00 to 100.00

Cookie jar, Kookie Kettle, 1960-77...............................15.00 to 20.00

Cookie jar, Lamb on Basketweave, white w/brown, 1956-57.....................48.00

Cookie jar, Lamp (Lantern), 1962-63....50.00

Cookie jar, Lazy Pig, 1978-79 ....40.00

Cookie jar, Lollipops, 1958-60 ....65.00

Cookie jar, "Mac" Dog, 1967-68 ....83.00

Cookie jar, Mammy, "Cookies" only, decorated dress, 1948-57 ....177.00

Cookie jar, Mammy, "Cookies" only, overall aqua glaze, 1948-57 ....295.00

Cookie jar, Mammy, "Cookies" only, yellow dress, 1948-57 ......500.00 to 550.00

Cookie jar, Mammy with Cauliflower, 1939 ....1,100.00 to 1,300.00

Cookie jar, Mary, Mary, Quite Contrary, 1970 ....45.00

Cookie jar, Milk Can, w/Gingham Flowers, No. 333 ....75.00

Cookie jar, Monk ("Thou Shalt Not Steal"), 1968-73 ....30.00

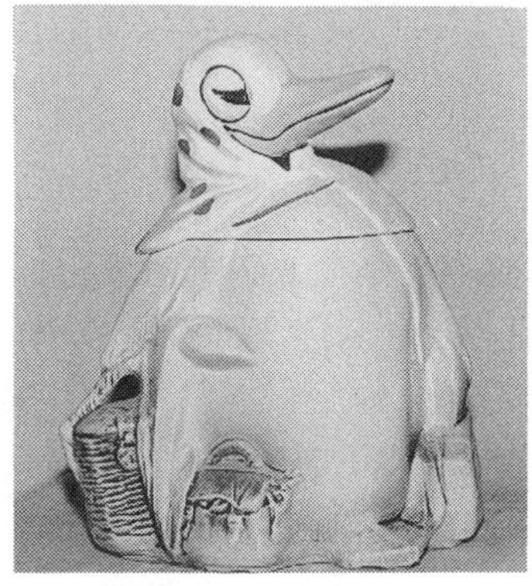

Mother Goose Cookie Jar

Cookie jar, Mother Goose, brown, 1948-52, (ILLUS.) 165.00

Cookie jar, Mushrooms on Stump, 1972 ....65.00

Cookie jar, Oaken Bucket, 1961-71 ....25.00

Old Auto Cookie Jar

Cookie jar, Old Fashioned Auto (Touring Car), 1962-64 (ILLUS.) ....70.00 to 80.00

Cookie jar, Owls (Mr. & Mrs. Owl), 1953-55 ....75.00 to 100.00

Cookie jar, Panda Bear (Upside Down Bear), 1978-79 ....35.00

Cookie jar, Peanut, 1976-77 ....30.00

Cookie jar, Pear, yellow, 1952-57 ....45.00

Cookie jar, Penguin, white, 1940-43 ....60.00

Cookie jar, Pepper, green, 1972-75 ....25.00 to 30.00

Cookie jar, Pepper, yellow, 1972-80 ....32.50

Cookie jar, Picnic Basket, 1962-63 ....45.00

Cookie jar, Pineapple, natural colors, 1955-57 ....73.00

Cookie jar, Pine Cones on Basket-weave, 1957 ....40.00

Cookie jar, Pirate's Chest, 1970 ....135.00

Cookie jar, Popeye, cylinder w/decal, 1971-72 ....180.00

Cookie jar, Pumpkin (Jack-O-Lantern), 1955 ....650.00 to 850.00

Cookie jar, Puppy (holding cookie sign), 1961-62 ....85.00

Cookie jar, Rabbit w/Cookie on stump, 1971 ....60.00

Cookie jar, Rag Doll (Raggedy Ann), 1972-75 ....75.00 to 100.00

Cookie jar, Rocking Chair (Dalmatians), 1961 ....400.00 to 425.00

Cookie jar, Snoopy on Doghouse, 1970 ....237.00

Cookie jar, Snow Bear, 1965 ....40.00

Cookie jar, Spaceship (Friendship 7), 1962-63 ....125.00 to 150.00

Cookie jar, Stagecoach, 1956 ....1,000.00 to 1,500.00

Cookie jar, Stove (Cook Stove), black, 1962-64 ....25.00

Cookie jar, Stove (Cook Stove), white, 1962-64 ....35.00

Cookie jar, Strawberry, white drip glaze, 1955-57 ....30.00

Cookie jar, Teddy Bear & Friend, 1986-87 ....40.00

Cookie jar, Teepee, 1956-59 (ILLUS. top next column) .300.00 to 350.00

Cookie jar, Time for Cookies (Mouse on Clock), 1968-73 ....35.00

Tepee Cookie Jar

Cookie jar, Turkey, brown, 1960 ....175.00 to 200.00

Cookie jar, Turkey, green, 1960 ....275.00 to 300.00

Cookie jar, W.C. Fields, 1972-74....157.00

Cookie jar, Wedding Jar, 1961 ....80.00

Cookie jar, Winking Pig, 1972 ....350.00

Cookie jar, Wishing Well, 1961-70 ....28.00

Cookie jar, Woodsy Owl, 1973-74....200.00 to 250.00

Wren House Cookie Jar

Cookie jar, Wren House w/brown bird on top, 1958-60 (ILLUS.) ...75.00 to 100.00

Cookie jar, Wren House w/pink bird on top, 1958-60....150.00 to 200.00

Cookie jar, Yosemite Sam, cylinder w/decal, 1971-72 ....100.00 to 125.00

Creamer, Daisy patt., matte pink & turquoise glaze 6.50

Creamer, Pine Cone patt.....10.00

Decanter, Apollo series, Astronaut,marked "Thomas 'n Sims Distillery," 1968 ....190.00

Decanter, Apollo series, missile, 1968....225.00

Decanter set, train locomotive, coal car marked "Jupiter" & two cars, 1969, the set 90.00

Fern box, oblong Butterfly patt., greenish-brown, glaze, 1940, 4½ x 8¾", 3¼" h....9.00

Flower holder, ball-shaped, scalloped top, green glaze, 1943 ....6.50

Flowerpot & saucer, embossed double beetle rim band decoration, orange glaze, 1961, 5" h., 2 pcs. 6.00

Flowerpot w/attached saucer, embossed icicle band around upper half above finely ribbed lower section, green & cream glaze, 1957, 3¾" h....3.50

Flowerpot w/attached saucer, Greek Key band decoration, green glaze, 1954, 4" h....5.00

Food warmer, El Rancho Bar-B-Que line, model of a Chuck Wagon w/rack,1960 ....150.00 to 175.00

Iced tea server, El Rancho Bar-B-Que line, barrel-shaped, 1960....175.00 to 200.00

Jardiniere, underglaze slip-painted tulips, brown glaze, marked "Loy-Nel-Art," 5" h. 165.00

Jardiniere, relief-molded flying birds around sides, ca. 1935, 7½" h. 18.00

Jardiniere, footed bulbous body w/fluted rim & foot, glossy dark green, 1959, 7¼" d., 5¼" h., ...7.00

Lamp base, modeled as a pair of cowboy boots, brown glaze, ca. 1956, small size 65.00

Mug, barrel-shaped, brown glaze, Nelson McCoy, 1926 ....4.00

Mugs, coffee, El Rancho Bar-B-Que line, 1960, set of 4 ....80.00

Planter, Arcature line, bird & foliage framed in base, 1951, 6½" h. (ILLUS. top next column) 28.00

Planter, Banana Boat, Calypso line, man holding banjo standing by boat, tan glaze 80.00

Planter, Chinese Man w/Wheel-barrow, yellow, 1950....10.00

Arcature Line Planter

Planter, model of frog & lotus blossom, gold trim, 1943....................22.00

Planter, model of a pheasant in grass, 1959..50.00

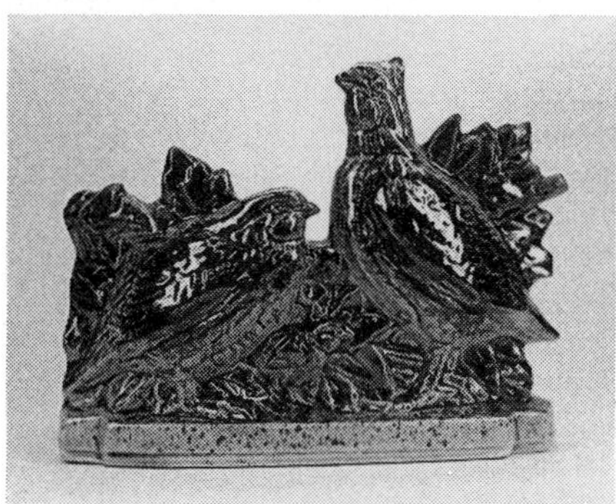

Quail Planter

Planter, model of two adult quail w/chick, brown & green glaze, 1955 (ILLUS.) 32.00

Planter, model of a rocking chair, 1954..38.00

Planter, model of a rolling pin w/Boy Blue seated on one end, 1952...........60.00

Planter, model of a rooster, grey glaze, red comb, ca. 1951, 7½" h. 25.00

Planter, model of a swan, rose glaze, 1943, 4⅝ x 6".....................................16.00

Planter, model of a wishing well, brown & green glaze, 7" h..................16.00

Planter, rodeo cowboy roping steer, tan & green, ca. 1950s.......................65.00

Planter, triple lily-type, three upright white blossoms above green leaves & a brown log, ca. 1950.....................22.00

Village Smithy Planter

Planter, Village Smithy, blacksmith standing under tree lettered "Under the spreading chestnut tree," horse standing to one side, ca. 1954 (ILLUS.) 22.00

Planters, model of the Stretch horse, yellow glaze, pr. 200.00

Salt & pepper shakers, model of a head of cabbage, pr. 40.00

Soup tureen, cov., El Rancho Bar-B-Que line, model of a sombrero, 1960, 5 qt.........................350.00 to 450.00

Sugar bowl, open, Daisy patt..................7.00

Sugar bowl, open, Pine Cone patt..........8.00

Teapot, cov. Daisy patt.........................32.50

Pine Cone Tea Set

Tea set: cov. teapot, creamer & sugar bowl; Pine Cone patt., 3 pcs. (ILLUS.) 65.00

Vase, bud, 6⅛" h., onyx glaze, streaked green, black & gold 28.00

Vase, double bud, 8½" h., a side by side large & small hexagonal upright on an oval base, white glaze, 1940..18.00

Wall pocket, conical, Mexican patt., molded peasant figures, bluish green glaze, ca. 1941, 7½" l. 25.00

Wall pocket, model of a lily, 1940, 6" h...22.00

MEISSEN

Ornate Meissen Candelabrum

The secret of true hard paste porcelain, known long before to the Chinese, was "discovered" accidentally in Meissen, Germany, by J.F. Bottger, an alchemist working with E.W. Tschirnhausen. The first European true porcelain was made in the Meissen Porcelain Works, organized about 1709. Meissen marks have been widely copied by other factories. Some pieces listed here are recent.

Basket, reticulated oval sides w/twisted handles, floral decoration & gilt trim, 19th c., 9¾" l $605.00

Bowl, 9" sq., the shaped square decorated w/floral sprays, 19th c. 330.00

Butter dish, cov., ornate mold, Blue Onion patt., crossed swords mark ...325.00

Butter pat, Blue Onion patt., crossed swords mark 45.00

Candelabra, three-light, the shaped circular base supporting an ornate standard w/floral encrustations, each curved arm terminating w/a candle socket resting on a leafy base, 11½" h., pr. (ILLUS. of one) 715.00

Charger, decorated overall w/raised gold flowers & foliage against a soft green ground, blue crossed swords mark, 11" d......................................275.00

Coffee cup & saucer, each piece w/a scale-patterned ground formed of overlapping puce quatrefoils & reserved on the front or in the center w/a rococo cartouche of yellow, blue, purple & green scrollwork heightened in gilding, issuing small floral sprigs, & colorfully painted w/a cluster of fruit (slight scratching on saucer) & flowers, the rim w/a gilt dentil edge, the elaborate scroll handle on the cup heightened in gilding, crossed swords marks in underglaze-blue, the saucer impressed "63," ca. 1750., 5⁵⁄₁₆" d., 2⅝" h. 575.00

Coffeepot, cov., 'Bataillenmalerei' patt., each piece painted in puce *camaieu* on either side w/a military skirmish or encampment scene within a puce-heightened gilt rocaillerie cartouche surrounded by shadowed insects painted in the manner of Klinger & on the pear-shaped pot sprigs of *Holzschnitt-blumen*, the gilt-edged rim w/*Alt-Ozier* molding interrupted on the pot by the gilt-heightened scroll-molded spout (firing crack) & wishbone handle, crossed swords mark in underglaze-blue, impressed "3," & gilder's numeral ".2," ca. 1740, 8¾" h. (knop replaced in gilt-metal) 3,450.00

Compote, 8¾" h., reticulated border, Indian Purple patt., blue crossed swords mark 550.00

Cup & saucer, demitasse, delicate, Blue Onion patt., crossed swords mark 65.00

Cup & saucer, decorated w/blue morning glory blossoms & gilded bands 90.00

Cup & saucer, Red Onion patt..............85.00

Dish, figural, shell-shaped w/figure of a young boy glazed in white, further decorated w/a green branch covered w/pale green flowers, marked on base "M-447," 7½" w., 8¾" h. 125.00

Ecuelle, cov., painted in underglaze-blue on the front of each piece w/a bird alighting on a flowering branch & on the reverse w/an insect near a similar branch between double lines encircling the rim & lower body of the bowl, double lines encircling the knop (damaged) & a trellis diaper border above the rim of the cover, the scroll handles at the sides w/blue dot motifs, crossed swords & letter "K" mark within a double circle in underglaze-blue, ca. 1740, 5¹¹⁄₁₆" w..2,013.00

Figure of a blackamoor, the exotic figure dressed in flowing robes, seated before a leafy bush w/one leg under him & the other fully extended to one side, a parrot perched on his right hand, glazed in pastel tones, modeled by Prof. Paul Scheurich, underglaze-blue crossed swords mark, incised "A1068," impressed "1530," 1922, 8½" h.....1,650.00

Figure of a cherub holding a scythe & wheat, blue crossed swords mark, ca. 1890s, 5" h. 575.00

Figure of Cupid holding an abalone shell, underglaze-blue double crossed swords mark, 8" h. 650.00

Lady with Fan Figure

Figure of a lady, the Flapper modeled in full relief wearing a low-cut gown w/side slit opposite long ruffles & w/her arms crossed holding a large feather fan, standing on a rectangular base, decorated in shades of gold, brown, pink, green & black, designed by Paul Scheurich, ca. 1929, marked "SCHEURICH 29," crossed swords & "A 1224 - 930," minor repair, 18¼" h. (ILLUS.) 7,475.00

Figure of a sculptress, young woman w/her skirts at her knees, modeling a bust on a plinth, on a low stepped base, polychrome enamels, 5⅛" h...192.50

Figure of a young gardener, modeled as a girl w/yellow bow (small chips) in her hair & on her shoulders, wearing a pink bodice w/a puce-striped stomacher above a turquoise-lined bustled blue skirt & a yellow-edged & turquoise-ruched blue underskirt, carrying a tan basket of colorful flowers over her right arm, her left hand (fingertips touched up) raised before her, & standing amid iron-red & yellow florettes & green leaves on a small mound base, crossed swords mark in underglaze-blue & impressed "14," ca. 1760, 4 11/16" h. 920.00

Figures, depicting a lady & gentleman in 18th c. dress, she holding a flower in one hand & he holding his hat, 19th c., 7" & 7⅜" h., pr. 1,210.00

Meissen Malabar Musicians Figures

Figures of Malabar Musicians, each wearing a puce-ribboned pale tan straw hat, hers w/green tassels (one restored), a fur-lined white coat, hers tied w/a gilt-striped & tasseled puce sash over a gilt-fringed white skirt patterned w/colorful *indianische Blumen* above white pantaloons & his tied w/a yellow sash affixed at the back w/a gilt-hinged tan wooden box above a puce skirt, the lady playing a black-edged ivory hurdy-gurdy, a chinoiserie-decorated lantern affixed to her back above a green leafy plant (restorations) in a gilt-edged urn, the singing man playing a mottled brown guitar (neck repaired), each standing amid colorful florettes & green leaves on a gilt-heightened scroll-molded mound base, modeled by Friedrich Elias Meyer, crossed swords marks in underglaze-blue, 19th c., 6¾" & 6⅞" h., pr. (ILLUS.) 3,450.00

Figure group, an amorous young man kneeling before a seated young maiden pushing him away, on a rococo base, polychrome enamel w/gilt trim, marked, 5¼" h. 203.50

Figure group, allegorical, composed of a craggy mountain background fitted along the slopes w/eleven separate classical male & female figures as well as model of Pegasus above a cascading spring, all raised on a scroll-molded base, late 19th c., 38" l., 27" h. 34,500.00

Model of a lady's shoe, slipper-type, turquoise, crossed swords mark, ca. 1860, 6" l. 285.00

Colorful Meissen Model of a Bird

Models of birds, colorful specimens perched on tall stumps, late 19th c., 15½" h., pr. (ILLUS. of one) 2,875.00

Plaque, pierced to hang, scene of cavalier pouring wine, No. 2621, 7⅝" d. 150.00

Plate, 8⁹⁄₁₆" d., *famille verte* palette, painted in iron-red, green, turquoise, blue, shades of puce, black & touches of gilding w/a songbird in flight near a chrysanthemum plant growing from swirling stylized rocks, the cavetto encircled by two iron-red lines & the rim w/three flowering chrysanthemum branches, crossed swords mark in underglaze-blue & impressed former's double-circle mark for Johann Kuhnel, Sr., ca. 1730 ....12,650.00

Plate, 8¾" d., "Zwiebelmuster," painted in underglaze-blue in the 'Onion' patt. w/a central flowering chrysanthemum plant within sprigs of fruit, flowers & leaves on the rim, the whole over-decorated in tooled gilding (slightly worn in center), the cavetto w/a scroll-edged wide gilt border & the rim w/a narrow gilt band at the edge (slight wear), Augsburg-decorated, crossed swords & three-dot mark in underglaze-blue & impressed "14," ca. 1740-50 ....2,080.00

Plate, 9" d., Blue Onion patt., 19th c. ...50.00

Plate Depicting the Goddess Diana

Plate, 9½" d., center decorated w/scene of the Goddess Diana, seated on a stone bench, carrying a club & wearing a boarskin & draped in a green & white toga, red & green w/gilt borders in a classical design, underglaze-blue crossed swords mark (ILLUS.) 935.00

Plate, 10⅛" d., scalloped rim, a wide band of relief-molded grape leaves across the center flanked by smaller molded leaves & grape clusters, heavy gold trim, late18th c. 325.00

Plate, 12" d., decorated w/butterflies & delicate flowers on a white ground amid a center & rim border of gilt leaves 250.00

Platter, 20" l., Blue Onion patt. 250.00

Potpourri, cov., the large inverted pear-shaped body raised on a short pedestal base, the sides heavily encrusted w/large & small colorful flowers framing a central figural panel, the pierced low-domed cover fitted w/a large, upright floral bouquet, the base applied w/a small figural putti & openwork basket, all trimmed w/gilt on a white ground, blue crossed swords mark, late 19th c., 30½" h. (damages)...........6,325.00

Sauce boat w/attached undertray, Blue Onion patt., crossed swords mark 200.00

Sauce boat w/attached underplate, double-spouted, decorated w/birds & insects, 10¼" l. 104.50

Tea set: cov. teapot, cov. sugar bowl, creamer, five cups, six saucers & 19" l. oval tray; white w/heavy gilt design at midsection & rim of each piece, gilt handles,15 pcs. 797.50

Tea tile, Blue Onion patt., crossed swords mark 195.00

Tureen, oval, Blue Onion patt., underglaze-blue crossed swords mark, 19th c., 9½ x 14", 10¼" h. 550.00

Vase, 6¾" h., Art Nouveau style, a wide flattened round base tapering to a tall very slender stick neck, a pale blue ground decorated w/white & grey *pate-sur-pate* poppy blossoms around the bottom w/the stems up the neck, blue crossed swords mark & stamped numbers, ca. 1898 ....1,320.00

Vase, cov., 10" h., baluster-form, painted on the front w/a sprig of grey-shaded white freesia & yellow-centered puce stock w/black-veined green leaves surrounded by small iron-red, black, yellow & puce insects including a spider spinning a web, the reverse w/an iron-red, yellow, rose & grey lily blossom, a bee drinking from an iron-red & yellow blossom, & scattered insects w/shadows painted in the manner of Klinger, the neck & footrim encircled w/gilt bands, the gilt-edged cover (repaired chip) w/three insects around the gilt-heightened teardrop-shaped knop, crossed swords mark in underglaze-blue & impressed "21," ca. 1740-45 ....4,888.00

Vegetable dish, cov., round, Blue Onion patt., crossed swords mark ...300.00

Waste bowl, the exterior painted on the front & reverse in naturalistic shades of brown, green, yellow & grey w/two animal vignettes: one depicting a black bear clinging to a falling branch as it breaks from a dead tree, the other a brown horse galloping in a landscape, the sides & the interior w/a colorful spray of *deutsche Bluemen* beneath the gilt-edged rim, crossed swords & dot mark in underglaze-blue, impressed "36," ca. 1765, 6⁷⁄₁₆" d. 1,725.00

Whistle, porcelain, Blue Onion patt., ca.1870 ....190.00

MERRIMAC POTTERY

The Merrimac Ceramic Company of Newburyport, Massachusetts, was initially organized in 1897 by Thomas S. Nickerson for the production of inexpensive garden pottery and decorated tile. Within the year, production was expanded to include decorative art pottery and this change was reflected in a new name, Merrimac Pottery Company, adopted in 1902. Early glazes were limited to primarily matte green and yellow but by 1903, a variety of hues, including iridescent and metallic lustres, were used. Marked only with a paper label until after 1901, it then bore an impressed mark incorporating a fish beneath "Merrimac." Fire destroyed the pottery in 1908 and this relatively short span of production makes the ware scarce and expensive.

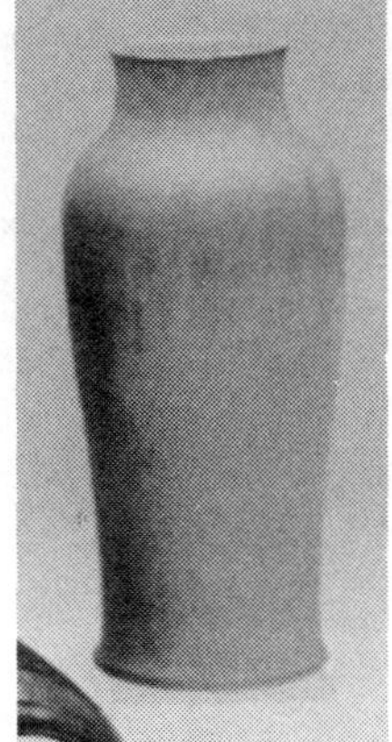

Merrimac Pottery Vase

Bowl, 5¾" d., 3½" h., single handle, canted base & flat wide shoulder, wide collared mouth, matte green glaze, unmarked (small repairs to rim) $110.00

Vase, 6½" h., 3½" d., iridescent mauve snakeskin fragmented glaze, marked 660.00

Vase, 7¼" h., 4½" d., slightly bulging form, decorated w/tooled & applied quatrefoils on long, sinewy stems, flanked by foliage, under a leathery deep cucumber green matte glaze, large paper label w/fish mark 3,630.00

Vase, 7½" h., wide cylindrical body w/rounded bottom edge & shoulder, a narrow flat rim band, greyish brown white-streaked matte glaze over red clay, impressed fish mark & "Merrimac" 330.00

Vase, 7½" h., 4¼" d., slightly swelled cylindrical body w/rounded shoulder to the closed mouth, applied w/long, curled broad leaves, matte dark green glaze, unmarked (restoration to rim, hairline)...........1,980.00

Vase, 8½" h., expanding cylindrical body w/rounded shoulder & raised rim, yellowish grey matte glaze streaked from top rim w/blue-green striations, paper label w/fish design on base (ILLUS.)..................440.00

Vase, 10½" h., 9¼" d., very wide ovoid body w/a wide shoulder to the slightly raised flat mouth, overall semi-matte mottled green glaze, paper label......................................522.50

Vase, 10¾" h., 5¼" d., tall ovoid body tapering to a flat rim, thick matte green glaze, die-stamped mark (small glaze nicks at base)..............550.00

METLOX POTTERIES

Figure of "Conchita"

Metlox Potteries was established in 1927 in Manhattan Beach, California. In 1932, dinnerware was introduced and within two years a complete line of Poppytrail was available. Carl Romanelli joined Metlox as an artware designer and became well-known for his miniature animals and novelties. However, it is the Romanelli figurines, especially nudes and nudes with vases, that are eagerly sought by collectors. After World War II, Evan K. Shaw bought Metlox and dinnerware became a staple for the success of the business. Poppets by Poppytrail are piquing the interest of collectors in today's market. They are stoneware flower-holders and planters created in doll-like fashion by Helen Slater. Metlox produced them during the 1960s and 1970s. The shelf sitters and the individual Salvation Army band figures are among the most popular. In 1989, Metlox ceased operations.

METLOX
MADE IN
U. S. A.

C Romanelli

Miniatures
by METLOX
MANHATTAN BEACH
CALIFORNIA

Cookie jar, model of the head & tall hat of a drummer boy or toy soldier, red collar, white face, black brim on hat & chin strap, blue hat, red knob on top, 10¾" h.......................$115.00

Cookie jar, model of an owl, dark & pale blue, 10½" h..............................45.00

Figure, Poppets' series, "Conchita," Mexican girl w/serape draped over her shoulders, open pot on her head & another pot beside her, open holes for her eyes, rough textured w/sand colored body, black hair, 8¾" h. (ILLUS.).................................18.00

Figure, Poppets' series, "Effie" standing w/her cymbals together, blue Salvation Army hat & coat, white skirt, yellow cymbals, 7¾" h...20.00

Figure, Poppets' series, "Huck," boy shelf sitter fishing, w/feet crossed, blue pants, brown shirt, yellow hat, 6½" h...26.00

Figure, Poppets' series, "Jenny," shelf sitter w/legs crossed at knees, yellow dress & bow in hair, 8¾" h...28.00

Figure, Poppets' series, "Nellie," bird on her head, holding vase, holes for eyes & five holes around top of her hair, black hair & blouse w/black & turquoise circles on skirt, turquoise bird & vase 8¼" h...............20.00

Flower holder, figural, woman standing on square base w/her arms behind her & wrapped around a cornucopia w/three openings, satin ivory woman w/satin pink cornucopia outside & satin green & brown inside, "C. Romanelli" signed on base rim & "Metlox Made in U.S.A. Des. Patent 122409" in stamped mark under the glaze, 8¼" h...........115.00

Metlox Figural Flower Holder

Flower holder, figural, nude woman standing on oval base, right leg out in front & bent at knee, right hand under left breast, left arm bent w/hand at neck, head turned to left, vase w/three openings behind her, satin ivory glaze, "C. Romanelli" signed on base rim & also incised in script on bottom, "Poppytrail Made in California" incised on bottom, design patent No. 125593, Model No. 1806, 9¼" h. (ILLUS.) 175.00

Figure of a woman standing on a stylized ovoid base & holding an urn to the right side of her head & her left arm over her head touching the urn, left leg slightly bent at knee & in front of right leg, satin ivory glaze, "C. Romanelli" signed on base rim & "patent no. 125594" on bottom, Model No. 1816, 9" h. 150.00

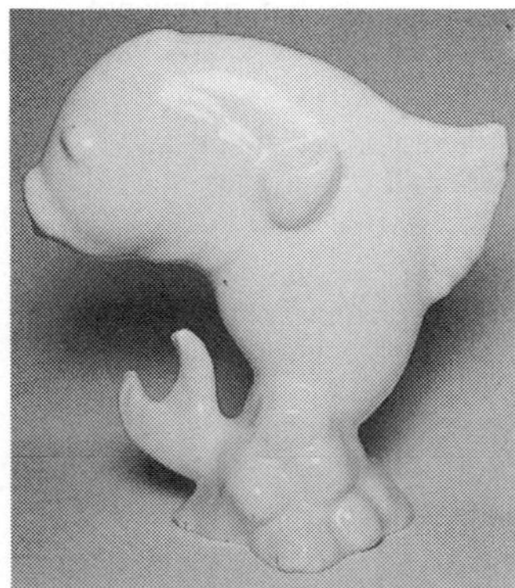

Miniature Model of a Fish

Model of a fish on a base, satin ivory glaze, paper label shows "Miniatures by Metlox Manhattan Beach, California," 4¼" h. (ILLUS.) 75.00

Metlox Model of a Stork

Model of a stork on a base, satin ivory glaze, stamp mark, "Metlox Made in U.S.A.," 6½" h. (ILLUS.) 65.00

Planter, model of a seal w/two front flippers hugging a round planter, pale blue satin matte, Model No. 456, 5¼" h. 18.00

METTLACH

Mettlach Plaque with Knight Scene

Ceramics with the name Mettlach were produced by Villeroy & Boch and other potteries in the Mettlach area of Germany. Villeroy and Boch's finest years of production are thought to be from about 1890 to 1910.

Ale set: 12" h., 9" d. jug-type pitcher & four tumblers; Art Nouveau floral decoration, No. 2098 pitcher & No. 2834 tumblers, 5 pcs. $1,650.00

Beaker, PUG, scene of gnomes drinking, No. 1032, ¼ liter 75.00

Charger, Art Nouveau style decoration w/floral cluster 'trees' in blue & gold around the rim separated by white leaf-shaped reserves around a central stylized 'flowerhead' in gold & blue, No. 2960, 14⅞" d. 440.00

Pitcher, 8½" h., birch handle, green leaves in relief on grey, ca. 1890 .....245.00

Pitchers, 12" h., Phanolith dancing scene, white on green ground, No. 7012, pr. 1,800.00

Plaque, pierced to hang, etched scene of a cavalier pouring wine, ca. 1903, No. 2621, 7½" d. 250.00

Plaque, pierced to hang, etched scene of a cavalier holding glass, blue ground, signed "Quidenus," No. 2622, 7½" d. 295.00

Plaque, pierced to hang, etched scene depicting cavalier dressed in blue playing mandolin, brick color ground, No. 2625, 7½" d. 295.00

Plaque, pierced to hang, Phanolith, white relief bust of a lady on green, No. 7032, ca. 1900, 7½ x 8¾" oval 485.00

Plaque, pierced to hang, rectangular, cameo, white relief detailed scene of two boys, one w/flute, one w/mandolin, playing for a girl holding a fan on green ground, No. 2445, ca. 1898, 7¼ x 10¼" 650.00

Plaque, pierced to hang, PUG, Oriental lady in yellow kimono, pink floral decoration on grey background, No. 1044, 14" d. 295.00

Plaque, pierced to hang, etched scene of a knight carrying a weapon, signed "Schultz," dated 1910, No. 1385, 14½" d. (ILLUS.) 1,195.00

Plaque, pierced to hang, etched scene of man & woman on horseback, jumping fence, signed "Stocke," No. 2041, 15" d. 800.00

Plaque, pierced to hang, etched scene of Bismarck on horseback, No. 2142, 15" d. 950.00

Plaque, pierced to hang, etched scene of knight trying to kiss a maiden & being pushed away, No. 2322, 15" d. (ILLUS.) 1,195.00

Plaque with Scene of Amorous Knight

Plaque, pierced to hang, Phanolith, rectangular, decorated w/white relief-molded figures in a scene from "The Flying Dutchman," No. 7046, mate to No. 7047, artist-initialed "JS," ca. 1901, w/original frame, 12 1/16 x 15¼" 1,250.00

Plaque, pierced to hang, Phanolith, rectangular, decorated w/white relief-molded figures in a scene from "The Flying Dutchman," No. 7047, w/original frame, 12 3/16 x 15 5/16" 1,250.00

Mettlach "Lohengrin" Scene Plaque

Plaque, pierced to hang, Phanolith, white relief-molded scene from the opera "Lohengrin," signed "Stahl," No. 7026, framed, 12 x 15½" (ILLUS.) 1,045.00

Plaque, pierced to hang, the center incised & decorated w/a profile bust of a young lady w/long brown hair w/a deep forest in the background, a border band of stylized flowers on a white ground, artist-signed, No. 2547, 15¾" d. 880.00

Plaque, pierced to hang, etched scene of castle above the Rhine River, gold edge, dated 1895, No. 1108, 17" d. 1,400.00

Plaque, pierced to hang, etched castle & river scene, No. 1365, 17" d. 1,400.00

Plaque, pierced to hang, etched design of woman holding flowers, signed "Warth," leather frame, No. 1488, 11 x 17" 1,750.00

Plaque, pierced to hang, etched design of woman picking grapes, signed "Warth," leather frame, No. 1489, 11 x 17" 1,750.00

Plaque, pierced to hang, decorated w/the incised bust portrait of a young woman w/long curling brown hair amid large pink & brown lilies w/green leafage & against a bluish grey ground, matte glaze, artist-signed, No. 2549, 17½" d. 990.00

Mettlach Plaque with Art Nouveau Woman

Plaque, pierced to hang, etched scene depicting an Art Nouveau woman sniffing a yellow rose, signed "R. Fournier," No. 2544, 19½" d. (ILLUS.) 805.00

Vase, 7¼" h., Mosaic, footed ovoid body tapering to a ringed trumpet neck, the body w/tapering stripes of stylized blossomhead alternating w/panels of an overall small diaper design, in shades of brown & blue, No. 1728 ....302.50

Vase, 7⅝" h., wide ovoid body w/a rounded shoulder to the short flaring neck, decorated w/two bands of confronting serrated leaf-form lappets flanking a narrow center band in shades of green, rust & blue w/similar bands of smaller lappets around the shoulder & base, all against a brick orange ground, ca. 1905, No. 1596 ....550.00

Vase, 8¾" h., ovoid body tapering to a short, wide neck w/flared rim, decorated w/a dark blue background glaze highlighted by small scattered leaf sprigs & tiny blossomheads in light blues & gold, the neck w/a brick orange band applied w/dark blue "jewels," ca. 1910, No. 2868 ....495.00

Vase, 8¾" h., wide bulbous footed body w/a wide shoulder to a ringed, slender cylindrical neck, the body w/a wide flattened center band of roundels w/stylized florals, lappet band around shoulder & small roundel band around the neck, in shades of blue & brown, No. 1681 ....357.50

Vase, 9½" h., Relief, bulbous body w/flaring mouth, full color geometric design, No. 1829 ....295.00

Vase, 12½" h., etched multicolored decoration w/four different scenes showing a boy in a tree shooting a bow or picking flowers, No. 1591 ....480.00

Vase, 13½" h., tall baluster-form body w/a cylindrical neck w/flared rim flanked by long loop handles from rim to shoulder, etched, large swirled scrolling leaves in soft colors on a blue ground, No. 2414 ....385.00

Vase, 13¾" h., 4½" d., tapering cylinder w/narrow shoulder & short collared neck, decorated w/incised flower pods in peacock blue & gold on a white ground, No. 2913, die-stamped marks 400.00

Vase, 14½" h., 5½" d., tapering cylinder w/narrow shoulder & scalloped rim, decorated w/large incised blossoms on tall stems, pink, ochre, brown & sage green on a bone ground, No. 2976, incised marks 700.00

Vase, 18⅞" h., tall slender baluster-form body, the tall neck decorated w/palmettes & looped band, the body w/a continuous design of exotic birds in bamboo, done in shades of blue & beige, No. 2457 ....522.50

Vases, 6¾" h., wide ovoid body w/a wide flared neck & raised on a conical foot, a wide body band of stylized florals in a diamond pattern in jewel-like colors on a teal green ground, No. 1573, pr. 330.00

Vases, 15" h., 6" d., tall baluster-form body w/a wide shoulder tapering to a short scalloped neck, decorated w/large etched stylized red & gold blossoms on long, flowing stems separated w/dark blue oval reserves w/a red heart at the base, the blossoms on an ivory ground, No. 2909, pr. 1,540.00

STEINS

Mettlach Stein No. 1403

No. 171, grey & tan w/blue band w/relief-molded white figures representing the twelve months, inlaid lid, 3½" d., 5¾" h., ¼ liter .... 150.00 to 175.00

No. 171, grey & tan w/blue band w/relief-molded white figures representing the twelve months, inlaid lid, ½ liter 200.00

No. 485, white relief-molded continuous scene of musicians & dancers on a tan background, inlaid lid, ½ liter 230.00

No. 675, relief-molded barrel w/hoops at top, base & middle, inlaid lid, ½ liter 150.00

No. 1005, relief-molded tavern scenes, inlaid lid, ½ liter...................325.00

No. 1005, relief-molded tavern scenes, inlaid lid, 1 liter....................375.00

No. 1146, etched scene of students drinking in a tavern, signed "C. Warth," inlaid lid, ½ liter 365.00

No. 1155, mosaic-type, wide center band w/scrolling leafy hop band flanked by narrow molded button bands, inlaid lid, ½ liter 220.00

No. 1403, etched scene depicting a man bowling in a tavern, signed "C. Warth," inlaid lid, ca. 1898, ½ liter (ILLUS.) ....375.00 to 450.00

No. 1642, tapestry, scene of man drinking, pewter lid, 1 liter 395.00

No. 1725, etched scene w/lovers & man holding a stein, signed "Warth," inlaid lid, ¼ liter 275.00

No. 1940, relief-molded Yale University emblem, pewter lid, 3 liter 1,150.00

No. 2036, character, model of an owl, the bird's head forming the lid, a crest at its feet inscribed "BIBITE," stoneware lid, ½ liter........................900.00

Mettlach Stein No. 2057

No. 2057, etched scene of dancing peasants, inlaid pewter lid, .3 liter (top repaired) 350.00

No. 2094, etched scene of lady playing fiddle & people dancing, inlaid lid, ½ liter 500.00

Steins No. 2126 (left) & 2102 (right)

No. 2102, etched, Germania stein, coats of arms around sides, signed "Schultz," pewter lid, 5.75 liter (ILLUS, right) 3,575.00

No. 2106, etched & relief monkeys in cage, monkey handle, inlaid lid, .4 liter ....3,500.00 to 4,000.00

Steins No. 2136 (left) & 2123 (right)

No. 2123, etched, scene of drinking knight, signed "Schlitt," inlaid lid, ½ liter (ILLUS. right) 1,485.00

No. 2126, etched, Symphonia stein, composers around body, signed "Schultz," pewter lid, 5½ liter (ILLUS. left) 3,850.00

No. 2134, etched scene of gnome in nest holding two steins, inlaid lid, .3 liter 2,970.00

No. 2136, etched & PUG, Anheuser Busch Brewery, inlaid lid, ½ liter (ILLUS. left) 3,190.00

No. 2248, relief scene depicting peasants dancing, inlaid lid, .3 liter 210.00

No. 2249, relief tavern scene, inlaid lid, .3 liter 275.00

No. 2278, relief-molded w/four panels of sports scenes on a colored ground, inlaid lid, ½ liter...250.00 to 300.00

No. 2359, relief four-panel decoration w/figures in each, inlaid lid, .3 liter 225.00

No. 2430, etched, scene of Cavalier drinking, inlaid lid, 3 liter 495.00

No. 2582, etched jester performing on table in front of tavern, signed "Quidenus," inlaid lid, 1 liter ....450.00 to 500.00

No. 2799, etched, overall Art Nouveau design, inlaid lid, 2.1 liter 675.00

No. 2808, etched, girl bowling, inlaid lid, ½ liter 475.00

No. 2917, etched & relief, Munich Child & scenes of Munich, signed

Steins No. 3156 (left) & 2917 (right)

"Heim," inlaid lid w/figural lion & shield, ½ liter (ILLUS. right).......3,300.00

No. 2921, etched, scene of hunter drinking in front of campfire, inlaid lid, 2.8 liter 900.00

Stein No. 2936

No. 2936, etched, Elk's Club stein, inlaid lid, ½ liter (ILLUS.) 495.00

No. 2966, tapestry, a scene of a man seated on an upright barrel & holding a stein of beer in one hand & a long cane under his other arm, pewter lid, ½ liter.............................357.50

No. 3000, etched, three panels w/women, pewter lid, ½ liter 300.00

No. 3156, etched, Chicago stein w/three buildings pictured, inlaid lid w/gold dome & eagle, ½ liter (ILLUS. left)...................................2,860.00

No. 3251, etched, hunter & young girl, inlaid lid, ½ liter 345.00

No. 3254, etched, a scene of people eating & drinking, inlaid lid,½ liter 302.50

MINTON

Minton Covered Vase

The Minton factory in England was established by Thomas Minton in 1793. The factory made earthenware, especially the blue-printed variety and Thomas Minton is sometimes credited with invention of the blue "Willow" pattern. For a time majolica and tiles were also an important part of production, but bone china soon became the principal ware. Mintons, Ltd., continues in operation today.

Garden seat, Chinese style, barrel-shaped, yellow glaze, ca. 1880, 21" h. $357.50

Garden seats, earthenware, barrel-shaped, transfer-printed in underglaze-blue around the sides & on the top w/wide borders of sinuous vines bearing blossoms & scrolling foliage between 'cracked-ice and prunus' bands flanking on the body a central pierced area of interlocking wickerwork ovals trimmed in underglaze-blue, the top w/a pierced 'cash medallion' patterned w/'cracked-ice and prunus', impressed "MINTON," & year mark for 1865, 17⅞" h., pr. 2,875.00

Plate, 8¾", square shape w/scalloped edges, white relief-molded flower garlands on Kelly green ground w/fancy molded edge & gold trim, ca. 1929 .... 50.00

Plate, 9" d., decorated w/h.p. large apple blossom spray tied w/russet ribbon, gold rim, retailed by Shreve Crump & Low - Boston 35.00

Plate, 9¼" d., center medallion w/landscape scene against a gold-trimmed white ground, rim decorated w/gold bands & gold trim alternating w/bands of raised gold dots 95.00

Plates, dessert, 8¾" d., scalloped rim, transfer-printed in puce & painted in rose, purple, yellow, turquoise, blue, brown & shades of green in the center w/a pair of ducks amid Oriental shrubbery & rocks at the edge of a stream within a gilt feather-edged band at the upper edge of the cavetto, & on the rococo scroll-molded rim w/three clusters of flowers & fruit or objects, or at the top of a cluster of flowers against a landscape w/a swimming swan, the scrolls at the edge trimmed in gilt, pattern number 436 in gold, 1830-35, set of 10 (one w/small hairline) 1,725.00

Plates, dessert, 9¼" d., each h.p. w/floral bouquets, decorated by J. Colclough, date "1883," set of 24 .. 5,750.00

Vase on stand, cov., 14" h., *pate-sur-pate*, elongated ovoid body, the front decorated w/a young woman in diaphanous drapery holding flowering branches w/butterflies against a chocolate ground, ending in a waisted base decorated w/beads & flowers, further raised on three scrolling legs on a flat disc base, the cover w/acorn finial, signed by the decorator Marc Louis Solon, printed Mintons mark, third quarter 19th c. 1,438.00

Vases, 4⅞" h., lily-of-the-valley-type, the body formed of overlapping green leaves applied w/three sprigs of yellow-centered white blossoms & three dark green leaves, the scroll-molded foot edged & dotted in gilding, ca. 1860, pr. (some leaftip repairs & touch-ups) 3,450.00

Vases, cov., 15" h., *pate-sur-pate*, each w/opposing allegorical scenes, on a teal blue ground, flanked by faux loop handles, the neck & base w/gilt highlights, raised on a square plinth, signed "Birks," the underside w/printed Mintons mark, ca. 1900, pr. 3,738.00

Vases, cov., 16" h., tall urn-form raised on a knopped pedestal base, the shoulder mounted w/two upright loop handles below the flaring neck supporting a low-domed cover w/oblong knob finial, the sides decorated w/oval medallions framing classical allegorical figures, gilt handles, cover & trim, impressed Minton & retailer's mark & "1073," late 19th c., pr. (ILLUS. of one) 6,900.00

MOCHA

Mocha Bowl with Seaweed Decoration

Mocha decoration is found on basically utilitarian creamware or yellowware articles and is achieved by a simple chemical reaction. A color pigment of brown, blue, green or black is given an acid nature by infusion of tobacco or hops. When this acid nature colorant is applied in blobs to an alkaline ground color, it reacts by spreading in feathery seaweed designs. This type of decoration is usually accompanied by horizontal bands of light color slip. Produced in numerous Staffordshire potteries from the late 18th until the late 19th centuries, its name is derived from the similar markings found on mocha quartz. In addition to the seaweed decoration, mocha wares are also seen with Earthworm and Cat's Eye patterns or a marbleized effect.

Bowl, 6" d., deep flaring & slightly rounded sides, wide center band decorated w/an undulating Earthworm patt. band, narrow dark bands at top & base, 19th c. (some discoloration) $550.00

Bowl, 6¼" d., 3¼" h., footed, deep gently flaring sides, a wide blue center band decorated w/a dark Earthworm patt., thin upper & lower black bands, 19th c. 275.00

Bowl, 6¼" d., 3¼" h., pearlware, a short wide pedestal base below the deep gently rounded sides, a wide blue band decorated w/brown Earthworm patt., narrow tan, white & brown bands around the top & embossed beaded bands, early 19th c., (small broken interior blister, small rim flake) 352.00

Bowl, 7¼" d., 3¾" h., deep flaring sides tapering to a high foot, bluish grey wide center band decorated w/a double-spiral Earthworm patt. in brown, tan & white, narrow blue stripe above & below center band (wear, small chips & hairlines) 412.50

Bowl, 9¾" d., 4" h., deep rounded sides above a footring, heavy molded rim, wide white center band w/blue seaweed decoration flanked by thin tan stripes (wear, stains, small chips) 110.00

Bowl, 9¾" d., 4⅜" h., footed, deep rounded sides, a wide blue center band decorated w/an undulating band of Earthworm patt. above a band of Cat's Eye patt. in tan, white & dark brown, narrow stripes & dark brown & blue at the top & bottom (bruise on foot, rim hairlines, cleaned) 770.00

Bowl, 11" d., 5" h., footed, a wide white center band decorated w/brown Earthworm patt., narrow green stripes at top & bottom, East Liverpool, Ohio, late 19th - early 20th c. (wear, stains) 687.50

Bowl, 12" d., 5¼" h., deep flaring rounded sides above a thick footring, w/a heavy molded rim, a wide white band w/blue seaweed decoration flanked by thin black stripes, East Liverpool, Ohio, late 19th - early 20th c. (wear, hairlines, small flakes) 247.50

Bowl, 12¼" d., 6" h., flaring sides w/rolled rim, wide white band w/seaweed decoration, flanked by blue stripes, minor wear (ILLUS.) 357.50

Bowl, 12½" d., 6¼" h., deep flaring rounded sides resting on a thick footring, a heavy molded rim, wide white band around the top half w/blue seaweed decoration & flanked by thin blue stripes (wear, small flakes) 275.00

Bowl, 12⅝" d., 5¾" h., deep rounded sides above a thick footring, a heavy molded rim, wide white center band w/green seaweed decoration & flanked by thin brown stripes (stains, hairline) 385.00

Chamber pot, miniature, yellowware w/a white center band flanked by thin brown stripes & decorated w/a blue seaweed band, 1¾" h. 192.50

Chamber pot, miniature, footed bulbous body w/a flattened flaring rim, yellowware w/a wide white center band decorated w/red seaweed design & flanked by narrow brown stripes, 6" d., 4" h. (edge wear, hairlines) 192.50

Creamer, jug-type, a wide white upper band w/green seaweed decoration & flanked by thin double brown stripes, another band of double brown stripes lower on the body, 4" h. (hairline in base of handle, chip on base) 412.50

Cup, footed rounded bowl w/molded rim, loop handle, white center band w/seaweed decoration in blue, on yellowware, 4¼" d. (hairline)............214.50

Flowerpot & detachable saucer base, the widely flaring trumpet body above a rimmed flaring base, pale salmon pink ground decorated w/dark rim & base bands & bold seaweed decoration in black, impressed mark "Creil," France, 19th c., 7¼" h. (wear, chips) 605.00

Flowerpots, flaring cylindrical body w/flattened rim, wide blue band flanked by narrow stripes of ochre & brown & decorated w/a looping Earthworm patt. in blue, white, brown & ochre, tooled blue rim, 4¼" h., pr. (wear, small chips & minor hairlines) 3,190.00

Mug, short cylindrical sides w/molded foot, wide pale blue band decorated w/blue Earthworm patt., thin white & dark brown rim & base bands, leaftip handle, 3⅛" h. (hairline, flake on base) 302.50

Mug, cylindrical w/molded base band, leaftip strap handle, wide white band edged w/thick black lines & decorated w/blue seaweed decoration, on yellowware, 3¾" h. (hairline) 412.50

Mug, squatty bulbous body w/small footring, C-scroll leaftip handle, a wide grey band flanked by orange stripes & decorated w/overlapping dot bands in white, brown & blue, tooled w/green glaze, 4¼" d. (chips on footring, wear, stains, hairline in handle) 522.50

Mug, cylindrical, ironstone w/blue & teal green bands w/black seaweed decoration divided by black stripes, marked "Pint," 4⅞" h. 357.50

Mug, cylindrical w/a wide pale orange band decorated w/several large striped white, tan & brown fan-shaped leaves, molded leaftip handle, 4⅞" h. (wear, chips) 2,200.00

Mug, tall cylindrical ironstone body decorated w/a dark blue wide center band w/black seaweed designs, thick teal blue, white & black rim & base bands, 5" h. 187.00

Mug, cylindrical w/embossed rim band & leaftip handle, narrow stripes & bands in blue, brown & chocolate brown w/wider bands of white decorated w/zigzag leaf bands, 5⅞" h. (wear, rim chips & hairline) ...220.00

Mug, tall, cylindrical form, molded leaf handle, orangish tan bands w/black seaweed decoration flanked by black & white stripes, incised green rim, 6" h. (wear & small flakes) 412.00

Mug, cylindrical, a wide pumpkin orange band decorated w/brown seaweed design, narrow black & white bands at the top & base, applied handle, 19th c., 6" h. (imperfections) 467.50

Mug, cylindrical body w/molded base, strap handle w/embossed leaftip end, wide blue band w/teal stripes & black seaweed decoration, applied white seal w/"Imperial," 6¼" h. (stains, crazing & minor rim hairlines) 192.50

Mug, cylindrical, the wide central band decorated w/the Earthworm patt., narrow dark pinstripe bands around the rim & base, 19th c., 6¼" h. (hairline, enamel loss).....................715.00

Mustard pot, cov., baluster-form body tapering to a flat rim & low-domed cover w/button finial, C-scroll handle, decorated w/thin stripes of orange, chocolate brown & white w/an embossed green band, leaftip handle, 3⅝" h. (chips, repair)...........467.50

Pitcher, 4¾" h., tapering cylindrical ironstone body decorated w/a wide dark blue center band w/black seaweed designs, thick white, teal blue & black edge & base bands, impressed "Pint" (minor wear)..........192.50

Pitcher, jug-type, 4¾" h., a wide white band around the upper half w/blue seaweed decoration & flanked by thin double brown stripes, another band of double brown stripes lower on the body (minor flake under base) 577.50

Pitcher, 6½" h., three bands of Cat's Eye patt. around the body on a banded ground, narrow dark bands around the top & base, 19th c. (imperfections) 1,210.00

Pitcher with Blue Seaweed Decoration

Pitcher, 6⅝" h., footed bulbous body tapering to a wide cylindrical neck w/a long, arched spout, yellowware w/a wide white band flanked by narrow brown stripes & decorated w/blue seaweed design, East Liverpool, Ohio (stains, hairlines, small flakes) 550.00

Early 19th Century Mocha Pitcher

Pitcher, 8" h., wide footed ovoid body tapering slightly toward the wide flat rim w/pointed spout, C-scroll handle, decorated w/incised green bands enclosing central bands of butternut, brown & white w/twig, wave & cat's eye decoration, molded foliate spout & handle, imperfections, early 19th c. (ILLUS.).............................2,750.00

Pitcher, 8½" h., wide ovoid body w/arched spout & applied strap handle, decorated w/two wide white bands trimmed w/black pinstripes, one band w/brown seaweed decoration, the other w/squiggled feathery blue bands, on yellowware, 19th c. (spout repaired)....................920.00

Pitcher, jug-type, 9¼" h., a wide white band around the shoulder decorated w/bold brown seaweed decoration & flanked by thin double brown stripes, another wide white band below decorated w/bands of thin brown stripes 1,210.00

Pitcher, jug-type, 9½" h., a wide band around the top w/brown Earthworm patt. & flanked by thin black double stripes, a band of thin double black stripes around the center above another wide band w/blue seaweed decoration & flanked by double thin black stripes, applied small tab handle under spout (wear, overall staining & crazing, chip on spout)...1,320.00

Salt dip, Earthworm patt. in blue & brown on an ochre ground, 2¾" d., 2⅛" h. (flake on rim).........................137.50

Mocha Salt Dip & Sugar Bowl

Salt dip, shallow cylindrical bowl raised on a short pedestal base, the sides w/a wide white band decorated w/green seaweed design, wear & stains, 2¾" d., 2⅛" h. (ILLUS. left).....................................357.50

Salt dip, wide squatty bulbous bowl raised on a short flaring foot, yellowware decorated w/a white band w/brown seaweed decoration, 3" d. (hairlines)................................225.50

Shaker, cov., footed baluster-form w/domed cap, narrow stripes of slate blue, tan, white & olive grey flanking a wide center band of Cat's Eye patt. in chocolate brown, 4¼" h. (damage & repair)...........................330.00

Shaker, cov., the footed cylindrical body tapering to a short flared neck fitted w/a pierced domed top, a wide blue band around the body flanked by black stripes & decorated in brown, white & black Earthworm patt., blue on the top, 4⅞" h. (chips) 632.50

Sugar bowl, cov., bulbous footed body tapering to a wide, rolled rim w/inset cover, a wide white center band decorated w/black seaweed design & flanked by thin blue bands, small chips, stains, 5¾" h. (ILLUS. right) 990.00

Waste bowl, footed w/deep flaring sides, wide blue band flanked by pairs of black stripes & decorated w/the Cat's Eye patt. in black, brown & white, 4½" d., 2½" h. (minor wear, pinpoint foot flakes) 550.00

MOORCROFT

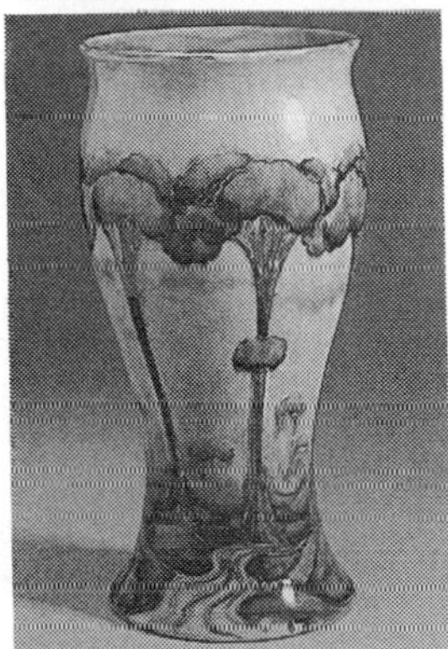

Hazledene Pattern Vase

William Moorcroft became a designer for James Macintyre & Co. in 1897 and was put in charge of their art pottery production. Moorcroft developed a number of popular designs, including Florian Ware *while with Macintyre and continued with that firm until 1913 when they discontinued the production of art pottery.*

After leaving Macintyre in 1913, Moorcroft set up his own pottery in Burslem and continued producing the art wares he had designed earlier as well as introducing new patterns. After William's death in 1945, the pottery was operated by his son, Walter.

MOORCROFT

W Moorcroft

Basket w/silver plate handle, decorated w/multicolored pomegranates on blue ground, 4" h. $365.00

Bowl, cov., 6½" d., pink & purple floral decoration on deep blue ground, signed 300.00

Bowl, 7" d., 2½" h., Claremont patt., decorated w/large mushrooms 450.00

Bowl, 9¾" d., Hibiscus patt., coral blossoms on green ground 310.00

Bowl, 10" d., Hibiscus patt., red & yellow blossoms on an ivory ground 310.00

Bowl, 12" d., wide shallow rounded sides, the interior decorated w/the African Lily patt. w/pink & yellow flowers & green foliage against a shaded green to blue ground, marked 220.00

Box, cov., Poppy patt., 3¾" h. 215.00

Creamer & sugar bowl, Pansy patt., cobalt blue ground, Macintyre period, ca. 1897-1913, creamer 3" h., sugar bowl 3¼" d., pr. 640.00

Ginger jar, cov., ovoid body w/domed cover, Hazledene patt., decorated w/a band of leafy trees in a gently rolling landscape, in shades of deep turquoise & dark blue on a cobalt blue ground, impressed mark & script signature, 11¼" h. (small chip to rim of base) 4,600.00

Jam jar w/silver plate cover, Pomegranate patt., 3" h. 475.00

Jar, cov., cylindrical w/a flat fitted cover, African Lily patt. w/yellow to light red blossoms in cloisonné against a clear bluish green ground, marked, 3½" d., 3¾" h. 192.50

Jar, cov., bulbous ovoid body fitted w/a domed cover, Anemone patt., decorated w/pink & purple flowers & green foliage against a cobalt blue ground, impressed initials & paper label, 4½" d., 6" h. 220.00

Jar, cov., wide ovoid body w/a short cylindrical neck fitted w/a domed cover, Wisteria patt., yellow, purple & warm red blossoms on a cobalt blue ground, marked "MOORCROFT - 269 - MADE IN ENGLAND," 6" d., 8¼" h. 715.00

Jar, cov., Cobridge Ware, Hazeldene patt., ovoid body w/flattened domical lid, decorated w/leafy trees in the foreground, w/gentle hillocks in the distance, glazed in shades of ochre, rose red, cobalt blue, green & tan, base impressed "MOORCROFT - MADE IN ENGLAND - 769," signed in cobalt blue "Moorcroft," lid impressed "MOORCROFT," ca. 1930, 9½" h. 3,788.00

Jar, cov., bulbous ovoid shouldered body w/a domed cover, decorated in low-relief w/stylized trees w/a red flambé glaze, impressed mark "MOORCROFT MADE IN ENGLAND 766" & glazed "MOORCROFT," 10½" h. 6,325.00

Lamp base, table model, tall ovoid body, Pomegranate patt., decorated w/red fruit w/cobalt centers & brown foliage against a cobalt blue ground, fitted for electricity, signed, 3½" d., 7½" h. 220.00

Lamp, cloisonné-style, decorated in the Poppy patt. w/large blossoms overall in red, yellow & blue, on low footed square metal base, w/two-light fittings, vase portion 5½" d., 8" h. 550.00

Lamp, cloisonné-style, decorated in the Fuchsia patt. w/large blossoms in red, yellow, pink & blue, in silver plated mount, marked "MOORCROFT" w/green smear, vase 11" h. 1,100.00

Lamp, table model, large iris blossoms in cloisonné-style in purple, red & yellow against a cobalt blue ground, brass fittings & foot, 6½" d., 14½" h. 660.00

Loving cup, wide slightly flaring cylindrical bowl flanked by long upright loop handles & raised on a short flaring pedestal foot, a round center medallion w/a swirled cloisonné design in blue & green on a glossy green ground, script signature mark, 7" w., 5¼" h. 165.00

Urn, decorated w/multicolored berries & leaves on a teal & green ground, 1940s mark, 3½" h. 175.00

Urn, decorated w/red & purple berries, large green, red, yellow leaves, dark teal green ground, artist-signed 225.00

Vase, 3¾" h., 3" d., cabinet-type, bulbous body tapering to a wide neck & slightly flaring mouth, cloisonné-style, Iris patt. w/blossoms in cloisonné in purple, yellow, green & cobalt blue, marked "MOORCROFT, MADE IN ENGLAND," ca. 1921-30 ....192.50

Vase, 4⅛" h., compressed globular form w/short slightly flaring neck, decorated w/large magnolia blossoms in pink, green & brown on a cobalt blue ground, signature & impressed marks 220.00

Vase, 4¼" h., Anemone patt., reds & purples on a blue ground, ca. 1949 ....185.00

Vase, 4½" h., Moonlit Blue line, landscape decoration, Macintyre period, ca. 1897-1913 ....1,120.00

Vase, 4½" h., 2½" d., ovoid shouldered body w/short, rolled neck, Anemone patt., white, pink & purple blossoms against a cobalt blue ground, die-stamped mark w/ink 220.00

Vase, 5" h., decorated w/pink, white & blue flowers on a shaded green ground, script mark & "Made in England - Potter to H.M. the Queen," ca. 1930-45 ....350.00

Vase, 5" h., Claremont patt., large mushrooms decoration, retailed by Liberty & Co., ca. 1910 ....1,895.00

Vase, 5" h., pomegranates on mottled yellow & green ground, W. Moorcroft green signature, ca. 1912 ....399.00

Vase, 6" h., decorated w/red poppies & blue forget-me-nots, ruffled rim, Macintyre period, ca. 1897-1913 ....1,320.00

Vase, 6" h., bulbous ovoid body tapering to a short wide flaring neck, Eventide patt., decorated w/a landscape scene w/a band of large mushroom-shaped trees in brown, yellow & greenish brown against a shaded yellow & red sunset background w/brown mountains, marked, ca. 1925 ....1,540.00

Vase, 7¼" h., Florian Ware, tulip blossoms & foliage in gold & green against a white ground, Macintyre period, ca. 1897-1913 ....1,005.00

Vase, 7½" h., baluster-form, Hazledene patt., tall trees w/clusters of foliage at the tops in shades of blue & green, printed factory marks, signed in green, retailed by Liberty & Co. (ILLUS.) 978.00

Vase, 8" h., 4" d., baluster-form w/wide, rolled rim, Pomegranate patt., large orangish gold & purple fruit against a cobalt blue ground, die-stamped mark w/ink, ca. 1910 ....605.00

Vase, 8½" h., cornflower, decoration, Macintyre period, ca.1897-1913 ...2,280.00

Vase, 8¾" h., bottle-shaped, Florian Ware, green & gold design of tulips, Macintyre period, ca. 1903 ....1,199.00

Vase, 8¾" h., decorated w/green & gold tulips, green mark "W.M. Des," Macintyre period, ca.1897-1913 ......995.00

Vase, 9" h., 5¾" d., baluster-form w/two small round handles, "Tudor Rose" patt., decorated in cloisonné-style w/round blue roses against a turquoise blue ground, ink signature "W. Moorcroft, des. - Rd. No. 431157," ca. 1904 (tight hairlines to base) 770.00

Vase, 11¾" h., Florian Ware, tall baluster-form body decorated w/raised trailed slip designs of ruffled iris blossoms & scrolling leafage, in various shades of cobalt blue, printed mark "Florian Ware - Jas. Macintyre & Co. Ltd. - Burslem - England," painted in slip "W.M. dectr.," ca. 1900...........................1,150.00

Vase, 12⅝" h., footed baluster-form body, decorated w/a band of stylized fruit in shades of rose, ochre, purple & blue on a cobalt blue ground, impressed mark & script signature 1,725.00

Vase, 13" h., ovoid body tapering to a short, rolled rim, decorated in low-relief w/a large band of fruits & leaves in deep orange & burgundy against a very dark blue ground, impressed & glazed "Moorcroft" marks 3,680.00

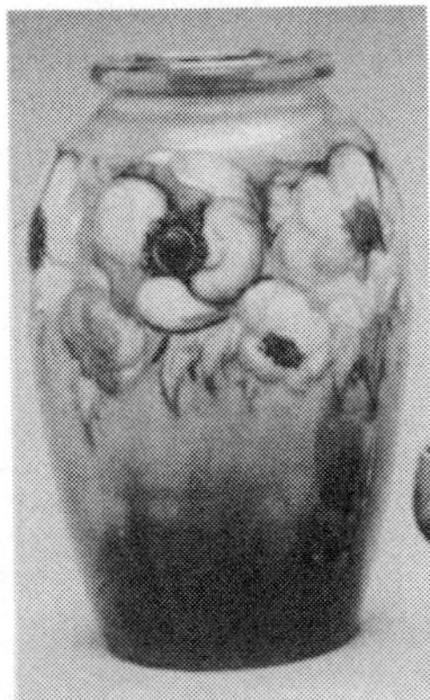

Vase with Poppy Decoration

Vase, 13⅛" h., ovoid w/rolled rim, decorated w/a band of poppy blossoms & leafage in raised slip in shades of cobalt blue, rose & green against a shaded ground of blue & green, impressed "W. Moorcroft - POTTER TO - H.M. THE QUEEN" & "MADE IN - ENGLAND," ca. 1925 (ILLUS.) 1,380.00

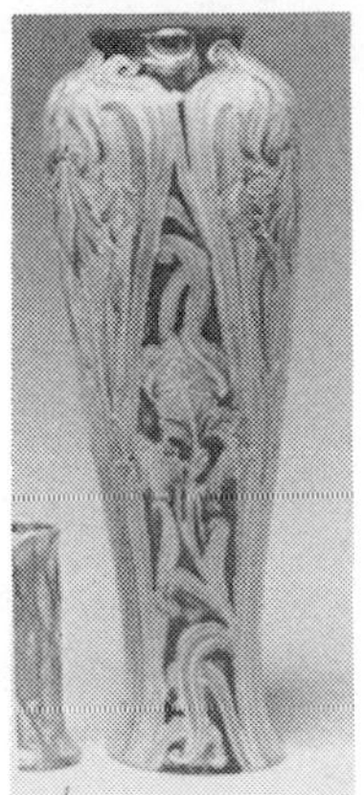

Early 20th Century Moorcroft Vase

Vase, 16¼" h., baluster-form, incised w/undulating iris blossoms & leafage & glazed in shades of green & blue, signed "W. Moorcroft" in green, early 20th c. (ILLUS.) 1,955.00

MULBERRY

Mulberry Jeddo Pattern Plate

Mulberry or Flow Mulberry wares were produced in the Staffordshire district of England in the period between 1835 and 1855 at many of the same factories which produced its close "cousin," Flow Blue china. In fact, some of the early Flow Blue patterns were also decorated with the purplish mulberry coloration and feature the same heavy smearing or "flown" effect. Produced on sturdy ironstone bodies, quite a bit of this ware is still to be found and it is becoming increasingly sought-after by collectors although presently its values lag somewhat behind similar Flow Blue pieces. The standard reference to Mulberry wares is Petra Williams' book, Flow Blue China and Mulberry Ware, Similarity and Value Guide.

Bowl, 10" l., rectangular, Rose patt., Edward Challinor $150.00

Chamber pot, cov., Udina patt., J. Clementson 350.00

Coffeepot, cov., Medina patt., Jacob Furnival 325.00

Coffeepot, cov., Montezuma patt., J. Godwin 295.00

Coffeepot, cov., Rhone Scenery patt., T.J. & J. Mayer 275.00

Coffeepot, cov., Vincennes patt., Samuel Alcock (finial replaced) 325.00

Creamer, Abbey patt., Wm. Adams & Sons 150.00

Creamer, Cyprus patt., Davenport......225.00

Creamer, Flora patt., Hulme & Booth 165.00

Creamer, Flora patt., Thomas Walker 175.00

Creamer, large, Loretta patt., Samuel Alcock 195.00

Creamer, Moss Rose patt., Jacob Furnival 225.00

Creamer, Ning Po patt., R. Hall & Co. 225.00

Creamer, Panama patt., Edward Challinor 225.00

Creamer, Rose patt., Thomas Walker 225.00

Creamer, Sydenhan patt., J. Clementson 190.00

Creamer, Vincennes patt., Samuel Alcock 275.00

Creamer, Washington Vase patt., Podmore, Walker & Co. 210.00

Creamer & cov. sugar bowl, Genoa patt., Davenport, pr. 395.00

Cup, handleless, Washington Vase patt., Podmore, Walker & Co. 40.00

Cup & saucer, Corean patt. 72.00

Cup & saucer, large, Corean patt. 95.00

Cup & saucer, handleless, Jeddo patt., Wm. Adams & Sons 75.00

Cup & saucer, handleless, Montezuma patt., J. Godwin 75.00

Cup & saucer, handleless, Neva patt., Edward Challinor 55.00

Cup & saucer, Pelew patt., Challinor....85.00

Cup & saucer, Percy patt., Francis Morley 65.00

Cup & saucer, handleless, Peruvian patt., John Wedge Wood 98.00

Cup & saucer, Rhone Scenery patt., Podmore, Walker & Co. 75.00

Cup & saucer, Tonquin patt., Heath 65.00

Cup & saucer, Udina patt., J. Clementson 65.00

Cup & saucer, Washington Vase patt., Podmore, Walker & Co. (tiny nick on base) 70.00

Cup plate, Athens patt., Wm. Adams & Sons 65.00

Cup plate, Corean patt., Podmore, Walker & Co. 60.00

Cup plate, Cyprus patt., Davenport 65.00

Cup plate, Loretta patt., Samuel Alcock 60.00

Cup plate, Shapoo patt., Boote 65.00

Cup plate, Vincennes patt., Samuel Alcock 65.00

Gravy boat, Jeddo patt., Wm. Adams & Sons 175.00

Honey dish, Cyprus patt., Davenport....65.00

Honey dish, Peruvian patt., John Wedge Wood 75.00

Ladle holder, Sydenhan patt., J. Clementson 95.00

Pitcher, 6¾" h., 1½ pt., Corean patt., Podmore, Walker & Co. 275.00

Pitcher, 8" h., Castle Scenery patt., J. Furnival (tiny repaired flake) 325.00

Pitcher, 8¼" h., Dresden patt., Edward Challinor 275.00

Pitcher, 8½" h., Peruvian patt., John Wedge Wood 335.00

Pitcher, 8¾" h., Corean patt., Podmore, Walker & Co., 1½ qt. (handle reset) 350.00

Pitcher, 9⅞" h., Hong patt., Thomas Walker, 2 qt. 425.00

Pitcher & bowl set, Corean patt., Podmore, Walker & Co., 2 pcs. (tiny nick on pitcher & ¾" fine hairline under bowl rim) 875.00

Plate, child's, 4⅛" d., Jeddo patt., Wm. Adams & Sons 95.00

Plate, 6½" d., Washington Vase patt., Podmore, Walker & Co. 65.00

Plate, 7" d., Alleghany patt., T. Goodfellow 35.00

Plate, 7" d., Corean patt., Podmore, Walker & Co. 50.00

Plate, 7" d., Washington Vase patt., Podmore, Walker & Co. 52.00

Plate, 7½" d., Delhi patt. 45.00

Plate, 7½" d., Tonquin patt., T. Heath 35.00

Plate, 7¾", Washington Vase patt., Podmore, Walker & Co. 47.00

Plate, 8" d., Corean patt., Podmore, Walker & Co. 45.00

Plate, 8" d., Temple patt., Podmore, Walker & Co. 45.00

Plate, 8½" d., Jeddo patt., Wm. Adams & Sons (ILLUS.) 60.00

Plate, 8½" d., Neva patt., Edward Challinor 45.00

Plate, 8½" d., Pelew patt., Edward Challinor 50.00

Plate, 8½" d., Washington Vase patt., Podmore, Walker & Co. 47.50

Plate, 8¾" d., Corean patt., Podmore, Walker & Co. 55.00

Plate, 8¾" d., Rhone Scenery patt., Podmore, Walker & Co. 45.00

Plate, 8¾" d., Washington Vase patt., Podmore, Walker & Co. 50.00

Plate, 9" d., Peruvian patt., John Wedge Wood 55.00

Plate, 9" d., Washington Vase patt., Podmore, Walker & Co. 60.00

Plate, 9¼" d., Cypress patt., Davenport 45.00

Plate, 9½" d., Flora patt., Thomas Walker 75.00

Plate, 9½" d., Pelew patt., Edward Challinor 70.00

Plate, 9½" d., Peruvian patt., John Wedge Wood 89.00

Plate, 9½" d., Rose patt., Thomas Walker 75.00

Plate, 9½" d., Tonquin patt., Heath 50.00

Plate, 9⅞" d., Corean patt., Podmore, Walker & Co. 85.00

Plate, 10" d., Bochara patt., John Edwards 75.00

Plate, 10" d., Corean patt., Podmore, Walker & Co. 65.00

Plate, 10" d., Washington Vase patt., Podmore, Walker & Co. 80.00

Plate, 10½" d., Cyprus patt., Davenport 75.00

Plate, 10½" d., Pelew patt., Edward Challinor 65.00

Plate, 10¾" d., Rhone Scenery patt., T.J. & J. Mayer 65.00

Plates, 9½" d., Washington Vase patt., Podmore, Walker & Co., set of 6 ....210.00

Plates, 9¾" d., Corean patt., Podmore, Walker & Co., set of 4 ....175.00

Platter, 10" l., Neva patt., Edward Challinor 95.00

Platter, 10 x 13½", Washington Vase patt., Podmore, Walker & Co. 150.00

Platter, 10½" l., Tonquin patt., Heath 75.00

Platter, 12 x 15½", Rhone Scenery patt., T.J. & J. Mayer 225.00

Platter, 13½" l., Heath's Flower patt., T. Heath 295.00

Platter, 13½" l., Hong patt., Thomas Walker 100.00

Platter, 13½" l., Rose patt., Thomas Walker 225.00

Platter, 13¾ x 18", Washington Vase patt., Podmore, Walker & Co. 200.00

Platter, 14" l., Washington Vase patt., Podmore, Walker & Co. 150.00

Platter, 15¼" l., Bochara patt., John Edwards 195.00

Platter, 15½" l., Athens patt., Charles Meigh 175.00

Platter, 15½" l., Cyprus patt., Davenport 195.00

Platter, 15½" l. Tavoy patt., Thomas Walker 190.00

Potato bowl, 10½" d., Tivoli patt., Charles Meigh 190.00

Relish dish, large, Vincennes patt., Samuel Alcock 195.00

Sauce boat, Corean patt., Podmore, Walker & Co. (hairlines) 95.00

Sauce dish, Alleghany patt., Thomas Goodfellow, 6½" d. 40.00

Sauce dish, Athens patt., Charles Meigh 45.00

Sauce dish, Corean patt., Podmore, Walker & Co., 4½" d. 45.00

Sauce dish, Cyprus patt., Davenport 27.50

Sauce dish, Flora patt., Thomas Walker 50.00

Sauce dish, Pelew patt., Edward Challinor, 4½" d. 55.00

Sauce dish, Pelew patt., Edward Challinor, 5¼" d. 65.00

Sauce dish, Rhone Scenery patt., T.J. & J. Mayer, 4½" d. 55.00

Sauce dish, Temple patt., Podmore, Walker & Co. 40.00

Sauce dish, Tonquin patt., T. Heath.....45.00

Sauce tureen, Corean patt., Podmore, Walker & Co. 295.00

Sauce tureen, cover & underplate, Bochara patt., John Edwards, the set 525.00

Sauce tureen, cover & underplate, Vincennes patt., Samuel Alcock, the set (finial reset & professional repair) 525.00

Soup plate w/flanged rim, Washington Vase patt., Podmore, Walker & Co., 9½" d., ...55.00

Sugar bowl, cov., Castle Scenery patt., Thomas Furnival 275.00

Sugar bowl, cov., hexagonal, Corean patt., Podmore, Walker & Co. 350.00

Sugar bowl, cov., hexagonal, Hyson patt., J. Clementson 275.00

Sugar bowl, cov., Jeddo patt., Wm. Adams & Sons 175.00

Teapot, cov., Corean patt., Podmore, Walker & Co. (finial reset) 490.00

Teapot, cov., Foliage patt., E. Walley (finial reset) 375.00

Teapot, cov., Jeddo patt., Wm. Adams & Sons 465.00

Teapot, cov., Tavoy patt., Thomas Walker (flakes on lid edge) 475.00

Teapot, cov., Washington Vase patt., Podmore, Walker & Co. (chip under finial) 465.00

Tea set: cov. teapot, cov. sugar bowl & creamer; Jeddo patt., Wm. Adams & Sons, 3 pcs. 595.00

Vegetable bowl, cov., Corean patt., Podmore, Walker & Co. 550.00

Vegetable bowl, cov., Cyprus patt., Davenport (finial reset) 450.00

Vegetable bowl, cov., Jeddo patt., Wm. Adams & Sons 495.00

Vegetable bowl, cov., Vincennes patt., Samuel Alcock, 10" d. (nick) 500.00

Vegetable bowl, cov., Washington Vase patt., Podmore, Walker & Co. (finial reset) 495.00

Vegetable bowl, open, Athens patt., Wm. Adams & Sons, 9" d. 125.00

Vegetable bowl, open, Pelew patt., Edward Challinor, 9¼" d. 175.00

Vegetable bowl, open, Temple patt., Podmore, Walker & Co., 7" d. 145.00

Waste bowl, Corean patt., Podmore, Walker & Co., 4 x 6½" (tiny faint hairline) 195.00

Waste bowl, Washington Vase patt., Podmore, Walker & Co. (tiny edge flake) 195.00

NEWCOMB COLLEGE POTTERY

Newcomb College Scenic Plaque

This pottery was established in the art department of Newcomb College, New Orleans, Louisiana, in 1897. Each piece was hand-thrown and bore the potter's mark and decorator's monogram on the base. It was always a studio business and never operated as a factory and its pieces are therefore scarce, with the early wares being eagerly sought. The pottery closed in 1940.

Bowl, 4" d., 3" h., decorated w/a band of green abstract foliage against a blue ground, matte finish, Sadie Irvine, 1933 ....$660.00

Bowl, 8¼" d., 3" h., wide squatty bulbous form w/a flat bottom, decorated around the upper half w/a continuous garland of large white stylized gardenias against a deep bluish green body, by Henrietta

Bailey, probably sold at the 1904 Louisiana Purchase Exposition, incised mark "NC - HB - JM - W - CX21" 4,675.00

Bowl-vase, footed squatty bulbous body tapering to a wide flat mouth, decorated around the upper half w/a wreath of white freesia & green foliage against a blue ground, by A.E. Simpson, impressed mark "NC - JM - GNS - AES '13 - 257," 1913, 5" d., 3" h. 935.00

Box, cov., round cylindrical low sides w/a flared rim & inset slightly domed cover w/button finial, decorated w/the Espanol patt., blue stripes & blue & white swags around the body, decorated by Sadie Irvine, 1925, 2¾" h. (firing separation at finial) 1,100.00

Candlestick, a wide squatty cushion base tapering sharply to a slender standard below a cupped drip pan & cylindrical candle socket, matte bluish green speckled glaze dripping over a matte blue ground, incised "NC - JM," 6½" d., 11" h..................412.50

Chamberstick, widely flaring conical base supporting a cupped small bowl centered by a candle socket, a C-scroll side handle on the base, decorated in the Espanol patt. of narrow blue & white bands against a dark blue ground, carved & decorated by Sadie Irvine, 1927, 3¾" h..715.00

Charger, a sculpted & painted border band of stylized chrysanthemum blossoms, pale green ground, potted by Joseph Meyer, decorated by Anna Frances Simpson, 1913, 8¾" d..1,760.00

Creamer, spherical body decorated w/thin blue stripes on a pale blue ground, the short cylindrical neck molded w/a band of small inverted pineapples in blue, dark blue angled handle, potted by Joseph Meyer, decorated by Alice R. Urquhart, 1904, 3⅝" h.....................................935.00

Jar, cov., wide bulbous ovoid body tapering slightly to a wide, low domed cover, the base w/a wide incised band of stylized sweet peas in pale blue against a deep blue ground, the cover w/the motto "Here are sweet peas on the tip toe for a flight" around a large central white blossom, glossy glaze, by Mazie T. Ryan, 1904, 6" d., 7¾" h.........10,450.00

Mug, cylindrical body flaring at the base, angled handle, decorated w/a wide upper band of stylized ivory flowers w/green stems above a cobalt blue band over the green base, cobalt blue handle, by Leona Nicholson, 1906, 3" d., 3" h...........1,870.00

Mug, C-form handle, incised mushroom decoration in high gloss green, against a light- & cobalt blue ground, Sara Levy, 1903, 5¼" d., 4" h., (professional restoration to handle)...1,210.00

Mug, bulbous pear-shaped body w/wide, flat rim, C-scroll handle, decorated around the rim w/a band of small stylized blue blossoms within blocks above the dark blue body, potted by Joseph Meyer, decorated by Desiree Roman, 1904, 4⅛" h..................................1,650.00

Mug, wide bell-shaped body, the upper half incised w/a band of trees in light bluish green on a yellow & ivory ground, the lower half in light bluish green, by H. Bailey, 1907, 5¼" d., 4¼" h. (invisible restoration to handle).....................................1,540.00

Pitcher, tankard, 6⅞" h., tall tapering cylindrical body w/pinched spout & long round strap handle, decorated w/a stylized band of bluebell blossoms & leaves suspended from the rim in dark blue & bluish green against a pale blue ground, potted by Joseph Meyer, decorated by Sarah B. Levy, 1903 (dark line inside rim does not come through) 2,750.00

Plaque, circular w/molded rim, relief molded across the center w/a large live oak tree draped in Spanish moss in dark blue-green against a shaded pale pink to yellow sky, carved & decorated by Sadie Irvine, 1927, 5½" d..................................1,540.00

Plaque, rectangular, "Palms," scene w/large palm trees in the foreground, the foliage in bluish green, trees & border in blue, the lower sky a pale pink changing to light blue, matte glaze, kiln particles, framed, incised & painted "NC," impressed "84," incised artist's cipher, "Shape No. 514" on reverse & paper label, ca. 1915, 5¾ x 9¾" (ILLUS.).........4,400.00

Plaque, rectangular, decorated w/a landscape of large cypress trees reflected in water in light yellow & periwinkle blue, w/original wide &

flat pickled wood frame, by Sadie Irvine, 1913, paper labels, tile 6 x 10" 3,080.00

Vase, miniature, 2" h., 1¾" d., footed ovoid body w/flared rim, decorated w/a matte blue glaze, impressed mark "NC - JM" 220.00

Vase, miniature, 2" h., 3" d., wide tapering cylindrical body molded in relief around the sides w/a band of stylized foliate design in mauve, green & grey matte glaze on a blue ground, incised "NC Sa 14 12" & artist's initials 715.00

Vase, 3¼" h., 4¼" d., squatty bulbous body w/a short, cylindrical neck flanked by loop handles to the shoulder, incised w/a wide band of quatrefoils in white w/yellow centers against a bluish green, blue & white body, glossy glaze, A. Urquhart, 1907 ....2,090.00

Vase, 3½" h., 3¾" d., spherical body tapering to a flat rim, decorated around the sides w/long green sinewy leaves on a light blue ground, marked "NC - JM - D71 - U," 1901 ....2,200.00

Vase, 3¾" h., bulbous ovoid body tapering to a flat mouth, decorated w/a repeating band of upright stems w/three-leaf clusters alternating w/round dark blue buds, dark blue rim band, pale blue ground, glossy glaze, potted by Joseph Meyer, decorated by Esther H. Elliot, 1902 ....4,180.00

Vase, 4" h., 3¼" d., tapering base & closed-in neck, incised blue berries on an ivory band, over a dark greenish blue ground, incised "NC - B - JM - FW52 - EAH - 204," by E. A. Horner, 1913 ....825.00

Vase, 4½" h., 5" d., squatty bulbous ovoid body tapering to a wide, flat mouth, decorated w/a night landscape w/a full moon shining through oak trees hung w/Spanish moss, in shades of light & dark blue w/a white moon, by Sadie Irvine, 1931 ....1,320.00

Vase, 5" h., squatty bulbous footed body tapering to a short neck w/flat rim, decorated around the wide shoulder w/a band of stylized white blossoms w/yellow centers along a dark blue band w/another dark blue band at the rim, all against a pale blue ground, potted by Joseph Meyer, decorated by Henrietta Bailey, 1916 (peppering around rim) 1,430.00

Vase, 5¼" h., 3¾" d., expanding cylinder w/narrow shoulder & wide mouth, decorated w/a night scene depicting Spanish moss & a full moon, dark blue, bluish grey & bluish green, decorated by A. F. Simpson, marked "NC, AFS, JH, SD83, 24," 1930 ....1,650.00

Newcomb College Vase with Poppies

Vase, 5½" h., globular w/short wide neck, matte bluish green glaze w/blue background at neck & shoulder, decorated w/pale blue & yellow poppy blossoms, green & yellow leafy stems & buds, impressed "JM," "176" & "B" in a circle, inscribed "GH27" & incised artist's cipher, Cynthia Littlejohn, ca.1912 (ILLUS.) 1,870.00

Vase, 5½" h., 3" d., spherical base & long stovepipe neck, lustered *sang-de-boeuf* glaze, incised "NC - JM" 715.00

Vase, 5½" h., 4" d., "Espanol" patt., bulbous body carved w/an arched, curtain-like design in matte blue & white against a blue ground, die-stamped mark 1,760.00

Vase, 5¾" h., wide ovoid body tapering to a wide, flat mouth, decorated w/a continuous landscape scene of Spanish moss-draped trees in blue-green, potted by Joseph Meyer, decorated by Sadie Irvine, 1922 ....1,320.00

Vase, 6" h., 5½" d., bulbous body, decorated w/carved bunches of white flowers w/tall greyish green foliage against a deep blue ground, incised or ink marks "NC - AFS - EH73 - JM - K," by A. F. Simpson, 1911 ....1,980.00

Vase, 6¼" h., 6¼" d., spherical body

w/short rim, upper portion decorated in high glaze w/large yellow freesia blossoms & bluish green foliage against an ivory ground, over a light green base, incised or ink marks "NC - M.W.B - UU97 - JM - X - Q," by M.W. Butler, 1904 ....7,150.00

Vase 6¼" h., 6¾" d., bulbous spherical body tapering toward the base & toward the wide, flat mouth, decorated around the shoulder w/a band of large bright pink roses w/green leaves against a smooth deep blue ground, matte glaze, Henrietta Bailey, 1927 ....2,310.00

Vase, 6⅜" h., bulbous ovoid body tapering to a flat mouth, decorated w/a continuous repeating band of upright green stems w/paired stylized yellow blossoms against a large spade-shaped leaf all against a pale yellow ground, a dark blue rim band & a pale green base band, potted by Joseph Meyer, decorated by Esther H. Elliot, 1906 ....6,600.00

Vase, 6½" h., slightly swelled cylindrical shouldered body tapering to a flat rim, decorated w/a carved moonlit landscape of moss hanging from live oak trees in shades of blue, probably decorated by Sadie Irvine, marked, ca. 1925..1,955.00

Vase, 6¾" h., 6" d., wide ovoid body tapering to a low flat rim, decorated around the shoulder w/a wide band of white & yellow gardenias w/green leafage against a deep blue ground, by Sadie Irvine, matte glaze, 1931 ...1,045.00

Vase, 7" h., 4" d., dimpled ovoid base below a wide tapering cylindrical neck, green & turquoise glossy glaze dripping over red clay, marked "NC - JM - F.H.C."..385.00

Vase, 7" h., 6½" d., spherical body tapering to a short flat neck, glossy glaze decorated w/a large band of floral sprigs w/ochre flowers framed by sage green leafy branches all on a white ground, possibly by Mary Reinfort, impressed mark "NC - X - J59 - MR," 1902 (hairline in rim).......4,400.00

Vase, 8" h., 5½" d., wide ovoid body on a narrow footring, the shoulder tapering to a short & wide cylindrical neck w/molded rim, decorated around the shoulder w/a band of white & yellow narcissus blooms against a ground of long green leaves separated by blue bands, matte glaze, A. F. Simpson, 1911 (minute chip on base) 6,600.00

Early Newcomb College Vase

Vase, 8¼" h., 5½" d., tapering ovoid body w/wide closed mouth, decorated w/a band of large stylized trees w/green foliage outlined in cobalt blue & w/blue trunks, by Grace Blethen, 1902, signed "NC - JM - V46 - Q" (ILLUS.)..................5,775.00

Vase, 8⅝" h., tapering ovoid body tapering to a wide, flat mouth, decorated w/a landscape scene of live oak trees draped in Spanish moss w/a full moon peeking through, shades of blue & green, potted by Joseph Meyer, decorated by Anna F. Simpson, 1924 ....3,520.00

Vase, 8⅞" h., wide ovoid body tapering to a wide, flat mouth, carved & decorated w/a continuous band of blue iris blossoms on tall leafy stems down the sides, dark blue-green leaves & cobalt blue above the blossoms, glossy glaze, potted by Joseph Meyer, decorated by Henrietta Davidson Bailey, 1908...14,300.00

Vase, 9" h., slender trumpet-form, decorated w/symmetrical stylized blue flowers w/yellow centers, within a band of foliage, against a blue & white ground, incised "C" & painted "D.R.C87" & w/firm's mark 3,450.00

Vase, 9" h., 4" d., tall waisted cylindrical body, decorated w/full-length stylized light blue dandelion seedlings on tall green stems w/cobalt blue bands around the top & bottom, glossy glaze, by M. H. Palfrey, impressed mark "NC - JM - Q - M.P. - V41," 1902...................4,125.00

Vase, 9" h., 5" d., footed squatty bulbous base below a tall conical neck w/a slightly flaring rim, decorated in light green w/wheat stalks against a blue sky & bluish green field, by C.P. Littlejohn, impressed mark "NC - JM - B - GJ51," 1914 ....1,870.00

Vase, 10½" h., 6" d., wide ovoid body tapering slightly to a wide, flat mouth, decorated around the shoulder w/large pink pine cones & green needles against a matte blue ground, by H. Bailey, 1919 ....3,960.00

Vase, 10¾" h., 5¼" d., gently ovoid body w/a flat rim, decorated w/a continuous moonlit scene of Spanish moss dripping from live oak trees in shades of blue w/a matte glaze, by S. Irvine, marked "NC - SI - 144 - RF81," 1928 ....5,775.00

Vase, 11" h., 6" d., carved scene of live oaks w/Spanish moss, in shades of blue & bluish green w/an ivory full moon rising behind the trees, incised "NC - 211 - JH - RU60 - FS," F. Simpson, 1929 .....7,700.00

Vase, 11½" h., cylindrical, painted w/stylized daffodils & foliage in yellow & lime against a cream ground, inscribed "C" & painted "B'60" & w/firm's mark...................4,600.00

Vase, 12⅛" h., tall slender ovoid body decorated w/a band of tall, slender oak trees in greenish blue against a cream & green ground, potted by Joseph Meyer, decorated by Maria de Hoa LeBlanc, 1909 ......25,300.00

Vase, 12½" h., tall slender waisted cylindrical form, decorated w/elongated stylized blue & white iris blossoms & green buds & spiked leaves, impressed marks "NC LN Cp-63 JM" & "W"...........................3,850.00

NILOAK

NILOAK

This pottery was made in Benton, Arkansas, and featured hand-thrown varicolored swirled clay decoration in objects of classic forms. Designated Mission Ware, this line is the most desirable of Niloak's production which was begun early in this century. Less expensive to produce, the cast Hywood Line, finished with either high gloss or semi-matte glazes, was introduced during the economic depression of the 1930s. The pottery ceased operation about 1946.

Niloak Candlesticks

Candlesticks, Mission Ware, wide flaring base tapering to a segmented shaft, bowl-shaped candlecup, swirled clays, marked & w/paper labels, 5½" d., 8¼" h., pr. (ILLUS.) $220.00

Candlesticks, Mission Ware, widely flaring base tapering to a slender shaft ending in a wide, rounded candlecup, swirled clays, 9" h., pr....275.00

Candy jar, cov., Mission Ware, marbleized swirls, w/paper label, 8½" h...2,550.00

Cornucopia-vase, feathered rim & crest, fluted tail, glossy light blue glaze, 7 x 8" 20.00

Cornucopia-vase, Hywood Line, pink glaze 12.00

Hatpin holder, Mission Ware, marbleized swirls, 6" h. 925.00

Jardiniere, Mission Ware, marbleized swirls, 7 x 8½"................................225.00

Jardiniere, Mission Ware, marbleized swirls, 8½ x 9½"..............................400.00

Pitcher, 5" h., bulbous w/rim spout, tannish ivory glaze 8.50

Planter, Hywood line, model of a camel, green glaze 40.00

Planter, Hywood Line, model of a canoe, brown glaze, 8" l.....................30.00

Planter, Hywood Line, model of an elephant, matte maroon glaze (ILLUS.) 35.00

Niloak Elephant Planter

Planter, Hywood Line, model of a monkey, pink glaze 22.00

Planter, Hywood Line, model of a rabbit, green glaze 25.00

Vase, 4¾" h., Mission Ware, rolled rim, blue, brown & cream marbleized swirls 55.00

Vase, 5" h., Mission Ware, burnt orange ground w/blue & brown marbleized swirls 145.00

Vase, 6" h., 3½" d., flaried rim w/wing shoulder handles, rose glaze, relief-molded mark 10.00

Vase, 6" h., 4" d., Mission Ware, marbleized shades of tan...................85.00

Vase, 6¼" h., Mission Ware, marbleized swirls of brown & blue, unmarked 125.00

Vase, 6½" h., bulbous melon-ribbed body w/a spiral twist neck w/scalloped rim, wing side handles, pea green glaze 10.00

Vase, 8" h., Mission Ware, blue & cream marbleized swirls 395.00

Vase, 8¾" h., 4½" d., Mission Ware, ovoid body tapering to a short neck w/a widely flaring rim, marbleized blue, brown & ivory clays, marked...165.00

Vase, 10¼" h., 5" d., Mission Ware, tall baluster-form body w/cupped rim, swirled multicolored clays, marked 220.00

NIPPON

"Nippon" is a term which is used to describe a wide range of porcelain wares produced in Japan from the late 19th century until about 1921. It was in 1891 that the U.S. implemented the McKinley Tariff Act which required that all wares exported to the United States carry a marking indicating the country of origin. The Japanese chose to use "Nippon," their name for Japan. In 1921 the import laws were revised and the words "Made in" had to be added to the markings. Japan was also required to replace the "Nippon" with the English name "Japan" on all wares sent to the U.S.

Many Japanese factories produced Nippon porcelains and much of it was hand-painted with ornate floral or landscape decoration and heavy gold decoration, applied beading and slip-trailed designs referred to as "moriage." We indicate the specific marking used on a piece, when known, at the end of each listing below. Be aware that a number of Nippon markings have been reproduced and used on new porcelain wares.

Important reference books on Nippon include: The Collector's Encyclopedia of Nippon Porcelain, Series One through Three, *by Joan F. Van Patten (Collector Books, Paducah, Kentucky) and* The Wonderful World of Nippon Porcelain, 1891-1921 *by Kathy Wojciechowski (Schiffer Publishing, Ltd., Atglen, Pennsylvania).*

Nippon Footed Ferner

Ashtray, rounded triangular form w/swelled sides, decorated on the interior w/sailboats, 5½" w. (green "M" in wreath mark)..........................$85.00

Basket w/overhead handle, pink roses on gold stippled ground, 7¾" d., 7½" h...285.00

Bowl, 5¼" sq., decorated w/a leafy branch heavily laden w/peaches, trimmed w/jeweled black tracery........65.00

Bowl, 7½" d., footed, relief-molded nuts decoration 145.00

Bowl, 7½" l., two-handled, footed, decorated w/h.p. pink roses, moriage border 30.00

Bowl, 8¾" d., two-handled, floral & geometric decoration, gold trim 65.00

Bowl, 9" d., turned-up gold handles, decorated w/a landscape scene, red & gold border 95.00

Bowl, 9½" d., ornate mold, "gaudy" floral decoration & lavish gold..........135.00

Bowl, 9½" d., two-handled, roses decoration w/gold trim & gold handles 55.00

Bowl, 9½" d., two-handled, decorated w/scene of house & tree beside a lake, gold handles...............................58.00

Bowl, 10" d., 2" h., white & raised gold chrysanthemums on pale peach & yellow ground, scalloped rim w/elaborate geometric decoration, gold beading, unmarked 75.00

Box, cov., decorated w/violets, 5" d. (green "M" in Wreath mark)................25.00

Butter bowl, cover & strainer, white w/light blue & green floral decoration, gold trim around rims, handles & finial (China E-OH mark)...60.00

Cake set: open-handled 9¾" d. plate & six matching 6½" d. plates; windmill & sunset scene, 7 pcs........120.00

Casserole, cov., decorated w/small pink flowers, 7½ x 10" oval 125.00

Celery set: oval handled tray & six tiny oval trays; h.p. plums on branch in almond, greens & brown w/geometric border design, 7 pcs. (green "M" in Wreath mark)...............................150.00 to 170.00

Cheese & cracker plate, blossom decoration w/gold trim, 8½" d. 44.00

Chocolate pot, cov., decorated w/water lilies & pads, trim & jewels in shades of purple & lavender w/gold accents, bud finial on cover..175.00

Chocolate set: cov. chocolate pot & five cups; decorated w/azaleas & lavish gold trim, 6 pcs. 185.00

Chocolate set: cov. chocolate pot & four cups & saucers; h.p. gold overlay design against a pale yellow ground, 9 pcs. (Double T Diamond in Circle mark).................................160.00

Chocolate set: cov. chocolate pot & four cups & saucers; pink floral decoration, 9 pcs. 325.00

Creamer & cov. sugar bowl, Nile River scene decoration, pr. 85.00

Demitasse set: cov. pot, creamer, cov. sugar bowl & four cups & saucers; decorated w/trees in a meadow, 11 pcs................................85.00

Dessert set: six cake plates, four cups & saucers, creamer, sugar bowl & 4" d. nut dish; gold tracery decoration on white ground, 17 pcs. 120.00

Dish, divided w/center basket handle, floral decoration, gold beading & trim, 5" d..85.00

Dresser set: 4½ x 6½" tray w/attached hatpin holder, stickpin holder & ring tree; decorated w/pastel green, yellow & orange florals, gold trim, unmarked 95.00

Dresser tray, woodland scene, 11" l. (green "M" in Wreath mark).............325.00

Ewer, bulbous, gold dragon decoration w/cobalt & green trim, 7½" h. (green Maple Leaf mark) 325.00

Ferner, quadrilobed body w/rim handles, h.p. desert scene of Arab on camel at an oasis, gold handles & feet, 10¾" w. across handles, 5¾" h. (ILLUS.) 310.00

Hatpin holder, woodland scene, 4¾" h. (blue Maple Leaf mark).........295.00

Hatpin holder, decorated w/green flowers around top, gold & white ground...65.00

Humidor with Carriage Scene

Humidor, cov., h.p. Victorian coaching scene around the sides, moriage Greek key rim band, 5½" h., Maple Leaf mark (ILLUS.) 525.00

Humidor, cov., barrel-shaped, sailboat scene around the sides, 6" h. (green "M" in Wreath mark) 350.00

Humidor, cov., cylindrical w/flared base & rim, decorated w/a three-quarter length portrait of an old accordion player against a shaded dark brown ground, 6" h. (green "M" in Wreath mark) 575.00

Humidor, cov., cylindrical w/flared rim, relief-molded owl on branch design, naturalistic coloring on a shaded tan to brown ground, 7" h. (green "M" in Wreath mark) 550.00

Humidor, cov., barrel-shaped, relief-molded bulldog head w/pipe in its mouth & framed by a shield against a shaded yellow & brown marbleized ground, 6" h. (green "M" in Wreath mark) 675.00

Humidor, cov., moriage scenic decoration w/tropical island, mountains, water & boats in earth tones, brown top & cover w/beading, 6½" d. (blue Maple Leaf mark)....485.00

Lemonade set: 7" h., 5¾" d. pitcher & three 3⅝" h. mugs; lakeside scene w/jeweled brown rims, 4 pcs....115.00

Mustard jar, cover & underplate, h.p. river scene, lavish gold trim (green "M" in Wreath mark) 50.00

Mustard jar & cover on attached undertray, h.p. lakeside sunset scene & gold beading 75.00

Pitcher, 9" h., jug-type, coralene design of roses on cobalt blue ground....425.00

Plaque, pierced to hang, decorated w/h.p. head of a dog, moriage decoration in blue on border, 8½" d. (green "M" In Wreath Mark)....425.00

Plaque, pierced to hang, rural road scene w/apple tree in foreground, 9" d. (green "M" in Wreath mark) 225.00

Plaque, pierced to hang, decorated w/pink wild roses, 9" d. 75.00

Plaque, pierced to hang, decorated w/matte-glazed windmill scene, narrow brown border, 10" d., (green "M" in Wreath mark)....120.00

Plaque, pierced to hang, landscape scene of shepherd & sheep, 10" d. (green "M" in Wreath mark)....225.00

Plaque, pierced to hang, decorated w/relief-molded squirrel, 10½" d. (green "M" in Wreath mark)....575.00

Plaque, pierced to hang, relief-molded scene of two buffalo grazing on a prairie, 10½" d. (green "M" in Wreath mark)....750.00 to 850.00

Plaque, pierced to hang, oval, relief-molded hanging dead Mallard drake, 9¼ x 18½" (green "M" in Wreath mark)....925.00

Plate, 10½" d., handled, hunt scene decoration (Maple Leaf mark)....120.00

Plates, 6½" d., decorated w/roses & gold beading, set of 6 ....60.00

Powder jar, cov., three-footed, elaborate gold scrolls & beaded medallions w/beaded green swags, gold trim, 3 x 4½" (blue Maple Leaf mark)....80.00

Powder jar, cov., spherical body on three legs, decorated overall w/gold flowers (Maple Leaf mark) 75.00

Relish dish w/pierced Indian head profile end handles, decorated w/a h.p. lakeside landscape, 8½" l. (green "M" in Wreath mark)....150.00

Sugar shaker, decorated w/grapes & gold leaves on a white ground (blue Maple Leaf mark)....55.00

Syrup pitcher, cover & underplate, decorated w/gold flowers & leaves, raised gold outlining & beading on white & ivory ground, 4¼" h., the set (Royal Nippon mark)....90.00

Tea set: cov. teapot, creamer, cov. sugar bowl & four cups & saucers; moriage dragon decoration, 11 pcs. 200.00

Tea set: cov. teapot, creamer, cov. sugar bowl & four cups & saucers; lakeside scene decoration, gold trim, 11 pcs. 220.00

Tea set: cov. teapot & six cups & saucers; decorated w/pink roses & gold beading ("RC" in Wreath mark) 13 pcs. 110.00

Tea set: cov. teapot, creamer, cov. sugar bowl, four tea plates & four cups & saucers; decorated w/jewels & gold butterflies, ornate butterfly finials, 15 pcs. 115.00

Toothpick holder, three-handled, sailboats decoration, 2" h....150.00

Toothpick holder, cylindrical w/three loop handles, lakeside landscape decoration, 2¼" h. (green "M" in Wreath mark) 60.00

Vase, 4½" h., 2½" d., flattened ovoid body on a funnel-form foot, tapering at the top w/a short flared neck flanked by D-form loop handles, central four-lobed reserve decorated w/a pink rose & surrounded by overall moriage loops & beading in blue, pink & green on a greyish green ground, unmarked 65.00

Vase, 5½" h., 4½" d., footed bulbous melon-lobed body tapering to a short ruffled neck flanked by small loop handles on the shoulder, h.p. large pink rose & green leaves on a shaded pink & blue ground, moriage trim around the neck, Cherry Blossom mark (ILLUS. top next column) 110.00

Vase, 5½" h., handled, scalloped rim, decorated w/roses, scrolls & gold tracery....70.00

Nippon Vase with Rose

Vase, 5½" h., handled, decorated w/chrysanthemums at neck & lakeside sunset scene on body, gold handles & trim, matte finish 95.00

Vase, 6" h., ovoid body tapering to a short neck flanked by small angled loop handles, decorated w/a camel rider in a desert scene (green "M" in Wreath mark) 200.00

Vase, 6" h., 4¾" d., decorated w/h.p. lavender flowers & leaves on yellow, stylized raised black enamel flowers & leaves outlined in gold & gold trim (green "M" in Wreath mark)..............110.00

Vase, 7" h., squatty bulbous body tapering to a short flared neck, overall relief-molded acorns & leaves (blue Maple Leaf mark) 450.00

Vase, 7½" h., decorated w/pink & blue floral design, lavish gold trim on white ground ("LFH" over Crown mark)..70.00

Nippon Vase with Molded Strawberries

Vase, 9¾" h., tall ovoid body tapering to a small short flared neck, overall relief-molded red strawberries & green leaves decoration, green "M" in Wreath mark (ILLUS.) 460.00

Vase, 10" h., footed ovoid body tapering to a short cylindrical neck w/flaring rim flanked by gold scrolled handles at shoulder, decorated w/jonquils & leaves on scenic background, gold outlined (blue Maple Leaf mark).............................250.00

Vase, 11¼" h., tall cylindrical body w/flared foot & scroll-molded & scalloped rim issuing long scrolling loop handles, decorated w/long clusters of purple & white wisteria against a shaded tan ground (Maple Leaf mark).......................................250.00

Vase, 11½" h., h.p. grapes & vines decoration, lavish gold trim (blue Maple Leaf mark) 190.00

Vase, 12⅜" h., two-handled, scenic design w/river, trees, fence, fields & narcissus decoration at base and top (green "M" in Wreath mark) 550.00

Vase, 15¼" h., 7½" d., h.p. woodland scene w/grouse, base & rim borders decorated w/relief gold pattern (green Maple Leaf mark) 325.00

NORITAKE

Azalea Pattern Plate

Noritake china, still in production in Japan, has been exported in large quantities to this country since early in this century. Though the Noritake Company first registered in 1904, it did not use "Noritake" as part if its backstamp until 1918. Interest in Noritake has escalated as collectors now seek out pieces made between the "Nippon" era and World War

II (1921-41). The Azalea pattern is also popular with collectors.

Ashtray, hexagonal, Art Deco style dancing couple in center, tan lustre ground, artist-signed, 3 x 3½" $125.00

Ashtray, figural pelican, blue on orange & white ground 145.00

Basket, Tree in Meadow patt., "Dolly Varden," No. 213, 2½ x 4⅜", overall 4" h. ....75.00 to 100.00

Berry set: 10½" d. master bowl w/ pierced handles & six 5¼" d. sauce dishes; Tree in Meadow patt., 7 pcs. 150.00

Bouillon cup & saucer, Azalea patt., No. 124 ....22.00

Bowl, cream soup, 5⅛" d., Azalea patt., No. 363 ....150.00

Bowl, 5¼" d., handled, Art Deco style, center medallion w/colorful Art Deco lady feeding parrot a cracker, scalloped black trimmed rim, tan lustre ground, artist-signed 160.00

Bowl, 7" d., two-handled, h.p. floral decoration, artist-signed 45.00

Bowl, 7" d., footed, Art Deco style, flower-shaped, decorated w/lavender flowers in orange circular panel, black diamond-shaped outlining 42.00

Breakfast set: sugar shaker & syrup pitcher on matching trivet; decorated w/colorful exotic birds on orange lustre ground, 3 pcs. 110.00

Butter (or cheese) dish, cov., Azalea patt., No. 314 ....125.00

Butter dish, cov., pearlized w/gold trim & handle, Nippon mark 60.00

Butter pat, Azalea patt., No. 312 ....85.00

Butter tub, Azalea patt., No. 54 ....40.00

Cake plate, handled, sunset scene w/tree, boat, water, purple sage & mountain, 8" d. (green "M" in Wreath mark) 45.00

Cake plate, colorful florals on lustre ground, 9½" d. 58.00

Cake plate, colorful landscape scene decoration, 9½" oval 48.00

Cake plate, pierced handles, Tree in Meadow patt., No. 45, 9¾" d. 65.00

Cake plate, handled, decorated w/exotic birds on pearlized ground, 9¾" d. 35.00

Candlesticks, flaring base w/cylindrical standard, sunset scene w/tree & water, 6½" h., pr. (green "M" in Wreath mark) 105.00

Candlesticks, decorated w/gold flowers & bird on blue lustre ground, 7½" h., pr. (green "M" in Wreath mark) 125.00

Candy dish, cov., stylized floral decoration on turquoise ground, 6½" d. 90.00

Candy jar, cov., Tree in Meadow patt., No. 318, 4" d., 5" h. 300.00

Casserole, cov., Azalea patt., No. 16, 10¼" d. 75.00

Coffee set, demitasse: round tray, cov. demitasse pot, creamer, cov. sugar bowl, two cups & saucers; decorated w/gold birds & flowers on orange & pearlized white ground, 8 pcs. 175.00

Coffee set, demitasse: cov. demitasse pot, creamer, cov. sugar bowl, four cups & saucers; Tree in Meadow patt.,11 pcs. 275.00

Compote, 6½" d., 2¾" h., Azalea patt., No. 170 ....85.00

Condiment set: salt & pepper shakers & cov. mustard jar w/spoon on handled tray; Tree in Meadow patt., No. 49, the set 45.00

Creamer & sugar bowl w/basket handle, Art Deco style, decorated w/two Japanese lanterns on a cobalt blue ground, pr. 40.00

Creamer & sugar shaker, Azalea patt., No. 122, creamer 5¾" h., shaker 6½" h., pr.............125.00 to 150.00

Cruet w/original stopper, Azalea patt., No. 190 ....180.00

Cruet set w/original stoppers, oil & vinegar, the two globular bottles at angles & joined at the base w/a covered handle joining them at the shoulder, Tree in Meadow patt., No. 319, tip to tip 6½" 125.00

Cup, demitasse, Azalea patt., No. 183 ....80.00

Cup & saucer, Tree in Meadow patt., No. 43 ....15.00

Dessert set: large cake plate & five individual plates; cobalt blue & gold decoration on white, 6 pcs. 85.00

Dresser box, cov., figural lady w/large full skirt which forms base, body forms cover, 4½" h. 245.00

Dresser set: cov. powder jar, pin tray, pair of candlesticks & large tray; geometric design in turquoise & gold, 5 pcs. 165.00

Dresser tray, handled, flamboyantly dressed Art Deco-style lady decoration, blue & green lustre finish, gold handles 275.00

Egg cup, Azalea patt., No. 120.............50.00

Hair receiver, cov., Art Deco style, geometric design on gold lustre ground, 3¼" h., 3½" d. (green "M" in Wreath mark) 50.00

Humidor, cov., cigar & matches decoration, 5½" h. (green "M" in Wreath mark) 250.00

Humidor, cov., decorated w/scene of lake, tree & windmill, 6½" h.............100.00

Jam jar, cov., decorated with flowers on side & figural pink rose finial (green "M" in Wreath mark)................42.00

Loving cup, pedestal base, scenic decoration in front medallion, enameling & moriage trim.................95.00

Mustard jar, cov., parrot decoration on pearlized ground 40.00

Mustard jar, cov., w/attached liner, decorated w/flowers, beading & gold 65.00

Napkin ring, Art Deco style, decorated w/a bust portrait of a girl in red fur-trimmed outfit, blue lustre ground, 2½" w. 40.00

Napkin ring, Art Deco style, decorated w/a bust portrait of a gentleman in top hat & cape, pale orange lustre ground, 2¼" w...................................55.00

Pitcher, milk, 5⅝" h., jug-type, Azalea patt., No. 100, 1 qt. 100.00

Place card holders, blue lustre base w/white stripe & figural butterfly, pr. (green "M" in Wreath mark)................35.00

Place card holders, gold lustre base w/white stripes & a figural bluebird, pr. (green "M" in Wreath mark) 35.00

Place card holders, orange lustre base w/white stripe & figural flower, pr. (green "M" in Wreath mark) 35.00

Plaque, pierced to hang, relief-molded w/three brown & white dog heads....595.00

Plate, bread & butter, 6½" d., Azalea patt., No. 8 ....9.00

Plate, 6" d., Tree in Meadow patt. 9.00

Plate, 8½" d., Azalea patt., No. 98 (ILLUS.) 15.00

Plate, dinner, 9¾" d., Azalea patt., No. 13 ....26.00

Plates, 7½" d., Tree in Meadow patt., No. 44, set of 6 ....75.00

Platter, 10¼ x 14" oval, Azalea patt., No 17 ....60.00

Platter, 14" l., Azalea patt., No. 17........98.00

Platter, turkey, 16" l., Azalea patt., No. 186 ....300.00 to 325.00

Refreshment set: shaped plate & cup; Azalea patt., No. 39, 2 pcs.................35.00

Refreshment set: tray w/cup; Tree in Meadow patt., 2 pcs..........................25.00

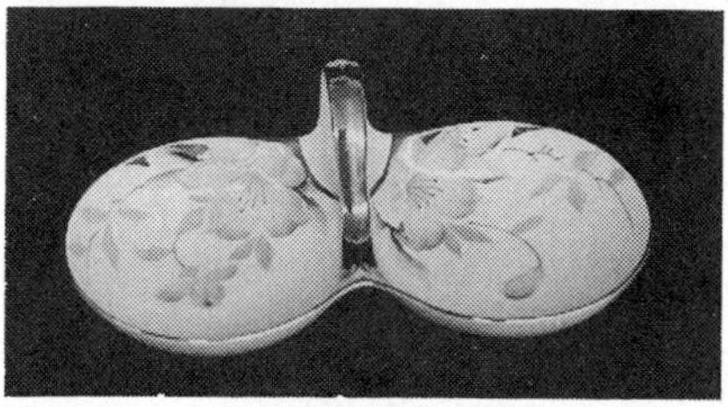

Noritake Relish Dish

Relish dish, two-lobed form w/center handle, Azalea patt., No. 450, 7½" l. (ILLUS.) 30.00

Relish dish, oval, Azalea patt., No. 18, 8¼" l. 20.00

Relish dish, w/figural orange bird in center (green"M" in Wreath mark)......95.00

Sandwich server w/center handle, decorated w/stylized fruit basket designs 58.00

Sandwich server w/center handle, decorated w/scene of gondolier poling his gondola.............................48.00

Sauce dishes, Azalea patt., No. 12, 5¼" d., set of 12..............................108.00

Soup plate, Azalea patt., No. 19...........25.00

Sugar bowl, basket-shaped, scenic decoration 38.00

Sugar bowl, cov., Azalea patt., No. 7 ...22.50

Sugar bowl, cov., Azalea patt., gold finial, No. 401 ....70.00

Syrup pitcher, cov., pansy decoration 25.00

Teapot, cov., Azalea patt., 5-cup size, No. 15, 4½" h. 175.00

Teapot, cov., Tree in Meadow patt. 90.00

Tea set, child's: cov. teapot, creamer, sugar bowl, two cups & saucers, six 4¼" d. plates; parrots on swing decoration, 13 pcs. 175.00

Tea set: cov. teapot, creamer, sugar bowl & six cups & saucers; Tree in Meadow patt., 15 pcs......................225.00

Tea tile, round, Azalea patt., No. 169 ....40.00

Toothpick holder, Azalea patt., No. 192 ....95.00

Toothpick holder, Tree in Meadow patt. 65.00

Tray, decorated w/large green & blue medallions on white ground, 8 x 11" (green "M" in Wreath mark)................65.00

Tray, handled, center decoration of rose & mauve flowers, cobalt blue border w/lavish gold beading & gold handles, 11¼" l. 85.00

Tray, Art Deco style, decorated w/a portrait of a brunette lady wearing a white dress w/blue design & a spray of pink flowers, orange lustre ground w/blue trim (green"M" in Wreath mark)..165.00

Tray for condiment set, Azalea patt., No. 14 (light gold wear)......................12.00

Vase, 5" h., gold lustre ground decorated w/scarlet birds & flowers in ovals, 1930s..................................35.00

Vase, double, 7" h., gate-form, two scalloped tapering tubes joined by two bars, a colorful orange parrot perched on the top bar....................225.00

Vase, 7 x 8", bulbous, stylized yellow & grey daisies decoration on crimson ground 75.00

Vegetable dish, cov., Art Deco style, decorated w/orange & black floral design on lustre ground, 9" d. (green "M" in Wreath mark) 40.00

Vegetable bowl, cov., Azalea patt., 10" d., No. 101 ....60.00

Vegetable bowl, open, oval, handled, Azalea patt., No. 101, 10½" h. 55.00

Wall pocket, flared, colorful Art Deco style landscape scene w/house, 7" h...125.00

Wall pocket, wooded scene w/house near water in a band, blue lustre ground, 8" h. 75.00

Wall pocket, decorated w/Art Deco flower on a white w/orange lustre ground (green "M" in Wreath mark) ...65.00

Wall pocket, Art Deco vase filled w/flowers decoration, blue lustre ground, slight wear on bottom (green "M" in Wreath mark)................65.00

NORTH DAKOTA SCHOOL OF MINES

North Dakota Vase

All pottery produced at the University of North Dakota School of Mines was made from North Dakota clay, In 1910, the University hired Margaret Kelly Cable to teach pottery making and she remained at the school until her retirement. Julia Mattson and Margaret Pachl were other instructors between 1923 and 1970. Designs and glazes varied through the years ranging from the Art Nouveau to modern styles. Pieces were marked "University of North Dakota - Grand Forks, N.D. - Made at School of Mines, N.D." within a circle and also signed by the students until 1963. Since that time, the pieces bear only the students' signatures. Items signed "Huck" are by the artist Flora Huckfield and were made between 1923 and 1949. Pieces were marked with the University name until 1963.

Bowl, 4½" d., matte brown glaze artist-signed $49.00

Bowl, 6" d., 2½" h., incised flower decoration, lime green to sand color, artist-signed 225.00

Bowl-vase, wide squatty bulbous body tapering to a wide flat rim, the sides decorated w/stylized Native American geometric bird & flower symbols in black & yellow against a dark red ground, marked & artist-signed, ca. 1935, 3⅝" h. 880.00

Bowl-vase, a squatty bulbous body w/a wide angled shoulder tapering to a wide, flat mouth, the shoulder carved w/a wide band of stylized flowers, artist-signed, 6¾" d., 5" h. .. 247.50

Humidor, cov., wide ovoid body tapering to a wide flat rim supporting a thick flat cover centered by a large mushroom finial, a wide deeply incised center band showing Native American dancers, overall brown glaze w/black highlights in the center band, marked, artist monogram & number "160," 7" h. 1,430.00

Jardiniere, straight sides, incised w/an Arts & Crafts design of blue & green stylized flowers against a matte green ground, by E.W. Wilker, ca. 1920, round ink mark, incised "EWW" 1,870.00

Vase, 3½" h., 4½" d., squatty bulbous form w/a rounded lower half below an incised medial band, the tapering upper half incised w/a band of large, swirling poppy blossoms, olive green glaze, stamped mark 385.00

Vase, 4⅞" h., wide slightly swelled cylindrical body w/flattened incurvate mouth, the sides divided into three large rectangular panels each showing a scene of a covered wagon pulled by oxen, crystalline matte glaze in shades of green, brown, yellow & ochre, marked & incised "Covered Wagon - FLH - 8 - HUCK - 2011," 1930 .... 1,980.00

Vase, 5" h., 4" d., cylindrical w/incurved rim, decorated w/a repeated incised design of a long-beaked bird on a branch over tall grasses, under a smooth matte green glaze, stamped "UNIVERSITY OF NORTH DAKOTA GRAND FORKS, N.D. - MADE AT SCHOOL OF MINES - N.D. CLAY," incised (S) FLH8-Huck-577," F.C. Huckfield, ca. 1926 (hairline to rim) 825.00

Vase, 5" h., 4½" d., bulbous ovoid body tapering to a short cylindrical neck, the shoulder incised w/a wide band of stylized Dutch girls (?) holding hands, brown matte glaze, artist-signed 412.50

Vase, 5¾" h., 3" d., incised "WhyNotMinot" w/a cowboy & lasso, blue high gloss glaze, ink-stamped mark & incised "JTT 175" 302.50

Vase, 6" h., 6" d., wide ovoid body w/a closed rim, decorated w/a wide band of incised ivy around the rim in green against a buff ground, artist-signed 440.00

Vase, 6¼" h., 4½" d., cylindrical w/narrow shoulder & wide mouth, decorated w/incised stalks of wheat, under a matte green glaze, by F.C. Huckfield, circular die-stamped & incised "No. Dak Wheat - Huck 47" 660.00

Vase, 6⅞" h., wide bulbous ovoid body tapering to a short wide cylindrical neck, decorated around the shoulder w/a wide band of carved & painted blue prairie rose plants flanked by pairs of blue bands, all against a pastel bluish green ground, satiny glossy glaze, marked & artist-signed & incised "PRAIRIE ROSE - 150" (few tiny glaze bubbles) 880.00

Vase, 7" h., 6" d., bulbous ovoid body tapering to a short neck w/flat rim, decorated w/a band of carved stylized flowers around the shoulder in a turquoise shaded to ivory matte glaze, marked & artist-initialed (ILLUS.) 275.00

Vase, 9" h., 5½" d., tapering cylinder w/short neck, decorated w/sgraffito iris blossoms & leaves in brown in a medium green ground, circular ink mark & incised "L.M. Barlow 1-11-50" 467.50

OHR (George) POTTERY

George Ohr Bowl

George Ohr, the eccentric potter of Biloxi, Mississippi, worked from about 1883 to 1906. Some think him to be one of the most expert throwers the craft will ever see. The majority of his works were hand-thrown, exceedingly thin-walled items, some of which have a crushed or folded appearance. He considered himself the foremost potter in the world and declined to sell much of his production, instead accumulating a great horde to leave as a legacy to his children. In 1972 this collection was purchased for resale by an antiques dealer.

GEO. E. OHR

BILOXI, MISS.

Bowl, 4½" d., 2¼" h., the squatty rounded footed body tapering to a widely flaring rolled, pinched & lobed rim, pink exterior w/green & blue sponged decoration, olive green interior, die-stamped mark "G.E. OHR - Biloxi, Miss." $1,320.00

Bowl, 6" d., 4" h., canted sides beneath angled shoulder, frothy mottled green, pink, blue & red glaze, die-stamped "G.E. OHR Biloxi, Miss.".................................1,045.00

Bowl, 8¾" w., 4" h., a footed, rounded body below a deeply folded & twisted rim, unglazed light beige clay, script signature (ILLUS.).......1,760.00

Candleholder, consisting of a floriform four-lobed ruffled receptacle covered in a gun-metal black glaze, on a flat square scalloped base covered in clear glaze, underneath is a die-stamped poem "A BILOXI WELCOME . . . .," die-stamped "G.E. OHR - Biloxi, Miss.," 1¾ x 4½"..880.00

Cup, two-handled, tall modified double gourd-form flanked by two dissimilar ear-shaped handles, dripping gun-metal & clear brownish green glaze, script signature, 6¼" w., 4½" h..............................1,980.00

Inkwell, modeled in buff clay as a perfectly detailed log cabin, covered in an olive green glossy glaze, die-stamped "G.E. OHR - BILOXI," 2¼ x 3¼"..412.50

Mug, footed cylindrical body w/a loop handle near the base, fine raspberry, green, white & purple mottled glaze, die-stamped mark "G.E. OHR - Biloxi, Miss. - 3/18/96," 4½" d., 4½" h. 797.50

Tall Ohr Mug

Mug, tall cylindrical body w/a band of pinched indentations around the middle & a deep twist the height of the sides, an angled loop handle, dead-matte dark green & black glaze, script signature, 4½" d., 4¾" h. (ILLUS.) 1,540.00

Mug, two-handled, compressed globular base & long cylindrical neck, low flared foot, one handle curved & the other angular, lustrous brown glaze w/green interior, inscribed "G E OHR," ca. 1895, 6" h...1,495.00

Pen holder, figural, a flat rectangular plaque incised w/squiggly lines & mounted w/a figural long-eared mule head w/a pen hole at the top of the head, overall mottled black glaze, base stamped "Geo. E. Ohr Biloxi, Miss.," 2⅝" l. (minor firing separation in base) 660.00

Pitcher, 3" h., 7" w., squatty low rounded pinched & scalloped irregular sides w/a pinched handle, unglazed light beige clay, script signature 770.00

Pitcher, 3¼" h., 5" w., footed, pinched spout, cut-out handle, covered in a light mottled clear green glaze w/sponged gun-metal accents, die-stamped "G.E. OHR - Biloxi, Miss" 1,650.00

Pitcher, 4" h., 4¼" w., cylindrical sides w/overall random dimpling & a flared rim w/pinched spout, long twisted loop handle, brown glossy speckled glaze, die-stamped mark "G.E. OHR - Biloxi, Miss." 1,540.00

Pitcher, 4" h., 6" w., a swelled & pulled body below a pinched & scalloped rim, a pinched-flat angled handle, glossy khaki glaze, die-stamped "G.E. OHR - BILOXI, MISS." 1,320.00

Pitcher, 4¼" h., 3¾" d., spherical pinched & dimpled body w/cut-out handle, horizontal gun-metal & brown striations under a clear caramel glaze, die-stamped "G.E. OHR Biloxi, Miss." 1,540.00

Pitcher, 4½" h., 3" d., flaring cylindrical lower body below tapering funnel-shaped shoulder below a bulbous cupped rim w/pinched spout, slender folded loop handle, gun-metal black glaze, die-stamped mark "G.E. OHR - Biloxi, Miss." 990.00

Pitcher, puzzle-type, 8¼" h., 8" d., w/groups of holes near the top, incised w/a gulf shore scene under a clear caramel glaze, script signature & die-stamped "Biloxi Miss - 1899" 2,970.00

Puzzle mug, slightly waisted cylindrical body pierced w/two rows of small holes near the rim, angled handle w/thin banding, clear brown speckled & gun-metal glaze, script signature, 5" w., 4" h. 605.00

Teapot, cov., spherical body w/a deep in-body twist band around the lower body, a deep galleried rim w/inset cover, swan's-neck spout & C-loop handle, clear dark blue glaze over an orange clay body, die-stamped mark "G.E. OHR - BILOXI," 7" l., 4¼" h. 3,300.00

Teapot, cov., "Right Hand Pot," the handle slightly to the front of the pot, snake-like spout, decorated w/an incised band around the shoulder, covered in a matte leathery purple & blue glaze, die-stamped "G.E. OHR - Biloxi, Miss." & loose paper label inside "Right Hand Pot," 7" d., 4½" h. 3,575.00

Vase, 3¼" h., 4¼" d., short straight neck over a slightly spherical base w/one deep in-body twist around center, covered in a copper brown glaze w/a band of gun-metal sponged decoration, die-stamped "G.E. OHR - Biloxi, Miss." 1,870.00

Vase, 3½" h., 4¼" w., bulbous body w/full-length folds & dimples around the sides, gun-metal brown glaze, die-stamped mark "G.E. OHR - Biloxi, Miss." (ILLUS.) 1,980.00

Squatty Ohr Vase

Vase, 3½" h., 4¾" d., squatty bulbous body raised on a low flaring foot, the wide four-lobed rim further scalloped, mottled satin red, white & black glaze exterior, clear glaze over orange clay interior, die-stamped mark "G.E. OHR - Biloxi, Miss." 3,300.00

Vase, 4¾" h., cylindrical body w/a bulbous swelled shoulder below the wide symmetrically folded & crimped flaring neck, glossy mottled black & brown glaze, base incised "GE Ohr" 990.00

Vase, 5 " h., 5½" d., spherical body on a narrow footring, the short flaring neck pinched & ruffled, the sides pinched w/dimples, unusual leathery bubbly matte pink & beige glaze w/sponged-on white & black sprig bands, die-stamped mark "G.E. OHR - Biloxi - Miss." 8,800.00

Vase, 5½" h., waisted cylindrical body w/a crumpled & folded double-handle on one side & an ear-shaped loop handle on the other, unglazed beige to orange clay, script signature 825.00

Bulbous Vase by Ohr

Vase, 5½" h., 6" d., ovoid body w/the sides crumpled & the rim flared &

pinched, superior leathery matte green, purple & red mottled glaze, script signature, restored (ILLUS.) 9,350.00

Vase, 6" h., 5" w., jack-in-the-pulpit form, the footed baluster-form body tapering to a very large, over-sized pinched & folded four-sided rim w/three of the folds pointed & pulled out, lustered brown glaze, impressed in one line mark "GEO. E. OHR, BILOXI, MISS." 1,430.00

Vase, 6½" h., 4" d., spherical base, cylindrical neck & deep flaring mouth, covered in a pigeon-feathered red & gun-metal brown glaze against a honey brown base, incised "OHR - BILOXI" 3,640.00

Vase, 7" h., 4½" d., footed w/spherical base & flaring neck, w/one inverted in-body twist on the shoulder, covered in a mottled gun-metal glaze w/green accents, script signature 2,750.00

Vase, 7" h., 4¾" d., barrel-shaped, short neck w/very deep in-body twist & cupped mouth, covered in clear glaze w/densely packed gun-metal brown speckles, die-stamped "G.E. OHR - Biloxi" 4,000.00

Vase, 8½" h., 5½" d., slightly globular w/large dimples in the sides & collapsed rim, covered in a pigeon-feathered olive, green, dark blue, rose & mustard glaze, clear glossy interior, marked "GEO. E. OHR - BILOXI, MISS." 14,300.00

Water jug, antique-style, bulbous ovoid body tapering sharply to a top center ring handle, a short angled cylindrical spout on one shoulder opposite a round knob, buff-colored w/bisque finish, marked "G.E. OHR - Biloxi, Miss.," 6¼" d., 9" h. (touch to nick on side) 357.50

OLD IVORY

Old Ivory china was produced in Silesia, Germany, in the late 1800s and takes its name from the soft white background coloring. A wide range of table pieces was made with the various patterns usually identified by a number rather than a name.

Old Ivory No. 16 Cracker Jar

Bacon platter, Thistle patt. $175.00

Berry set: master bowl & six sauce dishes; No. 15, 7 pcs. 295.00

Bowl, master berry, 9½" d., No. 75 ....75.00 to 100.00

Bowl, master berry, 9½" d., No. 84 ....100.00 to 125.00

Bun tray, No. 84................................125.00

Cake plate, open-handled, No. 10, 9½" d. 92.50

Cake plate, open-handled, No. 11, 10" d. 60.00

Cake plate, open-handled, No. 15, 10" d. ....125.00 to 150.00

Cake plate, open-handled, No. 84, 10" d. 95.00

Cake set: 10" d., cake plate & nine dessert plates; No. 16, 10 pcs. 250.00

Chocolate pot, cov., No. 16, 10" h. 495.00

Chocolate set: cov. chocolate pot & six cups & saucers; No. 15, pot, 10" h., 13 pcs. 825.00

Cracker jar, cov., No. 16 (ILLUS.) 400.00

Creamer, No. 118 ....85.00

Creamer & cov. sugar bowl, No. 16, pr. ....125.00 to 150.00

Cup & saucer, No. 16 ....65.00

Dresser tray, La Touraine patt., lily of the valley blossoms in shades of green w/gold trim, artist-signed, 6 x 11½" 165.00

Plate, 6" d., No. 16...............................22.50

Plate, 7½" d., No. 15...............25.00 to 50.00

Plate, 7½" d., No. 16 (ILLUS. top next column) 30.00

Plate, 7½" d., No. 84 ....50.00

Old Ivory No. 16 Plate

Plate, 8" d., No. 84 ....55.00

Plate, 8¼" d., No. 16 ....35.00

Plate, 8½" d., No. 28 ....65.00

Plate, dinner, 9¾" d., No. 7 ....70.00

Plate, chop, 13" d., No. 11 ....185.00

Plate, chop, 13" d., No. 15 ....295.00

Plate, chop, 13" d., No. 16 ....150.00

Platter, cold meat, 8 x 11½", open-handled, No. 15 ....115.00

Platter, 11¾" oval, No. 16...135.00 to 165.00

Platter, cold meat, oval, No. 21 ....95.00

Relish dish, oval, handled, No. 15, 4¼ x 6½" 45.00

Relish dish, No. 84, 8½" l. ....75.00 to 100.00

Salt & pepper shakers, No. 16, pr. 135.00

Sauce dish, No. 16, 5½" d. 48.00

Sauce dish, No. 84, 5" d. 65.00

Tea tile, No. 16 ....145.00

Toothpick holder, No. 16 ....250.00 to 300.00

Toothpick holder, No. 84 ....250.00 to 275.00

Tureen, cov., No. 84 ....700.00

OLD SLEEPY EYE

Sleepy Eye, Minnesota, was named after an Indian chief. The Sleepy Eye Milling Co. had stoneware and pottery premiums made at the turn of the century first by the Weir Pottery Company and subsequently by Western Stoneware Co., Monmouth, Illinois. On these items the trademark Indian head was signed beneath "Old Sleepy Eye," The colors were Flemish blue on grey. Later pieces by Western Stoneware to 1937 were not made for Sleepy Eye Milling Co. but for other businesses. They bear the same Indian head but "Old Sleepy Eye" does not appear below. They have a reverse design of tepees and trees and may or may not be marked Western Stoneware on the base. These items are usually found in cobalt blue on cream and are rarer in other colors. In 1952, Western Stoneware made a 22 oz. and 40 oz. stein with a chestnut brown glaze. This mold was redesigned in 1968. From 1968 to 1973 a limited number of 40 oz. steins were produced for the Board of Directors of Western Stoneware. These were marked and dated and never sold as production items. Beginning with the first convention of the Old Sleepy Eye Club in 1976, Western Stoneware has made a souvenir which each person attending receives. These items are marked with the convention site and date. It should also be noted that there have been some reproduction items made in recent years.

Sleepy Eye Stoneware Butter Jar

Butter jar, Flemish blue on grey stoneware, Weir Pottery Co., 1903 (ILLUS.) ....$450.00 to 500.00

Pitcher, 4" h., cobalt blue on white, w/small Indian head on handle, Western Stoneware Co., 1906-37 (half pint) 190.00

Pitcher, 5¼" h., cobalt blue on white, w/small Indian head on handle, Western Stoneware Co., 1906-37 (pint) 250.00

Pitcher, 6¼" h., cobalt blue on white, w/small Indian head on handle, Western Stoneware Co., 1906-37, quart (ILLUS. top next column) 325.00

Pitcher, 7¾" h., cobalt blue on white, w/small Indian head on handle, Western Stoneware Co., 1906-37 (half-gallon) ....225.00 to 275.00

Sleepy Eye Pitcher

Stein, brown on yellow, Western Stoneware Co., 7¾" h. 900.00

Stein, blue on white, Western Stoneware Co., 1906-37, 7¾" h.......600.00

Stein, Flemish blue on grey stoneware, Weir Pottery Co., 8" h....500.00

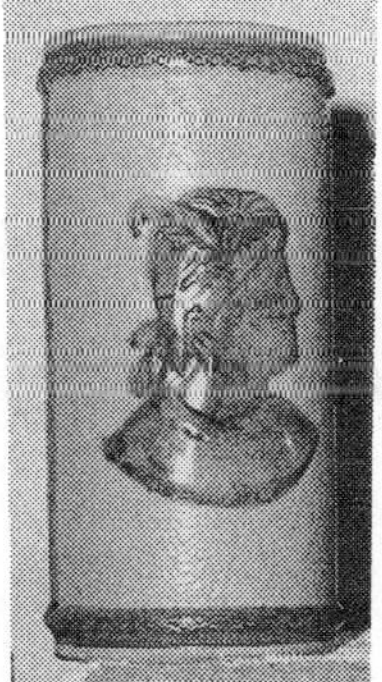

Sleepy Eye Stoneware Vase

Vase, 9" h., Flemish blue on grey stoneware, Indian head signed, dragonfly, frog & bulrushes reverse, Weir Pottery Co., 1903 (ILLUS.) ....350.00 to 375.00

OWENS

Owens pottery was the product of the J.B. Owens Pottery Company, which operated in Ohio from 1890 to 1929. In 1891 it located in Zanesville and produced art pottery from 1896, introducing "Utopian" wares as its first art pottery. The company switched to tile after 1907. Efforts to rebuild after the factory burned in 1928 failed and the company closed in 1929.

Jug, Art line, decorated w/poppy florals, glossy glaze, shape No. 820, 6" h. $175.00

Loving cup, three-handled, Utopian line, strawberries decoration on dark brown ground, artist-initialed, 6¾" h. (glaze flake on one handle) 495.00

Mug, Utopian line, leaves & berries decoration, dated 1908 ....95.00

Vase, 6" h., 7" d., Utopian line, two-handled, slip-decorated grapes & vines around body, artist-signed......250.00

Vase, 10" h., Utopian line, bulbous body, floral decoration, artist-signed (factory glaze bubbles on bottom) ...295.00

Vase, 11" h., Utopian line, pansies decoration on dark brown ground 135.00

Vase, 11¾" h., Utopian line, pillow-type, the footed wide flattened spherical body w/a long oval opening, decorated w/the bust portrait of a Native American warrior in shades of brown, tan & black against a slightly shaded black-brown to tan ground, marked, ca. 1900 (some chips on front feet) 1,980.00

Vase, 12" h., floral decoration w/profile of Indian on the back, glossy glaze 400.00

Vase, 10 x 13", pillow-type, Utopian line, decorated w/a shepherd & his dog herding his flock 1,650.00

Vase, 13½" h., 8½" d., Mission line, ovoid w/tiny mouth, slip-decorated scene of the Santa Barbara Mission in grey & brown against the evening sky, artist-signed & "Mission Pottery" 900.00

Vase, 15⅞" h., Utopian line, slender baluster-form body w/a flared rim, decorated w/two yellow chicks within a golden reserve against the overall black-brown background, stamped mark "Utopian J. B. Owens 1078" & artist-initialed, ca. 1900 (minor scratches, glaze bubbles & areas of cupped glaze) 1,540.00

PACIFIC CLAY PRODUCTS

Pacific Clay Candleholder

At the beginning of the 1920s William Lacy merged several southern California potteries to form the Pacific Clay Products Company in Los Angeles. However, it was not until the early 1930s that Pacific began producing tableware and artware that has piqued the interest of today's collectors. Ceramic engineer, Frank McCann, and designer and head of the art department, Matthew Lattie, were largely responsible for Pacific's success. Pottery production ceased in 1942. Today the company has a plant in Corona, California specializing in roofing tiles.

PACIFIC

PACIFIC 1500 MADE IN USA

PACIFIC 3010 USA

Candleholder, double, rectangular base w/rounded corners, curved pedestal the length of base arching upward at one end w/a round holder on the top, then slanting down to the base w/a low round holder, jade green, 4½" h., 6" l. (ILLUS.) $33.00

Plate, 10¼" d., pie w/rim, deep blue without clip-on handles 32.00

Platter, 15" d., round w/numerous rings, tab handles, yellow glaze.........40.00

Vase, 3¼" h., 3" d., model of a miniature cornucopia on a base w/six rings near middle of body & w/six rings at the narrow end, maroon glossy glaze, Model No. 3010, ca. 1930s (ILLUS. top next column) 18.00

Miniature Cornucopia

Vase, 4¼" h., baluster shape w/elongated molded handles from center to under rim, maroon glaze.....20.00

Small Pacific Clay Vase

Vase, 5" h., 6" d., bulbous body w/three horizontal rings near bottom & three horizontal rings at middle, jade green, Model No. 1500, raised circular mark, ca. late 1930s (ILLUS.) 55.00

Vase, 6½" h., oval base, straight sides flaring gently to pleated & tiered rim, Model No. 3050, ca. 1938..................35.00

Vase, 7¼" h., 2¾" d., bottle shaped w/molded handles on each side near middle, mint green, Model No. 886 ....28.00

PAIRPOINT - LIMOGES

The Pairpoint Manufacturing Company of New Bedford, Massachusetts, producers of fine plated silver, as well as glass items, had china especially made in Limoges, France for a short period of time. These tastefully decorated porcelains, often enhanced with plated silver, are in short supply.

Tall Pairpoint - Limoges Vase

Ewer, squatty bulbous base w/molded scrolls on small knob feet, the sides tapering to a tall slender neck w/arched spout & high graceful loop handle, each side decorated w/chrysanthemums on a wine red ground, brushed gold trim on the base scrolls, rim & handle, artist-signed, 16" h. $1,000.00

Vase, 13¼" h., tall cylindrical body w/a narrow shoulder tapering up to a flat rim flanked by small pierced scroll handles, decorated in the Crown Milano style w/a large Mideastern scene of Arabs & camels on one side & three flamingoes in flight on the other, stamped "Pairpoint Limoges - 2011-70," missing cover (ILLUS.) .1,650.00

PARIAN

Parian Figure of John A. Andrews

Parian is unglazed porcelain in the biscuit stage, and takes its name from its resemblance to Parian marble used for statuary. Parian wares were made in this country and abroad through much of the last century and continue to be made.

Bust of Charles Dickens, 10¼" h. $200.00

Bust of Lord Byron, raised on a socle base, late 19th c., 8⅛" h. 66.00

Bust of a young woman, looking down w/a pensive expression, scalloped edge, raised on a low footed base, base marked "C. Delpeoh Art Union of London 1855," 13" h. (minor edge chips) 330.00

Figure of John A. Andrews, standing stocky gentleman wearing a long cloak over his suit, atop a square base w/cut corners, printed verse on the back on the base, impressed marks "M. Milmore Sc." & "Publishers - J. McD & S Boston -copyright," England, ca. 1867, chips on base, 21" h. (ILLUS.) 1,210.00

Figure of Daniel Webster

Figure of Daniel Webster, full-bodied, standing upright w/right hand in coat next to a fabric-draped half pillar w/books propped below, on a square base w/fringed floor cover, marked on reverse "T. Ball, Sculptor, Boston, MA 1853 - Patent Assigned to G.W. Nichols, Boston," 26" h. (ILLUS.) 2,300.00

Figure group, a young woman in classical garb seated on a mound & holding a basket of fish, a young child seated at her side, 7¼" w., 6½" h. (ILLUS.) 175.00

Figure Group of Woman & Child

Pitcher, 5½" h., the body molded in relief w/holly berries & leaves, a twisted twig handle, Minton, 19th c. 110.00

Pitcher, 8" h., footed ovoid body tapering to a low arched spout, strap handle, the sides w/relief-molded foliage framing oval medallions w/figural representations of day and night, 19th c. 137.50

Pitcher, cov., 9⅛" h., molded leaf & grain design w/green & yellow enameling, pewter lid, English registry mark 181.50

Planter, oblong, molded in high-relief w/a young girl & two turkeys & chicks, 10½" l., 6" h..........................200.00

PARIS & OLD PARIS

Old Paris Bulb Pot

China known by the generic name of Paris and Old Paris was made by several Parisian factories from the 18th through the 19th century; some of it is marked and some is not. Much of it was handsomely decorated.

Bulb pots & covers, D-shaped, each colorfully painted on the front w/a lush floral cluster & on the sides w/a floral bouquet within slightly recessed panels between gilt sprig- and dot-patterned pilasters above the gilt swag-decorated bracket feet, the lower body & rounded rim w/gilt foliate borders & the upper edge of the rim enameled in green, the covers w/three everted bulb-holders & four pierced holes, all edged in worn gilding, probably the Rue Thiroux Factory, crowned "A" marks in green enamel, ca. 1820-30, 10 11/16" & 10 13/16" l., pr. (ILLUS. of one)..$7,475.00

Paris Porcelain Centerpiece

Centerpiece, a round flaring reticulated basket set atop a pedestal surrounded by kneeling figures of angels holding ring wreaths above a round ormolu base w/raised scrolls & lions' masks & raised on paw feet, artist-signed, ca.1810 (ILLUS.).........................29,700.00

Ecuelle & cover, each colorfully painted between gilt bands w/a wide border of birds beneath chaplets of roses suspending from their beaks gilt floral swags further suspended from foliate scrolls & octagonal panels framing smaller gold-ground panels of pink rose sprigs above further leaf scrolls suspending green laurel swags below the birds, the leaf-molded angular handles & loop knop heightened in gilding, ca. 1790, 7⅞ w. 460.00

Pots de creme (custard cups), cov., a pink border band decorated w/entwined ribbons & floral reserves, h.p. cups on scrolls in the center, by Boyer - Rue de la Paix, late 19th c., 3" h., set of 12 ....920.00

Paris Urn with Spigot

Urn, cov., shield-shaped, painted around the body in yellow, blue, brown, black & iron-red w/small scattered insects beneath a black-ground border of pink, yellow & white roses & shaded green leaves between *oeil-de-perdrix*-patterned gilt bands interrupted at the sides by the foliate-molded gold & white angular handles, the cover similarly decorated around the gilt seed-cluster knop (repaired) & the circular foot decorated w/gilt leaves & berries between *oeil-de-perdrix*-patterned bands around the ankle & upper edge, "LSX" monogram in gold for Louis Stanislaus Xavier, Comte de Provence, the lower body mounted w/a silver-gilt spigot, Clignancourt Factory, ca. 1790, 14½" h.(ILLUS.) 2,588.00

Urns, octagonal body, the neck decorated w/flowers above a panel boss base flanked by mask handles above a circular socle; raised on a step plinth decorated w/wreaths & the initial "B," mid-19th c., 14½" h., pr. (restorations) 1,150.00

Vases, 11¾" h., blue-ground ovoid body decorated around the shoulder w/a wide tooled gilt border of floral paterae between beads & leafage issuing whorls suspending grape clusters & blossoms interrupted at the sides by gilt swan-form handles, the lower body w/a further dot-and oval border above the gilt waisted foot & integral square base (slight wear), the trumpet-form neck fully gilded, incised numerals "6" & "11" or "S," ca. 1825, pr. 2,588.00

Vases, 13¾" h., baluster-form w/flaring rim, applied gilt swan handles, sides decorated w/scene of lovers in a country landscape, pr. 467.50

Paris Porcelain Vases

Vases, 14⅜" h., gold ground reserved on the front of the ovoid body w/a rectangular panel colorfully painted w/a cluster of flowers on a russet & white marble ledge against a shaded brown ground within a tooled foliate surround, the reverse tooled w/Gothic arches & tracery between tooled floral & foliate borders on the lower body (one w/three tiny chips), shoulder & trumpet-form neck, the sides w/gilt loop handles molded w/foliate scrolls (one w/tiny chip) & paterae, the circular foot on an integral square base molded around the edges w/blossoms & foliage, Darte Freres, Palais Royal No. 21 marks stenciled in iron-red, ca. 1820, 14⅜" h., pr. (ILLUS.) 19,550.00

Vases, 17" h., decorated w/a central floral panel surrounded by a scrolling gilt border on a cobalt blue ground flanked by scrolled handles, artist-signed, mid-19th c., pr. 2,875.00

Vases, 18½" h., wide baluster-form body w/broad, widely flaring neck, the shoulder mounted w/ornate pierced scroll gilt handles, the front decorated w/a large oval reserve w/two beautiful young ladies, a cobalt blue ground w/overall gilt scrolls & foliate designs, late 19th c., pr. 1,980.00

Ornate Paris Vases

Vases, 22½" h., tall baluster-form footed body flanked by large leaf- and blossom-form side handles, the ornate flaring rim molded w/scrolled leaves & large blossoms, each decorated on the front side w/a vignette scene of Victorian maidens, ornate gilt trim, mid-19th c., chip on one leaf handle, repaired, pr. (ILLUS.) 1,100.00

PAUL REVERE POTTERY

Paul Revere Pottery Bowl

This pottery was established in Boston, Massachusetts, in 1906, by a group of philanthropists seeking to establish better conditions for underprivileged young girls of the area. Edith Brown served as supervisor of the small "Saturday Evening Girls Club" pottery operation which was moved, in 1912, to a house close to the Old North Church where Paul Revere's signal lanterns had been placed. The wares were mostly hand decorated in mineral colors and both sgraffito and molded decorations were employed. Although it became popular, it was never a profitable operation and always depended on financial contributions to operate. After the death of Edith Brown in 1932, the pottery foundered and finally closed in 1942.

S.E.G.

Bowl, 6" d., 3¾" h., slightly canted sides & gently rounded shoulder, wide band at top of stylized incised blossoms in oyster white w/green foliage against an orange ground above a blue speckled body, ink marked "339-12-11 - S.E.G. - S.G., Sara Galner, 1911 .... $1,650.00

Bowl, 7⅜" d., deep rounded sides, the interior decorated w/a gun-metal black exterior glaze & a black over dark blue interior, original paper label on base reading "Paul Revere Pottery Price $2.50" 175.00

Bowl, 8½" d., 3" h., green-glazed w/sgraffito interior border of yellow nasturtium blossoms outlined in black below off-white band at rim, signed on base "S.E.G." & "SG" in circle (ILLUS.) 935.00

Bowl, 8⅞" d., shallow widely flaring sides w/a smooth rim, the interior decorated w/a mottled green, brown & gold crystalline flambé glaze, marked on the base (minor glaze bubbles in the bottom) 275.00

Box, cov., wide squatty bulbous body w/closed rim, low-domed cover w/button finial, overall bluish green glaze, dated "7/9/26," 5½" d., 4¼" h. 137.50

Canister, cov., upright hexagonal form w/low, flat cover, a blue band around the top & shoulder above a matte cream ground decorated w/a monogrammed round medallion in yellow & green w/a cream-colored rabbit, inscribed marks & artist-initialed, 4½" h. 550.00

Luncheon set: five mug-style cups, five dessert plates & five luncheon plates; cream ground decorated around the rim w/a repeating band of trees & sky in green & blue, designs outlined in black, signed & numbered, the set 1,650.00

Mug, decorated w/a well-dressed rabbit strolling in the grass in matte brown & blue on a cream ground w/a blue band, inscribed "John Fisk - Zueblin" below rim, & "Xmas - 1914 - S.E.G.," 3" h. (hairline)..........385.00

Mug, incised tree-filled landscape & solitary nightingale over the inscription "In the forest must always be a nightingale and in the soul a faith so faithful that it comes back even after it has been slain," glazed in greens, brown, blue, cream & yellow, decorated by Sara Galner, inscribed artist's initials & marks, ca. 1915, 4" h. 1,430.00

Paul Revere Pottery Floral Pitcher

Pitcher, tankard, 7¾" h., incised & decorated w/stylized yellow tulips & brown leaves outlined in black on yellow ground w/a white horizontal ring below spout, spout loss & hairline, signed "SEG/AM" (ILLUS.) 660.00

Plate, 8½" d., incised center monogram "HOS" in a circle for Helen Osbourne Storrow, the border decorated w/a band of running pigs in brown, yellow & green, signed "SEG - F.L." & numbered..............1,870.00

Vase, 4¼" h., 3¾" d., wide ovoid body w/closed rim, overall green volcanic glaze, impressed mark & "5/25".......220.00

Vase, 6" h., 4¾" d., ovoid body w/a closed mouth, decorated around the top w/a banded landscape decorated in green & black against a matte blue ground, marked (minor restoration to rim)............................990.00

Vase, 6½" h., 3½" d., slightly swelled cylindrical body w/a flat rim, decorated around the upper half w/a banded landscape of broad stylized trees in ochre & brown against a white ground & above the ochre lower body, marked 825.00

Vase, 6⅞" h., wide ovoid body w/closed rim, overall dark blue matte glaze, remnants of paper label 220.00

Vase, 7¼" h., cylindrical body w/slightly flared rim, decorated w/a continuous design of stylized trees in greyish green & brown w/black outlining, marked 440.00

Vase, 9" h., 4¾" d., swelled cylindrical body w/wide flat mouth, decorated w/stylized yellow tulips against a dark, light & teal blue mottled matte glaze, marked 2,200.00

Vase, 9⅛" h., expanding cylinder, decorated w/a stylized band in matte yellow, green & brown outlined in black, matte white & yellow band at shoulder & rim, all on a matte yellow ground, inscribed marks (two hairlines at rim) 522.50

Vase, 10½" h., 5½" d., tall ovoid body tapering to a wide flat mouth, glossy blue to teal blue drip glaze, impressed circular mark 385.00

PETERS & REED

In 1897 John D. Peters and Adam Reed formed a partnership to produce flowerpots in Zanesville, Ohio. Formally incorporated as Peters and Reed in 1901, this type of production was the mainstay until after 1907 when they gradually expanded into the art pottery field. Frank Ferrell, a former designer at the Weller Pottery, developed the "Moss Aztec" line while associated with Peters and Reed and other art lines followed. Though unmarked, attribution is not difficult once familiar with the various lines. In 1921, Peters and Reed became Zane Pottery which continued in production until 1941.

Basket, hanging-type, Moss Aztec line, 9¼" d., 4" h. $59.00

Basket, hanging-type, Moss Aztec line, 5" d., 2½" h. 30.00

Bowl, 2" h., marbleized red & black glaze 35.00

Bowl, 2" h., Persian Ware, decorated w/geometric designs 25.00

Bowl, 3" h., Pereco Ware, decorated w/geometric designs 25.00

Bowl, 8½" d., 3¼" h., Pereco Ware, dark blue glaze decorated w/berries, leaves & stems 45.00

Flowerpot, Florentine line, 4" h. 35.00

Jardiniere, decorated w/green lion heads on beige ground, bunting between lions, fluted around bases, 7½" d., 6½" h. 62.00

Mug, cavalier decoration, standard glossy glaze, 5" h. 50.00

Pitcher, jug-type, 6" h., decorated w/flower sprigs, standard glossy glaze 65.00

Vase, 4" h., Drip line, dark & light shades of blue & brown glaze 50.00

Vase, 4" h., 6" d., hexagonal w/crimped rim, molded flower medallions, glossy brown glaze 46.00

Vase, 5" h., 6" d., three-footed, three shoulder handles, decorated w/three pink & beige applied cavaliers, glossy streaked brown glaze 40.00

Vase, double bud, 7" h., Florentine line 35.00

Vase, 7" h., whiskey bottle-shaped w/wreath sprigging, standard glossy glaze 60.00

Vase, 8" h., 5½" d., Pereco Ware, corset-shaped, relief-molded ivy around upper half, stamped "Zane Ware" 28.00

Vase, 12" h., Drip line, blue & yellow glaze (drilled for lamp) 115.00

Wall pocket, flower sprigs decoration, standard glossy glaze, 5" h. 60.00

Wall pocket, Egyptian Ware, green glaze, 9" h. 75.00

PEWABIC

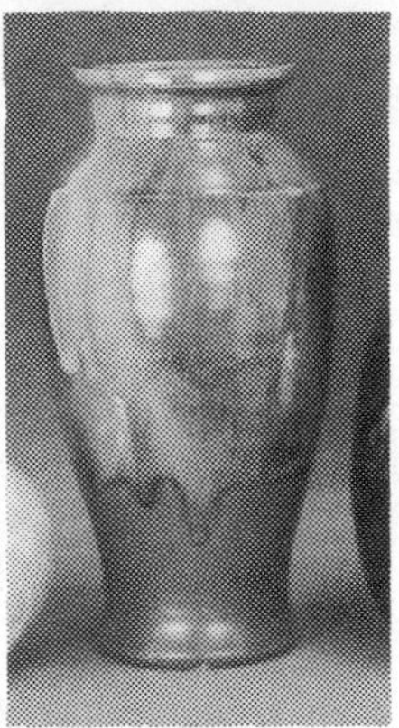

Fine Pewabic Vase

Mary Chase Perry (Stratton) and Horace J. Caulkins were partners in this Detroit, Michigan pottery. Established in 1903, Pewabic Pottery evolved from their Revelation Pottery, "Pewabic" meaning "clay with copper color" in the language of Michigan's Chippewa Indians. Caulkins attended to the clay formulas and Mary Perry Stratton was the artistic creator of forms & glaze formulas, eventually developing a wide range of colors for her finely textured glazes. The pottery's reputation for fine wares and architectural tiles enabled it to survive the depression years of the 1930s. After Caulkins died in 1923, Mrs. Stratton continued to be active in the pottery until her death, at age ninety-four, in 1961. Her contributions to the art pottery field are numerous.

Bowl, 1⅜" h., wide flat bottom & low incurved sides, a mottled glossy black glaze around the top half above a silvery green iridescent lower glaze, impressed mark & paper label w/original "$2.00" price $220.00

Bowl-vase, spherical body tapering to a low, flat molded rim, overall iridescent greyish blue glaze, impressed mark, ca. 1910, 3⅛" h. 302.50

Vase, miniature, 2¼" h., bulbous ovoid body w/a short cylindrical neck, overall mottled silver, grey, purple & blue iridescent glazing, marked on base 220.00

Vase, 3¾" h., wide ovoid body w/a very wide flat rim, a wide band of pale blue iridescent drip glaze around the rim above a silvery grey iridescent glazed body, marked on base 275.00

Vase, 3¾" h., 4¼" d., squatty w/rounded sides & slightly flaring rim, dark greyish green glaze w/red lustered patches, die-stamped "PEWABIC - DETROIT" 440.00

Vase, 3¾" h., 4¾" d., squatty bulbous body w/a wide shoulder to a short slightly flaring neck, matte cobalt blue glaze, incised mark 467.50

Vase, 4¾" h., 4" d., squatty bulbous base w/tapering cylindrical neck, mottled green & burgundy iridescent glaze, faint traces of impressed mark 550.00

Vase, 5" h., 5½" d., footed bulbous body w/short flaring rim, mottled bluish grey & gold iridescent glaze, impressed circular mark "PEWABIC - DETROIT" 715.00

Vase, 6" h., 4½" d., footed spherical body tapering to a short flaring neck, deep eggplant gun-metal glaze, impressed mark 990.00

Vase, 6½" h., 4½" d., bulbous ovoid body w/flaring rim, lustered gold, bronze, green, blue & purple glaze, impressed circular mark "PEWABIC - DETROIT" 550.00

Vase, 6¾" h., 3¼" d., slightly swollen body w/straight rim, iridescent blue glaze, impressed circular mark 330.00

Vase, 6¾" h., 3¾" d., ovoid body tapering to a flaring neck, iridescent burgundy & green glaze, w/paper label 715.00

Vase, 9" h., 7½" d., bulbous ovoid body tapering to a short wide & slightly flaring neck w/molded rim, iridescent copper glaze dripping over a cobalt blue body, w/paper label (restoration to rim) 1,210.00

Vase, 10" h., wide baluster-form body, iridescent silver volcanic glaze over a translucent blue glaze, impressed mark, ca. 1910 ....2,970.00

Vase, 10½" h., 5" d., baluster-form body w/sloping shoulder to a short cylindrical neck w/a flat molded rim, covered in a vibrant thick gold lustered glaze dripping over a matte dark blue body, die-stamped circular mark w/"PEWABIC - DETROIT" (ILLUS.) 3,850.00

PHOENIX BIRD & FLYING TURKEY PORCELAIN

Phoenix Bird Plate

The phoenix bird, a symbol of immortality and spiritual rebirth, has been handed down through Egyptian mythology as a bird that consumed itself by fire after 500 years and then rose again, renewed, from its ashes. This bird has been used to decorate Japanese porcelain designed for export for more than 100 years. The pattern incorporates a blue design of the bird, variously known as the "Flying Phoenix," the "Flying Turkey" or the "Ho-o," stamped on a white ground. It became popular with collectors because there was an abundant supply since the ware was produced for a long period of time. Pieces can be found marked with Japanese characters, with a "Nippon" mark, or a "Made in Japan" or "Occupied Japan" mark. Though there are several variations to the pattern and border, we have lumped them together since values seem to be quite comparable. A word of caution to the collectors, Phoenix Bird pattern is still being produced.

Casserole, cov., Phoenix Bird $45.00

Creamer, Phoenix Bird 12.50

Egg cup, Phoenix Bird 16.00

Plate, 7" d., Phoenix Bird (ILLUS.) 12.00

Plate, dinner, 10" d., Phoenix Bird 30.00

Phoenix Bird Sugar Bowl

Sugar bowl, cov., Phoenix Bird (ILLUS.) 18.50

Teapot, cov., one-cup size, Flying Turkey 35.00

PICKARD

Ornate Pickard Jug

Pickard, Inc., making fine hand-colored china today in Antioch, Illinois, was founded in Chicago in 1894 by Wilder A. Pickard. The company now makes its own blanks but once only decorated those bought from other potteries, primarily from the Havilands and others in Limoges, France.

Bowl, 6¼" d., 2¼" h., flowers & berries decoration, artist-initialed, pre-1915 mark $135.00

Bowl, 4½ x 7¼", 1¾" h., decorated w/nasturtiums & trailing stems, Haviland blank, ca. 1898 ....87.50

Bowl, 7½" d., handled, decorated w/strawberries, artist-signed 95.00

Bowl, 7¼ x 8¼" oval, 4½" h., decorated w/lilies & gold trim, artist-signed 225.00

Bowl, 9" d., shallow, single open handle, pastel scenic decoration w/two fully-leaved trees & bush in foreground, leafless woods in background w/meandering stream, wide gold border, ca. 1912, artist-signed 295.00

Bowl, 9¼" d., 4¾" h., pedestal base, Modern Conventional patt., artist-signed 300.00

Bowl, 9¾" d., h.p. strawberries & gold trim, artist-signed 195.00

Bowl, 10¾" d., open-handled, strawberries decoration w/heavy gold borders & design, artist-signed 275.00

Cake plate, open-handled, decorated w/gold-outlined multi-colored leaves, artist-signed 95.00

Candy dish, round, ball-footed, decorated w/currants & lavish gold trim, artist-signed, Willets Belleek blank, ca. 1905 ....135.00

Celery tray, oval, center decoration of bunches of grapes hanging down from each side, yellow & purple w/green, blue & yellow leaves on cream ground, heavy gold edge band w/maroon design, artist-signed, 1898-1904 mark, 6⅝ x 14", 2½" h. 225.00

Charger, h.p. scenic decoration w/farm & stream, gold trim, artist-signed, 12" d. 250.00

Charger, h.p. w/yellow flowers & green leaves, artist-signed, 12½" d. 175.00

Chocolate pot, cov., white w/gold trim, gold initials "C.E.," w/blue trim, ca. 1905 ....175.00

Coffeepot, cov., demitasse, Art Deco style, wide band of pastel water lilies, blue flowers & gold trim, artist-signed, Willets Belleek blank 195.00

Condensed milk can holder & underplate, h.p. iris decoration, gold trim, 6½" h., 2 pcs. (some gold wear) 78.00

Creamer, h.p. scenic decoration, artist-signed, 2¾" h. 125.00

Creamer & cov. sugar bowl, decorated w/red holly berries & green leaves, ornate gold handles & finial, artist-signed, Limoges blank, 1898-1904 mark, pr. 195.00

Creamer & cov. sugar bowl, decorated w/violets, artist-signed, ca. 1898-1904, Silesia blank, pr. 325.00

Creamer & cov. sugar bowl, h.p. decoration of plums & grapes, artist-signed, pr. 175.00

Creamer & cov. sugar bowl, 23k gold over floral etching, ca. 1940s, pr......110.00

Creamer, sugar bowl & tray, overall gold decoration, No. 486, 3 pcs. 75.00

Dresser set: 12" oval tray, 6" h. cov. powder jar, 5" d. hair receiver, 4" d. cov. jewelry box; decorated w/violets, tendrils, leaves, heavy gold trim, artist-signed, 1905-12 mark, impressed "B," Tresseman & Vogt, Limoges blank, the set 850.00

Dish, oval w/deep sides, h.p. daffodils, Limoges blank, ca. 1908, 12" l. 95.00

Gravy boat, decorated w/acorns, ca. 1905-10, artist-signed, M & Z - Austria blank 295.00

Jug w/original flat-topped stopper, tall waisted cylindrical body tapering to a short small neck, sharply angled handle from the neck to the shoulder, decorated w/ears of corn outlined in gold on a burgundy ground, 10¾" h. (ILLUS.) 550.00

Marmalade jar, cov., h.p. strawberries decoration w/gold trim & handles, ca. 1905 (slight wear on handles)......95.00

Mug, decorated w/strawberries & foliage, artist-signed, 1910 mark, 6" h. (gold wear on handle)................90.00

Nappy, scalloped rim, ring handle, decorated w/a center reserve of blackberries & blackberry blossoms framed by wide gold sides, artist-signed, ca. 1915, 9" d. 135.00

Pitcher, 4" h., "Aura Argenta Linear" patt., artist-signed 115.00

Pitcher, 7½" h., cylindrical, decorated w/white lilies & green leaves, heavy gilt trim, artist-signed........................250.00

Pitcher, 7½" h., cylindrical, h.p. water lilies w/roots in water, in shades of gold, green, blue, white, yellow & lilac, rainbow iridescent interior, artist-signed, 1905-10 mark 595.00

Pickard Pitcher with Cherries

Pitcher, 5¾" h., 7½" d., squatty bulbous shouldered body w/an angled handle, the wide shoulder band in gold decorated w/green & purple leaves & beige & gold flowers & a large cluster of yellow cherries w/green & purple leaves overhanging the lower body on a dark green satin ground, gold handles, artist-signed, ca. 1905-10 (ILLUS.) 395.00

Pitcher, 7½" h., 8½" d., overall decoration of lavender, yellow & orange spider mums, gold trim, artist-signed, ca. 1905-1910, Limoges blank..................................400.00

Pitcher, 8" h., pine cone decoration outlined in gold on rust ground, gold neck & handle, artist-signed 695.00

Pitcher, tankard, 11" h., decorated w/stylized trees, grapes & leaves, artist-signed 540.00

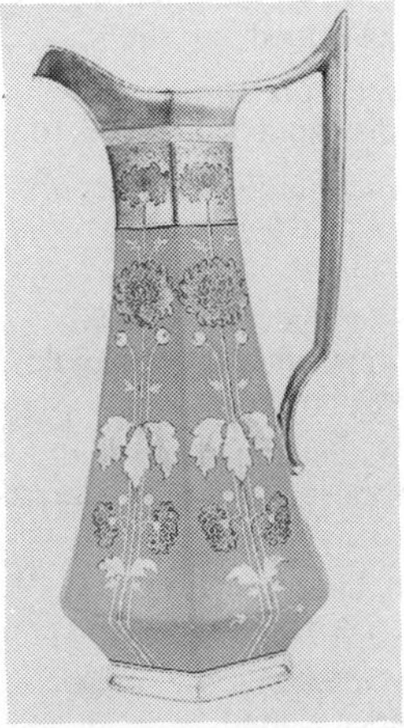

Pickard Tankard Pitcher

Pitcher, tankard, 16" h., tall footed tapering hexagonal body w/a high spout & long angular handle, each panel decorated w/tall stylized chrysanthemums in shades of purple w/gold stems & white leaves all against a deep reddish orange ground, gold rim, handle & base band, artist-signed (ILLUS.) 550.00

Plate, 6" d., decorated w/currants & foliage, artist-signed, ca. 1910 ....75.00

Plate, 6" d., Italian Gardens patt., artist-signed 135.00

Plate, 6½" d., gooseberry decoration, artist-signed, ca. 1905 ....85.00

Plate, 8" d., oak leaves decoration 85.00

Plate, 8" d., decorated w/tulips & lavish gold trim 150.00

Plate, 8" d., decorated w/walnuts, almonds & filberts in brown tones, artist-signed 145.00

Plate, 8" d., pastel Western landscape scene, artist-signed............................95.00

Plate, 8½" d., colorful tulips decoration, heavy gold trim, circle mark 95.00

Plate, 8½" d., decorated w/blackberries & leaves, gilt border 60.00

Plate, 8½" d., poppies decoration, artist-signed, ca. 1905 ....185.00

Plate, 8½" d., decorated w/russet apples & green leaves, wide gold border, artist-signed, ca. 1905 ....145.00

Plate, 8¾" d., blackberry decoration, artist-signed, ca. 1910 ....130.00

Plate, 8¾" d., decorated w/Easter lilies, artist-signed 138.00

Plate, 8¾" d., decorated w/red carnations, artist-signed, ca. 1905...........185.00

Plate, 9" d., decorated w/purple plums, artist-signed, ca. 1905-10.....175.00

Plate, 9" d., calla lilies decoration, platinum & gold finish, artist-signed 125.00

Plate, 10½" d., handled, scenic decoration w/farm & stream, gold trim, artist-signed 150.00

Plate, 12" d., decorated w/a landscape w/house, trees & lake, artist-signed 550.00

Relish dish, decorated w/floral decoration & gold trim, 9½" d............85.00

Sugar bowl, cov., stylized Art Deco design, artist-signed..........................65.00

Sugar bowl, cov., decorated w/roses, artist-signed 85.00

Tray, two-handled, decorated w/stylized flowers, gilt border, 9½" l. 40.00

Tray, three-section w/figural peacock center handle, overall gold w/engraved flower basket design, 10½" d. 70.00

Tray, handled, decorated w/garden scene, heavy gold trim, artist-signed, 15½" l. 245.00

Vase, 5½" h., scenic decoration of two mallards in flight, artist-signed 375.00

Vase, 7" h., two-handled, garden scene decoration, artist-signed........345.00

Vases, 7" h., decorated w/violets, gold trim, artist-signed, pr. 150.00

Vase, 7½" h., tiger lilies decoration on black ground, gold trim 125.00

Vase, 8" h., fluted top, decorated w/stylized poinsettias, w/gold trim, pearlized background, artist-signed, double circle mark...........................215.00

Vase, 8½" h., decorated w/yellow roses & green leaves on blue ground, gold collar & gold band at base, artist-signed, ca. 1905-1910 ....410.00

Vase, 12" h., cylindrical, palm trees decoration, artist-signed, ca. 1910...550.00

Vase, 12" h., handled, poinsettias & daisies decoration w/heavily decorated wide band of gold around top & scalloped free-form rim w/gold twisted handles, artist-signed, ca. 1905 ....325.00

Vases, 7½" h., gold pedestal base, double gold handles, floral medallions on black ground, gold rim, ca. 1925, pr. 650.00

PICTORIAL SOUVENIRS

These small ceramic wares, expressly made to be sold as a souvenir of a town or resort, are decorated with a pictorial scene which is usually titled. Made in profusion in Germany, Austria, Bavaria, and England, they were distributed by several American firms including C.E. Wheelock & Co., John H. Roth (Jonroth), Jones, McDuffee & Co., Stratton Co., and others. Because people seldom traveled in the early years of this century, a small souvenir tray or dish, picturing the resort or a town scene, afforded an excellent, inexpensive gift for family or friends when returning from a vacation trip. Seldom used and carefully packed away later, there is an abundant supply of these small wares available today at moderate prices. Their values are likely to rise.

Bowl, 5¼" d., reticulated rim, gold trim, "Prospect Point, Niagara Falls," Schwarzenburg, Bavaria blank $14.00

Dish, "New Meadow Inn, Bath, Maine," cut-out corners folded back, Wheelock, Germany blank, 4¾" d. 14.00

Model of "Ann Hathaway's Cottage," Goss, England, 6" w., 4¼" h. 40.00

Pitcher, "Boldt Castle on Heart Island, Alexandria Bay, 1000 Islands, New York," h.p. scene on bluish-green lustre, Germany (shows light wear) 8.00

Plate, 6" d., "Cooper Bldg., Newton, Kansas," Wheelock, Austria blank 10.00

Plate, 6½" d., "Village Free Library, West Gouldsboro, Maine," scalloped & beaded scroll purple lustre rim, gold tracery trim 15.00

Plate, 7½" d., "Plymouth, Massachusetts," six historical scenes in medallions, crown & circle marks, Jonroth, England blank 16.00

Plate, 9⅞" sq., "Rainbow Falls, Watkins Glen, New York," h.p. on ivory, thistle & camellia border decoration, scalloped corners, Jonroth, Adamo England blank 19.00

Plate, "Methodist Church, Forest Grove, Oregon," Homer Laughlin blank 20.00

Vase, 4¼" h., 2¾" d., pinched neck flanked by high handles, "Life Saving Station, South Haven, Michigan," h.p. scene medallion on cobalt blue ground 16.50

Vase, 4⅝" h., "Grand Canyon National Park, Arizona," colored scene on cream ground, Jonroth, Royal Winton, England blank.............17.00

PIERCE (Howard) CERAMICS

Howard Pierce began his studio in 1941 in Claremont, California. By 1950, he had national representation for all his products. From the beginning, wildlife and animals were the major output of Pierce's artware. In the early years, Pierce produced some polyurethane pieces but an allergic reaction forced him to stop using it. He also created a small amount of merchandise in a Wedgwood Jasper ware style. A few years later, Pierce designed porcelain bisque animals and plants that were placed in or near the open areas of high-glazed vases. When Mt. St. Helens volcano erupted, Pierce obtained a small quantity of the ash and developed a sandy, rough-textured glaze. There was also a 'lava' glaze unrelated to the Mt. St. Helens treatment. Mr. Pierce described 'lava' as "...bubbling up from the bottom." He created a few pieces in gold leaf; however, there was a 'gold' treatment of the 1950s which became known as 'Sears gold.' Sears, Roebuck & Company ordered a large quantity of assorted Pierce products but wanted them done in an overall gold color. Only a few of these pieces have the Howard Pierce mark. In the late 1970s, Mr. Pierce began incising a number in the clay of experimentally glazed products. From this numbering system he was successfully able to create various glazes in blues, deep greens, pinks, purples, yellows, and blacks which are highly collectible. In November 1992, due to health problems, Howard and Ellen Pierce destroyed all the molds they had created over the years. In 1993, Mr. Pierce began work on a very limited basis creating smaller versions of past porcelain items. These pieces are simply stamped "Pierce." Howard Pierce passed away in February, 1994.

Pierce

Howard
Pierce
Claremont
Calif.

Bowl, 9" d., 2½" h., round base w/flared, deep sides, dark brown outside, brown & white 'lava' treatment inside, signed in script "Pierce" $65.00

Bowl, nut, 5" l., 1¾" h., rectangular shape w/an irregular rim, glossy light green interior, mauve exterior, incised mark, "Howard Pierce P-6, Calif" 15.00

Stylized Figure of an Eskimo Man

Figure of an Eskimo man, standing, crude face features, arms indistinct against body, brown face & feet over white body, Model No. 206P, ca. 1953, 7" h. (ILLUS.) 85.00

Figure of a girl, kneeling w/bowl in left hand, right arm extended, palm raised & open, 'Sears gold,' no mark, 7" h. 15.00

Figure group of a black boy & girl holding hands, white glossy glaze, ca. 1985, 4½" h. 30.00

Model of a circus horse, head down, tail straight, leaping position w/middle of body attached to small, round center base, experimental blue, 7½" l., 6½" h. 85.00

Model of a duck, head turned slightly, 'Sears gold' stamped marked "Howard Pierce," 7¾" h. 48.00

Model of an egret, standing, feet & legs obscured by leaf base, neck long & curved, 9½" h. 75.00

Model of an elephant, seated, trunk raised, 'Mt. St. Helens' ash treatment, 4¾" h. 28.00

Model of an ermine, seated upright w/tail curled upward behind & against body, brown eyes, ears, nose & tip of tail w/white body, ca.early 1950s, 9" h. (ILLUS. top next column) 135.00

Model of a fawn, sitting, head & ears up, legs folded under body, dark brown eyes, experimental tan glaze, ca. 1985, 5½" h. 32.00

Model of a giraffe, head turned to side, modernistic design, legs slightly apart, no base, 12½" h. 42.00

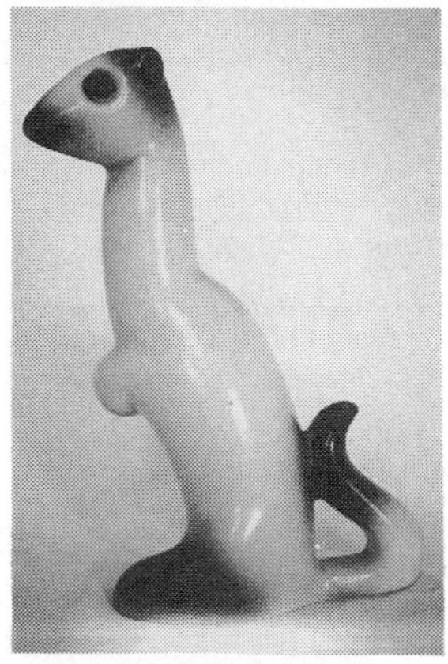

Model of an Ermine

Model of a goose, seated w/head stretched upward, mouth open, 'Sears gold,' no mark, 3¾" h. 7.00

Model of a leopard, pacing position, hand-painted spots, tawny body, dark brown spots, limited production, 11½" l., 2¾" h. 325.00

Model of a panther, pacing position, black glaze, 11½" l., 2¾" h. 75.00

Model of a raccoon, seated, head turned slightly, full face, brown glaze w/four stripes around tail, 9" l., 3½" h. 55.00

Model of a roadrunner, standing on wire legs, tail pointed upward, head held high, polyurethane, 8" h. 155.00

Model of a seal, seated, head up, black glaze, 5½" l., 5" h. 45.00

Model of a tiger, pacing position, cream body, brown hand-painted stripes, limited production, 11½" l., 2¾" h. 315.00

Pencil holder, nude women in relief around outside, one year limited production, 1980, 3½" d., 4¼" h. 25.00

Sign, dealer advertising, smooth surface, triangular shape, 'Pierce' at top in 1½" block letters, 'Porcelain' underneath Pierce in ½" letters, 6" l., 2½" h. 110.00

Sign, dealer advertising, rough surface resembling tree bark, 'Howard Pierce' in script on upper line, "Porcelain' in block letters on second line, gold leaf, 6" l., 2½" h. 80.00

Sign, dealer, advertising, rough surface resembling tree bark, 'Howard Pierce' in script on upper line, 'Porcelain' in block letters on second line, grey or brown glaze, 6" l., 2½" h. 65.00

Figural Vase by Pierce

Vase, 7½" h., rectangular black base w/straight-sided glossy vase on one end, white porcelain bisque fawn & tree on other end w/three tree branches attached to vase, underside of recessed base divided in half w/one side incised in script underglaze 'Howard Pierce' & the other side incised '302P Claremont, Calif.' (ILLUS.) 125.00

Whistle, bird shape w/hole at tail, brown w/white glaze, 3½" h. 20.00

PISGAH FOREST

Pisgah Forest Lamp Base

Walter Stephen experimented with making pottery shortly after 1900 with his parents in Tennessee. After their deaths in 1910, he eventually moved to the foot of Mt. Pisgah in North Carolina where he became a partner of C.P. Ryman. Together they built a kiln and a shop but this partnership was dissolved in 1916. During 1920 Stephen again began to experiment with pottery and by 1926 had his own pottery and equipment. Pieces are usually marked and may also be signed "W. Stephen" and dated. Walter Stephen died in 1961 but work at the pottery still continues, although on a part-time basis.

Creamer, Cameo ware, scene of a mountain man, his dog, a cabin & mountains $350.00

Cups & saucers, turquoise glaze, ca. 1950s, four sets 120.00

Lamp base, Cameo ware, baluster-form body decorated w/a white relief band of pioneers & covered wagons against a powder blue ground, signed "STEPHEN," 6" d., 10¾" h. (ILLUS.) 450.00

Pitcher, milk, 6" h., 4½" d., Cameo ware, covered wagon scene, matte green top & glossy glaze blue bottom, signed "Stephen" on side & "Cameo Stephen, Longpine, Arden, N.C., 195?" 425.00

Sugar bowl, cov., turquoise & pink glaze, 3½ x 3½" 25.00

Vase, 5" h., 3½" d., bell-shaped, light green crystalline glaze, pink interior ..75.00

Vase, 4" h., bulbous, blue crystalline glaze w/pink interior, dated "1938".....50.00

Vase, 4½" h., corset-shaped, turquoise glaze, ca. 1941 ....40.00

Vase, 5" h., 3" d., white & pink glaze, signed "Stephen," ca. 1946................85.00

Vase, 5¼" h., Cameo ware, wide baluster-form body w/a flaring mouth, Wedgwood blue ground decorated w/a white-relief central band of pioneers in covered wagons, marked, dated "1951" 550.00

Vase, 7" h., 4¾" d., Cameo ware, ovoid body below the wide slightly waisted neck, the neck decorated in white relief w/an Indian buffalo hunt scene on a dark green ground, a white crystalline lower body, rose pink interior, raised mark 1,210.00

Pisgah Forest Vase

Vase, 7¼" h., 4½" d., ovoid body tapering to a short slightly flared neck, covered in a glaze of tightly packed medium sized blue crystals against a clear sea green body, raised mark (ILLUS.)........................770.00

Vase, 7¾" h., 4½" d., Cameo ware, ovoid body w/a wide slightly flaring neck, decorated around the neck w/a white relief-molded wagon train scene against a deep blue ground, the body glazed in a green-over-brown crystalline glaze, impressed mark "W.B.S. 1941" 1,210.00

Vase, 8¼" h., 6½" d., wide ovoid body tapering slightly to a flat ring-molded mouth, covered in an unusual thick volcanic turquoise blue & brown glaze, raised mark, 1928 ....330.00

Vase, 8½" h., 5¼" d., ovoid body w/a rounded shoulder to the short cylindrical neck w/flat wide mouth, lustre glaze in blue & bluish green crystals over a gold body, rose pink interior, raised mark, 1943...............550.00

Vase, 10" h., 4¾" d., tall ovoid body tapering to a gently flared neck, overall tiger's-eye flambé glaze, rose pink interior, raised mark 220.00

Vase, 12¼" h., 7¼" d., Cameo ware, wide ovoid body tapering to a wide flat mouth, decorated around the shoulder w/a white relief-molded wagon train scene on a khaki ground, over a mottled turquoise body, impressed mark, 1929 ....1,540.00

Vase, 13¼" h., 7¾" d., Cameo ware, tall ovoid body tapering to a short cylindrical neck, a dark green band around the neck & shoulder decorated w/a white relief covered wagon scene, the lower body w/a periwinkle blue crystalline glaze, marked, artist-signed & dated 1939..1,430.00

POT LIDS

Collectible pot lids are decorated ceramic lids for commercial pots and jars originally containing soaps, shaving creams, hair pomade, and so on. The best-known lids were made by F. & R. Pratt in Fenton, England from about the middle of the 19th century.

"Lyman's Cherry Toothpaste, Imparts a Delightful Fragrance to the Breath, Montreal Canada," center depiction of a cherry & leaves, black transfer, Canada, ca. 1870-90, 3¼" d. $165.00

"Odontine or Rose Toothpaste, Prepared by Eugene Roussel, Philadelphia - Eugene Roussel - 114 Chestnut St. Philada'," black transfer, ca. 1830-40, 2¾ x 2¾".................61.50

Pratt, Dr. Johnson portrait, in a square frame...125.00

Pratt, "Hide and Seek," color transfer of children playing, in round wooden frame, 6" d. 55.00

Pratt, "War," polychrome scene of a fallen soldier & horse, w/jar, 4" d. (stains, minor chips).........................137.50

Royal Harbour, Ramsgate, multicolored scene of Royal Harbour, 4" d. (old minor rim chip)....................93.50

"Taylor's (H.P. & W.C.) Saponaceous Shaving Compound," black transfer, w/jar, 3¾" d. 82.50

PRATT WARES

The earliest ware now classified as Pratt ware was made by Felix Pratt at his pottery in Fenton, England from about 1810. He made earthenware with bright glazes, relief sporting jugs, toby mugs and commercial pots and jars whose lids bore multicolored transfer prints. The F. & R. Pratt mark is mid-19th century. The name Pratt ware is also applied today to mid and late 19th century English ware of the same general type as that made by Felix Pratt.

Prattware Model of a Cockerel

Creamer, slightly squared form, molded & decorated w/children in hearts, one side lettered "Sportive Innocence" & the other "Mischievious Sport," all in polychrome enamels, 4⅞" h. (small edge chips) $434.50

Figure of a lady, standing & wearing a brown hat & gloves & a brown-dotted dress, holding two sprigs of ochre roses & green leaves, standing barefooted on a green mound base dashed in ochre & brown, ca. 1815, 8⅛" h. (hat brim touched up, base footrim chips).......575.00

Model of a cockerel, the stylized bird w/ochre comb & wattles, a brown beak & eyes, incised plumage sponged or feathered in yellow, brown, ochre & blue, modeled perched astride a grassy scroll on a circular mound base washed in green, ca. 1800, 8¼" h. (ILLUS.) ..2,013.00

Model of a dog, seated hound hunched forward w/painted brown eyes, ears, mouth, forelegs, collar & spine, a dimpled coat spotted in brown, blue, yellow & ochre, on an oblong green-edged base w/his long tail curling around his left hind foot, ca. 1800-10, 2¾" h...........................690.00

Pratt Hawk & Eagle Figures

Model of an eagle, the stylized bird w/ochre beak & legs, a brown crest & plumage spotted in blue, yellow & ochre & sponged in brown, modeled w/raised wings (one repaired) & alighting from a green rocky perch above a tapering square base patterned w/blue squiggles & ochre dots on an incised ground between impressed bands of yellow & ochre lozenges, ca. 1810, 9⅝" h. (ILLUS. right)..2,875.00

Model of a hawk, the stylized bird w/brown eyes, legs & tail tip, an ochre-sponged neck & breast & yellow, ochre & blue wing & tail feathers, modeled perched on a green mound (chip at front) molded on either side w/a large ochre blossom above an ochre-sponged square base (some chips), 1800-10, 6⅝" h. (ILLUS. left) 2,300.00

Mug, portrait-type, modeled as the head of a smiling officer wearing a yellow-edged dark brown tricorn hat, a light brown collar above a ruffled jabot, a white waistcoat, ochre sash over a blue coat w/yellow & ochre frogging & epaulets, the brown queue of his hair looping up to form the handle, ca. 1800-10, 6 3/16" h. (small chips on hat, repaired hairline in handle) 633.00

Plaque, oval, pearlware, molded in relief in the center w/two lions decorated in blue, green & olive enamel, early 19th c., minor stains & wear w/hairlines, 9¾ x 11½" (ILLUS. top next column) 660.00

Prattware Oval Plaque

Pratt Fox & Swan Sauceboat

Sauceboats, each modeled as the head of an ochre fox w/an open mouth forming the spout & w/pricked ears (very small chips), conjoined w/the spread-winged body of a white swan w/an arched neck & yellow-beaked head forming the handle, the neck & wings (one repaired) lightly sponged in brown & interrupting at the back of the oval base a border of green & yellow leaves (one chipped) molded against a dimpled ground between blue bands, the rim (one chipped) also edged in blue, ca. 1800, 6⅞" & 7" l., pr. (ILLUS. of one) 805.00

QUIMPER

This French earthenware pottery has been made in France since the end of the 17th century and is still in production today. Because the colorful decoration on this ware, predominantly of Breton peasant figures, is all hand-painted and each piece is unique, it has become increasingly popular with collectors in recent years. Most pieces offered today date from about the mid-19th century to the present. Modern potteries continue to operate today and contemporary examples are available in gift shops.

Madonna & Child Figure

Figure of the Madonna & Child, titled on the round base "Ste. Vierge," decorated in cobalt blue, yellow & orange, decorated by Adolphe Porquier, Henriot, France, ca. 1930s, small chips on base, age lines, 10½" h. (ILLUS.)..................$302.50

Pitcher, 4⅛" h., cylindrical body w/flat rim & angled handle, the front decorated w/three vertical rectangular panels, the center h.p. w/the bust portrait of a sailor, the two flanking w/the heads of young ladies in costume, in shades of blue & white against a dark green ground, marked "HB Quimper Odetta 453-1145," ca. 1930s......................302.50

Plaque, pierced to hang, "Les Filets Bleus," in blue, orange & black central decoration & rim, inscribed marks, 12⅜" d.................................357.50

Plate, 9½" d., h.p. polychrome center scene of a standing soldier framed by floral sprigs, paired sprigs on the wide border w/scalloped rim, titled "Vive la Nation - 1789," marked "Henriot - Quimper, France" (edge chips) 165.00

REDWARE

Unique Redware Figure Group

Red earthenware pottery was made in the American colonies from the late 1600s. Bowls, crocks and all types of utilitarian wares were turned out in great abundance to supplement the pewter and handmade treenware. The ready availability of the clay, the same used in making bricks and roof tiles, accounted for the vast production. The lead-glazed redware retained its reddish color though a variety of colors could be obtained by adding various metals to the glaze. Interesting effects occurred accidentally through unsuspected impurities in the clay or uneven temperatures in the firing kiln which sometimes resulted in streaks or mottled splotches.

Redware pottery was seldom marked by the maker.

Bowl, 8¼" d., 5¼" h., squatty bulbous body on a thin footring, the sides tapering to a widely flaring rim, applied ribbed strap handles at the shoulders, brown sponged glaze (wear, glaze flakes & chips) $104.50

Cup, squatty wide bulbous body w/flared rim resting on a narrow footring, applied C-scroll handle, brown splotches on reddish ground, 5¼" d., 3½" h. (edge wear, chips)....110.00

Figure group, the small-scale grouping including a log cabin w/shingled roof & chimney, a bearded man w/whiskey flask & dog seated before them, all mounted on a shaped rectangular base, the roof inscribed "Sovineer (sic) of Strasburg, VA," J. Eberly & Co., Strasburg, Virginia, ca. 1894, 6½ x 9¼", 5½" h. (ILLUS.) 29,900.00

Flowerpot w/attached saucer base, finger crimped rims, tooled foliate band, greenish amber glaze, 5½" h. (wear & chips) 137.50

Jar, wide ovoid body w/a very wide flat molded rim, greenish amber glaze w/dark orange spots, 3⅝" h. (small chips).......................................44.00

Jar, ovoid body w/a wide molded rim, tan flecked glaze, impressed mark "W. Smith Womelsdorf," Pennsylvania, late 19th c., 5½" h. (minor chips & a hairline) 192.50

Jar, ovoid body tapering to a slightly flared rim, side strap handle, dark amber glaze w/brown splotches, 5⅞" h. (small flakes) 93.50

Jar, ovoid body w/a wide molded rim, greenish orange pebbly glaze, Galena, Illinois-type, 6¼" h. (hairline in base) 181.50

Jar, ovoid body tapering to a wide upright molded rim band, greenish amber glaze w/olive green speckled dots, Galena, Illinois-type, 7¼" h. (wear, chips) 192.50

Jar, ovoid, eared shoulder handles, tooled lines around shoulder, clear glaze w/dark brown splotches, 9" h. (wear, glaze chips & hairline)...........165.00

Jar, cov., wide bulbous body tapering to a wide mouth w/molded gallery rim w/side spout, side ribbed strap handle, tooled shoulder ring, wide brown sponged stripes down the sides, 9" h. (minor chips on pot, chipped mismatched cover).............467.50

Jug, ovoid w/ribbed strap handle, dark brown shiny glaze, attributed to Boughner, Greensboro, Pennsylvania, 13¼" h. (small glaze & edge flakes) 275.00

Model of a chest of drawers, miniature, a rectangular top overhanging a case w/three pairs of small drawers over the scalloped apron & bracket feet, yellow slip glaze w/overall brown speckles, the back incised "Annie Maria Marsden, 1884," 5¾ x 11¼", 10¼" h. (very minor edge chips) 825.00

Model of a rooster, a large stylized bird w/comb, wattle & arched tail all w/molded detailing, on a 'cole slaw' decorated oblong base, rich amber glaze w/green highlights, 12½" h. (damage, glaze flakes) 467.50

Pitcher, miniature, 3¼" h., simple ovoid body tapering to a flared rim w/pinched spout, applied loop handle, incised on base "W.W.C. 1906"..................................93.50

Pitcher, 5¾" h., wide ovoid body

tapering to a flared rim w/pinched spout, small ribbed loop handle, yellowish glaze w/amber spots (minor edge wear) 55.00

Pitcher, 10½" h., bulbous ovoid body tapering to a wide flaring neck w/pinched spout, small strap handle, clear glaze w/dark scattered manganese splotches, 19th c. (imperfections) 357.50

Rare Redware Sugar Bowl

Sugar bowl, cov., squatty bulbous body on a small footring & w/eared handles flanking the flaring rim, high stepped & domed cover w/ball finial, decorated overall w/marbleized white & black slip on a red ground, Pennsylvania, first half 19th c., cover & base cracked, 12" h. (ILLUS.) 4,600.00

RED WING

Various potteries operated in Red Wing, Minnesota from 1868, the most successful being the Red Wing Stoneware Co., organized in 1878. Merged with other local potteries through the years, it became known as Red Wing Union Stoneware Co. in 1894, and was one of the largest producers of utilitarian stoneware items in the United States. After a decline in the popularity of stoneware products, an art pottery line was introduced to compensate for the loss and this was reflected in a new name for the company, Red Wing Potteries, Inc., in 1930. Stoneware production ceased entirely in 1947, but vases, planters, cookie jars and dinnerwares of art pottery quality continued in production until 1967 when the pottery ceased operation altogether.

BRUSHED & GLAZED WARES

Red Wing Lion Vase

Lobby (sand) jar or umbrella stand, Brushed Ware, cylindrical, embossed stag & doe in mountainous landscape, shaded green glaze, 12" d., 15" h. $1,500.00

Vase, 10" h., Glazed Ware, embossed lion in landscape decoration, tan & grey glaze (ILLUS.) 80.00

Vase, 12" h., expanding cylinder w/squared handles rising from narrow shoulder to mouth, Grecian design, No. 155.................................80.00

Vase, 12½" h., squared handles, tapering cylinder, marked w/pre-1936 ink mark, No. 163......................75.00

DINNERWARES & NOVELTIES

Bean pot, cov., Village Green patt........25.00

Bowl, 5¼" d., Tampico patt.....................6.00

Bowl, salad, 6" d., Bob White patt. 35.00

Bowl, 8" d., Vintage patt. 10.00

Bowl, 9" d., two-handled, Bob White patt. 25.00

Bowl, 12" d., salad, Bob White patt., deep 45.00

French Chef Cookie Jar

Butter dish, cov., Bob White patt. 62.00

Butter dish, cov., Lute Song 32.50

Butter dish, cov., Vintage patt., 1/4 lb.....15.00

Cake stand, pedestal base, Tampico patt. 35.00

Casserole, cov., Village Green patt., 1 qt. 12.00

Console bowl, Magnolia patt. 60.00

Cookie jar, cov., Bob White patt. ....125.00 to 145.00

Cookie jar, cov., figural French Chef, blue or yellow glaze, h.p. details, stamped wing mark & "Red Wing Pottery," each (ILLUS.) 80.00

Cookie jar, cov., figural Katrina (or Dutch Girl), blue or yellow glaze, impressed "Red Wing U.S.A.," each 70.00

Cookie jar, cov., figural Monk, "Thou Shalt Not Steal," yellow or blue glaze, each 95.00

Creamer, Merrileaf patt. 8.00

Cup & saucer, Bob White patt. 19.00

Cup & saucer, Tampico patt. 12.50

Cup & saucer, Vintage patt. 7.00

Ewer, Magnolia patt., No. 1028 ....45.00

Figure of a lute player, deep maroon glaze, No. 2507 ....125.00

Figure of an Oriental man, standing wearing a tall hat & long robes w/long sleeves, green glaze, No. 1309, 10" h. 125.00

Gravy boat, cov., handled, Vintage patt. 15.00

Hors d'oeuvre holder, Bob White patt., model of a bird pierced for picks 40.00

Model of a badger on football, stump base, signed "Red Wing Potteries" & dated 1939 ....110.00

Model of a gopher on football, "Minnesota," dated 1939 ....85.00

Mug, cylindrical w/embossed banner reading "Hamm's Krug Klub" over embossed scene of a bird & animals in the forest around the body, brown glaze 70.00

Mug, Village Green patt. 9.00

Pitcher, 7" h., Bob White patt., 60 oz....18.00

Planter, model of a cornucopia, yellow outside, salmon pink inside, artist-signed 38.50

Plate, bread & butter, 6½" d., Bob White patt. 7.50

Plate, salad, 7½" d., Round Up patt. 17.50

Plate, dinner, 10" d., Vintage patt. 9.00

Plate, dinner, 10¼" d., Lute Song patt. 8.50

Plate, dinner, 10½" d., Bob White patt. 12.50

Plate, dinner, 10½" d., Round Up patt. 60.00

Plate, 11" d., Capistrano patt. 7.50

Platter, 12¾" oval, Vintage patt. 15.00

Platter, 13" oval, Bob White patt. 25.00

Relish dish, three-part, handled, Bob White patt. 18.00

Salt & pepper shakers, figural birds, Bob White patt., pr. 30.00

Salt & pepper shakers, tall, hourglass shape, Bob White patt., 6" h., pr. 20.00

Salt & pepper shakers Village Green patt., pr. 20.00

Sugar bowl, cov., Bob White patt. 22.50

Sugar bowl, cov., Rodeo patt. 65.00

Sugar bowl, cov., Vintage patt. 8.00

Teapot, cov., Bob White patt. 65.00

Toothpick holder, model of a gopher on a log, signed "Red Wing Potteries" & dated 120. 00

Vegetable bowl, open, divided & angled, Bob White patt. 35.00

Vegetable bowl, oval, divided, Lute Song patt. 20.00

Vegetable bowl, divided, Vintage patt., 12" d. 14.00

Wall pocket, model of a guitar, green glaze, No. M1484 ....35.00

Water jar, cover & stand, Bob White patt., 2 gal. 375.00

STONEWARE & UTILITY WARES

Red Wing Spongeware Bowl

Bowl, 6" d., Grey Line stoneware 165.00

Bowl, 6" d., paneled sides, spongeware (ILLUS.)....................................90.00

Bowl, 7" d., paneled sides, blue banding, spongeware 98.00

Bowl, 7" d., Grey Line, stoneware w/spongeband decoration, w/Wisconsin advertising 195.00

Bowl, 8" d., Grey Line, stoneware, w/ advertising...................................185.00

Bowl, 9" d., Grey Line, stoneware w/paneled sides & blue sponge band decoration ....100.00 to 125.00

Red Wing Stoneware Fruit Jars

Fruit jar w/screw-on lid, "Stone Mason Fruit Jar, Union Stoneware Co., Red Wing, Minn." printed in black on stoneware, qt. (ILLUS. right) 185.00

Fruit jar w/screw-on zinc lid, "Stone Mason Fruit Jar, Union Stoneware Co., Red Wing, Minn." printed in black (or blue) on stoneware, half gal. (ILLUS. left) 190.00

Jug, miniature, beehive shape, copy of the "little brown jug," symbol of football rivalry between Minnesota & Michigan, brown top half, grey bottom half printed in blue w/"Who Will Win?"..195.00

Pitcher, 5" h., spongeware, rust & green daubing on stoneware, unmarked..80.00

Pitcher, milk, 8" h., stoneware w/dark blue edging & crimped lip, logo on front...235.00

Pitcher, 8½" h., (so-called Russian milk pitcher without pouring spout), brown glaze, 1 gal.............................75.00

Red Wing Poultry Feeder

Poultry feeder (or waterer), stoneware, "Ko - Rec Feeder," half gal. (ILLUS.) 125.00

Refrigerator jar w/bail handle, white-glazed stoneware w/blue bands, No. 5 ....200.00

RIDGWAYS

Ridgway Ale Set

There were numerous Ridgways among

English potters. The firm J. & W. Ridgway operated in Shelton from 1814 to 1930 and produced many pieces with scenes of historical interest. William Ridgway operated in Shelton from 1830 to 1865. Most wares marked Ridgway that have been offered in this country were made by one of these two firms, or by Ridgway Potteries, Ltd., still in operation. Also see HISTORICAL & COMMEMORATIVE WARES

Ale set: 9½" h. tankard pitcher & six 4½" h. mugs on a 12¼" d., tray; Coaching Days & Ways series, caramel ground w/black transfer-printed coaching scenes, silver lustre rims & handles, 8 pcs. (ILLUS.) $295.00

Bowl, 10" d., Coaching Days & Ways series 50.00

Dessert service: a pair of shaped oval dishes, a pr. of shaped square dishes, three cruciform dishes & nine plates; each piece transfer-printed in green & trimmed in gilt w/an overall design of blossom clusters & berried branches within a gilt-edge scalloped & wave-molded rim, the dishes molded at either end w/a row of five gilt-trimmed rose blossoms, pattern number 323l, ca. 1835, dishes 9¾", 10½" & 11½" l., the set (some gilt wear) 1,035.00

Gravy boat, Coaching Days & Ways series, "Old England Ware," ca. 1920-50..25.00

Mug, Coaching Days & Ways series, 4" h..25.00

Mug, Coaching Days & Ways series, silver lustre trim, 4½" h. 38.00

Pitcher, 7½" h., Coaching Days & Ways series 80.00

Pitcher, 9" h., relief-molded stoneware, the sides molded w/a scene from "Tam O'Shanter," ca. 1835...150.00

Pitchers, jug-type, graduated set, 4¼" h., 4¾" d., 5" h., 5" d., 5½" h., 5½" d., Coaching Days & Ways

"Coaching Days" Pitchers

series, scenes in black on caramel background, silver lustre trim, "Racing the Mall," "Henry the Eighth" & "The Abbot of Reading," set of 3 (ILLUS.) 135.00

Plate, 9" d., Coaching Days & Ways series, marked "Old England Ware," ca. 1920-50..30.00

Plate, 10¼" d., "View from Ruggles House Newburgh," blue transfer-printed scene 55.00

Soup plate w/flanged rim, "Harper's Ferry from the American Side," blue transfer-printed scene, 9" d................65.00

Tea set: cov. teapot, open handled sugar bowl & creamer; spherical bodies, rich deep caramel background w/scenes in black, silver lustre top bands & handle trim, scenes based on Dickens' Mr. Pickwick character, teapot 4" d., 4½" h., sugar bowl 5½" d., 2⅜" h., creamer 3⅛" d., 2⅝" h., 3 pcs..........145.00

Tray, oval, Coaching Days & Ways series, 12½" l. 80.00

ROCKINGHAM WARES

Rockingham-Glazed Bowl

An earthenware pottery was first established on the estate of the Marquis of Rockingham in England's Yorkshire district about 1745 and occupied by a succession of potters. The famous Rockingham glaze of mottled brown, somewhat resembling tortoise shell, was introduced about 1788 by the Brameld

Brothers, and was well received. During the 1820s, porcelain manufacture was added to the production and fine quality china was turned out until the pottery closed in 1842. The popular Rockingham glaze was subsequently produced elsewhere, including Bennington, Vermont, and at numerous other U.S. potteries. We list herein not only wares produced at the Rockingham potteries in England, distinguishing porcelain wares from the more plentiful earthenware productions, but also include items from other potteries with the Rockingham glaze.

Bowl, 8½" d., 3½" h., deep rounded sides on a footring & flaring to a wide flattened rim, mottled brown glaze $60.50

Bowl, 9½" d., 4¼" h., deep rounded sides on a footring & a molded rim, tan & white horizontal bands beneath overall mottled dark brown glaze 132.00

Bowl, 11" d., 2¾" h., a wide round flat bottom & wide gently sloping low sides, mottled dark brown glaze 93.50

Bowl, 11" d., 4¾" h., deep rounded & flaring sides on a thick footring, a flaring rolled rim, mottled dark brown glaze, some wear (ILLUS.) 71.50

Bowl, 11½" d., 3¼" h., wide canted sides, overall mottled dark brown glaze 126.50

Bowl,11½" d., 3¼" h., wide flat bottom w/widely canted sides, mottled dark brown glaze (minor wear) 82.50

Cuspidor, hand-held, cylindrical mug-form w/strap handle, mottled dark brown glaze, 3½" h. 181.50

Dish, round flat bottom w/low flared sides, mottled dark brown glaze, 5" d. 44.00

Dish, squared & ruffled flaring sides w/the rounded corners molded w/ribbing, scroll bands at the rims, mottled dark brown glaze, 9" w. 44.00

Jar, cov., cylindrical sides w/a molded base band & wide flaring top, domed cover w/button finial, mottled dark brown glaze, 8" d. (chip on cover) 88.00

Lamp base, modeled in the form of a seated dog, mottled dark brown glaze, drilled at top & base for fittings, 8¼" h. 253.00

Models of lambs, reclining animal w/light curly coat, on a cobalt blue glazed oval base, 5½" l., pr..............495.00

Mug, cylindrical w/molded base, C-scroll handle, mottled dark brown glaze, 3" h. 44.00

Pie plate, wide round flat bottom w/low sloping sides, mottled dark brown glaze, 9" d. 82.50

Pie plate, wide flat bottom w/low flared sides, mottled dark brown glaze, 9½" d. 49.50

Pie plate, wide round flat bottom w/low sloping sides, mottled dark brown glaze, 10" d. ....75.00 to 100.00

Pie plate, wide flat bottom w/flat, flared sides, mottled dark brown glaze, 11¼" d. 93.50

Pitcher, 6⅜" h., footed bulbous base tapering to cylindrical sides, high arched spout & angled handle, molded Gothic Arch design on sides, mottled dark brown glaze 60.50

Pitcher, 8⅝" h., footed bulbous octagonal body w/incurved panels to the short neck w/scalloped rim & wide, arched spout, angled handle, overall mottled & streaky flint enamel glaze, mid-19th c. (small chips) 192.50

Pitcher, 9" h., footed bulbous ovoid body tapering to a flat rim w/arched spout, S-scroll handle, relief-molded deer & hanging game designs on the sides, mottled dark brown glaze 165.00

Pot, cov., a bulbous ovoid flat-bottomed container tapering to a wide flat rim w/large spout & a long stick handle to the side, the low domed cover w/a button finial, mottled dark brown glaze, 4⅝" h. 280.50

Soap dish, oval, mottled dark brown glaze, 4⅞" l. 49.50

Soap dish, deep rounded tapering sides w/molded rim, mottled dark brown glaze, 5¼" d. 38.50

Vegetable dish, open, oval, shallow flaring sides w/rolled rim, mottled dark brown glaze, 10" l. 71.50

Vegetable dish, open, octagonal w/wide flanged rim, boldly mottled dark brown glaze, 13½" l. 170.50

ROOKWOOD

Considered America's foremost art pottery, the Rookwood Pottery Company was established in Cincinnati, Ohio in 1880, by Mrs. Maria Nichols Longworth Storer. To accurately record its development, each piece carried the Rookwood insignia, or mark, was dated, and, if individually decorated, was usually signed by the artist. The pottery remained in Cincinnati until 1959 when it was sold to Herschede Hall Clock Company and moved to Starkville, Mississippi, where it continued in operation until 1967.

A private company is now producing a limited variety of pieces using original Rookwood molds.

Rookwood Limoges-type Dish

Book ends, figure of an Oriental lady seated in the lotus position, stepped sides on the back plate, matte brown glaze, No. 2362, 1919, William P. McDonald, 5¼" w., 7¾" h., pr. (minor roughness to top of headdresses) $220.00

Book ends, figural, model of an elephant, trunk up, glossy ivory glaze, No. 6124, 1957, pr. 350.00

Book ends, figural, model of an owl, matte blue glaze, No. 2655, 1935, pr. 350.00

Book ends, model of a rook standing in front of a flower-molded block, mauve glaze, over-sized weighted design, No. 2274, 1926, 6½" h., pr. 412.50

Bowl-vase, squatty bulbous body w/a closed rim, decorated w/large clusters of yellow roses on a dark brown ground, Standard glaze, No. 214C, 1903, Edith Noonan, 5½" d., 2¾" h. (crazing) 302.50

Bowl-vase, very compressed squatty bulbous body w/the wide shoulder tapering to a wide flat rim, decorated w/deep red, ochre & blue blossoms & green foliage on a dark purple & raspberry butterfat ground, Wax Matte glaze, No. 923, 1922, E. Lincoln, 6¼" d., 2½" h. 935.00

Bowl-vase, porcelain, globular w/a closed-in rim, decorated w/red & yellow pansies & green foliage against a dark bluish grey ground, 1946, E.T. Hurley, 5" d., 4" h. 495.00

Bowl-vase, wide squatty bulbous body w/a shoulder tapering to a low cylindrical neck w/flat rim, decorated around the shoulder w/a wreath of heart-shaped leaves in blue & green against a rose pink ground, No. 131, 1915, C.S. Todd, 8½" d., 5½" h. 935.00

Dish, low swirled sides, Uncle Remus series, center w/a line drawing of a man & child, lettered "Miss Sally Callin' - Better Run Along" on a pumpkin ground, gilded edge, No. 87G, 1885, E.P. Cranch, 6½" d. ...440.00

Dish, shallow rounded form molded on one side w/a large model of a frog, fine leathery matte peacock green glaze, No 2606, 1922, 7" l., 4" h. 330.00

Dish, shell-shaped, Limoges-type, decorated w/black sparrows & bamboo plants against a beige & brown ground, gilded edge, No. 222, 1883, William McDonald, 8½" w. (ILLUS.) 440.00

Ewer, flattened disc-form base tapering to a slender tall neck w/a trilobed rolled rim, loop handle from neck to shoulder, decorated w/orange nasturtiums on a bright orange shaded to dark brown ground, Standard glaze, No. 715E, 1898, 4½" d., 5" h. 165.00

Rookwood Ewer with Flowers

Ewer, squatty spherical body on a narrow footring w/a tall, slender cylindrical neck w/tricorner rim & long strap handle, decorated w/exotic yellow & white flowers on brown leafy stems, green Standard glaze, No. 101C, 1885, Matt Daly, crazing, 8½" h. (ILLUS.)....................385.00

Ewer, squatty bulbous base below a tall slender neck w/a trilobed rim & S-shaped handle, the base w/silver overlay Art Nouveau flowers & scrolling foliage, silver overlay on the rim & handle, the background h.p. w/sprigs of orange flowers & green foliage on a shaded brown ground, Standard glaze, No. 468CC, 1893, Josephine Zettel, silver marked "Gorham," 5½" d., 8½" h. 3,475.00

Ewer, bulbous ovoid shouldered body w/a cylindrical neck & tricorner rim, applied loop handle, yellow & green rose against a brown ground, Standard glaze, late 19th - early 20th c., 6" d., 8½" h..........................577.50

Rookwood Standard Glaze Ewer

Ewer, squatty spherical body on a narrow footring w/a tall, slender cylindrical neck w/tricorner rim & long strap handle, decorated w/yellow flowers & brown medallions against a sheer olive green ground, Standard glaze, No. 101A, 1888, Matt Daly, 6½" d., 11" h. (ILLUS.)....550.00

Ewer, globular base & long slender neck w/undulating rim, decorated w/fish & leaves incised & embossed under a clear green glaze, No. 101, 1882, H. Wonderoth, 7¼" d., 11½" h..825.00

Ewer, bulbous ovoid body tapering to a very slender tall neck flaring to a trefoil rim, applied S-form strap handle, decorated w/a school of fish in various shades of green, Sea Green glaze, 1894, A. R. Valentien, 13⅛" h. (restored)............................978.00

Jar. cov., Limoges-type, globular body w/dimpled sides & low collared neck, decorated w/snails & insects on a rust, sand & deep blue ground w/green foliage & gilded accents, 1882, Maria Longworth Nichols, 5" d., 6" h. (tight hairline in side) ...1,650.00

Mug, bisque, tapering sides w/three incised lines near base & top, temperance-oriented, "Wild Oats, Thistles," decorated w/drawn allegory of men drinking & its consequences, No. 587W, 1892, E.P. Cranch, 5½" d., 4½" h. 550.00

Mug, angular handle, depicting a stalk of corn in caramel brown & greens against a shaded dark brown shading to ochre ground, Standard glaze, 1898, Leonore Asbury, 5" d., 4¾" h..302.50

Paperweight, model of an elephant, green glaze, No. 6490, 1496 ....110.00

Pitcher, 4¼" h., 5" d., rounded tapering triangular body w/three pinched spouts, decorated around the lower half w/stylized red blossoms on a green ground, Matte glaze, No. 341E, 1902, A. R. Valentien...385.00

Pitcher, 4½" h., 6" w., swelled ovoid body w/a wide triple-spout rim, angular handle, decorated w/large orange cherries & green foliage against a deep green shaded to bright orange ground, No. 259D, 1892, C. Baker.................................165.00

Pitcher, 6⅜" h., simple ovoid body tapering to a short cylindrical neck w/long pinched spout, angled handle, decorated w/a long holly sprig in green & brown w/red berries highlighted in white against a shaded bluish grey ground w/ivory rim & interior, Standard glaze, No. 18, 1890, Edward Abel..............605.00

Pitcher, 7" h., Limoges-style, spherical body on a small footring & tapering to a short cylindrical neck, round loop handle, decorated w/silhouetted Oriental grasses against a green & beige background w/butterflies in shades of brown, gold trim in the scene & streaking at the rim, No. 36, 1883, Albert Valentien (ILLUS. top next column) 495.00

Limoges-Style Rookwood Pitcher

Rookwood Scenic Plaque

Plaque, rectangular, decorated w/a beach scene in half-light w/a blue sky, turquoise water & pink sand, in original wide, flat oak frame, 1916, Lenore Asbury, 5¼ x 8¼" (ILLUS.) 2,310.00

Hexagonal Rookwood Vase

Vase, 4¾" h., 4¼" w., hexagonal body on small tab feet, lightly molded in each panel w/a facing pair of small birds above a basket of fruit, dark bluish green Matte glaze, 1920, Arthur Conant (ILLUS.) 165.00

Vase, 5" h., 4½" d., barrel-shaped w/rolled rim, decorated w/stylized flowers outlined against a butterfat turquoise & navy blue ground, Wax Matte glaze, 1931 Kataro Shirayamadani 650.00

Vase, 5½" h., 3¼" d., bulbous w/short slender neck, decorated w/white & yellow flowers & greyish green foliage against a dark to light grey ground, Iris glaze, No. 905, 1908, Irene Bishop 605.00

Vase, 5¾" h., 4¾" d., bulbous ovoid shouldered body tapering to a short cylindrical neck, decorated around the top half w/a continuous branch of white & celadon green dogwood flowers & leaves on a shaded pink, cream & teal blue ground, Iris glaze, No. 531E, 1908, K. Van Horn 1,210.00

Vase, 6" h., globular body w/short slightly everted neck, decorated w/stylized cream floral garland, on a green ground, Standard glaze, No. 346B, 1899, Matt Daly...............440.00

Vase, 6" h., 3½ d., waisted cylindrical form, molded around the top w/a band of stylized chickens in purple, green & ochre, Matte glaze, No. 1358F, 1912, W. Hentschel.......550.00

Vase, 7½" h., 7" d., bisque, decorated w/a stylized underwater scene of crabs & plant life in heavy slip on a medium brown ground, die-stamped "ROOKWOOD 1884 94B"................770.00

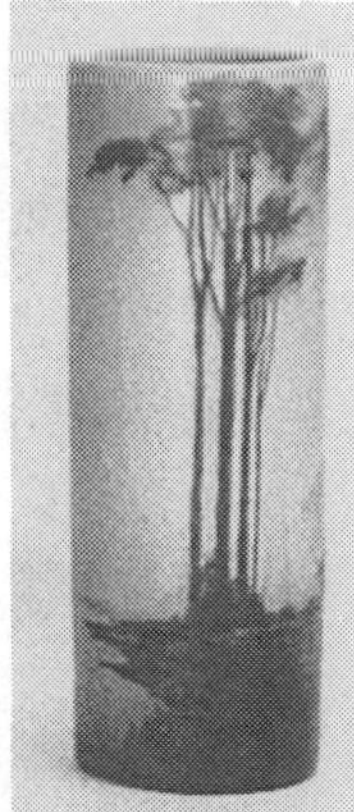

Rookwood Scenic Vellum Vase

Vase, 7¾" h., 2¾" d., cylindrical, decorated w/a continuous landscape w/tall trees by a lake against a twilight sky in soft colors, Vellum glaze, No. 2118, 1916. E. F. McDermott (ILLUS.) 2,860.00

Vase, 8⅛" h., slightly cylindrical body tapering to a flat rim, decorated w/a landscape in shades of green, blue, cream & brown, Vellum glaze, 1921, Frederick Rothenbusch.................1,495.00

Vase, 8¼" h., 4¼" d., bottle-shaped, decorated w/golden pine cones & green needles against a dark brown shaded ground, Standard glaze, 1903, Cecil Duell....................................412.50

Vase, 9" h., slightly swelled cylindrical body tapering gently to a short wide neck w/flat rim, decorated w/a large blue iris & leaves on a shaded grey to cream ground, Vellum glaze, No. 907E, 1905, Lenore Asbury ...1,610.00

Vase, 9" h., 6½" d., wide ovoid body tapering to a flat rim, incised decoration around the sides of water lilies in light lavender & large pads against a shaded periwinkle to green ground, Vellum glaze, No. 999C, 1907, Kataro Shirayamadani (firing lines on inside partially go through) 2,200.00

Vase, 9¼" h., 4¾" d., tall gently ovoid body tapering to a short flaring neck, decorated w/a landscape of dark green & blue trees against a stormy sky, Vellum glaze, No. 922C, 1918, E. Diers 2,530.00

Vase, 9¾" h., 3½" d., cylindrical, decorated w/a broad band of incised stylized purple grapes w/brown leaves against a deep bluish green ground, Vellum glaze, No. 952D, 1915, Sara Sax.................................935.00

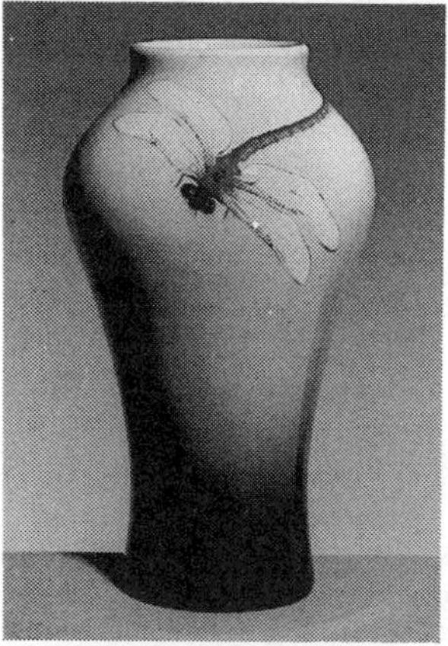

Rare Iris Glaze Vase

Vase, 10" h., baluster-form body swelled near the top, decorated w/a large dragonfly, Iris glaze, Carl Schmidt (ILLUS.) 15,400.00

Vase, 10½" h., 5½" d., ovoid, decorated w/a continuous landscape w/bluish green & ochre birch trees by a body of water, Vellum glaze, No. 614D, 1930, E. T. Hurley........2,860.00

Vase, 10¾" h., 4½" d., baluster-form, decorated w/brown leaves & blue berries against a turquoise & blue ground, Wax Matte glaze, No. 1667, 1929, Elizabeth Lincoln.................1,100.00

Vase, 11¾" h., 5" d., expanding cylinder w/narrow flared rim, decorated w/golden daffodils & green foliage against a shaded pink ground, Wax Matte glaze, No. 2790, 1928, Sallie Coyne.......1,540.00

Vase, 13¼" h., ovoid body w/an angled shoulder to the narrow molded mouth, an incised band of long geometric triangular devices below the shoulder, thick green Matte glaze, No. 886B, 1907 ....863.00

Vase, 14½" h., baluster-form w/everted rim, decorated w/chrysanthemums in amber, green, ochre & dark brown, Standard glaze, No. 816B, 1899, Amelia Sprague Browne..1,380.00

Vase, 14½" h., 6½" d., expanding cylinder w/narrow shoulder & rolled rim, decorated w/red flowers on tall brown stems, against a shaded deep purple to red to green ground, Wax Matte glaze, 1925, Elizabeth Lincoln 1,540.00

Vase, 14¾" h., 6¼" d., bulbous ovoid body tapering to a tall, slender neck w/a widely flaring rim, decorated w/large gold irises & green leaves against a shaded brown ground, Standard glaze, No. 303A, 1898, A.M. Valentien 1,320.00

Vase, 16" h., tall slender ovoid body tapering at the top to a small, short cylindrical neck, the sides molded in low-relief w/large iris blossoms & leaves, overall glossy yellow glaze, No. 6171, 1931, Harriet E. Wilcox ...770.00

Water jug, ovoid w/strap handle at top & circular spout at shoulder, Limoges-type, decorated w/gilded incised Moorish designs at shoulder & base & painted roses & insects in tones of brown & blue against a beige ground, die-stamped "ROOK-WOOD 1883 - Y41," dated 1883, 7" d., 9¾" h. 660.00

ROSELANE POTTERY

Roselane Pottery began in the home of William "Doc" Fields and his wife,

Georgia, in 1938. In 1940 the Fields moved the operation to Pasadena, California. The pottery successfully manufactured such items as vases, ashtrays, figurines, covered boxes, candlesticks, bowls, sculptured animals on wood bases, "Sparklers" and wallpockets. Roselane moved again in 1968 to Baldwin Park, California where it remained for six years. In 1977, the business closed. Several marks were used as well as paper labels.

Roselane Figure of a Boy

Roselane ©
U.S.A.

RoseLane

Bowl, 9" d., 2" h., high-glaze grey underneath, pink inside w/sgraffito-type grey "snowflakes" design, scroll mark, Model No. A-9 ....$35.00

Bowl, 15" d., 8" w., shallow rectangle form w/butterfly, bird, tulip & marigold in each corner in-relief underglaze & "Chinese Modern" footed base, deep purple inside w/light purple on decorations, scroll mark, Model No. 52 ....60.00

Candleholder, double "Chinese Modern" openwork base w/two lily shaped holders, one slightly higher than the other, deep purple glaze, 6½" l., 5¼" h......................................35.00

Figure of a boy, seated & holding open cookie jar w/cookies in it & left hand holding one cookie near mouth, legs folded under body w/right foot showing, satin matte beige & brown glaze, incised "Roselane U.S.A." w/copyright symbol, 3½" h. (ILLUS.) 24.00

Figure of a girl, kneeling, arms folded over chest w/hands together in prayer, head slightly raised, eyes closed, reverse of girl shows pony-tail & bottoms of feet & toes, satin matte beige & brown glaze, incised "Roselane U.S.A." w/copyright symbol, 4½" h. 22.00

Figure of a newsboy, standing, left hand in pocket, newspaper tucked under right arm, knee patch on left trouser, beige & brown, incised on back bottom of left pant leg, "Roselane" & incised on right pant leg bottom "USA" w/copyright symbol, 5" h. 26.00

Model of a bear, seated, head facing forward & tilted slightly, ears up, arms & hands in front of body but not touching, rough textured, light to dark brown glaze, Model No. 2635, 5½" h..28.00

Model of a bulldog, seated, glossy beige, brown, light blue, w/pink plastic eyes, "Sparkler" series, 2½" h...23.00

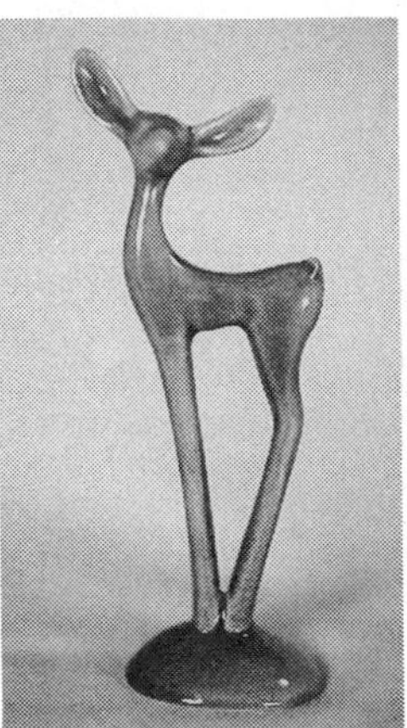

Roselane Deer

Model of a deer on oval base, stylized design, standing w/back legs together & bent, front legs together & straight, head turned, ears straight, weighs two ounces, glossy green glaze, 5" h. (ILLUS.) 35.00

Model of a duck, standing on round

base, wings back w/4" wing span, head turned to right, glossy light brown glaze, Model No. 126, 4" h. 18.00

Model of a goose, seated w/head & neck over back w/bill touching back, light & dark grey satin-matte glaze, incised "USA" w/copyright symbol, 2¼" l., 3½" h. 16.00

Model of an owl, modernistic design w/large head & tapering body, plastic eyes, semi-porcelain, "Sparkler" series, 6" h. 45.00

Model of a giraffe, seated, two front legs folded under, back legs not visible, tail up & over back, long neck twisted w/head turned to look behind, glossy cream glaze w/dark brown spots, Model No. 264, ca. 1960, 4¾" l., 9" h. 35.00

Model of a horse standing on oval base, stylized, light grey w/brown glaze, ca. 1949-53, 8½" h. 32.00

Model of a raccoon, seated, head turned, tail up, semi-porcelain w/brown & black glaze, "Sparkler" series, 4¼" h. 25.00

Sign, dealer advertising, scroll design, glossy light grey glaze, 12½" l., 3" h. 145.00

Vase, 6½" h., "Chinese Modern," openwork on small square base rising to straight sides w/tiny flare at rim, glossy grey exterior, maroon interior 15.00

ROSEMEADE

Laura Taylor was a ceramic artist who supervised Federal Works Projects in her native North Dakota during the Depression era and later demonstrated at the potter's wheel during the 1939 New York World's Fair. In 1940, Laura Taylor and Robert J. Hughes opened the Rosemeade-Wahpeton Pottery, naming it after the North Dakota county and town of Wahpeton where it was located. Rosemeade Pottery was made on a small scale for only about twelve years with Laura Taylor designing the items and perfecting colors. Her animal and bird figures are popular among collectors. Hughes and Taylor married in 1943 and the pottery did a thriving business until her death in 1959. The pottery closed in 1961 but stock was sold from the factory salesroom until 1964.

Ashtray, in the shape of the state of Oregon $40.00

Bank, model of a bear, brown glaze ...450.00

Book ends, model of a dog, aqua glaze, pr. 250.00

Flower frog, model of a deer....................35.00

Flower frog, model of a fawn jumping...65.00

Lamp, TV-type, model of a horse, black glaze 490.00

Model of a hippopotamus, blue glaze, 2 x 3" 135.00

Model of a rooster & hen, black & rust glaze, 5 x 7" 79.50

Model of a swan, black glaze 80.00

Models of a bear, small, pr. 18.00

Models of pheasants, crouching stance, pr. 100.00

Planter, model of a dove, wings folded in, white glaze, large 155.00

Planter, model of an elephant....................60.00

Plaque, pierced to hang, model of a trout....................110.00

Salt & pepper shakers, model of a Bloodhound, pr. 32.00

Salt & pepper shakers, model of a buffalo, pr. 75.00

Salt & pepper shakers, model of a California quail, pr. 30.00

Salt & pepper shakers, model of a deer, pr. 35.00

Salt & pepper shakers, model of a duck, blue glaze, pr....................35.00

Salt & pepper shakers, model of an English Setter dog, pr. 25.00

Salt & pepper shakers, model of a fawn, pr. 55.00

Salt & pepper shakers, model of a fish, pr. 39.50

Salt & pepper shakers, model of a Fox Terrier dog, pr. 22.50

Salt & pepper shakers, model of a hen & a rooster, white glaze, pr. 45.00

Salt & pepper shakers, model of a pelican, pr. 39.50

Salt & pepper shakers, model of a pheasant rooster, tail up, pr. 42.50

Salt & pepper shakers, model of a pheasant rooster, large, pr.................95.00

Salt & pepper shakers, model of a prairie dog, pr....................................40.00

Salt & pepper shakers, model of a Scottie dog, pr....................................20.00

Salt & pepper shakers, model of a skunk, large, pr. 45.00

Salt & pepper shakers, model of a tulip, pr. 22.00

Salt & pepper shakers, model of a turkey, miniature, pr. 60.00

Salt & pepper shakers, model of a windmill, pr. 200.00

Spoon rest, relief-molded prairie rose decoration 45.00

Vase, 4 x 5", model of a Dutch shoe, fluted, pearl & lime green glaze 35.00

Vase, 6½" h., model of a boot, matte blue glaze 50.00

Vase, 7½" h., model of a deer, matte turquoise glaze 38.00

ROSE MEDALLION - ROSE CANTON

Rose Mandarin Platter

The lovely Chinese ware known as Rose Medallion was made through the past century and into the present one. It features alternating panels of people and flowers or insects with most pieces having four medallions with a central rose or peony medallion. The ware is called Rose Canton if flowers and birds or insects fill all the panels. Unless otherwise noted, our listing is for Rose Medallion ware.

Basin, decorated w/panels of long-tailed birds & peony alternating w/figural court scenes, 19th c., 18½" d..$1,150.00

Bowl, 5¾" d...71.50

Bowl, 9" d., 3⅝" h. 187.00

Bowl, 9¼" d., shallow..........................195.00

Bowl, 11⅛" d., decorated w/a profusion of fruit, flower & bird panels alternating w/figural panels, 19th c. 518.00

Bowl, 11¼" d., Rose Mandarin variant, richly decorated w/a scene of mounted hunters before the chase & treeing the fox, a deep border & a hunting vignette on the interior, ca. 1785 ....1,093.00

Bowl, 11¾" d., 4½" h., flaring sides 495.00

Bowl, 13½" d., 5½" h. 1,045.00

Creamer, helmet-shaped....................225.00

Creamer, Rose Canton, helmet-shaped, 4" h.......................................93.50

Dish, cov., oval, 8" l 550.00

Dish, hexagonal, footed, 11" w...........302.50

Flowerpot, hexagonal, 4¾" h..............220.00

Plate, 7¾" d., Rose Canton, bird & butterfly border.................................148.50

Plate, 8½" d., Rose Canton, bird & butterfly border.................................148.50

Plates, 5¾" d., octagonal, set of 8......275.00

Platter, 15" l., orange peel glaze.........412.50

Platter, 14¾ x 18" oval, Rose Mandarin variant, three figural & three floral panel reserves around the sides, 19th c. (ILLUS.) 522.50

Punch bowl, deep rounded sides, decorated w/colorful panels of pavilions, flowers, birds & insects, w/wooden base, 16" d..................1,540.00

Soap dish, cover & drain insert, Rose Mandarin variant, 19th c., 4" w., 5½" l., 3 pcs. (imperfections) 412.50

Teapot, cov., Rose Mandarin variant the sides decorated w/figures in a lakeside garden viewing a passing junk flying a large banner, ca. 1785 ....403.00

Umbrella stand, 19th c., 24" h. 1,540.00

Vase, 8½" h., decorated w/two lizards, gold trim 265.00

Rose Medallion Vase

Vase, 14¼" h., baluster-form, the wide cylindrical neck w/a flaring rim & flanked by a pair of molded animal-head handles, 19th c. (ILLUS.) 440.00

Vase, 15½" h., flaring base, bulbous midsection & cylindrical top w/collared rim...................................489.50

Vegetable dish, cov., Rose Mandarin variant, 19th c., 8¼" w., 9½" l. 715.00

ROSENTHAL

Rosenthal Pan Figure

The Rosenthal porcelain manufactory has been in operation since 1880 when it was established by P. Rosenthal in Selb, Bavaria. Tablewares and figure groups are among its specialties.

Cake set: 8" w. octagonal platter & eight octagonal 8" w. plates; Phoenix patt., 9 pcs. $175.00

Cigarette set: 2½" h. oval urn a 4" d. underplate; each w/scalloped rims, Moss Rose patt., decorated w/rose buds & leaves w/gold trim, 2 pcs. 25.00

Coffee & tea set: cov. coffeepot, cov. teapot, creamer & cov. sugar bowl; Donatello patt., silver covers, marked "Rosenthal - Selb - Bavaria," 4 pcs. 95.00

Figure group, a slender standing Pan recoiling from a menacing crocodile wrapped around the base below him, 26" h. (ILLUS.) 1,600.00

Mug, h.p. fruit decoration......................45.00

Plate, 8½" d., decorated w/h.p. large yellow, blue & salmon flowers on a shaded ground..................................27.00

Plates, 8" d., scalloped edges, decorated w/pears, grapes & berries, gold trim, set of 4 ....195.00

ROSEVILLE

Roseville Pottery Company operated in Zanesville, Ohio from 1898 to 1954 after having been in business for six years prior to that in Muskingum County, Ohio. Art wares similar to those of Owens and Weller Potteries were produced. Items listed here are by patterns or lines.

Roseville

APPLE BLOSSOM (1948)

White apple blossoms in relief on blue, green or pink ground; brown tree branch handles.

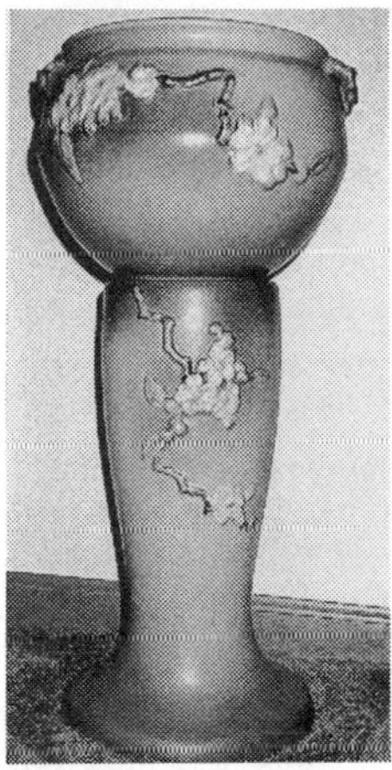

Apple Blossom Jardiniere & Pedestal

Basket w/low overhead handle, blue or green ground, No. 310-10", 10" h, each ....$175.00 to 225.00

Basket, hanging-type, pink ground.....125.00

Bowl, 6½" d., 2½" h., flat handles, blue or green ground, No. 326-6", each ....85.00 to 95.00

Candlesticks, pink ground, No. 352-4½", 4½" h., pr. 95.00

Console bowl, blue ground, No. 333-14", 8 x 18" oval 125.00

Console bowl, pink ground, No. 331-12", 12" l. 135.00

Cornucopia-vase, green ground, No. 321-6", 6" h. ....50.00 to 70.00

Creamer & open sugar bowl, blue ground, pr. 85.00

Ewer, pink ground, No. 318-15", 15" h. 395.00

Jardiniere, two-handled, No. 302-5", 5" h. 65.00

Jardiniere, pink ground, No. 302-10", 10" h. 395.00

Jardiniere & pedestal base, pink ground, No. 302-8" & No. 305-8", overall 24½" h., 2 pcs. (ILLUS.) 785.00

Jardiniere & pedestal base, green ground, No. 306-10", overall 31" h., 2 pcs. ....1,100.00 to 1,275.00

Vase, 6" h., pink ground, No. 342-6" 95.00

Vase, 7" h., green ground, No. 373-7" 80.00

Vase, bud, 7" h., base handles, flaring rim, blue, green or pink ground, No. 379-7", each ....60.00 to 75.00

Vase, 9½" h., 5" d., asymmetrical handles, cylindrical w/disc base, green ground, No. 387-9" 90.00

Vase, 10" h., two-handled, blue ground, No. 389-10" 140.00

Vase, 12½" h., base handles, blue ground, No. 390-12" 145.00

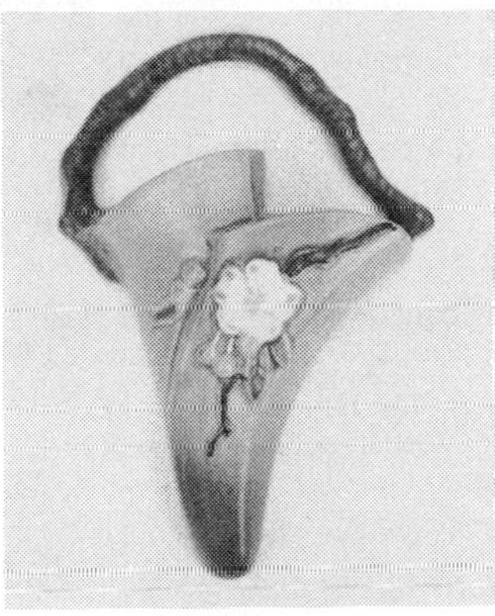

Apple Blossom Wall Pocket

Wall pocket, conical w/overhead handle, pink ground, No. 366-8¼", 8½" h. (ILLUS.) ....125.00 to 150.00

Window box, end handles, green or pink ground, No. 368-8", 2½ x 10½", each ....60.00 to 70.00

Window box, end handles, pink ground, No. 369-12", 12" l. ....125.00 to 150.00

AZTEC (1915)

Muted earthy tones of beige, grey, brown, teal, olive, azure blue or soft white with sliptrailed geometric decoration in contrasting colors.

Vase, 7½" h., 4½" d., tapering cylindrical body w/bulbous top, squeeze-bag decoration of stylized florals & swags in white & orange on a bluish grey ground 302.50

Vase, 10" h., white & tan decoration against a blue ground, artist-signed 350.00

Vase, 11" h., 4½" d., corseted form, blue & beige stylized florals against a tan ground 550.00

BANEDA (1933)

Band of embossed pods, blossoms and leaves on green or raspberry pink ground.

Bowl, 8" d., 2½" h., two-handled, green ground 255.00

Bowl, 9" d., 3¾" h., two-handled, green ground 295.00

Bowl, 10" d., 3½" h., two-handled, raspberry pink ground.......................270.00

Candlesticks, handles rising from flaring base to nozzle, green ground, pr.....................................400.00 to 425.00

Jardiniere, green ground, 7" h. 485.00

Jardiniere, raspberry pink ground, 9½" h...750.00

Jardiniere & pedestal base, raspberry pink ground, 8" h. jardiniere, 2 pcs. 1,850.00

Vase, 4½" h., tiny rim handles, sharply canted sides, raspberry pink ground, No. 603-4"...........................280.00

Vase, 6" h., two-handled, tapering cylinder w/short collared neck, green ground...225.00

Vase, 7" h., two-handles at shoulder, cylindrical, green ground..................250.00

Vase, 7" h., two-handled, bulbous, green ground, No. 605-7" 360.00

Vase, 8½" h., green ground................200.00

Wall pocket, flaring sides, raspberry pink ground, 8" h..........................1,200.00

BITTERSWEET (1940)

Orange bittersweet pods and green leaves on a grey blending to rose, yellow with terra cotta, rose with green or solid green bark-textured ground; brown branch handles.

Basket w/pointed overhead handle & conforming rim, grey ground, No. 809-8".......................................110.00

Basket, low overhead handle, shaped rim, green or grey ground, No. 810-10", 10" l., each..160.00 to 185.00

Book ends, green ground, No. 859, pr...185.00

Bowl, 6" d., grey ground 75.00

Candleholders, handles rising from conical base to midsection of nozzle, green ground, No. 851-3", 3" h., pr. 95.00

Cornucopia-vase, grey ground, No. 857-4", 4½" h..............................75.00

Cornucopia-vase, double, grey ground, No. 858-4", 4" h. 80.00

Ewer, green ground, No. 816-8", 8" h...75.00

Tea set: cov. teapot, cov. sugar bowl & creamer; green ground, No. 871-P, S & C, 3 pcs..................275.00

Vase, 7" h., base handles, squared form w/flaring rim, yellow ground, No. 874-7"......................................110.00

Vase, 7" h., green ground, No. 879-7"......................................115.00

Vase, 8" h., asymmetrical handles, bulging cylindrical form, grey ground, No. 883-8"............................67.50

Vase, 14" h., two-handled, yellow ground, No. 887-14"........................200.00

Wall pocket, curving conical form w/overhead handle continuing to one side, yellow ground, No. 866-7", 7½" h...170.00

BLACKBERRY (1933)

Band of relief clusters of blackberries with vines and ivory leaves accented in green and terra cotta on a green textured ground.

Basket, hanging-type, 6½" d. 4½" h...450.00

Console set, 13" l. bowl & pair of 4½" h. candleholders, 3 pcs............700.00

Jardiniere, two-handled, 8" d., 6" h.....325.00

Jardiniere, spherical body w/heavy molded rim & small loop rim handles, 16½" d., 12¼" h,............1,760.00

Jardiniere & pedestal base, overall 28" h., 2 pcs. 3,950.00

Vase, 4" h., two-handled, bulbous......175.00

Vase, 5" h., two handles at mid-section, bulbous base & wide neck..225.00

Vase, 5" h., tiny rim handles, canted sides 180.00

Vase, 6" h., semi-ovoid base continuing to wide neck 255.00

Vase, 6" h., two handles at midsection.......................................255.00

Vase, 10" h., waisted cylinder w/two handles at midsection 400.00

Vase, 12½" h., handles rising from shoulder to rim 635.00

Wall pocket, basket shaped w/narrow base & flaring rim, 6¾" w. at rim, 8½" h...580.00

BLEEDING HEART

Pink blossoms and green leaves on shaded blue, green or pink ground.

Bleeding Heart Vase

Basket w/circular handle, blue ground, No. 360-10", 10" h............................250.00

Candlesticks, conical base, curved handles rising from base to midsection, blue ground, No. 1139-4½", 5" h., pr. 80.00

Cornucopia-vase, blue ground, No. 141-6", 6" h.................................60.00

Cornucopia-vase, blue ground, No. 142-8", 8" h...............................160.00

Ewer, pink ground, No. 963-6", 6" h. ..165.00

Jardiniere, small pointed shoulder handles, blue ground, No. 651-3", 3" h...65.00

Vase, 8" h., base handles, blue ground, No. 969-8" (ILLUS.) 180.00

Vase, 15" h., two-handled, flaring hexagonal mouth, green ground, No. 976-15"......................................375.00

Wall pocket, angular pointed overhead handle rising from midsection, blue ground, No. 1287-8", 8½" h...........................250.00

BUSHBERRY (1948)

Berries and leaves on blue, green or russet bark-textured ground; brown or green branch handles

Basket w/asymmetrical overhead handle, russet ground, No. 369, 6½" h..170.00

Basket w/asymmetrical overhead handle, blue, green or russet ground, No. 370-8", 8" h., each ....125.00 to 150.00

Basket w/low overhead handle, asymmetric rim, blue ground, No. 372-11", 12" h..........................185.00.

Beverage set: 8½" h. ice lip pitcher & four 3½" h. handled mugs; blue ground, pitcher No. 1325, mugs No. 1-3½", 5 pcs. 600.00

Bowl, 4" h., two-handled, globular, blue ground, No. 411-4"....................65.00

Bowl, 6" d., russet ground, No. 412-6".......................................115.00

Candleholders, large flaring handles, russet ground, No. 1147, 2" h., pr......58.00

Console bowl, two-handled, russet ground, No. 414-10", 10" d. 130.00

Console bowl, russet ground, No. 415-10", 10" d...........................125.00

Cornucopia-vase, single handle, russet ground, No. 153-6", 6" h........125.00

Cornucopia-vase, green ground, No. 154-8", 8" h...............................135.00

Ewer, blue ground, No. 1-6", 6" h. 65.00

Ewer, cut-out rim, russet ground, No. 3-15", 15" h...............................285.00

Flowerpot w/saucer, green ground, No. 658-5", 5" h.................................60.00

Jardiniere, russet ground, No. 657-6", 6" h..245.00

Jardiniere & pedestal base, blue ground, No. 657-8", 2 pcs. 975.00

Mug, russet ground, No. 1-3½", 3½" h...90.00

Planter, handled, russet ground, No. 384-8", 8" l..................................90.00

Tea set: cov. teapot, creamer & sugar bowl; russet ground, No. 2, 3 pcs. ...275.00

Small Bushberry Vase

Vase, 4" h., conical w/tiny rim handles, blue ground, No. 28-4" (ILLUS.) 40.00

Bushberry Gate-form Bud Vase

Vase, double bud, 4½" h., gate-form, blue ground, No. 158-4½" (ILLUS.) ...70.00

Vase, 6" h., two-handled, blue or green ground, No. 30-6", each ....75.00 to 85.00

Vase, 7" h., two-handled, blue ground, No. 31-7" 90.00

Vase, bud, 7½" h., asymmetrical base handles, cylindrical body, russet ground, No. 152-7" 90.00

Vase, 8" h., pedestal base, squared side handles, compressed body w/wide neck, green ground, No. 157-8" 100.00

Vase, 9" h., two-handled, ovoid, green or russet ground, No. 35-9" ....100.00 to 125.00

Vase, 10" h., two-handled, russet ground, No. 37-10" 130.00

Vase, 18" h., floor-type, green or russet ground 450.00

Wall pocket, high-low handles, green or russet ground, No. 1291-8", 8" h. ....170.00 to 200.00

CARNELIAN I (1910-15)

Matte glaze with a combination of two colors or two shades of the same color with the darker dripping over the lighter tone or heavy and textured glaze with intermingled colors and some running.

Candleholders, simple disc base w/incised rings at base of candle nozzle, deep green & light green, 2½" h., pr. 40.00

Flower frog or candleholder, blue & rose, 3½" h. 55.00

Lamp, factory drilled w/original fittings, two-handled, mottled olive green & pink 425.00

Urn, light blue & dark blue, 7" h. 95.00

Vase, double bud, 5" h., thick olive green & blue 150.00

Vase, 6" h., pillow-type, light blue & dark blue 55.00

Vase, 7" h., deep green & light green...57.50

Vase, 8" h., two-handled, ovoid base & ringed neck, deep green & light green 55.00

Vase, 10" h., semi-ovoid base & long wide neck w/rolled rim, ornate handles, dark blue & light blue...........60.00

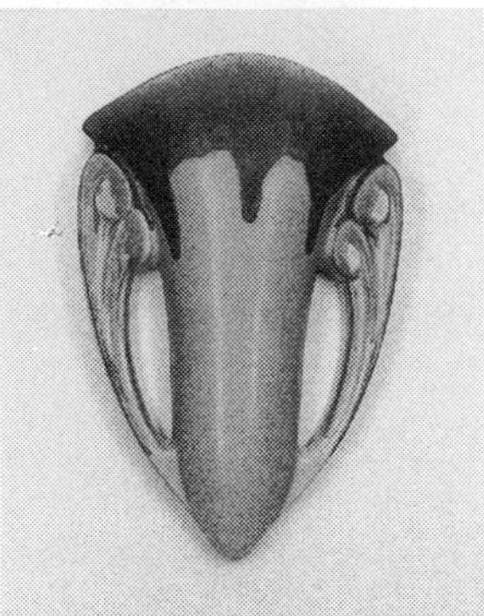

Carnelian I Wall Pocket

Wall pocket, ornate side handles, flaring rim, dark blue & grey, 8" h. (ILLUS.) 95.00

CARNELIAN II (1915)

Intermingled colors, some with a drip effect.

Carnelian II Floor Vase

Bowl, 9 x 12½", 5¼" h., flaring rim, intermingled shades of blue & purple 145.00

Ewer, intermingled shades of red, 15" h. 295.00

Flower frog, intermingled shades of red 90.00

Urn, ornate handles, compressed globular form, intermingled shades of blue, 8" h. ....175.00 to 225.00

Urn, ornate handles, compressed globular form, intermingled shades of green, 8" h. ....175.00 to 225.00

Vase, 5" h., rectangular w/rounded sides, pierced curved handles, intermingled shades of pink 115.00

Vase, 7" h., compressed globular base w/short wide neck, large handles, purple & rose 135.00

Vase, 7" h., expanding cylinder, sharply defined shoulder w/small handles, intermingled shades of raspberry pink 100.00

Vase, 8" h., cylindrical w/narrow shoulder & wide mouth, intermingled shades of blue & green 60.00

Vase, 8" h., intermingled shades of blue 185.00

Vase, 9" h., ovoid w/short collared mouth, intermingled shades of red...205.00

Vase, 10" h., canted sides w/short sharp shoulder, flat pierced handles rising from shoulder to rim, intermingled shades of green or red, each 145.00

Vase, 12" h., globular lower section & flaring top portion joined by straight handles, intermingled shades of pink & green 460.00

Vase, 16½" h., 10" d., floor-type, slightly compressed globular body w/wide flaring neck, intermingled shades of turquoise blue (ILLUS.) 1,045.00

CHERRY BLOSSOM (1933)

Sprigs of cherry blossoms, green leaves and twigs with pink fence against a combed blue-green ground or creamy ivory fence against a terra cotta ground shading to dark brown.

Basket, hanging-type, blue-green ground, 8" 450.00

Jardiniere, two-handled, terra cotta ground, No. 350-5", 5" h. 250.00

Jardiniere, two-handled, terra cotta ground, 9" h. 750.00

Lamp, factory-type w/fittings, two-handled, spherical, blue-green ground...900.00

Urn-vase, two-handled, globular w/short collared neck, terra cotta ground...225.00

Vase, 4" h., jug-type, two-handled, terra cotta ground 215.00

Vase, 5" h., two-handled, squatty jug-type, blue-green or terra cotta ground.............................200.00 to 225.00

Vase, 5" h., two-handled, slightly globular, terra cotta ground.............185.00

Vase, 8" h., handles at midsection, terra cotta ground 375.00

Vase, 8" h., two-handled, globular, terra cotta ground 450.00

Wall pocket, flaring rim, blue-green ground, 5½" w., 8¼" h.....................825.00

CHLORON (1907)

Molded in high-relief in the manner of early Roman and Greek artifacts. Solid matte green glaze, sometimes combined with ivory. Very similar in form to Egypto.

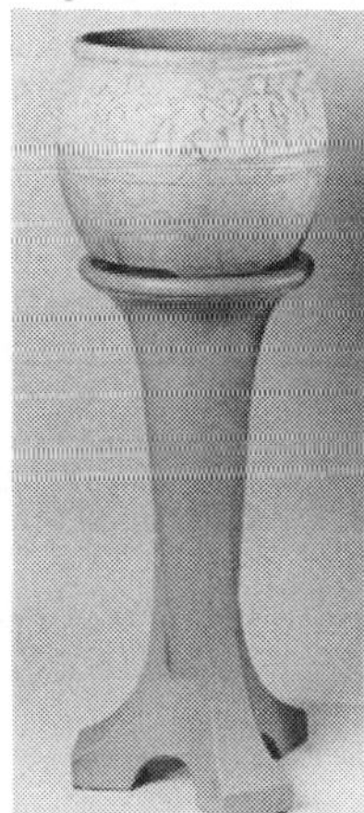

Chloron Jardiniere & Pedestal

Jardiniere & pedestal base, the wide ovoid jardiniere w/a molded band of dancing classical ladies around the top, the trumpet-form pedestal tapering toward the base then flaring to a tripod base w/blocky buttress feet, fine matte green glaze, chip to base, jardiniere 14½" d., overall 42½" h., 2 pcs. (ILLUS.)..................880.00

Planter, eared handles, relief-molded heart-shaped leaves in groups of three, matte green glaze, 7" d., 3" h..225.00

Umbrella stand, relief-molded poppies decoration, matte green ground, 22" h..750.00

Umbrella stand, octagonal, each panel decorated w/a relief-molded iris blossom, 23¼" h........................275.00

CLEMATIS (1944)

Clematis blossoms and heart-shaped green leaves against a vertically textured ground - white blossoms on blue, rose-pink blossoms on green and ivory blossoms on golden brown.

Clematis Basket

Basket w/ornate circular handle, waisted cylindrical body, brown ground, No. 387-7", 7" h. (ILLUS.)...115.00

Bowl, 10" d., two-handled, green ground, No. 6-10"...65.00

Console bowl, end handles, blue ground, No. 456-6", 9" l...75.00

Cornucopia-vase, brown ground, No. 190-6", 6" h...65.00

Creamer & sugar bowl, blue ground, Nos. 5C & 5S, pr...110.00

Ewer, squatty, brown ground, No. 16-6", 6" h...75.00

Ewer, blue ground, No. 17-10", 10" h...125.00

Flower arranger, base handles, three openings for flowers, brown ground, No. 102-5", 5½" h...55.00

Flowerpot w/saucer, blue ground, No. 688-5", 5½" h...75.00

Rose bowl, brown ground, No. 455-4", 4" d...35.00

Vase, 5" h., green ground, No. 192-5"...70.00

Vase, double bud, 5" h., two cylinders joined by a single clematis blossom, blue ground, No. 194-5"...65.00

Vase, 6" h., two-handled, urn-form, blue ground, No. 188-6"...75.00

Vase, 6" h., two-handled, urn-form, brown or green ground, No. 188-6", each...50.00 to 65.00

Vase, 8" h., two-handled, blue ground, No. 107-8"...82.50

Vase, 8" h., two-handled, globular base w/high collared neck, green ground, No. 108-8"...70.00

Vase, 10" h., two-handled, blue or brown ground, No. 111-10", each....145.00

Wall pocket, angular side handles, green ground, No. 1295-8", 8½" h...120.00

COLUMBINE (1940s)

Columbine blossoms and foliage on shaded ground - yellow blossoms on blue, pink blossoms on pink shaded to green and blue blossoms on tan shaded to green.

Basket w/elaborate handle rising from midsection, pink ground, No. 365-7", 7" h...105.00

Bowl, 3" h., squatty w/small handles at shoulder, tan ground, No. 655-3"...50.00

Bowl, 8" d., tiny end handles, pink or blue ground, No. 402-8", each...50.00 to 65.00

Console bowl, stepped handles rising from rim, tan ground, No. 404-10"...87.50

Console bowl, 12" d., irregular rim forming handles, pink ground, No. 405-12"...95.00

Flower frog, blue ground, No. 42, 5" h...60.00

Flowerpot w/saucer, tan ground, No. 656-5", 5" h...105.00

Jardiniere, tan ground, No. 655-3", 3" h...50.00

Jardiniere, two-handled, tan ground, No. 655-6", 6" h...165.00

Jardiniere, two-handled, blue ground, No. 655-10", 10" h...400.00

Vase, bud, 7" h., pink ground, No. 15-7"...80.00

Vase, 8" h., handles rising from base, tan ground, No. 19-8"...87.50

Vase, 9" h., two-handled, tan ground, No. 21-9"...160.00

Vase, 9½" h., angular side handles rising from pedestal base, blue ground, No. 22-9"...160.00

Vase, 10" h., ovoid body w/angular handles rising from base to mid-section, tan ground,No. 24-10"...145.00

Wall pocket, squared flaring mouth, conical body w/curled tip, blue ground, No. 1290-8", 8½" h....195.00

COSMOS (1940)

Embossed blossoms against a wavy horizontal ridged band on a textured ground - ivory band with yellow and orchid blossoms on blue, blue band with white and orchid blossoms on green or tan.

Cosmos Vase

Basket w/pointed overhead handle, pedestal base, tan ground, No. 358-12", 12" h. 285.00

Basket, hanging-type, handles rising from midsection to rim, blue ground, No. 361-5", 7" 275.00

Bowl, 6" d., two-handled, shaped rim, green ground, No. 369-6" 65.00

Candlesticks, loop handles rising from disc base, slightly tapering candle nozzle, tan ground, No. 1137-4½", 4½" h., pr. 95.00

Console bowl, end handles rising from base to rim, shaped rim, tan ground, No. 372-10", 10" l. 60.00

Flower frog, pierced globular body w/asymmetrical overhead handle, blue ground, No. 39, 3½" h. 60.00

Planter, rectangular w/shaped rim, blue ground, No. 381-9", 3 x 3½ x 9" 375.00

Vase, 4" h., two-handled, globular base & wide neck, blue ground, No. 944-4" 60.00

Vase, bud, 7" h., slender, slightly tapering cylinder w/large loop handles at base, blue ground, No. 959-7" 82.50

Vase, 8" h., two-handled, cut-out top edge, tan ground, No. 950-8" 185.00

Vase, 9" h., tapering cylinder w/shaped flaring mouth, curved handles at midsection, blue or tan ground, No. 953-9", each ....175.00 to 200.00

Vase, 12½" h., ovoid w/large loop handles, green ground, No. 956-12" (ILLUS.) 350.00

Vase, 18" h., floor-type, trumpet-shaped w/handles rising to flaring rim, tan ground, No. 958-18" ....650.00 to 750.00

Wall pocket, circular overhead handle, blue ground, No. 1285-6", 6½" h......300.00

Window box, tan ground, No. 381-9", 9" l. 165.00

CREMONA (1927)

Relief-molded floral motifs including a tall stem with small blossoms and arrowhead leaves, wreathed with leaves similar to Velmoss or a web of delicate vines against a background of light green mottled with pale blue or pink with creamy ivory.

Bowl, 8" sq. w/notched cut corners, turned in rim, pink ground, No. 177-8" 88.00

Vase, 4" h., rectangular mouth w/pointed ends, slightly canted sides, stepped foot, green or pink ground, No. 72-4", each.......40.00 to 50.00

Vase, 10½" h., ovoid w/pointed handles, green or pink ground, No. 350 10", each ....125.00 to 150.00

Vase, 12" h., baluster-form w/slender neck & flaring mouth, pink ground, No. 361-12" 180.00

CRYSTALIS, ROZANE (1906)

Heavy unusual shapes, some with intricate handles and many are three-footed. The name is taken from the glaze which is textured with scattered crystal flakes or smooth with grown crystals.

Vase, 12¼" h., three pierced buttress-like arms beneath rim, three stubby feet, triangular body, mottled green crystalline glaze, No. C-19 ....2,640.00

Vase, 14¾" h., 5½" d., shaped as an American Beauty vase w/three raised heads near the rim, dead matte frothy yellow & mustard glaze, Rozane Ware Egypto wafer..........2,000.00

DAHLROSE (1924-28)

Band of ivory daisy-like blossoms and green leaves against a mottled tan ground.

Basket, hanging-type, 7½".................175.00

Bowl, 6" d. 115.00

Bowl, 10" d., two-handled 195.00

Console bowl, 9" d. 82.50

Jardiniere, tiny rim handles, 7" d., 4" h. 160.00

Jardiniere, tiny rim handles, 6" h. 150.00

Jardiniere, tiny rim handles, 8" h. 225.00

Jardiniere, 10" h. 365.00

Dahlrose Jardiniere & Pedestal

Jardiniere & pedestal base, overall 25" h., 2 pcs. (ILLUS.) 675.00

Vase, 5" h., 7" w., pillow-shaped 100.00

Vase, double bud, 6" h., gate-form 100.00

Vase, triple bud, 6½" h., expanding cylinder flanked by tusk-form tubes ....100.00 to 125.00

Vase, bud, 8" h., ornate curving asymmetrical handle, mound base ..125.00

Vase, 8" h., two handles rising from midsection to rim 125.00

Vase, 9" h., No. 65-9" 175.00

Vase, 10" h., two-handled, ovoid w/wide flaring rim 165.00

Wall pocket, tiny rim handles, 9" h......155.00

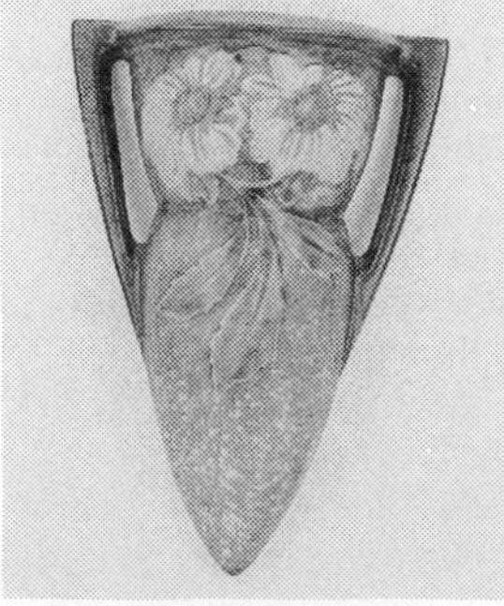

Dahlrose Wall Pocket

Wall pocket, two-handled, conical, 10" h., (ILLUS.) 175.00

Window box, 6 x 12½" 240.00

DELLA ROBBIA, ROZANE (1906)

Incised designs with an overall high-gloss glaze in colors ranging from soft pastel tints to heavy earth tones and brilliant intense colors.

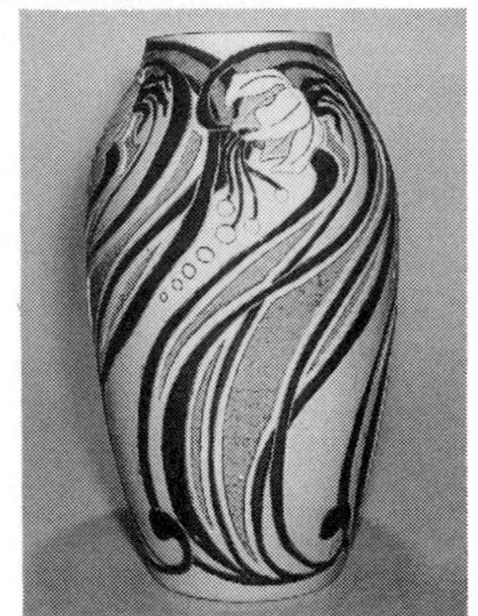

Monumental Della Robbia Vase

Teapot, cov., footed, compressed base & incurving tapered sides, high pointed handle, decorated in sgraffito w/stylized roses under a caramel & brown glaze, 5¼ x 8½" (small chip under lid) 605.00

Teapot, cov., tall tapering hexagonal body w/long graceful spout & loop handle, domed cover w/pointed finial, each panel carved w/an abstract design of roses & leaves in greyish green against dark bluish grey, wafer mark, 7" w., 8¼" h. 1,100.00

Vase, 8½" h., 6½" d., globular w/short neck, carved overall decoration of green tear-shaped medallions encompassing lavender stylized flowers, excised bands of stylized spades at top & bottom, a band of yellow crocuses around the rim, against a glossy burnt orange ground, Frederick Rhead, 1906, unmarked 5,225.00

Vase, 8½" h., 7" d., spherical w/small mouth, decorated w/five concentric excised bands w/incised white & orange daisies, w/tall green stems beginning at the base & extending upward against a honed blue sky 9,075.00

Vase, 11½" h., 4" d., footed & buttressed tapering cylindrical body, intricate incised & excised Wiener Werkstatte style design of a stylized cityscape in brown, yellow, pink &

grey w/tall square trees in grey w/yellow buds against a honed khaki ground, decorator-initialed by Frederick Rhead, 1906 ....10,450.00

Vase, 12" h., 4½" d., bullet-shaped, decorated w/incised & excised grapevines w/green leaves & olive green grape clusters against a grey ground, interspersed w/French blue 'honed' sections, incised initials "ETG" 3,575.00

Vase, 15⅛" h., decorated w/deeply cut back, incised & painted flowers in the Art Nouveau style, in shades of bluish grey, navy blue & peach, artist-initialed (ILLUS.) 14,850.00

DOGWOOD (1916-18)

White dogwood blossoms and brown branches against a textured green ground.

Bowl, 5" d...75.00

Bowl, 6½" d..125.00

Jardiniere, 10" h.................................270.00

Jardiniere, 12" d., 12" h. 295.00

Vase, 6½" h. 70.00

Wall pocket, cone-shaped, 9½" h.......155.00

DOGWOOD II (1928)

White dogwood blossoms and black branches against a smooth green ground.

Basket, 8" h. 125.00

Bowl, 6" d...70.00

Jardiniere, 6" h...................................150.00

Jardiniere & pedestal base, 2 pcs. 825.00

Vase, 10" h. 125.00

Wall pocket, double, 9" h...................150.00

Wall pocket, two handles in the form of blossoming branches, No. 1218-10", 10" h.........................165.00

DONATELLO (1915)

Deeply fluted ivory and green body with wide tan band embossed with cherubs at various pursuits in pastoral settings.

Basket w/high pointed overhead handle, globular body, 15" h. 450.00

Basket, hanging-type, 7" d., 5" h..................................175.00 to 200.00

Bowl, 8" d., 3½" h. 135.00

Bowl, 10" d., 3" h., rolled rim 65.00

Console bowl, oval, No. 60-8", 8" l. 85.00

Flower frog, No. 14-2½", 2½" d. 15.00

Flower frog, No. 14-3½", 3½" d. 18.00

Flowerpot w/saucer, flaring sides, 5" h..115.00

Flowerpot w/saucer, 7" h. 135.00

Jardiniere, No. 575-4", 4" h. 45.00

Jardiniere, 7" d., 6" h. 75.00

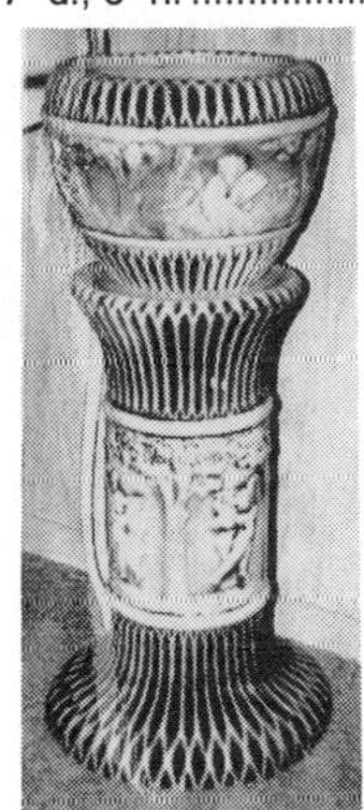

Donatello Jardiniere & Pedestal

Jardiniere & pedestal base, 8" h. jardiniere & 15" h. pedestal, 2 pcs. (ILLUS.) 650.00

Jardiniere & pedestal base, 10" h. jardiniere, overall 29" h., 2 pcs.........750.00

Pitcher, 6½" h. ....250.00 to 300.00

Plate, 8" d. 275.00

Vase, bud, 7" h. 55.00

Vase, 8" h., cylindrical 50.00

Vase, 8½" h., slightly canted lower section, cylindrical top half.................85.00

Vase, 9" h., two-handled 160.00

Vase, bud, 10" h., bottle-form, No. 115-10"......................................225.00

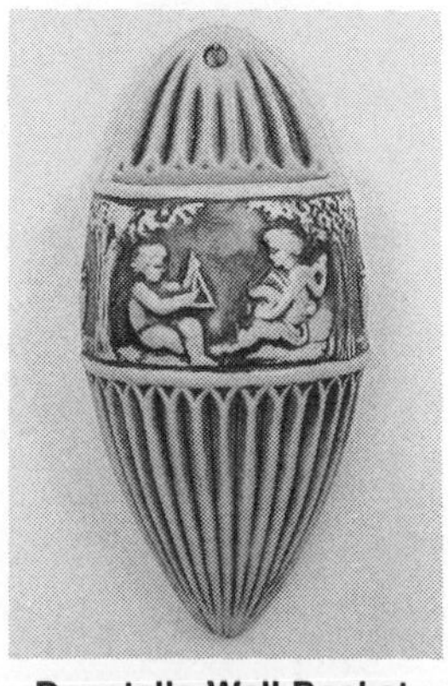

Donatello Wall Pocket

Wall pocket, ovoid, 9" h. (ILLUS.).......140.00

Window box, No. 60-12", 6 x 12"........135.00

DUTCH (pre-1916)

Creamware with colorful decal scenes of Dutch children and adults at various activities.

Ale set: large tankard pitcher & six mugs; 7 pcs. ....575.00 to 625.00

Chamber set consisting of 9" & 11" h. pitchers, cov. waste pot, cov. child's potty, cov. combinet, tumbler, toothbrush holder, drinking mug & two cov. soap dishes, 10 pcs...........715.00

Mug, long straight handle, three-footed, 5" h..75.00

EARLAM (1930)

Mottled glaze on various simple shapes. The line includes many crocus or strawberry pots.

Bowl, 4" d., two-handled, mottled blue, black & tan, No. 217-4"...........195.00

Candlestick, deep saucer base, interior oval loop handle, slightly tapering candle nozzle w/relief rings near top, mottled brown & green glaze, 4" h.......................................165.00

Planter, two-handled, rectangular w/shaped rim, curved end handles, mottled green & blue or mottled green glaze, No. 89-8", 5 x 10½", each 140.00

Urn-vase, two-handled, mottled blue green, No. 521-7", 7" h. 190.00

Vase, 5½" h., two handles rising from middle of globular base to rim, mottled green glaze, No. 517-5½" ...125.00

Vase, 6" h., two-handled, mottled green ground 125.00

Vase, 6" h., two-handled, semi-ovoid, mottled blue-green glaze, No. 518-6"......................................130.00

EARLY EMBOSSED PITCHERS (pre-1916)

Utility pitchers with various embossed scenes; high gloss glaze.

The Boy, 7½" h. (minor defects).........250.00

The Cow, 6½" h.................................230.00

The Cow, 7½" h.................225.00 to 250.00

The Grape, 6" h. ....100.00 to 125.00

Iris, 9" h..110.00

Landscape, 7½" h.............................125.00

The Mill, 8" h.......................325.00 to 350.00

EGYPTO (1905)

Classic shapes resembling those from ancient Egypt; soft deep green matte glaze.

Ewer, 10" h. 425.00

Lamp, oil-type, low body w/spout at each end, pointed overhead center handle, 5".......................................475.00

Pitcher, 5" h., globular body on low foot, narrow neck w/cupped mouth, curved pouring spout, shaped handle 140.00

Vase, 8" h., crisp leaves & buds w/thin frothy blue & white glaze (rare experimental piece) 595.00

FALLINE (1933)

Curving panels topped by a semi-scallop separated by vertical peapod decorations; blended backgrounds of tan shading to green and blue or tan shading to darker brown.

Bowl, 11" d., shallow, end handles, tan shading to brown 275.00

Urn-vase, loop handles, tapering sides, tan shading to blue & green, 8" h...650.00

Vase, 6" h., two-handled, ovoid, tan shading to blue & green..................410.00

Vase, 8" h., two-handled, bulbous, tan shading to blue & green..................475.00

Vase, 9" h., two-handled, horizontally ribbed lower section, tan shading to blue & green 465.00

Vase, 12½" h., 7¼" d., compressed globular stacked base, tall cylindrical neck w/wide mouth, two small handles rising from base to lower part of neck.....................................665.00

FERRELLA (1930)

Impressed shell design alternating with small cut-outs at top and base; mottled brown or turquoise and red glaze.

Bowl, 9½" d., 4¼" h., deep flaring sides w/rolled rim, on a flared foot, the bowl rim w/a band of small pierced triangles above a band of larger pierced ovals, pierced triangles also around the foot, turquoise & red glaze, w/flower frog, 2 pcs. 275.00

Console bowl w/attached flower frog, brown glaze, No. 87-8", 8" d. 250.00

Console set: 9½" d. bowl w/flower frog & pair of 4½" h. goblet-form candlesticks; turquoise & red glaze, the set 522.50

Urn-vase, compressed globular form w/tiny handles at midsection, recticulated foot & rim, turquoise & red glaze, No. 505-6", 6" h...............315.00

Vase, 4" h., squatty base w/exaggerated handles & narrow neck, turquoise & red glaze, No. 497-4"..265.00

Vase, 4" h., angular handles, bulbous, turquoise & red glaze, No. 498-4"....250.00

Vase, 6" h., handles rising from shoulder of compressed globular base to beneath the rim of the long tapering neck, brown glaze, No. 502-6"..250.00

vase, 9" h., sharply compressed globular base, large handles rising from midsectoin to below rim, brown glaze 405.00

Vase, 10" h., 6¼" d., ovoid body on flaring foot & tapering to a widely flaring mouth, low angular handles down the sides, the foot pierced w/a band of small squares, the mouth pierced w/two bands of small rectangles, brown glaze, No. 511-10"......................................550.00

FLORENTINE (1924-28)

Bark-textured panels alternating with embossed garlands of cascading fruit and florals; ivory with tan and green, beige with brown and green or brown with beige and green glaze.

Florentine Wall Pocket

Bowl, 8" d., shallow, beige....................68.00

Bowl, 9" d., low, beige 47.50

Compote, 5" d., brown 50.00

Jardiniere, brown, No. 130-4", 7" d., 4" h..63.00

Jardiniere, ivory, 8" d., 6¼" h..............130.00

Jardiniere, 14" h..................................435.00

Vase, 8" h., squared handles rising above rim, ovoid w/collared neck, ivory, No. 255-8" 95.00

Vase, 10" h., 6" d., footed, beige..........98.00

Wall pocket, conical, beige, 7" h..................................100.00 to 150.00

Wall pocket, semi-ovoid, brown, 9½" h. (ILLUS.) ....100.00 to 125.00

Wall pocket, tapering cylinder, brown, 12½" h...140.00

FOXGLOVE (1940s)

Sprays of pink and white blossoms embossed against a shaded matte finish ground.

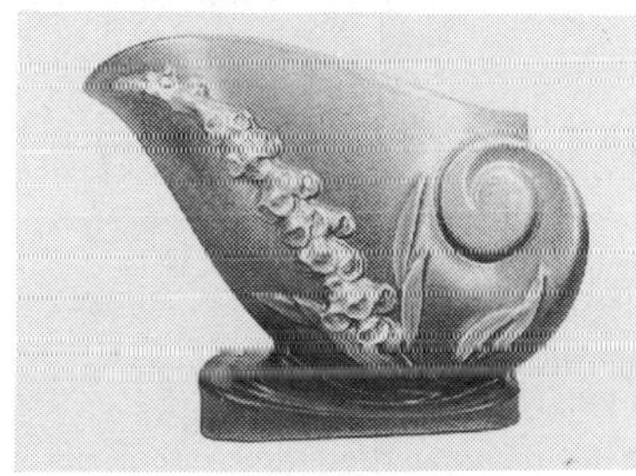

Foxglove Cornucopia-vase

Basket w/circular overhead handle, green ground, No. 373-8", 8" h. 175.00

Basket, hanging-type, blue or green ground, No. 466-5", 6½", each ....225.00 to 250.00

Book ends, pink ground, No. 10, pr. ...250.00

Console bowl, green ground, No. 421-10", 10" l..............................95.00

Console set: 12" l. bowl & pair of 2½" h. candleholders; pink ground, Nos. 423-12" & 1149-2½", 3 pcs......195.00

Cornucopia-vase, snail shell-type, blue ground, No. 166-6" (ILLUS.) 70.00

Ewer, blue ground, No. 6-15", 15" h................................300.00 to 325.00

Model of a conch shell, blue ground, No. 426-6", 6" l.................................78.00

Vase, bud, 5" h., pink ground, No. 159-5"...75.00

Vase, 7" h., handled, pink ground, No. 45-7"..65.00

Vase, 14" h., conical w/flaring mouth, four handles rising from disc base, blue ground, No. 53-14"....................250.00

Vase, 18" h., floor-type, blue ground ..625.00

Wall pocket, two-handled, blue ground, No. 1292-8", 8" h. 185.00

FREESIA (1945)

Trumpet-shaped blossoms and long slender green leaves against wavy impressed lines - white and lavender blossoms on blended green; white and yellow blossoms on shaded blue or terra cotta and brown.

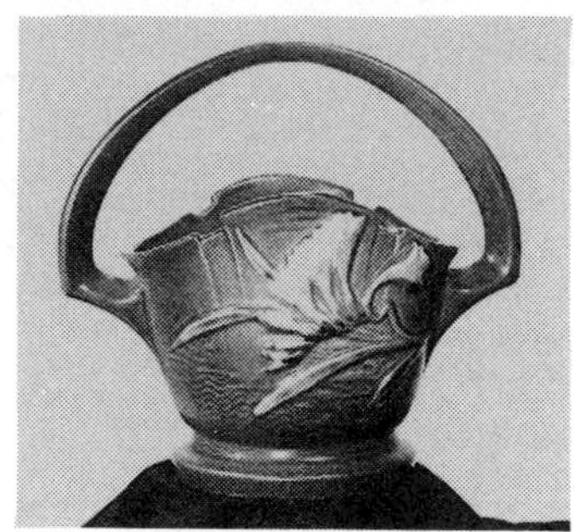

Freesia Basket

Basket w/low overhead handle, terra cotta ground, No. 390-7", 7" h............75.00

Basket w/overhead handle, blue ground, No. 391-8", 8" h. (ILLUS.)...110.00

Bowl, 10" d., green ground, No. 467-10"....................................135.00

Bowl, 16½" l., two-handled, blue ground, No. 469-14".........................110.00

Candleholders, tiny pointed handles, domed base, blue ground, No. 1160-2", 2" h., pr. 75.00

Ewer, terra cotta ground, No. 21-15", 15" h...300.00

Flowerpot w/attached saucer, blue ground, No. 670-5", 5½" h. 125.00

Jardiniere, tiny rim handles, terra cotta ground, No. 669-4", 4" h............45.00

Pitcher, 10" h., swollen cylinder, green or terra cotta ground, No. 20-10", each ....110.00 to 125.00

Vase, 7" h., base handles, long cylindrical neck, blue ground, No. 119-7"...95.00

Vase, 7" h., two-handled, slightly expanding cylinder, green ground, No. 120-7".......................................100.00

Vase, 7" h., two-handled, fan-shaped, green, No. 200-7"............................100.00

Vase, 8" h., two-handled, green ground, No. 121-8".............................95.00

Vase, 9½" h., pointed handles at midsection, terra cotta ground, No. 123-9"............................85.00 to 95.00

Vase, 10" h., blue ground, No. 126-10"......................125.00 to 150.00

Vase, 15" h., two-handled, blue ground, No. 128-15"..........................265.00

Vase, 18" h., blue ground, No. 129-18"......................................315.00

Wall pocket, angular handles, green or terra cotta ground, No. 1296-8", 8½" h., each.....................130.00 to 160.00

FUCHSIA (1939)

Coral pink fuchsia blossoms and green leaves against a background of blue shading to yellow, green shading to terra cotta or terra cotta shading to gold.

Fuchsia Bowl

Basket w/rounded overhead handle & flower frog, terra cotta ground, No. 350-8", 8" h................................280.00

Basket, hanging-type, green ground, No. 359-5"..310.00

Bowl, 4" d., two-handled, terra cotta ground, No. 346-4" (ILLUS.) ....85.00 to 95.00

Candlestick, domed base, tubular form raised on ring, blue ground, 5½" h...95.00

Console bowl, two-handled, terra cotta ground, No. 349-8", 8" l.............90.00

Jardiniere, two-handled, blue ground, No. 645-3", 3" h................................55.00

Jardiniere, two-handled, blue ground, No. 645-4", 4" h..............................100.00

Pitcher w/ice lip, 8" h., blue ground, No. 1322-8".....................................380.00

Vase, 6" h., two handles rising from bulbous base to neck, terra cotta ground, No. 891-6"...........................110.00

Vase, 8" h., handles rising from flat base to shoulder, blue ground, No. 897-8" 175.00

Vase, 8½" h., 6" w., pillow-type w/handles rising from base to midsection, green ground, No. 896-8" 150.00

Vase, 15" h., terra cotta ground, No. 904-15" ....400.00 to 450.00

Vase, 18" h., floor-type, blue ground, No. 905-18" 905.00

FUTURA (1928)

Varied line with shapes ranging from Art Deco geometrics to futuristic. Matte glaze is typical although an occasional piece may be high gloss.

Futura Vase

Bowl, 8" d., collared base, shaped flaring sides w/relief decoration, rose glaze, No. 187-8" 285.00

Jardiniere, angular handles rising from wide sloping shoulders to rim, sharply canted sides, tan w/multicolored leaves, No. 616-7", 7" h. 440.00

Pot, square body w/canted sides on a low footed square base, relief-molded flowering branch decoration, mottled blue & green, 3½" h. 230.00

Vase, 5" h., 6" w., rectangular, elongated triangles forming a fan-shaped design on sides in shades of blue, No. 81-5" 285.00

Vase, 6" h., stepped shoulders, square body w/canted sides, grey w/green & blue elongated triangles, No. 380-6" 265.00

Vase, 6" h., octagonal cone-shaped body on a conforming low base, bluish green, No. 397-6" 325.00

Vase, 6" h., squared buttressed form, mottled grey, No. 423-6" 260.00

Vase, 8" h., ovoid w/short collared neck, lightly embossed floral branch at shoulder, incised rings at midsection, deep rosy beige shading to sand white & back to beige w/touch of blue at branch, No. 428-8" 350.00

Vase, 8¼" h., 5" d., conical body on flat disc base, buttressed sides, orange w/green buttresses & blue base, No. 401-8" (ILLUS.)................375.00

Vase, 10¼" h., 5¼" d., small buttressed handles at disc base, slightly swollen cylindrical lower portion flaring to a wide mouth, decorated w/blue flowers on green stems against a shaded orange body, No. 431-10" 600.00

Vase, 14" h., 5½" d., two large handles at lower half, squat stacked base & faceted squared neck, matte glaze in three shades of brown, No. 411-14" 1,540.00

Wall pocket, canted sides, angular rim handles, geometric design in blue, yellow, green & lavender on brown ground, 6" w., 8¼" h.........................315.00

GARDENIA (1940s)

Large white gardenia blossoms and green leaves over a textured impressed band on a shaded green, grey or tan ground.

Basket w/overhead handle, shaped rim, tan ground, No. 608-8", 8" h. 125.00

Bowl, 8" d., two-handled, green ground, No. 627-8" 85.00

Candleholders, grey ground, No. 652-4", 4½" h., pr. 120.00

Cornucopia-vase, double, tan ground, No. 622-8", 8¾" h..............................85.00

Ewer, ovoid base, tan ground, No. 617-10", 10" h...........................135.00

Vase, 6" h., tan ground, No. 682-6"......40.00

Vase, 10½" h., large handles rising from base to shoulder, ornate rim, tan ground, No. 686-10"..................115.00

Wall pocket, large handles, green, grey or tan ground, No. 666-8", 9½" h., each....................175.00 to 185.00

Window box, green ground, No. 658-8", 8½" l...............................60.00

IMPERIAL I (1924)

Brown pretzel-twisted vine, green grape leaf and cluster of blue grapes in relief on green and brown bark-textured ground.

Bowl, 8" d., pierced rim handles, rounded sides, No. 71-8" 58.00

Planter, open-handled, 9" l., 2½" h.....180.00

Vase, bud, 8" h., cylindrical w/flaring base, long pierced side handles 75.00

Vase, triple bud, 8½" h., No. 30-8½" 60.00

IMPERIAL II (1924)

Varied line with no common characteristics. Many of the pieces are heavily glazed with colors that run and blend.

Candleholders, deep dished base, slender candle nozzle, No. 1077-4", 4" h., pr. 155.00

Vase, 5½" h., tapering cylinder w/horizontal ribbing above base, mottled green ground, No. 468-5" 155.00

Vase, 8⅛" h., two handles at shoulder, expanding cylinder w/light horizontal ribbing around lower quarter of body, slightly crystalline rust over caramel matte glaze, No. 478-8"......................................385.00

IRIS (1938)

White or yellow blossoms and green leaves on rose blending with green, light blue deepening to a darker blue or tan shading to green or brown.

Basket w/pointed overhead handle, compressed ball form, blue or rose ground, No. 354-8", each.................250.00

Bowl, 14" l., end handles, shaped rim, tan ground, No. 364-14"...................150.00

Candlesticks, flat disc base, cylindrical nozzle flanked by elongated open handles, tan ground, No. 1135-4½", 4½" h., pr. 150.00

Jardiniere, two-handled, rose ground, No. 647-3", 3" h................................65.00

Jardiniere, two-handled, tan ground, No. 647-4", 4" h................................95.00

Rose bowl, tan or blue ground, No. 357-4", 4" h., each.......................95.00

Pot, globular body w/wide mouth & tiny handles, on small circular foot, rose or tan ground, No. 647-3", 3" h., each...65.00

Vase, 4" h., base handles, tan ground, No. 914-4"..60.00

IXIA (1930s)

Embossed spray of tiny bell-shaped flowers and slender leaves - white blossoms on pink ground; lavender blossoms on green or yellow ground.

Ixia Centerpiece

Bowl, 7" d., pink or yellow ground, No. 329-7", each................................65.00

Candleholder, two-light, green ground, No. 1127, 3" h.......................50.00

Centerpiece, one-piece console set w/six candleholders attached to center bowl, green ground, 13" l. (ILLUS.) 170.00

Flower frog, pink ground, No. 34 ....60.00

Flowerpot w/saucer, green ground, No. 641-5", 5" h.................................65.00

Vase, 7" h., closed handles, ovoid, green ground, No. 854-7" 75.00

Vase, 10½" h., closed pointed handles at shoulder, cylindrical w/short neck, green ground, No. 862-10".....130.00

JONQUIL (1931)

White jonquil blossoms and green leaves in relief against textured tan ground; green lining.

Jonquil Jardiniere & Pedestal

Basket w/pointed overhead handle rising from base, waisted body, No. 323-7", 7" h...............................325.00

Basket w/tall pointed overhead handle, bulbous body, No. 324-8", 8" h..315.00

Basket, hanging-type..........................345.00

Bowl, 3" h., large down-turned

handles, No. 523-3" 85.00

Jardiniere, two-handled, No. 621-9", 9" h. 300.00

Jardiniere & pedestal base, overall 29" h., 2 pcs. (ILLUS.)..................1,045.00

Urn, 5½" h..135.00

Vase, 4½" h., globular, No. 93-4½" 175.00

Vase, 7" h., base handles..................150.00

Vase, 8" h., tapering cylinder w/elongated side handles, No. 528-8"........200.00

JUVENILE (1916 on)

Transfer-printed and painted on creamware with nursery rhyme characters, cute animals and other motifs appealing to children.

Juvenile Feeding Dish

Dinner set: four 8¼" d. plates, four 6¾" d. plates, four mugs, one cereal bowl & one creamer; sitting rabbit, 14 pcs. (tight hairline to bowl) 440.00

Feeding dish w/rolled edge, chicks, 7" d. 81.00

Feeding dish w/rolled edge, chicks, 8" d. 90.00

Feeding dish w/rolled edge, seated dog, 8" d. 95.00

Feeding dish w/rolled edge, sitting rabbits, 8" d. (ILLUS.) 100.00

Pitcher, 3½" h., sunbonnet girl............105.00

Plate, 8" d., chicks 69.00

LAUREL (1934)

Laurel branch and berries in low-relief with reeded panels at the sides. Glazed in deep yellow, green shading to cream or terra cotta.

Bowl, 7" d., shallow, green ground 120.00

Urn, green, No. 250-6", 6½" h. 175.00

Vase, 6" h., tapering cylinder w/wide mouth, closed angular handles at shoulder, terra cotta, No. 667-6".......................120.00 to 135.00

Vase, 7¼" h., tapering cylinder w/pierced angular handles at midsection, deep yellow, No. 671-7¼"...................................165.00

Vase, 8" h., deep yellow, No. 672-8" ..180.00

Vase, 9¼" h., angular side handles, globular base w/wide stepped mouth, deep yellow, No. 674-9¼" 260.00

Vase, 14½" h., base handles rising from stepped disc base to midsection of slightly flaring cylindrical body, terra cotta, No. 678-14½" 495.00

LUFFA (1934)

Relief-molded ivy leaves and blossoms on shaded brown or green wavy horizontal ridges.

Candlesticks, two-handled, bell-shaped base, brown ground, 5" h., pr. 150.00

Jardiniere, green ground, 5¼" base d., 7" h. 100.00

Jardiniere, green ground, 8" h. 495.00

Vase, 6" h., brown ground 125.00

Vase, 8" h., green ground....................95.00

Vase, 8½" h., tapering cylinder w/two handles rising from shoulder to beneath rim, brown ground.............185.00

Vase, 13" h., two-handled, flaring base, brown ground 500.00

Wall pocket, conical w/tiny angular handles beneath rim, brown or green ground, 8½" h., each 550.00

MAGNOLIA (1943)

Large white blossoms with rose centers and black stems in relief against a blue, green or tan textured ground.

Basket w/ornate overhead handle, green ground, No. 384-7", 7" h. 85.00

Basket w/fan-shaped overhead handle, blue ground, No. 384-8", 8" h. 125.00

Basket, hanging-type, green ground, No. 469-5" 125.00

Bowl, 10" d., two-handled, tan ground, No. 450-10", 10" l. 110.00

Candlesticks, angular handles rising from flat base to midsection of stem, tan ground, No. 1157-4½", 5" h., pr. 90.00

Cornucopia-vase, blue or tan ground, No. 184-6", 6" h., each.........55.00 to 75.00

Ewer, blue or green ground, No. 13-6", 6" h., each...........85.00 to 95.00

Ewer, green ground, No. 15-15", 15" h...275.00

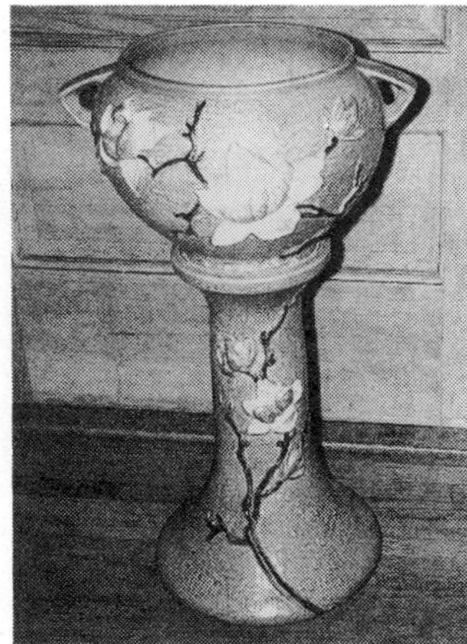

Magnolia Jardiniere & Pedestal

Jardiniere & pedestal base, blue ground, 2 pcs. (ILLUS.)....725.00 to 825.00

Pedestal base, green ground, 16" h. ..300.00

Planter, shell-shaped w/angular base handles, green ground, No. 183-6", 6" l..66.00

Planter, rectangular w/angular end handles, green ground, No. 388-6", 8" l..57.00

Rose bowl, tan ground, No. 446-4", 4" d......................................55.00 to 65.00

Vase, 6" h., two-handled, green ground, No. 87-6"..............................65.00

Vase, 6" h., angular pointed handles from base to midsection, blue or green ground, No. 88-6" 67.00

Vase, 8" h., two-handled, green ground, No. 91-8".............................155.00

Vase, 9" h., two-handled, blue ground, No. 93-9"..135.00

MING TREE (1949)

Embossed twisted bonsai tree topped with puffy foliage — pink-topped trees on mint green ground, green tops on white ground and white tops on blue ground; handles in the form of gnarled branches.

Basket w/overhead branch handle, rounded body w/shaped rim, blue or white ground, No. 508-8", 8" h., each.................................85.00 to 100.00

Candleholders, squat melon-ribbed body w/angular branch handles at shoulder, blue ground, No. 551, pr. ...45.00

Console set: 10" l. bowl & pair of candleholders, No. 551; blue ground, 3 pcs. 180.00

Ewer, green or white ground, No. 516-10", 10" h., each.................125.00

Vase, 8" h., asymmetrical branch handles, green ground, No. 582-8"....85.00

MONTACELLO (1931)

White stylized trumpet flowers with black accents on a terra cotta band — light terra cotta mottled in blue or light green mottled and blended with blue backgrounds.

Basket w/pointed overhead handle, tall collared neck, terra cotta ground, No. 332-6", 6½" h.............425.00 to 450.00

Vase, 4" h., sharply compressed globular base, handles rising from shoulder to rim, blue ground, No. 555-4"..95.00

Vase, 7" h., ovoid w/shoulder handles & collared neck, terra cotta ground, No. 562-7".......................................325.00

MOSS (1930s)

Spanish moss draped over a brown branch with green leaves against a background of ivory, pink or tan shading to blue.

Basket, hanging-type, tan ground, No. 353-5".......................................325.00

Bowl, 6" d., tan ground, No. 291-6" 145.00

Console set: 10" d. bowl & pair of 4½" h. candlesticks; pink ground, bowl No. 193-10", 3 pcs..................195.00

Vase, 6" h., large open angular handles, tan ground, No. 774-6" 90.00

Vase, 7" h., ivory ground, No. 777-7".......................................150.00

Wall pocket, bucket-shaped, pink ground, No. 1279, 10" h..................475.00

MOSTIQUE (1915)

Incised Indian-type design of stylized flowers, leaves or geometric shapes glazed in bright high-gloss colors against a heavy, pebbled ground.

Bowl, 7" d., low rounded sides, floral design, sandy beige ground..............67.50

Jardiniere, geometric design, tan ground, 18" h. 175.00

Vase, 6" h., glossy yellow stylized flowers, grey ground, green glazed interior 50.00

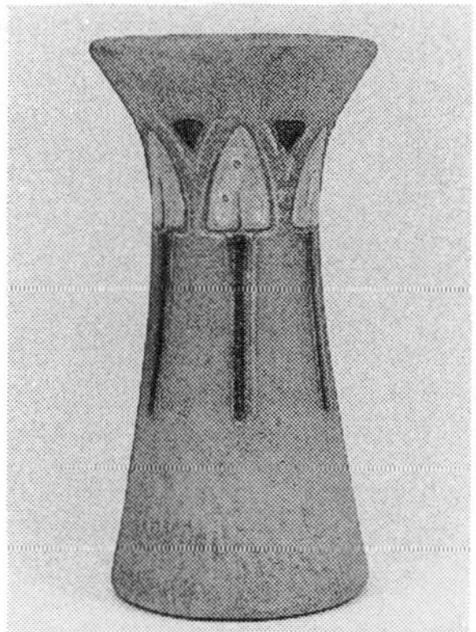

Mostique Vase

Vase, 10" h., slightly waisted cylinder w/flaring mouth, arrowhead designs, grey ground (ILLUS.) 80.00

Vase, 15" h., corset-shaped, geometric floral design, grey ground 275.00

ORIAN (1935)

Art Deco-style shapes, bladelike slender leaf-shaped handles; high-gloss glaze, often in a two-tone color combination.

Candlestick, cylindrical shaft flanked by narrow buttress handles on a wide, flaring foot, blue, 4½" h.............65.00

Vase, 6" h., flared foot below a cylindrical body w/a spherical top & short cylindrical neck, long & low loop handles down the sides, turquoise, No. 733-6 ....95.00

Vase, 10" h., yellow 135.00

Vase, 10½" h., baluster form w/slender handles rising from low foot to shoulder, yellow 135.00

Wall pocket, double, two cylindrical tubes, one slightly longer & wider than the other, joined by two swirls, green, 8" h. 325.00

PANEL (1920)

Recessed panels decorated with embossed naturalistic or stylized florals or female nudes.

Candleholders, dark brown ground, 2½" h., pr. 125.00

Urn, dark green ground, 4" h. 65.00

Vase, 6" h., pillow-shaped, small rim handles, orchid blossoms decoration, dark green ground 105.00

Vase, 6" h., cylindrical w/short collared neck, stylized florals, dark brown ground 92.00

Vase, 6" h., pillow-shaped, dark brown ground 120.00

PEONY (1942)

Peony blossoms in relief against a textured swirling ground — yellow blossoms against rose shading to green, brown shading to gold or gold with green; white blossoms against green.

Peony Double Candleholders

Basket w/overhead handle, gold ground, No. 377-8", 8" h. 85.00

Basket, hanging-type, green ground, No. 467-5".......................................120.00

Book ends, gold ground, No. 11, 5½" h., pr. 135.00

Bowl, 13" d., rose ground, No. 432-12".......................................95.00

Candleholders, double, green ground, No. 1153, 5" h., pr. (ILLUS.) 66.00

Candlesticks, gold or green ground, No. 1152-4½", 4½" h., each pr...........60.00

Cornucopia-vase, rose ground, No. 171-8", 8" h.................................76.00

Ewer, gold ground, No. 8-10", 10" h. ..135.00

Ewer, gold or rose ground, No. 9-15", 15" h., each......................250.00 to 300.00

Flower frog, fan-shaped w/angular base handles, rose ground, No. 47-4", 4" h..................................58.00

Jardiniere, rose ground, No. 661-4", 4" h..65.00

Jardiniere & pedestal base, rose ground, overall 30" h., 2 pcs. 725.00

Pedestal base, gold ground, 20½" h.............................300.00 to 325.00

Planter, rectangular w/angular end handles, slightly canted sides, green ground, No. 387-8", 10" l...................85.00

Rose bowl, two-handled, gold ground, No. 427-6", 6" d...............................135.00

Teapot, cov., gold ground, No. 3 ....135.00

Tray, single rim handle, rose ground, 8" sq...................................55.00 to 65.00

Vase, 8" h., urn-form, rose ground, No. 169-8" 100.00

Vase, 9" h., green ground, No. 65-9"..190.00

Vase, 14" h., angular handles at midsection, rose ground, No. 68-14" 235.00

Vase, 15" h., floor-type, gold ground, No. 69-15" 335.00

Wall pocket, two-handled, green ground, No. 1293-8", 8" h. 265.00

Water set: ice lip pitcher & 4 mugs; green ground, No. 1326-7½ & No. 2-3½, 5 pcs. 275.00

PERSIAN (1916)

Geometric shapes and angular floral designs in bright colors against creamware.

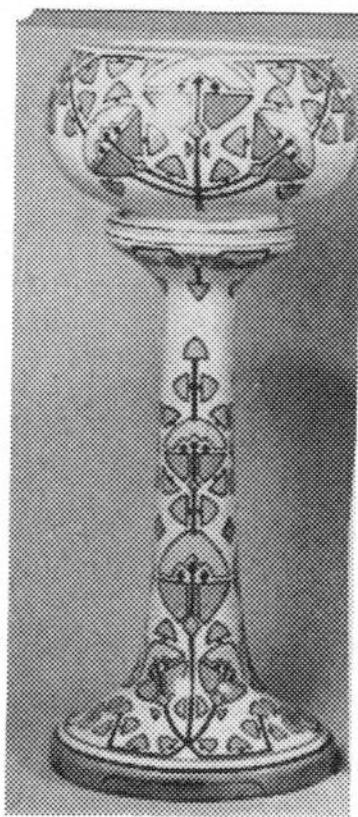

Persian Jardiniere & Pedestal

Jardiniere, wide ovoid body w/incurved wide mouth, on thin molded feet, decorated w/h.p. stylized three-petal purple flowers & whiplash leaves around the top half on a creamy white ground, 10½" d., 9¼" h. 275.00

Jardiniere & pedestal base, overall colorful geometric design, 13" jardiniere, overall 30½" h., 2 pcs. (ILLUS.) 715.00

Tea & coffee service: cov. teapot, cov. coffeepot, cov. sugar bowl & creamer; squared form w/incurved tapering sides, angular handles, decorated w/purple & green arabesques on a white ground, 4 pcs. (very minor chipping to coffeepot) ...550.00

PINE CONE (1931)

Realistic embossed brown pine cones and green pine needles on shaded blue, brown or green ground. (Pink extremely rare.)

Pine Cone Bowl

Ashtray, blue or green ground, No. 499, 4½" l., each ....85.00 to 95.00

Basket w/overhead branch handle, brown ground, No. 409-8", 8" h. ....425.00 to 450.00

Basket w/overhead branch handle rising from midsection of cylindrical body w/shaped base, disc foot, brown ground, No. 353-11", 11" h....325.00

Bowl, 4½" h., two-handled, shaped rim, brown ground, No. 320-5" 75.00

Bowl, 6¼ x 9½", 4" h., oval w/pleated ends, twig handles, green ground, No. 279-9" (ILLUS.) 125.00

Candleholders, flat disc base supporting candle nozzle in the form of a pine cone flanked by needles on one side & branch handle on the other, blue ground, No. 1123, 2½" h., pr. 235.00

Cornucopia-vase, blue ground, No. 126-6", 6" h. 100.00

Ewer, brown ground, No. 851-15", 15" h. 500.00

Flower frog, blue ground, No. 20-4"....150.00

Flower frog, brown or green ground, No. 21-5", each 175.00

Jardiniere, two-handled, globular, green ground, No. 632-3", 3" h. 95.00

Jardiniere, blue ground, No. 632-4", 4" h. 170.00

Jardiniere, two-handled, globular, blue or green ground, No. 632-5", 5" h., each ....325.00 to 350.00

Jardiniere, two-handled, blue or green ground, No. 632-6", 9" d., 6½" h., each ....225.00 to 250.00

Jardiniere & pedestal base, green ground, overall 25" h., 2 pcs. 950.00

Pedestal, blue ground, No. 406-10" ...800.00

Planter, single side handle rising from base, blue or brown ground, No. 124-5", 5" h., each.......80.00 to 100.00

Planter, green ground, No. 456-6", 6" l. 95.00

Rose bowl, green ground, No. 278-4", 4" h. 225.00

Rose bowl, blue ground, No. 261-6", 6" d. 395.00

Tray, double, center handle in the form of pine needles & cone, blue, brown or green ground, 6½ x 13", each ....250.00 to 275.00

Tumbler, green ground, No. 414, 5" h. 130.00

Urn, blue ground, No. 745-7", 7" h. 275.00

Vase, 6" h., brown ground, No. 838-6" 110.00

Vase, 7" h., asymmetrical handles, footed, brown ground, No. 121-7"....160.00

Vase, 7" h., brown or green ground, No. 704-7" ....150.00 to 175.00

Vase, 7" h., spherical body w/flat mouth, raised on a small square foot, small loop twig handles, green ground, No. 745-7" 165.00

Vase, 8" h., pillow-type, green ground, No. 845-8" 225.00

Vase, 9½" h., brown or green ground, No. 705-9" ....150.00 to 200.00

Vase, 10½" h., conical w/base handles, brown or green ground, No. 747-10", each ....155.00 to 180.00

Vase, 12" h., brown ground, No. 911-12" 325.00

Vase, 15" h., two-handled, ovoid w/waisted neck & flaring mouth, brown ground, No. 807-15" 675.00

Vase, 18½" h., floor-type, two-handled, low foot, ovoid w/short neck & flaring rim, No. 913-18" 660.00

Wall pocket, double, brown or green ground, No. 1273-8", 8½" h., each ....275.00 to 300.00

Triple Pine Cone Wall Pocket

Wall pocket, triple, green ground, No. 466-8½", 8½" w. (ILLUS.)..........350.00

Wall bracket, brown ground, 5 x 8", No. 1 ....350.00

POPPY (1930)

Embossed full-blown poppy blossoms, buds and foliage — yellow blossoms on green, white blossoms on blue or soft pink blossoms on a deeper pink.

Poppy Rose Bowl

Basket w/pointed overhead handle, slender ovoid body on disc base, green ground, No. 348-12", 12½" h. 215.00

Bowl, 5" d., two-handled, pink ground, No. 336-5" 110.00

Bowl, 8" d., two-handled, irregular rim, blue ground, No. 337-8" 100.00

Ewer, ornate cut-out lip, green or pink ground, No. 876-10", 10" h., each ....150.00 to 175.00

Flower frog, pink ground, No. 35 ....105.00

Jardiniere, tiny handles at rim, pink ground, No. 642-4", 4" h. 80.00

Jardiniere & pedestal base, green ground, 8" h. jardiniere, 2 pcs. 825.00

Rose bowl, two-handled, pink ground, No. 334-4", 4" h. (ILLUS.) 72.50

Poppy Vase

Vase, 7½" h., two-handled, green ground, No. 869-7" (ILLUS.) 105.00

Vase, 7½" h., two-handled, expanding cylinder w/slightly waisted neck & wide mouth, green ground, No. 868-7" 65.00

Vase, 10" h., two-handled, semi-ovoid, cut-out rim, green ground, No. 875-10" 225.00

Wall pocket, triple, tapering center section flanked by small tapering cylinders, green ground, No. 1281-8", 8½" h..........................310.00

PRIMROSE (1932)

Cluster of long-stemmed blossoms and pod-like leaves in relief on blue, pink or tan ground.

Basket, hanging-type, two-handled, globular, tan ground, No. 354-5"......185.00

Jardiniere, pink ground, No. 634-4", 4" h...75.00

Jardiniere & pedestal base, pink ground, No. 634-10", 2 pcs. 1,500.00

Vase, 6½" h., angular handles, pink ground, No. 761-6"............................80.00

Vase, 7" h., two-handled, blue ground, No. 762-7"..77.50

Vase, 8" h., fan-shaped, blue ground, No. 765-8"......................................125.00

Vase, 10" h., shoulder handles, pink or tan ground, No. 770-10", each ....150.00 to 175.00

RAYMOR (1952)

Modernistic design oven-proof dinnerware.

Raymor Dinnerware

Bean pot, cov., individual size, Contemporary white, No. 195..................35.00

Bowl, soup, lug-type, Autumn brown, No. 155 ....18.00

Celery & olive dish, Beach gray, No. 177 ....35.00

Coffee tumbler, handled, Beach gray, No. 179 (small inner rim flake)...........18.00

Coffee tumbler, handled, Terra Cotta, No. 179 ....30.00

Corn servers, individual size, long slender form w/section for butter, one each Autumn brown, Avocado green, Terra Cotta, Beach gray & Contemporary white, 12½" l., set of 5...200.00

Cup, Autumn brown, No. 150 ....12.00

Cup & saucer, Autumn brown, Nos. 150 & 151, set 18.00

Cup & saucer, Beach gray, Nos. 150 & 151, set...25.00

Dinner service for five: dinner plates, cov. ramekins & cups & saucers; Beach gray, 20 pcs. 200.00

Plate, bread & butter, Autumn brown, No. 154 ....6.50

Plate, salad, Beach gray, No. 154........15.00

Plate, salad, Terra Cotta, No. 154........15.00

Platter, rectangular, Avocado green, No. 163 ....50.00

Teapot, cov., black, No. 174..............125.00

ROSECRAFT HEXAGON (1924)

Six-sided form decorated with a simple impressed circular medallion enclosing an elongated stylized flower.

Bowl, 7½" d., sharply compressed sides, brown....................................150.00

Pin tray, green 115.00

Vase, 4" h., brown 250.00

Vase, double bud, 5" h., gate-form, dark green.......................................200.00

Wall pocket, slender w/flaring rim, brown, 8½" h. 195.00

ROSECRAFT VINTAGE (1924)

Curving band of brown and yellow grapevine with fruit and foliage at top, usually on a dark brown ground.

Rosecraft Vintage Vase

Bowl, 6" d., low, compressed sides......40.00

Bowl, 7" d..85.00

Candlesticks, circular flaring base, expanding cylindrical stem, 8" h., pr. 175.00

Jardiniere, 6" h. 140.00

Vase, 4" h., small rim handles, barrel-shaped 95.00

Vase, 5" h., expanding cylinder (ILLUS.) 65.00

Vase, 8½" h., small rim handles, expanding cylinder 145.00

Wall pocket, two-handled, conical w/shaped rim 185.00

ROZANE (early 1900s)

Underglaze slip-painted decoration on dark blended backgrounds.

Rozane Vase with Dog Portrait

Jardiniere, squeeze bag decoration of flying geese & stylized trees, artist-signed, 10" d., 6" h. 605.00

Jug, floral decoration, artist-signed, No. 888, 4½" h. 215.00

Vase, 8¼" h., 5" d., tall ovoid body, decorated w/burnt orange poppies on green stems & w/green leaves in a glossy glaze against a creamy bisque ground, glossy-glazed interior 1,540.00

Vase, 9" h., 6" d., ovoid w/tiny mouth, decorated w/pink, white & green raspberries w/green foliage against a shaded brown ground, artist-signed 425.00

Vase, 9½" h., pillow-type w/scalloped rim, decorated w/a scene of a hunting dog w/a pheasant in its mouth, artist-signed (ILLUS.) 660.00

Vase, 10¼" h., 6¼" d., a wide domed base on tab feet tapering sharply to a bulbous knob at the base of the tall slender cylindrical neck w/a widely flaring rim, slender straight handles running from rim to top of knob, squeeze-bag decoration w/dark bands trimmed in delicate scrolls around the base & on the knob, the base further decorated w/a large cluster of chestnuts & leaves in bluish grey & brown against a light ground, artist-signed (two tight horizontal hairlines in handles) 1,320.00

Vase, 10½" h., 4" d., tall waisted cylindrical form w/short flared neck, decorated w/sprigs of white & grey flowers against a shaded greyish green ground, artist-signed & numbered "36" 440.00

Vase, 13" h., 6" d., tall footed ovoid body tapering to a short wide slightly flaring neck, decorated w/a bust portrait of an Indian warrior against a dark shaded ground, artist-signed & die-stamped "A (?) PPC - D" 660.00

Vase, 13½" h., decorated w/a dog portrait against a dark shaded ground, signed M. Timberlake 1,400.00

Vase, 14" h., decorated w/the portrait of an Indian brave 1,870.00

Vase, 18" h., blueberry decoration against a grey ground 1,870.00

Vase, 21¼" h., 12" d., floor-type, tall footed ovoid body tapering to a short narrow neck w/flared rim, golden & brown irises on a dark brown ground, artist-signed (very minor rim chip) 1,320.00

Vase, 22" h., portrait of Indian in full headdress, signed A. Dunlavy 5,225.00

ROZANE (1917)

Clusters of delicately tinted roses and green leaves against a honeycomb background in blue, ivory, light green, pink or yellow.

Basket w/overhead handle, ivory ground, 7" h. 60.00

Bowl-vase, ivory ground, 9" d. 60.00

Candleholder, cone-shaped, 7¾" h. 70.00

Compote, 6½" h., ivory ground 75.00

Wall pocket, semi-ovoid, 7½" h. 100.00

RUSSCO (1930s)

Narrow perpendicular panel front and back, stacked handles and octagonal rim openings; solid matte glaze or matte glaze with crystalline overglaze.

Russco Lamp Base

Cornucopia-vase, white glaze, No. 100-8", 8" h. 95.00

Jardiniere, brown glaze, 6" h. 155.00

Lamp base, urn-shaped, two slender elongated handles, crystalline orange glaze, 10½" h. (ILLUS.) 220.00

Vase, 7" h., urn-shaped, low foot, angular handles at shoulder, aqua glaze 140.00

Vase, 8¼" h., 6¾" d., urn-shaped, the bulbous base w/small molded buttress handles below the wide slightly tapering octagonal upper section w/a flared rim, raised on a flaring pedestal base, gold glaze 110.00

Vase, double bud, 8½" h., tall slender cylinder attached by a narrow strip to a shorter & wider cylinder, octagonal base, tan glaze 65.00

Vase, 8½" h., footed, brown & bronze w/crystalline overglaze 125.00

Vase, double bud, 9" h., blue glaze 50.00

Vase, 12½" h., low foot, slightly bulbous base, closed handles at midsection, blue glaze 115.00

Vase, 12½" h., footed, slightly globular base tapering to a wide neck, buttressed handles at midsection, turquoise glaze 115.00

SILHOUETTE (1952)

Recessed shaped panels decorated with floral designs or exotic female nudes against a combed background.

Ashtray, square w/indentations at corners, rose, No. 799 ....45.00

Basket w/asymmetrical rim & overhead handle, florals, rose, tan or white w/turquoise blue panel, No. 709-8", 8" h., each ....90.00 to 110.00

Basket w/curved rim & asymmetrical handle, florals, white w/turquoise blue panel, No. 710-10", 10" h. 125.00

Basket, hanging-type, florals, turquoise blue ....80.00 to 110.00

Bowl, 10" d., florals, white, No. 730-10" 70.00

Bowl, 12" l., florals, tan, No. 729-12" 75.00

Ewer, bulging base, florals, turquoise blue, No. 716-6", 6" h. 55.00

Ewer, sharply canted sides, florals, rose, No. 717-10", 10" h. 80.00

Planter, florals, turquoise blue, No. 769-9", 9" l. 80.00

Rose bowl, female nudes, rose or tan, No. 742-6", 6" h., each ....285.00 to 315.00

Urn, female nudes, rose, No. 763-8", 8" h. 400.00

Vase, 5" h., florals, turquoise blue, No. 779-5" 65.00

Vase, 6" h., small angular handles between compressed globular base & tall wide neck, turquoise blue, No. 780-6" 275.00

Vase, 6" h., rectangular curved body on a wedge-shaped base, rose or white, No. 781-6", each 55.00

Vase, 7" h., florals, double wing-shaped handles above low footed base, cylindrical w/asymmetrical rim, white, No. 782-7" 95.00

Vase, 7" h., fan-shaped, florals, white w/turquoise blue panel, No. 783-7" 230.00

Vase, 8" h., urn-form, tapering ovoid body raised on four angled feet on a round disc base, wide slightly flaring mouth, turquoise blue, No. 763-8" 330.00

Vase, 9" h., double, base w/canted sides supporting two square vases w/sloping rims, joined by a stylized branch-form center post, florals, rose, No. 757-9" 85.00

Vase, 9" h., flat closed handles between domed base & body, florals, white, No. 785-9" 165.00

Vase, 12" h., florals, turquoise blue, No. 788-12" 125.00

Vase, 12" h., florals, white, No. 788-12" 125.00

Wall pocket, bullet-shaped w/angular pierced handles, florals, white w/turquoise blue panel, No. 766-8", 8" h. 120.00

SNOWBERRY (1946)

Clusters of white berries on brown stems with green foliage over oblique scalloping, against a blue, green or rose background.

Snowberry Sugar Bowl

Basket w/low pointed overhead handle, shaded blue ground, No. 1BK7", 7" h. 115.00

Basket w/curved overhead handle, disc base, shaded rose ground, No. 1BK-10", 10" h. 150.00

Basket w/overhead handle curving from base to beneath rim on opposite side, curved rim, shaded rose ground, No. 1BK-12", 12½" h. 195.00

Basket, hanging-type, shaded rose ground, No. 1HB5", 5" h. 175.00

Book ends, shaded blue or rose ground, No. 1BE, each pr. 145.00

Bowl, 6" d., shaded blue ground, No. 1BL2-6" 75.00

Bowl, 10" d., footed, shaded blue ground, No. 1FB-10" 145.00

Bowl, 14" d., green ground, No. 1BL14" 65.00

Candlesticks, angular side handles, shaded rose ground, No. 1CS2-4½", 4½" h., pr. 75.00

Console bowl, pointed end handles, shaded rose ground, No. 1BL1-10", 10" l. 75.00

Console set: 12" l. bowl & pair of candleholders; shaded blue ground, No. 1BL2-12", 3 pcs. 175.00

Cornucopia-vase, shaded blue, green or rose ground, No. 1CC-6", 6" h., each 48.00

Cornucopia-vase, shaded blue ground, No. 1CC-8", 8" h. 115.00

Creamer & sugar bowl, angular side handles, shaded blue ground, Nos. 1C & 1S, pr. (ILLUS. of sugar bowl) 95.00

Ewer, sharply compressed base w/long conical neck, shaded blue ground, No. 1TK-10", 10" h. 145.00

Ewer, flaring base, oval body, shaded green or rose ground, No. 1TK-15", 16" h., each ....250.00 to 300.00

Flower holder, shaded blue ground, No. 1FH-7", 7" h. 85.00

Jardiniere, two-handled, shaded rose ground, No. 1J-4", 4" h. 62.00

Jardiniere, shaded rose ground, No. 1J-6", 6" h. 115.00

Jardiniere & pedestal base, shaded blue ground, overall 25" h., 2 pcs. 600.00

Snowberry Pillow Vase

Vase, 6½" h., pillow-type, shaded blue ground, No. 1FH-6" (ILLUS.) 100.00

Vase, bud, 7" h., single base handle, asymmetrical rim, shaded green ground, No. 1BV-7" 52.50

Vase, 9" h., base handles, shaded rose ground, No. 1V1-9" 95.00

Vase, 18" h., shaded blue ground, No. 1V-18" ....575.00 to 600.00

Window box, shaded blue or rose ground, No. 1WX-8", 8" l. 75.00

SUNFLOWER (1930)

Long-stemmed yellow sunflower blossoms framed in green leaves against a mottled green textured ground.

Sunflower Vase

Candlestick, 4" h. 250.00

Urn, globular w/small rim handles, 4" h. 210.00

Urn, straight sided, 5" h. 280.00

Vase, 5" h., two-handled, bulbous (ILLUS.) 240.00

Vase, 5½" h., 5½" d., bulbous ovoid body tapering to a wide flat mouth, small loop handles at the shoulder ..385.00

Vase, 6" h., cylindrical w/tiny rim handles 235.00

Wall pocket, curved openwork double handle, 7½" h. 600.00

TEASEL (1936)

Gracefully curving long stems and delicate pods.

Basket w/low overhead handle, cut-out rim, pale blue, No. 349-10", 10" h. 85.00

Flower frog, pale blue, No. 36, 4" d., 3" h. 65.00

Rose bowl, beige shading to tan, No. 342-4", 4" h. 52.50

Rose bowl, beige shading to tan, No. 343-6", 6" h. 95.00

Vase, 6" h., closed handles at midsection, cut-out rim, beige shading to tan, No. 881-6" 55.00

THORN APPLE (1930s)

White trumpet flower and foliage one side, reverse with thorny pod and foliage against shaded blue, brown or pink ground.

Basket w/pointed overhead handle, conical w/low foot, shaded brown ground, No. 342-10", 10" h. 135.00

Basket, hanging-type, shaded brown ground, No. 355-5", 7" d. ....175.00 to 225.00

Bowl, 7" d., 3" h., pointed handles, shaded pink ground, No. 308-7" 145.00

Jardiniere, shaded blue ground, No. 638-5", 5" h. 55.00

Urn, stepped handles, disc foot, shaded pink ground, No. 305-6", 6½" h. 200.00

Vase, 6" h., shaded blue ground, No. 810-6" 70.00

Vase, 6" h., shaded blue or pink ground, No. 811-6", each 75.00

Vase, 7" h., shaded pink ground, No. 815-7" 75.00

Vase, 8½" h., semi-ovoid body flanked by slender columns, on low disc base, shaded pink ground, No. 816-8" ....115.00 to 135.00

Vase, 10" h., shaded pink ground, No. 821-10" 175.00

Vase, 12" h., curved base handles, flaring cylinder, shaded pink ground, No. 823-12" 250.00

Vase, 15" h., floor-type, shaded pink ground, No. 824-15" 350.00

Wall pocket, triple, shaded blue or brown ground, No. 1280-8", 8" h., each ....275.00 to 300.00

TOPEO (1934)

Four evenly spaced vertical garlands beginning near the top and tapering gently down the sides.

Bowl, 11½" d., 3" h., wide low sides w/angled flat shoulder to a wide, low rim, molded around the shoulder w/four small "snails" in pink & blue on a mottled matte blue ground 165.00

Console set: 13" l. bowl & pair of 5" h., double candlesticks; green crystalline glaze shading to blue, the set ...575.00

Vase, 6" h., glossy deep red glaze 185.00

Vase, 7" h., slightly bulbous base & straight tapering sides, short collared mouth, glossy deep red glaze 185.00

Vase, 7" h., globular base & flaring mouth, green crystalline glaze shading to blue 240.00

TOURMALINE (1933)

Produced in various simple shapes and a wide variety of glazes including rose and grey, blue-green, brown or azure blue with green and gold, and terra cotta with yellow.

Bowl, 8" d., low, mottled blue or green ....60.00 to 70.00

Console bowl w/flower frog, mottled blue, No. 241-12", 12" l. 175.00

Cornucopia-vase, semi-gloss medium blue glaze, No. 106-7", 7" h. 45.00

Flower frog, oval, mottled green, 1¾ x 4¼" 10.00

Ginger jar, cov., baluster-form, domed cover w/flaring rim, mottled terra cotta & yellow, 10" h. 275.00

Urn, compressed globular base

w/short collared neck, mottled turquoise or terra cotta, No. A-200-4", 4½" h., each....................................82.50

Urn, globular w/embossed lines around shoulder, mottled blue or green, No. 238-5", 5½" h., each.........75.00

Vase, 5½" h., globular w/loop handles rising from midsection to rim, mottled turquoise blue, No. A-517-6".......72.00

Vase, 6" h., two-handled, globular base & short wide neck, mottled blue...85.00

Vase, 6" h., handles rising from globular base to top of short slightly flaring neck, mottled terra cotta & yellow..60.00

Vase, 6" h., pillow-type, two-handled, horizontally ribbed lower half, mottled blue, No. A-65-6"..................85.00

Vase, 7" h., cylindrical w/low flaring foot, slightly flared rim, mottled pink & blue, No. A-308-7"..........................70.00

Vase, 8" h., base handles, bulbous tapering to flared rim, mottled blue, No. A-332-8"...................................225.00

Vase, 8" h., two-handled, urn-form, mottled blue....................................125.00

Vase, 10⅜" h., hexagonal body tapering toward the base, four sides molded w/diminishing circular designs, glazed in striated & streaked blue over pale green & blue, No. 616-10"........................132.00

TUSCANY (1927)

Gently curving handles terminating in blue grape clusters and green leaves.

Bowl, 7" d., two-handled, mottled pink...54.00

Candlesticks, domed base w/open handles rising from rim to beneath candle nozzle, mottled grey or pink, 3" h., each pr....................................87.50

Console bowl, mottled grey, 14½" l......85.00

Flower arranger, pedestal base, flaring body, open handles, mottled pink, 5" h...80.00

Flower frog, mottled pink, 3" h.............32.50

Urn-vase, mottled pink or grey, 5" h.....................................60.00 to 75.00

Vase, 8" h., two-handled, mottled grey...135.00

Vase, 10" h., shoulder handles, bulbous, mottled pink......................100.00

Wall pocket, long open handles, rounded rim, mottled pink, 8" h........175.00

VELMOSS (1935)

Embossed clusters of long slender green leaves extending down from the top and crossing three wavy horizontal lines. Some pieces reverse the design with the leaves rising from the base.

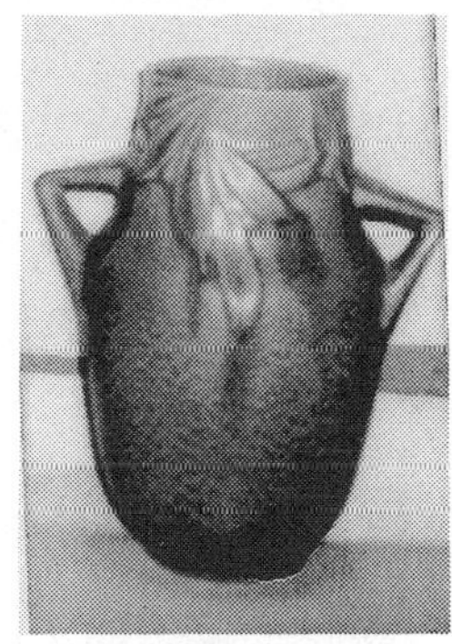

Velmoss Vase

Cornucopia-vase, double, mottled blue, No. 117-8", 8½" h...................100.00

Urn-vase, angular pointed side handles, mottled blue, No. 264-5", 8½" d., 5" h..110.00

Urn-vase, angular pointed side handles, mottled pink, No. 265-6", 6" h...175.00

Vase, 5" h., angular handles, mottled green..65.00

Vase, 6" h., cylindrical w/angular pointed handles, mottled green, No. 714-6"...........................50.00 to 60.00

Vase, 7" h., angular side handles at midsection, cylindrical w/low foot, mottled blue or raspberry red, No. 715-7", each.............135.00 to 150.00

Vase, 8" h., angular pointed handles at midsection, footed, mottled raspberry red, No. 717-8"................160.00

Vase, 9½" h., angular handles, mottled green, No. 719-9" (ILLUS.).......250.00

VISTA (1920s)

Embossed green coconut palm trees and lavender blue pool against grey ground.

Basket, hanging-type, wide low-sided cylindrical form w/three low strap handles along the sides, 8" d., 4" h. (two bruises on the rim)..................302.50

Jardiniere, 6½" h. 185.00

Jardiniere, 9" h. 295.00

Vase, 10" h., cylindrical w/flaring base 265.00

Wall pocket ....450.00 to 500.00

WATER LILY (1940s)

Water lily blossoms and pads against a horizontally ridged ground. White lilies on green lily pads against a blended blue ground, pink lilies on a pink shading to green ground or yellow lilies against a gold shading to brown ground.

Water Lily Cookie Jar

Basket, hanging-type, gold shading to brown ground, No. 468-5", 9" h. 160.00

Bowl, 6" d., blended blue ground, No. 439-6" 75.00

Console bowl, pointed end handles, blended blue ground, No. 443-12", 12" l. 118.00

Cookie jar, cov., angular handles, blended blue ground, No. 1-8", 8" h. (ILLUS.) ....250.00 to 300.00

Ewer, flared bottom, blended blue ground, No. 10-6", 6" h. 92.00

Ewer, compressed globular base, pink shading to green ground, No. 11-10", 10" h. 150.00

Ewer, swollen cylindrical form on flat base, blended blue ground, No. 12-15", 15" h. (ILLUS. top next column) 260.00

Flower holder, two-handled, fan-shaped body, gold shading to brown or pink shading to green ground, No. 48, 4½" h., each ....45.00 to 50.00

Jardiniere, two-handled, gold shading to brown ground, No. 663-3", 3" h. 45.00

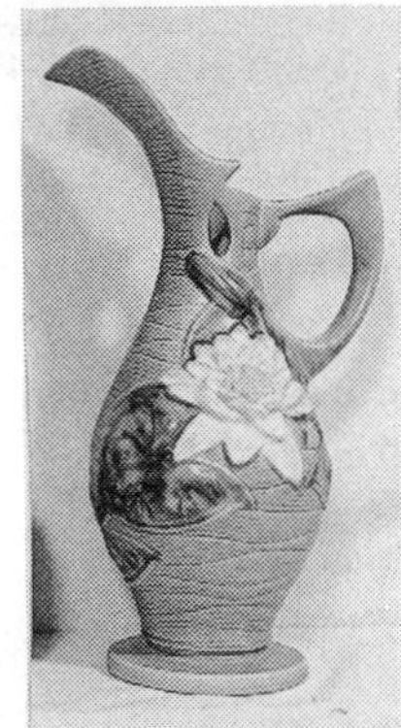

Large Water Lily Ewer

Jardiniere & pedestal base, blended blue ground, 2 pcs. 895.00

Model of a conch shell, gold shading to brown or pink shading to green ground, No. 438-8", 8" h., each 150.00

Pedestal base, blended blue ground, 17" h. 275.00

Rose bowl, two-handled, gold shading to brown or pink shading to green ground, No. 437-4", 4" h., each ....50.00 to 75.00

Rose bowl, two-handled, gold shading to brown ground, No. 437-6", 6" d. 100.00

Urn-vase, pink shading to green ground, No. 175-8", 8" h. 80.00

Vase, 4" h., blended blue ground, No. 71-4" 47.00

Vase, 8" h., two-handled, blended blue ground, No. 76-8" 80.00

Vase, 14" h., angular side handles, gold shading to brown or pink shading to green ground, No. 82-14", each ....250.00 to 275.00

Vase, 15" h., gold shading to brown ground, No. 83-15" 200.00

WHITE ROSE (1940)

White roses and green leaves against a vertically combed ground of blended blue, brown shading to green or pink shading to green.

Basket w/low pointed overhead handle, blended blue ground, No. 362-8", 7½" h. 125.00

Basket w/low pointed overhead handle, pink shading to green ground, No. 362-8", 7½" h. 150.00

Basket w/pointed circular handle, blended blue ground, No. 363-10", 10" h. 195.00

Basket w/pointed circular handle, brown shading to green or pink shading to green ground, No. 363-10", 10" h., each ....135.00 to 165.00

Basket w/sweeping handle rising from base to rim at opposite side, blended blue ground, No. 364-12", 12" h. 190.00

Basket, hanging-type, blended blue, brown shading to green or pink shading to green ground, No. 463-5", each ....150.00 to 175.00

Book ends, blended blue ground, No. 7, pr. ....165.00 to 195.00

Bowl, 10" d., two-handled, blended blue ground, No. 392-10" 100.00

Console bowl, elongated pointed handles, pink shading to green ground, No. 393-12", 16½" l. 125.00

Console set: bowl, pair of candle-holders & flower frog w/overhead handle; pink shading to green ground, No. 392-10", No. 1141 & No. 41, the set 245.00

Ewer, compressed globular base, blended blue or pink shading to green ground, No. 981-6", 6" h., each ....65.00 to 75.00

Jardiniere, two-handled, blended blue ground, No. 653-3", 3" h. 60.00

Jardiniere, brown shading to green ground, No. 653-5", 5" h. 80.00

Jardiniere & pedestal base, pink shading to green ground, 10" h. jardiniere, 2 pcs. (minor chips) 1,095.00

Vase, 4" h., cylindrical w/slightly sloping shoulder, blended blue ground, No. 978-4" 30.00

Vase, double bud, 4½" h., two cylinders joined by an arched bridge, blended blue ground, No. 148 ....115.00

Vase, 6" h., cylindrical w/short collared neck, angular handles at shoulder, blended blue or pink shading to green ground, No. 979-6", each 75.00

Vase, 7" h., pink shading to green ground, No. 983-7" 65.00

Vase, 8" h., base handles, brown shading to green ground, No. 984-8" 100.00

Vase, 8½" h., handles rising from globular base to rim, blended blue, No. 985-8" 125.00

Vase, 9" h., blended blue ground, No. 986-9" 135.00

Vase, 18" h., two-handled, blended blue ground, No. 994-18" 465.00

Wall pocket, swirled handle, flaring rim, pink shading to green ground, No. 1288-6", 6½" h. 175.00

WINCRAFT (1948)

Shapes from older lines such as Pine Cone, Cremona, Primrose and others, vases with an animal motif, and contemporary shapes. High gloss glaze in bright shades of blue, tan, yellow, turquoise, apricot and grey.

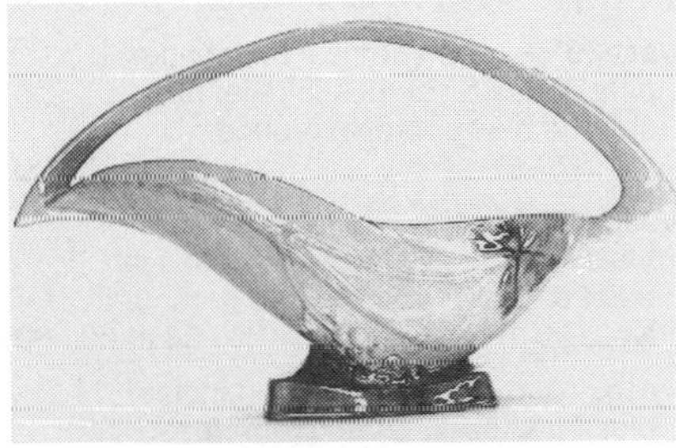

Wincraft Basket

Basket w/low overhead handle, shaped rim, narcissus-type blossoms & foliage in relief on blue ground, No. 208-8", 8" h. 105.00

Basket w/low overhead handle, shaped rim, berries & foliage in relief on green ground, No. 209-12", 12" h. (ILLUS.) 85.00

Basket, hanging-type, lime green or tan, 8" h., each 110.00

Book ends, yellow, No. 259, 6½" h., pr. 60.00

Bowl, 8" d., blue, No. 226-8" 75.00

Candleholders, brown, No. 251, pr. 92.50

Cigarette box, cov., rectangular, blue, No. 240, 4½" l. 95.00

Console bowl, brown, No. 228-12", 12" l. 165.00

Cornucopia-vases, low rectangular base, relief florals against a mottled blue ground, No. 221-8", 9" l., 5" h., pr. 90.00

Ewer, stepped lower portion & long slender neck w/flaring mouth, leaves in relief on shaded lime green ground, No. 218-18", 18" h. (ILLUS. top next column) 350.00

Tall Wincraft Ewer

Vase, 6" h., asymmetrical fan shape, pine cones & needles in relief on shaded blue or brown ground, No. 272-6", each 75.00

Vase, 10" h., cylindrical, tab handles, black panther & green palm trees in relief on shaded lime green ground, No. 290-10"......................250.00 to 300.00

Vase, 10" h., cylindrical, tab handles, black panther & green palm trees in relief on shaded green ground, No. 290-10"......................................435.00

Vase, 12" h., tan, No. 275-12"............160.00

Vase, 18" h., floor-type, blue, No. 289-18"......................400.00 to 425.00

Wall pocket, horizontally ribbed square body, shaded brown, No. 266-4, 8½" h..............................125.00

WINDSOR (1931)

Stylized florals, foliage, vines and ferns on some, others with repetitive band arrangement of small squares and rectangles, on mottled blue blending into green or terra cotta and light orange blending into brown.

Vase, 5" h., globular base w/short wide neck, two handles rising from midsection to below rim, geometric design against mottled terra cotta ground...190.00

Vase, 6" h., canted sides, handles rising from shoulder to rim, geometric design against mottled terra cotta ground, No. 546-6".................175.00

Vase, 7" h., large handles, globular base, stylized ferns against mottled blue ground, No. 548-7"..................320.00

Vase, 7½" h., 10" widest d., two handles rising from shoulder of compressed globular base to rim of short wide mouth, stylized ferns against mottled terra cotta ground...295.00

Vase, 9" h., two handles rising from globular base to rim of wide neck, stylized ferns against mottled terra cotta ground....................................400.00

Vase, 10¼" h., 7" d., ovoid body tapering to a wide conical neck, curved handles from neck to shoulders, orange ground w/lightly molded green leaves at neck, silver paper label......................................302.50

WISTERIA (1933)

Lavender wisteria blossoms and green vines against a roughly textured brown shading to deep blue ground, rarely found in only brown.

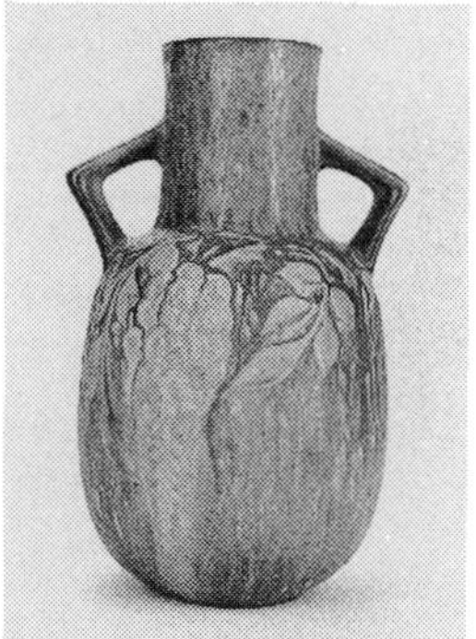

Wisteria Vase

Bowl, 4" h., angular rim handles, brown ground, No. 242-4"................145.00

Candleholders, high domed base w/angular pointed handles, No. 1091-4", 4" h., pr. 450.00

Planter, rectangular w/angular end handles, brown ground, No. 243, 5 x 9"...225.00

Vase, 4" h., squatty, angular handles on sharply canted shoulder, No. 629-4"..195.00

Vase, 6" h., two-handled, pear-shaped w/wide mouth, No. 631-6"...235.00

Vase, 6½" h., globular w/angular rim handles, No. 637-6½" 430.00

Vase, 7" h., angular handles at shoulder, brown ground, No. 634-7".........210.00

Vase, 8" h., 6½" d., wide tapering cylindrical body w/small angled handles flanking the flat rim, No. 633-8"..450.00

Vase, 8½" h., slender base handles, conical body bulging slightly below rim, brown ground, No. 635-8"........................275.00 to 325.00

Vase, 9½" h., cylindrical body w/angular handles rising from shoulder to midsection of slender cylindrical neck, No. 638-9" (ILLUS.) 450.00

Wall pocket, flaring rim, 8" h. 575.00

ZEPHYR LILY (1946)

Deeply embossed day lilies against a swirl-textured ground. White and yellow lilies on a blended blue ground; rose and yellow lilies on a green ground; yellow lilies on terra cotta shading to olive green ground.

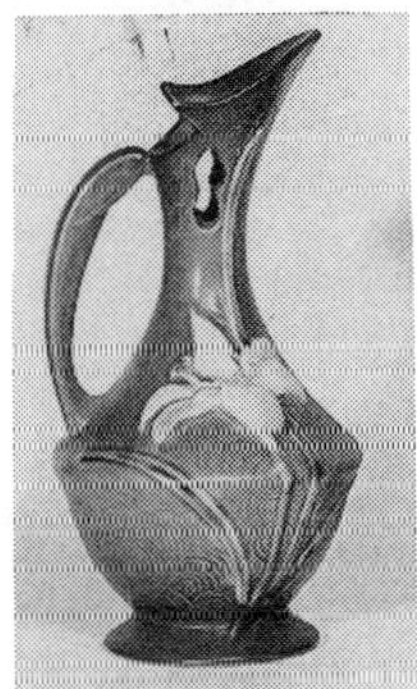

Zephyr Lily Ewer

Basket w/asymmetrical overhead handle & rim, terra cotta ground, No. 394-8", 8" h...............................115.00

Basket w/low, wide overhead handle, disc foot, cylindrical body flaring slightly to an ornate cut rim, terra cotta ground, No. 395-10", 10" h......175.00

Basket, hanging-type, blue, green or terra cotta ground, No. 472-5", 7½", each ....125.00 to 150.00

Book ends, green ground, No. 16, pr...135.00

Bowl, 8" d., terra cotta ground, No. 474-8"..80.00

Candleholders, two-handled, blue ground, No. 1162-2", 2" h., pr. 55.00

Candlesticks, terra cotta ground, No. 1163-4½", 4½" h., pr. ....75.00 to 95.00

Console bowl, end handles, terra cotta ground, No. 474-8", 8" l............80.00

Console bowl, raised shaped sides, terra cotta ground, No. 475-10", 10" l...125.00

Cornucopia-vase, blue ground, No. 204-8", 8½" h.................75.00 to 85.00

Cornucopia-vase, green or terra cotta ground, No. 204-8", 8½" h., each ....65.00 to 75.00

Creamer, blue or terra cotta ground, No. 7-C, each.......................50.00 to 60.00

Ewer, terra cotta ground, No. 23-10", 10" h. (ILLUS.) 110.00

Jardiniere, two-handled, terra cotta ground, No. 671-4", 4" h. 80.00

Rose bowl, blue ground, No. 471-6", 6" h...100.00

Teapot, cov., terra cotta ground, No. 7T 190.00

Tea set: cov. teapot, creamer & sugar bowl; green ground, Nos. 7C, S & T, 3 pcs. 225.00

Vase, 6½" h., fan-shaped, base handles, blue ground, No. 205-6" 85.00

Vase, bud, 7½" h., handles rising from conical base, slender expanding cylinder w/flaring rim, blue ground, No. 201-7" 95.00

Vase, 8" h., green ground, No. 134-8" 85.00

Vase, 8½" h., handles rising from flat disc base to midsection of cylindrical body, No. 133-8" 135.00

Vase, 9" h., green or terra cotta ground, No. 136-9", each ....125.00 to 150.00

Vase, 12" h., conical w/base handles, green ground, No. 139-12" 125.00

Vase, 18" h., terra cotta ground, No. 142-17"....................................350.00

(End of Roseville Section)

ROSE WARES

Three different gaudy-type patterns of rose-decorated wares, once popular with the Pennsylvania "Deutsch" (Germans) that settled in the southeastern part of that state, are sought out by collectors who are willing to pay high prices for these early wares made in England, circa 1810-30. King's Rose pattern has an orange-red rose placed off center and green to yellow leaves and is quite a bold design. Queen's Rose pattern has a pink bloom and the remaining portions of the design are more delicate. Adams' Rose, named after its maker, William Adams (which see), has a border of two red roses and is a later production. The superb shapes and the vivid decoration of this scarce and expensive ware has a cheery appeal entirely its own.

Creamer, footed boat-shaped body w/C-scroll handle, molded ribs at front & back, King's Rose patt., 4¾" h. (minor stains & wear) $187.00

Cup & saucer, handleless, King's Rose patt. (wear, pinpoint flakes) 82.50

Cup plate, King's Rose patt., solid pink border, 3½" d. (wear, small old chips) 110.00

Plate, 7¼" d., King's Rose patt. (wear, flaking & pinpoint flakes) 159.50

Plate, 8½" d., King's Rose patt. 165.00

Teapot, cov., footed boat-shaped body w/molded ribs at front & back & on base of spout, angled handle, inset domed cover w/knob finial, King's Rose patt., 6" h. (professional repair) 302.50

Toddy plate, King's Rose patt., solid border, 5¼" d. 93.50

ROYAL BAYREUTH

Good china in numerous patterns and designs has been made at the Royal Bayreuth factory in Tettau, Germany, since 1794. Listings below are by the company's lines, plus miscellaneous pieces. Interest in this china remains at a peak and prices continue to rise. Pieces listed carry the company's blue mark except where noted otherwise.

CORINTHIAN

Box, cov., curved front, classical figures on black ground, 4" sq. $40.00

Creamer, classical figures on black ground 52.50

Mug, classical figures, 4¾" h. 55.00

Pitcher, 5½" h., classical figures on orange ground 65.00

Corinthian Pitcher

Pitcher, 5½" h., classical figures on black ground, yellow bands w/leaf decoration around neck & base (ILLUS.) 75.00

Pitcher, 7⅛" h., 4⅜" d., classical figures on black ground 135.00

Smoke set: cov. cigarette jar, a jar w/striker for matches, a jar for spent matches & kidney-shaped tray; 4 pcs. 195.00

Tea set: cov. teapot, creamer & open sugar bowl; classical figures on red ground, 3 pcs. 150.00

Toothpick holder, classical figures on black ground 100.00

Vase, 3½" h., classical figures on green ground 125.00

DEVIL & CARDS

Devil & Cards Candy Dish

Ashtray, full-figure devil 450.00

Ashtray, figural devil's head,

red ....550.00 to 650.00

Ashtray w/match holder & striker.....1,000.00

Candleholder, low..............350.00 to 400.00

Candlestick, 8" h.............................3,000.00

Candy dish, 7" d. (ILLUS.)..300.00 to 350.00

Creamer, 4" h. ....225.00 to 275.00

Dresser tray........................500.00 to 600.00

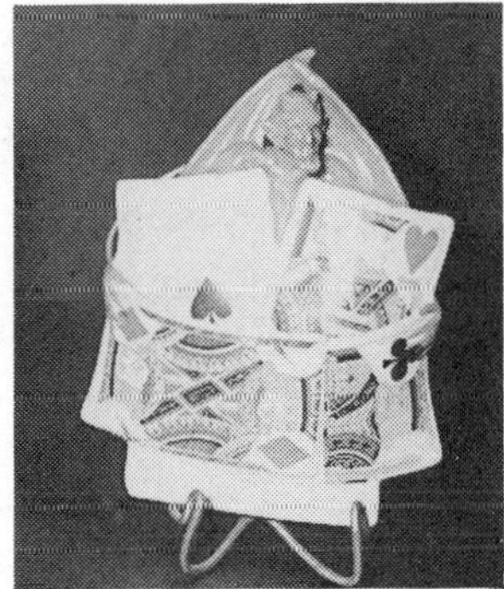

Devil & Cards Match Holder

Match holder, wall-type (ILLUS.) 525.00

Match holder, wall type, full figure style 1,800.00

Mug, beer-type 425.00

Pitcher, milk, 5" h...............350.00 to 400.00

Pitcher, water, 7¼" h. ....550.00 to 600.00

Stamp box, cov., 3½" l.......................800.00

MOTHER-OF-PEARL FINISH

Bowl, 9" d., conch shell mold, pearlized white w/black highlights.............50.00

Bowl, nut, poppy mold, pearlized finish 110.00

Cracker jar, cov., grape cluster mold, pearlized white finish ....425.00 to 450.00

Creamer, grape cluster mold, pearlized finish.................................145.00

Creamer, Oyster & Pearl mold 335.00

Creamer, poppy mold, lavender pearlized finish.................................150.00

Gravy boat & underplate, conch shell mold, pearlized white w/black highlights, 2 pcs. 60.00

Hatpin holder, octagonal, scalloped rim w/gold scroll trim, pearlized finish 135.00

Marmalade jar, cov., grape cluster mold, pearlized yellow finish...........350.00

Nappy, Oyster & Pearl mold, large.....250.00

Pitcher, 4" h., 2¾ x 6¼", Murex Shell patt., pearlized finish exterior (unmarked) 79.00

Plate, 5½" d., oak leaf mold.................80.00

Platter, 5 x 7", grape & leaf mold, white pearlized finish 135.00

Salt & pepper shakers, figural grape cluster, white satin finish, pr............120.00

Salt & pepper shakers, grape cluster mold, pearlized red finish, pr...........160.00

Sugar bowl, cov., grape cluster mold, pearlized finish................................165.00

Sugar bowl, cov., poppy mold, white pearlized finish................................575.00

ROSE TAPESTRY

Rose Tapestry Chocolate Pot

Basket, three-color roses, 4½" w., 4" h...285.00

Basket, two-color roses, 4¼" w., 3¾" h..............................350.00 to 375.00

Basket, footed, drapery chain of buds on base w/handle & base cut-outs, 5½" h...455.00

Bell w/wooden clapper, pink roses decoration on white background, gold handle 395.00

Box, cov., oval, one-color roses, 4" l..235.00

Box, cov., three-color roses, 2½" sq..275.00

Box, cov., two-color roses, 3¼" d., 2¼" h...275.00

Cake plate, three-color roses, free-form fancy rim w/gold beading, 9½" w. 365.00

Cake plate, pierced gold handles, three-color roses, 10½" d................450.00

Chocolate pot, cov., footed, four-color roses, gold trim, 8½" h. (ILLUS.)...2,000.00

Clock, two-color roses, German works (runs) 1,200.00

Creamer, pinched spout, three-color roses, 3" h. 195.00

Creamer, three-color roses, 3¼" h. 175.00

Creamer, pinched spout, two-color roses, 3½" h. 195.00

Creamer, corset-shaped, three-color roses, 3¾" h. 195.00

Creamer, pinched spout, three-color roses, 4" h. 275.00

Dish, leaf-shaped, three-color roses...195.00

Dresser tray, rectangular, two-color roses, 10" l. 325.00

Rose Tapestry Dresser Tray

Dresser tray, rectangular, three-color roses, 8 x 11½" (ILLUS.)..................350.00

Hair receiver, cov., one-color rose......225.00

Rose Tapestry Hair Receiver

Hair receiver, cov., three-color roses (ILLUS.) ....250.00 to 300.00

Hatpin holder, two-color roses, scrolled base, 4½" h. 275.00

Hatpin holder, three-color roses, scrolled base, 4½" h. ....400.00 to 450.00

Pitcher, milk, 4" h., three-color roses..185.00

Rose Tapestry Pitcher

Pitcher, 4¼" h., pinched spout, three-color roses (ILLUS.) 285.00

Pitcher, water, 5⅞" h., pinched spout, three-color roses 610.00

Plate, 6" d., red roses & daisies..........125.00

Plate, 6" d., three-color roses 180.00

Powder box, cov., one-color rose, 4" d.................................175.00 to 200.00

Sauce dishes, red roses & green & yellow leaves, 5¾" d., pr. 250.00

SAND BABIES

Creamer, spherical body w/narrow, short neck, decorated w/three children running, pastel ground, gold handle, 2¼" d. 3" h.............................75.00

Dish, clover-shaped, 4¼" w. 159.00

Dish, diamond-shaped, 4¼" w. 135.00

Dish, star-shaped, 4¼" w....................155.00

Feeding dish, 7¼" d...........................145.00

Plate 125.00

Vase, miniature, 3" h., babies running, silver collar...98.00

SNOW BABIES

Candleholder, shield-back, handled ....225.00 to 250.00

Creamer, squatty 135.00

Inkwell, cov., w/original paper label....375.00

Nappy, handled, curled-in sides, 3½ x 5" 110.00

Plate, 9" d. 140.00

Sugar shaker, scene of children sledding 125.00

Teapot, cov. 225.00

Vase, 3¼" h., footed, shell-molded around top......................................100.00

Vase, 3¾" h., three-handled, silver rim 130.00

SUNBONNET BABIES

Sunbonnet Babies Plate

Candlestick, babies mending, 4¼" h..325.00

Candy dish, 5" d. 265.00

Creamer, babies ironing, 4" h..................................150.00 to 175.00

Creamer, babies mending, 4" h. 200.00

Creamer, babies washing, 4" h..................................150.00 to 175.00

Creamer, tankard-type, babies washing, 4" h. 290.00

Creamer & open sugar bowl, babies washing & mending, pr. 395.00

Dish, cov., club-shaped, babies fishing 265.00

Hatpin holder, bulbous body w/saucer base, babies cleaning 495.00

Mug, babies cleaning, 2¾" h. 195.00

Pin tray, babies cleaning, 4" sq. 15.00

Plate, 6" d., babies cleaning 110.00

Plate, 8¼" d., babies washing (ILLUS.) 100.00

TOMATO ITEMS

Tomato box, cov., 3¾" d.......................51.00

Tomato box, cov., 4½" d.......................45.00

Tomato creamer, cov., small 65.00

Tomato creamer, cov., large...............115.00

Tomato cup, demitasse 65.00

Tomato gravy boat...............................95.00

Tomato mustard jar, cov.......................85.00

Tomato Mustard Jar & Underplate

Tomato mustard jar, cover, leaf-shaped, spoon & underplate, 4 pcs. (ILLUS.) 150.00

Tomato pitcher, water.........................425.00

Tomato salt & pepper shakers, pr. 110.00

Tomato Sugar Bowl

Tomato sugar bowl, cov. (ILLUS.) 70.00

Tomato teapot, cov., large..................195.00

Tomato teapot, cov., small ....250.00 to 275.00

Tomato tea set: large cov. teapot, creamer & cov. sugar bowl; footed, 3 pcs. ....325.00 to 375.00

MISCELLANEOUS

Ashtray, cows in pasture decoration, 5½" d...95.00

Ashtray, figural clown ....325.00 to 350.00

Ashtray, figural eagle w/talons extending upward, grey 525.00

Ashtray, figural elk.............175.00 to 200.00

Ashtray, flying goose holding a frog in its mouth decoration, blues & orange, unmarked............................475.00

Ashtray, round, hunt scene w/woman riding a horse & hounds, naturalistic colors, 4⅝" d.......................................55.00

Basket, "tapestry," scenic decoration of mountain, cove & cottage, 4½" d., 5" h...395.00

Bell, girl w/dog scene..........................198.00

Bowl, 5½" d., "tapestry," lady portrait, gold trim 145.00

Figural Lobster Bowl

Bowl, 4¾ x 8", figural red lobster (ILLUS.) ....350.00 to 450.00

Bowl, 9" d., figural pansy 295.00

Bowl, 10½" d., figural orchid, decorated w/fuchsia, yellow & gold trim..165.00

Box, cov., egg-shaped w/a four-footed ring base, scenic decoration of mountain buildings & a waterfall, unmarked, 2¾" w., 4" l., 2½" h.........150.00

Boxes, cov., spade-shaped, fox hunt scene w/man & woman...................195.00

Cake plate, open handles, figural orange poppy, 10½" d.....................395.00

Calling card holder, figural clown, red, 6 x 7"...125.00

Candleholder, figural basset hound, black w/red trim...............................450.00

Candleholder w/tray, figural owl 1,000.00

Candlestick, figural clown in seated position, red 1,900.00

Candlestick, figural monk in grey robes holding a jug & candle, unmarked.....................................1,200.00

Candlestick, figural red poppy 850.00

Candlestick, handled, Jack & the Beanstalk decoration 150.00

Candy dish, figural clown...................395.00

Chamberstick, cows in field decoration on green ground............110.00

Chamberstick, shield-back, Ring Around the Rosy decoration 225.00

Chamberstick w/center grip handle & three-footed base, shaded green & yellow ground decorated w/large orange roses 195.00

Charger, Cavalier Musicians decoration, grey ground, 14" d.........425.00

Charger, stag & does winter scene decoration, 12¾" d..........................185.00

Chocolate pot, cov., decorated w/man & dog hunting scene 275.00

Creamer, two-handled, Brittany Girl decoration, 4" h...............................175.00

Creamer, cows scene decoration ....75.00 to 100.00

Creamer, scene of schooner on ocean, black ground, gold handle....195.00

Creamer, pinched spout, goats decoration, 4" h...............................210.00

Creamer, hunting scene decoration, 4½" h...115.00

Creamer, corset-shaped, rooster & hen decoration, 5" h........................125.00

Creamer, figural alligator ....350.00 to 400.00

Creamer, figural apple ....150.00 to 175.00

Creamer, figural bear, brown ....700.00 to 750.00

Creamer, figural bellringer ..250.00 to 300.00

Creamer, figural Bird of Paradise...........................250.00 to 300.00

Creamer, figural bull's head, brown & white 240.00

Creamer, figural bull's head, grey.................................175.00 to 200.00

Creamer, figural butterfly w/closed wings...............................425.00 to 475.00

Creamer, figural butterfly w/open wings...............................350.00 to 400.00

Creamer, figural cat, black ....175.00 to 200.00

Creamer, figural cat handle ....250.00 to 300.00

Creamer, figural chimpanzee, black w/rose beige face, crossed arms & interior..700.00

Figural Chimpanzee Creamer

Creamer, figural chimpanzee, grey (ILLUS.) ....425.00 to 475.00

Creamer, figural chrysanthemum 395.00

Creamer, figural clown, red w/black buttons 225.00

Creamer, figural coachman wearing red coat ....250.00 to 300.00

Creamer, figural cockatoo 550.00

Creamer, figural cow, grey ....225.00 to 250.00

Creamer, figural cow, red 275.00

Figural Crow Creamer

Creamer, figural crow, black w/red beak (ILLUS.)..................200.00 to 250.00

Creamer, figural crow, black w/yellow beak 300.00

Creamer, figural Dachshund dog........200.00

Creamer, figural duck ....150.00 to 200.00

Creamer, figural eagle, black ....300.00 to 325.00

Creamer, figural eagle, brown ....150.00 to 175.00

Creamer, figural elk head, shades of brown & cream, 3½" d., 4¼" h. 125.00

Figural Fish Head Creamer

Creamer, figural fish head (ILLUS.) ....175.00 to 200.00

Creamer, figural flounder....................450.00

Creamer, figural frog...........175.00 to 200.00

Creamer, figural geranium..................495.00

Figural Girl with Basket Creamer

Creamer, figural girl w/basket (ILLUS.) ....750.00 to 850.00

Creamer, figural girl w/pitcher, blue ....700.00 to 750.00

Creamer, figural grape cluster, green 125.00

Creamer, figural grape cluster, purple ....100.00 to 125.00

Creamer, stirrup-type, figural ibex head 700.00

Creamer, figural iris 950.00

Creamer, figural ladybug 675.00

Creamer, figural lamplighter, green, 5½" h. ....300.00 to 325.00

Creamer, figural lemon ....150.00 to 200.00

Creamer, figural lettuce leaf w/figural lobster handle, unmarked 150.00

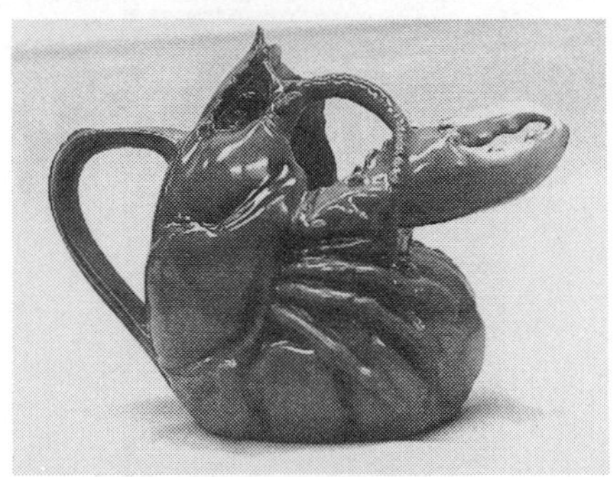

Figural Lobster Creamer

Creamer, figural lobster (ILLUS.) .... 100.00 to 125.00

Creamer, figural maple leaf 350.00

Creamer, figural melon w/morning glory 350.00

Figural Monk Creamer

Creamer, figural monk, brown (ILLUS.) .... 800.00 to 825.00

Creamer, figural monkey, brown .... 375.00 to 400.00

Creamer, figural monkey, green .... 450.00 to 475.00

Creamer, figural mountain goat .... 300.00 to 375.00

Creamer, figural oak leaf 300.00

Creamer, figural Old Man of the Mountain .... 75.00 to 100.00

Creamer, figural orange...... 200.00 to 250.00

Creamer, figural owl .... 375.00 to 400.00

Creamer, figural pansy, dark pink....... 250.00

Creamer, figural parakeet... 225.00 to 250.00

Creamer, figural pear.......................... 475.00

Creamer, figural pelican ..... 325.00 to 350.00

Creamer, figural penguin.... 450.00 to 500.00

Creamer, figural pig, grey 650.00

Creamer, figural pig, red, unmarked... 700.00

Creamer, figural platypus .... 900.00 to 1,000.00

Figural Poodle Creamer

Creamer, figural Poodle dog (ILLUS.) .... 200.00 to 225.00

Creamer, figural poppy, pink 195.00

Creamer, figural poppy, red.................................... 150.00 to 175.00

Creamer, figural red parrot handle, 5" h.. 250.00

Creamer, figural robin......................... 175.00

Creamer, figural rooster, black 325.00

Creamer, cov., figural rose, pink .... 400.00 to 450.00

Creamer, figural St. Bernard dog.................................. 175.00 to 200.00

Creamer, figural Santa Claus 2,900.00

Creamer, figural seal .... 325.00 to 350.00

Creamer, figural seashell w/coral handle, tall .... 125.00 to 150.00

Creamer, figural seashell w/lobster handle .... 100.00 to 125.00

Creamer, figural seashell w/seahorse handle .... 250.00 to 275.00

Creamer, figural straw-berry................................ 175.00 to 225.00

Creamer, figural trout, 4" h. 175.00

Creamer, figural turtle......................... 600.00

Creamer, figural water buffalo, grey .... 225.00 to 275.00

Creamer, figural water buffalo, black w/orange horns & trim, 3½ x 6", 4" h.. 150.00

Creamer & cov. sugar bowl, figural pansy, lavender, pr. 375.00

Creamer & cov. sugar bowl, figural

Creamer & cov. sugar bowl, figural parrot, pr. 265.00

Creamer & cov. sugar bowl, Brittany Girl decoration, pr. 85.00

Creamer & cov. sugar bowl, cows decoration on shaded lavender ground, pr. 125.00

Cup & saucer, demitasse, figural apple 175.00

Cup & saucer, demitasse, figural rose, gold ....400.00 to 475.00

Cup & saucer, demitasse, figural shell 150.00

Cup & saucer, stag & doe in winter scene 65.00

Dish, cov., figural turtle, 6"..................325.00

Dish, canoe-shaped, handled, stag & doe in winter scene, 9½" l.................95.00

Dish, spade shaped, stag & doe in winter scene, 5¼" l.............................65.00

Dish, three rolled-up sides, stag & doe in winter scene, 5½" w.......................75.00

Dresser tray, "tapestry," courting couple decoration, 7 x 11" 475.00

Dresser tray, "tapestry," raging waterfall scene, 7 x 11"....................550.00

Ewer, bulbous base tapering to small mouth, scenic design of four sheep on hillside, green background, 4" h....95.00

Ewer, "tapestry," scene of castle on mountain w/ladies by pond at mountain base, blue & green ground, gold trim, unmarked, 2¼" d., 3½" h. 225.00

Humidor, cov., "tapestry," scene of a woman leaning on horse, 6½" h...1,675.00

Match holder, hanging-type, candle girl decoration 250.00

Match holder, hanging-type, figural red clown ....300.00 to 325.00

Match holder w/striker, figural Santa Claus (slight damage)..................2,200.00

Match holder, hanging-type, figural stork 260.00

Match holder, hanging-type, man working w/two horses scene on cup, cottage scene background..............150.00

Match holder, hanging-type, nursery rhyme scene & verse w/Little Miss Muffet..325.00

Match holder, hanging-type, "tapestry," Cavalier Musicians scene.........345.00

Mayonnaise dish, cover & underplate, figural red poppy, the set 525.00

Model of a lady's shoe, "tapestry," courting couple scene decoration....600.00

Model of a lady's shoe, "tapestry," decorated w/violets, original shoe lace 750.00

Figural Elk Beer Mug

Mug, beer, figural elk, 5¾" h. (ILLUS.) 650.00

Mug, nursery rhyme scene w/Jack and the Beanstalk 95.00

Mug, nursery rhyme scene w/Jack & Jill, 3" h. 150.00

Mug, peacock in foliage decoration, 3½" h...75.00

Mustard jar, cov., figural apple, green...............................200.00 to 225.00

Mustard jar, cov., figural lobster 165.00

Mustard jar, cov., figural pansy...........250.00

Mustard jar, cov., figural poppy 200.00

Mustard jar, cov., figural shell............145.00

Nappy, clover-shaped, ring handled, "tapestry," scene of cottage, waterfall w/rocks, mountains, gold trim.....235.00

Nappy, handled, spade-shaped, nursery rhyme scene w/Little Jack Horner...135.00

Nut cup, master size, figural poppy 150.00

Pin dish, figural turtle 500.00

Pin dish, cov., heart-shaped, scene of sheep decoration, 4¾" d. 50.00

Pin tray, Brittany Girl decoration, 3½ x 5"..50.00

Pin tray, rectangular w/cut corners, Hunt scene w/rider & hounds, 3½ x 5"..50.00

Pitcher, 2¾" h., 2¼" d., ovoid body w/short cylindrical neck, gold handle, scene of Dutch boy flying

Small Royal Bayreuth Pitcher & Vase

kite w/dog at his heels, blue & brown ground (ILLUS. left) 55.00

Pitcher, 3⅜" h., 1⅛" d., tapering cylindrical body, double-handled, scene of lady in purple dress walking w/gentleman, pastel cream, blue & green ground 55.00

Pitcher, 4" h., Brittany Girl decoration...95.00

Pitcher, 4" h., decorated w/a scene of fisherman in boat 135.00

Pitcher, 4¼" h., pinched spout, scene of two cows 90.00

Pitcher, 5½" h., stork decoration on yellow ground....................75.00

Pitcher, 5½" h., decorated w/a scene of hounds pursuing a stag in a marshy landscape against a green ground....................185.00

Pitcher, lemonade, 7¾" h., figural lemon 395.00

Pitcher, milk, figural alligator....................550.00

Pitcher, milk, figural apple 225.00

Pitcher, milk, figural coachman....................775.00

Pitcher, milk, 4½" h., figural clown, yellow....................600.00 to 650.00

Pitcher, milk, figural elk....................235.00

Pitcher, milk, 5½" h., figural fish head....................185.00

Pitcher, milk, 4¾" h., figural oak leaf ..295.00

Pitcher, milk, 4" h., figural owl ....400.00 to 500.00

Pitcher, milk, 5¼" h., figural Santa Claus (ILLUS. top next column) 3,500.00

Pitcher, milk, figural St. Bernard dog, unmarked....................300.00

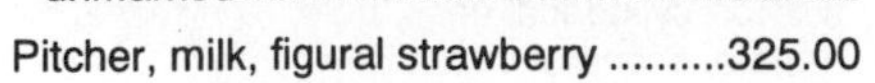

Pitcher, milk, figural strawberry 325.00

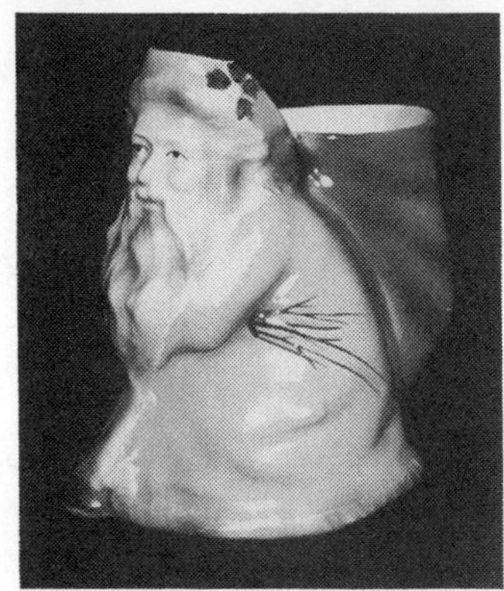

Rare Santa Claus Milk Pitcher

Cavalier Musicians Pitcher

Pitcher, milk, Cavalier Musicians scene decoration (ILLUS.) 225.00

Pitcher, milk, 5½" h., Hunt scene decoration 165.00

Pitcher, water, 6" h., figural apple.......875.00

Pitcher, water, 6½" h., figural clown ...895.00

Pitcher, water, figural coach-man ....750.00 to 800.00

Pitcher, water, 7¼" h., figural conch shell 225.00

Pitcher, water, figural eagle 1,900.00

Pitcher, water, 7" h., figural elk ....400.00 to 450.00

Pitcher, water, 7" h., figural orange....................700.00 to 800.00

Pitcher, water, 6½" h., figural red parrot handle....................550.00

Pitcher, water, 6½" h., figural poppy...795.00

Pitcher, water, 7" h., figural Santa Claus....................3,100.00

Pitcher, water, 7" h., Jester pictured & "Never say die - Up man and try".....375.00

Pitcher, water, 8" h., three cows & calf scene 295.00

Pitcher, 7" h., fighting cocks scene decoration 90.00

Pitcher, 7" h., sheep scene.................110.00

Pitcher, 8" h., pinched spout, Hunt scene decoration w/rider & hounds 110.00

Planter, handled, horsemen decoration 55.00

Planter, figural oak leaf, small 155.00

Planter, "tapestry," woodland & mountain scene w/deer in a stream & gazebo in background, small........175.00

Plate, 4½" d., full figure red devil against a black clock face................575.00

Plate, 4½" d., full figure red devil against a white clock face w/black Roman numerals 575.00

Plate, 6" d., Hunt scene decoration......75.00

Plate, dessert, 6" d., stag & doe in winter scene.......................................45.00

Plate, 6½" d., nursery rhyme scene w/Little Bo Peep & rhyme 125.00

Plate, 7" d., ring-handled, figural apple leaf in green w/yellow blossoms at edge 33.00

Plate, 7½" d., figural purple pansy......225.00

Plate, 7½" d., scene of girl w/dog on leash 100.00

Plate, 8" d., nursery rhyme scene w/Jack & Jill 135.00

Plate, 9" d., scenic decoration of man resting w/draft horse 110.00

Plate, 10½" d., pierced handles, stag & doe winter scene 165.00

Ramekins w/underplates, decorated w/pink roses w/leaves, wide embossed gold trim, six sets, 12 pcs. 175.00

Relish dish, open-handled, courtship scene decoration, 4 x 8¼" 200.00

Salt & pepper shakers, figural apple, pr...75.00

Salt & pepper shakers, figural elk head, pr...160.00

Salt & pepper shakers, figural grape cluster, purple, pr. 110.00

Salt & pepper shakers, figural lobster, pr...110.00

Salt & pepper shakers, figural radish, pr...185.00

Salt & pepper shakers, figural seashell, multicolored glaze, pr. 170.00

Salt dip, figural pansy ....100.00 to 125.00

Salt dip, figural lobster claw.................90.00

Salt dip, four reticulated panels & one w/a scene depicting a woman feeding chickens, 3" d. 125.00

Salt shaker, figural bellringer (unmarked) 250.00

Salt shaker, figural lemon (unmarked) 85.00

Shaving mug, figural elk .....450.00 to 550.00

Stirrup cup, figural elk head................550.00

Rooster String Holder

String holder, hanging-type, figural rooster head (ILLUS.) 350.00

Sugar bowl, cov., figural apple, 3½" h...100.00

Sugar bowl, cov., figural grape cluster, purple ....125.00 to 150.00

Sugar bowl, cov., figural pansy...........235.00

Sugar bowl, cov., figural strawberry (unmarked) 95.00

Table set: creamer, cov. sugar bowl, salt & pepper shakers; figural grape cluster, purple, artist-signed, 4 pcs. 325.00

Teapot, cov., "tapestry," Arab & horses scene, blue ground, 5" h. 149.00

Teapot, cov., scene of girl w/dog on leash, 5½" h. 180.00

Teapot, cov., decorated w/cottage & cow scene, 7" h...............................245.00

Teapot, cov., side handle, boy & donkey decoration, 7¼" h. 125.00

Teapot, cov., scenic decoration of hunter w/turkeys 95.00

Tea strainer, figural poppy, red (unmarked) 300.00

Tea tray, nursery rhyme scene w/Little Boy Blue, verse & holly border, 7¾ x 11" 325.00

Toothpick holder, basket-shaped w/square mouth & overhead handle, Dutch children in sailboat scene 145.00

Toothpick holder, dice-shaped, table tennis scenes on sides, 2½" h. 950.00

Toothpick holder, figural bell ringer, 3" h. 425.00

Toothpick holder, figural elk head ....125.00 to 175.00

Toothpick holder, Goose Girl decoration (unmarked) 125.00

Toothpick holder, spherical body w/applied gold handles, Hunt scene w/man & woman on horses w/hounds, 2¾" d., 3¾" h. 125.00

Toothpick holder, three-footed, jester pictured & "More than enough is too much" (unmarked) 600.00

Toothpick holder, pedestal base, decorated w/lavender roses & butterflies 145.00

Toothpick holder, three-handled, Goose Girl decoration 145.00

Toothpick holder, three-handled, Hunt scene w/rider & hounds 78.00

Toothpick holder, three-handled, moose & dogs scene decoration 300.00

Toothpick holder, urn-shaped, three-handled, scene of Dutch girl walking w/little white dog 135.00

Tumbler, "tapestry," castle by the lake scene, 3¾" h. 200.00

Tumbler, "tapestry," wooded scene w/deer in stream & gazebo in background 225.00

Vase, 3" h., 2½" d., spherical body tapering to a short cylindrical neck, lady dressed in pink & white & holding a candlestick decoration, silver rim 75.00

Vase, 3" h., 2⅝" d., conical body tapering to a silver rim, small loop handles at the shoulder, decorated w/a scene of a Dutch lady carrying a basket, a sailboat in the distance, shaded blue to white to brown ground (ILLUS. right top next column) 55.00

Small Royal Bayreuth Vases

Vase, 3½" h., 2" d., conical body w/flared rim issuing four small loop handles, Hunt scene w/rider & hounds (unmarked) 45.00

Vase, 3½" h., 2" d., footed conical body tapering to a swelled neck flanked by four loop handles, decorated w/a scene of two peasant women & lambs by a lake, natural colors (ILLUS. w/pitcher, right) 55.00

Vase, 3½" h., 2" d., footed conical body tapering go a swelled neck flanked by four loop handles, decorated w/a Hunt scene, lady on horseback w/hounds (unmarked) 45.00

Vase, 3½" h., 4¼" d., ring-handled, ruffled rim, nursery rhyme scene w/Little Miss Muffet 165.00

Vase, 4" h., 4½" d., squatty bulbous base flanked by small loop handles, a tall slender swelled cylindrical neck w/silver rim, scene of two sheep on a shaded green to grey ground (ILLUS. left) 60.00

Vase, 4" h., bulbous base, "tapestry" castle scene 110.00

Vase, 4¼" h., nursery rhyme scene w/Little Boy Blue decoration 160.00

Vase, 4¼" h., scenic decoration of man w/dog hunting ducks 225.00

Vase, 4½" h., footed, handled, "tapestry," boy & turkeys decoration 250.00

Vase, 5½" h., decorated w/a scene of a fisherman 110.00

Vase, 6" h., handled, "tapestry," castle scene decoration 310.00

Vase, 6¾" h., two-handled, lady w/hat decoration 140.00

Wall pocket, figural grape cluster, pink 175.00

Wall pocket, pictures a jester & "Penny in Pocket," 9" h. 550.00

ROYAL BONN & BONN

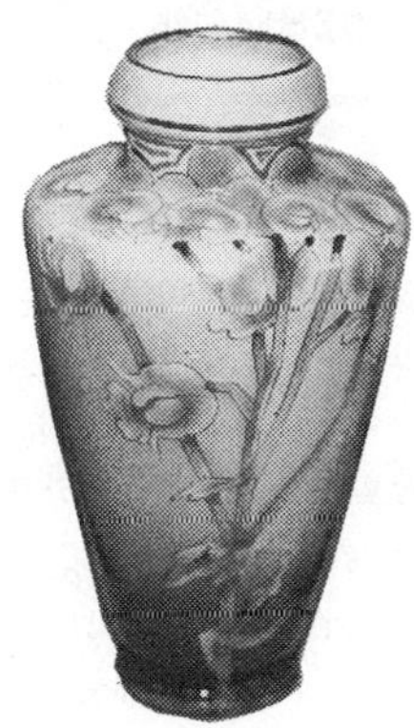

Floral Decorated Royal Bonn Vase

Bonn and subsequently Royal Bonn china were produced in Bonn, Germany, in a manufactory established in 1755. Later wares made there are often marked Mehlem or bear the initials FM or a castle mark. Most wares were of the hand-painted type. Clock cases were also made in Bonn.

Ewer, scrolled gold handle, decorated w/large multicolored flowers on front & back, raised gold veins & outlining, 4" d., 10½" h. $155.00

Ewer, decorated w/pink & blue flowers & gold tracery on a cream ground, gold trim around neck & handle, 13" h. 485.00

Pitcher, 6½" h., decorated w/pink & gold flowers & leaves 65.00

Sardine box, cov., floral decoration w/figural sardine handle 75.00

Umbrella stand, cylindrical w/flaring base, decorated w/large iris blossoms & foliage in shades of blue, yellow & green base & top relief-molded w/a scrolling foliate design, 11" d., 18" h. (professional touch-up) 395.00

Vase, 5½" h., decorated w/colorful pansies on a maroon shaded to yellow ground 75.00

Vase, 6⅝" h., tapering rounded cylindrical body w/low molded rim, decorated overall w/Art Nouveau stylized colorful floral sprigs in red, orange, yellow & green against a pale blue & reddish orange ground, ca. 1905, base marked "Royal Bonn Old Dutch Germany - 265 - 1997 - 12"...385.00

Vase, 7½" h., 4" d., tapering ovoid body w/a short closed neck, soft gold flowers on a pale blue & pink ground, gold trim, late 19th c. 75.00

Vase, 7½" h., 7½" d., wide ovoid body tapering to a wide flat mouth, molded handles, decorated w/flower garden scene, cast-iron fence & two large cast-iron pots filled w/flowers sitting on the two posts 395.00

Vase, 8" h., 3⅞" d., expanding cylinder w/sharply angled shoulder, short wide neck, decorated w/golden yellow flowers against a pink shading to blue ground, gold trim (ILLUS.) 65.00

Vase, 11¼" h., decorated w/pink & yellow roses against a green & yellow ground, gold trim, ca. 1900, red crown mark, Franz Anton Mehlem Porcelain Factory 275.00

Vase, 12" h., 6¼" d., tall footed ovoid body w/a flaring scalloped rim, small double-loop handles, decorated w/Worcester-style pink & blue flowers w/gold trim on a beige satin ground, gold handles, late 19th c.....175.00

Vase, 27" h., baluster-form body w/applied gilt dragon handles, raised on molded gilt scroll feet, decorated w/a scene of three gentlemen observing an artist painting in his studio, the reverse w/a formal garden landscape w/a marble stairway, artist-signed 1,980.00

Vase, 50" h., slender elongated baluster-form body w/a tall flaring neck, the bottom fitted into a leafy petal-form gilt cup above a short pedestal w/an everted ring over the flaring foot set in a gilt molded base w/four scroll feet, a flaring & scroll-molded rim on the neck & applied, knotted cord gilt handles on the shoulder, the sides decorated w/large pink & yellow roses against

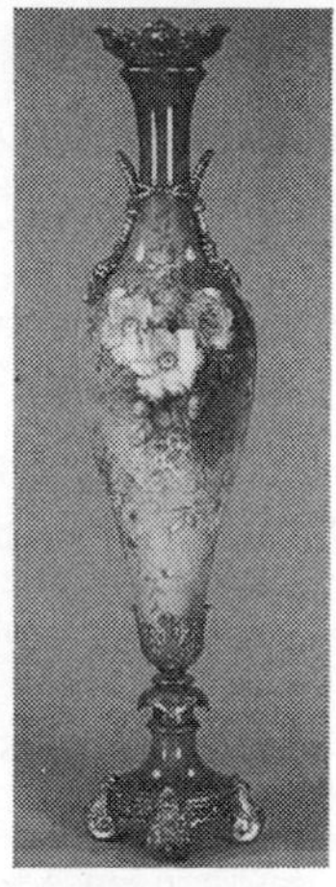

Very Large Royal Bonn Vase

a shaded green ground, artist-signed, late 19th c. (ILLUS.) 3,300.00

Vases, 10¾" h., flask-form w/applied reticulated gold handles, the creamy ground decorated w/blossoms on gilt stems, pr. 121.00

Vases, 18" h., baluster-form, decorated w/farm scenes, stamped & impressed marks, pr. 880.00

ROYAL COPENHAGEN

Large Royal Copenhagen Vase

This porcelain has been made in Copenhagen, Denmark, since 1715. The ware is hardpaste.

Figure of a boy whittling, No. 905.....$195.00

Figure of a boy w/a ball, No. 3542........95.00

Figure of a boy w/a calf, No. 772........290.00

Figure of a boy w/a gourd, No. 4539..225.00

Figure of a boy w/a horn, No. 3689....108.00

Figure of a farm girl, No. 815..............375.00

Figure of a faun & bear wrestling, No. 648 ....350.00

Figure of a faun on a pedestal, No. 433 ....275.00

Figure of a faun playing pipes, No. 1736 ....265.00

Figure of a faun riding a bear, No. 1804 ....585.00

Figure of a faun w/lizard on column, No. 433, 8½" h. 303.00

Figure of a girl w/a calf, No. 779.........290.00

Figure of a little girl w/doll, No. 3539, 5¾" h...40.00

Figure, Goose Girl, No. 528, 7" h. 150.00

Figure of a mermaid, artist-signed, No. 4431 ....390.00

Figure of a milkmaid, No. 899............425.00

Figure of a nude on a rock, No. 4027 ....140.00

Figure of young Pan w/his goat, No. 1012-498 ....225.00

Figure, Sandman, No. 1129 ....250.00

Figure group, two doves on a branch, 5¾" h...60.00

Model of a calf, brown & white, No. 1072 ....140.00

Model of an Icelandic falcon, No. 263 ....300.00

Model of a kitten lying on back playing w/tail, grey & white, No. 727 ....47.00

Model of a koala bear, No. 5402 ....275.00

Model of a polar bear, No. 1137.........180.00

Model of a rabbit, No. 4676................245.00

Model of a seal, No. 1441, 5" h. 110.00

Teapot, cov., Flora Danica patt. 1,475.00

Vase, cov., 29¼" h., wide footed ovoid body w/the wide shoulder tapering to a short neck supporting a high domed pierced cover w/a crenelated finial, the body cast around the shoulders w/clusters of lilacs & modeled in low-relief w/chestnut leaves, the pierced lid w/carved foliage, decorated on the lower sides w/a scene of a swan family on each side, cobalt blue base, decorated by Vilhelm T. Fischer, ca. 1910, marked, restorations (ILLUS.) 8,050.00

Vase, "Langlelinie" (Girl on Rock), No. 4576 ....185.00

ROYAL CROWN POTTERY

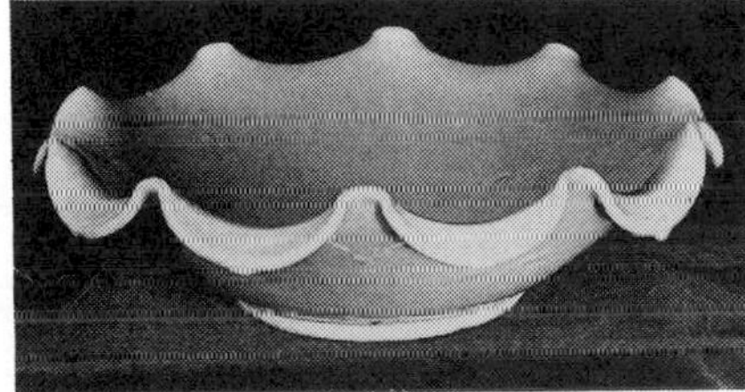

Royal Crown Bowl

The Royal Crown Pottery and Porcelain Company, Merry Oak, North Carolina was in business from 1939-1942. Victor and Henry Obler were Russian immigrants who became silversmiths in New York but it was Victor who pursued the pottery business. Despite the name of his company, there have been no records found proving that any porcelain products were made and no examples have been found. However, Victor was able to create some remarkable glazes for his pottery with the help of Jack Kiser, Charlie Craven and Leslie Stanley. Many colors were used: black, blue, Colonial cream, enamel green, golden brown, maroon, moss green, Spanish moss, turquoise, white, and yellow. Harder to find glazes are light blue or pink and also 'rainbow' finishes on blue, white, turquoise or black backgrounds. Vases were the biggest money maker for Royal Crown due, in part, to Obler furnishing vases to the New York Florist Association. Some of Obler's vases, especially the handled pieces, are similar to George Ohr products. Catalogs have been found indicating Royal Crown also made miniatures but, because they were probably not marked, none have been attributed to this company. Almost all the other pottery items were marked.

Basket, footed, flared sides w/crimped rim ends, center handle, yellow glaze, 8½" d., 11" h. $68.00

Bowl, 10" d., 2½" h., round w/oblong handles, yellow glaze, Model No. 34 ....34.00

Bowl, 14" d., 4" h., deep sides w/crimped edges, moss green glaze (ILLUS.) 85.00

Ewer, bulbous body tapering to short neck w/three bands, twig handle from center of body & rising slightly above rim, Colonial cream glaze, 16" h. 185.00

Pitcher, milk, 6" h., bulbous, maroon glaze 27.00

Royal Crown Vase

Vase, 5" h., bulbous body tapering gently to a short neck w/scalloped rim, moss green glaze (ILLUS.) 45.00

Vase, 7" h., conical w/handles at bottom, maroon glaze 38.00

Vase, 9" h., 4½" d., classic shape w/four rings at base tapering to a tall neck, handles from center of body to rim, Model No. 1210 ....85.00

Vase, 11" h., globular w/thin, flat rim, molded ring handles, rainbow finish 125.00

Vase, 15" h., 5½" d., baluster shape, twisted shoulder handles 110.00

Vase, 16" h., 7" d., baluster shape w/shoulder to rim handles, golden brown glaze 95.00

ROYAL DUX

This factory in Bohemia was noted for the figural porcelain wares in the Art Nouveau style which were exported around the turn of the century. Other notable figural pieces were produced through the 1930s and the factory was nationalized after World War II.

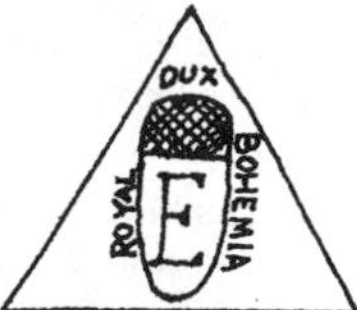

Bust of a Victorian woman, lavish lace trim on hat & dress, pastel decoration, parian finish, 16" h. $550.00

Centerpiece, figural, the oblong bulbous bowl molded in high-relief pods w/long undulating leaves, centered by a large full-figure model of a seated classical maiden w/a dove on one arm, pierced branch-form base band, glazed in solid olive green & pink w/gold & beige trim, triangular tag & impressed marks, ca. 1900, 13¼" h. 880.00

Centerpiece, figural, a large oblong shell-form shallow bowl fitted at one end w/a large seated figure of an Art Nouveau maiden w/flowing hair & robe, raised on a blossom & branch pedestal base w/another full-figure maiden clinging to one side, cream glaze trimmed in gold & grey, triangular tag & impressed marks, ca. 1900, 15" h. 770.00

Centerpiece, figural, shallow cobalt blue bowl w/gilt trim supported on the shoulders of a maiden & putti on a circular swirling base, 20" h. 500.00

Centerpiece, figural, a tall full-figure running classical maiden in flowing robe centering a pair of large, deep bowl-form lotus leaves on long stems flanking a tall lily-form blossom at the back, all on an oval base, cream glaze trimmed w/gilt & grey, triangular tag & incised marks, ca. 1900, 21" h. 715.00

Centerpiece, figural, cast as a young maiden seated on the edge of a large shell carried by two long-haired tritons over cresting waves & water foliage, glazed in tones of olive green, pale puce & ivory trimmed w/gold, applied triangular mark & impressed numbers, ca. 1900, 23¼" h. 1,725.00

Dish, figural, molded as a harem lady in an elaborate costume w/decorated bodice, openwork midriff & flaring skirt, her arms lifted as she dances on tip-toe, long lengths of ribbons trailing into the clover leaf-form dish below, its edges molded in full-relief w/clusters of blossoms, glazed in tones of mustard yellow, cotton-candy pink, lavender, charcoal grey & ivory, trimmed w/gilt, applied triangular mark & impressed & incised numbers, ca. 1900, 10⅞" h. 690.00

Figure of a seated nude girl w/a butterfly on her knee, pink triangle mark, 8½" h. 165.00

Figure of a girl at a waterfall, the lovely young woman dressed in flowing robes, pink triangle mark, 12½" h. 995.00

Figure of a sheepherder, pink triangle mark, 16½" h. 895.00

Figure of Cupid, bisque, depicted w/his arm in a sling, 21" h. 550.00

Figure group, depicting two children w/basket, matte finish, pink triangle mark, 8½" h. 450.00

Figure group, mother w/child near woven basket, pink triangle mark, 8½" h. 425.00

Figure group, two coachmen converse w/a lady in a coach, raised on an oval plinth, trimmed in green, gold & pink, 15½" h. 220.00

Figure group, woman w/basket on one arm, the other arm raised to her shoulder, a young child standing to one side, on an oval base, pink triangle mark, 16" h. 695.00

Figure group, model of a sea shell w/a woman seated at the top & another clinging to the side of the shell, 17½" 500.00

Figure group, cloaked Harlequin

male dancer enfolding matching female, artist-signed, No. 294/72, 15 x 20" 875.00

Jardiniere, figural, rectangular, the tapering sides molded in high-relief w/a young girl dressed in a diaphanous pale olive green gown w/a pink shawl about the shoulders, reclining against a blossoming pink poppy, the sides & reverse further molded w/full-blown green & pink poppies, against an off-white ground heightened w/gilt, worn applied triangular mark, impressed & inscribed numerals, ca. 1900, 12" h. 575.00

Model of a cockatoo on limb, white w/pink head, marked, 15" h. 175.00

Model of a dog, German Shepherd, pink triangle mark, No. 458, 8¼" h. 119.00

Model of a dog, Setter, w/pheasant in mouth, "Sportsman's Dream," pink triangle mark, 19" h. 350.00

Model of a polar bear, 10½ x 12½" 575.00

Model of a stallion, black, Art Deco style, pink triangle mark, 6 x 7" 110.00

Vase, 14⅜" h., figural, a long-haired maiden nude but for a flowing length of dusty-rose drapery falling from her neck, astride a moss green & pale pink conch shell, sea-foam green waves & pale pink, ivory & green lotus blossoms & leaves swirling below, applied triangular mark & impressed & incised numbers, ca. 1900 .... 920.00

Vases, 15½" h., ovoid body w/square foot, Art Nouveau style, molded olive tree swirling branches forming two levels of handles, pink triangle mark, pr. 437.00

Vide poche (figural dish), the standing figure of a maiden w/arms folded across her breast wearing a voluminous green gown continuing to form a dish at her feet, glazed in pink & cream, heightened in gilt, impressed applied factory mark, numbered "1313," ca. 1900, 14¾" h. 920.00

ROYAL RUDOLSTADT

This factory began as a faience pottery established in 1720. E. Bohne made hard paste porcelain wares from 1852 to 1920, when the factory became a branch of Heubach Brothers. The factory is still producing in what was East Germany.

Bowl, 6" d., low sides, handled, decorated w/chestnuts on gold to green shaded ground, gilt handles $55.00

Bowl, 6½" d., pierced handles, h.p. floral decoration 20.00

Ewer, gold dragon handles, decorated w/delicate flowers edged w/gold beads, 12" h. 140.00

Figure of young woman w/hands behind back, dressed in peacock blue & pink costume w/lavishly detailed gold decorations, marked "2920 RW" in blue, 18" h. 1,295.00

Plate, 8" d., h.p. flowers w/large rose in center, gold rim 40.00

Plate, serving, 8½" d., decorated w/a border band of light & dark red roses, gilt edging 35.00

Vase, 5" h., two-handled, medallion scene of a castle 50.00

Vase, 9" h., handled, decorated w/pastel wildflowers 65.00

Vase, 9½" h., circular disc-form lower section beneath a tall slender cylindrical neck, the reticulated pale pink front w/a gold center design, the reverse decorated w/purple flowers against a creamy white ground, applied gold handles rising from shoulder to midsection of neck, ca. 1887 .... 195.00

Vase, 14" h., handled, decorated w/roses on a cream & pink ground .. 175.00

ROYAL VIENNA

The second factory in Europe to make hard paste porcelain was established in

Vienna in 1719 by Claud Innocentius de Paquier. The factory underwent various changes of administration through the years and finally closed in 1865. Since then, however, the porcelain has been reproduced by various factories in Austria and Germany, many of which have reproduced also the early beehive mark. Early pieces, naturally, bring far higher prices than the later ones or the reproductions.

Royal Vienna Covered Urn

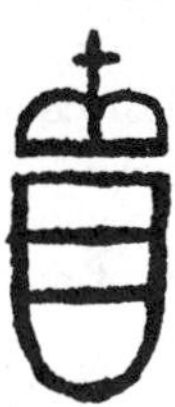

Candlesticks, scenic medallions on maroon & gold ground, signed "Angelica Kauffmann," blue beehive mark, 5½" h., pr. $550.00

Charger, cupid & a maiden surrounded by six cherubs, pseudo beehive mark in black enamel & stamped "CARL KNOLL CARLSBAD 29," ca. 1900, 16½" d. 1,725.00

Charger, central scene depicting a young woman w/children & putti, within a border of gilt-bronze scrolls & latticework, mounted within a circular gilt-bronze foliate frame, signed "Corner," late 19th c., 28½" d. 1,495.00

Cup, three-handled, urn-shaped w/undulating gilt rim, decorated w/children at play within three gilt-dot rimmed medallions on a cream ground, dark green & gilt-patterned foot, applied gilt scroll handles, 20th c., 4" h. 88.00

Demitasse set: cov. pot, cov. creamer, cov. sugar bowl, cups w/deep saucers & a rectangular tray w/cut corners; each of cylindrical form w/angled handles, white decorated w/delicate floral bouquets & wavy ribbon edge bands, late 19th c., tray 11" l., the set 660.00

Figure group, a pair of lovers in 18th c. costume seated beneath a leafy tree w/a lamb at their side, 11" l. 247.50

Figure group, two cherubs representing the Arts studying & reading beneath a palm tree, 12½" h. 302.50

Plaque, decorated w/h.p. white water lilies on shaded ground, narrow gold rim, gold palette mark & green crown mark, 9½" d. 45.00

Plate, 9½" d., the center decorated w/a female figure representing "Spring," framed by a gilt border of medallions & griffins, artist-signed ...330.00

Plate. 9½" w., octagonal, decorated in the center w/a scene of Venus & Adonis, the maroon & gilt patterned paneled rim w/small classical nymphs, artist-signed....................467.50

Plates, 6⅛" d., chocolate brown, gold, blue & pink lustre w/center decoration of two cherubs, beehive mark, Austria, set of 6....................300.00

Urns, cov., each decorated w/a continuous allegorical band surmounted by a removable waisted neck & domed cover, raised on triform legs ending in paw feet, pseudo shield mark in blue enamel, 17½" h., pr. (ILLUS. of one) 5,463.00

Urns, cov., one entitled "Romischer Siegeszug" (Rome under Siege), the other "Romischer Triumphzug" (Rome Triumphant), the foot, neck & lid adorned w/gilt scrolls & animal figures on wine red ground, lionesque applied ormolu handles & pineapple finial, each scene finely painted on a gilt-dot ground, on ormolu mounted square base on four paw feet, each decorated by K. Willnert, 27" h., pr. 17,000.00

Vase, 5" h., 4½" w., triangular, decorated w/a brown bird perched on the corner, green foliate decoration on the front, against a beige satin ground, gold trim, marked "Turn" 95.00

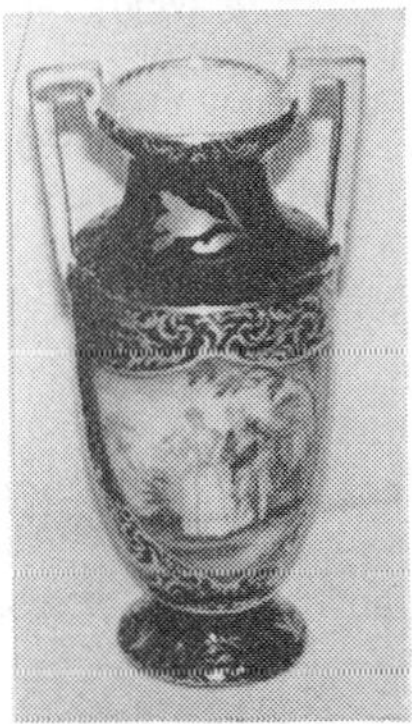

Royal Vienna Scenic Vase

Vase, 6½" h., 3" d., two-handled, low foot, scene of a gentleman & lady reserved within a lacy gilt border against a cobalt blue ground, lavish gold trim & gold handles, underglaze-blue beehive mark (ILLUS.) ...195.00

Vase, 21½" h., ovoid w/short neck & flaring rim, decorated w/a continuous allegorical scene against a cream ground, the neck & base heightened w/gilt, signed "Gorney," pseudo beehive mark in blue enamel & title in black enamel, late 19th c. 4,025.00

Vase, 33¼" h., ovoid w/narrow neck & flaring rim, w/an oval panel depicting a fair-skinned young lady w/hands crossed at her breast, w/gilt highlights on a lustre brown ground, signed "Schmidt," pseudo 'Vienna' beehive mark in blue enamel, titled in red enamel, late 19th c. 6,900.00

Royal Vienna "Bachantan" Vase

Vase, 38" h., "Bachantan," ovoid body raised on a pedestal base, slender neck w/flaring rim, decorated w/a scene of a classically garbed reclining woman on front, the reverse a scene of putti in a garden, gilt decorated dark green lustre ground, 19th c. (ILLUS.)..........................18,700.00

ROYAL WORCESTER

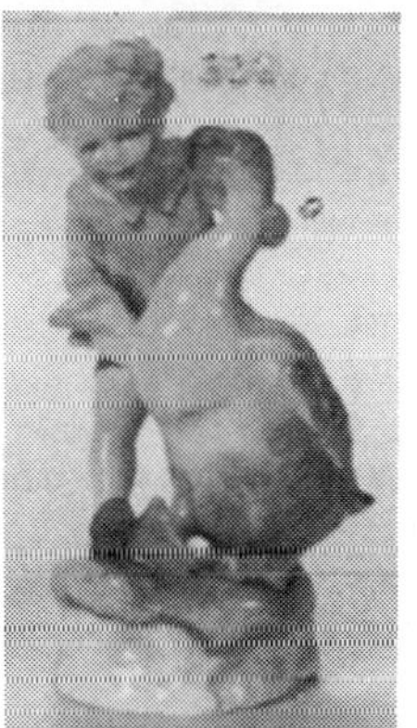

"Goosie Goosie Gander"

This porcelain has been made by the Royal Worcester Porcelain Co. at Worcester, England, from 1862 to the present. For earlier porcelain made in Worcester, see WORCESTER. Royal Worcester is distinguished from those wares made at Worcester between 1751 and 1862 that are referred to as only Worcester by collectors.

Candle snuffer, figural monk.............$115.00

Celery tray, decorated w/apples & purple grapes, gold border, artist-signed, 4¼ x 10" 275.00

Cracker jar, cov., cobalt blue leaves on a white molded bamboo background, matching cover, 5¾" d., 7" h..355.00

Creamer & sugar bowl w/gold wreathed lyres, beribboned lanterns & scrolls, ca. 1906, 4" d., pr. 24.00

Cup & saucer, demitasse, h.p. gold scenes commemorating the state of Maryland against a cream ground, No. RD 117963 ....195.00

Cup & saucer, decorated w/pink, yellow & blue flowers w/gold trim on beige satin ground, cup 3⅜" d., 2½" h., saucer 5⅝" d..........................85.00

Dish, square, decorated w/apples & purple grapes, gold border, artist-signed, 5 x 7" 225.00

Ewer, applied gold leaves & flowers on cream ribbed body w/scrolling, gold spout & handle, ca. 1880, 7" h..450.00

Ewer, melon-form, decorated w/applied gold leaves, gold spout & handle, 7" h....................................435.00

Ewer, overall floral decoration, handle molded as a stalk of bamboo, artist-signed, 10¼" h. 275.00

Ewer, tusk-form w/closed spout & branched antler-form handle, decorated w/gilt & iron-red chrysanthemums & gilt bands, No. 1116, artist-initialed, 11" h. 330.00

Ewer, salamander handle, decorated w/pastel pink blossoms, ivory ground shading to green, impressed mark, No. 226/6 ....175.00

Figure, "The Dandelion," 4¼" h. 100.00

Figure, "Duchess's Dress," designed by F. Doughty, No. 3106..................300.00

Figure, "January" 175.00

Figure, "Sir Walter Raleigh," tan, lavender & ecru, dated 1885, 6½" h...190.00

Figure, "Tommy," designed by F. Doughty, No. 2913, 4½" h...............110.00

Figures, a Mideastern lady playing a tambourine & a companion man w/a stringed instrument, each signed "Hadley," 12½" h., pr.......................825.00

Figure group, "Goosie Goosie Gander," playful young curly-haired child w/one hand on the goose's neck, the goose w/one wing raised & its beak near the child's face, 5½" h. (ILLUS.) 150.00

Jar, cov., footed bulbous ovoid body w/a short wide cylindrical neck supporting a domed reticulated cover w/a bulbous lobed finial w/a pointed tip, the cover & neck w/a molded basketweave design & the lower body & foot also w/molded basketweave, the shoulder & sides h.p. w/a large flock of flying swallows & clusters of colorful wildflowers, gilt trim on the basketweave section & the finial, marked, No. 1286, late 19th c. 8¼" d., 11½" h. 550.00

Model of a Great Tit, No. 335, artist-signed 50.00

Model of a Kingfisher, No. 2666 ....125.00

Model of a Nuthatch, No. 3334, artist-signed 50.00

Model of a Sparrow, No. 3236, artist-signed 50.00

Pitcher w/ice lip, 5¾" h., chased gold w/floral decoration, ca. 1887...........235.00

Royal Worcester Melon-Form Pitcher

Pitcher, 8½" h., melon-form body w/a wide cylindrical leaf-molded neck & spout, gilt leaves continuing to vine handle, the body decorated w/pastel floral sprigs, No. 1369, ca. 1889 (ILLUS.) ....400.00 to 450.00

Pitcher, ice water, 10" h., tusk-form, yellow ground w/stylized gilt florals, No. 1116, ca. 1885 ....265.00

Plate, 9⅛" d., h.p. bird decoration w/red & gold embossed gilded border, artist-signed, No. W-202, ca. 1880 ....75.00

Plate, 10¾" d., h.p. Tewkesbury village scene, artist-signed, ca. 1953...225.00

Plates, 8" d., Granada patt., set of 7 ..100.00

Plates, luncheon, 9¼" d., decorated w/flowers against a pink border, gilt foliate designs, printed mark, ca. 1920, set of 12 ....660.00

Plates, dinner, 10" d., floral center, cobalt blue rim w/scrolling gilt trim, artist-signed, set of 12 ....400.00

Platter, 12½" l., Blue Willow patt...........75.00

Spill vase, Japanese-style, square tapering sides applied w/a model of a climbing frog & molded w/ivy vines, No. 499, ca. 1875, 3½" h. 295.00

Teapot, cov., molded melon-form in the Japanese taste, the lobed creamy body decorated w/gilt & iron-red leaf & stalk forms, 6" h. 247.50

Vase, 2½" h., miniature, decorated w/flowers & gold enameling, cranberry ground 85.00

Vase, 4" h., center decoration of bird in flight, beige ground w/black enamel borders, artist-signed 375.00

Vase, 5½ x 6", sack-shaped, tightly crimped neck w/applied twisted rope & large bow, bulbous base, decorated w/h.p. flowers, leaves & stems on cream ground, gold rim & trim, ca. 1886 ....185.00

Vase, 6½" h., two-handled, reticulated sides w/floral decoration, artist's initials on base, No. 982, ca. 1883 ....225.00

Vase, 7¾" h., ovoid body molded w/a basketweave design & decorated w/applied leafy vines in gold & iron-red, Crown & Circle mark..........302.50

Vase, 8" h., ovoid body on circular foot & applied handles, pale blue w/gilt & iron-red floral decoration, Crown & Circle mark, No. 1654, ca. 1893 ....302.50

Vase, 10¼" h., bulbous body w/a slender tapering neck & applied handles, creamy ground decorated w/flowers in pink, yellow & gold, Crowned Circle mark 247.50

Vase, 13¾" h., bulbous body supporting a cylindrical neck w/reticulated lip, applied gilt handles, decorated w/purple & lavender flowers on gilt branches, Crown & Circle mark, artist-initialed 825.00

ROZENBURG DEN HAAG

This Dutch earthenware and porcelain factory was established in 1855 at The Hague. It is noted for the exceptionally thin earthenware made in the late 19th and early 20th centuries. Subtle shapes and fine enameled decoration combine to make it an exquisite production greatly influenced by the Art Nouveau movement. The ware was marked Rozenburg den Haag with a stork and crown.

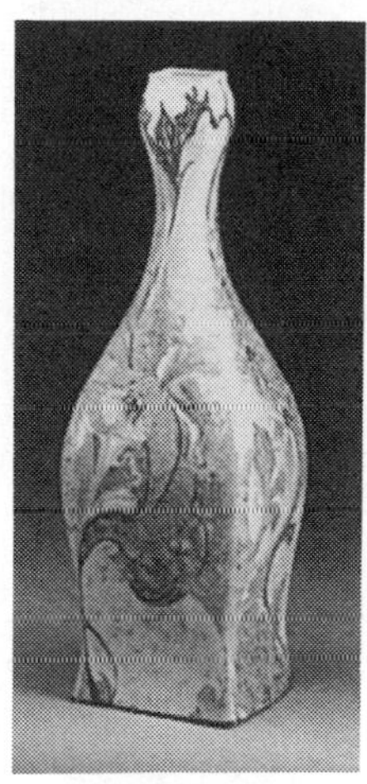

Rozenburg Vase

Cups & saucers, each paneled cup & octagonal saucer finely painted w/various spring flowers including crocuses, irises & lilies, one w/a bird, in rich shades of yellow, blue, lavender & green, decorated by J.M. Van Rosson & J. Schellink, stamped & enameled factory marks, ca. 1904, set of 6 (minor chips) $3,300.00

Plaque, round, decorated w/a symmetrical Art Nouveau design of stylized florals in yellow & grey trimmed w/maroon & brown against a blue ground, inscribed marks & monogram, ca. 1900, 17⅝" d........1,760.00

Vase, 4⅛" h., 2⅝" w., squared base below a swelled slender neck w/a flared square rim, decorated w/yellow flowers trimmed w/red & brown & stylized green leaves all on a white ground, stamped & monogrammed, ca. 1903 (minor staining) 1,980.00

Vase, 10¼" h., baluster-shaped of square section tapering to a slender swelled neck, delicately painted w/polychrome stylized orchid blossoms & leaves in shades of pale green, amber, yellow & burgundy against a green & white ground, printed mark & yearmark for 1901 (ILLUS.) 3,220.00

Vase, 11½" h., wide bulbous baluster-form body w/a narrow neck below a widely flaring cupped rim, decorated overall w/abstract decoration in shades of green, brown & blue, marked "Rosenburg - L. - 401 - Den Haag," ca. 1894 ....1,650.00

R.S. PRUSSIA & RELATED WARES

Ornately decorated china marked "R.S. Germany" and "R.S. Prussia" continues to grow in popularity. According to Clifford J. Schlegelmilch in his book, Handbook of Erdmann and Reinhold Schlegelmilch — Prussia – Germany and Oscar Schlegelmilch – Germany, *Erdmann Schlegelmilch established a porcelain factory in the Germanic provinces at Suhl, in 1861. Reinhold, his younger brother, worked with him until 1869 when he established another porcelain factory in Tillowitz, upper Silesia. China bearing the name of this town is credited to Reinhold Schlegelmilch. It customarily bears also the phrase "R.S. Germany." Now collectors seek additional marks including E.S. Germany, R.S. Poland and R.S. Suhl. Prices are high and collectors should beware the forgeries that sometimes find their way to the market . Mold names and numbers are taken from Mary Frank Gaston's books on R.S. Prussia.*

We illustrate three typical markings, however, there are several others. The "R.S. Prussia" mark has been reproduced in decal form so buy with care.

R.S. GERMANY

Bowl, 9½" d., Cabbage or Lettuce mold (Mold 126), rose decoration on a green ground $225.00

Bowl, 7 x 10½" oval, floral decoration...55.00

Celery tray, Bird of Paradise decoration, 10½" l....................................195.00

Celery tray, two-handled, floral decoration, 13" l. 32.50

Cracker jar, cov., handled, decorated w/yellow roses & greenery, 5" h.......115.00

Creamer & cov. sugar bowl, cobalt blue floral decoration w/gold highlights, 3" h., pr. 75.00

Creamer & cov. sugar bowl, cream & apricot shaded feathery tulips on beige to grey blended ground w/gold trim, pr...47.50

Dessert set: master bowl & six 7" d. matching bowls; Lettuce mold (Mold 12), interior floral decoration, pearlized lustre finish, 7 pcs. 165.00

Dresser tray, snowball floral decoration, gold trim, 8½" d. 100.00

Hatpin holder, Mold 777, decorated w/pink & white roses on earthtone ground, 4½" h. 60.00

Hatpin holder, pussy willow decoration 90.00

Mustard pot, cov., white floral decoration on pastel ground, 3" h. 28.00

Pitcher, tankard, 11½" h., Mold 520, h.p. pink & yellow roses 495.00

Snack set: tray w/cup; parrot decoration, 6¼ x 7½" 150.00

Snack set: tray w/cup; pheasants decoration, 9½" l., 2 pcs. 135.00

Vase, 4" h., scenic decoration of windmill w/stream, house in trees, boy walking in the grass, shadow leaves in background......................125.00

R.S. PRUSSIA

Mold 82 Cake Plate

Basket, Scallop & Fan mold, triple handle, nine scalloped feet w/each further scalloped, roses decoration, glossy finish, 8½" d., 8" h. 450.00

Berry set: 9" l. leaf-shaped master bowl & six sauce dishes; Leaf mold (Mold 10), decorated w/flowers, unmarked, 7 pcs. 495.00

Berry set: 10½" d. master bowl & six sauce dishes; Acorn or Nut mold, pink & red roses decoration, 7 pcs. 495.00

Bowl, 7" d., three-footed, Carnation mold (Mold 28), ivory, blue & pink florals 165.00

Bowl, 8½" d., Icicle mold (Mold 7), decorated w/pears, grapes & plums 300.00

Bowl, 9½" d., Fleur-de-lis mold (Mold 9), fruit decoration 175.00

Bowl, 10" d., Iris mold (Mold 25), Summer Season decoration 4,600.00

Bowl, 10" d., Mold 90, fruit decoration 275.00

Bowl, 10¼" d., 3" h., Mold 95, center decorated w/pink poppies, cobalt blue florals surround the sides 965.00

Bowl, 10½" d., Mold 105, Countess Potocka portrait in center 1,050.00

Bowl, 10½" d., Mold 252, Swans & Gazebo decoration 775.00

Bowl, 10¾" d., Mold 53, Reflecting Water Lilies decoration, satin finish 345.00

Bowl, 11" d., Mold 405, Swans & Evergreens decoration on a shaded lavender ground 395.00

Bowl, 8 x 12½" oval, Mold 343, center floral decoration w/beaded rim, cobalt blue ground, unmarked 450.00

Bun tray, Icicle mold (Mold 7), Sitting Basket decoration 200.00

Cake plate, open-handled, Mold 155, barnyard decoration w/swallows, chickens & duck, 9¾" d. 1,005.00

Cake plate, open-handled, Icicle mold (Mold 7), swan decoration, 10" d. 600.00

Cake plate, open-handled, Mold 259, pink & white roses w/lavender Tiffany coloring, 10" d. 300.00

Cake plate, open-handled, Mold 82, decorated w/flowers on a blue ground, 10¼" d. (ILLUS.) 175.00

Cake plate, open-handled, decorated w/floral center & Tiffany finish on border & inner ring, six cupids on border & two scenes of reclining women w/cupids, 10½" d. (unmarked) 475.00

Cake plate, open-handled, Fleur-de-lis mold (Mold 9), Spring Season decoration, 11" d. 1,400.00

Cake plate, open-handled, Lily mold (Mold 29), large Madame Recamier portrait, green ground w/gold trim, 11" d. 1,095.00

Cake plate, open-handled, Mold 276, decorated w/yellow & brown roses, 11½" d. 50.00

Celery tray, Stippled Floral mold (Mold 23), decorated w/roses, 12" l. 80.00

Celery tray, Mold 304, Man in the Mountain decoration, 6 x 12" 795.00

Celery tray, Lily mold (Mold 29), decorated w/florals, 12½" l. 150.00

Celery tray, Plume mold (Mold 16), Reflecting Poppies & Daisies decoration, green shading, 12½" l. 80.00

Celery tray, Medallion mold (Mold 14), Reflecting Poppies & Daisies decoration, portraits of Diana the Huntress & Flora on each side, 7" w., 14" l. 650.00

Chocolate pot, cov., Iris mold (Mold 25), decorated w/poppies 160.00

Chocolate pot., cov., Mold 454, decorated w/green roses on yellow ground, 11" h. 295.00

Chocolate pot., cov., Mold 501, decorated w/blue florals on a white ground, 10" h. 195.00

Chocolate pot., cov., Mold 520, white snowballs & pink roses decoration on a pale green ground, 10½" h. 325.00

Mold 644 Chocolate Pot

Chocolate pot., cov., Mold 644, floral decoration, 11" h. (ILLUS.) 595.00

Coffeepot, cov., Mold 474, floral decoration, 9" h. (unsigned).............375.00

Cracker jar, cov., Lily mold (Mold 29), decorated w/pink & yellow roses (unmarked) 295.00

Cracker jar, cov., Sunflower mold (Mold 626), footed, pearly white w/green trim, 6½" h...........................275.00

Cracker jar, cov., Mold 933, decorated w/white roses on a fuchsia ground...295.00

Creamer & cov. sugar bowl, Mold 452, swans decoration, satin finish, pr..600.00

Dessert set, child's: six cups & saucers & handled cookie plate; Mold 550, pink & white floral decoration on pastel blue & white ground (unsigned)............................135.00

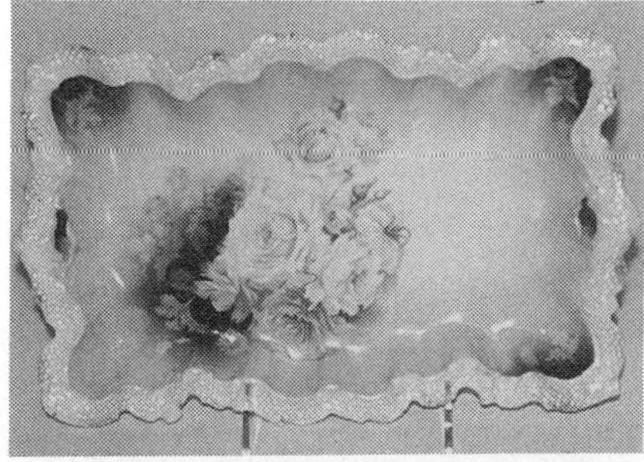

Stippled Floral Dresser Tray

Dresser tray, Stippled Floral mold (Mold 23), rectangular, decorated in the center w/a large cluster of pink & red roses & green leaves against a shaded green ground, white & yellow border band, 7⅛ x 10¾" (ILLUS.). 195.00

Dresser tray, Icicle mold (Mold 7), swans in lake decoration, 7 x 11½"..485.00

Dresser tray, Icicle mold (Mold 7), heavy gold tapestry w/hanging baskets in relief, 7½ x 11½".............595.00

Dresser tray, Ribbon & Jewel mold (Mold 18), Melon Eaters & Dice Players decoration, 12" l...............1,375.00

Dresser tray, Mold 78, floral decoration, 7½ x 12"..................................75.00

Dresser tray, Mold 327, rose floral decoration, 12" l..................................80.00

Ewer, Mold 640, roses decoration, artist-signed, 5" h. 125.00

Nut set: 5¾" d., 3" h. master bowl & seven 1½" h. individual bowls; Mold 107 variation, decorated w/peach-colored roses, 8 pcs.........................560.00

Carnation Mold Pitcher

Pitcher, tankard, 11½" h., Carnation mold (Mold 526), roses decoration (ILLUS.) 895.00

Pitcher, tankard, 11½" h., Mold 508, decorated w/red & white roses, satin finish (unmarked) 495.00

Pitcher, tankard, 12½" h., Carnation mold (Mold 526), decorated w/pink roses 650.00

Pitcher, tankard, 13½" h., Carnation mold (Mold 526), poppies decoration, satin finish.............................960.00

Plate, 7" d., Icicle mold (Mold 7), water lily decoration 60.00

Plate, 8½" d., Mold 90, mill scene decoration 425.00

Plate, 8½" d., Mold 300, Castle scene 425.00

Plate, 8½" d., Mold 303, swan decoration, lavender & blue satin finish (unmarked) 195.00

Plate, 9" d., Carnation mold (Mold 28), decorated w/roses on teal blue ground...165.00

Plate, 10" d., Point & Clover mold (Mold 82), Melon Eaters & Dice Players decoration 950.00

Lily Mold Plate

Plate, 12" d., Lily mold (Mold 29), large center portrait of Madame Recamier against a shaded yellow to dark green ground, Tiffany finish greenish bronze panels around the border (ILLUS.) 1,650.00

Relish dish, Mold 82, decorated w/roses on pale yellow ground, 9½ x 14½"......................................120.00

Shaving mug w/beveled mirror, Stippled Floral mold (Mold 525), roses decoration on green ground...550.00

Tea set, child's: cov. teapot, creamer, cov. sugar bowl, five cups & saucers & five 6" d. plates; Mold 517, decorated w/pink poppies w/blue trim, 18 pcs. 2,150.00

Urn, cov., ovoid body on a pedestal base, two large gold loop handles, Mold 932, molded jewels & scrolls & rope chains w/small jewels around the shoulder, decorated w/Melon Eaters & Dice Throwers scenes, 7" d., 12" h. 3,000.00

Vase, 4½" h., handled, scene of a girl & a boy..450.00

Vase, 4½" h., Melon Eaters decoration w/mountain background.........495.00

Vase, 4½" h., Mold 914, woman in swing decoration..............................550.00

Vase, 5" h., two-handled, cartouches w/small pink roses, unusual gold handles, cobalt blue ground.............425.00

Vase, bud, 6⅛" h., multicolored floral decoration on "tapestry" body..........195.00

Vase, 6½" h., baluster-shaped, decorated w/landscape of swans in the foreground & Old Man of the Mountain in the distance..................695.00

Vase, 9½" h., tall urn-form body w/swelled top & serrated, jeweled rim flanked by long loop handles, raised on a domed & jeweled pedestal base, decorated w/rose florals & lovely colors w/a satin finish 575.00

OTHER MARKS

Bowl, 10" d., cameo portrait of lady holding roses, green w/gold trim (E.S. Germany) 130.00

Celery tray, Chief Spotted Horse decoration, 5½ x 12" (E.S. Germany - Royal Saxe) 225.00

Celery tray, decorated w/roses, 12½" l. (P. K. Silesia) 95.00

Coffee set: 9" h. cov. coffeepot, creamer, sugar bowl & six cups & saucers; figural scenes on all pieces, some marked "Angelica Kauffmann," 15 pcs. (R.S. Suhl) ...1,675.00

Creamer, Mold 645, molded swags & jewels, barnyard animals scene (Wheelock).......................................400.00

Cuspidor, decorated w/roses (E.S. Germany - Prove. Saxe) 395.00

Ewer, Lebrun portrait, red & pink decoration on pale cream ground, 6½" h. (O.S. St. Kilian) 145.00

Ewer, lady w/swallows decoration, pink & lavender iridescent finish, 7⅜" h. (Prov. Saxe - E.S. Germany) 250.00

Hair receiver, cov., Ribbon & Jewel mold (Mold 8), water lilies decoration (Wheelock Prussia)........200.00

Ice cream set: tray & five plates; pheasant decoration, 6 pcs. (E.S. Germany) 195.00

Jar, cov., floral "tapestry" decoration (E.S. Germany) 875.00

Plate, 7½" d., the Cage scene, cobalt blue ground w/lavish gold trim (R.S. Suhl) 695.00

Plate, 8¼" d., full frontal portrait of Queen Louise, iridescent w/gold decoration (E.S. Germany) 195.00

Shaving mug, scene of swallows over mountain & lake (E.S. Germany) 85.00

Vase, 5⅜" h., parrot decoration on a lavender ground w/lavish gold (Prove. Saxe - E.S. Germany) 295.00

Vase, 10½" h., swallows on cream ground w/gold highlights (E.S. Germany) 165.00

Vase, 11" h., decorated w/poppies, green leaves & gold trim on dark green ground (R.S. Poland) 295.00

RUSSEL WRIGHT DESIGNS

The innovative dinnerwares designed by Russel Wright and produced by various companies beginning in the late 1930s were an immediate success with a society that was turning to a more casual and informal lifestyle. His designs, with their flowing lines and unconventional shapes, were produced in many different colors which allowed the hostess to arrange a creative table. Although not antique, these designs, which we list below by line and manufacturer, are highly collectible. In addition to dinnerwares, Wright was also known as a trend-setter in the design of furniture, glassware, lamps, fabrics and a multitude of other household goods.

AMERICAN MODERN (Steubenville Pottery Company)

Ashtray, coaster-type, seafoam blue ..$10.00

Ashtray, coaster-type, white 21.00

Bowl, fruit, lug handle, bean brown 20.00

Bowl, fruit, lug handle, coral 10.00

Bowl, salad, cedar green 65.00

Bowl, salad, chartreuse 50.00

Bowl, salad, coral 45.00

Bowl, salad, granite grey 51.00

Bowl, soup, lug handle, cedar green 26.00

Bowl, soup, lug handle, chartreuse 7.00

Bowl, soup, lug handle, granite grey 11.00

Bowl, soup, lug handle, seafoam blue..15.00

Carafe w/stopper, bean brown 200.00

Carafe w/stopper, granite grey 140.00

Casserole, cov., stick handle, black chutney (deep brown) 71.00

Casserole, cov., stick handle, coral 46.00

Casserole, cov., stick handle, glacier blue 145.00

Casserole, cov., stick handle, seafoam blue 51.00

Celery tray, slender oblong shape w/asymmetrical incurved sides, bean brown, 13" l. 60.00

Celery tray, slender oblong shape w/asymmetrical incurved sides, black chutney, 13" l. 36.00

Celery tray, slender oblong shape w/asymmetrical incurved sides, cedar green, 13" l. 18.00

Celery tray, slender oblong shape w/asymmetrical incurved sides, coral, 13" l. 22.00

Celery tray, slender oblong shape w/asymmetrical incurved sides, granite grey, 13" l. 30.00

Celery tray, slender oblong shape w/asymmetrical incurved sides, seafoam blue, 13" l. 25.00

Coffeepot, cov., demitasse, black chutney 90.00

Coffeepot, cov., demitasse, chartreuse 60.00

Coffeepot, cov., chartreuse 65.00

Coffeepot, cov., granite grey 100.00

Creamer, chartreuse..............................7.00

Cup & saucer, demitasse, chartreuse 23.00

Cup & saucer, demitasse, coral............19.00

Cup & saucer, demitasse, granite grey 20.00

Cup & saucer, bean brown 25.00

Cup & saucer, black chutney................20.00

Cup & saucer, granite grey.....................9.00

Gravy boat, black chutney 15.00

Gravy boat & underplate, coral, 2 pcs. 30.00

Hostess set w/cup, chartreuse 62.00

Hostess set w/cup, white 85.00

Mug, white 85.00

Pickle dish, black chutney 18.00

Pitcher, water, 12" h., black chutney 67.00

Pitcher, water, 12" h., chartreuse 55.00

Pitcher, water, 12" h., coral..................75.00

Pitcher, water, 12" h., seafoam blue.....80.00

Plate, bread & butter, 6¼" d., coral.........4.00

Plate, salad, 8¼" d., granite grey............8.00

Plate, dinner, 10" d., black chutney 16.00

Plate, dinner, 10" d., cedar green 12.00

Plate, dinner, 10" d., glacier blue..........20.00

Plate, chop, 13" sq., bean brown..........45.00

Plate, chop, 13" sq., black chutney 31.00

Plate, chop, 13" sq., chartreuse...........17.00

Plate, chop, 13" sq., coral 25.00

Plate, chop, 13" sq., seafoam blue 30.00

Platter, 13¾" l., oblong, coral 14.00

Ramekin, cov., black chutney............165.00

Ramekin, cov., chartreuse 145.00

Refrigerator jar, cov., chartreuse 195.00

Relish dish, divided, bean brown........250.00

Salt & pepper shakers, black chutney, pr. 15.00

Salt & pepper shakers, granite grey, pr. 12.00

Salt & pepper shakers, seafoam blue, pr. 10.00

Teapot, cov., bean brown 135.00

Teapot, cov., coral 55.00

Teapot, cov., granite grey 65.00

Teapot, cov., seafoam blue 40.00

Vegetable bowl, cov., coral, 12" l..........45.00

Vegetable bowl, open, oval, black chutney, 10" l. 21.00

Vegetable bowl, open, oval, coral, 10" l. 17.00

Vegetable dish, divided, black chutney 85.00

Vegetable dish, divided, cedar green...65.00

Vegetable dish, divided, charteuse......50.00

Vegetable dish, divided, coral.............55.00

Vegetable dish, divided, granite grey 60.00

Vegetable dish, divided, white 87.50

CASUAL CHINA (Iroquois China Company)

Bowl, cereal, 5" d., avocado yellow 6.00

Bowl, cereal, 5" d., canteloupe (orange) 14.00

Bowl, cereal, 5" d., pink sherbet 6.00

Bowl, fruit, 5½" d., pink sherbet 6.00

Butter dish, cov., avocado yellow 40.00

Butter dish, cov., ice blue 70.00

Butter dish, cov., lemon yellow 75.00

Butter dish, cov., lettuce green (chartreuse) 60.00

Butter dish, cov., pink sherbet 67.00

Butter dish, cov., ripe apricot 60.00

Carafe, cov., avocado yellow, 10" h...125.00

Carafe, cov., ice blue, 10" h...............105.00

Carafe, cov., lettuce green, 10" h. 92.00

Carafe, cov., sugar white, 10" h.........150.00

Casserole, cov., divided, pink sherbet, 1½ qt. 76.00

Casserole, cov., divided, avocado yellow, 1½ qt. 32.50

Casserole, cov., divided, nutmeg brown, 1½ qt. 45.00

Creamer, pink sherbet 12.00

Creamer, stack-type, avocado yellow.....5.00

Creamer, restyled, sugar white.............24.00

Creamer & sugar bowl, stack-type, cantaloupe, pr. 31.00

Creamer & sugar bowl, stack-type, ice blue, pr. 15.00

Creamer & sugar bowl, stack-type, nutmeg brown, pr. 25.00

Creamer & sugar bowl, stack-type, pink sherbet, pr. 25.00

Creamer & sugar bowl, stack-type, sugar white, pr. 55.00

Cup & saucer, restyled, canteloupe......20.00

Cup & saucer, tea, avocado yellow 8.00

Cup & saucer, tea, oyster grey 10.00

Cup & saucer, tea, pink sherbet 9.00

Gumbo soup bowl, handled, charcoal ..22.00

Gumbo soup bowl, handled, ice blue ...25.00

Gumbo soup bowl, handled, sugar white 20.00

Mug, nutmeg brown, 13 oz. 50.00

Mug, restyled, ice blue.........................40.00

Mug, restyled, pink sherbet 48.00

Plate, salad, 7½" d., lemon yellow..........4.00

Plate, salad, 7½" d., pink sherbet...........8.00

Plate, luncheon, 9" d., ice blue 5.00

Plate, dinner, 10" d., avocado yellow......6.00

Plate, dinner, 10" d., canteloupe 16.00

Plate, dinner, 10" d., ice blue..................6.00

Plate, dinner, 10" d., pink sherbet...........8.50

Plate, dinner, 10" d., sugar white..........12.00

Platter, 12¾" l., oval, aqua....................30.00

Platter, 12¾" l., oval, nutmeg brown.....16.00

Platter, 14" l., oval, forest green 18.00

Salt & pepper shakers, stack-type, ice blue, pr. 16.00

Soup bowl, cov., canteloupe.................10.00

Soup bowl, cov., ice blue, 18 oz. 15.00

Soup bowl, cov., pink sherbet, 18 oz....18.00

Sugar bowl, cov., restyled, nutmeg brown 12.00

Sugar bowl, cov., restyled, sugar white 39.00

Sugar bowl, stack-type, forest green 7.00

Teapot, cov., small, parsley green, 4½" h..80.00

Teapot, cov., restyled, nutmeg brown 75.00

Teapot, cov., restyled, sherbet pink......95.00

Teapot, cov., restyled, sugar white.....150.00

Vegetable bowl, open, canteloupe, 8" d..36.00

Vegetable bowl, open, lettuce green, 8" d..13.50

Vegetable bowl, open, divided, lettuce green, 10" d. 24.00

SALTGLAZED WARES

This whitish ware has a pitted surface texture, which resembles an orange skin as a result of salt being thrown into the hot kiln to produce the glaze. Much of this ware was sold in the undecorated state, but some pieces were decorated. Decorative pieces have been produced in England and Europe since at least the 18th century with later production in the United States. Most pieces are unmarked.

Saltglazed Leaf-Shaped Dishes

Basket & undertray, oval basket w/rolled & scalloped rim & branch end handles, the sides w/pierced diamond lattice panels & cartouche-shaped panels edged w/ molded fruit & nuts on a basketweave ground, a matching oval undertray, Staffordshire, England, ca. 1765, undertray 10⅝" l., 2 pcs. (crack in undertray) $2,860.00

Butter tub, cover & undertray, the oval cylindrical body molded on the exterior, cover & rim of the undertray w/a pattern of 'rice' molding interrupted at the ends w/a molded leaf, its stem forming the tab handles on the tub or issuing from the flower-head knop on the cover, its tip extending to the cover's rim notched, & the cover pierced on either side w/two diamond devices, Staffordshire, ca. 1760, tub 4¾" l., undertray 6½" l., the set (small chip on knop, one cover notch chipped)....1,495.00

Candlestick, figural, modeled as two large standing cranes on either side of a cylindrical bamboo-form candleholder & raised on a decagonal-shaped mound base molded & applied w/flowers, Staffordshire, England, ca. 1755, 11¾" h. (one head & neck restored, three ankles cracked)........................110,000.00

Candle snuffer, figural, modeled as a lady standing & wearing a long dress & frilly cap, one hand at her side the other at her waist, Staffordshire, England, ca. 1750, 3¾" h. (cracked & restored) 1,980.00

Dish, scalloped & reticulated sides, England, 18th c., 9" d......................770.00

Dish, pierced shaped cartouches around the edges w/foliage on a basketweave-molded ground &

alternating panels of diaper & basketweave, Staffordshire, England, ca. 1760, 9½" d. 308.00

Dish, leaf-shaped w/tightly fluted edges, molded in the center w/a bird perched on a branch w/leaves & berries against a veined ground, Staffordshire, England, ca. 1760, 9½" l. (minute rim chips) 2,090.00

Dish, leaf-shaped, press-molded as a fluted leaf w/a feathered rim (small chips & pierced at the top w/a tiny suspension hole) & a ground of circlets superimposed w/a bird perched on a berried leafy branch issuing from the integral stem handle, Staffordshire, ca. 1760, 9¹¹⁄₁₆" l. (ILLUS. right) 690.00

Dish, shallow round sides w/a scalloped rim & molded w/cartouche-shaped diaper & trellis panels on a herringbone ground & smaller panels centering a circular cross-hatched ground, Staffordshire, England, ca. 1760, 12" d. (hairline) 1,045.00

Dishes, leaf-shaped, each press-molded w/a network of veining within a ruffled & serrated edge (tiny chip), the end w/a gnarled stem handle, the underside w/three blossom-form feet, Staffordshire, ca. 1760, 7⅝" l., pr. (ILLUS. of one left) 805.00

Figure of a lady, agateware, modeled standing w/her hands at her sides, in brown & buff clays, Staffordshire, England, ca. 1755, 5¾" h. (cracked at bodice) 990.00

Figure of a woman, modeled wearing a bodice w/a 'Watteau' panel at the back over a lacy stomacher & wide panniered skirt, holding a fan & standing before a grassy mound base behind her feet, Staffordshire, ca. 1750-55, 3⁹⁄₁₆" h. (chips on base, repaired through waist & neck) 575.00

Model of a seated cat, molded features & painted blue eyes, Staffordshire, England, ca. 1760, 5⅞" h. 9,350.00

Mug, "scratch-blue" type, the cylindrical body incised on the front & picked out in cobalt blue w/the initials "JG" above two flowering branches rising from the ridged & slightly flaring foot (hair crack becoming a star crack on the base), & he reverse affixed w/a strap handle terminating in an applied heart, the base incised w/a flower, "LO" (or 07)

Staffordshire Saltglazed Mug

& letter "C," Staffordshire, 1750-55, 4⅝" h. (ILLUS.) 2,013.00

Mug, tall cylindrical body w/loop handle, painted inscription "Aaron and Mary Heaward - In Godley 1763," within pink, blue, yellow & green scrolling foliage bands, Staffordshire, England, ca. 1763, 5" h. (cracks at handle) 1,540.00

Pitcher, cov., milk, 5¾" h., jug-type, the hexagonal pear-shaped body molded w/six different panels of figures, animals, birds & flanking the spout coats of arms above an ogee-shaped hexagonal foot, the loop handle notched at the thumbpiece, & the domed cover molded w/six ropework-edged panels of animals, one being ridden by a putto, encircling the slightly conical knop, Staffordshire, 1745-50 (small chips on foot, hairlines & repaired chips in handle, knop repaired) 1,265.00

Pitcher, cov., 6¼" h., jug-type, footed bulbous body tapering to a cylindrical neck w/pointed spout & fitted w/a flattened cover w/crabstock finial, looped crabstock handle at the back, the drabware body w/applied white flower, scroll & beaded decoration, England, ca. 1755 (spout chipped & w/small crack at base of handle) 3,520.00

Plate, 9" d., wide scalloped rim molded w/scroll-framed reserves w/diapering & the inscription "Success to the - King of Prussia - And His Forces," & w/his portrait, martial trophies & an eagle, England, ca. 1770 ....1,870.00

Sauceboat, oblong boat-shaped body w/loop handle, the spout molded w/a leaf & enameled in color w/a lady playing the harpsichord, the reverse w/a house within molded scrolling foliage trimmed in blue reserved on the ermine-molded ground w/maroon edge, Staffordshire, England, ca. 1760, 7⅞" l. 3,850.00

Scent bottle, book-form, realistically modeled as a small book w/a crossed pattern of zigzag rouletting on the spine, similar rouletted borders on the covers enclosing a dotted diamond device & four stars picked out in dark brown iron slip, w/incised pages pierced on the front edge w/a circular threaded aperture for a stopper, Staffordshire, ca. 1725, 2 1/16" h. (restored chips on cover, stopper missing) 1,439.00

Scent bottle w/stopper, flattened ovoid body molded on the front & back w/a naked lady reclining amid clouds over a unicorn walking between shrubbery above a basket of fruit & a small shell device interrupting a sawtooth border on the canted sides, the neck w/a screw-on stopper, Staffordshire, ca. 1750, 2¾" h. (small neck chips, stopper damaged) 1,955.00

Soup tureen, cov., oval squatty bulbous body tapering to a flared base & flared rim supporting a low-domed cover w/large knop handle, the body molded on either side w/a central flowerhead device between fruiting grapevines concealing a kneeling naked boy, the cover molded on either side & on the knop (reglued) w/extended & reduced versions of the boy & grapevine, Staffordshire, ca. 1750, 11½" l. (repaired chips & cracks) 1,840.00

Soup tureen, cover & undertray, lozenge-shaped, each piece press-molded on the body, dome or rim w/foliate-scroll-edged cartouches of dot- and star-diaperwork alternating w/panels of basketweave, the handles (one repaired) & knop formed as angular branches, & the tureen (some discolored crackling) raised on three grotesque-mask-and-paw feet (one w/a small chip), Staffordshire, ca. 1750, tureen 13⅛" l., undertray 16½" l., the set (small chips on cover rim & border of undertray) 1,840.00

Spoon tray, quatrefoil-form, press-molded in the center w/stylized flowers issuing from the scroll motifs within beadwork & ropework bands beneath scalloped panels on the scalloped & barbed rim, small chips, firing cracks & slight speckling,

Saltglazed Quatrefoil-Form Spoon Tray

Staffordshire, 1750-60, 6½" l. (ILLUS.) 805.00

Stand, shallow circular dish w/a narrow flat rim raised on three scrolling Chinese-style T-shaped feet, Staffordshire, ca. 1750, 4 11/16" d. 1,150.00

Sweetmeat dish, leaf-shaped, molded as a finely fluted & scrolled trifid leaf w/a short stem & three short bracket feet, Staffordshire, ca. 1760, 5 7/16" l. 920.00

Teapot, cov., quatrefoil 'pectin-shell' type, the bulbous pear-shaped body molded w/overlapping shells & trailing oak branches & enameled in colors w/Charles II in the branches above the shells, the leaves & roses trimmed in green & red, raised on three paw feet headed by lions' masks, Staffordshire, England, ca. 1760, 5¼" h. (tip of spout, one foot & chip on cover restored, crack at base of handle) 8,250.00

SAN ILDEFONSO (Maria) POTTERY

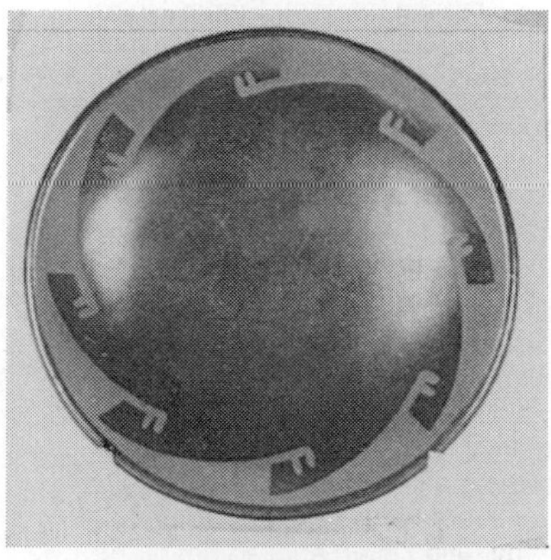

Dish by Maria & Julian

A thin-walled and crudely polished blackware has been made at most Rio Grande Pueblos. Around 1918 a San Ildefonso Pueblo woman, Maria Montoya Martinez and her husband, Julian, began making a thicker walled blackware with a finely polished gun-metal black sheen. It was fired in the traditional manner using manure to smother the firing process and produce the black coloration. The following is a chronology of Maria's varied signatures: Marie, mid to late teens-1934; Marie & Julian, 1934-43; Maria & Santana, 1943-56; Maria & Popovi, 1956-71 and Maria Poveka, used on undecorated wares after 1956. Maria died in July of 1980. Rosalia, Tonita, Blue Corn and other signatures might also be found on pottery made at the San Ildefonso Pueblo. Considered a true artistic achievement, early items signed by Maria, or her contemporaries, command good prices. It should be noted that the strong pottery tradition is being carried on by current potters.

Dish, shallow, blackware w/matte geometric design around the rim, glossy center, signed "Maria & Julian," 5¾" d. (ILLUS.)..................$550.00

Jar, squatty bulbous form w/a sloping shoulder, blackware w/a matte & shiny spearhead design on the upper half, signed "Marie & Julian," ca. 1940, 4⅝" d., 2⅞ " h. (minor wear)...313.50

Jar, ovoid body w/a wide, flat mouth, blackware w/a finely polished feature design around the upper half, signed "Donicia Tafoya," 4⅜" d., 3¼" h. (faint rub line at shoulder).......93.50

Jar, blackware, wide rounded base below a tapering funnel-shaped upper half, finely polished w/a feather design around the shoulder, signed "Pauline," Pauline Martinez, granddaughter of Maria, 3¼" d., 3½" h...104.50

Jar, squatty bulbous form w/steeply angled shoulder to flat mouth, black on black w/a geometric avian design around the shoulder, signed "Mama-Popovi 669," ca. 1960s, 5" d., 4" h. (small repaired rim chips) 286.00

Jar, blackware, squatty glossy globular body w/three matte lines, the sloping shoulder decorated in a glossy & matte feather design, signed "Santana & Adam" (ILLUS. top next column).............2,970.00

San Ildefonso Feather Design Jar

Plate, 5¾" d., black on black w/a feather border design, signed "Maria & Santana" (very minor wear)..........192.50

SARREGUEMINES

Sarreguemines Majolica Pitcher

This factory was established in Lorraine, France, about 1770. Subsequently Wedgwood-type pieces were produced as was Mocha ware. In the 19th century, the factory turned to pottery and stoneware.

Basket, Etna line, leopard skin crystals, quilted green ground, marked "Etna," 9" h........................$215.00

Cup & saucer, majolica, cup modeled in the form of an orange, leafy saucer..125.00

Dish, cov., majolica, strawberries in basket decoration 175.00

Humidor, cov., molded high-relief figures & forest scene around body.....125.00

Pitcher, 5⅜" h., 4⅜" d., majolica, figural bulbous man's head, color trim w/red cheeks & nose, aqua lining, marked (ILLUS.) 65.00

Plate, 7½" d., majolica, molded grapes & leaves 50.00

Plate, pierced to hang, French peasant scene, F. Richard, marked "PV" 40.00

Stein, w/pewter top, decorated w/colored scene of men drinking beer on front, cream exterior & white interior, 9½" h..................................195.00

Vase, 5" h., Etna line, the squatty bulbous body tapering to a wide cupped rim, overall green crystalline glaze w/the crystals forming concentric circles, marked on base "Sarreguemines - Etna - 4072 - 227 - G - E," early 20th c. 605.00

Vase, 6½" h., squatty bulbous base tapering to a tall trumpet-form neck, shaded amber to rich brown glaze, blue-glazed interior, impressed mark 33.00

SASCHA BRASTOFF

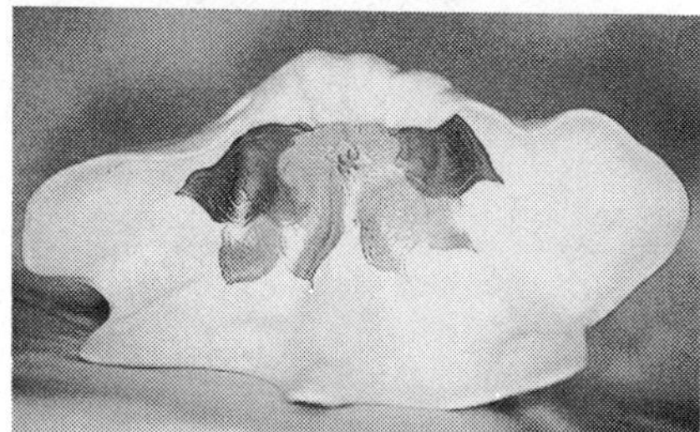

Sascha Brastoff Bowl

Even though Sascha Brastoff experimented with different materials and had a natural talent for sculpting, it was not until November, 1953 that he felt his unique ability in ceramic design was recognized. His friend, Winthrop Rockefeller, backed him in a large, newly constructed showplace encompassing a full block on Olympic Boulevard in downtown Los Angeles, California. Brastoff designed each piece personally and the Brastoff-trained employees produced them. He created a full line of hand-painted china in about twelve designs. A pottery dinnerware line named 'Surf Ballet,' a marbleized treatment usually in gold and pink or silver and blue, was marketed. Artware items with patterns such as 'Star Steed,' a leaping fantasy horse and 'Rooftops,' a village scene with a batik look, are popular items. Hard-to-find resin items are an example of Brastoff's diversified talents. A line of enamels on copper was also made. Pieces signed "Sascha B." were done by his artisans; those with the full "Sascha Brastoff" signature were personally hand-painted by him. The chanticleer was a Brastoff trademark used as a backstamp in conjunction with the signature marks. Because of health problems Brastoff left his company in 1963; it would be another ten years before the business closed. Sascha Brastoff died February 4, 1993.

Sascha Brastoff

Sascha B.

Ashtray, rectangular w/six cigarette rests at one end, house motif in black, grey, maroon & white glaze, 7½" w., 10" l. $65.00

Bowl, 3½" d., 5" h., three small round feet, "Surf Ballet," blue & silver marbleized glaze...............................20.00

Bowl, 12" d., 4½" h., shell-shaped white matte glaze w/gold & platinum glossy leaves in bottom of shell (ILLUS.) 95.00

Candleholder, yellow resin, 4" d., 7¼" h...27.00

Cigarette holder, pipe-shaped, overall gold glaze, Model No. 080, 4¼" h...45.00

Cigarette holder, round w/straight sides, turquoise w/abstract flower design, 2½" h. 22.00

Cigarette lighter, white w/pink glaze w/blue & purple flowers, 2" h. 25.00

Cup & saucer, peacock design w/tan, gold, light blue & white over brown background, saucer 5½" d., cup 3½" d., 3" h. 25.00

Model of a bear, seated w/legs straight, head slightly raised, arms across chest, dark green resin, 10½" h...250.00

Obelisk w/lid, horizontal stripes in brown, blue & tan over white background, full signature, 22" h. 310.00

Sascha Brastoff Pitcher

Pitcher, 6" h., 5½" d., bulbous ovoid body tapering to a rim slightly raised forming angular spout, brown glossy background w/tan & rust fruits & leaves trimmed in green & gold (ILLUS.) 95.00

Sugar bowl, cov., "Surf Ballet," pink & gold marbleized glaze, 4½" d., 3¾" h. 40.00

Tray, angular free-form shape, white background, platinum & gold flowers & leaves, Model No. F3, 9¾" l., 5½" w. 35.00

Tray, shallow oval, enamel on copper, abstract design w/blue, black, yellow & green glazes, 4" l., 3½" w. 28.00

Vase, 9" h., figural model of a high-buttoned shoe, blue, brown, tan stripes over white background, ca. 1959 ....85.00

SATSUMA

These decorated wares have been produced in Japan since the end of the 18th century. The early pieces are scarce and high-priced. Later Satsuma wares are plentiful and, with prices rising, as highly collectible as earlier pieces.

Bowl, miniature, 4" d., flattened form, decorated w/mon, flowers & foliage in colors & gilt, signed "Kinkozan," early 20th c. (ILLUS. top next column) ....$1,000.00 to 1,500.00

Miniature Satsuma Bowl

Bowl, 4" w., squared form, the interior decorated w/Kannon flying & holding a lotus blossom amid clouds, each interior side decorated w/a flying crane, a small applied figure on the exterior peeks over the corner of the rim, the exterior decorated w/fan & heart-shaped panels depicting geisha, dancers & samurai, a fluted leaf border near the base, signed 330.00

Bowl, 5⅛" d., decorated w/an urn in a garden w/birds & a large chrysanthemum in enamel & gilt, the exterior w/a gilt border at the top & base 137.50

Bowl, 6" d., a shallow rounded form, the interior decorated w/a scene of water fowl in a hanging garden, the exterior w/panels of birds amid flowers separated by cobalt blue & gilt borders from the rim to the base, on a wooden base, signed 660.00

Bowl, 6" d., lotus-form, polychrome & gilt design of Rakan & their attributes, late 19th c. ....400.00 to 600.00

Bowl, 6¾" d., decorated on the exterior w/a scene of men in a two-story pavilion w/mountains & a waterfall in the background, the interior rim decorated w/flying cranes 220.00

Bowl, 15½" d., deep, the center depicting a pair of cockerels & hens in a garden w/blooming wisteria & bellflowers, the scene surrounded by a border of alternating patterned panels beneath the barbed rim edged in gilt, the exterior painted w/beribboned cash designs & paulownia crests, on a later carved wood stand, late 19th c. (slightly rubbed) 1,725.00

Box, cov., cover w/Foo dog finial, decorated overall w/beautiful ladies & scholars, w/stamped signature, 3 x 3¼" 650.00

Box, cov., square form w/canted corners, decorated w/a procession of samurai reserved on a ground of chrysanthemums, the interior decorated w/irises, 3¼" w. 330.00

Box, cov., cover w/Foo dog finial, decorated overall w/beautiful ladies & scholars, w/stamped signature, 3 x 3¼" 650.00

Box, cov., square form w/canted corners, decorated w/a procession of samurai reserved on a ground of chrysanthemums, the interior decorated w/irises, 3¼" w. 330.00

Buttons, floraform w/designs of butterflies, 1¼" d., ca. 1925, set of 7 ....100.00 to 175.00

Dish, motif of Kannon astride a dragon, signed "Kinkozan," ca. 1910, 10" d. (repairs to rim) ....1,050.00 to 1,500.00

Figure of a man seated on a tatami mat & holding a pipe, late 19th c., 6" l. ....1,200.00 to 1,500.00

Ornate Satsuma Jar

Jar, cov., wide ovoid body w/a four-lobed scalloped base, figural drum handles on the shoulders flanking the short flaring neck supporting a high domed & reticulated cover w/a double pod finial, the sides decorated overall w/Immortals & attendants on a ground of gold dots, signed, 11¼" h. (ILLUS.) 825.00

Koro (censer), globular, Rakan & dragon in relief, three stump feet, 7" h. (finial restored) ....400.00 to 600.00

Plates, 7" d., h.p. scene of geisha & master, moriage trim, ca. 1920s, set of 5 ....150.00

Sake cup, 1000 Butterflies patt., exterior w/panels of flowers, ca. 1900, 2" d. ....500.00 to 600.00

Sake pot, teapot-shaped, floral decoration w/lappets, 19th c., 2½" h. 675.00

Teapot, cov., decorated w/flowers & butterflies, 19th c. 250.00

Teapot, cov., overall decoration of irises in colors & gilt, ca. 1920, 4½" h. ....400.00 to 600.00

Vase, 4¼" h., baluster-form w/dragon handles, decorated w/Ebisu & panels of flowers, gilt & colors, signed "Dai Nihon Satsuma Hozan," ca. 1910 ....800.00 to 1,000.00

Vase, 4½" h., 1000 Flowers patt., colors & gilt, ca. 1920 ......250.00 to 350.00

Vase, 5" h., overall floral decoration, orange, gold & white, ca. 1920s 75.00

Vase, 5½" h., globular form w/panels of Samurai, late 19th c. .....500.00 to 700.00

Vase, 6" h., black ground w/gold scenic decoration, signed "Satsumayaki," ca. 1930 ....200,00 to 300.00

Vase, 9" h., gourd-shape, design of cranes & flowers below a lappet border, colors & gilt, ca. 1910 ....800.00 to 1,200.00

Vase, 10¼" h., decorated w/a detailed landscape of mountain, bridge & pagodas 70.00

Vase, cov., 11" h., three-footed, decorated w/scene of warriors, Foo dog handles & finial 85.00

Vase, 11½" h., figural medallions on brocade ground, colors & gilt late 19th c. ....800.00 to 1,200.00

Vase, 14½" h., ovoid, four panels w/birds on flowering branches, ca. 1910, signed "Satsuma yaki" ....1,000.00 to 1,500.00

SCHAFER & VATER

Founded in Rudolstadt, Thuringia, Germany in 1890, the Schafer and Vater Porcelain Factory specialized in decorative pieces of porcelain usually in white or colored bisque. They produced many novelty figural items such as creamers, toothpick holders, boxes and hatpin holders and also produced a line of jasper ware with white relief decoration in imitation of the famous Wedgwood jasper wares. The firm also decorated white ware blanks.

The company ceased production in 1962 and collectors now seek out their charming pieces which may be marked with a crown over a starburst containing the script letter "R."

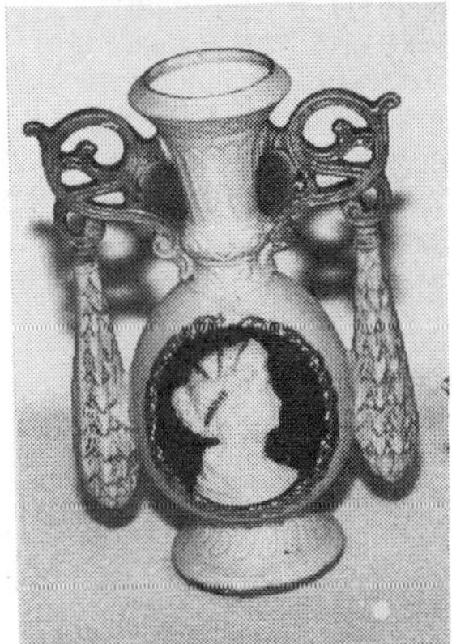

Schafer & Vater Vase

Box, cov., cameo-like white relief bust profile of Art Nouveau lady, No. 3177, 4" d. $115.00

Creamer, bisque, figural orange 35.00

Hatpin holder, bisque, figural, Egyptian woman's head, pink, 4½" h. 170.00

Humidor, cov., man w/pipe decoration, lavender 550.00

Match holder w/attached tray, jasper ware, white relief roses on a light green ground 50.00

Pitcher, 3½" h., figural maid w/jug & keys, multicolor trim 98.00

Pitcher, 5½" h., figural Mother Goose, blue trim 98.00

Pitcher, milk, 6½" h., figural cow dressed as a woman........................195.00

Vase, 4¾" h., 3" d., bisque, baluster-form w/the tall trumpet neck flanked by looped scroll handles suspending long pendent swags, the front centered by an oval reserve w/a white relief cameo portrait of a classical lady against a dark green ground, the body & handles washed in pale green (ILLUS.) 55.00

Vase, 6½" h., jasper ware, white relief scene of a man, woman & cupid against a blue ground, No. 593........150.00

Wall pocket, jasper ware, decorated w/white relief roses on green ground...48.00

SEVRES & SEVRES-STYLE

Sevres-Style Candelabra

Some of the more desirable porcelain ever produced was made at the Sevres factory, originally established at Vincennes, France, and transferred, through permission of Madame de Pompadour, to Sevres as the Royal Manufactory about the middle of the 18th century. King Louis XV took sole responsibility for the works in 1759 when production of hard paste began. Between 1850 and 1900, many biscuit and soft-paste porcelains were again made. Fine early pieces are scarce and high-priced. Many of those available today are late productions. The various Sevres marks have been copied and pieces listed as "Sevres-Style" are similar to actual Sevres

wares, but not necessarily from that factory. Three of the many Sevres marks are illustrated below.

Cache-pots, Sevres-Style, gilt-bronze mounted, the cylindrical sides decorated w/a figural panel of lovers in a garden, framed by gilt scrolling, the reverse w/a floral panel, all on a *bleu celeste* ground, mounted at the top w/a pierced flaring gilt-bronze band, fitted at the sides w/lion mask handles w/rings & raised on a round tapered gilt-bronze base w/scrolled feet, late 19th c., 11½" h., pr.......$6,325.00

Cache-pots, Sevres-Style, straight sided w/scrolling handles, decorated w/two panels depicting birds, leafy trees & flowers, pr.........................1,500.00

Candelabrum, Sevres-Style, six-light, each of vase-form painted w/a figural panel on the obverse & birds & flowers on the reverse, on a cobalt ground w/gilt highlights, raised on a gilt-bronze square base fitted w/painted porcelain plaques & supporting tiers of foliate-scrolled branches, late 19th c., 28¾" h., pr. (ILLUS. of one) 6,900.00

Centerpiece, Sevres-Style, gilt-bronze mounted, a wide & deep rounded bowl decorated on the exterior w/oval panels of putti framed by gilt scrolls against a cobalt blue ground, the interior w/colorful flowers on a white ground, the rim fitted w/a pierced gilt-bronze 'crown' band joining gilt-bronze scroll handles down the sides, raised on a gilt-bronze connector above a domed cobalt blue & white porcelain foot resting upon a pierced domed gilt-bronze footed base, late 19th c., 18" h...5,175.00

Centerpieces, Sevres-Style, oval bowl w/figural panels flanked by ram's heads, the rim & base fitted w/foliate scrolled mounts, late 19th c., 13" l., 10" h., pr. 3,163.00

Cup & saucer, Sevres-Style, cobalt blue decorated w/scenic panels of young lovers & landscapes, gilt trim..60.00

Garniture set: large centerpiece bowl & a pair of cov. potpourris; all fitted w/pierced gilt-bronze top bands joining figural caryatid-topped handles, the exteriors w/oval panels decorated w/18th c. couples in landscapes or landscape scenes each w/gilt scroll borders against a cobalt blue ground, the centerpiece interior in white, the potpourris w/domed covers w/pineapple-form gilt-bronze finials & gilt scroll trim, all raised on gilt-bronze connectors to domed cobalt blue porcelain bases & raised on ornate gilt-bronze footed plinths, late 19th c., artist-signed, centerpiece 21" h., 3 pcs. 26,450.00

Potpourri, cov., urn-form body on a ringed pedestal base, bell-form domed cover w/gilt-bronze pineapple finial, the sides decorated w/a large oval panel of an 18th c. couple walking in a garden, the reverse w/a landscape panel, framed by a gilt scroll border w/further gilt scroll bands on the cover & domed base, all against a cobalt blue ground, the rim fitted w/a pierced gilt-bronze band connecting the raised figural caryatid-topped handles continuing down to the base of the body, raised on a gilt-bronze ornately embossed & footed plinth base, late 19th c., 28½" h., pr.....10,350.00

Late 19th Century Tea Service

Tea service: cov. teapot, cov. sugar bowl, creamer, six cups & saucers; Sevres-Style, each decorated w/figural panels on a cobalt blue ground, w/circular "sevres," crowned interlacing "L" mark & Chateau mark, late 19th c., teapot 18" h., 15 pcs. (ILLUS. of part).................4,313.00

Sevres-Style Covered Urn

Urn, cov., Sevres-Style, globular body raised on an octagonal gilt-bronze base & domed foot, the sides painted w/a figural & landscape scene, signed "M. Demonceaux," flanked by gilt-bronze putti term handles, late 19th c., 25" h. (ILLUS.)..........2,875.00

Urn, cov., Sevres-Style, gilt-bronze mounted, the tall baluster-form body decorated on the front w/a large oval panel depicting the coronation of Napoleon based on the David painting, the reverse w/a panel of a landscape scene, each panel within gilt laurel border, the flaring neck decorated w/a spread-winged eagle & the domed cover w/a gilt crown, the base decorated w/gilt athenium & scrolls, all against a cobalt blue ground, fitted w/gilt-bronze mounts & a bracket plinth, artist-signed, late 19th c., pseudo "Mre. Imple de Sevres" mark in red, 4' 10" h.......36,800.00

Urns, the tall baluster-form body decorated w/a large oval panel depicting a glorified war scene, the reverse w/a landscape scene, all within gilt scroll borders on a cobalt blue ground, flanked by gilt-bronze foliate scroll handles, raised on a bracket plinth gilt-bronze base, late 19th c., 35" h., pr.........................17,250.00

Urns, cov., Sevres-Style, gilt-bronze mounted, the tall baluster-form body decorated w/a continuous classical scene of a maiden & cupids among flowers against a white ground, the flaring neck, domed cover & ringed pedestal base in *bleu celeste* w/gilt scroll trim, fitted at the sides w/gilt-bronze scroll handles & on a footed gilt-bronze square plinth w/cut corners, late 19th c., now mounted as a lamp, 38" h., pr. (damages) 4,025.00

Urns, cov., Sevres-Style, the tall baluster-form body decorated on the front w/a large oval panel depicting a classical allegorical scene of semi-nude females & putti, the reverse w/a landscape panel, both panels framed by gilt banding & scrolls, the domed cover w/a pineapple finial & heavy gilt trim, all on a cobalt blue ground, mounted w/gilt-metal slender scroll handles from the rim to the shoulder & ending in masks, raised on a bracket gilt-bronze plinth base, artist-signed, late 19th c., pseudo 'sevres' chateau mark & 'sevres' circular mark, 44½" h., pr...35,650.00

Urns, cov., Sevres-Style, palace-type, each w/an oval figural panel depicting 18th century style figures within a garden, signed "Bertren," the opposing side depicting a landscape within gilt borders, the neck & base further heightened w/gilt on a *bleu celeste* ground, the neck flanked by gilt-bronze cherubs, continuing to foliate scrolled & lyre-cast handles, the socle raised on a tassel & drapery-cast bracket base centered by fleur-de-lis decorated shield, the domed cover fitted w/lovebirds, pseudo interlacing "L's" mark in blue enamel enclosing the letter "E," late 19th c., 5' h., pr. 74,000.00

Vase, 13½" h., commemorative, tall ovoid body tapering to a short cylindrical neck, the waist w/four *pate-sur-pate* roundels enclosing athletes at various pursuits in white slip on grey within lime green borders reserved against a rich blue ground trimmed w/gilt laurel leaves, made to commemorate the 1924 Olympic Games in Paris, factory marks, artist-signed 10,350.00

Vase, 20" h., Sevres-Style, slender baluster-form body raised on a pedestal w/a lobed metal foot, gilt-metal scroll handles flanking the tall neck & shoulder, decorated on the front w/a long reserve w/an elegant 18th c. couple in a garden, the reverse w/a landscape reserve, all on a cobalt blue ground, 19th c. 467.50

Vase, cov., 15" h., Sevres-Style, slender ovoid body w/flaring trumpet neck & pointed cover, slender pedestal base w/gilt metal foot, large decorated reserve w/full-length portrait of woman & cupid in garden, background of blue & gold, artist-signed 495.00

Vase, cov., 33½" h., the wide ovoid body raised on a knop on a ringed pedestal set on an octagonal foot, the shoulder tapering w/a flaring neck & flanked by ram's head handles, the high domed cover w/an acorn finial, decorated on the front w/a large reserve showing a young man leaving a basket of flowers for a sleeping girl as a cupid observes, the reverse w/a wide landscape w/large hollyhocks in the foreground, all against a cobalt blue ground w/gilt trim, artist-signed, marked w/gilt interlaced "L's," 19th c. 4,620.00

SHAWNEE

Dutch Girl Cookie Jar

The Shawnee pottery operated in Zanesville, Ohio, from 1937 until 1961. Much of the early production was sold to chain stores and mail-order houses including Sears, Roebuck, Woolworth and others. Planters, cookie jars and vases, along with the popular "Corn King" oven ware line, are among the collectible items which are plentiful and still reasonably priced. Reference numbers used here are taken from Mark E. Supnick's book, Collecting Shawnee Pottery, The Collector's Guide to Shawnee Pottery *by Duane and Janice Vanderbilt, or* Shawnee Pottery - An Identification & Value Guide *by Jim and Bev Mangus.*

Shawnee
U.S.A.

Ashtray/coasters, heart-shaped w/three-section interior, No. 411, various colors, set of 4 .... $38.00

Bank, figural Bulldog 125.00

Bank-cookie jar combination, figural Smiley Pig, No. 61 .... 325.00

Bank-cookie jar combination, figural Winnie Pig, chocolate-colored base 395.00

Bank-cookie jar combination, figural Winnie Pig, caramel-colored base ... 550.00

Batter pitcher, embossed Snowflake patt., yellow glaze 50.00

Bowl, 6" d., "Corn King" line, No. 92 ..... 32.50

Bowl, soup or cereal, "Corn King" line, No. 94 .... 32.50

Bowl, 9" d., "Corn King" line, No. 95 ..... 45.00

Bowls, nest-type, "Corn King" line, set of 3 .... 85.00

Butter dish, cov., "Corn King" line, No. 72 .... 52.50

Casserole, individual size, "Corn King" line, No. 73, 9 oz. 55.00

Casserole, cov., "Corn King" line, 1½ qt., No. 74 .... 62.00

Casserole, cov., model of fruit basket, No. 81, 5½" h. 40.00

Cookie jar, "Corn King" line, figural ear of corn, No. 66 .... 145.00

Cookie jar, "Corn Queen" line, figural ear of corn, No. 66 .... 195.00

Cookie jar, figural Cottage, "USA 6" .... 1,000.00 to 1,500.00

Cookie jar, figural Dutch boy, blue tie, striped pants .... 100.00 to 150.00

Cookie jar, figural Dutch Girl, marked "Great Northern, No. 1026" (ILLUS.) 150.00

Cookie jar, figural Dutch Girl, decorated w/a tulip 114.00

Cookie jar, figural Elephant, marked "Lucky" on the front, w/gold trim & floral decals 695.00

Cookie jar, Fernware line, octagonal, green glaze 75.00

Cookie jar, figural Jug, blue glaze 150.00

Cookie jar, Little Chef patt., hexagonal w/molded chefs in three panels & "Cookies" in others, cream ground 65.00

Cookie jar, figural Mugsey Dog, w/blue bow .... 350.00 to 450.00

Cookie jar, figural Owl .... 125.00 to 175.00

Cookie jar, figural Owl, gold trim .... 250.00 to 300.00

Cookie jar, figural Puss 'n Boots 145.00

Cookie jar, figural Puss 'n Boots, gold trim .... 500.00 to 550.00

Cookie jar, figural Sailor Boy .... 100.00 to 125.00

Cookie jar, figural Sailor boy, gold trim & decals 295.00

Cookie jar, figural Smiley Pig, blue collar, gold trim 348.00

Cookie jar, figural Smiley Pig, decorated w/pink flowers & gold trim, red kerchief .... 275.00 to 325.00

Cookie jar, figural Winnie Pig, decorated w/clover leaves 290.00

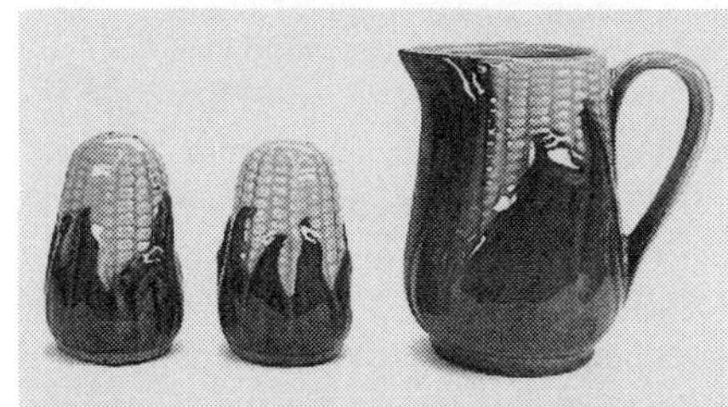

Corn King Salt & Pepper & Creamer

Creamer, "Corn King" line, No. 70, 5" h. (ILLUS. right) 29.00

Creamer, "Corn Queen" line, No. 70, 5" h. 25.00

Creamer, figural Elephant, gold trim ....125.00 to 150.00

Creamer, figural Puss 'n Boots, white w/color trim, 5" h. 45.00

Creamer, figural Smiley Pig, colored trim 40.00

Creamer, Heart & Tulip patt. 45.00

Creamer, embossed Snowflake patt., green glaze 15.00

Ewer, tall slender footed ovoid body, angled handle w/gold trim, No. 1168, 8" h. 15.00

Figurine, model of a Pekinese dog 39.50

Figurine, model of a puppy dog 30.50

Mixing bowl, "Corn King" line, No. 5, 5" d. 45.00

Mixing bowl, "Corn King" line, No. 6, 6½" d. 37.50

Model of a gazelle, recumbent, mottled brown glaze 50.00

Pie bird, pink glaze, 5¼" h. ....35.00 to 40.00

Corn King Pitcher

Pitcher, tankard, "Corn King" line, 1 qt., No. 71 (ILLUS.) 76.00

Pitcher, 5½" h., ball-shaped, embossed Flower & Fern patt., yellow glaze 45.00

Pitcher, ball-type, Fruit patt., No. 80 ....65.00

Pitcher, ball-type, Pennsylvania Dutch patt. ....150.00 to 175.00

Pitcher, ball-type, Sunflower patt. ....50.00 to 75.00

Pitcher, ball-type, Valencia line, yellow glaze, 2 pt. 60.00

Pitcher, figural Chanticleer Rooster, w/flower decals & gold trim 125.00

Pitcher, figural Little Bo Peep, peach trim ....50.00 to 75.00

Pitcher, figural Little Boy Blue, No. 46 ....90.00

Pitcher, figural Smiley Pig, red clover decoration ....150.00 to 175.00

Planter, figural, boy standing beside stump, wearing a pale turquoise cap & shorts & a large bow tie, No. 533 ....12.00

Planter, figural clown lying on his back, w/gold trim, No. 607 ....19.00

Planter, model of an alarm clock, No. 1262 ....12.00

Planter, model of a bull, brown glaze, No. 668 ....45.00

Planter, model of a large chick pulling a spherical cart, No. 720 ....19.00

Planter, model of a doe & log, lime green base, No. 766, 7" h. 28.00

Planter, model of a fish w/wide open mouth, tail curled up & touching back of head, blue glaze 40.00

Planter, model of a frog on lily pad, No. 726 ....59.00

Planter, model of gazelle & baby heads, glossy black glaze, No. 841 ....48.00

Planter, model of a globe, 7" h. 25.00

Planter, model of a goose flying, No. 820 ....25.00

Planter, model of a horse, standing, red glaze w/white mane & tail, No. 506 ....20.00

Planter, model of a hound & Pekinese, No. 611 ....18.00

Planter, model of a hound next to green keg, No. 610 ....12.00

Planter, model of a pig, No. 760 ....16.00

Planter, model of a ribbed conch shell, No. 655 ....10.00

Planter, model of an upright piano, No. 528 ....25.00

Planter, model of a watering can, 5½ x 8" 10.00

Planter, model of a windmill, white w/gold trim, No. 715 ....35.00

Train Planter Set

Planters, train set composed of locomotive, coal car, box car & caboose, 4 pcs. (ILLUS.) 99.00

Plate, 8" oval, "Corn King" line, No. 93 ....26.00

Plate, 10" d., "Corn King" line, No. 65 ....37.00

Plate, 10" oval, "Corn King" line, No. 68 ....36.50

Platter, 12" oval, "Corn King" line, No. 96 ....45.00

Relish tray, "Corn King" line, No. 79 ....35.00

Relish tray, "Corn Queen" line, No. 79 ....18.00

Salt & pepper shakers, Basket of Fruit line, No. 82, small, pr. 19.00

Salt & pepper shakers, Basket of Fruit line, No. 82, large, pr. 35.00

Salt & pepper shakers, "Corn King" line, No. 76, 3¼" h., pr.(ILLUS. left) 20.00

Salt & pepper shakers, "Corn King" line, large range size, No. 77, 5¼" h., pr. 28.00

Salt & pepper shakers, embossed Fernware line, green glaze, large, pr. 28.00

Salt & pepper shakers, Sunflower patt., large, 5" h., pr. 45.00

Salt & pepper shakers, figural Chanticleer Rooster, small, pr. 35.00

Salt & pepper shakers, figural Chanticleer Rooster, gold-decorated, large, pr. 45.00

Salt & pepper shakers, figural duck, 3¼" h., pr. 35.00

Salt & pepper shakers, figural Dutch Boy & Girl, small, pr. 45.00

Salt & pepper shakers, figural Dutch Boy & Girl, large, pr. 60.00

Salt & pepper shakers, figural lobster claw, Lobster Ware, Kenwood Line, pr 35.00

Salt & pepper shakers, figural Little Bo Peep, pr. 15.00

Salt & pepper shakers, figural Mugsey Dog, small, pr. 48.00

Salt & pepper shakers, figural Mugsey Dog, large, pr. 108.00

Salt & pepper shakers, figural Owl, pr. 35.00

Salt & pepper shakers, figural Sailor Boy, 3½" h., pr. 15.00

Salt & pepper shakers, figural Smiley Pig, green scarf, small, pr 30.00

Salt & pepper shakers, figural Swiss Boy & Girl, large, pr. 45.00

Salt & pepper shakers, figural Winnie & Smiley Pig, large, 5" h., pr. ....100.00 to 115.00

Sugar bowl, cov., Clover Flower patt. 75.00

Sugar bowl, cov., "Corn King" line, No. 78 ....40.00

Sugar bowl, cov., "Corn Queen" line, No. 78 ....38.00

Sugar bowl, cov., figural water bucket..25.00

Sugar bowl, cov., Lobster Ware, Kenwood line, domed white cover w/red lobster finial 30.00

Teapot, cov., Blue Leaves patt. 39.00

Corn King Teapot

Teapot, cov., "Corn King" line, 30 oz., No. 75 (ILLUS.) 77.00

Teapot, cov., embossed Flower & Fern patt., green glaze 38.00

Teapot, cov., Embossed Rose patt. 48.00

Teapot, cov., embossed Snowflake patt., blue glaze, small 35.00

Teapot, cov., embossed Snowflake patt., blue glaze, medium 45.00

Teapot, cov., embossed Snowflake patt., green glaze 25.00

Teapot, cov., Fernware line, yellow glaze 19.00

Teapot, cov., Pennsylvania Dutch patt. 45.00

Teapot, cov., Sunflower patt., 6½" h. 44.00

Teapot, cov., figural Granny Ann, coral apron 85.00

Utility jar, cov., Basketweave patt., green trim 58.50

Vase, bud, 8" h., tall cylindrical footed body w/gold trimmed handles, No. 1178 ....18.00

Vase, bulbous body tapering to a flaring neck flanked by short open handles, overall diamond-quilted embossed design w/small flowers, grey glaze, No. 287 ....25.00

Vegetable bowl, open, "Corn King" line, 9" oval, No. 95 ....45.00

Wall pocket, model of a birdhouse & birds, No. 830 ....28.00

Wall pocket, model of a bowknot, No. 434 ....22.00

Wall pocket, model of a grandfather clock, No. 1261 ....25.00

SHELLEY

Shelley Cake Plate

Members of the Shelley family were in the pottery business in England as early as the 18th century. In 1872 Joseph Shelley formed a partnership with James Wileman of Wileman & Co. who operated the Foley China Works. The Wileman & Co. name was used for the firm for the next fifty years, and between 1890 and 1910 the words "The Foley" appeared above conjoined "WC" initials.

Beginning in 1910 the Shelley family name in a shield appeared on wares, although the firm's official name was still Wileman & Co. The company's name was finally changed to Shelley in 1925 and then Shelley China Ltd. after 1965. The firm changed hands in the 1960s and became part of the Doulton Group in 1971.

At first only average quality earthenwares were produced but in the late 1890s new shapes and better quality decorations were used.

Bone china was introduced at Shelley before World War I and these fine dinnerwares became very popular in the United States and are increasingly popular today with collectors. Thin "eggshell china" teawares, miniatures and souvenir items were widely marketed during the 1920s and 1930s and are sought-after today.

Shelley
CHINA
ENGLAND

Bouillon cup,Old Sevres patt. $55.00

Cake plate, Regency patt., 9½" d. 65.00

Cheese dish, cov., Rosebud patt. 90.00

Coffeepot, cov., Regency patt., 8½" h. 125.00

Coffee set: large cov. coffeepot, creamer & cov. sugar bowl; Dainty White patt., 3 pcs. 250.00

Creamer & sugar bowl, demitasse, Regency patt., pr. 30.00

Creamer & cov. sugar bowl, all white w/gold trim, Dainty shape, small, pr. 80.00

Creamer & cov. sugar bowl, Dainty Blue patt., small, pr. 78.00

Creamer & cov. sugar bowl, Pansy patt., Dainty shape, medium, pr. 85.00

Creamer & cov. sugar bowl, Regency patt., pr. 45.00

Cup & saucer, demitasse, Begonia patt. 45.00

Cup & saucer, demitasse, Blue Rock patt., six-flute shape 38.00

Cup & saucer, demitasse, Harebell patt., blue & white 55.00

Cup & saucer, demitasse, Rosebud patt. 45.00

Cup & saucer, demitasse, The Georgian patt. 20.00

Cup & saucer, demitasse, Thistle patt. 50.00

Cup & saucer, Begonia patt., six-flute shape 45.00

Cup & saucer, Bridal Wreath patt. 48.00

Cup & saucer, Charm patt. 48.00

Cup & saucer, Dainty Blue patt., six-flute shape 45.00

Cup & saucer, Dainty White patt. 35.00

Cup & saucer, Daffodil Time patt. 32.50

Cup & saucer, Fantasy patt. 45.00

Cup & saucer, Harebell patt. 43.00

Cup & saucer, Lilac patt., six-flute shape 46.50

Cup & saucer, Lily of the Valley patt. 35.00

Cup & saucer, Old Mill patt. 45.00

Cup & saucer, Oleander shape 50.00

Cup & saucer, Polka Dot patt., aqua 48.00

Cup & saucer, Rambler Rose patt. 48.00

Cup & saucer, Regency patt., Dainty shape 35.00

Cup & saucer, Rock Garden patt. 55.00

Cup & saucer, Shamrock patt., six-flute shape 44.00

Cup & saucer, Stocks patt. 35.00

Cup & saucer, Wildflowers patt. 45.00

Cup & saucer, Woodland patt. 28.00

Dessert set: cup & saucer & dessert plate; Red Daisies patt., 3 pcs. 75.00

Dessert set: cup, saucer & 5" d. plate; Stocks patt., 3 pcs. 65.00

Dessert set: cake plate, four dessert plates, cups & saucers; Queen Anne shape, 13 pcs. 350.00

Dessert set: large creamer, sugar bowl, cake plate, four dessert plates & cups & saucers; Gainsborough shape, 15 pcs. 370.00

Dessert set: 8 x 9½" cake plate, six 6¼" d. plates, six cups & saucers; Tall Trees & Sunrise patt., 19 pc. (ILLUS. of cake plate) 650.00

Egg cup, Rosebud patt., six-flute shape, small 42.50

Jam jar, cov., Rosebud patt., six-flute shape 70.00

Luncheon set: 8" plate, cup & saucer; Bridal Rose patt., 3 pcs. 125.00

Luncheon set: 8" plate, cup & saucer; Daffodil Time patt., 3 pcs. 110.00

Luncheon set: 8" plate, cup & saucer; Rosebud patt., 3 pcs. 80.00

Mug, Rosebud patt., six-flute shape, 4" h. 60.00

Mustard jar, cov. & underplate, Dainty Pink patt., 2 pcs. 80.00

Nut dish, Regency patt. 15.00

Plate, 6" d., Dainty Blue patt., six-flute shape 22.50

Plate, 7" d., Wildflowers patt. 22.00

Plate, 7¾" d., Dainty Blue patt., six-flute shape 35.00

Plate, 8" d., Old Sevres patt. 90.00

Plate, 9½" d., Wildflowers patt. 30.00

Plate, dinner, 10½" d., Dainty Blue patt., six-flute shape 50.00

Plates, 8" d., Begonia patt., six-flute shape, set of 6 ....150.00

Plates, luncheon, Dainty White patt., six-flute shape, set of 6 ....195.00

Saucer, 5½" d., Dainty Blue patt., six-flute shape 13.50

Sugar bowl, cov., handleless, Dainty Blue patt., six-flute shape 22.50

Teapot, cov., Dainty White patt. 300.00

Teapot, cov., Regency patt., small 75.00

Tea set: cov. teapot, creamer & sugar bowl; Daffodil Time patt., 3 pcs. 350.00

Tea set: cov. teapot, creamer & sugar bowl; Woodland patt., 3 pcs. 395.00

Vase, 7½" h., stylized butterflies decoration on black glaze 110.00

SHENANDOAH VALLEY POTTERY

Monkey & Dog Figure Group

The potters of the Shenandoah Valley in Maryland and Virginia turned out an earthenware pottery of a distinctive type. It was the first earthenware pottery made in America with a varied, brightly colored glaze. The most notable of these potters, Peter Bell, Jr., operated a pottery at Hagerstown, Maryland and later at Winchester, Virginia, from about 1800 until 1845. His sons and grandsons carried on the tradition. One son, John Bell, established a pottery at Waynesboro, Pennsylvania in 1833, working until his death in 1880, along with his sons who subsequently operated the pottery a few years longer. Two other sons of Peter Bell, Jr., Solomon and Samuel, operated a pottery in Strasburg, Virginia, a town sometimes referred to as "pot town" for six potteries were in operation there in the 1880s. Their work was also continued by descendants. Shenandoah Valley redware pottery, with its colorful glazes in green, yellow, brown and other colors, and the stoneware pottery produced in the area, are eagerly sought by collectors. Some of the more unique forms can be considered true American folk art and will fetch fantastic prices.

Dish, oval tub-form w/molded lines & applied small rope handles at the top edge of the ends, white slip w/mottled green & brown, impressed "J. Bell & Sons, Strasburg, Va.,"8" l. (rim glaze chips) $2,310.00

Figure group, redware, the standing figure of a dog w/a basket in its mouth, supporting a monkey wearing a cap, mottled green & yellow, monkey lacks arm & one hand, monkey's head reattached, some glaze exfoliation, attributed to the Bell Pottery, Strasburg, Virginia, mid-19th c., 9½" l., 10" h. (ILLUS.) 23,000.00

Flowerpot w/attached saucer base, tapering cylindrical body w/everted rim & dished circular base w/single bead & footring, tin-glazed, marked by John Bell, Waynesboro, mid-19th c., rim 6½" d. 690.00

Food mold, redware, sides w/light horizontal lines, conical center stem, coggled rim, creamy white slip w/green & clear glaze, impressed "Solomon Bell, Strasburg, Va.," 7¾" d., 3½" h. (wear & glaze flakes) 1,200.00

Food mold, Turk's turban-style, sponged green & brown glaze, impressed "Upton M. Bell, Waynesboro, Pa.," 5¾" d. (rim chip) 330.00

Jar, ovoid w/molded rim, brown sponged glaze, impressed label "John W. Bell, Waynesboro, Pa.," 6½" h. (chips) 400.00

Jar, ovoid w/wide flat molded rim, brown glaze w/matte exterior & glossy interior, impressed mark "John Bell, Waynesboro," 7¼" h. (hairline in base) 82.50

Model of a Dog by John Bell

Model of a dog, redware, the standing figure w/a basket in its mouth & tail curled over back, the body incised to simulate fur, the oblong base decorated w/an incised & punchwork-decorated human face, decorated overall w/manganese splotches on an orange ground, attributed to John Bell, Pennsylvania, mid-19th c., 8½" l., 9" h. (ILLUS.) 26,540.00

Model of a dog, Whippet in reclining position on an oblong base, overall reddish tan glaze w/brown highlights, inside lip of base incised "S.B. Anno 1878, by F.C. 150," 9" l. 445.50

Covered Pitcher by Bell

Pitcher, cov., 9" h., redware, spherical footed body tapering to a wide cylindrical neck, thick strap handle, domed cover w/button finial, overall finely spattered green & blue on a cream-glazed ground, stamped "J. Bell" twice, ca. 1860 (ILLUS.) 7,150.00

Shenandoah Valley Redware Pitcher

Pitcher, 9¾" h., redware, cylindrical body, squared rim w/pinched spout, white slip w/green & brown glaze, impressed "S. Bell & Son, Strasburg," wear, chips & glaze flakes (ILLUS.) 3,350.00

SLIPWARE

Slipware-Inscribed Charger

This term refers to ceramics, primarily redware, decorated by the application of slip, or semi-liquid paste made of clay. Such wares were made for decades in England and Germany and elsewhere on the Continent, and in the Pennsylvania Dutch country and elsewhere in the United States. Today, contemporary copies of early Slipware items are featured in numerous decorator magazines and offered for sale in gift catalogs.

Charger, redware w/a stylized petaled flower center, dash border, in yellow, pale orange & brown, 11½" d., (wear, flakes, hairlines & small old rim repairs) $632.00

Charger, round w/gently sloping sides & a coggled rim, a triple-line wavy yellow slip band across the center & yellow slip groups of dashes around the interior, 11¾" d. (wear, scratches & old surface flakes) 693.00

Charger, round dished form w/crimped rim, the interior decorated w/a yellow slip inscription reading "Temperance - Health - Wealth" flanked by squiggled lines in yellow & green slip, New England, 19th c., 13¾" d. (ILLUS.) 19,500.00

Dish, round w/shallow canted sides, the interior decorated w/a single blossomhead in the center & angled bands extending from the rim, all in rust slip on the yellow ground, scattered green splotches, Pennsylvania, 19th c., 6" d. (rim flakes) 1,495.00

Dish, round w/deep double-tapered sides, the interior decorated w/sgraffito-incised tulips, flowers & leaves on a yellow ground w/green splotches, Pennsylvania, ca. 1800, 11¼" d. (some minor flakes) 9,775.00

Dish, round, notched rim, yellow slip decoration of four concentric rings of large dots or dots & dashes, 19th c., 11½" d. (chips) 1,045.00

Flasks, footed spherical form w/flattened front & back sides, small flaring mouth, each flat side decorated w/a yellow slip bull's-eye design on orangish red, Pennsylvania, 3¾" h. (two minor flakes)....1,035.00

Jug, flattened cylindrical sides tapering to a wide slightly flared mouth, each side w/a yellow slip inscription "JS(?) 1794" flanked by leafy vines up the edges, Pennsylvania, 8½" h. (numerous chips, handle missing)............................1,265.00

Loaf dish, rectangular w/rounded corners, crimped edge, the center decorated w/an abstract design of trailed & scrolled slip in shades of green & yellow on an orangish red ground, Pennsylvania, 19th c., 10½ x 13⅞" 6,325.00

Milk bowl, shallow rounded sides, greenish amber glaze w/white slip bands around the interior, 9" d., 3" h. (old surface chips) 247.50

Pie plate, redware w/straight & wavy yellow lines, 8¼" d. (hairlines, minor wear & chips) 302.50

Pie plate, coggled rim, three-line wavy band of yellow slip across the center flanked by pairs of yellow slip "pine tree" designs, 9" d. (minor wear, old flakes & crazing) 375.00

Pie plate, round w/crimped rim, decorated w/eight bold yellow slip lines across the middle flanked by wavy trailed slip bands, scattered green splotches, Pennsylvania, ca. 1850, 9¼" d...................................8,050.00

Pie plate, coggled edge, decorated w/small scattered yellow slip "pine tree" devices, 9⅝" d. (small chips)...385.00

Slipware Pie Plate

Pie plate, round w/coggled rim, decorated w/a row of triple-line yellow slip "S" scrolls, rim chips, Pennsylvania, mid-19th c., 10⅝" d. (ILLUS.) 805.00

Pie plate, shallow round form w/crimped edge, the interior decorated w/an incised depiction of a man on horseback, possibly George Washington, shown holding a sword & horn, the border decorated w/stylized leaves, the whole glazed in green, blue & red on a yellow ground, attributed to Johannes Neesz, Tyler's Port, Montgomery County, Pennsylvania, ca. 1800, 10⅝" d. (two very minor flakes) 24,150.00

Pie plate, oval w/crimped edge, the interior decorated w/trailed slip in green, yellow & brown on a rust ground, Pennsylvania, 19th c., 10¾" l. (minor glaze flake) 5,750.00

Pie plate, round w/crimped edge, the center inscribed in yellow slip "Lafayette" between two long yellow slip S-scrolls, all on an orangish red ground, Pennsylvania, 19th c., 12⅛" d. 1,955.00

SNUFF BOTTLES (Chinese Porcelain)

Reticulated Snuff Bottle

Blue & white, cylindrical, design of seven monkeys, 19th c. .... $800.00 to 1,200.00

Blue & white, bell-shaped, design of five red bats & clouds, 19th c. ....750.00 to 1,000.00

Blue & white, melon-ribbed, painted w/Buddhistic lions & meandering foliage, 19th c.(air bubbles, neck crack) ....500.00 to 700.00

Famille rose, ovoid, painted w/figures in a landscape, Daoguang (Tao Kuang 1821-50) ....1,500.00 to 2,000.00

Famille rose, heart-shaped, painted on one side w/two ladies seated under a tree, the edges w/a blue band, four-character Qianlong (Ch'ien Lung) pseudo-mark, 19th c. ....800.00 to 1,200.00

Famille rose, square form w/a continuous scene of a scholar & ladies in a garden, iron-red & blue borders, Jaiqing (Chia Ching 1796-1820) ....3,000.00 to 4,000.00

Famille rose, slender ovoid form, painted on each side w/roosters upon rockwork, late 19th c. ....500.00 to 600.00

Famille rose, cylindrical, scene of water buffalo in a landscape, mid-19th c. ....400.00 to 600.00

Flambé-glazed, rounded shape w/purple & blue splashes, late 19th c. (damaged).........900.00 to 1,000.00

Green teadust-glazed, rounded shape w/mottled glaze, 19th c. ....1,000.00 to 1,500.00

Green-splashed white-glazed, pear-shaped, five-clawed dragon chasing a flaming pearl above waves............................900.00 to 1,500.00

Grisaille-decorated, pear-shaped, painted w/peony blossoms & foliage amid rockwork, 19th c......500.00 to 700.00

Iron-rust glazed, cylindrical , even mottling, 19th c. ....1,000.00 to 1,500.00

Molded & reticulated, flattened ovoid form w/desigh of *shou* characters & bats on a green ground, late 19th c. ....700.00 to 1,000.00

Robin's-egg blue-glazed, cylindrical, 19th c. ....400.00 to 700.00

Turquoise-glazed (faux turquoise), flattened spade-shape, the matrix painted to simulate feathery inclusions, 18th c. ....1,500.00 to 2,500.00

White-glazed, molded & reticulated, flattened ovoid form w/a design of bats & auspicious characters enclosing a roundel of butterflies, late 18th - early 19th c. (ILLUS.) ....1,000.00 to 1,500.00

SPATTERWARE

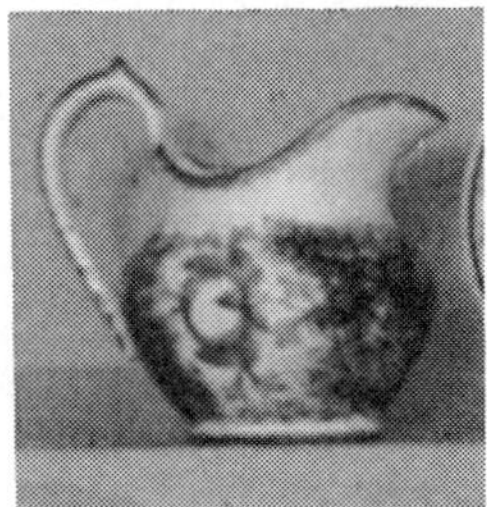

Rose Pattern Creamer

This ceramic ware takes its name from the "spattered" decoration, in various colors, generally used to trim pieces hand-painted with rustic center designs of flowers, birds, houses, etc. Popular in the early 19th century, most was imported from England.

Related wares, called "stick spatter," had free-hand designs applied with pieces of cut sponge attached to sticks, hence the name. Examples date from the 19th and early 20th century and were produced in England, Europe and America.

Some early spatter-decorated wares were marked by the manufacturers, but not many. 20th century reproductions are also sometimes marked, including those produced by Boleslaw Cybis in the 1940s which sometimes have "CYBIS" impressed.

Creamer, squatty bulbous footed body tapering to a wide arched shoulder, C-scroll handle, Rose patt., free-hand blossom in red, black & green, brown & black spatter ground, 4" h. (ILLUS.) $247.50

Creamer, tall footed waisted & paneled body w/a wide arched spout & C-scroll handle, Rose & Cornflower patt., free-hand flowers in red, blue, green & black, red & blue spatter ground, 5⅜" h. (stains, hairlines) 143.00

Cup, handleless, Vine & Berry patt., free-hand red berries on a yellow vine, green spatter ground...............357.50

Cup & saucer, handleless, free-hand central cluster of four buds on saucer & three buds on cup, red & blue spatter borders, impressed "Harvey" 110.00

Cup & saucer, handleless, Peafowl patt., free-hand bird in red, blue, yellow & black, red spatter borders..412.50

Rooster Cup & Saucer

Cup & saucer, handleless, Rooster patt., free-hand bird in blue, red, black & yellow ochre, blue spatter rims, stains & minor wear, small flakes on table ring of cup, saucer marked "T" (ILLUS.) 440.00

Cup & saucer, handleless, Star patt., free-hand six-point star on cup & saucer in red, green & ochre, blue spatter rims 275.00

Cup & saucer, handleless, Tulip patt., free-hand red, green & black flower, yellow spatter borders (minor stains & pinpoint flakes, short hairline in cup)....................852.50

Pitcher, 7⅝" h., footed bulbous ribbed body tapering to a flaring rim w/high arched spout, S-scroll handle, free-hand daisy-like flower in yellow, green, pink & black within a squared bordered reserve on the side surrounded by blue spatter (stains, wear)....................330.00

Pitcher & bowl set, footed tall paneled tapering pitcher w/high arched spout & angled handle & matching bowl, Rose patt., free-hand flowers & leaves in red, green & black w/blue spatter background, bowl 13¾" d., pitcher 12" h., pr. (hairlines, small chips & stains)....................880.00

Plate, 8⅝" d., Rainbow spatter, a red & blue spatter blossom-form cross in the center & alternating bands of red & blue spatter around the border (wear, small flakes)....................302.50

Plate, 8¾" d., Peafowl patt., free-hand bird in blue, green, yellow ochre & black, red spatter border....................467.50

Plate, 9" d., blue & green overall spatter w/a black rim band....................104.50

Plate, 9½" d., Star patt., free-hand six-point star in red, blue & green in the center, blue spatter border band......110.00

Sauce dish, Peafowl patt., free-hand bird in red, blue, green & black, red spatter border, 5" d....................170.50

Toddy plate, Peafowl patt., free-hand bird in red, yellow, blue & black, yellow spatter background, 6" d. (professional repair)....................467.50

Toddy plate, Thistle patt., free-hand thistle in red & green, yellow spatter border, 6¼" d....................1,595.00

STICK OR CUT-SPONGE SPATTER

Cut-Sponge Creamer, Sugar & Mug

Bowl, 9" d., shallow, center decorated w/large, gaudy blossoms within a border of cut-sponge design, blue & white, marked "Villeroy & Boch".......137.50

Creamer & cov. sugar bowl, bulbous body w/loop handle, each decorated w/a band of cut-sponge blue blossoms above a wide band of free-hand yellow & green leaves w/small blue cut-sponge blossoms, marked "Maastricht," Holland, early 20th c., pr. (ILLUS. left)....................165.00

Cup & saucer, handleless, miniature, a band of paired leaves in blue around the rim of the cup & saucer, flanked by red pinstripes, impresed mark "Tunstall" (stains)....................71.50

Cup & saucer, handleless, rounded cup & deep bowl each w/free-hand green leaf sprigs w/triple cut-sponge red blossoms, black trim.......38.50

Mug, miniature, cylindrical, decorated w/a free-hand colorful flower & leaf band w/small cut-sponge blossoms, 2¼" h. (ILLUS. right)....................38.50

Mug, decorated w/green & yellow striping over a central band of black cut-sponge diamond design, 3" h. ...110.00

Rabbit Pattern Stick Spatter

Mug, slightly tapering cylindrical body, Rabbit patt. transfer-printed top & bottom bands flanking a wide center band w/free-hand & cut-sponge polychrome flowers & leaves, edge chips, 5½" h. (ILLUS. center)........1,210.00

Plate, 7¾" d., ten-sided, decorated w/three tightly packed rows of diamonds w/dots, diamond-petaled flowerhead in the center, in red, blue & green (underrim chip)....................104.50

Plate, 9" d., wide border band of polychrome leaves w/tiny cut-sponge blossoms, marked on back "Maastricht," Holland, late 19th - early 20th c....................22.00

Plate, 9¼" d., Rabbit patt., transfer-printed center design, a wide border band w/polychrome free-hand leaves & large & scattered small cut-sponge blossoms (ILLUS. left).........467.50

Plate, 9¼" d., Rabbit patt., transfer-printed center design w/a wide border band of free-hand poly-chrome leaf bands & large blossoms & clusters of three small cut-sponge blossoms, stains, rim hairlines (ILLUS. right)....................440.00

Plate, 9¼" d., Rabbit patt. transfer-printed border center design w/a wide border band of free-hand polychrome leaf & cut-sponge blossoms, circle of small cut-sponge blossoms in the very center (rim hairline) 330.00

Platter, 14" l., oval, a wide "chain" design border band, the center w/large polychrome leafy sprigs w/small cut-sponge blossoms, marked on back "Auld Heather Ware, Scotland" 412.50

SPONGEWARE

Spongeware Crock

Spongeware's designs were spattered, sponged or daubed on in colors, sometimes with a piece of cloth. Blue on white was the most common type, but mottled tans, browns and greens on yellowware were also popular. Spongeware generally has an overall pattern with a coarser look than Spatterwares, to which it is loosely related. These wares were extensively produced in England and America well into the 20th century.

Bowl, 13" d., 6½" h., deep rounded sides w/molded rim band, overall blue on white (crazing, hairline) $192.50

Cheese keeper, cov., Cockscomb patt., red, brown, blue & yellow..........85.00

Creamer, octagonal, grape leaf decoration on panels, scalloped rim, sponged rim & handle, blue on white, 3" h. 54.00

Crock, straight-sided, overall coarse blue sponging on white, rim chip & hairline, 10¾" d., 15" h. (ILLUS.) 440.00

Cup & saucer, ring-handled, over-sized, heavy dark blue on white.......390.50

Pitcher, milk, 6" h., bulbous body tapering to a shaped rim w/wide arched spout, C-form handle, overall heavy dark blue on white (minor stains) 247.50

Pitcher, 6¾" h., cylindrical body w/pointed rim spout, squared handle, overall blue on white (minor hairline, tiny flakes) 247.50

Pitcher, 7¾" h., bulbous ovoid body tapering to a wide tall spout, C-form handle, a narrow blue center band flanked by narrow white bands & surrounded by overall blue on white (short hairline & crow's foot) 385.00

Pitcher, 8½" h., tall barrel-shaped body w/small rim spout, C-form handle, overall heavy blue on white (rim chips) 302.50

Pitcher, 8⅞" h., cylindrical w/pinched rim spout & C-form handle, relief-molded flower sprig on the sides highlighted in dark blue, coarse blue sponged bands at the rim & base, white ground (small chips) 495.00

Pitcher, 9" h., ovoid body tapering to a flat rim w/a pinched spout, C-form handle, overall coarse blue sponging on white, dark brown Albany slip interior (surface & edge chips) 330.00

Pitcher, 9¼" h., bulbous body tapering to a wide, flaring neck w/pinched spout, small C-form handle, overall finely spattered blue on white, dark brown Albany slip interior 385.00

Pitcher, 10" h., 7" d., cylindrical, embossed Old Fashioned Garden Rose patt., blue on white 750.00

Pitcher, 11⅜" h., footed baluster-form body w/a high & wide arched spout & long S-scroll handle, overall coarse light blue sponging on white (stain, chips on base).......................385.00

Pitcher, embossed decoration of girl & dog, blue on white...........................445.00

Spongeware Slop Jar

Slop jar, cov., slightly waisted form, wire bail handle w/wooden grip, blue band near base flanked by white bands, repeated on cover, overall blue on white, hairline & chips, 12½" h. (ILLUS.) 247.50

Syrup jug, bulbous ovoid body w/rim

spout & filler opening, wire bail handle w/wooden hand grip, blue on white w/oval reserve on the front printed "GRANDMOTHER'S MAPLE SYRUP OF 50 YEARS AGO," 7" d., 6½" h. 800.00

Tray, rectangular w/rounded corners & slightly flared edges, heavy blue on white, 10½" l. (small edge chips) 137.50

STAFFORDSHIRE FIGURES

Equestrian Figure of St. George

Small figures and groups made of pottery were produced by the majority of the Staffordshire, England potters in the 19th century and were used as mantel decorations or "chimney ornaments," as they were sometimes called. Pairs of dogs were favorites and were turned out by the carload, and 19th century pieces are still available. Well-painted reproductions also abound and collectors are urged to exercise caution before investing.

Cat, miniature in seated position, white coat w/orange & black spots, green trim, 2⅞" h. $181.50

Cat, miniature, in seated position w/bow around neck, white & orange w/blue & green trim, 3⅞" h. (small edge flakes) 247.50

Cat, standing animal w/tail curled over its back, black & tan sponging, glass eyes, 5¼" h. 275.00

Cat, seated, large black spots on white w/painted facial features, on a green & red pillow w/a rectangular base, gilt trim, 19th c., 7¼" h. (enamel wear) 357.50

Cats, seated w/tail curled around legs, brown spatter decoration w/black & yellow trim, 5⅛" h., pr. (hairline, small chips) 715.00

Doe, reclining figure on a grassy base, pearlware w/tan & green enameling, 6¼" l., 5⅜" h. (stains & minor wear) 522.50

Dog, Pug, miniature, creamware, seated animal w/a brown muzzle & eyes & a streaky brown & ochre coat wearing a collar fastened at the back w/an incised florette, seated on a mound base washed in green, ca. 1770-80, 3" h. (tail restored) 1,265.00

Dog, hound w/a slender body seated on a stepped oval base, creamware splashed w/brown & green spots, ca. 1760, 8¾" h. (chip on base) ..11,000.00

Dog, Poodle, miniature, in a playful position w/front legs bent & tail in the air, white sanded coat w/red & black spots, green trim, 2⅝" h. 302.50

Dog, Spaniel, miniature, in seated position & holding the handle of a small basket in its mouth, sanded coat w/worn gilt trim, 3" h. 192.50

Dog, Spaniel in seated position, white w/sanded coat & black & yellow enameling, 3⅝" h. 143.00

Dog, Spaniel in seated position, molded fur, white w/black & yellow, worn gilt trim, 14¾" h. 275.00

Dogs, Pekingese, orange & white, 9" h., pr. 835.00

Dogs, Spaniel, white w/brown muzzle, 10" h., pr. 450.00

Equestrian figure, miniature, man in soldier's uniform astride a prancing white horse, on oval base, poly-chrome enamel trim, 4⅝" h. (wear to paint) 258.00

Equestrian figure, man in tricorn hat astride a prancing horse, oval base marked "T. King," 10" h. 522.50

Equestrian figure, St. George, his plumed helmet splashed in ochre & green w/green drapery, yellow tack on his brown-spotted horse, a green dragon at his feet, Ralph Wood-type, spear broken, chips to right foot, his left foot & horse's tail restuck, ca. 1780, 11" h. (ILLUS.) 2,090.00

Equestrian figure, man w/plumed hat astride a horse w/head down & left front leg raised, ca. 1850, 13¾" h. ...325.00

Equestrian figure, Scotsman on horseback w/slain deer, polychrome enameling, 14¼" h. (minor hairlines) 247.50

Equestrian figure, creamware, William III or the Duke of Cumberland, the man wearing classical garb w/a blue cloak, green & blue armor, astride a rearing brown charger supported by moss-encrusted rockwork on a waisted rectangular base w/green laurel, ca. 1785, 14¾" h. (one hoof missing, his left foot reglued, chip to reins) 13,200.00

Equestrian figures, Scotsman on horseback, late 19th c., 14½" h., pr. 467.50

Ewe & lamb, creamware, the recumbent ewe splashed in brown, her lamb at her side on a shaped base molded & applied w/flowers splashed in green & brown, ca. 1775, 6" l. (ears, tail & three flowers restored, cracked) 880.00

Figure of a Highlander, standing man wearing traditonal kilt holding a staff in one hand & w/elbow resting on tree stump to one side, 15¼" h. 440.00

Figure of "The Lion Slayer," man in Scots outfit holding a dead lion by one rear paw, oval base w/title molded, late 19th c., 16¼" h. 357.50

Figure of an old woman seated in a chair, holding a jug & glass, polychrome enamels & pink lustre, 6⅜" h. 225.50

Figure of a woman standing & holding a rose to her bosom, wearing a large feathered hat & a long dark blue coat & ruffle-trimmed gown, polychrome detailing, 19th c., 5½" h. 192.50

Bull-Baiting Figure Group

Figure group, pearlware, bull-baiting scene, the iron-red-spotted salmon bull (right rear leg hair cracked) w/grey head & horns (left restored), spine, tail tuft (repaired), hooves & tether (touched up), tossing a black-spotted white dog (repainted & extremities restored) over his shoulder while another yellow-spotted dog (feet & tail restored) barks at the bull's head & a showman (reconstructed in plaster) wearing a russet jacket, grey waistcoat & yellow breeches stands to one side, one a green serpentine-fronted rectangular base above a black-sponged apron molded on the front w/an iron-red, blue & green floral garland & raised on four ridged bracket feet, Obadiah Sherratt-type, ca. 1830, 11¼" l. (ILLUS.) 1,725.00

Figure group, a girl wearing flowered dress & small hat seated on a large, horned goat w/shaggy fur, oval base, late 19th c., 12" h. 605.00

Figure group, Highland lad & lassie w/deer, bright polychrome enameling, 7⅝" h. (minor wear & flaking) 275.00

Figure group, two milkmaids, each carrying a milk pail, polychrome enamel decoration, 8½" h. (minor wear) 236.50

Figure group, "St. John" depicted w/goose, white w/enamel & gilt trim, 11¼" h. (crazed) 214.50

Figure group, "Tenderness," a man & woman standing w/a lamb before a leafy tree, on a scrolled base, back impressed "Walton," 7" h. (edge chips & minor damage) 522.50

Figure group, woman holding baby in her arms, a young child standing at one side clutching her skirt & another child standing at her other side, pearlware w/polychrome enameling, 7⅜" h. 412.50

Figure group, pearlware, the standing young shepherdess wearing a yellow-trimmed white hat on her grey hair, a yellow-buttoned white bodice, yellow-trimmed blue dress & skirt & yellow shoes, holding a fleecy lamb under her left arm & standing amid blue plants on a green-glazed mound base, her cheeks trimmed w/dots of manganese-brown, 1785-95, 10¼" h. (hat plume restored, chip on edge of dress, base repaired) 805.00

Figure group, a youth & maiden, he standing to one side wearing a large feathered hat, jacket, waistcoat, kneebreeches & black boots, she standing to other side wearing peasant costume & carrying a load on her head, polychrome decoration, 19th c., 12½" h. 220.00

Goat, recumbent animal on an oval base, polychrome enamel trim, 2¾" l. 137.50

Hen on nest, polychrome feather detail, yellow basketweave base, 9¾" l. (minor chips & wear) 225.50

Hen on nest, white hen on a basketweave base, trimmed in orange, green & black, 3¼" h. 110.00

Hen on nest, large white hen w/red comb & black eyes on a green grass & brown basket base, 10½" l. 302.50

Staffordshire Figures of Horses

Horses, earthenware, bocage-type, modeled affronté, one w/black spots (legs hair cracked & left ear chipped), the other w/brown spots, each standing before a leafy green tree (first partially missing) applied w/yellow-centered iron-red & blue blossoms, on a bright green mound base (first hair cracked) decorated at the front w/blue dashes, 1820-30, 5½" h., pr. (ILLUS.) 4,888.00

Lamb, white animal w/sanded coat on four free-standing legs, 2¼" h. 258.50

Nun pigeon on nest sauce tureen, cov., the body of the bird forming the cover & decorated w/a salmon & iron-red beak, iron-red-encircled black eyes & grey & white plumage, the oval nest base in mottled brown & yellow, pearlware, ca. 1820, 7¼" l. (enamel chips, rim chips, hairline in breast) 316.00

Rabbit, reclining black & white animal on a red & green "coleslaw" grass base above an underglaze-blue band, 3½" l. (crazed, hairlines) 247.50

Rooster, jar, cov., the removable head forming the cover & decorated w/iron-red comb & wattles & yellow beak, his body & arched tail in yellow, iron-red & grey & his wings & tail in shades of grey, perched on a turquoise grassy scroll on a green & brown mottled mound base applied w/small mounds of 'moss,' ca. 1820-30, 8⅜" h. (enamel chips, restoration to neck rims, flange & right spur) 920.00

Sheep, standing animal on an oval base, polychrome enamel trim, 3" h. 159.50

Staffordshire Pearlware Squirrel

Squirrel, pearlware, modeled nibbling a nut, his incised coat spotted all over in mocha- and chocolate brown, seated on a chamfered rectangular base streaked in green, chips, some restored, two small hair cracks on the base & left ear tip restored, 1790-1800, 6¾" h. (ILLUS.) 1,955.00

Stag w/bocage, the brown deer w/black eyes, mouth & hooves standing before a green leafy tree applied w/a central yellow blossom & two yellow-centered puce blossoms, on a green-topped rectangular base w/black-edged iron-red sides molded w/a yellow foliate border, ca. 1820-30, 7" h. (right foreleg repaired, small chips & repairs on tree, central blossom touched-up) 2,530.00

Vase, 8¾" h., figural, maiden & deer above a rockwork arch enclosing a swan in front of a tree trunk vase, polychrome trim 255.50

Vase, spill-type, 11" h., figural Robert Burns & his Mary 375.00

Vases, 10¾" h., model of a cow w/a nursing calf standing in front of a tree stump vase, on a grassy mound base, pr. 935.00

STAFFORDSHIRE TRANSFER WARES

Early Cup & Saucer

The process of transfer-printing designs on earthenwares developed in England in the late 18th century and by the mid-19th century most common ceramic wares were decorated in this manner, most often with romantic European or Oriental landscape scenes, animals or flowers. The earliest such wares were printed in dark blue but a little later light blue, pink, purple, red, black, green and brown were used. A majority of these wares were produced at various English potteries right up till the turn of the century but French and other European firms also made similar pieces and all are quite collectible. The best reference on this area is Petra Williams' book Staffordshire Romantic Transfer Patterns - Cup Plates and Early Victorian China *(Fountain House East, 1978). Also see ADAMS, CLEWS and other makers and HISTORICAL & COMMEMORATIVE WARES. Also see ABC PLATES.*

Basket & undertray, deep oval flaring reticulated sides w/end loop handles, light blue design of Roman ruins, matching oval underplate, impressed "Rogers," ca. 1840, 9¾" l., 2 pcs. $852.50

Basket & undertray, the basket w/reticulated oval loops forming the sides below a flaring rim w/end handles, the oval undertray w/a reticulated rim, each decorated w/English country landscapes w/a vintage border, medium blue, ca. 1830, tray 10¼" l., 2 pcs. 632.50

Coffeepot, cov., Italia patt., blue, Davenport 165.00

Coffeepot, cov., Scroll Frond Border patt., blue, Charles Meigh & Son, 1850s 350.00

Creamer & cov. sugar bowl, Coysh patt., blue, Spode, pr. 135.00

Cup & saucer, handleless, Cologne patt., red 49.50

Cup & saucer, handleless, oversized, large basket of flowers design, dark blue (wear, small colored-in rim flakes) 181.50

Cup & saucer, handleless, pearlware, decorated w/cows in a landscape, blue, ca. 1810 (some damage) 77.00

Cup & saucer, handleless, transfer-printed figure of a man w/symbols & inscription "The Great Advocate for TEMPERENCE - Father Matthews," black (tiny hairline under base line) 65.00

Cup & saucer, Roselle patt., blue, John Meir & Son 75.00

Cup & saucer, handleless, pearlware, Salopian polychrome enameled transfer of birds & flowers, early 19th c., chips on saucer, wear on 6 cup (ILLUS.) 93.50

Cup & saucer, handleless, scene entitled "Washington," red (minor edge flakes) 137.50

Cup plate, Canova patt., brown 35.00

Cup plate, central scene of a landscape w/a large lake & arched bridge in the distance, dark blue, impressed "Wood," 3¾" d. 159.50

Cup plate, Oriental scenery, Fakeer's Rock, fruit & flower border, dark blue, Hall & Sons, 4¼" d. 140.00

Cup plate, Oriental village w/willow tree, man & boy, medium to dark blue, Enoch Wood, 4¾" d. 130.00

Ladle holder, Columbia patt., blue, J. Wedgwood, ca, 1845 ....95.00

Mug, cylindrical, pearlware, black scene of a military surrender titled "Cornwallis," pink lustre trim, 2⅛" h. (wear, small chips) 467.50

Mug, motto-type, black transfer-printed scene illustrating "Dr. Franklin - Poor Richard" maxim "Constant dropping wears away stones...." 2½" h. (wear, chip on bottom)...104.50

Mug, cylindrical body, the lip & base w/a black band & transfer-printed w/a verse entitled "Bachelor's Wish" enclosed by floral garlands, mid-19th c., 4" d., 6" h............................437.00

Pitcher, 8" h., Medici patt., blue, Mellor, Venables & Co., ca. 1835-50.....195.00

Pitcher, 11¼" h., Roselle patt., blue, John Meir & Son 350.00

Pitcher, 12¼" h., Lausanne Villa patt., blue 295.00

Pitcher & bowl set, tall paneled tapering pitcher w/scalloped rim & angled handle, matching bowl, Byzantium patt., light blue, bowl 13" d., pitcher 10" h., 2 pcs. (stains, hairlines) 275.00

Plate, 5⅞" w., octagonal, black transfer-printed center scene titled "Robinson Crusoe" & trimmed in polychrome enamel, ca. 1830 (small edge flakes) 93.50

Plate, 6⅜" d., Quadrupeds patt., dog depicted, dark blue 165.00

Plate, 6⅝" d., landscape scene w/dog & bird, dark blue, E. Wood & Sons (minor stains) 93.50

Palestine Pattern Plate

Plate, 7" d., Palestine patt., blue, Adams, ca. 1850 (ILLUS.) 45.00

Plate, 7⅛" d., black center scene entitled "The Sluggard," enhanced w/blue, orange, yellow & green enamel, purple lustre rim 104.50

Plate, 7½ d., Florentine patt., blue, T. Mayer 35.00

Plate, 7⅝" d., Quadrupeds patt., gazelle depicted, dark blue 247.50

Plate, 7⅞" d., Oriental scenes, dark blue, Clews 60.50

Plate, 8" d., Wild Rose patt., dark blue (wear) 55.00

Plate, 8¼" d., Siam patt., blue, J. Clementson, mid-19th c. 45.00

Plate, 8⅞" d., Castle of Furstenfel scene, dark blue 115.50

Plate, 8⅞" d., English river scene w/fishermen, dark blue, Clews (very minor wear) 170.00

Plate, 9" d., Clyde Scenery patt., purple, ca. 1840 ....38.50

Plate, 9½" d., Baronial Halls patt., blue, T. Mayer 55.00

Plate, 9½" d., Columbia patt., blue, Adams 75.00

Plate, 9½" d., Florentine patt., blue, T. Mayer 65.00

Plate, 9½" d., a central scene of an Indian landscape w/elephant & temple, floral border, light medium blue, ca. 1840 (wear) 93.50

Plate, 9¾" d., pearlware, the center w/an Oriental landscape w/river & temple similar to the Willow design, bracketed scroll border, blue, early 19th c. (flake on back rim, minor glaze wear on rim) 82.50

Plate, 10" d., Castle Scenery patt., blue, J. Furnival 75.00

Plate, 10" d., Lozere patt., blue, E. Challinor 75.00

Plate, 10" d., central round reserve w/a large fruit cluster, wide border w/flower & leaf reserves, dark blue, marked "Stubbs," ca. 1830s (small flakes on table ring) 132.00

Plate, 10" d., Italian Buildings patt., light blue, R. Hall 44.00

Plate, 10¼" d., Carolina patt., purple, R. Hall, ca. 1840 ....60.50

Plate, 10½" d., Cambrian patt., black, George Phillips 72.00

Plate, 10½" d., Delaware patt., blue, Ridgways 25.00

Plate, 10½" d., Palestine patt., dark blue, R. Stevenson, ca. 1830s 82.50

Platter, 7¼ x 10", Isola Bella patt., blue, W. Adams 125.00

Platter, 9½ x 12½", Ivanhoe patt., blue, Podmore, Walker & Co. 125.00

Platter, 9¾ x 12½", Florentine patt, blue, T. Mayer 225.00

Platter, 10 x 13¼", Ontario Lake Scenery, blue, Heath, ca. 1845-53 ..130.00

Platter, 10⅛ x 13⅛", Geneva patt., blue, Heath 225.00

Platter, 10¼ x 13½", Montilla patt., blue, Davenport 250.00

Platter, 10¾ x 13", Pantheon patt.,

polychrome center scene w/green transfer border, Ridgway & Morley, ca. 1840 .... 150.00

Platter, 11" l., oval w/scalloped edge, Fountain Scenery patt., red, impressed "Adams," ca. 1830 .... 126.50

Platter, 13½" oval, an overall scene of rabbit hunters on horseback, design runs to outer border, medium blue, ca. 1840 (minor stains) 225.00

Platter, 14" l., Oriental patt., Ridgway 175.00

Platter, 11 x 14", Cypress patt., mulberry, anchor mark, Davenport .. 200.00

Platter, 11¼ x 14¾", Priory patt., blue, E. Challinor 275.00

Platter, 15" l., oval w/slightly scalloped rim, large Oriental landscape in the center & small oval landscape reserves & round floral reserves around the rim, green, ca. 1840 .... 192.50

Platter, 12 x 15½", Ontario Lake Scenery patt., blue, Heath, ca. 1845-53 .... 350.00

Platter, 15¾ l., oval, Canova patt., light blue (stains) 192.50

Platter, 16" l., Ardennes patt., Edward Challinor, 1842-67 .... 195.00

Platter, 17" l., oval, India Temple patt., blue, J. & W. Ridgway, first quarter 19th c. 247.50

Platter, 17" l., oval, central Middle Eastern castle in landscape scene, wide border w/scenic cartouche reserves alternating w/oval floral reserves, purple 275.00

Platter, 14½ x 17", Canova patt., blue, T. Mayer 325.00

Platter, 17¼ l. oval, lightly scalloped rim, Oriental patt., green w/gilt rim, ca. 1840 .... 165.00

Platter, 20" l. oval, Lucerne patt., light blue, ca. 1840 (wear, glaze chips on back) 187.00

Soup plate w/flanged rim, a center scene of a fisherman w/his wife & child, a wide floral border, medium blue, 10" d. 82.50

Soup plate w/flanged rim, Japan patt., blue transfer-printed florals w/polychrome enamel decoration (wear, traces of gilt) 49.50

Soup plate, Palestine patt., medium blue, 10¼" d. 38.50

Soup plates, pastoral design w/cows in a meadow, grapevine border, dark blue, William Adams, early 19th c., 10¼" d., set of 5 (minor imperfections) 825.00

Sugar bowl, cov., oblong boat-shaped body w/raised & angled rim, angled end handles, slightly domed inset cover w/knob finial, medium blue design of a hunter w/two dogs, ca. 1830, 4⅞" h. (minor chips inside cover, hairline in one handle) 148.50

Sugar bowl, cov., oblong bulbous body w/closed rim & inset domed cover w/knob finial, Salopian polychrome transfer of a lad grooming a cow in a landscape, ca. 1800, 5" h. (stains, inner flange chipped) 302.50

Toddy plate, Cologne patt., lavender, ca. 1830s 60.00

Toddy plate, English ruins scene, medium blue, 5" d. 82.50

Toddy plate, dark blue transfer-printed design of a lady at an upright piano in a garden, 5" d. (stains) 137.50

Toddy plate, the center w/a design of a young woman & a goat, a wide looped design around the rim, brown, ca. 1830, 5" d. 82.50

Toddy plate, motto-type, a blue center scene of a farmer & two horses plowing a field surrounded by the motto "He that by the plough would thrive...," polychrome enameled rim w/lustre trim, 5" d. (stains & small flakes) 82.50

Tureen, cov., deep bulbous oblong body w/loop end handles & tapering to small pad feet, the wide flat rim supporting a stepped, domed cover w/loop handle, decorated w/European castle scenes, blue, ca. 1840, 13½" l. (hairline in cover handle & some damage) 220.00

Vegetable bowl, cov., Dorothy patt., Johnson Bros. 150.00

Vegetable dish, cov., Spoletto patt., dark blue, 13" l. (minor stains) 137.50

Waste bowl, Cobridge patt., blue, Brownfield, ca. 1850 .... 125.00

Waste bowl, decorated w/birds & flowers, medium blue, ca. 1840, 6" d., 3½" h. (wear, pinpoint flakes) 115.50

Waste bowl, footed, overall florals, dark blue, 6¼" d. (wear, small flakes) 137.50

STANGL POTTERY

Johann Martin Stangl, who first came to work for the Fulper Pottery in 1910 as a ceramic chemist and plant superintendent, acquired a financial interest and became president of the company in 1926. The name of the firm was changed to Stangl Pottery in 1929 and at that time much of the production was devoted to a high grade dinnerware to enable the company to survive the Depression years. One of the earliest solid-color dinnerware patterns was their Colonial *line, introduced in 1926. In the 1930s it was joined by their* Americana *pattern. After 1942 these early patterns were followed by a wide range of hand-decorated patterns featuring flowers and fruits with a few decorated with animals or human figures.*

Around 1940 a very limited edition of porcelain birds, patterned after the illustrations in John James Audubon's "Birds of America," was issued. Stangl subsequently began production of less expensive ceramic birds and these proved to be popular during the war years, 1940-46. Each bird was handpainted and each was well marked with impressed, painted or stamped numerals which indicated the species and the size.

All operations ceased at the Trenton, New Jersey plant in 1978.

Two reference books which collectors will find helpful are The Collectors Handbook of Stangl Pottery *by Norma Rehl (The Democrat Press, 1979), and* Stangl Pottery *by Harvey Duke (Wallace-Homestead, 1994).*

BIRDS

Bird of Paradise, No. 3408, 5½" h. ....$100.00 to 125.00

Bluebird, No. 3276-S, 5" h. ......85.00 to 90.00

Blue-Headed Vireo, No. 3448, 4¼" h. 75.00

Bobolink, No. 3595, 4¾" h. 135.00

Brewer's Blackbird, No. 3591, 3½" h. ....125.00 to 150.00

Broadbill Hummingbird, No. 3629, 6½" l., 4½" h. ....100.00 to 125.00

Canary facing right - Rose Flower, No. 3746, 6¼" h. 150.00

Cardinal, No. 3444, 6" h. ....100.00 to 125.00

Chat, No. 3590, 4¼" h. ....100.00 to 150.00

Chestnut-Backed Chickadee, No. 3811, 5" h. ....50.00 to 70.00

Chestnut-Sided Warbler, No. 3812.......95.00

Cockatoo, No. 3405-S, 6" h. 52.00

Stangl Cockatoo

Cockatoo, No. 3484, 11⅜" h. (ILLUS.) 275.00

Cock Pheasant, No. 3492, 6¼ x 11" ....155.00 to 175.00

Double Wren, No. 3410D .....75.00 to 100.00

Drinking Duck, No, 3250-E, 3¾" h. 75.00

Feeding Duck, No. 3250-C, 1¾" h. 40.00

Flying Duck, No. 3443, 9" h. ....225.00 to 275.00

Gazing Duck, No. 3250-D, 3¾" h. 60.00

Golden Crowned Kinglet, No. 3848, 4" h. 92.50

Goldfinch, No. 3849 ....92.50

Grosbeak, No. 3813, 5" h. ..100.00 to 125.00

Group of Goldfinches, No. 3635, 4 x 11½" ....200.00 to 225.00

Hummingbirds, pr., 3599-D, 8 x 10½" 215.00

Indigo Bunting, No. 3589, 3¼" h. 60.00

Kingfisher, No. 3406, 3½" h. 65.00

Kingfisher, No. 3406-S, 3½" h. 80.00

Oriole, No. 3402-S, 3¼" h. 55.00

Painted Bunting, No. 3452, 5" h. 90.00

Pair of Hummingbirds, No. 3599-D, 8 x 10½" ....225.00 to 250.00

Pair of Love Birds, N0. 3404-D, 4½" h. ....100.00 to 125.00

Pair of Parakeets, No. 3582, 7" h. 245.00

Pair of Wrens, No. 3401-D, 8" h. ....100.00 to 125.00

Paraquet, No. 3449, 5½" h. 125.00

Preening Duck, No. 3250-B, 2¼" h. 85.00

Quacking Duck, No. 3250-F, 2¼" h. 60.00

Red-Breasted Nuthatch, No. 3851 ....50.00

Red-Headed Woodpecker (Double), No. 3752-D, 7¾" h. ....300.00 to 350.00

Rieffers Hummingbird, No. 3628, 4½" h. 125.00

Rivoli Hummingbird, No. 3627, 6" h....150.00

Rooster, yellow, No. 3445, 9" h. 185.00

Rufous Hummingbird, No. 3585, 3" h...35.00

Scarlet Tanager (Double), No. 3750-D, 8" h. 395.00

Wren, No. 3401, 3½" h. 60.00

Wren, No. 3401S 42.00

Yellow Warbler, No. 3850 ....65.00

DINNERWARES & ARTWARES

Ashtray, Cosmos patt., 5½" d. 25.00

Ashtray, square, Mallard Duck patt., Sportsmen's Giftware line, 9" sq. 45.00

Ashtray, oval, Mallard Duck patt., Sportsmen's Giftware line, No. 3921, 10⅝" oval 38.00

Ashtray, oval, Pheasant patt., Sportsmen's Giftware line, No. 3926 ....50.00 to 60.00

Ashtray, oval, Quail patt., Sportsmen's Giftware line, No. 3926 ....49.00

Ashtray, crescent-shaped, Tropical Fish patt., Sportsmen's Giftware line, No. 3927 ....55.00

Ashtray, Tulip patt., 4" d. 15.00

Ashtray/coaster, Blossom Time patt., No. 3886 ....12.00

Bowl, cereal, 5½" d., Apple Delight patt. 10.00

Bowl, cereal, 5½" d., Fruits & Flowers patt. 6.00

Bowl, cereal, 5½" d., Starflower patt.....10.00

Bowl, cereal, 5½" d., Thistle patt. 12.00

Bowl, 6¼" d., Bittersweet patt. 7.00

Bowl, 8" d., Country Garden patt. 30.00

Bowl, soup, w/lug handles, Americana patt., red 4.00

Bowl, soup, 5¼" d., w/lug handles, Apple Delight patt. 12.00

Bowl, soup, w/lug handles, Blueberry patt. 15.00

Bowl, soup, w/lug handles, Thistle patt. 18.00

Bread tray, Thistle patt., 15¼" l. 22.00

Butter dish, cov., Thistle patt. 32.00

Candy dish, cov., Terra Rose patt. 22.00

Celery tray, Wild Rose patt. 18.00

Chamberstick, ring handle, motto around base, medium blue flambé glaze, artist-signed, 5¼" h. 35.00

Cigarette box, cov., Blossom Time patt., No. 3886 ....38.00

Cigarette box, cov., Garden Flower patt., 4 x 5" 36.00

Coaster, Country Garden patt., 5" d. 7.00

Coaster, Orchard Song patt., 5" d. 5.00

Coffeepot, cov., Blue Tulip patt., Terra Rose finish, 8-cup 65.00

Coffee server, cov., Amber Glo patt. ....40.00 to 50.00

Coffee warmer, Golden Harvest patt. ...12.00

Creamer, Fruits & Flowers patt. 6.00

Creamer, Thistle patt. 4.50

Creamer, Wild Rose patt. 10.00

Creamer & cov. sugar bowl, Bittersweet patt., pr. 15.00

Creamer & cov. sugar bowl, Golden Harvest patt., pr. 10.00

Cup & saucer, Apple Delight patt. 13.00

Cup & saucer, Bittersweet patt. 10.00

Cup & saucer, Country Garden patt. 10.00

Cup & saucer, Dahlia patt., blue, green & white 4.50

Cup & saucer, Fruits & Flowers patt.....10.00

Cup & saucer, Golden Harvest patt. 7.50

Cup & saucer, Provincial patt. 10.00

Cup & saucer, Thistle patt. 11.00

Egg cup, Golden Blossom patt. 8.00

Gravyboat & underplate, Thistle patt., 2 pcs. 32.00

Mug, Pheasant patt., Sportsmen's Giftware line, large, 2 cup 30.00

Pitcher, cov., Colonial patt., aqua glaze 40.00

Pitcher, Chicory patt., 2 qt. 40.00

Plate, 6" d., Apple Delight patt................5.00

Plate, 6" d., Blueberry patt......................7.00

Plate, 6" d., Dahlia patt...........................2.00

Plate, 6" d., Fruit & Flowers patt............4.00

Plate, 6" d., Golden Harvest patt............3.00

Plate, 6" d., Orchard Song patt...............2.00

Plate, 6" d., Starflower patt.....................4.00

Plate, 6¼" d., Thistle patt........................6.00

Plate, 8" d., Blueberry patt......................6.00

Plate, 8" d., Blue Daisy patt....................6.50

Plate, 8" d., Fruits & Flowers patt. 8.00

Plate, 8" d., Golden Blossom patt...........5.00

Plate, 8" d., Rooster patt.......................28.00

Plate, 8" d., Town & Country patt., blue glaze 20.00

Plate, luncheon, 8¼" d., Apple Delight patt. 3.50

Plate, 9" d., Little Bo Peep patt., Kiddieware line 78.00

Plate, 9" d., Star Flower patt..................7.00

Plate, dinner, 10" d., Apple Delight patt...15.00

Plate, dinner, 10" d., Blue Daisy patt......8.00

Plate, dinner, 10" d., Fruits & Flowers patt...10.00

Plate, dinner, 10" d., Golden Harvest patt..7.50

Plate, dinner, 10" d., Magnolia patt.........8.00

Plate, dinner, 10" d., Star Flower patt...10.00

Plate, chop, 12½" d., Colonial patt., blue glaze 12.00

Salt & pepper shakers, Bittersweet patt., pr...8.00

Salt & pepper shakers, Country Garden patt., pr.................................14.00

Salt & pepper shakers, Thistle patt., pr...14.00

Server, center-handled, Bella Rosa patt...10.00

Server, center-handled, Fairlawn patt...10.00

Server, center-handled, Orchard Song patt. 2.00

Smoke set: cov. cigarette box & round ashtray; Mallard patt., Sportsmen's Giftware line, the set 110.00

Snack set: cup & saucer & 8" d. plate; Orchard Song patt., 3 pcs. 6.00

Sugar bowl, cov., Carnival patt............22.00

Sugar bowl, cov., Thistle patt. 15.00

Vase, Tulip patt., Terra Rose line, yellow glaze, No. 3613.......................50.00

Vegetable bowl, open, divided, Country Garden patt. 24.00

Vegetable bowl, open, divided, Thistle patt., 10½" l.......................................32.00

Wig stand, stylized lady's head, brown hair, No. 5168, w/ceramic base, 15" h...425.00

STONEWARE

Stoneware Crock with Bird

Stoneware is essentially a vitreous pottery, impervious to water even in its unglazed state, that has been produced by potteries all over the world for centuries. Utilitarian wares such as crocks, jugs, churns and the like, were the most common productions in the numerous potteries that sprang into existence in the United States during the 19th century. These items were often enhanced by the application of a cobalt blue oxide decoration. In addition to the coarse, primarily salt-glazed stonewares, there are other categories of stoneware known by such special names as basalt, jasper and others.

Bank, model of a seated spaniel dog, molded fur & details, covered w/a dark cobalt blue glaze, coin slot in underside, 19th c., 9" h. $4,025.00

Batter jug, ovoid w/short wide neck, brushed cobalt blue floral & foliate decoration & impressed label "Cowden & Wilcox, Harrisburg," wire bail handle w/wooden handgrip & tin lids, 9" h. (in the making hairline in base) 1,705.00

Batter jug, cylindrical body w/rounded top, incised label "James Holloway" highlighted in cobalt blue w/blue feather foliate designs & incised rope spiral handle, glaze has dark drips of brown glaze, 10⅜" h. (rare filler hole lid is glued, minor chips & blue has bubbled) 1,320.00

Bird feeder, beehive form w/an arched & hooded side opening, a ball final on the top, decorated around the hood & the top w/brushed cobalt blue leaf sprigs, impressed mark of Richard C. Remmey, Philadelphia, late 19th c., 10" h. (two small flakes near base) 2,530.00

Bottle, miniature gemel-type, the conjoined ovoid bottles tapering to small mouths, a wide applied strap handle centered at the back, splotches of cobalt blue on the necks, impressed "NEW - HAVEN," possibly from the shop of Absalom Stedman, New Haven, Connecticut, ca. 1830, 3" h. 3,163.00

Bottle, figural, molded as a spread-winged eagle, the body tapering down to a round foot, decorated on its breast w/an American shield, blue & mahogany glazes, impressed mark "M & W, Gr," head-form cap, 10½" h. (small chips on base of head) 330.00

Butter churn, wide semi-ovoid body w/molded flared rim & eared handles, slip-quilled cobalt blue large crested peacock-like bird perched on a stump, impressed label "Cowden & Wilcox, Harrisburg, PA," ca. 1860, 14½" h. (cracked, some chips) 9,200.00

Butter churn, slightly swelled cylindrical body w/eared handles, slip-quilled cobalt blue large rose blossom on a leafy stem & a "4," ca. 1860-80, 4 gal., 15¾" h. (some spots of discoloration) 209.00

Butter churn, semi-ovoid body w/molded rim & eared handles, slip-quilled cobalt blue scene of a Gothic-style cottage flanked by fir trees & w/a picket fence in the yard, marked by Haxton Edmund & Co., Fort Edward, New York, ca. 1860, w/Albany slip-covered cover, 19" h. (cover cracked & chipped) 12,650.00

Butter crock, low cylindrical sides w/thick molded rim flanked by eared handles, brushed cobalt blue stylized flowers & leaves below a dashed leaf band under the rim, impressed "1," 1 gal., 9¼" d. (hairline, chips) 286.00

Butter crock, cov., wide cylindrical form w/eared handles & molded rim, low domed cover w/flat button finial, brushed cobalt blue stylized leaf & blossom band, impressed "1½," 19th c., 1½ gal., 12" d. (hairline in base, minor chip inside lid flange) ...412.50

Butter crock, wide cylindrical form w/eared rim handles, brushed cobalt blue large fanned leaf sprigs around the sides, 12" d., 7" h. (small chips) 275.00

Butter crock, cov., short cylindrical sides w/eared handles, flat cover w/knob handle, brushed cobalt blue two-leaf sprigs around the top edge, 12" d., 7½" h. (minor chips, lid not exact fit) 484.00

Butter crock, slightly swelled cylindrical sides, upturned loop handles at sides, brushed cobalt blue blossom & leaf cluster, blue trim on handles, New York, 19th c., 12½" d., 7" h. 242.00

Chicken waterer, high domed shape w/button finial at top, molded w/a large oval opening, white glaze, 5½" h. 137.50

Crock, slightly waisted cylindrical body w/molded rim & eared handles, impressed label. "F.-----& Son, Taunton, Mass" over brushed cobalt blue florals, 8" d., 7" h. 247.50

Crock, slightly tapering cylindrical body w/protruding lip & applied eared handles, the front decorated w/a slip-quilled cobalt blue pecking chicken, all on a rosy-beige ground, America, late 19th c., 8¾" d., 8" h....575.00

Crock, cylindrical w/molded rim & eared handles, impressed label "New York Stoneware Co. Fort Edward N.Y. 6" over slip-quilled cobalt blue stylized bird, 9" d., 8" h. (minor chips on handles) 396.00

Crock, slightly ovoid, cobalt blue stenciled marking "From W.D. Cooper & Bro, No. 7 Diamond, Pittsburgh," below brushed cobalt blue bands on the front, ca. 1870-80, ½ gal., 8⅛" h. 385.00

Crock, cylindrical w/eared handles & molded rim, brushed cobalt blue stylized bird on leafy scroll branch, impressed label at top "C.L. & A.K. Ballard - Burlington, VT - 2," second half 19th c., 2 gal., 8¼" h. (cracked) 633.00

Crock, cov., wide cylindrical body w/eared handles & a flattened overhanging cover w/flat knob finial, brushed cobalt blue zigzag leafy band around the body, leaf sprigs on the cover, Pennsylvania, ca. 1860, 8¾" h. (cover cracked & chipped)....403.00

Crock, cylindrical w/eared handles & molded rim, brushed cobalt blue large "3" above a "bull's-eye" design, late 19th c., 3 gal., 10¼" h. (old chips) 55.00

Crock, cylindrical w/rolled lip & eared handles, decorated on the front w/a slip-quilled cobalt blue bird perched on a flowering branch, indistinctly stamped w/the maker's name & "3," America, 19th c., 3 gal., 11¼" d., 10¼" h. (some cracks) 575.00

Crock, ovoid w/flared mouth & eared handles, slip-quilled cobalt blue stylized flower w/a bulbous upright blossom on a horizontal leafy stem, impressed "John B. Caire & Co., Main St., Po-keepsie, NY," 1845-52, 10½" h. (flakes) 330.00

Crock, cylindrical w/eared handles & molded rim, brushed cobalt blue large floral sprig w/pointed leaves & a "3," late 19th c., 3 gal., 10½" h. (stains on lower half).......................159.50

Crock, tall cylindrical body w/rounded shoulders tapering to a low molded rim, brushed cobalt blue large leafy sprig w/a droopy flowerhead, late 19th c., now mounted as a lamp, 10⅝" h...288.00

Crock, cylindrical w/molded rim & eared handles, slip-quilled cobalt blue bird on a large scalloped leaf, stamped mark "Fulper Bros. - Flemington, NJ 4," late 19th c., 4 gal., old rim chips, 11½" d., 11¼" h. (ILLUS.)................460.00

Crock, cylindrical w/eared handles, slip-quilled cobalt blue decoration of a rooster eating, mid-19th c., 12" h...230.00

Crock, cylindrical body tapering in slightly to the molded rim, eared handles, slip-quilled cobalt blue bird on branch, impressed label "White & Wood - Binghamton, N.Y. - 4," 1882-88, 4 gal., 13¾" h. (hairlines) 412.50

Crock, cylindrical w/eared handles, slip-quilled cobalt blue "6 - Butter - 1870" over a squiggle, 6 gal., 13¾" h...385.00

Rare Stoneware Crock

Crock, wide ovoid body w/ringed neck & applied strap handles, incised & cobalt blue- and ochre-decorated large flower & leaf bouquet w/a butterfly, impressed rim mark "N. Clark & Co. Lyons," Lyons, New York, ca. 1845, minor spider crack on side, 14½" h. (ILLUS.)..........16,500.00

Crock, tall cylindrical sides w/eared handles & molded rim, stenciled cobalt blue large label "8 - E.S. & B. - Newbrighton - PA," late 19th c., 8 gal., 16" h...................................126.50

Cuspidor, cylindrical waisted sides, top center opening & oblong drainage hole at top of one side, grey salt glaze w/brown highlights, 19th c., 8½" d. (minor chips) 55.00

Food mold, Turk's turban-form, interior w/molded fluted design w/a decorative border & brown Albany slip, exterior w/grey salt glaze, 12¾" d...330.00

Jar, cov., slightly ovoid body w/gently flared rim & eared handles, inset cover w/flat knob finial, brushed cobalt blue large flower sprig on the front & a "1," impressed mark "Lyons," Lyons, New York, late 19th c., 1 gal., 10¼" h. (small chips) 302.50

Jar, wide ovoid body w/molded rim & small side strap handle, brushed cobalt blue stylized floral design on the front, 8¾" d., 7" h. 412.50

Jar, wide ovoid body w/a wide molded rim, brushed cobalt blue large lobed leaf, impressed label "Sipe Nichols & Co., Williamsport, Pa.," 8" h. (surface flakes) 275.00

Jar, ovoid w/molded rim, cobalt blue brushed wavy & straight lines & "1½," 1½ gal., 9" h. 220.00

Jar, ovoid w/tab handles, slip-quilled cobalt blue swagged & dot-trimmed curled bands joining flowerheads around the shoulder below a zig-zag neck band, probably New Jersey, ca. 1835, 9½" h. (minor base flake) 920.00

Jar, ovoid body tapering to a short, flared rim, overall two-tone grey & brown banded glaze, impressed mark "Boston 1804," attributed to Frederich Carpenter, 9½" h. (minor firing chips) 1,210.00

Stoneware Jar & Jug

Jar, ovoid body swelling to a wide molded rim, cobalt blue stenciled label w/"A.P. Donaghho - Frederickstown, Pa." above a stenciled spread-winged eagle, late 19th c., 9¾" h. (ILLUS. left).............962.50

Jar, slightly ovoid w/rolled rim, stenciled cobalt blue label "McIntire & Brand - 4208 - Butler St - Pitts, Pa - 2," 2 gal., 10" h. (hairlines)...............165.00

Jar, ovoid body w/wide, molded mouth, eared handles, brushed cobalt blue large leaf sprig & blossom, impressed label "Cowden & Wilcox 2," Harrisburg, Pennsylvania, 1870-81, 2 gal., 10" h. 440.00

Jar, slender cylindrical body w/sloping shoulders tapering to a flaring rim, brushed cobalt blue humorous anthropomorphic bird w/oversized head & a flowering tree, Indiana, mid-19th c., now mounted as a lamp, 10¼" h. 978.00

Jar, slightly ovoid w/molded rim, eared handles, slip-quilled cobalt blue stylized floral design, impressed "2," 2 gal., 10¾" h. 247.50

Jar, cylindrical sides tapering gently to a thick flaring rim, brushed cobalt blue bold leaf sprig w/two large stylized blossoms, late 19th c., now mounted as a lamp, 11" h. 345.00

Jar, semi-ovoid, flared rim, eared handles, brushed cobalt blue tulip blossom & leaf sprig below a "2," impressed mark "Burger & Co., Rochester, N.Y.," 1867-71, 2 gal., 11" h. (lip chips) 247.50

Jar, semi-ovoid w/molded wide mouth, cobalt blue slip-quilled scroll flourish below "2," 2 gal., 11" h. (wear, small chips) 93.50

Jar, cylindrical slightly tapering sides w/a flat, flared mouth, brushed cobalt blue bands around the top & a "2" & lines at the base, the center stenciled in cobalt blue w/a very large marking reading "Hamilton & Jones - Star Pottery - Greensboro - PA" & centered by a star, late 19th c., now mounted as a lamp, 2 gal., 11¾" h. (some cracks) 518.00

Jar, ovoid w/molded rim & eared handles, cobalt blue brushed tulip & leaves, impressed "T. Reed 3," Ohio, mid-19th c., 3 gal., 13¼" h. 550.00

Jar, ovoid w/eared handles & flaring rim, brushed cobalt blue roundel filled w/dots & trimmed w/arched swirls, a downward pointing arrow forming the stem, ca. 1830, 13½" h. (rim chips) 690.00

Jar, ovoid w/eared handles, cobalt blue brushed tulips & foliage on both sides, impressed "Hamilton & Pershing, Johnstown 3," 3 gal., 13" h. 715.00

Jar, slightly ovoid body w/molded rim & eared handles, brushed cobalt blue band of zigzag dashes around the top & a large "3" at the base, cobalt blue stenciled marking in the center reading "Haught & Co., Shinnston, W.Va.," 3 gal., 13" h. (small chips)....................................632.50

Jar, cylindrical w/molded rim & eared handles, brushed cobalt blue sideways leafy floral sprig near the top on each side, impressed mark "W.H. Lehew & Co. Strasburg, Va. 3," late 19th c., 3 gal., 13¼" h. (slightly out-of-round, old chip, hairline) 275.00

Jar, semi-ovoid w/eared handles, brushed & stenciled cobalt blue label "Hamilton & Jones, Greensboro, Pa. 3," late 19th c., 3 gal., 13¾" h. 330.00

Jar, cylindrical w/tooled lines beneath molded rim, eared handles, cobalt blue stenciled label "Jas Hamilton & Co, Greensboro, Pa 4," 4 gal., 15" h. (hairlines) 181.50

Jar, ovoid, stenciled cobalt blue label "Zanesville Stoneware Co., Zanesville, O. 4," late 19th c., 4 gal., 15" h. (small chips) 93.50

Jar, slightly ovoid w/eared handles, cobalt blue stenciled & free-hand label "Williams & Reppert, Greensboro, Pa. 4," 4 gal., 15" h. 220.00

Jar, cylindrical w/rounded shoulders & molded rim, eared handles, impressed "New York Stoneware Co., Fort Edward, NY. 5" above slip-quilled cobalt blue stylized foliage, 5 gal., 14½" h. (white lime deposits) 302.50

Jar, wide ovoid body w/molded rim & eared handles, incised large tulip & leaf design & impressed label "C.E. Felton - 5," Newton Township, Muskingum County, Ohio, ca. 1850, 5 gal., 14¾" h. (chips, hairlines) 550.00

Jar, ovoid w/short collared rim, eared handles, incised lines & brushed cobalt blue stylized florals & foliage, incised "5," 5 gal., 16¼" h. 330.00

Jar, slightly ovoid w/rolled rim, eared handles, stenciled cobalt blue label w/three shields & "L.B. Milliner, New Geneva, PA 6," 6 gal., 16½" h. 715.00

Jug, squat semi-ovoid body w/strap handle, impressed label "J. Matheis" & incised bird & branch w/cobalt blue wash & "1869," blue stripes on handle, 6¼" h. (small chips & short hairline in base) 3,327.50

Jug, Bellarmine-type, bulbous ovoid body tapering to a short cylindrical neck w/molded rim, impressed bearded mask on neck & armorial medallion on the front, dark glaze, Germany, 19th c., 8½" h. 440.00

Jug, cylindrical w/canted shoulders, strap handle, cobalt blue brushed label "J.F. Weiler, Allentown, Pa., 9" h. 275.00

Jug, baluster-shaped ovoid body w/applied strap handle, brushed cobalt blue decoration on the circular base, stamped identification "Confederate Relief Bazaar - Baltimore, April 7, 1885," probably Maryland, 9¾" h. 2,760.00

Jug, semi-ovoid, brushed cobalt blue leaf sprig, impressed mark "M.J. Madden - Grocers - Rondout, NY," ca. 1870-80, 10½" h. 214.50

Jug, semi-ovoid, brushed cobalt blue man's profile w/"leafy" style hair, impressed mark "E. Wear...& Co., Elmira, NY," 19th c., 11½" h. 2,185.00

Jug, ovoid, strap handle, the front decorated w/an incised & cobalt blue-washed depiction of a grotesque half-man/half-beast, possibly the devil, w/protruding belly & long tail, shown smoking a pipe w/a bubble coming from its mouth incised "MONEY," probably New York, ca. 1820, 11½" h. (minor flakes on base) 12,650.00

Jug, shouldered cylindrical body w/arched strap handle, impressed label "Ottman Bros. Fort Edward, N.Y." above cobalt blue slip-quilled foliate design w/ flourish, 11¾" h. 181.50

Jug, cylindrical dome-topped form w/small neck & rim handle, overall dark brown Albany slip-glazed exterior, impressed mark "Fort Dodge's Stoneware Co., Fort Dodge, Iowa," ca. 1885-1906, 12" h. (lip chip) 38.50

Jug, semi-ovoid, stenciled cobalt blue label arched at the top & bottom & reading "Amos Meller, Dealer in Groceries, etc. - Little Falls NY," impressed "White's Utica," New York, 1865-77, 12" h. 203.50

Jug, ovoid, brushed cobalt blue scalloped band around the shoulder, impressed mark "C. Crolius New York," ca. 1820-30, 2 gal., 12¾" h. 880.00

Jug, semi-ovoid, slip-quilled cobalt blue bird perched on scroll branch, probably Albany, New York, 1830-40, 13" h. 220.00

Jug, ovoid, strap handle, brushed cobalt blue inscription around the shoulder "Geo. Washington," early 19th c., 13" h. (imperfections) 990.00

Jug, semi-ovoid w/angular strap handle, impressed label "Whites, Utica 2" & cobalt blue slip-quilled bird on a branch, 2 gal., 13½" h. 330.00

Jug, ovoid tapering to a small cylindrical neck, cobalt blue stenciled decoration of a large spread-winged eagle w/a banner in its beak reading "Star Pottery" above a brushed cobalt blue "2" near the base, Elmserdorf, Texas, 1888-1914, small chips on lip, 2 gal., 13¾" h. (ILLUS. right) 1,265.00

Jug, ovoid, slip-quilled cobalt blue feathered wreath framing a "2," impressed mark "Burger Bros. & Co., Rochester," New York, 1867-71, 2 gal., 13¾" h. (some glaze flakes)......................................55.00

Jug, ovoid body w/small loop handle at the shoulder, impressed "2," 2 gal., 14" h. (small chips)..................71.50

Jug, semi-ovoid, brushed cobalt blue tall leafy stalk & flower design, impressed mark "N.A. White & Son, Utica, N.Y. 2," 1882-86, 2 gal., 14" h. (short hairline in base)...........302.50

Jug, semi-ovoid, brushed cobalt blue large cluster of grapes on a leafy stem, impressed mark "M. & T. Miller, Newport, Pa. 2," 2 gal., 14" h. (chip on bottom edge).........3,520.00

Jug, baluster-form w/molded lip, applied strap handle, Bellarmine-type w/grimacing bearded mask & beaded rondel, orange peel glaze, Continental, 18th c., 14" h................550.00

Jug, semi-ovoid, cobalt blue script inscription "E. A. & H. Hildreth, Southampton, N.Y.," 2 gal., 14" h...880.00

Jug, ovoid, brushed ochre large tulip-like blossom & leaves on the front, early 19th c., 14" h. (surface imperfections & rim flakes) 247.50

Jug, semi-ovoid, simple brushed cobalt blue floral design w/"3," 3 gal., 13¼" h..................................115.50

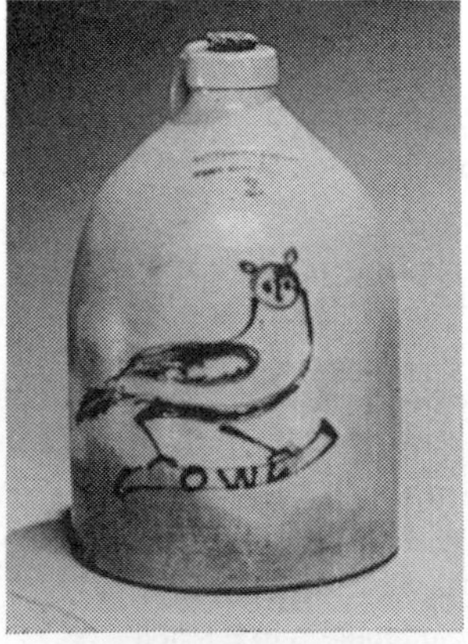

Stoneware Jug with an Owl

Jug, semi-ovoid tapering to a molded rim & strap handle, slip-quilled cobalt blue stylized owl perched on a banner w/"OWL," impressed mark for Satterlee & Mory, Fort Edward, New York above a "3," ca. 1865, 3 gal., 15" h. (ILLUS.) 3,163.00

Jug, semi-ovoid w/applied strap handle, slip-quilled cobalt blue large long-necked dotted bird perched on a long, vining scrolly-leaf branch, impressed mark "Bergan & Foy 3," 19th c., 3 gal., 15" h......................1,072.50

Jug, ovoid, brushed cobalt blue tulip design, 15½" h. (minor chips on base)..250.00

Jug, ovoid, ribbed strap handle, brushed cobalt blue stylized blossom on front shoulder, impressed mark "S.S. Perry & Co., W. Troy," ca. 1827-31, 15½" h.........247.50

Jug, ovoid w/strap handle, brushed cobalt blue stylized floral design w/"3," 3 gal., 16½" h. (chip on lip) 330.00

Jug, semi-ovoid, slip-quilled cobalt blue flower w/two large bulbous blossoms filled w/dots & raised on a single stem above a clump of long, dotted leaves, impressed mark "John Young & Co., Harrisburg, PA 3," 19th c., 3 gal., 17" h...................935.00

Jug, ovoid, brushed cobalt blue & incised fish & flower spray on the front & sides centering the inscriptions "...Addington...Utica," Samuel H. Addington, Utica, New York, ca. 1825, 18½" h. 3,163.00

Stoneware Jug with an Eagle

Jug, slightly ovoid tapering to a molded rim & strap handle, slip-quilled cobalt blue large spread-winged eagle w/a banner in its beak reading "1876 - 1776," impressed mark of New York Stoneware Co., Fort Edward, New York below a "5," flakes, 5 gal., 19½" h. (ILLUS.) 1,540.00

Milk pan w/eared handles, deep canted sides w/a rim spout on the edge, cobalt blue brushed scroll decoration, impressed "H. Smith & Co.," 19th c., 11" d. 1,100.00

Pitcher, 7" h., bulbous body w/pinched spout, the front decorated w/an incised & cobalt blue-filled bird on a branch w/flowers & leaves, incised & blue-trimmed inscription below the handle "R.C. Remmey, 1872," Richard C. Remmey, Philadelphia, Pennsylvania 17,250.00

Pitcher, 7" h., ovoid body tapering to a wide cylindrical neck w/pinched spout, applied strap handle, brushed cobalt blue crude floral sprig, 19th c. (minor hairline) 635.00

Pitcher, 8" h., ovoid body tapering to a gently flared rim, strap handle, brushed cobalt blue stylized leaf & blossom sprig (chips on base) 715.00

Pitcher, 8¾" h., ovoid body tapering slightly to a cylindrical neck w/pinched spout, strap handle, brushed cobalt blue stylized flower sprig on the front & leaf sprigs around the neck (small chip on base) 825.00

Pitcher, 9½" h., ovoid body tapering to a cylindrical neck w/pinched spout, applied strap handle, brushed cobalt blue bird perched on a large leafy branch, dot clusters around the neck, Pennsylvania, ca. 1845 ....4,888.00

Pitcher, 10½" h., ovoid body tapering slightly to a tall cylindrical neck w/pinched spout, applied strap handle, brushed cobalt blue squiggly bands around all the body & neck, Pennsylvania, ca. 1860 (flakes on rim) 2,185.00

Pitcher, 10½" h., ovoid body tapering to a wide cylindrical neck w/pinched spout, applied strap handle, brushed cobalt blue fanned three-leaf sprigs around the sides & dashed lines at the spout, impressed "1" in a circle, 19th c., 1 gal. 687.50

Pitcher, 10¾" h., ovoid w/wide short neck, strap handle, brushed cobalt blue floral decoration w/two long drips of Albany slip from spout to base 412.50

Pitcher, 10¾" h., wide ovoid body tapering slightly to a wide cylindrical neck w/pinched spout & applied strap handle, brushed cobalt blue bold feathery leafy branches w/blossoms around the front & leaf sprigs around the neck, Pennsylvania, second half 19th c., (base chips) 1,610.00

Pitcher, 12¼" h., bulbous ovoid body tapering to a short cylindrical neck w/molded rim & pinched spout, strap handle, large brushed cobalt blue tulip & leaves on the front, impressed mark "Sawyer & Smith, Akron, O. 2," mid-19th c., 2 gal. (wear, chip, repaired hole in center of base) 1,265.00

Large Stoneware Pitcher

Pitcher, 14½" h., tall wide ovoid body tapering to a cylindrical neck w/pinched spout, applied ribbed strap handle, brushed cobalt blue leafy floral band around the shoulder & wavy line around the neck (ILLUS.) 1,760.00

Pitcher, 15½" h., wide ovoid body tapering to a wide cylindrical neck w/pinched spout, applied strap handle, brushed cobalt blue leafy vines & blossoms up the front & leaf sprigs around the neck, impressed "3" at front, Pennsylvania, ca. 1850 (two small flakes on base, one flake on rim) 4,313.00

Preserving jar, slightly ovoid w/molded rim, brushed cobalt blue bands around the rim & base & cobalt blue stenciled label "J.H.---, St. Clairsville, Ohio," 6½" h. (small edge chips) 302.50

Preserving jar, slightly ovoid w/molded rim, stenciled cobalt blue label w/leaf sprigs reading "From Richard Nolan - Wheeling, W. Va.," late 19th c., 8" h. 247.50

Preserving jar, slightly cylindrical body tapering to a thick molded rim, stenciled cobalt blue label for "E.B. Taylor, Richmond, Va.," 8" h. 132.00

Preserving jar, diagonal cobalt blue stenciled label "A.P. Donagho, Parkersburg, W.Va," 8¼" h. 137.50

Preserving jar, slightly ovoid tapering to molded rim, brushed cobalt blue bold undulating flower & leaf vine around the middle & blue bands at the neck & base, 8¼" h. (wear, chips) 451.00

Preserving jar, ovoid body tapering to a short neck w/molded flared rim, cobalt blue stenciled inscription "A. Conrad, New Geneva, Pa.," late 19th c., 8½" h. 220.00

Preserving jar, slightly ovoid body w/molded flaring rim, brushed cobalt blue bands at the top & base & a cobalt blue stenciled label reading "E.J. Miller & Co....Alexandria, Va.," 19th c., 9½" h. 412.50

Preserving jar, tapering cylindrical sides, cobalt blue stenciled label "Jas. Hamilton & Co., Greensboro, Pa.," 9½" h. 192.50

Preserving jar, slightly ovoid body tapering to a flared neck w/molded rim, cobalt blue stenciled label w/a large rose blossom, "Wilkinson & Fleming, Shinnston, W.Va.," late 19th c., 10" h. 275.00

Preserving jar, slightly ovoid body w/wide molded mouth, stenciled cobalt blue label "Hamilton & Co. - Greensboro, Pa.," ca, 1880-1915, 10" h. 187.00

Preserving jar, cylindrical w/sloping shoulders & strap handle, simple brushed cobalt blue design, 10½" h. 154.00

Punch bowl, deep rounded bowl on a flaring foot, the sides molded w/three large shields w/cobalt blue-trimmed incised inscription "Bardwell's Root Beer," each shield separated by clusters of grapes & leaves tied w/bowknots all trimmed in blue & all on a dotted ground, the base w/a leafy band & Greek key band trimmed in blue, probably New York state, ca. 1890, 19½" d., 10½" h. 3,450.00

Water cooler, brushed cobalt blue leaves on each side, fitted strap handles, the front centering a circular spigot w/cork, Pennsylvania, ca. 1850, 14¾" h. (two small flakes inside rim) 1,035.00

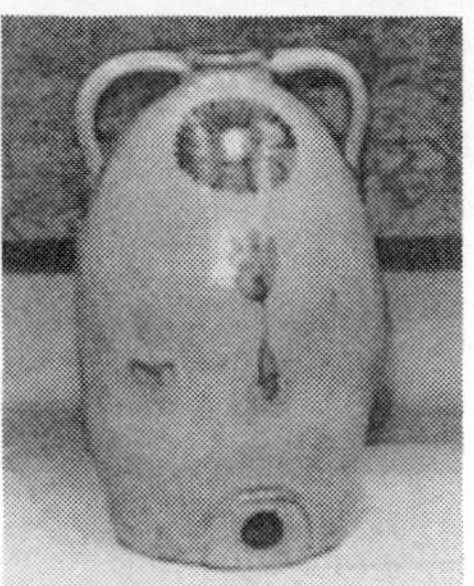

Large Stoneware Water Cooler

Water cooler, ovoid w/large eared handles & tooled lines at shoulder, impressed label "Westhafer Lambright 1865," brushed cobalt blue decoration w/daisy-like flower on one side, cockscomb-like flower on the other w/meandering line stem w/leaves & dots & repeated impressed date "1865," very minor chips, 26" h. (ILLUS.) 3,740.00

SUMIDA GAWA WARES

Contrary to some popular stories heard in the collecting world, these heavy porcelain wares were not produced in Korea nor on a mythical island of Poo. They were Japanese products made in the Tokyo region where the Sumida River (gawa = river) flows.

It was in the late 1890s that these wares apparently were first decorated with thick, often drippy-looking, "flambé" glazes and applied with small molded figures around the sides. Earliest wares usually had red, green or black grounds but later, in the 1920s, orange, brown, blue and lavender appeared. These unique and charming pieces are today highly collectible. For further information, see Sandra Andacht's Oriental Antiques & Art, An Identification and Value Guide *(Wallace-Homestead).*

Basket, applied w/three people on front & one person looking through an open handle, 9" h. $395.00

Creamer, decorated w/relief-molded scene of a boy taking eggs from bird 295.00

Pitcher, jug-form, 9" h., applied frog decoration, artist-signed 450.00

Vase, 6¼" h., 3¾ d., slender footed cylindrical body w/flared ear-like handles near the base, the front relief-molded w/the figure of an

Oriental man in white, blue & green, orangish red w/grey ground & green & dark brown mottling 75.00

Vase, 6⅞" h., 3⅜" d., slender waisted cylindrical body, relief-molded w/a figure of a boy wearing green & a rock, orangish red ground w/grey & dark brown mottling 135.00

Vase, 7" h., 2⅞" d., baluster-form body w/small, short neck, relief-molded figure of a boy wearing green on a rock, orangish red ground w/grey & dark brown mottled top 135.00

Vase, 7" h., 3⅛" d., squared bulbous base tapering to a tall cylindrical neck, relief-molded figure of an Oriental man in white, blue & green, orangish red ground w/grey & dark brown mottling 145.00

Vase, 12" h., 3¾" d. at rim, decorated w/relief-molded flowers & branches, 19th c. 600.00

TECO POTTERY

Teco Vases

Teco Pottery was actually the line of art pottery introduced by the American Terra Cotta and Ceramic Company of Terra Cotta (Crystal Lake), Illinois in 1902. Founded by William D. Gates in 1881, American Terra Cotta originally produced only bricks and drain tile. Because of superior facilities for experimentation, including a chemical laboratory, the company was able to develop an art pottery line, favoring a matte green glaze in the earlier years but eventually achieving a wide range of colors including a metallic lustre glaze and a crystalline glaze. Though some hand-thrown pottery was made, Gates favored a molded ware because it was less expensive to produce. By 1923, Teco Pottery was no longer being made and in 1930 American Terra Cotta and Ceramic Company was sold. A book on the topic is Teco: Art Pottery of the Prairie School, *by Sharon S. Darling (Erie Art Museum, 1990).*

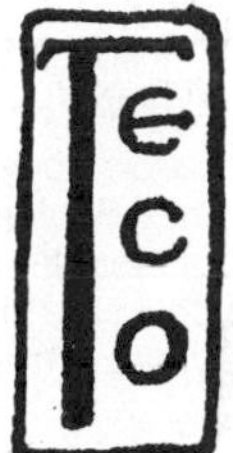

Ashtray, novelty figural-type, the flattened oblong shape formed as the body of a grumpy man w/his head extending from one end & his feet from the other, his arms going down the sides, semi-gloss light green glaze, marked, 5½" l. $275.00

Bowl, 8" d., 2½" h., shallow bulbous form w/a wide scalloped & slightly angled shoulder to a wide, flat mouth, smooth matte green & black glaze, marked 467.50

Bowl, 10½" d., 2½" h., saucer-shaped body, resting on a cross-shaped foot, smooth matte green glaze, die-stamped "Teco," w/paper label & original price tag 1,540.00

Lamp base, kerosene table-type, a squatty bulbous lower body tapering in slightly to a wide cylindrical upper body molded w/four wide buttress handles from the rim to the shoulder, overall matte green glaze, w/metal kerosene canister insert, Model No. 288, ca. 1905, impressed mark, 8⅛" h. 1,650.00

Vase, 3½" h., 4" d., footed spherical body w/a small molded mouth, smooth matte green veined glaze, Model No. 246, marked 385.00

Vase, 3¾" h., 3½" d., bulbous base, stovepipe neck & angular handles, smooth matte green glaze, die stamped mark 522.50

Vase, bud, 4½" h., 3" d., footed ovoid body tapering to a tiny mouth, fine veined smooth matte green glaze, impressed mark 467.50

Vase, 4½" h., 3" d., baluster-form body w/the rim of the flaring neck pulled into four wide "leaves" curling back & down to attach to the shoulder, matte green glaze, impressed "Teco - 61," 5½" h. 990.00

Vase, 5" h., 4½" d., bulbous base, wide neck w/undulating rim, matte green glaze, die-stamped mark 357.50

Vase, 5½" h., 3" d., cylindrical body contained in two full-length buttresses, smooth matte green glaze, die-stamped mark 660.00

Vase, 5½" h., 3" d., ovoid body tapering to a flat rim & flanked by square, pierced buttress rim handles w/ribs continuing down the sides, smooth matte grey glaze, marked (ILLUS. right) 770.00

Vase, 5½" h., 4¾" d., compressed globular base & long slender neck flaring slightly at rim, light matte green glaze, die-stamped mark & "#50" 440.00

Vase, 6" h., 8½" w., bulbous footed body pulled out at the sides to form heavy handles looping up & continuing into the flared rim of the short neck, smooth matte black & green glaze, designed by N. Forester, stamped "Teco - (2X) - 297" 605.00

Vase, 6¼" h., a wide tapering domical form w/alternating wide & narrow twisted panels up the sides, the narrow panels w/narrow grooves, the top w/a small incurvate opening, overall dark green glaze, stamped mark & paper label & number "319," ca. 1905 ....3,080.00

Vase, 6½" h., 2" d., cylindrical body w/small buttress handles & ribs, smooth matte brown glaze, marked (ILLUS. left) 495.00

Tall & Bulbous Teco Vases

Vase, 6½" h., 5¾" d., bulbous gently melon-lobed body w/four pierced oval openings & small pierced openings flanking the short neck & flat mouth, smooth matte dark green glaze, designed by F. Albert, Shape No. 113, stamped mark, firing nick at one corner (ILLUS. right) 990.00

Vase, 6¾" h., 4" d., pear-shaped w/two square buttressed handles flush w/the rim, smooth matte green glaze, die-stamped "Teco" twice......770.00

Vase, 7¼" h., 4½" d., tapering body w/four long upright buttressed handles, smooth matte green glaze, die-stamped mark (hairline to one handle) 825.00

Vase, 8½" h., a footed wide squatty bulbous body below a slender tall stick neck w/flared rim, overall mottled red, gold & black crystalline glaze, marked, ca. 1915 ....825.00

Vase, 9" h., slightly flaring cylindrical & gently lobed lower body tapering to form four elongated upright oblong knobs which extend past the top opening, an orange matte glaze on the lower half & a textured green & orange glaze on the upper half, marked, ca. 1910 (small base chip) 1,980.00

Vase, 11" h., 5" d., tall slightly tapering cylindrical body w/two full-length buttressed handles, green & black leathery matte glaze, die-stamped mark, designed by W.B. Mundy, Shape No. 266 (ILLUS. left) 935.00

Vase, 11½" h., 4¼" d., footed baluster-form body w/a trumpet-form neck, a band of narrow upright pierced leaves extending from the base to the shoulder & bent at right angles to attach to the neck, overall green glaze, stamped "Teco 85" (chip on one leaf, two touched-up nicks at top) 4,400.00

Vase, 12¼" h., 6¼" d., cylindrical flaring slightly at top, covered in an Aventurine glaze, the top half midnight blue metallic flowing into a bright orange crystalline base, die-stamped "TECO"........................13,200.00

Vase, 13⅞" h., tall slightly flaring cylindrical body w/four oblong pierced openings connected w/short straps to the arched closed rim, leathery yellow matte glaze, ca. 1905 ....1,870.00

Vase, 14" h., cylindrical w/four broad inset handles at shoulder, matte mustard yellow glaze, designed by Fritz Albert, impressed "TECO" twice 2,530.00

Vase, 16¾" h., 8¼" d., squatty bulbous base below a very tall slender four-lobed neck w/flaring rim, green matte glaze, marked 1,760.00

TEPLITZ - AMPHORA

Large Amphora Bust

These wares were produced in numerous potteries in the vicinity of Teplitz in the Bohemian area of what is now The Czech Republic during the late 19th and into the 20th century. Vases and figures, of varying quality, were the primary products of such firms as Riessner & Kessel (Amphora), Ernst Wahliss and Alfred Stellmacher. Although originally rather low-priced items, today collectors are searching out the best marked examples and prices are soaring.

Bust of a young woman wearing an elaborate off-the-shoulder dress in lavender & green, her hair curled & coiffed w/flowers & a large plume, Turn-Teplitz marking, 17¼" h.........$852.50

Bust of a serene maiden in a stylized medieval gown & headdress, raised on a tapering rectangular base molded w/a frieze on the front of a maiden on horseback in a forested meadow, the sides w/branching handles, all in shades of tan, brown & olive green trimmed w/gold, impressed Amphora marks & numbers, ca. 1900, minor chips, 18¾" h. (ILLUS.) 2,200.00

Candlestick, the cylindrical rib-molded stem-form shaft molded w/a thistle bud candle socket, the shaft flanked around the base w/three curled leaves looped down to the round, flaring base, overall bluish green glaze, Alfred Stellmacher company mark, early 20th c., 8¼" h. 495.00

Figure group, three cherubs struggle to carry three heavy baskets draped w/floral garlands, in pale pink & lavender glaze, impressed Amphora mark, 9½" h....................................385.00

Jardiniere, wide slightly tapering cylindrical body, boldly relief-molded around the sides w/a continuous scene of a man & wagon being pulled by two horses, trimmed in pale green, brown & tan, pearlized interior, Imperial - Amphora mark, 10" d., 13" h. 975.00

Model of a bird of prey, perched on a rockwork base, decorated in grey, brown & white, impressed "Amphora 38 - 17" & initialed "M.Z.," 15" h. 825.00

Pitcher, 10" h., 4¼" d., figural, modeled as a cream colored laughing cat w/grey spotting, wearing a red bow tie, black tail forms handle, marked "Amphora - Austria" 145.00

Plaque, figural, cast as the bust of a dour maiden w/flowing hair peering through a head of cabbage, glazed in cream, green & purple, heightened in gilt, impressed "AMPHORA," numbered "1270/9," "TURN-TEPLITZ-BOHEMIA - RSTK - MADE IN AUSTRIA" printed in red, inscribed "Ed. Stellmacher," ca. 1900, 8⅛" h. (chips to edges of leaves) 1,495.00

Tray, figural, the shaped rectangle cast w/the torso of a maiden at either end & decorated w/garlands of blossoms, glazed in pale blue & trimmed in gold, printed marks of Ernst Wahliss & impressed "MADE IN AUSTRIA - 4684," numbered in red overglaze "4684 - 223 - 12," ca. 1900, 11¼" l. 805.00

Vase, 5½" h., squat bottle-form w/short tiny neck, Art Nouveau style portrait & landscape decoration in olive green w/gold highlights on a cream ground, stamp, impressed numbers & "Amphora - Turn," ca. 1915 ....550.00

Vase, 8⅛" h., cast as a ripe ribbed melon w/vining leafy stem, a nude maiden perched on the upper edge, glazed in green & matte gilt, printed factory mark "DEPOSE' - EW - Turn Wien - Made in Austria," impressed "MADE IN AUSTRIA - 1754 - C," painted in overglaze "4755./28./7.," ca. 1900 (minor repairs to rim) 920.00

Vase, 9⅛" h., a square tapering vase below a bulbous swelled top w/a curled four-sided rim, the top reticulated w/leafy vines in cobalt blue w/gold trim & w/gold leaves at the corners, the sides of the base w/cobalt blue gold-trimmed borders framing narrow, round-topped panels decorated w/orange poppies against a pale green ground & trimmed w/gold crown & shield decal of Ernst Wahliss marked "EW Turn Austria," also numbers "5967 - 2649 - 31" ca. 1910..302.50

Vase, 9¼" h., the cylindrical body swelling to a bulbous wide shoulder w/a small short rolled neck, decorated overall w/large blue & white iris & leaves on a green ground all trimmed w/gold, marked "Turn - Teplitz - Bohemia - RStK - Made in Austria," ca. 1920s 385.00

Vase, 10⅜" h., Art Deco-style, bulbous ovoid body w/a rolled thick rim, the sides decorated w/two large round reserves, one w/a polychrome scene of an old man w/a walking stick, the other w/a scene of a young woman on a white horse, the reserves joined by wide center bands w/tan Art Deco scrolls all against a pebbled bluish green ground & w/dark blue borders & rim, ink-stamped on the base "Imperial Amphora Decoré A la Main" in a shield w/"LE" above, also "Modele Deposé - Czechoslovakia" & "46 - III" 330.00

Vase, 10⅝" h., wide ovoid body tapering to a rolled rim flanked by small loop handles, decorated w/a scene in polychrome of large black & dark blue ravens flying in the foreground w/trees & small houses in the distance, against a tan pebbled ground, ink-stamped on base "Amphora - Made in Czecho-Slovakia," numbered "3014 - 12190 - 6" 440.00

Vase, 11½" h., wide rounded conical base tapering to a tall slender stick neck w/flared rim, decorated w/a wide base band in ivory & blue w/gold trim of large blossoms alternating w/an insect, the upper body & neck w/a landscape scene of the sun through trees in blue & green w/gold trim, stamped "Turn - Teplitz - Bohemia - RStK - Made in Austria" & impressed "467/6" 467.50

Vase, 12" h., Symbolist-style, the baluster-form body decorated w/the bust of a maiden rising out of still waters w/a tranquil forest in the distance, in shades of cobalt blue, deep green, cream, tan, black, white & pink, trimmed in gold, printed Teplitz marks & impressed "446," ca. 1900 (drilled) 805.00

Vase, 12⅞" h., bulbous ovoid body tapering to a slender neck flanked by flattened "wing" tabs below a four-lobed mouth, shiny gold ground decorated on the front w/a profile bust portrait of an Art Nouveau lady w/white blossoms in her long hair, the reverse w/a woodland scene, base stamped "RStK Turn - Teplitz - Bohemia - Made in Austria," & "Amphora - Turn" shield mark, also marked "1326" & "HH," & "Amphora" in an oval, early 20th c. 1,210.00

Vase, 15¾" h., double sinuous handles rising above rim, elongated ovoid body w/relief-molded stylized octopus & crab decoration w/matte mottled green glaze highlighted by gold & maroon, impressed marks, ca. 1918 ....4,125.00

Vase, 16" h., Art Deco-style, tall cylindrical body w/closed rim, polychrome decoration of stylized florals in dark red, blue, green, gold & white against a pebbled blue ground, ink-stamped on base "Made in Czecho-Slovakia Amphora," ca. 1920s (slight glaze scratches on rim) 440.00

Jeweled Amphora Vase

Vase, 19¼" h., tall slender ovoid body w/flat rim, decorated w/ the bust profile of a crowned maiden w/the rising sun on the horizon, against a mottled blue & green ground, her crown & head ornaments decorated w/'jewels,' the whole trimmed w/gold, impressed & printed marks of Riessner & Kessel, Turn, Teplitz (ILLUS.) 4,600.00

Vase, 19⅜" h., the bulbous body w/elongated cylindrical neck pulled at one side w/a small looped handle, decorated w/pendent clusters of wisteria blossoms & leaves in shades of blue, purple & green against a ground shaded w/tan & ochre, trimmed in gold, printed Teplitz marks & impressed numbers, ca. 1900 ....460.00

Vase, 20" h., bulbous ovoid body decorated w/incised designs including a large condor fronting a band of intertwining vines & pendent clusters of grapes between geometric borders, in shades of dark blue, medium blue, green, brown, tan, purple & pink, printed factory mark "Czechoslovakia - AMPHORA" & numbered "813," ca. 1925.........1,725.00

Vase, 21¼" h., 6¾" d., Art Deco style, tall ovoid body tapering to a small mouth flanked by heavy, small loop rim handles, carved & polychromed scene of brightly colored birds on branches against a mottled tan & white matte ground, die-stamped "Amphora - Czechoslovakia," ca. 1920s 550.00

Vide poche (figural dish), a lovely maiden seated on furling lily pads w/flowers strewn about her flowing hair, wearing a long gown continuing to form an irregular tray at her feet, glazed in shades of blue & cream heightened in gilt, impresed "AMPHORA, 778/4," w/red printed factory mark "TURN-TEPLITZ-BOHEMIA - RStK - MADE IN AUSTRIA," ca 1900, 11¼ h. 1,725.00

Vide poche (figural dish), the standing figure of a maiden dancing in flowing gown glazed in mottled ochre & green, waving a long length of drapery about her & forming two small trays, glazed in iridescent cream shaded w/blue & grey & heightened in gilt, impressed "AMPHORA - 776," printed "TURN-TEPLITZ-BOHEMIA - RSTK - MADE IN AUSTRIA," ca. 1900, 19¼" h. 4,313.00

Vide poche (figural dish), in the form of a young Art Nouveau style maiden w/flowing pale & deep blue gown, her hair cascading down her back, her hips supporting two spade-form leaves forming trays, the base further cast w/the head of another Art Nouveau style maiden, the whole heightened w/gilt, printed & impressed factory marks & numbers, ca. 1900, 20¼" h...........4,600.00

TERRA COTTA

Figures of Chinese Maidens

This is redware or reddish stoneware, usually unglazed. All kinds of utilitarian objects have been made for centuries as have statuettes and large architectural pieces.

Busts of a young boy & girl, each in 18th c. attire w/curled wigs, one inscribed "Gir,Paris - 1755," on later marble socle bases, France, 13½" h., pr. $2,415.00

Figures of Chinese maidens, standing, the first holding a dove resting upon a cage w/an open door, the other also holding a dove & w/a flower-filled basket, France, 19th c., 14¾" h., pr. (ILLUS.) 1,495.00

Humidor, cov., squatty bulbous body w/a molded upright neck inset w/a flat cover, black printed classical Greek figures around the sides, a Greek key band around the neck, nickel-plated knob on cover, England, 19th c., 4¾" h......................55.00

Jar, cylindrical body w/a rounded shoulder tapering to a cylindrical neck w/a molded lip, decorated w/grisaille hunt scenes, diamond registry mark, England, late 19th c., 4" h..33.00

Medallion, round, centered w/a relief bust profile of Benjamin Franklin inscribed "B. Franklin, Americain," shown wearing a beaver fur hat, signed "Nini," France, dated 1777, framed, 4¼" d. 575.00

TIFFANY POTTERY

Tiffany Pottery Bowl-Vase

In 1902 Louis C. Tiffany expanded Tiffany Studios to include ceramics, enamels, gold, silver and gemstones. Tiffany pottery was usually molded rather than wheel-thrown, but it was carefully finished by hand. A limited amount was produced until about 1914. It is scarce.

Bowl-vase, squatty oviform body decorated w/an overall molded swirl design, glazed in shades of mottled amber, inscribed "L.C.T.," 7" h. (ILLUS.) $2,185.00

Vase, 6¼" h., 6" d., three full-length relief-molded leaves alternating w/curved handles each ending in a lobed foot, dead white matte glaze, glossy green interior, incised "LCT, 7"...2,200.00

Vase, 12⅝" h., cylindrical, molded in low-relief w/boughs of trumpet vines, blossoms & leafage, glazed in mottled shades of light green, inscribed "LCT - 192 - A-COLL. - L.C. Tiffany - Favrile Pottery," 1910...3,738.00

Vase, 14" h., 9" d., tall deeply waisted cylindrical form w/boldly molded large white lilies & leafy stems covered in a pea green lustered glaze, incised "LCT" (restoration to rim)..1,100.00

TILES

Marblehead Scenic Tile

Tiles have been made by potteries in the United States and abroad for many years. Apart from small tea tiles used on tables, there are also decorative tiles for fireplaces, floors and walls and this is where present collector interest lies, especially in the late

19th century American-made art pottery tiles.

American Encaustic Tiling Company, Zanesville, Ohio, molded in low-relief w/a scene of a reclining Bacchus holding a wine goblet & clothed only in a grapevine around his waist, clear caramel glaze, marked, 6 x 16" $330.00

American Encaustic Tiling Company, multicolored scene of shepherdess, 6 x 18" 550.00

American Encaustic Tiling Company, incised scene of a woman & pig, 6" d. 190.00

California Faience Company, Berkeley, California, decorated w/a blue basket w/pink & yellow flowers against a white ground, marked, 5¼" d. 77.00

California Faience Company, cloisonné decoration of a Spanish galleon, in a matte mustard & brown & glossy turquoise glaze, incised mark, 5¾" sq. 88.00

DeMorgan (William), London, England, stylized scrolling floral design in green & blue against a white ground, signed, framed, 6" sq. 385.00

DeMorgan, William, large & bold stylized floral sprays in bluish green & purple on a white ground, marked, 9" sq. 440.00

Grueby Faience & Tile Company, Boston, Massachusetts, decorated in cuenca w/a pair of brown & ivory ducks on a green water background in front of an orange setting sun & blue sky, circular mark & rectangular paper label, painted "MCM," 4" sq. 412.50

Grueby Faience & Tile Company, square, depicting a yellow tulip w/green leaves on a green ground, unmarked, 6" sq. 550.00

Grueby Faience & Tile Company, a stencil-designed figure of a monk playing the cello, rich & thick blue & ochre glaze, marked "659," 6" sq. 165.00

Grueby Faience & Tile Company, square, decorated w/a green chamberstick & a half-burnt yellow candle against a green ground, mounted in a four-footed hammered brass frame marked "HANDICRAFT SHOP, Boston, 6" sq. 990.00

Grueby Faience & Tile Company, each w/a galleon-type ship w/wind-filled sails & banners flying, polychrome on a red clay body, impressed "82," 8" sq., pr. 495.00

Grueby Faience & Tile Company, rectangular, decorated w/a group of three slip-trailed mottled brown elephants on dark greenish yellow ground & below pale blue skies, wide black wood ogee frame, paper & fabric label, artist-initialed, 5⅜ x 8½" 4,510.00

Grueby Faience & Tile Company, a two-tile frieze w/a continuous scene of a scrolling Viking-style longboat w/figure, dark ochre & gold w/scrolling cream sail, swirling cream clouds & waves w/pale green banding, blue sky, recently framed, 8½ x 17", pr. (small edge repair) 2,200.00

Low (J. & G.) Art Tile Works, Chelsea, Massachusetts, bust portrait of Shakespeare's Shylock holding a bag of coins, impressed inscription in upper corner, glossy shaded glaze, signed, framed, 6" sq. 220.00

Low (J. & G.) Art Tile Works, molded in low-relief w/a bust profile portrait of a bearded man in Renaissance costume, clear green glaze, marked "Copyright 1882," framed, overall 7½" sq. 220.00

Marblehead Pottery, Marblehead, Massachusetts, incised design of a tall sailing ship in brown & green on blue water w/light green clouds, in wide flat oak frame, rare paper label, tile 5¾" sq. 605.00

Marblehead Pottery, scene depicting a Boston house in ochre, blue & grey against a light grey speckled ground, matte finish, in an oak Arts & Crafts style frame, tile 6" sq. (ILLUS.) 1,430.00

Marblehead Pottery, incised woodland scene glazed in shades of green, impressed mark & paper label, 6⅛" sq. (chips) 385.00

Marblehead Pottery, decorated w/a scene of a white ship on blue ground 360.00

Mosaic Tile Company, Zanesville, Ohio, Medusa head, stork decoration, 4" d. 95.00

Paul Revere Pottery, Boston, Massachusetts, a round central reserve decorated w/a scene of a cottage by a lake in green, brown, white & orange outlined in black, on a light blue ground, signed & numbered, 5¾" d. 412.50

Pewabic Pottery, Detroit, Michigan, hexagonal, the center w/a stylized view of the Detroit skyline in blue & silver beige iridescent glazes, border band inscribed "Detroit," stamped mark & paper label on reverse, 2⅞" w. 220.00

Pewabic Pottery, souvenir-type, round, the center w/a stylized skyline view of Detroit in dark red & greenish blue iridescent glazes, dark red border band impressed "Detroit - GF-W-C - 1935," impressed mark on the back, 3⅛" d. 247.50

Rookwood Pottery, Cincinnati, Ohio, relief-molded stylized blossoms w/a matte purple, turquoise blue & pink glaze, framed, tile 5¾" sq. 220.00

Rookwood Pottery, oval, bas-relief design of a large kneeling putto amid blue & yellow flowers & green foliage against a burgundy ground, matte glaze, No. 9375DD, 13¾ x 23½" (two rim chips) 880.00

Spanish pottery, a bas-relief design of an old stone bridge w/rounded arches in front of a cityscape, in blues & brown, designed by Daniel Zuolagaa & impressed w/his name, Spain, framed, 6¼ x 8½" 220.00

Trent Tile Company, Trenton, New Jersey, rectangular, scenic, decorated w/a molded landscape scene of cows walking across a hillside toward a distant sunset, overall dark brownish green glossy glaze, designed by Isaac Broome, incised on the front "Broome 1882," framed, 10¼ x 12⅛".....................1,100.00

Viennese Art Nouveau Tile

Viennese pottery, Art Nouveau design w/a flowing decoration of stylized blossoms, leaves & berry clusters in French blue, orange, pink & green against a white ground, Vienna, Austria, early 20th c., unmarked, framed, 10½ x 16½" (ILLUS.) 440.00

TOBY MUGS & JUGS

Ralph Wood-Type Toby

The Toby is a figural jug or mug usually delineating a robust, genial drinking man. The name has been used in England since the mid-18th century. Copies of the English mugs and jugs were made in America.

For listings of related Character Jugs see DOULTON & ROYAL DOULTON.

Evans (Alfred), Napoleon, white background w/colored decoration, marked "Napoleon Jug - Alfred Evans, Phila. Pa.," 9¾" h. (some wear & crazing) $247.50

Melba Ware Toby, Henry VIII seated, H. Wains & Sons, Ltd., England, after 1951 ....99.00

Prattware Toby, seated Mr. Toby wearing a brown tricorn hat above his brown hair & eyebrows, a streaky teal blue coat, blue waistcoat, ochre breeches & brown shoes, supporting on his lap a blue-spotted jug & seated on a brown chair w/a fishscale patterned handle, a pipe between his feet on the stepped & chamfered rectangular base, the whole covered in a speckly blue glaze, England, 1790-1800, 7$\frac{9}{16}$" h. 460.00

Rockingham-glazed Toby, half-length figure of Mr. Toby wearing a tricorn hat, mottled dark brown glaze, 6" h...55.00

Staffordshire creamware Toby, seated Mr. Toby wearing a brown tricorn hat over his light brown hair & face, a blue coat, white waistcoat, yellow breeches & brown shoes, holding in his right hand a beaker, in his left a light brown jug of ale, seated on a brown chair above a brown chamfered rectangular base, England, ca. 1780, 6⅜" h. (hat & right wrist repaired, small chips on base) 575.00

Staffordshire creamware Toby, seated Mr. Toby wearing a brown tricorn hat on his grey hair, a green-washed coat, very pale green waistcoat & breeches & brown shoes, holding a pale manganese jug in his left hand, raising a beaker in his right, seated on a pale manganese chair above a chamfered rectangular base, England, ca. 1780, 6 7/16" h. (right hand restored) 575.00

Staffordshire creamware Toby, seated Mr. Toby wearing a brown tricorn hat on his greyish brown hair, a brown coat, white waistcoat, yellow breeches & brown shoes, holding a beaker in his right hand & a tan jug in his left, seated on a brown chair above a chamfered rectangular base, England, 1780-90, 6⅝" h. (hat abrasions & touch-ups, wrist repair, edge of jug rough, handle restored) 460.00

Staffordshire creamware Toby, Ralph Wood-type, seated Mr. Toby wearing a black tricorn hat, dark blue coat & yellow breeches, holding a frothing jug of ale & a beaker, a pipe between his feet, ca. 1780, pipe stem broken, 9¼" h. (ILLUS.) 1,100.00

Early Creamware Toby

Staffordshire creamware Toby, seated Mr. Toby wearing a dark brown tricorn, amber coat & shoes & mustard yellow breeches, holding a foaming jug of ale, seated on a scroll-footed chair above a rectangular base w/cut corners, ca. 1820, restored hat chips, shallow chip & star crack on base, 9½" h. (ILLUS.) 345.00

Staffordshire creamware Toby, seated gentleman wearing long coat & tricorn, holding a mug, underglaze sponging in brown, black, yellow & tan, 10" h. (small edge chips) 440.00

Staffordshire creamware "Thin Man" Toby, seated man wearing a brown tricorn hat on his long brown hair, a white coat w/green cuffs & sprinkles of brown on his sleeves, a green waistcoat & brown breeches, smoking a pipe & holding a brown slip-glazed jug, seated on a green-washed & brown-sprinkled chair, brown-shod feet, on a brown-fronted base, England, ca. 1780, 9⅝" h. (hat restored, star crack in back, various repairs, cracks & regluing) 690.00

Staffordshire earthenware Toby, seated Mr. Toby wearing a brown tricorn hat on his grey hair, a green coat, white waistcoat, pale yellow breeches & brown slip-covered shoes, holding a foaming mocha-ware beaker & a foaming brown jug, seated on a brown chair w/a pipe by his right leg, England, ca. 1830, 10" h. (hat edge rubbed) 460.00

'King Hal' Toby

Staffordshire pearlware "King Hal" Toby, seated figure wearing a black tricorn hat (chip & repair) w/a yellow-plumed removable crown forming the cover (repaired), an iron-red jacket w/yellow cuffs, shoulders &

slashes in the chest & sleeves, olive drab breeches, black shoes & a green belt suspending a brown scabbard (repaired) from which he draws his sword (missing), his left hand clasping a yellow shield (repaired) molded w/a royal profile portrait initialed "GR," & seated on a brown tree stump (chip, hairline) rising from a green mound base (cracked) applied around the edges w/iron-red & yellow floral clusters & green 'moss,' (some abrasions), ca. 1835, 15¼" h. (ILLUS.) 3,450.00

Staffordshire pearlware "Rodney's Sailor" or "Planter" Toby, the seated man wearing a brown flattened tricorn hat on his grey hair, a green waistcoat, manganese brown jacket, trousers & shoes, holding a beaker in his right hand & a green jug in his left supported on a manganese chest beneath his green chair, a loop handle issuing from its back, on a green-washed base molded w/rocks & grasses, England 1775-85, 11 11/16" h. (repaired hat, abrasions, chip on back edge).........805.00

Staffordshire pearlware "Squire" Toby, seated man wearing a brown tricorn hat on his long brown hair, a blue coat over a white waistcoat & breeches & blue-tied brown shoes, holding a foaming brown jug in his right hand, smoking a long-stemmed brown pipe in his left hand, seated on a green-washed corner chair issuing an ear-shaped handle up to the back of his head, inscribed on back "I. Hardin," the arrowhead-shaped base w/an underglaze-blue trellis diaper border, England, 1790-1800, 11" h. (repaired chips, tips of finger & jug handle repaired, repaired pipe & back handle, base w/hairline crack, chips & reduced) ...805.00

Staffordshire pearlware Toby, miniature, seated rotund man wearing tricorn, polychrome enamel, 3¾" h. (chips on hat rim).................165.00

Staffordshire pearlware Toby, seated Mr. Toby wearing a grey tricorn hat on his grey hair, a coat sponged in manganese & blue, an ochre waistcoat, ochre-bow-knotted grey breeches & shoes, holding a brown slip-decorated jug on his left knee, seated w/a pipe propped by his left heel & a small grey barrel between his feet, England, 1780-90, 9 15/16" h. (repairs, chips, small hairline, plaster foam on jug, slightly discolored crackling) 345.00

Staffordshire Toby, seated Mr. Toby wearing tricornered hat, decorated in underglaze blue & polychrome enamel, 8½" h. 440.00

Staffordshire Toby, seated Mr. Toby holding a pitcher & cup & decorated w/orange, yellow, black & grey, unmarked, 19th c., 9½" h. 330.00

Staffordshire yellowware Toby, seated man holding a jug in one hand, white slip decorated in black, tan, brown & blue glaze, 10¼" h. (old professional repair) 385.00

Syracuse China Toby, Herbert Hoover, ca 1928 ....115.00

TORQUAY POTTERIES

Torquay Creamer & Sugar Bowl

In the second half of the 19th century several art potteries were established in the South Devon region of England to take advantage of a belt of fine red clay. The coastal town of Torquay gives its name to this range of wares which often featured incised sgraffito *decoration or colorful country-style decoration with mottos.*

The most notable potteries operating in the Torquay area were the Watcombe Pottery, The Torquay Terracotta Company and the Aller Vale Art Pottery, which merged with Watcombe Pottery in 1901 and continued production until 1962. Other firms whose wares are collectible include Longpark Pottery and The Devonmoor Art Pottery.

Basket, round w/the sides pinched in at the middle & joined by a handle, Motto Ware, Cottage patt., "Aisy on the Sugar," 3¾ x 5¼", 4" h. $65.00

Cheese scoop, dustpan-shaped, Motto Ware, Sailboats patt., "Take a little cheese," 4¼ x 5", 2¾" h. 60.00

Creamer, bulbous ovoid body tapering to a flared rim & pinched spout, Motto Ware, Cottage patt., "Look Before You Leap," 2⅜" d., 3" h. 30.00

Creamer, bulbous ovoid body tapering to a short cylindrical neck, Motto Ware, Cottage patt., "Take a Little Cream," 3" d., 3" h. 28.00

Creamer, wide slightly tapering cylindrical body w/short cylindrical neck, Motto Ware, Cottage patt., "Hope Well and Have Well," 2⅞" d., 3⅛" h. 30.00

Creamer, bulbous ovoid body tapering to a flared rim, Motto Ware, Cottage patt., "Lands End" & "Guid volks be scarce, take care o' me," 3⅜" d., 3⅛" h. (ILLUS. left) 40.00

Creamer, bulbous body tapering to a flared rim, Motto Ware, Cottage patt., "Help Yourself to cream," 3¼" d., 3¼" h. 35.00

Creamer, barrel-shaped, Motto Ware, Cottage patt., "No Path of Flowers Leads to Glory," 3½" d., 3½" h. 38.00

Creamer, cylindrical, Motto Ware, Cottage patt., "Never Say Die, Up Man and Try," 3½" d., 3¾" h..............45.00

Cup & saucer, Motto Ware, Cottage patt., "Wookey Hole" & "It's better to wear out than rust out," saucer 5⅜" d., cup 3⅜" d., 3" h. 45.00

Cup & saucer, Motto Ware, Cottage patt., "Have another cup full," saucer 6" d., cup 3⅜" d., 3¼" h. 45.00

Egg cup, Motto Ware, "Still Waters Run Deep" 35.00

Hatpin holder, Shamrock patt...............98.00

Torquay Jam Dish

Jam dish, rounded fan-shaped ruffled bowl w/loop handle, Motto Ware, Cottage patt., "Canterbury" & "Take a little Jam," cobalt blue edging, 4⅜" w., 2⅝" h. (ILLUS.) 45.00

Jam jar, cov., cylindrical, Motto Ware, Cottage patt., "Widecombe" & "Guid volks be scarce take care of me," 3⅛" d, 4" h. 55.00

Torquay Mug & Jam Jar

Jam jar, cov., cylindrical, Motto Ware, Cottage patt., "Isle of Wight" & "Go aisy wi' it now," 2⅞" d., 4¼" h. (ILLUS. right) 55.00

Mug, cylindrical, Motto Ware, Cottage patt., "Look before you leap," 2¾" d., 3⅛" h., (ILLUS. left) 35.00

Mug, cylindrical, Motto Ware, Cottage patt., "Make hay while the sun shines," 3¼" d., 3¾" h.......................45.00

Mug, bulbous base below cylindrical sides, Motto Ware, Cottage patt., "Princetown" & "Up to the lips and over the gums - Look out tummy, Here it comes," 3⅝" d., 3⅞" h. 45.00

Mug, cylindrical, Motto Ware, Cottage patt., "Looe" & "Drink and be Merry," 3⅜" d., 4⅜" h. 65.00

Pitcher, child's, 2" h., 2" d., spherical body, Motto Ware, Cottage patt., "Castleton" & "Little Tommy Tucker"..45.00

Pitcher, child's, 2" h., 2" d., spherical body, Motto Ware, Cottage patt., "Llandudno" & "For my dolly" 45.00

Pitcher, 4¾" h., 3⅝" d., barrel-shaped, Motto Ware, Cottage patt., "No road is long with good company" 45.00

Pitcher, 4⅛" h., 3½" d., slightly tapering cylindrical body, Motto Ware, Cottage patt., "Cheddar Gorge - Help Yourself to Milk" 45.00

Plate, 8¼" d., Cottage patt., marked DMW, Made in England" 55.00

Torquay Salt & Pepper Shakers

Salt & pepper shakers, footed, egg-shaped, Motto Ware, Cottage patt., "Kind words never die" on one, "Hope well have well" on other, 3" h., pr. (ILLUS.) 70.00

Sugar basin, open, bulbous body w/flared rim, Motto Ware, Cottage patt., "Be aisy with the sugar," 3⅞" d., 2¾" h. (ILLUS. right, with creamer) 40.00

Sugar bowl, open, pedestal base, Motto Ware, Cottage patt., "Do good in time of need," 3½" d., 2⅞" h. 45.00

Torquay Teapot & Sugar Bowl

Sugar bowl, open, pedestal base, Motto Ware, Cottage patt., "Lands End" & "Help yourself to sugar," 3⅜" d., 3" h. (ILLUS. right) 45.00

Teapot, cov., squatty bulbous body, Motto Ware, Cottage patt., "Daunt'ee Worry but 'ave a cup of tay," 5" d., 4¾" h. 95.00

Teapot, cov., ovoid body, Motto Ware, Cottage patt., "You're very welcome," 3⅜" d., 5¼" h. (ILLUS. left) 85.00

Trivet, round, Motto Ware, "Except the kettle boiling B - Filling the teapot spoils the T," Longpark mark, 5¾" d. (ILLUS. top next column) 40.00

Longpark Motto Trivet

Vase, 6" h., relief-molded peacock on blue ground, ca. 1917 ....165.00

VAN BRIGGLE

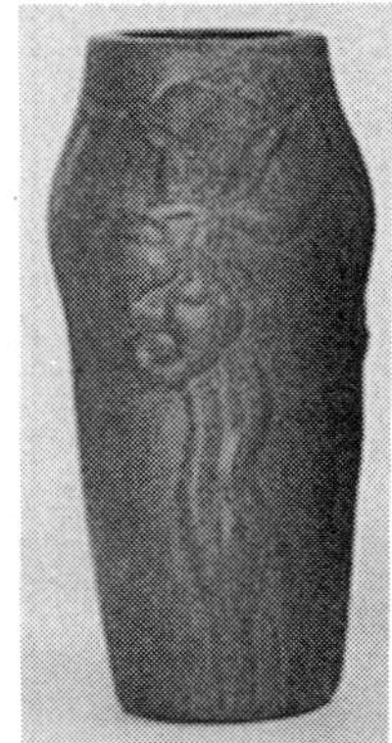

Early Van Briggle Vase

The Van Briggle Pottery was established by Artus Van Briggle, who formerly worked for Rookwood Pottery, in Colorado Springs, Colorado, at the turn of the century. He died in 1904 but the pottery was carried on by his widow and others. From 1900 until 1920, the pieces were dated. It remains in production today, specializing in Art Pottery.

Book ends, model of a squirrel, Persian Rose glaze, ca. 1930, pr. $275.00

Bowl, 6¼" d., 3½" h., tapering sides, large embossed heart-shaped leaves under a fine thick mottled matte brown glaze, marked "AA1914," 1914 ....450.00

Bowl, 6⅜" d., 2⅛" h., molded stylized leaves, Turquoise Ming glaze, Shape No. 776, ca. 1920 ....135.00

Bowl, 7" d., 3½" h., wide footed & lobed lower body below a wide, sloping shoulder to a flat mouth, molded around the shoulder w/stylized blossoms, their stems forming the ribs on the lower body, matte robin's-egg blue & purple glaze, Shape No. 513, 1906 ....467.50

Bowl, 8" d., 3¼" h., squatty bulbous body tapering to a small closed mouth, molded around the mouth w/a band of stylized flowers, leathery turquoise blue & purple glaze against a matte turquoise ground, Shape No. 22, incised "1902 - III 22" 935.00

Bowl, 8¼" d., 3¼" h., deep flat sides above a tapering bottom, the sides molded w/a continuous band of wide spade-shaped leaves, matte robin's-egg blue glaze, Shape No. 579, incised mark & "1907 - 579".............440.00

Bowl-vase, spherical body tapering to a flat mouth, molded around the top half w/stylized flower buds above a band of fine ribbing, overall ochre matte glaze, Shape No. 147, 1903, 4½" d., 3½" h. 605.00

Bowl-vase, squatty bulbous body w/a wide shoulder to the closed rim, molded around the shoulder w/oak leaves & acorns, crystalline bluish green glaze w/clay showing through, Shape No. 670, 1908-11, 5¼" d., 3½" h...385.00

Bowl-vase, footed squatty bulbous body w/a gently angled shoulder to the flat wide rim, the shoulder molded w/short arrowroot leaves glazed in dark blue, the lower body molded w/stem ribs & glazed in light blue, 1918, 5" h.(unobtrusive firing lines around rim) 605.00

Bowl-vase, squatty bulbous body w/closed mouth, molded in relief on each side w/large pairs of pine cones & pine sprigs, purple matte glaze w/dark blue highlights, Shape No. 762, 1915, 5¼" h. 825.00

Bowl-vase, spherical w/wide mouth, decorated w/embossed stylized peacock feathers under a shaded white, bluish grey to deep purple matte glaze, incised "AA - VAN BRIGGLE - 1903 - 231 - III," 6" d., 5½" h...2,000.00

Bowl-vase, wide squatty bulbous body w/a closed rim, molded w/clusters of large pine cones & needles, fine matte green & brown mottled glaze, marked, 1908-11, 9½" d., 5¾" h. ..1,430.00

Lamp base, figural, kneeling Indian woman holding urn on shoulders, purple & lavender glaze, 19" h.........275.00

Plate, 8¼" d., molded overall w/swirling vines & a poppy blossom in the center, matte bluish grey glaze, Shape No. 20, 1908-11 ....605.00

Plate, 8½" d., molded w/large poppy blossoms & swirled leaves & vines, apple green matte glaze, Shape No. 20, incised "Van Briggle 1903 - 20," 1903..825.00

Urn, footed bulbous spherical body tapering to a short, flared neck, loop handles angling from the shoulders, molded around the sides w/a band of upright spearpoint devices, robin's-egg blue shaded to dark blue glaze, incised "AA - 191(7)," 14" w., 11" h..440.00

Urn, tall footed classical form w/angled handles from the flaring rim to the edge of the shoulder, molded w/a staggered band of long, pointed leaves, dark purple shaded to raspberry pink matte glaze, ca. 1920s 137.50

Vase, 3½" h., 4½" d., squatty w/canted sides & wide mouth, decorated w/crisply embossed crocuses, textured frog-skin matte green glaze, incised "145 - AA - 1904 - V," 1904 ....1,200.00

Vase, 4⅛" h., spherical body w/a low, molded flat rim, molded w/a repeating design of stylized rayed hearts, variegated matte green glaze, Shape No. 148, 1904 ....880.00

Vase, 4⅝" h., spherical body w/a short, wide cylindrical neck, the sides molded in low-relief w/four Native American symbols including a large spider, bright green over yellow matte glaze w/red highlights, Shape No. 15, early 20th c. 770.00

Vase, 5⅜" h., spherical body tapering to a short molded flat rim, the shoulder molded w/a repeating design of large stylized peacock feathers, mottled dark green matte glaze, Shape No. 231, 1904 ....990.00

Vase, 5½" h., cylindrical body w/a swelled shoulder tapering to a closed rim, molded around the shoulder w/large stylized mistletoe clusters, overall slightly crystalline blue glaze, 1902 ....1,760.00

Vase, 5¾" h., 3¾" d., simple tapering ovoid body w/ molded flat mouth, overall robin's-egg blue glaze, Shape No. 417, 1906 ....330.00

Vase, bud, 6¼" h., 3¾" d., squat base & long swollen neck, veined chartreuse matte glaze, incised "AA - VAN BRIGGLE - 1902 - III - 88," 1902 ....500.00

Vase, 6⅝" h., wide bulbous body w/a narrow shoulder tapering to a wide, flat mouth, molded around the shoulder w/stylized morning glory blossom clusters, the stems continuing down the sides, overall olive green matte glaze w/darker green highlights, Shape No. 284, 1905 ....825.00

Vase, bud, 7" h., 2½" d., tapering sides w/globular mouth, decorated w/embossed long, sinewy leaves under a feathered matte bluish green glaze, incised "AA - VAN BRIGGLE - 1903 - III - 129," 1903....700.00

Vase, 7½" h., 3½" d., cylindrical w/narrow shoulder & short wide neck, band of embossed poppy pods around the neck, the long sinewy stems continuing to base, dark blue matte glaze, incised "AA - VAN BRIGGLE - COLO.SPGS. - 830", ca. 1908-11 ....700.00

Vase, 7¾" h., ovoid body w/a rounded shoulder to a short neck w/flat rim, overall bright yellow matte glaze, Shape No. 269, 1906........................467.50

Vase, 7⅞" h., slightly waisted cylindrical body molded w/narrow stripes below a squatty bulbous rim w/closed neck molded w/rounded, overlapping leaves, dark red matte glaze streaked w/green highlights, Shape No. 171, 1903....................1,760.00

Vase, 8" h., 4" d., expanding cylindrical body tapering slightly to a wide mouth, molded w/raised flowing poppies & poppy pods on swirling stems, matte raspberry glaze, incised "AA - VAN BRIGGLE - 1902," 1902 (ILLUS.) 2,310.00

Vase, 8" h., 4½" d., slightly tapering cylindrical body w/a swelled squatty bulbous top & closed rim, the main body molded w/a continuous band of long slender stylized leaves & stems, overall matte ochre glaze, Shape No. 171, 1903...............................1,100.00

Vase, 8⅜" h., cylindrical body swelled slightly around the flat rim, molded around the top w/daffodil blossoms w/the swirled leaves & stems down the sides, mottled crystalline bluish green matte glaze w/yellow & red highlights, Shape No. 127, dated 1903 (small rim bruise) 1,430.00

Vase, 9" h., 6¼" d., bulbous base & long wide neck, molded w/elongated leaves, curdled apple green glaze, Shape No. 797, mark obliterated under glaze......................................605.00

Vase, 9⅜" h., simple ovoid body tapering to a short cylindrical neck, molded around the shoulder w/a band of poppy pods atop slightly swirled stems down the sides & w/broad leaves around the base, mottled light blue glaze over red body, Shape No. 173, dated 1905..1,100.00

Vase, 9¾" h., 8" d., bulbous ovoid body tapering to a flat rim, molded w/large swirling poppies & stems around the sides in matte ochre against a brown & green 'hammered' ground, Shape No. 143, 1904..11,000.000

Vase, 9⅞" h., slender cylindrical body w/a swelled, incurvate flat rim, molded around the top w/stylized tulip-like flowers & leaves, the stems down the sides, overall mottled dark green glaze, Shape No. 649 (minor glaze bruise on base) 550.00

Vase, 10" h., 7½" d., ovoid body tapering to a thick cylindrical neck flanked by small thick loop handles, molded around the neck & shoulder w/small flowers, the body w/large oblong leaves, mottled deep purple & green matte glaze, Shape No. 49, 1903..1,760.00

Vase, 10¼" h., 4" d., slender cylindrical body slightly swelled near the top then tapering to a wide, flat mouth, molded w/columbine blossoms around the top w/the stems down the sides, matte periwinkle blue glaze on a light grey ground, Shape No. 25, 1903 ....1,870.00

Vase, 10⅜" h., cylindrical body swelled at the shoulder then angled & tapering to a flat mouth, molded around the shoulder w/curled & pointed leaves atop long swirled stems continuing down the sides, crystalline brown matte glaze w/pale green & yellow highlights, Shape No. 289, dated 1906 (very faint line inside the rim) 1,100.00

Vase, 10½" h., 4" d., tapering cylinder w/cup-form mouth, heavily embossed stylized narcissus blossoms & long twisting sinewy leaves, olive green to lighter green matte glaze, incised "AA - VANBRIGGLE - 1902 - III - 40," 1902 ....2,300.00

Vase, 10½" h., 11" w., "Lady of the Lily," modeled in the form of a reclining female figure against an oversized trumpet lily, matte burgundy & blue glaze, marked "VAN BRIGGLE, Colo. Spgs., " late 1920s 1,210.00

Vase, 11½" h., 5" d., slightly tapering cylinder, rich mottled bluish green feathered matte glaze over heavily embossed daisies, incised "Van Briggle Colo Spgs. 10,145," 1907-12 ....1,800.00

Vase, 12¾" h., 5½" d., tall cylindrical body swelled at the top & w/a closed rim, molded w/full-length dandelion blossoms around the rim on slender stems & leaves down the sides, mottled apple green glaze, ShapeNo. 650, 1908-11 (two hairlines) 825.00

Vase, 14" h., 5" d., tall bullet-form body, smooth burgundy matte glaze, marked "Van Briggle - 1903 - III - 134," 1903 ....1,100.00

Vase, 15" h., 6¾" d., wide ovoid body w/the swelled shoulder tapering to a short, flaring neck, molded geometric design around the shoulder w/spaced ribs down the sides, shaded blue & red matte glaze, Shape No. 632, incised "Van Briggle - Colo. Spgs.," pre-1930 ....605.00

Vase, 16¼" h., 7" d., tall conical body molded in relief w/tall yucca plants, dark blue & purple matte glaze, Shape No. 157, early 20th c. 467.50

Vase, 17" h., tall tapering cylindrical body, each side molded in relief w/a spray of three tulips, dappled blue & green glazes, incised mark "Van Briggle 1905 - V," ca. 1905 (ILLUS.) 2,640.00

Tall Van Briggle Vase

VERNON KILNS

The story of Vernon Kilns Pottery begins with the purchase by Mr. Faye Bennison of the Poxon China Company (Vernon Potteries) in July 1931. The Poxon family had run the pottery for a number of years in Vernon, California, but with the founding of Vernon Kilns the product lines were greatly expanded.

Many innovative dinnerware lines and patterns were introduced during the 1930s, including designs by such noted American artists as Rockwell Kent and Don Blanding. In the early 1940s items were designed to tie in with Walt Disney's animated features "Fantasia" and "Dumbo." Various commemorative plates, including the popular "Bits" series, were also produced over a long period of time. Vernon Kilns was taken over by Metlox Potteries in 1958 and completely ceased production in 1960.

DINNERWARES

Ashtray/coaster, Organdie patt., blue plaid, 4" d. $10.00

Ashtray/coaster, Tam O'Shanter patt 8.00

Bowl, 5½" d., Early California line, brown 3.00

Bowl, 5½" d., Gingham patt. 6.00

Bowl, 5½" d., Homespun patt. 3.00

Bowl, 5½" d., Tickled Pink patt. 7.50

Bowl, 8½" d., Gingham patt. 9.00

Bowl, 9" d., Organdie patt. 15.00

Bowl, 9" d., Tickled Pink patt. 16.00

Bowl, cereal, Heavenly Days patt. 8.50

Butter dish, cov., Tam O'Shanter patt., ¼ lb. 20.00

Butter dish, cov., Tickled Pink patt. 35.00

Carafe & stopper, Organdie patt. 35.00

Carafe & stopper, Raffia patt. 30.00

Carafe & stopper, Tam O'Shanter patt. 35.00

Casserole, cov., Modern California patt., blue 200.00

Casserole, cov., Tam O'Shanter patt., 8" d. 40.00

Chowder bowl, lug-handled, Vernon 1860 patt 10.00

Creamer, Heavenly Days patt. 10.00

Creamer, Native California line, yellow 10.00

Creamer, Tickled Pink patt. 9.00

Creamer & cov. sugar bowl, Homespun patt., pr. 15.50

Creamer & cov. sugar bowl, Monterey patt., pr. 15.00

Creamer & cov., sugar bowl, Ultra California line, pr. 25.00

Creamer & sugar bowl, Chintz patt., pr. 45.00

Creamer & sugar bowl, May Flower patt., pr. 40.00

Cup & saucer, demitasse, Early California line, red 25.00

Cup & saucer, demitasse, Early California line, cobalt 25.00

Cup & saucer, demitasse, Tam O'Shanter patt. 50.00

Cup & saucer, Gingham patt. 8.50

Cup & saucer, Homespun patt. 10.00

Cup & saucer, Tickled Pink patt. 7.00

Dinner service: complete service for eight including large platter, large round chop plate, vegetable bowl, gravy pitcher, salt & pepper shakers, creamer & cov. sugar bowl; Dolores patt., 49 pcs. 460.00

Egg cup, Homespun patt. 15.00

Gravy boat, Gingham patt. 6.00

Gravy boat, Homespun patt. 18.00

Gravy boat, May Flower patt. 45.00

Gravy boat, Raffia patt. 16.00

Mixing bowl, Organdie patt., blue, 5⅛" d. 15.00

Mixing bowl, Homespun patt., 6" d. 8.00

Mixing bowl, Homespun patt., 8" d. 10.00

Mixing bowls, Homespun patt., nested set of 3, 5", 8" & 9", the set 75.00

Mixing bowls, Early California line, nested set of 4 ....150.00

Mixing bowls, Organdie patt., nested set of 4, 6", 7", 8" & 9", the set 85.00

Pitcher, 5" h., Homespun patt. 15.00

Pitcher, Organdie patt., 2 qt. 30.00

Plate, bread & butter, 6½" d., Early California line, brown 3.00

Plate, bread & butter, 6½" d., Vernon 1860 patt. 7.50

Plate, 7" d., Heavenly Days patt. 7.00

Plate, 7" d., Homespun patt. 4.00

Plate, 7" d., Organdie patt. 5.50

Plate, salad, 7½" d., Tickled Pink patt. ...7.00

Plate, luncheon, 9½" d., Homespun patt. 9.50

Plate, luncheon, 9½" d., Organdie patt. 8.50

Plate, dinner, 10" d., Brown Eyed Susan patt. 11.00

Plate, dinner, 10" d., Heavenly Days patt. 9.50

Plate, dinner, 10½" d., Organdie patt. 7.00

Plate, chop, 12" d., Homespun patt. 12.00

Plate, chop, 12" d., Modern California line, green 25.00

Plate, chop, 12" d., Modern California line, ivory 25.00

Plate, chop, 12" d., Tam O'Shanter patt. 35.00

Plate, chop, 12" d., Ultra California line, yellow 20.00

Plate, chop, 14" d., Frontier Days (Winchester 73) patt. 145.00

Plate, chop, 14" d., Vernon 1860 patt...75.00

Plate, chop 17" d., Early California line, red 145.00

Plate, chop, 17" d., Modern California line, orchid 145.00

Platter, 10" l., Organdie patt. 12.00

Platter, 11" l., Tam O'Shanter patt........15.00

Platter, 11" l., Tickled Pink patt............18.00

Platter, 12" l., Gingham patt.................15.00

Platter, 12" l., Hibiscus patt..................25.00

Platter, 12½" l., Organdie patt. 15.00

Platter, 12¾" l., Homespun patt............18.00

Platter, 13" l., Heavenly Days patt........24.00

Platter, 13" l., Tam O'Shanter patt........19.00

Platter, 13" l., Tickled Pink patt............24.00

Platter, 14" l., Homespun patt...............15.50

Relish, divided, Tickled Pink patt..........22.00

Salt & pepper shakers, Chintz patt., pr...18.00

Salt & pepper shakers, Homespun patt., pr...14.00

Salt & pepper shakers, May Flower patt., pr...23.00

Salt & pepper shakers, Organdie patt., pr...10.50

Salt & pepper shakers, Raffia patt., pr...12.00

Salt & pepper shakers, Tam O'Shanter patt., pr..............................16.00

Salt & pepper shakers, Ultra California line, pr...............................10.00

Salt & pepper shakers, Vernon 1860 patt., pr...12.00

Sugar bowl, cov., Gingham patt. 9.50

Sugar bowl, cov., Heavenly Days patt..14.00

Sugar bowl, cov., Ultra California line 10.00

Teapot, cov., Arcadia patt....................65.00

Teapot, cov., Chintz patt....................110.00

Teapot, cov., Dolores patt. 28.00

Teapot, cov., Heavenly Days patt.........48.00

Teapot, cov., May Flower patt. 75.00

Teapot, cov., Tam O'Shanter patt. 45.00

Tea set: cov. teapot, creamer & sugar bowl; Chintz patt., 3 pcs....................75.00

Tea set: cov. teapot, creamer & sugar bowl; Monterey patt., 3 pcs...............75.00

Tidbit tray, three-tier, Gingham patt......35.00

Tumbler, Frontier Days (Winchester 73) patt., 5½" h. 45.00

Tumbler, Modern California line 20.00

Tumbler, Organdie patt.........................18.00

Tumblers, Early California line, set of 6...90.00

Tureen, cover & underplate, Vernon 1860 patt., tureen 13" d., underplate 15" d., 3 pcs...................................195.00

Vegetable bowl, cov., Gingham patt.....25.00

Vegetable bowl, cov., handled, Tam O'Shanter patt...................................55.00

Vegetable bowl, open, divided, Gingham patt., 11½" oval 15.00

Vegetable bowl, open, divided, Heavenly Days patt...........................18.00

Vegetable bowl, open, Native California line 9.00

Vegetable bowl, open, Organdie patt. 9.00

Vegetable bowl, open, divided, Tickled Pink patt. 20.00

Vegetable bowl, open, Vernon 1860 patt., 10" oval 22.00

Vegetable bowl, open, divided, Tam O'Shanter patt., 11" d........................22.50

"BITS" SERIES

Pitcher, Bits of the Old West, "Blue Ridge Betsy" 65.00

Plate, 8½" d., Bits of Old England, No. 6 ....6.50

Plate, 8½" d., Bits of Old England, No. 8 ....20.00

Plate, 8½" d., Bits of the Old South, "The Old Mill" 12.00

Plate, 8½" d., Bits of the Old Southwest, Santa Barbara Mission 45.00

Plate, 8½" d., Bits of the Old West, "The Stage Arrival"............................30.00

Plate, 8½" d., Bits of the Old West, "The Train Robbers" 30.00

Plate, chop, 14" d., Bits of Old New England, "Tapping for Sugar" 60.00

CITIES SERIES - 10½" d.

Plate, "Atlanta, Georgia".......................12.00

Plate, "Chicago, Illinois".......................15.00

Plate, "Greenville, South Carolina," blue 13.00

Plate, "Long Beach California," blue.....11.00

Plate, "Los Angeles, California"............17.00

Plate, "Memphis, Tennessee"..............15.00

Plate, "Natchez, Mississippi" 15.00

Plate, "Omaha, Nebraska"...................25.00

Plate, "Portsmouth, New Hampshire"...15.00

Plate, "Riverside, California"................12.00

Plate, "Rochester, Minnesota - 1954 Centennial" 35.00

Plate, "St. Augustine, Florida," red 13.00

Plate, "St. Mary's, Nevada"..................25.00

Plate, "San Francisco, California".........26.00

Plate, "Tri-Cities of Davenport, Iowa & Rock Island & Moline, Illinois," red.....13.00

Plate, "Tucson, Arizona".......................15.00

Plate, "Wichita, Kansas," blue 7.00

Plate, "Williamsburg, Virginia," multicolored 13.00

Plate, "Yakima, Washington," blue 12.50

DISNEY "FANTASIA" & OTHER ITEMS

Bowl, 10½" d., 3" h., Sprite design, blue, No. 125 ....225.00

Bowl, 12" base d., 2½" h., Winged Nymph design, pink, No. 122..........275.00

Figure of an elephant ballerina, No. 27 ....525.00

Figure of a hippopotamus ballerina, No. 32, 5½" h. 595.00

Figure of a satyr, No. 2, 4½" h...........225.00

Figure of a satyr, No. 5, 4½" h...........225.00

Pepper shaker, model of a mushroom, No. 36, 3¼" h. 75.00

Plate, 9½" d., Nutcracker patt............175.00

Vase, 10" h., Diana, Goddess of the Moon depicted in high relief, glossy white glaze, ca. 1940 (minor staining) 275.00

DON BLANDING DINNERWARES

Bowl, fruit, 5½" d., Hawaiian Flowers patt., maroon....................................12.00

Bowl, fruit, 5½" d., Leilani patt. 12.00

Chowder bowl, lug-handled, Hawaiian Flowers patt., maroon 35.00

Coffeepot, cov., Coral Reef patt., 6-cup 150.00

Cup & saucer, demitasse, Hawaiian Flowers patt., blue 18.00

Plate, 7½" d., Coral Reef patt., yellow..20.00

Plate, 9" d., Hawaiian Flowers patt., maroon 22.50

Plate, 9½" d., Coral Reef patt., blue & white 21.00

Plate, chop, 12" d., Coral Reef patt. 45.00

Plate, chop, 12" d., Hawaiian Flowers patt., blue 65.00

Plate, chop, 12" d., Leilani patt. 45.00

Plate, chop, 16½" d., Hilo patt., multicolored floral decoration 115.00

Platter, 13" l., Leilani patt......................85.00

Soup bowl w/flanged rim, Hawaiian Flowers patt., maroon 45.00

ROCKWELL KENT DESIGNS

Bowl, 8" d., Moby Dick patt. 125.00

Plate, 9½" d., Moby Dick patt. 55.00

Plate, chop, 12" d., Moby Dick patt.....155.00

Plate, chop, 16½" d., Salamina patt., ca. 1939 ....220.00

Plate, chop, 17" d., Moby Dick patt., brown 280.00

STATES SERIES - 10½" d.

Plate, "Alabama"..................................15.00

Plate, "Arizona" map, maroon...............16.50

Plate, "Arkansas," blue 7.00

Plate, "Colorado," red 10.00

Plate, "Connecticut," red.......................13.00

Plate, "Florida" 12.50

Plate, "Georgia, Empire State of South," blue 15.00

Plate, "Historical South Carolina," brown 13.00

Plate, "Idaho," multicolored..................11.50

Plate, "Iowa," maroon 7.00

Plate, "Maine" 8.00

Plate, "Michigan," maroon 12.00

Plate, "My Maryland," blue...................13.00

Plate, "Nevada"....................................25.00

Plate, "New Hampshire" 12.00

Plate, "North Carolina," multicolored 12.00

Plate, "Oregon," blue 21.00

Plate, "Rhode Island," brown 13.00

Plate, "Texas," blue 11.00

Plate, "West Virginia"...........................10.00

Plate, "Wisconsin," blue..........................7.00

Plate, "Wyoming," red...........................13.00

MISCELLANEOUS COMMEMORATIVES

Ashtray, "Glen Iris Inn, URC"..................8.00

Ashtray, "Michigan State College".........12.00

Plate, 8½" d., "Baltimore Harbor," blue..11.00

Plate, 8½" d., "Carroll Mansion - Homewood," blue...............................11.00

Plate, 8½" d., "Ft. McHenry," blue 11.00

Plate, 8½" d., "Historic Baltimore, Johns Hopkins Hospital," blue 11.00

Plate, 8½" d., "Old Shot Tower"............13.00

Plate, 8½" d., "University of Maryland School of Medicine," blue 11.00

Plate, 10½" d., "Baker's Chocolate 175th Anniversary"............................20.00

Plate, 10½" d., "Chinatown," San Francisco, California, maroon..............7.00

Plate, 10½" d., "Knott's Berry Farm," blue 20.00

Plate, 10½" d., "Mount Rushmore Memorial," dark red & white, ca. 1950s 15.00

Plate, 10½" d., "Northwestern University," dark red & white, ca. 1950s 15.00

Plate, 10½" d., "Statue of Liberty," multicolored 25.00

Plate, 10½" d., "University of Chicago" 12.00

Plate, 10½" d., "Will Rogers," dark red & white, ca. 1950s 15.00

Plate, "Convair" airplane.......................75.00

Plate, "50th Anniversary Bluemke & Sons, Rosendale, Wisconsin," multicolored 35.00

Plate, "Seattle - Ernst Hardware," maroon..22.50

Plate, "Supreme Forest Woodman," maroon..22.50

Plate, "Virginia Truckee Railroad".........25.00

Plate, "Washington Monument," blue ...11.00

Plate, "Western Colorado Wonderland" 16.00

WARWICK

Numerous collectors have turned their attention to the productions of the Warwick China Manufacturing Company that operated in Wheeling, West Vriginia, from 1887 until 1951. Prime interest would seem to lie in items produced before 1914 that were decorated with decal portraits of beautiful women, monks and Indians. Fraternal Order items, as well as floral and fruit decorated items, are also popular with collectors.

Chocolate pot, cov., decorated w/florals on a brown ground, 11" h..$125.00

Chocolate set: 10¾" h. tankard cov. chocolate pot & five matching cups & saucers; wild roses & daisies decoration, much gold & embossing, chocolate pot w/ornate handle & finial & scalloped base, 11 pcs. 245.00

Mug, decorated w/scene of a monk drinking ale, 4" h. 45.00

Mug, commemorative, "Detroit Foundry Mens Assn.," fisherman decoration 50.00

Mug, commemorative, Elk lodge emblem, 5½" h...................................90.00

Pitcher, 7" h., monk decoration...........200.00

Pitcher, 7¼" h., swirl-molded body decorated w/h.p. large yellow & pink flowers, sponged gold scalloped rim & handle..55.00

Pitcher, tankard, 12" h., ornate mold, poppies decoration 165.00

Pitcher, tankard, 13" h., monk decoration, IOGA mark 185.00

Pitcher, lemonade, plums decoration, IOGA mark......................................135.00

Syrup pitcher w/original spring lid, decorated w/orange poppies, artist-signed (slight age crazing) 85.00

Vase, 4¾" h., pine cone decoration on light background, IOGA mark 35.00

Vase, 8" h., pillow-shaped, portrait of a young brunette girl wearing a white bonnet 145.00

Vase, 9" h., two-handled, seagulls decoration on white ground 225.00

Vase, 10½" h., twig handles, portrait of lovely lady w/blue hair ribbon in brunette hair, IOGA mark................145.00

Vegetable dish, open, decorated w/lavender roses, 10" l.......................35.00

WATT POTTERY

Apple Bean Pots

Founded in 1922, in Crooksville, Ohio, this pottery continued in operation until the factory was destroyed by fire in 1965. Although stoneware crocks and jugs were the first wares produced, by 1935 sturdy kitchen items in yellowware were the mainstay of production. Attractive lines like Kitch-N-Queen (banded) wares and the hand-painted Apple, Cherry and Pennsylvania Dutch (tulip) patterns were popular throughout the country. Today these hand-painted utiltarian wares are "hot" with collectors.

A good reference book for collectors is Watt Pottery, An Identification and Value Guide, *by Sue and Dave Morris (Collector Books, 1933).*

Apple bowl, Apple patt., No. 73, 9½" d., 4" h. $85.00

Apple bowl, Apple patt., w/advertising, No. 73, 9½" d., 4" h.........................115.00

Baker, cov., Apple patt., No. 96, 8½" d., 5¾" h. 85.00

Batter bowl, Esmond line, orange & black glaze.......................................55.00

Bean pot, cov., tab handles, American Red Bud (Tear Drop or Bleeding Heart) patt., No. 76, 7½" d., 6½" h...132.00

Bean pot, cov., tab handles, Apple patt., No. 76, 7½" d., 6½" h. (ILLUS. left)...175.00

Bean pot, cov., tab handles, Double Apple patt., No. 76, 7½" d., 6½" h....775.00

Bean pot, cov., Apple patt., w/advertising, No. 502, rare oversized version (ILLUS. right).......................900.00

Bean pot, cov., Peedeeco line, 8" d., 6¾" h...45.00

Bean server, individual, American Red Bud (Tear Drop or Bleeding Heart) patt., No. 75, 3½" d., 2¼" h.....40.00

Bowl, 4" d., ribbed, Apple patt., No. 04 ....50.00 to 75.00

Bowl, cov., ribbed, 5" d., 4" h., Apple patt., No. 05 ....175.00

Bowl, 5" d., 2½" h., ribbed, Double Apple patt., No. 05 ....110.00

Bowl, 5½" d., 2" h., individual cereal, Eagle patt., No. 74 ....69.50

Bowl, 5½" d., 2" h., Mexican patt., shaded brown, No. 603.....................95.00

Bowl, berry, 5¾" d., 1½" h., Starflower patt 60.00

Bowl, 6" d., ribbed, American Red Bud pat., No. 06 ....55.00

Bowl, 6" d., 3" h., Apple patt., No. 06 ...40.00

Bowl, 6" d., 3" h., ribbed, Double Apple patt., No. 06 ....110.00

Bowl, 6½" d., 2½" h., cereal or salad, Starflower patt., No. 52 ....45.00

Bowl, ribbed, 7" d., 3¾" h., American Red Bud (Tear Drop) patt., No. 07.....65.00

Bowl, cov., 7½" d., 5½" h., Apple patt., No. 66 ....65.00

Bowl, cov., 7½" d., 5½" h., Rooster patt., No. 66 ....275.00

Bowl, cov., 7¾" d., ribbed, Apple patt., No. 600 ....135.00

Bowl, cov., 8½" d., Apple patt., No. 67 ....50.00

Bowl, cov., 8½" d., 6½" h., Rooster patt., No. 67 ....240.00

No. 96 Apple Pattern Bowl

Bowl, 8½" d., Apple patt., No. 96 (ILLUS.) 35.00

Bowl, cov., 8¾" d., 6½" h., ribbed, Apple patt., No. 601 ....132.00

Bowl, cov., 8¾" d., 6½" h., ribbed, Tulip patt., No. 601 ....150.00

Bowl, salad, 9½" d., Apple patt., w/green stripe, No. 73........................85.00

Bowl, salad, 9½" d., Autumn Foliage patt., No. 73 ....70.00

Bowl, 9½" d., 4" h., brown Basket-weave patt., No. 102 ....20.00

Bowl, salad, 9½" d., Double Apple patt., No. 73 ....175.00 to 200.00

Bowl, salad, 9½" d., Tulip patt., No. 73 ....150.00

Bowl, 11¾" d., Starflower patt., No. 55 ....75.00 to 100.00

Bowl, serving, 15" d., 3" h., Bull's-eye w/Cut Leaf Pansy patt......................155.00

Canister, cov., Tulip patt., No. 72, 7" d., 9½" h. 380.00

Dome Top Apple Canister

Canister, dome-top, Apple patt., No. 91, 7½" d., 20¾" h. (ILLUS.) ..2,300.00

Canister set: four-section on wooden base, w/wooden cover; Esmond line, each section labeled: "Flour," "Sugar," "Coffee," "Tea," 6 pcs. ....250.00 to 275.00

Casserole, cov., individual, French-type w/stick handle, Apple patt., No. 18, 8" l., 4" h.............225.00 to 275.00

Casserole, cov., individual, French-type w/stick handle, Dutch Tulip patt., No. 18, 8" l., 4" h.....275.00 to 325.00

Casserole, cov., individual, French-type w/stick handle, Pansy (Cut Leaf) patt., No. 18, 7½" l., 3¾" h........98.00

Casserole, cov., individual, French-type w/stick handle, raised Pansy patt., No. 18, 7½" l., 3¾" h...............................125.00 to 150.00

Casserole, cov., individual, French-type w/stick handle, Rooster patt., No. 18, 8" l., 4" h. 295.00

Casserole, cov., individual, French-type w/stick handle, Starflower patt., No. 18, 8" l., 4" h. 180.00

Casserole, cov., individual, French-type w/stick handle, Starflower patt., green, No. 18, 8" l., 4" h..................132.00

Casserole, cov., individual, tab-handled, Starflower patt., No. 18, 5" d., 4" h. 106.00

Casserole, cov., Dutch oven-type, Apple patt., No. 73, 9½" d., 6" h.................................250.00 to 300.00

Casserole, cov., brown Basketweave patt., No. 128, 8½" d., 6½" h.............40.00

Casserole, cov., Cherry patt., No. 54, 8½" d., 6" h. 95.00

Casserole, cov., oval, Rooster patt., No. 86, 10" l., 5" h.........................1,400.00

Chip & dip set w/metal rack, Apple patt., No. 120 bowl, 5" d., 2" h., No.110 bowl, 8" d., 3¾" h., the set.....90.00

Chip & dip set w/metal rack, Autumn Foliage patt., No. 120 bowl, 5" d., 2" h., & No. 110 bowl, 8" d., 3¾" h., the set 179.00

Cookie jar, cov., Apple patt., No. 503, 8¼" d., 8¼" h. 325.00

Cookie jar, cov., Cherry patt., No. 21, 7" d., 7½" h. 139.00

Cookie jar, cov., marked "Goodies" on the side, No. 76, 7½" d., 6½" h. 400.00

Cookie jar, cov., Starflower patt., No. 21, 7" d., 7½" h.........175.00 to 200.00

Cookie jar, cov., Tulip patt., No. 503, 8¼" d., 8¼" h. 410.00

Cookie jar, cov., barrel-shaped, Woodgrain line, marked "Cookie Barrel," No. 617, 8" d., 11" h. 150.00

Creamer, American Redbud (Tear Drop or Bleeding Heart) patt., No. 62, 4¼" h. 130.00

Creamer, Apple patt., No. 62, w/advertising, 4¼" h.........................115.00

Creamer, Autumn Foliage patt., No. 62, 4¼" h..................150.00 to 175.00

Creamer, Double Apple patt., No. 62, 4¼" h...80.00

Creamer, Pansy (Cut Leaf) patt., 6" w., 2¾" h.....................................130.00

Creamer, Rooster patt., No. 62, 4¼" h..............................125.00 to 150.00

Creamer, Tulip patt., No. 62, 4¼" h. ...275.00

Creamer & open sugar bowl, molded Morning Glory patt., creamer, No. 97 & sugar bowl, No. 98, creamer 4¼" h., sugar 4¼" h., pr. 385.00

Cup & saucer, Pansy (Cut Leaf) patt. 265.00

Grease jar, cov., Apple patt., No. 01, 5¼" d., 5½" h. 250.00

Ice bucket, cov., American Red Bud (Tear Drop or Bleeding Heart) patt. 185.00

Ice bucket, cov., Apple patt., No. 72, 7½" d., 7¼" h. 250.00

Ice bucket, cov., Rooster patt., No. 72, 7½" d., 7¼" h. 300.00

Ice bucket, cov., Starflower patt., No. 72, 7½" d., 7¼" h. ....250.00 to 300.00

Mixing bowl, American Red Bud patt., No. 5, 5" d., 2¾" h. 55.00

Mixing bowl, Apple patt., No. 5, 5" d., 2¾" h. 50.00

Mixing bowl, ribbed, Apple patt., w/advertising, No. 5, 5" d., 2¾" h. 80.00

Mixing bowl, Double Apple patt., No. 5, 5" d., 2¾" h. 200.00

Mixing bowl, Rooster patt., No. 5, 5" d., 2¾" h. 85.00

Mixing bowl, Starflower patt., No. 5, 5" d., 2¾" h. 60.00

Mixing bowl, ribbed, Starflower patt., No. 5, green on brown, 5" d. 55.00

Mixing bowl, American Red Bud patt., No. 6, 6" d. 55.00

Mixing bowl, ribbed, Green/White Banded patt., No. 6, 6" d., 3½" h. 28.00

MIxing bowl, Rooster patt., No. 6, 6" d. 95.00

Mixing bowl, ribbed, Starflower patt., No. 6, green on brown, 6" d. 55.00

Mixing bowl, Apple patt., No. 7, w/advertising, 7" d. 40.00

Mixing bowl, ribbed, Apple patt., No. 7, 7" d., 4" h. ....40.00 to 60.00

Mixing bowl, Cherry patt., No. 7, 7" d., 4" h. 50.00

Mixing bowl, Rooster patt., No. 7, 7" d., 4" h. 69.00

Mixing bowl, ribbed, Rooster patt., No. 7, 7" d., 4" h. 100.00

Mixing bowl, Starflower patt., No. 7, green on brown, 7" d. 65.00

Mixing bowl, ribbed, Apple patt., No. 8, 8" d., 4½" h. 60.00

Mixing bowl, Apple patt., No. 8, w/advertising, 8" d., 4½" h. 100.00

Mixing bowl, Rooster patt., No. 8, 8" d., 4½" h. 150.00

Mixing bowl, Starflower patt., pink on green decoration, No. 8, 8" d., 4½" h. 90.00

Mixing bowl, Pansy (Cut Leaf) patt., No. 9, 9" d., 4½" h. 95.00

Mixing bowl, ribbed, Starflower patt., w/advertising, No. 9, 9" d., 5" h. 95.00

Mixing bowl, brown band decoration, No. 12, 12" d. 100.00

Mixing bowl, Kitch-N-Queen line, No. 14, 14" d. 75.00

Mixing bowl, Dutch Tulip patt., No. 63, 6½" d. 50.00

Mixing bowl, Apple patt., No. 63, w/advertising, 6½" d. 35.00

Mixing bowl, Rooster patt., No. 63, 6½" d. 95.00

Mixing bowl, Apple (three leaf) patt., No. 64, 7½" d., 5" h. 60.00

Mixing bowl, Starflower patt., No. 64, 7½" d., 3" h. 65.00

Mixing bowl, Apple patt., No. 65, 8½" d., 5¾" h. 90.00

Mixing bowl, Apple (two-leaf) patt., No. 65, 8½" d., 5¾" h. 85.00

Mixing bowl, Tulip patt., No. 65, 8½" d., 5¾" h. ....125.00 to 150.00

Mug, barrel-shaped, American Red Bud (Tear Drop or Bleeding Heart) patt., No. 501, 2¾" d., 4½" h. 90.00

Mug, Starflower patt., No. 501, 4½" h. ....150.00 to 200.00

Pepper shaker, Rooster patt., hourglass shape, w/advertising 280.00

Pie plate, black band decoration, No. 33, 9" d. 45.00

Pie plate, Rooster patt., No. 33, 9" d. 525.00

Pie plate, Starflower patt., w/advertising, No. 33, 9" d. 155.00

PItcher, 5½" h., American Red Bud (Tear Drop or Bleeding Heart) patt., No. 15 ....56.00

Pitcher, 5½" h., Apple patt., No. 15 ....50.00 to 75.00

Pitcher, 5½" h., Autumn Foliage patt., No. 15 ....55.00

Pitcher, 5½" h., Double Apple patt., No. 15 ....425.00

Pitcher, 5½" h., Dutch Tulip patt., No. 15 ....130.00

No. 15 Rooster Pitcher

Pitcher, 5½" h., Rooster patt., No. 15 (ILLUS.) ....75.00 to 100.00

Pitcher, 5½" h., Starflower patt., No. 15 ....75.00 to 100.00

Pitcher, 6¾" h., Apple patt., No. 16 ....125.00 to 150.00

Pitcher, 6¾" h., brown & white drip glaze, No. 16.....................................59.50

Pitcher, 6¾" h., Dutch Tulip patt., No. 16 ....150.00 to 185.00

Pitcher, 6¾" h., Rooster patt., No. 16 ....125.00 to 150.00

Pitcher, 6¾" h., Rooster patt., w/advertising, No. 16 ....150.00 to 200.00

Pitcher, 6¾" h., Starflower patt., No. 16 ....100.00 to 150.00

Pitcher, 6¾" h., Tulip patt., No. 16 ....150.00 to 200.00

Pitcher, 7" h., Kla Ham'rd patt. 45.00

Pitcher w/ice lip, 8" h., Apple patt., No. 17 ....275.00 to 325.00

Pitcher w/ice lip, 8" h., Esmond line, No. 17 ....95.00

Pitcher w/ice lip, 8" h., Starflower patt., No. 17 ....275.00

Pitcher w/ice lip, 8" h., Tulip patt., No. 17 ....200.00 to 250.00

Pitcher, plain lip, 8" h., Dutch Tulip patt., No. 17 ....85.00

Pitcher w/ice lip, 8" h., molded Morning Glory patt., No. 96.............450.00

Pitcher, refrigerator-type, 8" h., Apple patt., No. 69 ....350.00 to 400.00

Pitcher, refrigerator-type, 8" h., Dutch Tulip patt., No. 69 ....625.00

Plate, dinner, 10" d., Apple patt., No. 101 ....450.00 to 550.00

Plate, dinner, 10" d., brown glaze, No. 101 ....55.00

Plate, dinner, 10" d., Pansy patt., No. 101 ....155.00

Platter, 15" d., Apple patt., No. 31 ....550.00 to 600.00

Platter, 15" d., Cherry patt., No. 31.....165.00

Platter, 15" d., Pansy (Cut-Leaf) patt., No. 31 ....100.00

Platter, 15" d., Starflower patt., No. 31 ....150.00 to 175.00

Platter, 15" d., Starflower patt., green on brown, No. 31 ....110.00

Salt & pepper shakers, hour-glass shape, Apple patt., 4½" h., pr....................................250.00 to 300.00

Salt & pepper shakers, hour-glass shape, w/raised "S" & "P," Apple patt. (two-leaf), w/advertising, 2½" d., 4½" h., pr. 400.00

Salt & pepper shakers, Autumn Foliage patt., pr...............................275.00

Salt & pepper shakers, barrel-shaped, Starflower patt., 4" h., pr....................................125.00 to 175.00

Spaghetti bowl, Apple patt., No. 39, 13" d., 3" h. 75.00

Spaghetti bowl, Cherry patt., No. 39, 13" d., 3" h. ....125.00 to 150.00

Spaghetti bowl, Pansy (Cut-Leaf) patt., No. 39, 13" d., 3" h......................................65.00 to 85.00

Spaghetti bowl, Pansy (Old) patt., No. 39, 13" d., 3" h...........150.00 to 175.00

Spaghetti bowl, Starflower patt., No. 39, 13" d., 3" h...........................118.00

Sugar bowl, cov., Apple patt., No. 98, 4½" h...115.00

Sugar bowl, cov., Autumn Foliage patt., No. 98, w/advertising, 4½" h. 85.00

Sugar bowl, cov., Rooster patt., w/advertising, No. 98, 4½" h. 250.00

Tumbler, round-sided, Starflower patt., No. 56, 4½" h. 350.00

WEDGWOOD

Reference here is to the famous pottery established by Josiah Wedgwood in 1759 in England. Numerous types of wares have been produced through the years to the present.

WEDGWOOD

CREAMWARE

Plate, 9⅛" d., "Buns! Buns! Buns!," man selling buns to lady & child h.p. center scene, gold border, artist-signed "E Lessore,"........................$395.00

Teapot, cov., Chintz patt., spherical body decorated w/four wide panels centering an iron-red & green flowerhead & purple foliage within an iron-red scalloped cartouche reserved on a black fish-red & scalework ground interrupted at the top & bottom w/iron-red, purple & yellow triangles, all between green, purple & yellow vertical bands edged w/black scalloped lines, the cover similarly decorated around the pierced ball knop, & the handle & spout patterned w/iron-red & black chevrons, possibly painted by David Rhodes, ca. 1770, 5⁵⁄₁₆" h., (body cracked & w/restored chip, repaired chip on cover, handle terminal chipped off) 4,025.00

JASPER WARE

Jasper Ware Cracker Jar

Bowl & underplate, 4½" d., white relief classical figures on blue, underplate w/white relief floral band, 2 pcs........375.00

Candlesticks, white relief classical figures on a dark blue ground, 5½" h...175.00

Cracker jar, cov., barrel-shaped, white relief classical figures on dark blue, silver plate rim, cover & bail handle, marked "Wedgwood" only, 5" d., 6" h. (ILLUS.) 225.00

Cracker jar, cov., cylindrical, white relief classical ladies & cupids on dark blue, replated silver cover, ball-footed base & bail handle, marked "Wedgwood" only, 5½" d., 6⅝" h. 225.00

Cup & saucer, demitasse, white relief classical ladies in oval medallions on the black ground, colored enamel & gold trim, marked "Wedgwood" only, cup 2" d., 2" h., saucer 4½" d..425.00

Jasper Ware Flowerpot

Flowerpot, white relief garlands of grapes & leaves w/lion's heads & small figures of classical women under each lion head on dark blue, marked "Wedgwood England," 3⅝" h., 4" d. (ILLUS.) 175.00

Mug, three-handled, white relief classical figures in an oval vignette on blue, late 19th c., 4½" h. 325.00

Mug, white relief classical figures on dark blue w/hallmarked silver top rim, impressed "Elkington & Co." on base, marked "Wedgwood" only, 3¾" d., 5" h. 135.00

Pitcher, 5¾" h., globular base tapering to a wide neck, white relief classical figures on salmon, marked "Wedgwood - Made in England" 192.50

Pitcher, 6" h., bulbous body, white relief classical figures on crimson, marked "Wedgwood - England".......895.00

Pitcher, tankard, 6½" h., 3¾" d., white relief classical figures on sage green, marked "Wedgwood - England" 165.00

Pitcher, 7" h., white relief classical figures on dark blue, ca. 1930 ....185.00

Pitcher w/silver plate hinged lid, 7¼" h., white relief classical figures on dark blue, lid w/engraved decoration & small lion finial, marked "Wedgwood" only (ILLUS. top next column) 185.00

Jasper Ware Covered Pitcher

Pitcher w/pewter cov., 9" h., jug-type, white relief classical figures on blue, white relief scene of "Sacrifice to Love" on the front, late 19th c. 180.00

Plate, 10" d., white classical figures on green, marked "Wedgwood" only 325.00

Portland vase, 5" h., white relief classical figures on dark blue, marked "Wedgwood - England" 350.00

Sweetmeat jar, cov., white relief classical figures on sage green, resilvered lid, rim & handle, marked "Wedgwood" only, 4½" h., 3¾" d. 195.00

Teapot, cov., oval form, white classical figures on blue, marked "Wedgwood England," 4" h. 110.00

Teapot, cov., bulbous body, white classical figures on salmon, marked "Wedgwood - Made in England," 5" h. 247.50

Teapot, cov., squatty bulbous body w/domed cover, white relief classical figures on dark blue, marked "Wedgwood England," 6½" h., 6½" d. 295.00

Tray, oval, white relief classical figures on green, marked "Wedgwood - England," 9" l. 165.00

Tray, octagonal, white relief classical figures on blue, early 20th c., 10½" w. 225.00

Vase, 4⅞" h., 3¾" d., baluster-form, white relief classical ladies at altar scene around the body on dark blue, marked "Wedgwood" only (ILLUS. top next column) 125.00

Vases, 5¼" h., 2½" d., footed ovoid body tapering to a small flaring neck, white relief scene of man w/a dog on one side of one & a girl w/a dog on

Small Jasper Ware Vase

the other, both w/white relief scene of cupids on the backs, all on dark blue, marked "Wedgwood" only, pr...175.00

Vase, 6⅝" h., four-color, the tapering cylindrical body w/flared foot & wide, rolled rim, green ground applied w/four white pilasters surmounted by lion's-mask-and-ring capitals suspending yellow floral garlands & interrupting yellow ribbon-entwined ivy & cable borders between white bands, the interstices w/lilac & white oval medallions, the rim & foot w/a white foliate border, impressed mark "WEDGWOOD" only & date letters for December 1882 (small rim chips) 2,013.00

MISCELLANEOUS

Small Dragon Lustre Bowl

Bowl, 2¾" d., 1¾" h., Dragon Lustre, mottled orange exterior, blue interior 80.00

Bowl, 4½" d., 2½" h., Dragon Lustre, mottled blue w/gold dragons decoration exterior, mother-of-pearl lustre w/Three Jewels & gold trim interior, pattern No. Z4829, Portland Vase mark (ILLUS.) 195.00

Bowl, 9" w., octagonal, Dragon Lustre,

gold dragons & trim on green shading to purple exterior, orange interior 545.00

Parian Bust of Milton

Bust of Milton, parian, by W.E. Wyon, bolted base, marked "Wedgwood" only, 8½" d., 14½" h. (ILLUS.) 850.00

Cup & saucer, Appledore patt. 28.00

Dish, pearlware, footed oblong form w/incurved edges & notched corners, mauve rim band h.p. w/flowers & leafy vines in green, red, yellow & black, impressed "Wedgwood" only, early 19th c., 8½ x 11" (pinpoint flakes, chip on underside of foot)....................192.50

Pin dish, center decoration of gold bull on blue ground, lustre finish, decorated gold rim, 3¾" d. 165.00

Plate, 6" d., bread & butter, Appledore patt....................18.00

Plate, 7¾" d., majolica, grape leaf decoration, green....................135.00

Plate, 9" d., scene of "Old Meeting House, Bingham, Mass.," blue & white 40.00

Plate, 10" d., pink lustre trim, Fallow Deer patt., Etruria, England................75.00

Plate, 10½" d., commemorative, "Old State House, Boston," blue transfer on white, Etruria, England 60.00

Plate, 10½" d., commemorative, "Old Ironsides," blue transfer on white 35.00

Plate, dinner, Appledore patt.................26.00

Soup plate w/flanged rim, Ivanhoe Series, "Wamba & Gurth," blue transfer on cream, ca. 1882................75.00

Tile, "April," blue transfer on white, 6" sq. 145.00

Tile, "October," brown transfer on white, framed, 6" sq.........................135.00

Toothpick holder, Butterfly Lustre, pearlized gold & orange, 3" h. 250.00

Tray, Lustre, center decoration of snake, snail & bamboo rod, scalloped, gold trimmed rim, marked "Wedgwood, England," 7 x 11¾"......285.00

WELLER

This pottery was made from 1872 to 1945 at a pottery established originally by Samuel A. Weller at Fultonham, Ohio, and moved in 1882 to Zanesville. Numerous lines were produced and listings below are by the pattern or lines.

Reference books on Weller include The Collectors Encyclopedia of Weller Pottery, *by Sharon & Bob Huxford (Collector Books, 1979) and* All About Weller *by Ann Gilbert McDonald (Antique Publications, 1989).*

WELLER

Weller Pottery

ARDSLEY (1928)

Various shapes molded as cattails among rushes with water lilies at the bottom. Matte glaze.

Candlesticks, blossom-shaped, 3" h., pr....................$70.00

Console bowl, 12" l., 2" h....................175.00

Console bowl w/figural fish flower frog, bowl 16½" d., 3½" h., 2 pcs. (frog professionally repaired) 250.00

Vase, bud, 7½" h. 35.00

AURELIAN (1898-1910)

Similar to Louwelsa line but brighter colors and a glossy glaze.

Charger, decorated w/a scene of baby chicks amid straw, brown glaze, artist-signed, 13" d.......................4,400.00

Clock, the long domed case w/flattened & incurved sides tapering to a flared footed &

scalloped base, decorated overall w/blackberry vines in green & gold against a shaded black, brown & gold ground, signed, 10⅞" h. (two glaze chips at edge of clock dial, minor glaze scratches) 1,320.00

Vase, 8⅞" h., squared form flaring out at base, decorated w/orange flowers 275.00

Vases, 8½" h., corseted form, flowers & leaves decoration, one unmarked, pr. 485.00

Vase, 8⅞" h., tall slender squared body w/flared base, leaf decoration 275.00

Tall Aurelian Vases

Vases, baluster-form, brilliant orange & yellow splashes amid similarly colored pansies & foliage, swirling on a deep brown ground, artist-signed, pr. (ILLUS.) 12,100.00

BALDIN (about 1915-20)

Rustic designs with relief-molded apples and leaves on branches wrapped around each piece.

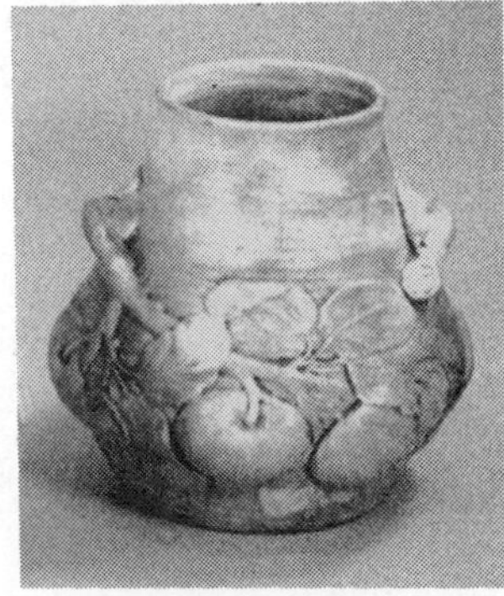

Baldin Vase

Bowl, 7½" d., 4" h., brown ground 160.00

Jardiniere & pedestal base, overall 39" h., 2 pcs. 1,250.00

Vase, 6" h., bulbous base 45.00

Vase, 7½" h., blue ground 275.00

Vase, 9½" h., squatty base w/wide tapering neck, branches forming flat handles (ILLUS.) 600.00

Wall pocket 95.00

BARCELONA (late 1920s)

Colorful Spanish peasant-style designs on buff ground.

Bowl, 9" d. 145.00

Candlesticks, single handle rising from base to midsection of tapering shaft, pr. 260.00

Pitcher, 8" h., ovoid w/strap handle 160.00

Vase, 6" h., two-handled, compressed base, incurving neck & flaring rim 150.00

Vase, 7" h. 175.00

Vase, 8" h. 185.00

Vase, 14" h., three-handled, matte green, red & yellow glaze 275.00

BLOSSOM (mid-late 1930s)

Pale pink flowers & green leaves on blue or green matte glazed ground.

Blossom Bowl-Vase

Basket, bulbous body w/uneven rim & scrolled, arched handle, 6" h. 45.00

Bowl-vase, footed squatty bulbous lobed body below a short flaring & ruffled neck, small eared handles on the shoulder, green ground, 5½" h. (ILLUS.) 35.00

Cornucopia-vase, 6" h., flared rim 25.00

Pitcher, 12½" h. 135.00

Vase, 7½" h., two-handled, blue ground..45.00

BLUEWARE (before 1920)

Classical relief-molded white or cream figures on a dark blue ground.

Jardiniere, slightly flared cylindrical form on three short feet, dancing ladies w/trees & birds, 6½" h. 155.00

Jardiniere, slightly flared cylindrical form on three short feet, dancing ladies w/trees & birds, 7½" d., 8½" h.......................................245.00

Jardiniere & pedestal base, the wide footed tapering ovoid bowl w/a widely flaring rolled rim molded in white relief w/leafy scrolls & florettes flanking grotesque masks above a band of acanthus leaves all against the dark blue ground, the matching footed baluster-form pedestal w/similar scrolls & masks & leaves around the bottom & on the feet, signed, overall 32¼" h., 2 pcs. (minor glaze nicks & scuffs)..........1,980.00

Vase, 8" h., slightly tapering cylinder..185.00

Vase, 10" h., 4⅜" d., slightly ovoid slender body, white relief, lady w/leg raised & holding a bunch of grapes over her head.................................250.00

BONITO (1927-33)

Hand-painted florals and foliage in soft tones on cream ground.

Bowl, 4" d., pedestal base, ring handles (some crazing) 95.00

Flowerpot & saucer...............80.00 to 100.00

Rose bowl, two-handled 52.00

Vase, 4¾" h., small upturned handles, bulbous body 55.00

Vase, 5" h., waisted cylinder w/wide flaring top 125.00

Vase, 6" h., segmented lower portion w/flat curved handles at midsection, wide slightly tapering cylindrical neck (very light crazing)....................95.00

Vase, 9¼" h., decorated w/small h.p. blue & lavender flowers 170.00

Vase, 10" h., slightly tapering cylindrical body w/flaring foot & rim, small scroll loop handles at rim, artist-signed 185.00

BOUQUET (late 1930s)

Various molded flowers in color against a light blue, green or ivory ground on simple shapes often accented by lightly molded ribbing.

Bouquet Vase with Tulips

Bowl, three-lobed sides, blue ground ...35.00

Pitcher, tankard, 9½" h., ivory ground ..50.00

Vase, 5" h., ovoid body w/flared rim flanked by tiny loop handles, No. B-15..25.00

Vase, 12" h., tall egg-shaped body w/four lobe rim & molded w/tall tulips issuing from the base, light green ground (ILLUS.) 125.00

BURNT WOOD (1910)

Etched designs on a light tan ground with dark brown trim. Similar to Claywood but no vertical bands.

Basket, hanging-type, 4 x 9".................65.00

Desk caddy, footed, 11" l., 4" h. 40.00

Vase, 9" h., Wise Men decoration 405.00

Vase, 11" h., etched birds 110.00

CAMEO (1935 - late 1930s)

White relief-molded flower and leaf bouquets on pastel blue, green or deep buff ground.

Basket w/ornate asymmetrical overhead handle, rounded sides, low foot, buff ground, 7½" h. 30.00

Baskets, hanging-type, fluted floral form, 5" h., pr. 110.00

Bowl, 10" d...25.00

Vase, 7½" h., two-handled...................40.00

Vase, 9¾" h., green ground.................35.00

Vase, 10" h., upright square body, buff ground.......................................20.00

CHASE (late 1920s)

White relief fox hunt scenes usually on a deep blue ground.

Ginger jar, cov. ....350.00 to 400.00

Vase, 6" h., white relief scene on a blue ground 125.00

Vase, 8" h., orange ground.................325.00

Vase, 11¾" h., blue ground 475.00

CHENGTU (1925-36)

Simple graceful shapes covered with an overall deep Chinese red glaze.

Ginger jar, cov., 12" h. 150.00

Vase, 9" h. 50.00

Vase, 12" h. 125.00

CLAYWOOD (ca. 1910)

Etched designs against a light tan ground, divided by dark brown bands. Matte glaze.

Claywood Jardiniere

Basket, hanging-type, etched floral decoration, 10½" h. 125.00

Bowl, 3" d., etched butterflies 12.50

Jardiniere, cylindrical sides tapering at the base, a series of panels each w/a different scene of a California Mission, the Mission name in a band at the top, unmarked, 9¾" d., 8" h. (ILLUS.) 137.50

Jardiniere, decorated w/a band of Greek figures, 10" h. 225.00

Jardiniere, 9½" x 11" 300.00

Mug, cylindrical, etched floral decoration, 5" h. 42.50

Vase, 3" h., etched panels of butterflies 35.00

Vase, 7½" h., etched floral decoration..65.00

COPPERTONE (late 1920s)

Various shapes with an overall mottled green glaze. Some pieces with figural frog or fish handles. Models of frogs also included.

Candleholders, model of a turtle beside a water lily blossom, 3" h., pr. ....450.00 to 475.00

Console bowl, shallow oblong lily pad-form w/a figural frog seated at one end, 11" l., 4½" h. 330.00

Model of a frog, 4" h. 275.00

Vase, 8¼" h., 9" w., fan-shaped top molded w/reeds above a low squatty bulbous base composed of lily pads & molded w/a pair of figural frogs on the shoulder, ink mark 700.00

Vase, 8½" h., bulbous base w/wide, flaring neck, heavy strap handles 200.00

Vase, 8½" h., 5¼" d., waisted cylinder 180.00

Watering device, model of a frog w/hole in mouth, 6" h. 565.00

DICKENSWARE 2nd LINE (1900-05)

Various incised "sgraffito" designs usually with a matte glaze.

Dickensware Turk's Head Humidor

Humidor, cov., figure of a military man's head, called "The Captain," dark blue collar & hat w/red trim, ca. 1905, 6¾" h. 550.00

Humidor, cov., figural, Turk's head, dark-skinned man w/black beard & mustache wearing a multicolored turban, ca. 1905, chips on cover, turban repaired, 7⅛" h. (ILLUS.)......385.00

Mug, tapering cylindrical body w/ring-molded flaring base, etched elk head decoration, 6" h. 385.00

Pitcher, jug-type, 5½" h., scene of a bridge across a river & "The Mt Vernon Bridge Co, Mt Vernon, O"....375.00

Vase, 8½" h., bust portrait of Indian wearing full headdress, "Black Bear" 1,450.00

Vase, 9" h., 4½" d., expanding cylinder w/rolled rim, scene of golfer preparing to address the ball, against a tree-lined ground in shades of blue, green & brown, marked "DICKENSWARE - WELLER" 1,100.00

Vase, 9½" h., scene w/football players 1,250.00

Vase, 9½" h., decorated w/a bold, outlined design of a fully-rigged galleon w/crosses on the sails on a rough dark green sea & a shaded yellow to pink sky, glossy glaze, signed (minor glaze scratches) 990.00

Vase, 9½" h., 5½" d., ovoid bottle-form w/short narrow neck & tiny mouth, "Domby and Son," decorated w/the figure of a gentleman seated next to a young boy, marked "DICKENSWARE WELLER, 54(?), 12D" 440.00

Vase, 12" h., woman walking the dog scene 750.00

Vase, 16" h., decorated w/scene of four cats 2,750.00

DUPONT (late Teens)

Embossed rose bushes or rose trees in planters joined by swags against fine net-embossed ground.

Basket w/liner, hanging-type, 2 pcs....120.00

Bowl, 3" d., Roma glaze 45.00

Bowl, 9" d., 2" h. 55.00

Planter, square sides w/a reticulated rim band, 5" h...................................75.00

Wall pocket, 9" h.................................90.00

EOCEAN (1898-1925)

Early art line with various hand-painted flowers on shaded grounds, usually with a glossy glaze.

Pitcher, tankard-type, 12" h., decorated w/berries, artist-signed....750.00

Vase, 7⅛" h., pilgrim flask-shaped, the flattened round body raised on thick flared feet, a squared rectangular neck at the top flanked by angled handles, decorated w/a single wading white stork against a shaded grey ground w/ribbon-like clouds & ripples, artist-signed, numbered "21" & "90," ca. 1905....1,100.00

Vase, 7⅛" h., simple ovoid body tapering to a flat mouth, decorated around the middle w/a cluster of small stylized pink & yellow blossoms & large green leaves against a shaded black to pale blue ground, ca. 1920 ....247.50

Vase, 7¼" h., wide cylindrical body tapering slightly to a wide, flat mouth, decorated around the shoulder w/large cluster of Virginia creeper leaves & berries in pink, green & dark blue, a cobalt blue rim band & a pale blue ground, ca. 1925 ....550.00

Vase, 8" h., simple ovoid body w/closed flat rim, decorated w/a cluster of black berries & shaded green leaves against a shaded dark green to grey-green ground, ca. 1900 (minor glaze dimples) 412.50

Vase, 10⅛" h., wide ovoid body tapering to a short narrow neck w/flat rim, decorated w/large stylized undulating leafy vines w/berries in dark greyish blue & pink against a shaded pale greyish blue to cream ground, signed, ca. 1905 ....1,430.00

Vase, 12¼" h., wide ovoid body tapering to a short neck w/widely flaring rim, decorated w/large stylized pink blossoms & green leaves around the shoulder against a shaded dark to pale blue ground, ca. 1925 (small glaze skip at base) 440.00

FLEMISH (mid-Teens to 1928)

Clusters of pink roses and green leaves, often against a molded light brown basketweave ground. Some pieces molded with fruit or small figural birds. Matte glaze.

Chamberstick, dished base centered by a blossom socket, ring handle at edge, No. 45 ....185.00

Jardiniere, wide slightly swelled cylindrical body, the sides divided into panels w/large molded red flowers & green leaves, 7½" h. 100.00

Jardiniere, deep slightly flared sides on three short legs, pink flowers & green leaves around the base, 6" d., 8" h...165.00

Jardiniere & pedestal, cream ground w/rose-colored flowers, 26½" h., 2 pcs. 550.00

Towel bar, a narrow horizontal oblong backplate molded in relief at the top w/two bluebirds & at the bottom center w/a cluster of red roses, a thick arched bar runs from end to end, marked, ca. 1915, 11⅝" l. 1,210.00

FLORALA (about 1915-20)

Embossed colored flowers in square panels on a cream ground. Matte finish.

Candleholders, 5" h., pr. 120.00

Console bowl, 11" d. 60.00

Wall pocket, 9½" h. 90.00

FLORETTA (1904)

Low-relief molded flowers and fruit decorated in underglaze brown & pastel colors. Glossy glaze.

Pitcher, tankard, 15" h., overall dark brown glaze, artist-signed on base 75.00

Vase, 6½" h., tri-cornered rim, molded grapes 135.00

Vase, 7" h., footed ovoid body tapering to a swelled neck, small handles on the shoulder, shaded brown glaze 100.00

FOREST (mid-Teens - 1928)

Realistically molded and painted forest scene.

Forest Jardiniere & Pedestal

Basket, hanging-type, w/chains, 10" d. ....225.00 to 250.00

Jardiniere, 4½" h. ....100.00 to 125.00

Jardiniere & pedestal, the tapering cylindrical jardiniere resting upon a cylindrical pedestal flaring at the top & bottom, overall 29" h.(ILLUS.) 990.00

Planter, tub-shaped, loop rim handles, 4" h. 95.00

Planter, tub-shaped, loop rim handles, 6" h. 125.00

Vase, 8" h., waisted cylinder w/flaring rim 125.00

Vase, 8" h., cylindrical w/slightly flared rim 60.00

FROSTED MATTE (about 1915)

Simple rounded forms decorated with overall mottled metallic iridescent glazes in green, yellow, purple, blue or pink.

Vase, 6" h., footed ovoid body 145.00

Vase, 12½" h., 5¾" d., baluster-form, apple green glaze 330.00

GARDEN ORNAMENTS (Figural)

Gnome, flattened profile figure of a seated long-nosed gnome wearing a peaked cap & pointed shoes, on a molded oblong base, wearing an orange coat & cap w/blue feather, 14¼" l., 9½" h. 2,310.00

GLENDALE (early to late 1920s)

Various relief-molded birds in their natural habitats, life-like coloring.

Vase, 8½" h., cylindrical, two parakeet-like birds on branch 325.00

Vase, 11¼" h., bulbous body tapering to a tall cylindrical neck, decorated w/a nesting marsh bird among cattails, marked 467.50

Wall vase, double bud, pierced to hang, tree trunk-form vases flank a panel w/a bird & nest w/four eggs, 7" h. 225.00

GREORA (early 1930s)

Various shapes with a bicolor orange shaded to green glaze splashed overall with brighter green. Semigloss glaze.

Strawberry pot, ovoid body w/wide flat mouth & pinched openings around the shoulder, 5" h. 85.00

Strawberry pot, baluster-form, 8½" h. 150.00

Vase, 5" h., bulbous, footed base below a tall, widely flaring neck 65.00

Vase, 9" h., ovoid body tapering to a flat rim flanked by angled handles ...160.00

Vase, 11½" h., tall cylindrical body slightly flared at the base & rim........225.00

HOBART (early to late 1920s)

Figural women, children and birds on various shaped bowls in solid pastel colors. Matte glaze.

Figure of Bacchus, a nude boy holding aloft a grape cluster, blue glaze 235.00

Vase, 11" h., figural lady holding her skirt out at the sides 225.00

Wall pocket, figural nude, turquoise glaze, 8" h. 135.00

HUDSON (1917-34)

Underglaze slip-painted decoration.

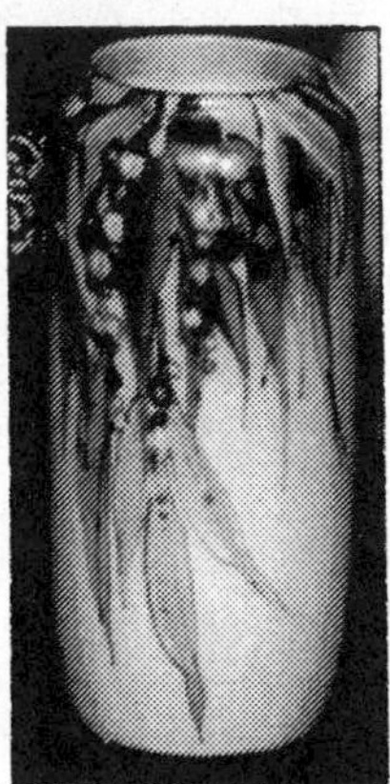

Hudson Vase with Leaves & Berries

Vase, 6" h., 3½" d., swelled cylindrical body tapering slightly to a wide flat rim, decorated w/pink & white cherry blossoms against a shaded lavender ground, signed & artist-initialed 275.00

Vase, 6¾" h., 3¾" d., ovoid body tapering to a flat wide mouth, decorated w/pink, white & yellow dogwood blossoms against a shaded blue to pink ground, artist-signed & marked 330.00

Vase, 6⅞" h., slightly swelled cylindrical body w/incurvate rim, decorated w/a band of long slender drooping green leaves & dark red berries suspended from the top, against a pale shaded yellow to pink ground, marked, minor glaze discoloration, ca. 1930 (ILLUS.) 605.00

Vase, 8⅜" h., plain cylindrical body w/flat rim, decorated w/a continuous landscape scene including a red-roofed cottage near a poplar tree, in shades of green, yellow, red & blue below a pastel blue & pink sky, marked & artist-signed, ca. 1925..2,200.00

Vase, 8⅝" h., wide ovoid body tapering to a swelled section at the base of the short tapering neck w/a flaring rim, decorated w/large pastel blue & pink orchids & green leaves against a shaded pink to pale green ground, marked & artist-signed, ca. 1925 ....440.00

Vase, 8¾" h., 4" d., gently ovoid body tapering to a small flat mouth, decorated around the upper half w/a cluster of pink & yellow roses on a shaded blue, pink & yellow ground, artist-signed & marked 440.00

Vase, 10" h., 5¼" d., shouldered gently ovoid body tapering to a flat mouth, decorated around the shoulder & upper half w/a cluster of pink & white nasturiums on a shaded blue to yellow ground, artist-signed & marked 5,225.00

Vase, 11⅝" h., tall hexagonal body w/a widely flaring cushion base, decorated w/delicate white dogwood blossoms & leaves around the top against a pale shaded blue to green ground, marked 275.00

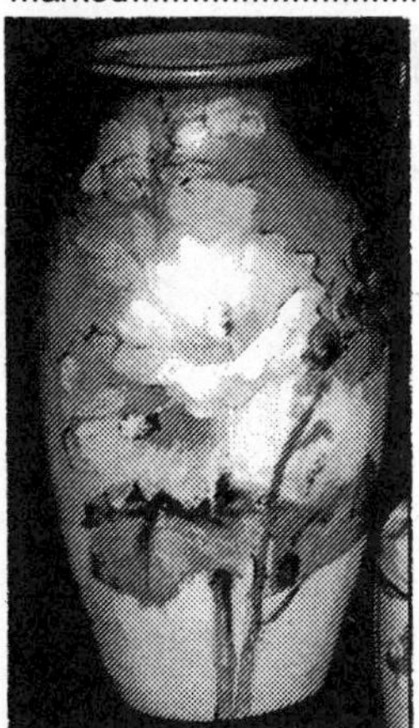

Large Hudson Vase

Vase, 11⅞" h., baluster-shaped body tapering to a short neck w/rolled rim, decorated w/large pink & white rose-of-sharon on tall green leafy stalks, against a pale green shaded to yellow ground, artist-signed & marked, ca. 1930 (ILLUS.)....................990.00

Vase, 13⅞" h., wide bulbous ovoid body tapering to a short cylindrical neck w/thick rolled rim, wide strap handles from neck to sides, decorated w/a large colorful macaw on a flowering jungle vine against a shaded bluish grey to pink ground, artist-signed, ca. 1920 ....6,875.00

Vase, 14¾" h., tall ovoid body tapering to a short neck w/flaring rim, decorated w/large irises in pink & yellow & blue w/green leaves against a shaded pale green to pink ground, marked & artist-signed, ca. 1920 .... 1,430.00

Vase, 15¼" h., 7" d., baluster-form, decorated w/multicolored irises in lavender, white, blue & brown against a shaded green to lavender ground, artist-initialed, ink-stamped "WELLER POTTERY" 1,100.00

Wall pocket, decorated w/black-berries, white ground,10" h. 1,500.00

IVORY (1910 to late 1920s)

Ivory-colored body with various shallow embossed designs with rubbed-on brown highlights.

Ivory Jardiniere & Pedestal

Jardiniere & pedestal, jardiniere w/angled shoulder on a tapering cylindrical body w/four raised feet, the sides molded w/four full-length Art Nouveau style women against stylized trees, on a matching decorated cylindrical pedestal, unsigned, 18" d., 35" h. (ILLUS.) 2,090.00

Vase, 9" h., bottle-shaped, decorated w/molded women's faces around the rim, molded fruit clusters around the base 95.00

Vase, 10" h., waisted cylindrical form, ornate winged scroll design 79.00

Vase, 10" h., cylindrical, molded w/nude caryatid figures around the top above ribbed columns & swags 125.00

JEWEL & CAMEO JEWEL (about 1910-15)

Similar to the Etna line but most pieces molded with a band of raised oval 'jewels' or jewels and cameo portraits in color against a light or dark shaded ground.

Mug, footed cylindrical body w/angled handle, lady head cameo framed by oak leaves, dark purple ground, 6½" h. 395.00

Vase, 9" h., sea horse decoration 300.00

KLYRO (early to late 1920s)

Most pieces feature molded wood framing around panels topped by double pink blossoms and dark purple berries against a finely ribbed ground, often trimmed in tan, brown, cream or olive green.

Bowl, 8" d., brown ground..................... 79.00

Vase, 8" h., circle-type, flattened upright sides on small feet, lattice openwork on the upper half 185.00

Wall pocket, 7½" h. 95.00

KNIFEWOOD (late Teens)

Pieces feature deeply molded designs of dogs, swans and other birds and animals or flowers in white or cream against dark brown grounds.

Bowl, 6½" d., 3¾" h., decorated w/daisies 125.00

Tobacco box, cov., round w/upright tab in center of the top, fox & chicken scene around the sides, 3½" h. 250.00

Tobacco jar, cov., cylindrical, low domed cover w/large button knob, hunting dog scene around the sides, 7" h. 450.00

Vase, 8" h., moon & owls decoration.. 425.00

Vase, 11" h., slightly swelled cylindrical body, etched design of a large squirrel among acorn branches 250.00

Wall pocket, figural girl, two-color glaze 265.00

L'ART NOUVEAU (1903-04)

Various figural and floral-embossed Art Nouveau designs.

Jardiniere, molded blossoms in dark green shading to light green, 8½" h. 245.00

Vase, 9" h., tall slender square form

flared at the base & w/a swelled rim molded w/blossoms, figures of Art Nouveau ladies on the side panels ....225.00 to 250.00

Vase, 11¾" h., tall cylindrical body swelled at the top & tapering to a closed rim, molded at the top w/ large orange poppy blossoms against a shaded grey-green ground, matte glaze, signed, ca. 1905 ....522.50

LASA (1920-25)

Various landscapes on a banded reddish and gold iridescent ground.

Vase, 5¼" h., 2¾" d., stick-type, rocky lakeside landscape w/pine trees, rose, gold, green & blue iridescent glaze 250.00

Vase, bud, 7½" h., scenic decoration of two pine trees, clouds, green, rose & gold iridescence 275.00

Vase, 9" h., 4¼" d., swelled cylindrical body tapering to a short, flaring rim, decorated w/poppies in purple & blue against a gold & orange iridescent ground (fine scratches on inside rim) 330.00

Vase, 11½" h., scenic decoration of sunset over water & trees 500.00

Vase, 11⅝" h., simple ovoid body gently tapering to a wide flat mouth, decorated w/an underwater scene of yellow & red fish among brown seaweed against a gold ground, all in iridescent glazes (few glaze scratches & rubs) 550.00

LOUWELSA (1896-1924)

Hand-painted underglaze slip decoration on dark brown shading to yellow ground; glossy glaze.

Clock, mantel or shelf, a wide domed case flattened at the front & back, swelled sides tapering down to rounded feet & an undulating front base, the round white enameled dial w/black Arabic numerals framed by a brass bezel, the case decorated overall w/wild roses & leafy vines in shades of gold, green, orange, brown & black, marked, ca. 1905 (bit of loose glaze near dial)...................385.00

Pitcher, 5½" h., yellow floral decoration on brown ground...................125.00

Pitcher, tankard, 11½" h., decorated w/long stemmed flowers 175.00

Umbrella stand, h.p. portrait of an Indian in full headdress, artist-signed, 23" h. 1,210.00

Vase, 2⅝" h., jug-type, spherical body w/small neck, small shoulder spout opposite a loop handle, flowers on a shaded brown ground 185.00

Vase, 10" h., tall square form, decorated overall w/a dark red glaze w/a light & dark pink Virginia creeper vine & berries climbing around the sides, marked & artist-signed, ca. 1905 (minor glaze scratches, small firing flaw at base) 990.00

Vase, 10½" h., 7" d., wide ovoid body tapering to a short flared neck, decorated w/a large bust profile portrait of an Indian chief wearing a headdress, artist-signed 1,760.00

Vase, 16¾" h., tall ovoid body tapering to a flaring neck, decorated w/large bold dogwood blossoms & leaves in yellow, gold & burnt orange against a shaded dark brown to reddish brown ground, artist-signed, ca. 1902 ....990.00

MARVO (mid-1920s-33)

Molded overall fern and leaf design on various matte-background colors.

Pitcher, 8" h., green 125.00

Plate w/rolled edge, rabbit decoration ..55.00

Umbrella stand, green, 19½" h..............................300.00 to 325.00

Vase, bud, 9" h., slender cylindrical body, green 75.00

MATT GREEN (ca. 1904)

Various shapes with slightly shaded dark green matte glaze and molded with leaves and other natural forms.

Vase, 12½" h., 5½" d., tall ovoid body molded in bold relief w/two full-length maidens embracing the sides at the top, fine mottled green glaze, unmarked 2,530.00

Vase, 13⅝" h., tall slightly tapering cylindrical body, a cluster of large poppy pods molded in high-relief at the rim w/a thin band & leaves wrapping around & over pierced slots near the rim, overall dark green glaze, ca. 1910, unmarked (minor griding of chips on base)..............1,540.00

MELROSE (about 1920)

Molded flowers or fruit clusters with branches on simple forms often molded with swirled ribs or indentations and with pale tan, grey or pink matte backgrounds.

Basket, 8½" h., flaring cylindrical sides w/high branch handle from rim to rim, molded grape cluster & vines 85.00

Vase, 7" h., cylindrical body w/twists below a ruffled rim, applied open branch handles wrap around the lower half & suspend apples 150.00

MUSKOTA (1915-late 1920s)

Figural pieces with human figures, birds, animals or frogs. Matte glaze.

Figure of a seated nude lady on rocks w/a swan below ....375.00 to 400.00

Figure of a standing nude boy holding a drape across his waist, No. 107, 5¼" h. 225.00

Flower frog, molded w/a dragonfly 135.00

Flower frog, model of two geese w/wings spread, 6½" h. 300.00

Flower frog, model of a lobster, 2" h. 115.00

Model of a rabbit, brown, 13" l., 7¾" h. 1,200.00

PANELLA (late 1930s)

Pansies or nasturtiums in relief on various shaded background colors. Matte glaze.

Basket, footed ovoid body, pointed loop handle from side to side, 7" h. 65.00

Vase, 6½" h., footed baluster-form body w/small loop handles near base, shaded blue ground 40.00

ROMA (1912-late 1920s)

Cream-colored ground decorated with embossed floral swags, bands or fruit clusters.

Comport, open, an oblong bowl w/shaped rim & scroll end handles raised on a low pedestal, 11" l., 4½" h. 156.00

Jardiniere, octagonal, white ground w/blue floral medallions, 8" d., 7" h. 150.00

Vase, bud, 6½" h., slender square upright body on a flared base 40.00

Wall pocket, conical, decorated w/floral basket & swags in Dupont motif, 10" h. ....125.00 to 150.00

ROSEMONT - 1st Line (late Teens - late 1920s)

Incised and colored birds on branches or flowers against a solid black or white background all with a glossy glaze.

Jardiniere, slightly tapering cylindrical form, bluebird decoration on black ground, 7" h. ....300.00 to 350.00

Vase, 9½" h., 4½" d., baluster-form, decorated w/blue jays on ivory & green branches against a black ground 220.00

SICARDO (1902-07)

Various shapes with iridescent glaze of metallic shadings in greens, blues, crimson, purple or copper tones decorated with vines, flowers, stars or free-form geometric lines.

Very Large Sicardo Vase

Bowl, 2⅜" h., wide flat bottom w/low upright sides molded w/four thin buttresses, iridescent glaze w/silvery clover leafs against a dark reddish purple ground, signed, early 20th c. (small chips on base) 550.00

Bowl, 8" d., 3¾" h., waisted flaring sides w/a shaped rim, the sides molded w/stylized scrolling flowers, green & purple iridescent glaze, signed in script "Sicard Weller" 605.00

Box, cov., squatty five-pointed star shape, conforming low pyramidal cover w/button finial, overall iridescent glaze decorated w/repeating gold fleur-de-lis & random dots on a crimson & blue ground, signed, 5¼" w., 2¾" h. 550.00

Jardiniere, very wide squatty bulbous hexagonal body raised on short arcaded feet, tapering to a low flared

& scalloped rim, the sides boldly embossed overall w/repeating scrolling vine & shell Moresque-style designs, reddish purple & dark bluish green iridescent glaze, signed, 12⅛" h. (small chip on one foot) 4,400.00

Plaque, rectangular, molded in relief w/a bust profile portrait of Saint Cecilia, after Donatello, iridescent glaze w/gold, reddish purple, blue & green highlights, marked, ca. 1902-07, 16½" w., 21" h. (minor chips at edge, repair to top right corner) 3,630.00

Vase, 4⅞" h., swelled base below tapering twisted cylindrical body w/a thick ruffled rim, iridescent glaze in shades of purple & dark green decorated w/stylized scrolling leaves, signed, No. 2039, ca. 1902-07 ....770.00

Vase, 5¾" h., 3" d., a bulbous base below gently tapering conical sides, decorated w/peacock feathers in a gold & burgundy iridescent glaze, signed 385.00

Vase, bud, 5¾" h., 3" d., globular base & long tapering neck, decorated w/gold clover leaves in a burgundy lustred glaze, unmarked 300.00

Vase, 6" h., 2½" d., swollen shoulder & corseted base, decorated in a lustred glaze w/silver blue stars on a burgundy ground, signed in script "Weller Sicard" 550.00

Vase, 6⅛" h., squatty bulbous base below a tall ovoid body tapring to a flat mouth, iridescent glaze in shades of green decorated w/scattered shamrocks, marked & incised "X 453," ca. 1902-07 ....990.00

Vase, 6¼" h., 4" d., waisted cylindrical body swelled near the top then tapering to a small mouth, decorated w/stylized flowers in gold, blue & purple lustre glaze, signed 770.00

Vase, 6¼" h., 5¼" d., corseted-form w/a broad flaring base, decorated w/a multitude of gold stars on an orange shading to green lustred ground, signed "Weller Sicard" 1,000.00

Vase, 6⅜" h., flaring cylindrical sides w/a rounded & flattened shoulder to the short molded neck, iridescent purple & green glaze decorated w/overall berries & leaves, signed 660.00

Vase, 7⅛" h., simple ovoid body tapering to a flat molded mouth, decorated w/iridescent green leafy scrolls & blossoms against a reddish purple iridescent ground, signed, ca. 1902-07 (some kiln burn & blistering near base) 660.00

Vase, 7⅛" h., tall slightly waisted slender cylindrical body w/a widely flaring base, iridescent greenish gold glaze w/blue highlights decorated w/stylized scattered florals, signed ...660.00

Vase, 7¼" h., compressed squatty base on thin footring tapering to tall cylindrical sides, iridescent glaze w/overall swirled whiplash blossoms & vines in green against a dark purple ground, marked & numbered (some kiln burn near base) 770.00

Vase, 7⅜" h., gently ovoid body tapering to a wide flat rim, iridescent glaze in shades of green depicting grasses on the lower half below stylized trumpet-form blossoms on the upper half, signed 1,045.00

Vase, 8¾" h., simple ovoid body tapering to a wide flat mouth, iridescent glaze in shades of purple & green decorated w/overall scattered stylized blossoms, signed (grinding chips on base) 770.00

Vase, 9½" h., tall slender ovoid body w/a flared rim, iridescent glaze in shades of blue & green decorated w/swirling whiplash blossoms & vines, marked & incised "X 39" (minor grinding to back nicks)........1,540.00

Vase, 11⅛" h., tapering cylindrical body w/a swelled shoulder below a short cylindrical neck, molded in relief around the shoulder w/large poppy blossoms, the stems undulating down the sides, overall purple & green iridescent glaze, marked 3,850.00

Vase, 24¼" h., very tall & wide baluster-form body tapering to a short neck w/widely flaring & flattened rim, decorated w/iridescent green & blue glazes w/kingfishers perched on leafy branches against a swirling & undulating background, gold, red, green, blue & purple highlights, signed 8,800.00

Vase, 27¾" h., very large baluster-form body w/a short neck & widely flaring rim, decorated w/iridescent glazes forming wild swirling & crashing waves in blues, greens & golds against a dark reddish purple ground, signed, possibly an exhibition piece at the 1904 St. Louis World's Fair, tiny glaze nick at rim, some minor crazing (ILLUS.) 9,625.00

SILVERTONE (1928)

Various flowers, fruits or butterflies molded on a pale purple-blue matte pebbled ground.

Console bowl, wide everted sides molded w/small birds & birds' nests among leaves & branches decorated in naturalistic colors, stamped mark & artist's initials "L.C.," 16" d., 3½" h. 467.50

Jardiniere, wide ovoid body tapering sharply at the foot, w/a wide flaring flat rim, molded w/large lilac-like purple flowers & green leaves w/white, yellow & brown trim, stamped mark & artist's initials "N.I." 357.50

Vase, 6⅞" h., ovoid body swelled at the top below the wide, flared mouth, bumpy ground h.p. w/a three-masted galleon w/large crosses on the sails in purples, blues & browns on a pale blue sea w/sea gulls flying above, possibly experimental, unmarked 880.00

Vase, 8" h., baluster-form body w/heavy loop handles below a short neck w/ruffled rim, large molded pink poppy blossom on green stem & a pale blue butterfly ....185.00 to 200.00

SYDONIA (1931)

Pleated blossom or fan shapes on a leaf-molded foot. Mottled blue or dark green glaze.

Cornucopia-vase, fan-shaped vase on leaf-molded domed foot, green, 8½" h. 98.00

Vase, double, two joined fan-shaped holders, blue, 9½" h..........................150.00

Vase, 10½" h., double, two conical bases, one tall & one short, curve up from a round foot, blue 95.00

WARWICK (1929)

Molded brown tree bark ground molded with dark brown branches with small pink blossoms and green three-leaf sprigs.

Basket, 3" d., 6" h.................................85.00

Console set: 10½" d. console bowl & pair of candlesticks, 3 pcs. 200.00

Flower frog, molded branch handle across the top, 5½" h..........75.00 to 100.00

Vase, 4½" h., two-handled, footed ovoid body tapering to a flared rim flanked by loop handles 50.00

Window box, 3½ x 12½".....................225.00

WILD ROSE (early to mid-1930s)

An open white rose on a light tan or green background. Matte glaze.

Basket, tan ground, 5½" h. 65.00

Basket, round bulbous footed body w/sides continuing to form strap handle across top, this handle topped by second smaller arched handle, green ground, 5½" h. 45.00

Cornucopia-vase, tan ground, 5½" h.....30.00

Vase, 7" h. 30.00

WOODCRAFT (1917)

Rustic designs simulating the appearance of stumps, logs and tree trunks. Some pieces are adorned with owls, squirrels, dogs and other animals.

Woodcraft Planter with Foxes

Basket, hanging-type, molded fox face & apples, 9" d., 4½" h...............................225.00 to 250.00

Bowl, 7" d., 5½" h., squatty round base w/molded branch, leaves & acorns around rim & figural squirrel seated on rim 110.00

Candelabra, two-light, a curved pair of branch-like uprights joined by looping apple-laden branches, each arm w/a petal-form bobeche, a small figural owl between the sockets at the top, marked, pr...........................660.00

Jardiniere, acorn-shaped w/deep sides 170.00

Planter, cylindrical tree trunk form w/three small foxes peeking out at side, 4½" h. (ILLUS.)........................135.00

Planter, log-form w/molded leaf & narrow strap handle at top center, 9" l., 4" h. ....50.00 to 75.00

Vase, 8½" h., cylindrical tree trunk form molded w/a branch of pink dogwood blossoms around the sides 110.00

Vase, 9" h., footed slender cylindrical body slightly flaring to the scalloped rim, molded w/tall slender trees w/leaf & fruit clusters around the top 120.00

Vase, 12" h., cylindrical smooth tree trunk-form w/molded leafy branch from rim down the sides & suspending cherries 165.00

Wall pocket, conical tree trunk-form w/relief-molded branch down front & figural squirrel seated at base, 9" h. ....200.00 to 225.00

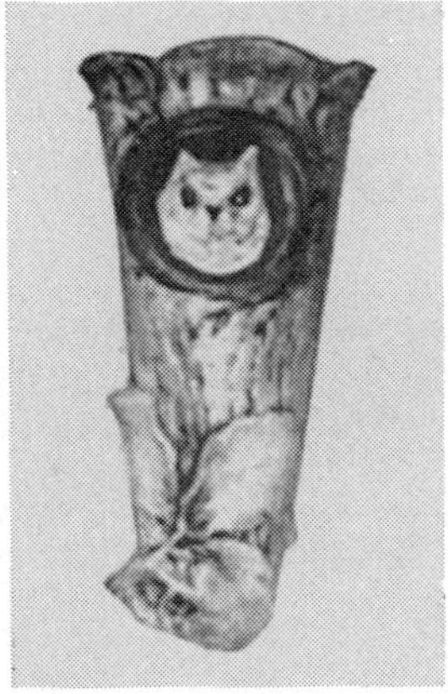

Woodcraft Wall Pocket

Wall pocket, conical, molded owl head in trunk opening, 10" h. (ILLUS.) ....150.00 to 195.00

ZONA (about 1920)

Red apples and green leaves on brown branches all on a cream-colored ground; some pieces with molded florals or birds with various glazes.

A line of children's dishes was also produced featuring hand-painted or molded animals. This is referred to as the "Zona Baby Line."

Comport, open, 5½" h., deep rounded bowl molded around the sides w/a band of large pink blossoms & green leaves on a wood-grained ground, raised a flaring pedestal base 125.00

Creamer, ovoid body w/twig handle, dinnerware line, 3½" h. 35.00

Pitcher, 7" h., cylindrical body, paneled splashing duck decoration 155.00

Pitcher, 8" h., cylindrical, paneled colored kingfisher decoration on a cream ground, brown branch handle 220.00

Pitcher, 8" h., cylindrical, paneled kingfisher decoration w/overall dark green glaze 125.00

Pitcher, 8" h., cylindrical body, paneled kingfisher decoration w/overall dark pink glaze, branch handle 145.00

Zona Umbrella Stand

Umbrella stand, cylindrical, decorated w/a row of tall, standing maidens in long dresses holding a continuous garland of pink roses, green ivy vines around the top, all on a cream ground, glossy glaze, 20½" h. (ILLUS.) ....1,000.00 to 1,400.00

WHIELDON-TYPE WARES

The Staffordshire potter, Thomas Whieldon, first established a pottery at Fenton in 1740. Though he made all types of wares generally in production in the 18th century, he is best known for his attractive, warm-colored green, yellow and brown mottled wares molded in the form of vegetables, fruit and leaves. He employed Josiah Spode as an apprentice and was briefly in partnership with Josiah Wedgwood. The term Whieldon ware is, however, a generic one since his wares were unmarked and are virtually indistin-

guishable from other similar wares produced by other potters during the same period.

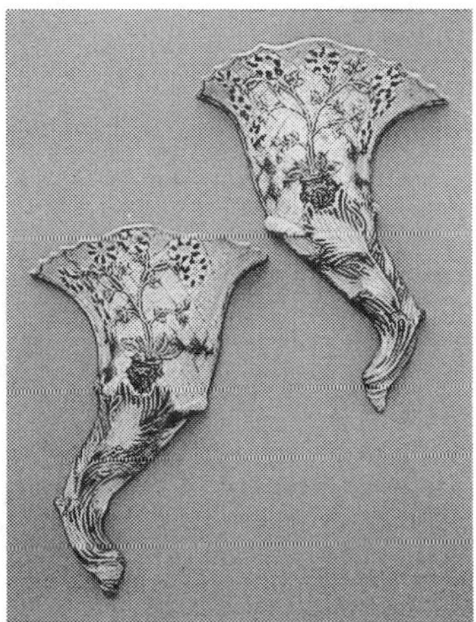

Whieldon-Type Wall Pockets

Basket, low widely-flaring scalloped & reticulated sides pierced w/interlocking circlets, covered overall w/a streaky brown tortoiseshell glaze, 1755-60, 11⅛" d.(small chips, hairlines) $2,875.00

Basket & undertray, oval basket, end loop handles & flaring reticulated sides spashed in mottled blue, green & ochre glaze on a brown ground, the matching undertray w/a reticulated border band, ca. 1760, undertray 9⅝" l., 2 pcs. (one handle reglued).......................................6,050.00

Plate, 9" d., commemorative-type, the scalloped wide rim molded w/a diaper pattern & reserved w/panels inscribed "Success to the - King of Prussia - And His Forces," his portrait, martial trophies & an eagle, splashed overall w/a mottled green, ochre, blue, brown & grey, ca. 1770 ....2,640.00

Plate, 9⅝" d., scalloped rim molded w/a narrow beaded band, mottled tortoiseshell glaze in black, green, blue & brown (minor wear & scratches) 214.50

Plates, 8⅝" w., octagonal, splashed overall w/mottled green & yellow on a grey ground within a reeded rim band, ca. 1770, set of 4 ....3,080.00

Platter, 18" l., oval w/scalloped wide rim molded w/a diaper, basketweave & scroll design & splashed overall w/a mottled green, ochre, grey & brown glaze, ca. 1770...................7,700.00

Soup plates w/flanged rims, the scalloped wide rim molded w/paneled ermine borders, splashed overall w/mottled ochre, brown, grey & green, ca. 1770, 8¾" d., pr. (rim chips) 3,850.00

Teapot, cov., spherical body w/inset cover w/knob finial, swan's-neck spout & loop handle w/thumb tab, overall mottled brown, yellow & green tortoiseshell glaze, Little Fenton, England, mid-18th c., 5¼" h...385.00

Vase, 6½" h., ovoid tapering body w/a short cylindrical neck, splashed overall w/a mottled brown, blue & grey glaze, ca. 1770 (rim chip) 3,520.00

Wall pockets, creamware, cornucopia-form, molded on the front w/a pot of ochre & brown flowers w/green trailing leaves on the diaper-molded ground above a scrolling leaf-molded base in yellow & green, ca. 1765, some restoration to both, 9½" h., pr. (ILLUS.) 7,700.00

WILLOW WARES

Ridgways Willow Platter

This pseudo-Chinese pattern has been used by numerous firms throughout the years. The original design is attributed to Thomas Minton about 1780 and Thomas Turner is believed to have first produced the ware during his tenure at the Caughley works. The blue underglaze transfer print pattern has never been out of production since that time. An Oriental landscape incorporating a bridge, pagoda, trees, figures and birds, supposedly tells the story of lovers fleeing a cruel father who wished to prevent their marriage. The gods, having pity on them, changed them into birds enabling them to fly away and seek their happiness together.

Also see BUFFALO POTTERY.

BLUE

Bouillon cup, Ridgway, England $25.00

Bowl, 5" d., deep, England 14.00

Bowl, 5¼" d., Homer Laughlin 3.50

Bowl, 5½" d., Royal China Co. 3.00

Bowl, cereal, 6" d., Adams, England 12.00

Bowl, cereal, 6½" d., Flair, Japan 12.00

Bowl, soup, 8½" d., Royal China Co.......8.50

Bowl, soup, 8⅞" d., Maddocks, England..22.00

Butter dish, cov., Allerton, England 190.00

Cake plate, Moriyama, Japan.............125.00

Canister, cov., marked "Sugar," Japan 55.00

Compote, open, low, ca. 1880s, W.T. Copeland, England 120.00

Condiment set: oil cruet w/stopper, vinegar cruet w/stopper, cov. mustard pot & salt in wire rack, Japan, 5 pcs. 110.00

Cracker jar, cov., barrel-shaped, 9" h...125.00

Creamer & cov. sugar bowl, Allerton, England, pr. 100.00

Creamer & cov. sugar bowl, Ridgway, England, pr. 100.00

Cup, lithophane base w/portrait of Geisha, Japan...................................25.00

Cup & saucer, demitasse, Booth's, England..45.00

Cup & saucer, W.T. Copeland, England..45.00

Cup & saucer, Japan 12.00

Cup & saucer, Meakin, England 12.00

Cup & saucer, Occupied Japan...........15.00

Cup & saucer, Royal China Co..............5.00

Cups & saucers, demitasse, Japan, set of 6 ....100.00

Cup plate, Staffordshire, England, mid-19th c., 4" d...............................33.00

Demitasse set, cov. coffeepot, creamer & six cups & saucers, 14 pcs. 175.00

Dinner set: six dinner plates, one large platter, two medium cov. vegetable bowls, open round vegetable bowl, open square vegetable bowl, two relish dishes, gravy boat, creamer & cov. butter dish w/drain; Wedgwood, England, 16 pcs. 1,400.00

Egg cup, Japan....................................15.00

Gravy boat, Ridgway, England 50.00

Mug, interior design & on handle, Japan 12.00

Plate, child's, 4½" d. 9.00

Plate, 5¾" d., Allerton, England.............8.00

Plate, 6" d., Japan 2.00

Plate, 6¼" d., Homer Laughlin................4.00

Plate, 6" d., Meakin, England 5.00

Plate, 6⅜" d., Royal China Co. 3.00

Plate, dessert, 7" d., J. & G. Meakin.....15.00

Plate, 8" d., Maddocks, England 7.00

Plate, 8½" d., Alfred Meakin, England..15.00

Plate, 8¾" d., Japan 4.50

Plate, 9" d., Japan 8.00

Plate, 9" d., Royal China Co. 5.50

Plate, 9" d., Shenango China Co............6.00

Plate, grill, 9¾" d., Japan......................12.00

Plate, 10" d., Johnson Bros., England..12.00

Plate, 10" d., Homer Laughlin...............10.00

Plate, dinner, 10" d., J. & G. Meakin, England..30.00

Plate, 10" d., Ridgway, England 15.00

Plate, 10½" d., Wm. Adams & Sons, England, made for Fisher Bruce & Co., Philadelphia...............................30.00

Plate, 12" d., Royal China Co. 15.00

Plates, 9" d., Allerton, England, pr. 30.00

Plates, 10" d., ca. 1930s, Adderley, England, set of 4 ....180.00

Plates, 10" d., ca. 1880s W.T. Copeland, England, set of 8 ....200.00

Platter, 9⅛ x 11¼", Allerton, England..100.00

Platter, 11½" l., ca. 1880s, W.T. Copeland, England 45.00

Platter, 11½" l., Homer Laughlin...........16.00

Platter, 11½" l., Ridgway, England 65.00

Platter, 12½ " l., Japan 25.00

Platter, 13" l., ca. 1880s, W.T. Copeland, England 60.00

Platter, 13" l., Ridgways, England (ILLUS.) 110.00

Platter, 15" l., Homer Laughlin..............45.00

Platter, 15 x 18", "Ye Old Willow," gold trim, Booths, England (shows a little wear) 150.00

Sauce dish, Ridgway, England 5.00

Sauce dishes, Burleigh Ware, Burgess & Leigh, England, set of 8 ...40.00

Soup bowl, coupe-style, 7½" d., Ridgway, England 22.00

Soup plate w/flanged rim, J. & G. Meakin, England 15.00

Soup plate w/flanged rim, 8¾" d., Ridgway, England 24.00

Soup plate w/flanged rim, Allerton, England..22.00

Teapot, cov., Japan 75.00

Teapot, cov., "Ringtons Limited Teas Merchants" on base, 8" h. 85.00

Teapot, cov., Woods Ware, England....85.00

Toothpick holder, unmarked 85.00

Vegetable bowl, cov., ca. 1880s, W.T. Copeland, England 150.00

Vegetable bowl, cov., handled, Ridgway, England 60.00

Vegetable bowl, open, Allerton, England...60.00

Vegetable bowl, round, Moriyama,Japan 40.00

OTHER COLORS

Butter dish, cov., red, ca. 1890, Societe Ceramique, France 90.00

Creamer & cov. sugar bowl, Mandarin patt., red, Spode, England, pr..........150.00

Cup, red, ca. 1890, Societe Ceramique, France 20.00

Egg cup, pink, Allerton, England 25.00

Ginger jar, cov., green, Mason's Patent Ironstone China, England, made for R. Twining & Co. Ltd., London, England................................65.00

Gravy boat w/attached undertray, red, ca. 1890, Societe Ceramique, France..125.00

Platter, 10½ x 13¾", red, ca. 1890, Societe Ceramique, France 175.00

Platter, 11½ x 16¾", red, ca. 1890, Societe Ceramique, France 225.00

Relish tray, red, ca. 1890, Societe Ceramique, France 5 x 8¾" 75.00

Salt & pepper shakers, red, pr.............20.00

Sugar bowl, cov., large, red, ca. 1890, Societe Ceramique, France 80.00

Vegetable bowl, cov., two-handled, large, red, ca. 1890, Societe Ceramique, France 275.00

Vegetable bowl, open, oval, red, ca. 1890, Societe Ceramique, France 65.00

WOOD (ENOCH) WARES

Enoch Wood established a pottery in Burslem, England, about 1784, which continued in business after 1790 as Wood & Caldwell and in 1818 as Enoch Wood & Sons. The last named company exported large quantities of ceramics to this country until around 1846. Also see HISTORICAL & COMMEMORATIVE WARES.

Cup plate, dark blue transfer-printed scene of a boat w/its sails half down, impressed "Wood," 4¾" d. $170.00

Mug, creamware, molded in the form of a grimacing satyr face w/brown beard, trimmed w/green leaves & border bands, ca. 1770, 4¼" h. (chips, base crack)...........................385.00

Plate, 8½" d., blue transfer-printed center design of a hunting dog in a landscape, floral & scrolls border, impressed mark (wear, minor glaze flakes, crazing on back) 110.00

Toasting cup, creamware, modeled as the faces of Dr. Johnson & Boswell in inverted positions, ca. 1770, 4" h...3,300.00

Toddy plate, medium blue transfer-printed design of a family of sheep in a landscape, flower & scroll border, impressed "Enoch Wood & Sons," 6½" d. 200.00

WORCESTER

The famed English factory was established in 1751 and produced porcelains. Earthenwares were made in the 19th century. Its first period is known as the "Dr. Wall" period; that from 1783 to 1792 as the "Flight" period; that from 1792 to 1807 as the "Barr and Flight & Barr" period. The firm became Barr, Flight & Barr from 1807 to 1813; Flight, Barr & Barr from 1813 to 1840; Chamberlain & Co. from 1840 to 1852, and Kerr and Binns from 1852 to 1862. After 1862, the company became the Worcester Royal Porcelain Company, Ltd., known familiarly as Royal Worcester, which see. Also included in the following listing are examples of wares from the early Chamberlains and early Grainger factories in Worcester.

Flight Barr & Barr

Fruit stand, the spirally-fluted dish & foot painted on the interior & exterior w/blue vines issuing gold- or black-delineated iron-red blossoms & bright green leaves forming a ground reserved in the center w/a gold- and iron-red-edged blue roundel depicting an iron-red & gold stylized kylin amid vines, & the worn gilt-edged rim w/six floral vignettes, Chamberlain's, ca. 1800, 12½" l. $770.00

Mug, tall footed pear-shaped body, decorated w/the "Beckoning Chinaman" patt., painted in shades of purple, iron-red, yellow, green, rose, blue & black on one side w/a Chinaman beckoning to a young boy w/raised arms running by a stylized rock, the reverse w/an Oriental flowering branch extending to the front, the back w/a ridged loop handle, ca. 1758, 5 11/16" h. (restored hole on the side) 1,955.00

Sweetmeat dishes, in the form of deep scallop shells, the interiors painted in colors w/loose bouquets & scattered sprays within green molded edges, ca. 1760, 5⅛" w., pr. (one repaired & cracked) 825.00

Teapot, cov., chinoiserie-style, spherical footed body finely printed in black & painted in green, rose, iron-red, black, yellow, white, blue & gold on either side w/two Oriental servant ladies & a small boy standing before a table at which is seated a Chinaman beside another standing lady, a tall table behind them, the domed cover w/a reduced version of the scene flanking the rose & green floral-sprig knop, the pot shoulder & cover rim w/an iron-red & gilt scallop-and-dot border, ca. 1770, 5½" h. (two small chips on spout)..990.00

Vases, 13⅝" & 13 5/16" h., bulbous ovoid body w/a cylindrical neck flanked by figural gold stag heads, raised on a short knopped pedestal on a square foot, each side of the body reserved w/a gilt-edged shaped oval cartouche colorfully painted w/a cluster of summer flowers against a drab green ground, the shoulder w/a border of gilt palmettes & foliate scrolls interrupted by the stag's head handles (some restoration to the antler tips) between molded gilt bands, the cylindrical neck w/a gilt flared rim decorated on the interior w/a bronze-ground border of gilt palmette & florette designs, the bronze-bordered square base (one w/shallow repaired chip) decorated on the upper corners w/gilt palmettes on a gilt-stippled ground, impressed crowned "FBB" marks & "Flight, Barr & Barr - Royal Porcelain Works. - Worcester - London House 1 Coventry Street," 1825-35, pr...19,800.00

Waste bowl, deep rounded sides raised on a footring, decorated w/the "Japan" patt., the exterior painted in underglaze-blue, iron-red, green, turquoise, shades of pink & gold w/a panel of a bird & a rock in a fenced garden, a second panel of a tree & flowers in a fenced garden, & a third panel of flowers, all separated by blue-ground narrower panels patterned w/gilt trelliswork & reserved w/iron-red & gilt *mons* beneath the gilt-edged rim, incised letter "B" mark of Flight & Barr, ca. 1800, 6⅝" d. (slight rim wear) 460.00

YELLOW-GLAZED EARTHENWARE

In the past this early English ware was often referred to as "Canary Lustre," but recently a more accurate title has come into use.

Produced in the late 18th and early 19th centuries, pieces featured an overall yellow glaze, often decorated with silver or copper lustre designs or black, brown or red transfer-printed scenes.

Most pieces are not marked and today the scarcity of examples in good condition keeps market prices high.

Mug, child's, cylindrical, transfer-printed scene of a boy rolling a hoop & the inscription "A Present for my Dear Boy," 2" h. (minor imperfections) $330.00

Mug, child's, cylindrical, transfer-printed scene of a girl in a landscape & the inscription "A Present for my Dear Girl," early 19th c., 2" h. (imperfections) 385.00

Mug, child's, cylindrical, decorated w/a red transfer-printed scene of a young boy with his dog & playing a recorder in a landscape, pink lustre rim band, early 19th c., 2½" h. (small chips, hairline, lustre wear) 104.50

Mug, child's, cylindrical, black transfer-printed design of cows in a landscape, silver lustre trim, 2⅝" h. (wear, small flakes) 253.00

YELLOWWARE

Yellowware is a form of utilitarian pottery produced in the United States and England from the early 19th century onward. Its body texture is less dense and vitreous (impervious to water) than stoneware. Most, but not all, yellowware is unmarked and its color varies from deep yellow to pale buff. In the late 19th and early 20th centuries bowls in graduated sizes were widely advertised. Still in production, yellowware is plentiful and still reasonably priced.

Bowl, 6" d., girl w/sprinkling can decoration $45.00

Canning jar, cov., cylindrical body tapering to a short flaring neck, inset flat cover w/knob finial, 7" h. (stains, rim & cover chips) 66.00

Medallion, oval, the center relief-molded w/a white profile bust of George Washington, 6¼" l. 253.00

Mixing bowl, footed, deep rounded sides w/a flared rim, wide white center band flanked by narrow brown stripes, 14¼" d., 7" h. 110.00

Pitcher, milk, w/blue stripe, "EC" 50.00

Rolling pin, long cylindrical body 265.00

ZSOLNAY

Zsolnay Figural Vase

This pottery was made in Pecs, Hungary, in a factory founded in 1862 by Vilmos Zsolnay. Utilitarian earthenware was originally produced but by the turn of the century ornamental Art Nouveau style wares with bright colors and lustre decoration were produced and these wares are especially sought today. Currently Zsolnay pieces are being made in a new factory.

ZSOLNAY PÉCS

Chargers, pink flowers center on a cobalt blue ground, repeated on the border amid yellow & green reticulated scrolls, 17" d., pr. $330.00

Figure group, modeled as a seated little boy w/a cat on his shoulder eating from his plate, peacock blue iridescent glaze, stamped company mark & artist's name incised on side, 6" h. 403.00

Vase, 5⅞" h., simple ovoid body tapering to a flat rim, overall iridescent gold & blue swirled glaze, raised medallion mark, ca. 1903 ......320.50

Vase, 6⅞" h., double-gourd shape w/four molded handles, red & ochre iridescent glaze decorated w/four mice, impressed company mark & "6020" (hairline in neck) 748.00

Vase, 8¼" h., 7" d., reticulated side handles, squatty-form, overall reticulated Arabic scrollwork design, cream & gold w/horizontal beaded bands, incised "Zsolnay - PECS," "2771" & impressed tower mark.......275.00

Vase, 8⅞" h., squatty bulbous body tapering to a short neck w/molded rim, the wide shoulder molded in full relief w/a large mermaid & merman & fish, peacock blue iridescent glaze, impressed company mark & "MADE IN HUNGARY" (ILLUS.) ...1,610.00

Vase, 9½" h., double-gourd shape w/three scrolled handles, the textured yellow-glazed body w/three applied medallions w/openwork in yellow, black & red, impressed "ZSOLNAY" 115.00

Vase, 10½" h., wide bulbous spherical body w/incurvate rim raised on a low flaring foot, decorated w/stylized foliage in regular geometric patterns in green, gold, grey, silver & burgundy lustres against a black ground, printed factory mark, ca. 1900 ....2,300.00

Vase, 14¾" h., cylindrical base supporting a compressed globular middle section beneath a long slightly waisted slender neck, elaborately decorated w/flowering peony, butterflies & leaves against a spotted ground, in rich colors heightened w/gilding, stamped w/the firm's trade-mark & "872" (ILLUS. top next column) 1,725.00

Elaborate Zsolnay Vase

Vase, 17" h., figural, a footed cushion base w/a wide shoulder to a tall, tapering cylindrical body, the base molded w/wild waves below the tall full-figure of a standing maiden w/diaphanous gown & long hair clutching the sides, iridescent gold, green & brown glaze, raised medallion mark, ca. 1903 (minor glaze chip) 2,640.00

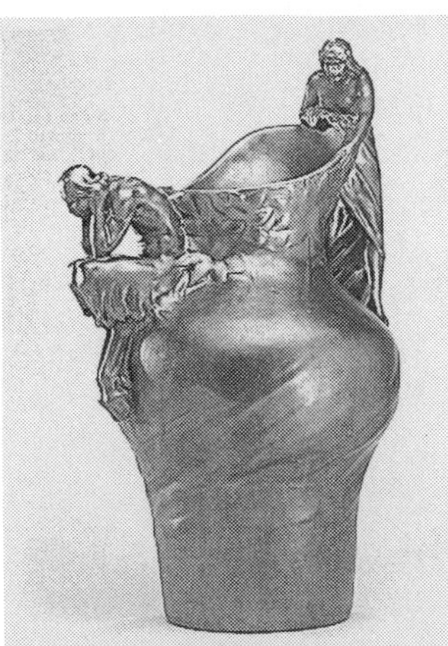

Large Zsolnay Vase

Vase, 17¾" h., baluster-form w/irregular rim, modeled w/a partially draped maiden & satyr around the rim, in a purple lustre glaze, impressed "ZSOLNAY PECS 6129 23 1" (ILLUS.) 4,025.00

GLOSSARY OF SELECTED CERAMICS TERMS

Abino Ware - A line produced by the Buffalo Pottery of Buffalo, New York. Introduced in 1911, this limited line featured mainly sailing ship scenes with a windmill on shore.

Agate Ware - An earthenware pottery featuring a mixture of natural colored clays giving a marbled effect. Popular in England in the 18th century.

Albany slip - A dark brown slip glaze used to line the interiors of most salt-glazed stoneware pottery. Named for a fine clay found near Albany, New York.

Albino line - A version of Griffen, Smith and Hill's Shell & Seaweed majolica pattern with an off-white overall color sometimes trimmed with gold or with pink or blue feathering.

Albion Ware - A line of majolica developed by Edwin Bennett in the 1890s. It featured colored liquid clays over a green clay body decorated with various scenes. Popular for jardinieres and pedestals.

Bas relief - Literally "low relief," referring to lightly molded decorations on ceramic pieces.

Bisquit - Unglazed porcelain left undecorated or sometimes trimmed with pastel colors. Also known as **bisque.**

Bocage - A background of flowering trees or vines often used as a backdrop for figural groups which were meant to be viewed from the front only.

Bone china - A porcelain body developed in England using the white ashes of bone. It has been the standard English porcelain ware since the early 19th century.

Coleslaw - A type of decoration used on ceramic figurines to imitate hair or fur. It is finely crumbled clay applied to the unfired piece and resembling coleslaw cabbage.

Crackled glaze - A glaze with an intentional network of fine lines produced by uneven contracting of the glaze after firing. First popular on Chinese wares.

Crazing - The fine network of cracks in a glaze produced by uneven contracting of the glaze after firing or later reheating of a piece during usage. An unintentional defect usually found on earthenwares.

Creamware - A light-colored fine earthenware developed in England in the late 18th century and used by numerous potters into the 19th century. Josiah Wedgwood marketed his version as **Queensware.**

Crystalline glaze - A glaze containing fine crystals resulting from the presence of mineral salts in the mixture. It was a popular glaze on American art pottery of the late 19th century and early 20th century.

Eared handles - Handles applied to ceramic pieces such as crocks. They are crescent or 'ear' shaped, hence the name.

Earthenware - A class of fine-grained porous pottery fired at relatively low temperature and then glazed. It produces a light and easily molded ware that was widely used by the potteries of Staffordshire, England in the late 18th and early 19th century.

Faience - A form of fine earthenware featuring a tin glaze and originally inspired by Chinese porcelain. It includes early Dutch Delft ware and similar wares made in France, Germany and other areas of Europe.

Fairyland Lustre - A special line of decorated wares developed by Susannah 'Daisy' Makeig-Jones for J. Wedgwood & Sons early in the 20th century. It featured fantastic or dreamlike scenes with fairies and elves in various colors and with a mother-of-pearl lustre glaze. Closely related to **Dragon Lustre** featuring designs with dragons.

Flambé glaze - A special type of glaze featuring splashed or streaked deep reds and purples, often dripping over another base color. Popular with some American art pottery makers but also used on porcelain wares.

Flint Enamel glaze - A version of the well known brown mottled Rockingham pottery glaze. It was developed by Lyman Fenton & Co. of Bennington, Vermont and patented in 1849. It featured streaks and flecks of green, orange, yellow and blue mixed with the mottled brown glaze.

Glaze - The general term for a vitreous (glass-like) coating fired on to pottery and porcelain to produce an impervious surface and protect underglaze decoration.

Hard-paste - Refers to 'true' porcelain, a fine, white clay body developed by the Chinese and containing **kaolin** and **petuntse** or china stone. It is fired at a high temperature and glazed with powdered feldspar to produce a smooth, shiny glaze.

Lead glaze - A shiny glaze most often used on cheap redware pottery and produced using a dry powdered or liquid lead formula. Since it would be toxic, it was generally used on the exterior of utilitarian wares only.

Lithophane - A panel of thin porcelain delicately molded with low-relief patterns or scenes which show up clearly when held to light. It was developed in Europe in the 19th century and was used for decorative panels or lamp shades and was later used in the bottom of some German and Japanese steins, mugs or cups.

Majolica - A type of tin-glazed earthenware pottery developed in Italy and named for the island of Majorca. It was revived in Europe and America in the late 19th century and usually featured brightly colored shiny glazes.

Mission Ware - A decorative line of pottery developed by the Niloak Pottery of Benton, Arkansas. It featured variously colored clays swirled together and was used to produce such decorative pieces as vases and candlesticks.

Moriage - Japanese term for the slip-trailed relief decorations used on various forms of porcelain and pottery. Flowers, beading and dragon decoration are typical examples.

Pâte-sur-pâte - French for 'paste on paste,' this refers to a decorative technique where layers of porcelain slip in white are layered on a darker background. Used on artware produced by firms like Mintons, Ltd. of England.

Pearlware - A version of white colored creamware developed in England and widely used for inexpensive earthenwares in the late 18th and early 19th century. It has a pearly glaze, hence the name.

Pillow vase - A form of vase designed to resemble a flattened round or oblong pillow. Generally an upright form with flattened sides. A similar form is the **Moon vase** or **flask,** meant to resemble a full moon.

Porcelain - The general category of translucent, vitrified ceramics first developed by the Chinese and later widely produced in Europe and America. Hard-paste is 'true' porcelain, while soft-paste is an 'artificial' version developed to imitate hard-paste using other ingredients.

Pottery - The very general category of ceramics produced from various types of clay. It includes redware, yellowware, stoneware and various earthenwares. It is generally fired at a much lower temperature than porcelain.

PUG - An abbreviation for "printed under glaze," referring to colored decorations on pottery. Most often it is used in reference to decorations found on Mettlach pottery steins.

Relief-molding - A decorative technique, sometimes erroneously referred to as "blown-out," whereby designs are raised in bold relief against a background. The reverse of such decoration is hollowed-out, giving the impression the design was produced by 'blowing' from the inside. Often used in reference to certain Nippon porcelain wares.

Rocaille - A French term meaning 'rockwork.' It generally refers to a decoration used for the bases of ceramic figurines.

Salt-glazed stoneware - A version of stoneware pottery where common rock salt is thrown in the kiln during firing and produces hard, shiny glaze like a thin coating of glass.

Sanded - A type of finish usually on pottery wares. Unfired pieces are sprinkled or rolled in fine sand, which, when fired, gives the piece a sandy, rough surface texture.

Sang-de-boeuf - Literally French for "ox blood," it refers to a deep red glaze produced with copper oxide. It was first produced by the Chinese and imitated by European and American potters in the late 19th and early 20th century.

Sgrafitto - An Italian-inspired term for decorative designs scratched or cut through a layer of slip before firing. Generally used on earthenware forms and especially with the Pennsylvania-German potters of America.

Slip - The liquid form of clay, often used to decorate earthenware pieces in a process known as **slip-trailing** or **slip-quilling.**

Soft-paste - A term used to describe a certain type of porcelain body developed in Europe and England from the 16th to late 18th centuries. It was used to imitate true hard-paste porcelain developed by the Chinese but was produced using a white clay mixed with a grit or flux of bone ash or talc and fired at fairly low temperatures. The pieces are translucent, like hard-paste porcelain, but are not as durable. It should **not** be used when referring to earthenwares such as creamware or pearlware.

Sprigging - A term used to describe the ornamenting of ceramic pieces with applied relief decoration, such as blossoms, leaves or even figures.

Standard glaze - The most common form of glazing used on Rookwood Pottery pieces. It is a clear, shiny glaze usually on pieces decorated with florals or portraits against a dark shaded background.

Stoneware - A class of hard, high-fired pottery usually made from dense grey clay and most often decorated with a salt glaze. American 19th century stoneware was often decorated with slip-quilled or hand-brushed cobalt blue decorations.

Tapestry ware - A form of late 19th century porcelain where the piece is impressed with an overall linen cloth texture before firing. The Royal Bayreuth firm is especially known for their fine "Rose Tapestry" line wherein the finely textured ground is decorated with colored roses.

Tin glaze - A form of pottery glaze made opaque by the addition of tin oxide. It was used most notably on early Dutch Delft as well as other early faience and majolica wares.

Underglaze-blue - A cobalt blue produced with metallic oxides applied to an unfired clay body. Blue was one of the few colors which does not run or smear when fired at a high temperature. It was used by the Chinese on porcelain and later copied by firms such as Meissen.

APPENDIX I

CERAMICS CLUBS & ASSOCIATIONS For Ceramic Collectors

American Art Pottery Association
125 E. Rose Ave.
St. Louis, MO 63119

Pottery Lovers Reunion
4969 Hudson Dr.
Stow, OH 44224

Bauer News
P.O Box 91279
Pasadena, CA 91109-1279

Belleek Collectors Society, The
c/o Reed & Barton Co.
144 West Britannia St.
Taunton, MA 02780

Blue & White Pottery Club
224 12th St., NW
Cedar Rapids, IA 52405

Camark Collectors Newsletter
1529 Kempton Court
Longmont, CO 80501

Clarice Cliff Collector's Club
Fantasque House
Tennis Drive, the Park
Nottingham NG1 IAE England

The Dedham Pottery Collectors Society Newsletter
248 Highland St.
Dedham, MA 02026

Heartland Doulton Collectors
P.O. Box 2434
Joliet, IL 60434

Mid-America Doulton Collectors
P.O. Box 483
McHenry, IL 60050

Flow Blue International Collectors' Club
P.O. Box 205
Rockford, IL 61105

Goss Collectors Club
4 Khasiaberry
Walnut Tree
Milton Keynes MK7 7DP England

National Autumn Leaf Collectors Club
7346 Shamrock Dr.
Indianapolis, IN 46217

Haviland Collectors Internationale Foundation
P.O. Box 423
Boone, IA 50036-0423

Hull Pottery News (Newsletter)
466 Foreston Place
St. Louis, MO 63119-3927

Hull Pottery Newsletter
11023 Tunnell Hill NE
New Lexington, OH 43764

Foundation for Historical Research of Illinois Potteries
704 E. Twelfth St.
Streator, IL 61364

Collectors of Illinois Pottery & Stoneware
1527 East Converse St.
Springfield, IL 62702

Majolica International Society
1275 First Ave., Suite 103
New York, NY 10021

Our McCoy Matters (Newsletter)
P.O. Box 14255
Parkville, MO 64152

Arkansas Pottery Collectors Society (Niloak)
12 Normandy Rd.
Little Rock, AR 72207

New England Nippon Collectors Club
64 Burt Rd.
Springfield, MA 01118

Long Island Nippon Collectors Club
145 Andover Pl.
West Hampstead, NY 11552

Lakes & Plains Nippon Collectors Club
4305 W. Beecher Rd.
P.O. Box 230
Peotone, IL 60468

International Nippon Collectors Club
112 Ascot Dr.
Southlake, TX 76092

Noritake News (Newsletter)
1237 Federal Ave. East
Seattle, WA 98102

North Dakota Pottery Collectors Society
P.O. Box 14
Beach, ND 58621

Old Ivory Newsletter
P.O. Box 1004
Wilsonville, OR 97070

Phoenix Bird Collectors of America
685 S. Washington
Constantine, MI 49042

Pickard Collectors Club
300 E. Grove St.
Bloomington, IL 61701

Roseville's of the Past Pottery Club
P.O. Box 681117
Orlando, FL 32868-1117

International Association of R.S. Prussia Collectors Inc.
22 Canterbury Dr.
Danville, IN 46122

Shawnee Pottery Collectors Club
P.O. Box 713
New Smyrna Beach, FL 32170-0713

Southern Folk Pottery Collectors Society
1224 Main St.
Glastonbury, CT 06033

Blue Ridge Collectors Club
Rte. 3, Box 161
Erwin, TN 37650

American Stoneware Association
930 Country Lane
Indiana, PA 15701

Red Wing Collectors Society, Inc.
P.O. Box 124
Neosho, WI 53059

Susie Cooper Collectors Group
P.O. Box 48
Beeston
Nottingham NG9 2 RN England

Tea Leaf Club International Membership
324 Powderhorn Dr.
Houghton Lake, MI 48629

Tile Heritage Foundation
P.O. Box 1850
Healdsburg, CA 95448

North American Torquay Society
P.O. Box 397
Dalton, GA 30722

Torquay Pottery Collectors Society
P.O. Box 373
Schoolcraft, MI 49087-0373

Uhl Collectors Society
233 E. Timberlin Lane
Huntingburg, IN 47542

Vernon Views Newsletter
P.O. Box 945
Scottsdale, AZ 85252

Watt Pottery Collectors
P.O. Box 26067
Fairview Park, OH 44126

Wedgwood Society
The Roman Villa
Rockbourne, Fordingbridge
Hants SP6 3PG England

Wedgwood Society of New York
5 Dogwood Ct.
Glen Head, NY 11545

Willow Society
39 Medhurst Rd.
Toronto
Ontario M4B IB2 Canada

International Willow Collectors
2903 Blackbird Rd.
Petoskey, MI 49770

APPENDIX II

Museums & Libraries with Ceramics Collections

BELLEEK

Museum of Ceramics at
East Liverpool
400 E. 5th St.
East Liverpool, OH 43920

BENNINGTON

Bennington Museum, The
W. Main St.
Bennington, VT 05201

CERAMICS (AMERICAN)

Everson Museum of Art of Syracuse
& Onondaga County
401 Harrison St.
Syracuse, NY 13202

CERAMICS (AMERICAN ART POTTERY)

Cincinnati Art Museum
Eden Park
Cincinnati, OH 45202

Newcomb College Art Gallery
1229 Broadway
New Orleans, LA 70118

Zanesville Art Center
620 Military Rd.
Zanesville, OH 43701

CHINESE EXPORT PORCELAIN

Peabody Museum of Salem
East India Square
Salem, MA 01970

COWAN POTTERY CO.

Cowan Pottery Museum at the
Rocky River Public Library
1600 Hampton Rd.
Rocky River, OH 44116-2699

DEDHAM

Dedham Historical Society
612 High St.
Dedham, MA

PENNSYLVANIA GERMAN

Hershey Museum
170 W. Hersheypark Dr.
Hershey, PA 17033

GENERAL COLLECTIONS:

The Bayou Bend Collection
#1 Wescott
Houston, TX

Greenfield Village and
Henry Ford Museum
Oakwood Blvd.
Dearborn, MI 48121

Museum of Early Southern
Decrotive Arts
924 Main St.
Winston-Salem, NC 27101

Abby Aldrich Rockefeller
Folk Art Collection
England St.
Williamsburg, VA 23185

The Margaret Woodbury
Strong Museum
700 Allen Creek Rd.
Rochester, NY 14618

Henry Francis DuPont
Winterthur Museum
Winterthur, DE 19735

APPENDIX III

References to Pottery and Porcelain Marks

DeBolt's Dictionary of American Pottery Marks - Whiteware & Porcelain
Gerald DeBolt
Collector Books,
Paducah, Kentucky, 1994

Encyclopaedia of British Pottery and Porcelain Marks
Geoffrey A. Godden
Bonanza Books,
New York,New York , 1964

Kovel's New Dictionary of Marks, Pottery & Porcelain, 1850 to the Present
Ralph & Terry Kovel
Crown Publishers,
New York, New York, 1986

Lehner's Encyclopedia of U.S. Marks on Pottery, Porcelain & Clay
Lois Lehner
Collector Books,
Paducah, Kentucky, 1988

Marks on German, Bohemian and Austrian Porcelain, 1710 to the Present
Robert E. Röntgen
Schiffer Publishing, Ltd.,
Atglen, Pennsylvania

APPENDIX IV
English Registry Marks

Since the early 19th century, the English have used a number of markings on most ceramics wares which can be very helpful in determining the approximate date a piece was produced.

The 'registry' mark can be considered an equivalant of the American patent number.This English numbering system continues in use today.

Beginning in 1842 and continuing until 1883, most pottery and porcelain pieces were printed or stamped with a diamond-shaped registry mark which was coded with numbers and letters indicating the type of material, parcel number of the piece and, most helpful, the day, month and year that the design or pattern was registered at the Public Record Office. Please note that a piece may have been produced a few years after the registration date itself.

Our **Chart A** here shows the format of the diamond registry mark used between 1842 and 1867. Accompanying it are listings of the corresponding month and year letters used during that period. In a second chart, **Chart B**, we show the version of the diamond mark used between 1868 and 1883 which depicts a slightly different arrangement. Keep in mind that this diamond registry mark was also used on metal, wood and glasswares. It is important to note that the top bubble with the Roman numeral indicates the material involved; pottery and porcelain will always be Numeral IV.

After 1884, the diamond mark was discontinued and instead just a registration number was printed on pieces. The abbreviation "**Rd**" for "Registration" appears before the number. We list here these design registry numbers by year with the number indicating the **first** number that was used in that year. For instance, design number 494010 would have been registered sometime in 1909.

CHART A

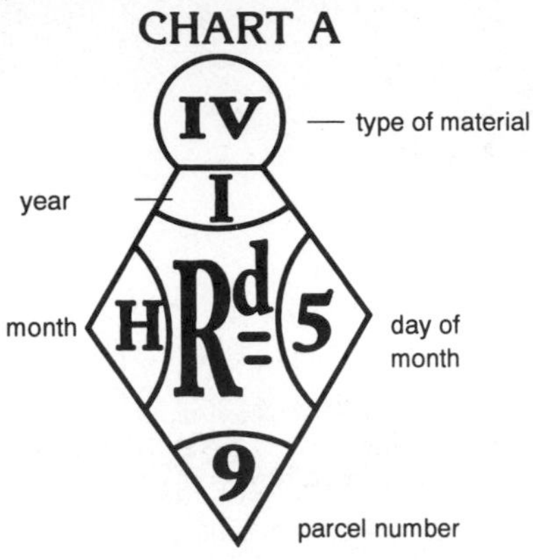

Registration for
April 5, 1846

CHART B

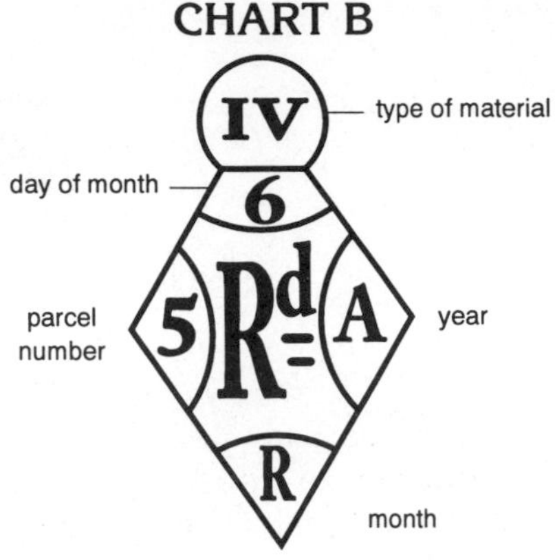

Registration for
August 6, l871

LIST 1

Month of the Year of Registration

C—January
G—February
W—March
H—April
E—May
M—June
I—July
R—August
D—September
B—October
K—November
A—December

LIST 2

Year of Registration — 1842-1867

1842—X
1843—H
1844—C
1845—A
1846—I
1847—F
1848—U
1849—S
1850—V
1851—P
1852—D
1853—Y
1854—J
1855—E
1856—L
1857—K
1858—B
1859—M
1860—Z
1861—R
1862—O
1863—G
1864—N
1865—W
1866—Q
1867—T

LIST 3

Year of Registration — 1868-1883

1868—X	1874—U	1879—Y
1869—H	1875—S	1880—J
1870—C	1876—V	1881—E
1871—A	1877—P	1882—L
1872—I	1878—D	1883—K
1873—F		

LIST 4

DESIGN REGISTRY NUMBERS — 1884-1951

Jan. 1884—1	1907—493900	1929—742725
1885—20000	1908—518640	1930—751160
1886—40800	1909—535170	1931—760583
1887—64700	Sep. 1909—548919	1932—769670
1888—91800	Oct. 1909—548920	1933—779292
1889—117800	Jan. 1911—575817	1934—789019
1890—142300	1912—594195	1935—799097
1891—164000	1913—612431	1936—808794
1892—186400	1914—630190	1937—817293
1893—206100	1915—644935	1938—825231
1894—225000	1916—635521	1939—832610
1895—248200	1917—658988	1940—837520
1896—268800	1918—662872	1941—838590
1897—291400	1919—666128	1942—839230
Jan. 1898—311677	1920—673750	1943—839980
1899—332200	1921—680147	1944—841040
1900—351600	1922—687144	1945—842670
1901—368186	1923—694999	Jan. 1946—845550
1902—385180	1924—702671	1947—849730
1903—403200	1925—710165	1948—853260
1904—424400	1926—718057	1949—856999
1905—447800	1927—726330	1950—860854
1906—471860	1928—734370	1951—863970

1994 CERAMICS PRICE GUIDE

INDEX